S0-CNC-471

THE BEST PLAYS OF 1933-34

THE BEST PLAYS OF 1933-34

AND THE
YEAR BOOK OF THE DRAMA
IN AMERICA

EDITED BY
BURNS MANTLE

DODD, MEAD AND COMPANY
NEW YORK

PRINTED IN THE U. S. A.

INTRODUCTION

THERE is a phrase that occurs frequently in the comments of those experts of the theatre called critics which, although pregnant with meaning to the writers, must remain fairly puzzling to many of their lay readers.

This play, or that scene, the critic will insist, is "good theatre." A scene or a play, he is trying to say, or so I assume, that represents the theatre and the things the theatre normally stands for with especial credit.

This season of the great rally has been a season in which all the better plays have represented "good theatre." Most of them have been simple excursions in romance or adventure stimulating to the commoner emotional reactions. And it has long been the contention of this particular commentator that it is emotional satisfaction for which playgoers pay most cheerfully and most consistently in the theatre.

Argument and debate stirred by the awarding of the Pulitzer prize was centered on two plays—Maxwell Anderson's "Mary of Scotland," a better type historical romance, and "Men in White," a conventionally plotted but highly effective melodrama concerned with a young medic's struggle 'twixt love and duty. It is significant, I think, that while the specialists of the jury selected "Mary of Scotland" the playgoers of the larger Pulitzer committee reversed their decision and substituted "Men in White."

The Theatre Guild's two outstanding successes were the essentially simple "Ah, Wilderness!" and that same romantic "Mary of Scotland." The most consistently popular box office attraction, in the dramatic list, was the "Dodsworth" which Sidney Howard extracted from the Sinclair Lewis novel of the same title. A typical American family life drama in which a cheating and selfish wife is given a whipping.

The leading comedy successes were Clare Kummer's "Her Master's Voice," revealing the homely readjustment of a potential radio crooner's domestic problem, and "No More Ladies," which carries a pair of young sophisticates representing the menacing generation through marriage to threatened divorce and leaves them prepared to try a compromise.

Another comedy success was a simple tale of revolutionary days exposing the happy custom of bundling. This was called "The Pursuit of Happiness." And the "Wednesday's Child" that was full of woe was a young man of 10 whose divorced parents could find no place for him in either of their new homes and were reluctantly forced to send him to a military academy.

Those plays from which playgoers extracted a greater intellectual than emotional satisfaction, such as Sidney Howard's "Yellow Jack," Eugene O'Neill's "Days Without End," Philip Barry's "The Joyous Season," Clemence Dane's "Come of Age" and Dan Totheroh's "Moor Born," struggled ineffectually against a relieved people's drift toward the simpler entertainments.

This is not a playgoing reaction that may be said to be peculiar to this particular season. The intellectual drama must always be content with small audiences in the people's theatre. But it was a reaction peculiarly noticeable in this first season following a five-year depression.

I again submit the ten plays from which excerpts are printed in this sixteenth volume of "The Best Plays" series as being fairly representative of the theatre season's output. They may be the best plays in fact, or only in the estimation of the editor who selected them and the public that supported them, but they are worthily representative.

The play that this year clamored most persistently for inclusion was the "Yellow Jack" Mr. Howard dramatized from the Walter Reed chapter in Paul de Kruif's "The Microbe Hunters." It was an outstanding novelty in its staging, a sincerely and strongly written history-drama of one of the brightest pages in the records of the medical profession. But it also must be classed as laboratory drama in the sense that it represents a definite departure from conventional play forms and is dependent upon a special and expensive production which will probably confine its showing to New York playgoers alone.

The year book of the drama in America, I feel, should be principally concerned with those plays that represent the whole theatre rather than with laboratory experiments of special types in which the larger playgoing public is seldom interested. At the moment it seems to me to be the duty of a year book editor to report trends rather than to attempt to direct them.

If I were to write that all ten of these selected plays were generously supported by the public that makes the theatre possible I should be forced to qualify in only two instances. John Wexley's "They Shall Not Die" did get sixty-two performances with the Theatre Guild, but, like all controversial dramas, it was not a popular choice. I have included it because I believe it to be the best of the propaganda plays of the year, because I believe those forces now expressing themselves in this changing world through the theatre are entitled to representation, and because of the nation-wide interest in the Scottsboro case which is the play's inspiration.

As a second instance Leopold Atlas's "Wednesday's Child" was not a popular success, though it was played for seven weeks. In this instance a personal conviction that the tragedy of the child of divorced parents is not only one of the most poignant tragedies of our time, but also a problem of the greatest social importance in this divorce-ridden country, influenced my selection. It is an interesting and a human play, and though it is dependent to a considerable extent upon the skill of the boy actor who plays the hero we fortunately are blessed with a number of these. Frank Thomas, Jr., played the rôle in New York with happy results.

Eight of the ten plays are of American authorship. The other two come from England. Keith Winter's "The Shining Hour" represents the London stage much as "Men in White" represents the New York stage, as an outstanding sample of the conventionally plotted play that is builded into an impressive dramatic exhibit by the skillful employment of theatre art.

"The Green Bay Tree" is another of those dramas designed for a special public that, by reason of its sensitive writing and perfect staging, overcame the handicap of a decadent inspiration. It is an example of high art in the theatre as well as a revealing study of one of those spiritually bankrupt dilettantes who stand, or should stand, as a warning to youth and as an amusingly ignoble failure to age.

"Mary of Scotland," I think, represents the historical romance-drama at its best. O'Neill's "Ah, Wilderness!" particularly with George M. Cohan lending his 100 per cent American quaintness and skill to the chief rôle, is a simple and authentically reminiscent American comedy; a shallow work of art, perhaps, but for American audiences a moving entertainment.

"Dodsworth" digs a bit deeper into the private lives of those rugged individualists who were the foundation of our most expansive industrial years. It, too, is thoroughly American in theme and expression. Walter Huston, playing the name part, unquestionably added much to the vitality of the Dodsworth character as drawn, but it is so firmly foundationed in truth that it can be, and doubtless will be, played successfully by a variety of rugged American actors before it is put aside.

For the rest, "The Best Plays of 1933-34" retains those features and departments which its reading public has been kind enough to endorse.

I trust the sixteen volumes have not become an embarrassing library problem by inconsiderately spilling off the end of your own five-foot shelf. If they have I can supply you with the name of an excellent carpenter.

B. M.

Forest Hills, L. I., 1934.

CONTENTS

	PAGE
Introduction	v
The Season in New York	3
The Season in Chicago	16
The Season in San Francisco	20
The Season in Southern California	24
Mary of Scotland, by Maxwell Anderson	29
Men in White, by Sidney Kingsley	76
Dodsworth, by Sidney Howard	115
Ah, Wilderness!, by Eugene O'Neill	159
They Shall Not Die, by John Wexley	203
Her Master's Voice, by Clare Kummer	256
No More Ladies, by A. E. Thomas	292
Wednesday's Child, by Leopold Atlas	317
The Shining Hour, by Keith Winter	352
The Green Bay Tree, by Mordaunt Shairp	381
The Plays and Their Authors	415
Plays Produced in New York, 1933-34	420
Statistical Summary	535
Long Runs on Broadway	536
Pulitzer Prize Winners	537
Previous Volumes of Best Plays	538
Where and When They Were Born	546

PAGE

Necrology 557

The Decades' Toll 564

Index of Authors 565

Index of Plays and Casts 570

THE BEST PLAYS OF 1933-34

THE BEST PLAYS OF 1933-34

THE SEASON IN NEW YORK

EACH year I find myself, in beginning the season's review intended for this annual record, wondering what might reasonably be the conclusions of a young reporter of the theatre sent by his editor fifty years from now to make a digest of the Mantle "Best Plays" series. What, for instance, would be his reactions to the happenings of this particular season of 1933-34?

Of this much we may be sure: It will be recorded as one of the outstanding years of the theatre's history. Because it marks the emergence of the theatre from one of those periodical depressions during which the drama was given up a little sadly but quite positively as approaching a state of rigor mortis.

This particular season was begun in the very depths of a depression that had continued the better part of five years. There was little hope for the theatre even among the more optimistic of its followers. Its leading producers had lost all their money. Its more dependable angels were in a state of bankruptcy. Its better playwrights and its better actors had deserted to the motion pictures. Its theatre properties were, for the most part, in the hands of mortgagor bankers who could not, for the life of them, think of anything to do with them.

This was the beginning, in late August. Six weeks later there had occurred such a definite reawakening of interest in the theatre as to amount practically to a rebirth. Within a week four of the new plays had scored outstanding hits. Within a fortnight thereafter literally thousands of playgoers who had lost contact with if not interest in the theatre were back inquiring the cost of seats and the earliest date on which they might hope to be admitted to the luckier playhouses.

Optimism and prairie fires have something in common. They spread rapidly and fasten on everything inflammable in their path. This new theatre interest fed on the long-developing weariness of older theatregoers with the set pattern plays of the movies. It fed on the curiosity of the growing younger public that had been brought up on the movies and were eager for a change. It fed on the interest that followed the return of actors and actresses who had been popular in the theatre, had deserted to Hollywood and were now coming home to what they tactfully referred to as their first love.

But it was buoyed and sustained in greatest measure by the consistent excellence of many of the early-season plays. The drama had again justified itself as an art apart from its appeal as entertainment. It was proving that it had something to offer that no form of mechanical reproduction of entertainment could satisfactorily replace.

And so, though there were the expected letdowns, and though the season, by the time it had reached its concluding weeks, had consistently settled to a reasonably common average in the quality of plays produced, that early season glow of enthusiasm was never completely dimmed.

The effects of the depression, however, were still noticeably in evidence. The two actors' charities, the Stage Relief Fund and the Actors' Dinner club, had been continued to meet the needs of long lists of unemployed. Of the 300,000 meals served in three seasons by the former 200,000 were served free to members of the profession. The work of the Fund included the collection and disbursement of $96,000 and quantities of food and clothes among 6,000 theatre dependents in this theatre capital alone. I have no exact record of the number of benefits given for various causes, but I venture to say they averaged at least two a week the season through.

It was a season of short runs. Only twenty-three of the one hundred and twenty-five musical and dramatic plays produced were given for more than a hundred performances, which, in the old days, was accepted arbitrarily as the line dividing a success from either a moderate or a complete failure. This, obviously, indicates the shrinkage in size of the normal playgoing public. The fact that the mortgagor bankers were prohibited by law from gambling with the chances of an attraction, i.e., the forcing of a run of three or four weeks in the hope of interesting the playgoing public by word of mouth reports telling the virtues of the play, also had its effect in shortening the lives of many plays that might, in other seasons, have lived, and eventually prospered.

Reports from those minor theatrical centers to the west of New York, however, were a little depressing. Neither Chicago, Philadelphia nor Boston has ever gone through so disastrous a year insofar as its legitimate theatres are concerned as it did last year. Western theatre centers are normally a year later than the theatre capital of the country in reflecting conditions. By the same token this year should see a marked and sustained revival in theatre interest.

Katharine Cornell, who devoted the season to touring the country with a repertory of three plays, "The Barretts of Wimpole Street," "Romeo and Juliet" and "Candida," covered 18,000 miles and visited seventy towns and cities, playing to a succession of enthused audiences. Eva Le Gallienne, making a similar tour, traveled 12,000 miles and visited forty-seven cities, playing five plays, "Romeo and Juliet," "Hedda Gabler," "A Doll's House," "The Master Builder" and "Alice in Wonderland," also to large attendance.

These two actresses returned to New York entirely convinced that the road is waiting eagerly, even impatiently, for the predicted renaissance of the spoken drama, insisting only that it shall be worthy in quality and honestly sold according to the advertising promises of its promoters.

The Theatre Guild, still America's most important producing unit in the theatre, scored outstanding successes with its first two plays, Maxwell Anderson's "Mary of Scotland" and Eugene O'Neill's "Ah, Wilderness!" and a moderate success with Lawrence Langner's and Arthur Guiterman's adaptation of Molière's "School for Husbands." Wexley's "They Shall Not Die" ran for eight weeks, O'Neill's "Days Without End" for seven and Dawn Powell's "Jig Saw" for five. It was so unexpectedly good a season for the Guild that even its directors were surprised.

Repeal may have had some slight effect upon the increased attendance at the theatres, but no one believes it did. There were speakeasies before there were taverns. New York was never exactly athirst in the dryest days of prohibition, and there were just as many theatre parties arriving late to disturb audience and actors in the old days as there are in the new. The conviviality of the new-deal drinking salons is as likely to lead to dancing as it is to playgoing. And there circumstantial evidence ceases. Several of the theatre managers tried to induce the liquor board heads to permit the introduction of bars in the theatres, but refusal was quick and flat.

Going back to the beginning of the season in those bad, black depression days, nothing worth recording filtered through the summer months except a few revivals. In early September Earl Carroll tried combining mystery drama with his familiar exhibit of legs, lingerie and license in his annual "Vanities." The result was sufficiently popular to keep "Murder at the Vanities" running for 207 performances.

Two weeks later or thereabouts one of the newer and younger producing firms, the Messrs. Potter and Haight, offered "Double Door," a shivery melodrama that caught the fancy of those who like shivery melodramas, and the season was on.

The Joe Cook show, "Hold Your Horses," came into the Winter Garden, struggled none too confidently through ten weeks and left. The Group Theatre, chief of the experimental producing associations next to the Theatre Guild and the Civic Repertory, produced "Men in White" at the Broadhurst and the young men who write reviews for the newspapers were delighted. Three days later, Courtenay Burr, also a newcomer among the producers, offered "Sailor, Beware!" a rowdy but funny farce, at the Lyceum, and there was more cheering. Two days after this Sam H. Harris released "As Thousands Cheer" at the Music Box, a revue written by Irving Berlin and Moss Hart, and played principally by Clifton Webb, Marilyn Miller, Helen Broderick, Leslie Adams and Ethel Waters. Again the reviewers rushed to their typewriters and filled their columns with superlatives of praise. By this time Broadway was reeling a bit under the impact of three over-night hits. Before it could recover balance the Guild offered O'Neill's "Ah, Wilderness!" with George M. Cohan as its featured player and the celebration of a reborn theatre achieved a new peak.

The following week brought "The Pursuit of Happiness," an amusing comedy in which report is made of the old-time American custom of bundling, a Puritan compromise with conscience that saved firewood. When a young man called upon a young lady in revolutionary days, and stayed beyond the time when the log fire burned out, he was invited to sit up in bed with his girl friend with a saw-toothed bundling board between them. The Lawrence Langners were the authors and the comedy ran through the better part of the season.

Two other Langner enterprises, "Champagne Sec," in which Lawrence was assisted by Robert Simon, who wrote the lyrics, and "School for Husbands," in which Arthur Guiterman did the book in verse, were moderate successes in October, the first an adaptation of "Die Fledermaus" and the second a rewriting of Molière's comedy.

"Ten Minute Alibi," a fascinatingly ingenious mystery murder play from London; a pleasant little comedy called "The Curtain Rises," in which a youthful spinster experiences the thrill of engaging an actor to make love to her; and "The Green Bay Tree," an exquisite production concerned with the lives of certain exquisites, were in the October list.

So, too, were "Let 'Em Eat Cake," an eagerly awaited sequel to "Of Thee I Sing" of the year before, by the same Kaufman-Gershwin-Ryskind trio, which suffered the common fate of sequels, and "Her Master's Voice," which brought the brighter and better Clare Kummer of "Good Gracious Annabelle" days back into the theatre after she had suffered an early season failure with "Amourette." With "Her Master's Voice" came Roland Young, Mrs. Kummer's gifted son-in-law, and Laura Hope Crews, both of whom had been five years away from Broadway helping the picture makers in the West. These two and Elizabeth Patterson, also a popular comedienne, helped to lift the Kummer comedy to the "Best Play" class, as more fully appears later in this volume.

Now for a stretch the plays were what might be termed interestingly unimportant. Item, a play called "Spring in Autumn," in which Blanche Yurka, as a slightly eccentric prima donna, displayed the parlor trick of singing a bar or two of an aria while standing on her head; item, "The World Waits," a fairly audacious dramatization of Admiral Byrd's first Little America adventure; item, "The Divine Drudge," a pattern comedy introducing Mady Christians, a German-American actress whose fame and reputation have been made in Germany, and who has just come home to stay, and "Thunder on the Left," a sensitive little comedy made by Jean Ferguson Black from Christopher Morley's novel. The Morley story of the little boy who wishes he could project himself into the future and have a peep at what life is going to mean for him as an adult, and who is pretty sadly disappointed when he finds grown-ups acting as grown-ups do, suffered from a mixture of moods that it is harder to reconcile on the stage than in a book.

Approaching the holidays with practically everybody happier than the year before Max Gordon produced a new Jerome Kern-Otto Harbach operetta, "Roberta." Its start was slow, but after five weeks it built rapidly into one of the season's most successful musical comedies. Thanks in part to a cast that included that old favorite, Fay Templeton, come again to the stage; Tamara, a Russian singer of songs ("Smoke in Your Eyes" was her chief contribution to "Roberta"); Lyda Roberti, a popular lady clown, and Bob Hope, a smart fellow familiar with the patter of the master of ceremonies.

A second hilarious evening with the robust and rowdy type of farce, played on an ingeniously contrived double-deck stage, was "She Loves Me Not," which Howard Lindsay fashioned from an Edward Hope story. So contagious was the broad humor of this one that it played through the season, with a little middle Westerner, Polly Walters, making the chief hit as a night club girl escaped from Philadelphia in dancing trunks and a brassière and seeking sanctuary, in a manner of speaking, in Princeton college.

"The Drums Begin" was an elaborate mixture of motion picture technique and imaginative drama in which a company engaged to make a picture called "No More War" in both French and German finds itself starting a new war during rehearsals. The significance of the title was found in a prophecy that already the drums begin to roll for a conflict that is coming. Rather a pity "The Drums Begin" was weakened by its elaborations and muddled plot. Good idea. Howard Irving Young wrote it.

A second melodrama, "The Dark Tower," written by Alexander Woollcott and George Kaufman, played for seven weeks and apparently entertained its audiences as thoroughly as it entertained this writer, but the audiences were not large enough to make the play pay, despite outstanding performances by Basil Sydney, Margalo Gillmore and others.

Now came the Theatre Guild's second sensation, Anderson's "Mary of Scotland," with little Helen Hayes stretching her five feet two to the stature of a queen, more of which appears elsewhere in these pages. And a few days after "Mary" a production of what was literally a "dirty" play in that its locale was a shack alongside a dirt road in the depths of Georgia, and its characters a group of white trash slimy with the soil, of animal-like instincts and reactions. This was a piece called "Tobacco Road" after the novel by Erskine Caldwell from which it was taken by Jack Kirkland. As Miss Hayes had done in "Mary of Scotland," Henry Hull, playing the chief character of "Tobacco Road," a shiftless, adulterous Georgia Cracker named Jeeter Lester, scored the hit of his recent career. His performance of old Jeeter was graphic and compelling. It became town talk and the fortunes of the play were immeasurably brightened. When failure threatened, first audiences turning away from the dirt play feeling a bit soiled by the contact, Matthew Zimmerman, a far-seeing head of the Leblang cutrate ticket agency in New York, took the play over and nursed it into a success that continued the season through. When Mr. Hull was called to the cinema James Barton, the dancer, took up the rôle and also scored a hit in it. Going to prove something or other in the age-old controversy as to whether the part makes the actor or the actor the part.

The Theatre Union, a group of young stage enthusiasts determined that the drama of social propaganda shall have a chance in New York, presented an anti-war play by George Sklar and Albert Maltz, "Peace on Earth," at the Civic Repertory Theatre, which Eva Le Gallienne had left vacant to go touring. With the support of hundreds of radical and political groups it achieved a run of 143 performances. It was followed later by a second play of propaganda, "Stevedore," by Mr. Sklar and Paul Peters, which enjoyed a similar experience.

Guthrie McClintic brought Miriam Hopkins back from the coast to play the heroine of Owen Davis's "Jezebel," the story of a fiery young Southerner who thought to be revenged for her hurt pride when the lover she left married another girl. Tallulah Bankhead had been cast and rehearsed in the part, but her health failed. Miss Hopkins gave a good performance, but the play was not for her.

The same month, which was December, Katharine Hepburn, whose pictures had been filling the cinema cathedrals with excited audiences and the motion picture fans with thrill upon thrill, thought also to make her reëntrance on Broadway as a legitimate dramatic actress. Jed Harris provided a play called "The Lake," written by two English players, Dorothy Massingham and Murray MacDonald. In it Miss Hepburn appears as a high-strung, sensitive young English girl who thought she was in love with a married neighbor and who, becoming affianced to a second suitor to break the charm, discovers that she really prefers the new love. As the now happy couple start gaily on their honeymoon their car skids into a lake and the boy is killed. For a time the heroine contemplates suicide, and you may take your choice as to whether or not she carries out the threat when she leaves the house at the last curtain.

Miss Hepburn's reception on her reappearance was warmly enthusiastic. It probably was the most difficult task any actress of the winter had faced. Did this young woman, shot spectacularly from an exceedingly limited stage experience to the very peak of acclaim as a super-star of the movies—did she or did she not deserve that success? Naturally, the actress, being conscious of this silent but ominous appraisal of her work, was nervous, strident and fairly unhappy her opening night. But she gave the best she had to give. Her newspaper critics were kindly non-committal for the most part. Her audiences continued enthusiastic and the advance sale of seats had been tremendous. When it ran out and there was talk of a road tour Mr. Harris suddenly decided to give Miss Hepburn back to the screen. By rumor he was paid $100,000 to do this by the picture company that thought thus to maintain the Hepburn picture popularity in those minor theatre centers of which "the road" is composed.

Eddie Dowling took a simple domestic comedy that Sophie Kerr and Anna Steese Richardson had written and produced it with J. C. Nugent in the name part and Elizabeth Risdon playing opposite, the same being "Big Hearted Herbert." It was extravagant as farce, but its foundations had a solid comedic value. A pompously self-made man tries to bring up his family on the theory that what was good enough for him is good enough for them. They turn the tables on him effectively by giving him what he asks for and he pleads to go back to the reëstablished standards of the rising generation.

Early in the new year, Billie Burke Ziegfeld having transferred the use of her late husband's name as the master of the "Ziegfeld Follies" to the Messrs. Shubert, his bitter rivals of other days, there was a new "Ziegfeld Follies" produced at the Winter Garden. It was, with Fannie Brice and Willie Howard featured, a lively and amusing burlesque and continued successfully for 174 performances.

A play on which Eugene O'Neill had been working feverishly for months, a psychological study of the mental conflict that may assail a sincere religionist who strays from his faith, entitled "Days Without End," was produced in January by the Theatre Guild and suffered a comparatively quick failure, though it ran through the subscription list with a week added, a net of fifty-seven performances. As drama it was extravagantly praised by Catholic reviewers as being the greatest of the O'Neill contributions to the theatre. Others found it, as did Brooks Atkinson of the *New York Times,* one of the few blunders committed by the first dramatist. "The story-telling is sophomoric; the writing is no match for the theme," wrote Mr. Atkinson. "Mr. O'Neill has tremendous brute power when he is crowding the night sky with 'strange images of death.' But when there is need of exaltation and rhapsody he is unequal to the emergency."

The story is of one who had come to doubt God and then, in his hour of need, flew back to the religion of his youth and sought forgiveness and regeneration at the foot of the crucifix. As a result of his spiritual rebirth his baser self was destroyed and his wife, who had been dying as a result of her discovery of his broken faith, was saved.

The character of the leading protagonist was played by two actors, the real man by Earl Larimore, the baser self, half masked and invisible to the other players, by Stanley Ridges. It was a reapplication, on the playwright's part, of the dual personality theme of "The Great God Brown," and the spoken thoughts of "Strange Interlude."

It was a year of simple reactions in the theatre. There was little or no interest in striking novelties and subtle themes. About this time a delicately sensitive and profoundly sincere play, "Come of Age," written in rhymed prose by the Clemence Dane whose "A Bill of Divorcement" was a success of other years, was produced by the Delos Chappell who had much to do with the establishment of the Central City drama festivals in Colorado. This was the story of the poet, Thomas Chatterton, taken out of life at the untimely age of seventeen and returned, in the play, through a compact with Death to be permitted to come of age normally before he is compelled to keep his rendezvous with eternity. In life young Chatterton would sing his songs of beauty and life and love. His meeting with a modern lady of passion disturbs and finally disgusts him and he is content, in the end, to return to that other world from which he has fled.

A small public delighted in "Come of Age" and the performances of Judith Anderson and Stephen Haggard, a young Englishman imported to play the Chatterton rôle. But the larger public would not buy. Less than five weeks and the play was gone.

A sensitively fine little drama woven about the tragedy of the children of divorced parents, "Wednesday's Child," of which further report is hereinafter made; an unhappy dramatization of the tragedy that followed the career of old John Brown of Ossawatomie, with George Abbott miscast in the name part, were also January productions. So was the A. E. Thomas comedy, "No More Ladies," which set the town laughing cheerfully again after a spell of serious drama, and which also is included with the best plays of this issue.

It was at this time that Arthur Hopkins, who previously had taken no part in the activities of the season, took charge of the production of Philip Barry's "The Joyous Season." This was the comedy that Mr. Barry had written hoping it would serve Maude Adams as a medium for her return to the stage. Miss Adams, unwisely I think, did not agree with Mr. Barry and the leading rôle, that of a Mother Superior who, pausing briefly at the home of troubled kin folk, helps them straighten out their family problems, was given to Lillian Gish. Miss Gish performed it sympathetically and well, but there were divided opinions in the reviews, and divided audiences in attendance during the two weeks the engagement lasted.

In February the chief theatre excitements were caused by three English plays with, for the most part, imported English companies. These were a pleasant comedy of medical student life in Edinburgh called "The Wind and the Rain," written by Merton Hodge; "The Shining Hour," a domestic drama by Keith Winter which brought Gladys Cooper, long a popular leading woman in London, to America for her first professional appearance, and "Richard of Bordeaux," a robust historical drama which dealt revealingly with the life of the rather precious Edward II of England. It was written by the Agnes MacIntosh who prefers to be known under her pen name of Gordon Daviot and played by Dennis King.

"The Shining Hour," with Raymond Massey and Adrianne Allen supporting Miss Cooper, proved an immediate success and played successfully for ten weeks. "Richard of Bordeaux" closed in five, but went on to a more definite success in Chicago. "The Wind and the Rain" struggled along for twelve weeks, proving greatly to the liking of those who approve the sentimental drama, but missing by just that much the approval of those who prefer stronger meat in their theatre.

An amusing experiment about this time was the production of an opera called "Four Saints in Three Acts." A perfectly mad text had been supplied by Gertrude Stein, who flatters herself that she writes perfectly by ear, even though no one can make sense of what she writes, and to this a really beautiful score was fitted by Virgil Thompson. Because of the score, and the curious interest attaching to the production as a novelty, "Four Saints" continued for four weeks and later came back for a return engagement of two more.

A late February success that stimulated interest in the entire list of late season plays was the Max Gordon production of "Dodsworth," being the Sinclair Lewis story as dramatized by Sidney Howard. Walter Huston came in from the cinema studios to score his greatest Broadway success in the name part, and Fay Bainter, playing opposite him, was also happily cast. "Dodsworth" ran till midsummer, and was then suspended for four weeks to let Mr. Huston play Othello in Central City.

A few weeks later a second and, to the author, a much more

important play, Howard's dramatization of Paul de Kruif's chapter on Walter Reed's search for the yellow-fever-bearing mosquito in Cuba, called "Yellow Jack," was given an impressive production by Guthrie McClintic at the Martin Beck Theatre. Admittedly a history rather than a drama, played for two hours without an intermission, with the historical scenes flashed on and off in motion picture sequence, the play won the extravagantly worded praise of most of the drama reviewers. The public, however, being difficult to win to the support of the laboratory drama, no matter how exalted and fine the sample, was not responsive. Eight weeks and this really fine play was withdrawn. During the run a solid individual success was won by John Miltern, an actor of other years who left the stage to become a broker, and returned to play the Reed part with impressive dignity. He was abetted by such good actors as Robert Keith, Barton MacLane and Eduardo Cianelli.

In March there arrived at the Fulton Theatre a revue called "New Faces." It was, according to the legend of the hoardings, a production sponsored by Charles B. Dillingham, years back the proud possessor of great honor and reputation as a producer of plays. The arrangement with Mr. Dillingham had been engineered by an erstwhile star of his, Elsie Janis, who, coming on from the Pacific coast for a visit, found, first, Leonard Sillman, Nancy Hamilton, Imogene Coca, James Shelton and perhaps twenty other youngsters raring to reconstruct a revue Sillman had staged on the coast the year before, and, second, Mr. Dillingham, depressed by the depression, without an occupation to keep his mind off his worries. These two, said Elsie, should be brought together and they were.

"New Faces" proved fresh and original. Its youthful cast was filled to its eyelashes with pep and eagerness, and the show, though small-time in the matter of physical settings and artistic limitations, had snap and humor. The crowd liked it. With the aid of a cöoperative payroll arrangement it played on through the spring.

An incident of the spring was the production of two new plays by John Howard Lawson in the same week. One was "The Pure in Heart," reciting the adventure of a village Annabelle who approaches the Big City ready to make such sacrifices as she may be asked to make to further her success. Her adventures being unhappy, she finally turns to a boy who has inadvertently taken to crime. They are shot trying to escape the law and manage a new start. It ran a week.

The second, "Gentlewoman," revealing the frustrations of a variety of groping souls, offers the experience of Gwyn, wife of a wealthy broker who kills himself. At loose ends, Gwyn turns to a radical writing man, living with him until his passion for the open road and complete liberty of thought and action draw him again into the world and leaves her carrying his child and still mystified with life. It ran a week and a half.

If any would know Mr. Lawson's opinion of the gentlemen who write dramatic criticisms for the New York papers, and who were, he believes, responsible for the failure of his two plays, he may read it in the preface to the printed versions of the plays called "Reckless Preface" published by the Messrs. Farrar and Rinehart.

An item also of the late spring was the production of the first of many Brontë plays promised New York to reach this territory. This was "Moor Born," written by Dan Totheroe. Helen Gahagan, home from the coast with her actor husband, Melvyn Douglas, who staged the play while he was himself acting in "No More Ladies," played Emily Brontë, Frances Starr was the Charlotte and Edith Barrett the Anne. It was an agreeably satisfying performance and of real interest to Brontë worshipers. But here again literary history failed to produce a cohesive drama and the play was withdrawn in four weeks.

The death of Milton Aborn having taken out of the theatre its finest and most devoted Gilbert and Sullivan enthusiast, there was fear expressed by the faithful for the future of their beloved repertory. A young man named Chartoc, S. M. Chartoc, who had been an Aborn assistant, elected to carry on the tradition and there were the usual spring revivals of the Gilbert-Sullivan repertory. Very well supported, too. "The Mikado," "The Pirates of Penzance," "Pinafore," "Trial by Jury" and "Iolanthe" were all given.

The Theatre Guild produced a sixth play to keep its record clean with the subscribers, but it need not have troubled. "Jig Saw," a brightly written but fairly wobbly comedy of the sex issue in a penthouse, barely lasted out the subscription period. Dawn Powell, novelist, wrote it, and is pretty sure to write a better one next time. Reaching out for more guest stars the Guild took Ernest Truex and Spring Byington over to play the leads.

A reasonably interesting mystery, "Invitation to a Murder," was on the spring list; also a prize-fighter farce, "The Milky Way," in which a shifty but dumb driver of a Borden milk wagon was accidently lifted into a middleweight championship. Hugh O'Connell played it.

Asadata Defora, whose great-great-grandfather was slave to a Nova Scotia family, and who has made a study of authentic African dance rhythms, arranged a dance opera called "Kykunkor, or Witch Woman." It was produced obscurely in a hall, caught the attention of the town's dance authorities and was moved into a theatre with exciting results for several weeks.

And that about ended this particular season. Statistically it offers no startling changes from the figures of depression years. But it always should be known as the year in which a theatre that was dead came again to life and lived on happily, probably forever after.

There were less than 130 productions, both dramatic and musical, depending on how you think revivals should be classified. The average of failures was, however, less than usual. Many weak plays have been weeded out and a good deal of "angel money" has been lost to the discouragement of its contributors, the last few years. This has served to turn show business back to its older and more experienced directors.

THE SEASON IN CHICAGO

By Charles Collins
Dramatic Critic of the *Chicago Tribune*

THE picture darkens.

The year that brought a vigorous renaissance into the theatrical life of New York City found the Chicago stage on a steepening descent into the shadows of collapse. Conditions, not only in the supply of plays but also in the public reaction at the box-office, have been so discouraging that the breakdown of the drama in this capital city of the populous midlands has become a matter of general comment. The man on the street talks about it and wonders why.

The element of time-lag may have been a factor in the situation, for in general the Chicago stage, being almost entirely dependent upon New York as a source of material, runs a year behind the fountain-head in its catalogue of offerings. This year's Broadway hits are usually Chicago's long runs for next season.

Another point to take into consideration in analyzing Chicago's alarming failure to give consistent and enthusiastic patronage to the relatively few first-class theatrical productions of the past year is the concentration of its attention during the period upon the great exposition called A Century of Progress. The city has contained an over-abundance of entertainment which competed with the stage. An amazing efflorescence of cabaret amusement all over the city preceded and accompanied the World's Fair sessions; and the cost of an evening in one of these show-giving cafés, if conservatively managed, would be no more of an extravagance than a theatre party. During the year, therefore, Chicago has been World's Fair conscious, night club conscious, jazz band conscious; but its recognition of the re-creative value of the legitimate theatre has become correspondingly vague.

The statistics which tell the story without generalizations should be submitted as evidence at this point. The total number of engagements was 43 from June 1, 1933, to June 1, 1934. Compare this figure with the returns for other years: 1932-1933 had 50; 1931-1932 had 75; 1930-1931 had 85; the pre-depression years always had more than 100.

Moreover, of these 43 engagements, only about fifty per cent (21, to be exact) deserved serious consideration as representing satisfactory work in the arts of playwrighting, acting and stage direction. The others ranged from badly disguised amateurism to small-town incompetence. The dramatic critics who had to record their impressions of this shoddy stuff reached the end of the year in a state of nerves resembling shell-shock. The fact that nearly all of these painful examples of theatrical illiteracy were "made-in-Chicago" affairs, launched with the laudable hope of giving the city an independent position in stage affairs, added to the embarrassment of the resident drama historians.

I shall now call the roll of the 21 offerings that served to keep the art of the drama alive in Chicago during this distressful year, letting the titles run in historical order:

Lenore Ulric in "Angel"; "Dinner at Eight," with the original New York cast; Katharine Cornell in "Alien Corn"; Pauline Frederick in "Her Majesty the Widow"; "Gay Divorce," with Joseph Santley, Dorothy Stone and Luella Gear; "Take a Chance," with Ole Olsen and Chic Johnson; "Dangerous Corner"; Ina Claire in "Biography"; "Sailor, Beware!" with a second cast; "Music in the Air," with the original New York company; "The Curtain Rises," with Louise Groody; Eva Le Gallienne in "Alice in Wonderland" and "Hedda Gabler"; Walter Hampden in "Richelieu," "Hamlet" and "The Servant in the House"; "Hold Your Horses," with Joe Cook; "Autumn Crocus," with Madge Kennedy and Rollo Peters; "Ten Minute Alibi," with the original cast; Dennis King in "Richard of Bordeaux"; "The Shining Hour," with Violet Heming and Conrad Nagel; "Annina," with Mme. Jeritza; "All the King's Horses," with Guy Robertson and Nancy McCord; and "Big Hearted Herbert," second company with Taylor Holmes.

The other productions may be consigned to oblivion. They were mildewed ears, blighting their wholesome brothers.

Two unclassified affairs, however, call for honorable mention. They were Cornelia Otis Skinner's programs of dramatic sequences, including "Loves of Charles II," and the engagements at the Auditorium Theater of the Monte Carlo Ballet Russe. The latter formed the highlight of the year in attendance and general interest.

The Russian ballet's relation to drama may be slight, and its appeal may be primarily to the class called music-lovers rather than to playgoers, but it has an important place in the theatre arts. Therefore I wish to call attention to the fact that Chicago, in the year during which it neglected the conventional theatre in a depressing manner, went mad over the company of young Russian émigrés who, under the direction of Col. De Basil, are reviving the great tradition of the historic Diaghileff troupe. The Auditorium was sold out to its enormous seating capacity for almost every performance of the two one-week engagements. The dancers became the talk of the town.

The incident proves, I believe, that Chicago is still eager to go to the theatre, when it is offered something that arouses its curiosity and admiration. Secondly, I believe that it indicates plainly the value of able management. The Monte Carlo Ballet Russe, successful everywhere on tour, was managed with skill and aggressiveness by an impresario (S. Hurok) who apparently was not afflicted with defeatism. He had the grand old Morris Gest enthusiasm and drive, and a staff of first-class men.

This was in striking contrast with the feebleness, the tiredness, the hopelessness of theatrical exploitation in general during the year, as I have glimpsed its workings. It has been my impression that the theatres in Chicago, and the touring companies that came to Chicago, have been operated by members of a financial suicide club. The business side of the theatre on tour appears to have lost its heart and its will-to-live. And if this is an exaggerated view, it is undeniable that the will-to-plan and power of decision have become dormant, so far as the theatres of Chicago are concerned. Up to the date of the writing of this chapter (June 29, 1934) not a single resident management has made formal announcement of plans for next season. The Muse of the Drama has become, for me, a distracted and neurotic lady who can't make up her mind.

The partial collapse of the professional theatre in Chicago has been accompanied by an acceleration of activity among the amateurs. The little theatre movement has expanded, and the young folks who are always just dying to act have been having a high old time. Several of the abler groups, such as the Uptown Players, and the Players Guild, came down-town with their productions and gave creditable semi-pro performances. A staging of "Girls in Uniform," with a cast largely recruited from the amateurs of the Jewish People's Institute, reached professional value through the able direction of Charles K. Freeman, and also revealed, in the heroine's rôle, a gifted girl named Shaindel Kalish, about whose happy future the prophets were unanimous.

The engagements during the year were generally brief, for Chicago has returned, from the booking agents' point of view, to its status of thirty years ago as a "two weeks' stand." However, "Dinner at Eight" lasted through the first World's Fair summer; Dennis King in "Richard of Bordeaux" had a rousing six weeks; and on a cut-rate basis "The Curtain Rises" won the year's record with fourteen weeks.

THE SEASON IN SAN FRANCISCO

By George C. Warren

Drama Editor of *The San Francisco Chronicle*

SAN FRANCISCO theatregoers lived on a thin diet in its playhouses during the year that began June 1, 1933, and ended May 31, 1934. The starvation point was reached several times when none of the half dozen theatres was open. There is a happier prospect for the new year.

Six touring companies visited the city, were well received and did good business. Ten productions were made by Henry Duffy or Belasco and Curran, and four others by various individuals. A meager array of attractions, surely. However, the plays presented were well done in most cases, several of them extraordinarily well presented.

The year began with "Dinner at Eight" still running at the Curran Theater. The cast was headed by Hedda Hopper, Louis Calhern, Alice White, Jobyna Howland, Martha Sleeper, Huntly Gordon and Georgia Caine. The run lasted several weeks.

Five of the traveling companies played at the Columbia Theater, and the sixth, Maurice Schwartz and his Yiddish company in "Yoshe Kalb" at the Tivoli Theater, the only legitimate attraction to be seen at that house. Attendance was light.

Katharine Cornell made her return in "Romeo and Juliet," with Basil Rathbone as her Romeo. Her Juliet, then new in her repertoire, showed great promise when she grows easy in the part and used to the conventions of poetic drama. The production was excellent, filled with youth and action, and played with only one intermission. "Candida" and "The Barretts of Wimpole Street" were also done.

The largest audiences for "Romeo and Juliet" and "Candida" on Miss Cornell's tour attended the play here.

Eva Le Gallienne followed shortly afterward at the Columbia, presenting a repertoire of Ibsen plays, "Hedda Gabler," "A Doll's House," and "The Master Builder." Egon Brecher joined the company here to play Solness in "The Master Builder," which was added to the repertoire in San Francisco. In "A Doll's House" Josephine Hutchinson was the Nora, and played the part brilliantly. Miss Le Gallienne contented herself with the rôle of Mrs. Linde.

Walter Hampden presented four plays, making his first appearance here in "Richelieu." Other plays were "Hamlet," "Macbeth" and "The Servant in the House."

Podrecca's "Teatro dei Piccoli" came for a week and remained for two more. The town liked his marionettes. He was on his way to Hollywood for the purpose of making his "little people" part of the Fox Films' picture, "I Am Suzanne," which starred Lilian Harvey.

Olsen and Johnson brought their production of "Take a Chance" to the Columbia, with Lillian Miles singing the Ethel Merman songs. A single week was enough for the show.

A production of S. N. Behrman's "Biography," sponsored in Los Angeles, played two weeks at the Columbia to fair business. Alice Brady had the Ina Claire rôle. Ada May played the ingénue part, and Huntly Gordon, Douglas Wood and Hardie Albright were others in the cast.

Guy Robertson, Charlotte Lansing, Wyndham Standing and Roland Woodruff were principals in a revival of Victor Herbert's "The Only Girl," done at the Columbia Theater for a short run.

One of the last productions made by Belasco and Curran before the breaking up of that producing firm, was "Music in the Air," in which the principals were Vivienne Segal, Walter Woolf, Montagu Shaw and Christian Rub. The operetta had a short run.

Perhaps the highlight of the season was the appearance of Will Rogers in Eugene O'Neill's "Ah, Wilderness!" at the Curran Theater. Henry Duffy was the producer who induced Rogers to play his first part in a straight play. His success was enormous. The engagement of two weeks was stretched to three, and business was very big. William Janney, Anne Shoemaker and Helen Flint were in the cast.

The two big New York farce successes of the year, "Sailor, Beware!" and "She Loves Me Not" failed to please San Francisco playgoers, and had short runs. Homer Curran was the producer. For "Sailor" he had Regis Toomey, Muriel Kirkland, John Alexander—Robert Mantell's leading man—and Ray Cooke of the films. Dorothy Lee, Russell Hopton, Philip Faversham, son of William; John Arledge, and W. P. Carleton, who used to sing leading baritone rôles in comic operas, were in the cast of "She Loves Me Not."

Duffy brought Francis Lederer here to act in "Autumn Crocus."

He was enthusiastically received, and devoted much time to talking on his favorite theme, "Peace." Lederer is to come back in the autumn to play at the Greek Theater in Berkeley.

"Twentieth Century" with many of the New York cast was produced by Duffy and Curran at the Curran Theater. Eugenie Leontovich, Moffat Johnston, Matt Briggs, Ray Roberts, James Spottswood and James Burtis played the leads.

Henry Duffy's last production at the Alcazar Theater was Sidney Howard's "The Late Christopher Bean," in which Charlotte Greenwood was starred as Abby. She played the rôle straight, showing she is something more than a clown. Reginald Mason and Craufurd Kent were in the supporting cast.

Homer Curran put on "Show Boat" with an extravagant production, but it did not draw. His principals were Perry Askam, who was starred; Estelle Taylor, Charlotte Lansing, Nina Olivetti, William Kent and Cecil Cunningham.

Amateur and semi-professional groups in and around San Francisco were busy. One of the important events was the appearance of Mimi Aguglia, the Sicilian actress who some years ago made a sensation in New York in a folk play called "Malia," at the Greek Theater, Berkeley, in Oscar Wilde's "Salome." Mme. Aguglia played the rôle in English. Afterwards the play was done at the Columbia Theater in San Francisco. Also at the Greek Theater there was an excellent student production of Aristophanes' "The Birds," which was dressed with unusual beauty from costume designs by Betty Bates, a young Oakland girl.

The Little Theater of the University of California did several notable things under the direction of Edwin Duerr. These included a stylized performance of "The Merry Wives of Windsor"; a production on an architectural stage of Andre Obey's "Lucrece" and a well-acted performance of "The Brothers Karamazov."

Palo Alto, a nearby city in which Stanford University is located, was given a fully equipped playhouse by Mrs. Louis Stern. The house was opened by the Community Players with a production of "Grumpy," Cyril Maude's old play. During the year Aurania Rouverol's comedy of adolescence, "Growing Pains," which was done later in Pasadena and New York, had its première. Maxwell Anderson's "Night Over Taos" was another of the group's good productions.

The Playmakers of Berkeley, a group ten years old, gave its usual four performances of original one-act plays. This body has produced 160 of these short dramas in the course of the years.

Martin Flavin's drama of the industrial age, "Amaco," was produced at Carmel-by-the-Sea, and Martin S. Rosenblatt's bedroom farce, "It Takes a Frenchman," had its first performance at Reginald Travers' Playhouse in San Francisco.

Andre Ferrier offered a beautiful production of Maeterlinck's "Pelleas and Melisande" in his small theatre, and later in the Memorial Opera House, gave an elaborate performance of Molière's "Le Bourgeois Gentilhomme."

THE SEASON IN SOUTHERN CALIFORNIA

By Edwin Schallert

A SINGULAR theatrical season, during which an ever-prevalent monotony of doomed attractions was broken here and there by a phenomenal success, has been recorded in Southern California. While recovery of the show world is chronicled in the East, the western part of the Continent is slow to feel the benefits of a similar revivification. Play-giving in the great majority of cases has, if anything, sunk to an unhappier estate, what with rabid price-cutting on tickets, give-aways and other undermining customs in vogue.

Henry Duffy has stood firm through it all as the only regularly surviving producer of class entertainment. Even the Belasco-Curran offerings, so representative in the past, have been sporadic. Other undertakings have been fitful, and, for the most part, of mediocre quality. Only the community theatres continue their budding and blooming, with the Pasadena Community Playhouse still in the forefront, and the Beverly Hills Theatre for Professionals, the Gateway, the Spotlight and one or two others evidencing increase in scope and activity.

Some of these theatres now correspond virtually to the summer try-out institutions around New York, operating, however, all the year round. Here the ambitious writer of plays has the chance to exhibit his wares. The object is not so much a Broadway production, but a sale to the movies. And though the actual closing of a deal is somewhat rare, there have been a few. "The Human Side" done at the Gateway, was purchased, and its author, Christine Ames, engaged by one of the studios, while the Hollytown, managed by Mrs. Lela Rogers, mother of Ginger Rogers, provided a film subject in "Let Who Will Be Clever," which emerged on the screen as "Arabella."

The Pasadena Community Playhouse achieved its tour de force in the staging of "Cavalcade" for the first time in America. It also presented a roster of plays that were in many respects unusual, like Gogol's "Inspector General" with Leonid Snegoff and Bradley Page; "The Playboy of the Western World," with Douglass Montgomery; "The Moon and Sixpence," with Ian

Keith; "St. Joan" by George Bernard Shaw, with Violette Wilson and Irving Pichel; "The Fan" by Goldoni, and "Alien Corn" by Sidney Howard. Premières included "Man of Wax," with Lloyd Corrigan and Moroni Olsen, and "Growing Pains," with Junior Durkin and Charlotte Henry.

Outstanding in the professional realm were two curiously contrasted enterprises—one the brilliant production of "Ah, Wilderness!" by Duffy, with Will Rogers starred in the George M. Cohan rôle, and the other that most amazing antique melodrama, "The Drunkard," which went into its second year.

"Ah, Wilderness!" was the most impressive step forward taken in the Coast drama in a number of years. It is the expectation of Duffy to do other productions of this sort, with the admission price raised as in the instance of the O'Neill play.

"The Drunkard" is a curiosity and a freak, associated with the psychological change contingent on repeal, and the revival of the old music hall mood. Given in a theatre not seating more than 100 persons, it has drawn capacity weeks on end, audiences delightedly entering into the spirit of a blood-and-thunder divertisement of yesteryear, while sipping lager, nibbling pretzels and munching popcorn. The novelty of the thing appealed, and not the least of the entertainment's facets of interest was the olio, which so often engaged guest talent from the Hollywood actor's colony.

How much of a revenue may be reaped in show-giving of the right kind in this locality is shown not only by the success of "The Drunkard," which was exceptionally well done, but also notably by the fact that the Rogers engagement in San Francisco and Los Angeles over a period of eight weeks grossed in the neighborhood of $100,000. Fine things are appreciated on the Coast, but theatregoers have so often been disappointed in the quality of productions that they want to be absolutely assured of the best before they will venture forth en masse.

They do that, of course, in the instance of Katharine Cornell, who again visited during the past season. However, in her case audiences gave their preference to "The Barretts of Wimpole Street" and "Candida" rather than "Romeo and Juliet." Shakespeare does not seem to exert much charm at the present time.

Altogether only about fifty productions of the (more or less) professional order were offered during the season, which is assuredly a low ebb. Three only out of Mr. Mantle's selection of the ten best plays were given during the season. These included "Men in White," with Roger Pryor, Miriam Jordan and Henry

Kolker; "Ah, Wilderness!" and "The Green Bay Tree." With Jane Cowl starred, "The Shining Hour" appeared officially during the 1934-35 season, the deadline between the two seasons always being more or less mythical.

"Mary of Scotland" also hovers on the horizon with Helen Gahagan, Ian Keith and Violet Kemble Cooper, but of "Dodsworth," "They Shall Not Die," "Her Master's Voice," "No More Ladies" and "Wednesday's Child" there is scant indication.

Other interesting and successful productions included "Counsellor-at-Law," with Otto Kruger; "Autumn Crocus," with Francis Lederer and Julie Haydon; "The Late Christopher Bean," which, curiously enough, starred Charlotte Greenwood; "Ten-Minute Alibi," and—a fair hit—"Sailor, Beware!" with Regie Toomey and Muriel Kirkland. Alice Brady essayed "Biography," but rather unfortunately. Ditto for Helen Morgan in a play called "Memory." "There's Always Juliet" furnished charm with Violet Heming and Conrad Nagel, though that really belongs beyond the seasonal line. "Double Door" was played with Nance O'Neill, Genevieve Hamper, Hardie Albright and Martha Sleeper, and "One Sunday Afternoon" with Lyle Talbot, Anita Louise, Lola Lane, Hobart Cavanaugh and others.

Besides Katharine Cornell, the following visiting stars appeared: Eva Le Gallienne in "Hedda Gabler" and "The Master Builder," with Josephine Hutchinson starred in "A Doll's House"; Maurice Schwartz, immensely favored for a short engagement in "Yoshe Kalb," and Walter Hampden playing "Richelieu," "Hamlet," "Macbeth" and "The Servant in the House." Le Gallienne drew very fairly and will probably return again.

The most interesting première was "Bitter Harvest" by Katherine Turney, originally produced at the Beverly Hills Community Playhouse, and then later staged professionally, with Leslie Fenton and Lilian Bond in the leading parts. This play delved into the romance between Lord Byron and his half-sister, Augusta Leigh, legendary and real, and had the merit of being well-written.

"Low and Behold," which, much revised, became "New Faces" in New York held forth during the summer of 1933. Others that may be mentioned en passant included "The Ghost Train," "Louder Please," "Elizabeth Sleeps Out" by Leslie Howard; "The Hairy Ape" and "White Cargo," "The Whispering Gallery," "Love Chiselers," "On the Cuff," and a few others. Some negligible revivals may be noted among these.

One new evolvement is quite hopeful. The studios have been giving private performances of plays, which may eventually become public in a large way. "All Good Americans" was offered for cinema executives alone, and then at two benefit performances. That presentation belongs to the new season, however. "Double Door" and "The Pursuit of Happiness" were privately presented at another studio.

The urge to do plays, which will give opportunities to members of the stock companies in the film plants, is growing. Provided they call on the better talent of the picture colony for directorial supervision, these undertakings should come to thrive. The matter of staging such productions has been talked of for several years, but nothing has been actually done until within the past year. The royalty question has to some extent been a stumbling block, as concerns public presentations. However, that may be overcome.

Practically nothing was done with musical shows, outside of a semi-revue entertainment under the supervision of Frederick Hollander at a new intimate little showhouse, called the Tingel-Tangel Theatre. Hollander succeeded in creating a true continental atmosphere about this attraction, which enjoyed a very good run. "Take a Chance," with Olsen and Johnson, played a short engagement. Florine McKinney and Lillian Miles were the feminine leads.

"The Drunkard" was not alone as an ancient-vintage show. A theatre called Tony Pastor's was opened with "The Ticket-of-Leave Man," which continued for sundry weeks. "The Streets of New York" was elsewhere performed. Refreshments have been a feature with practically all such attractions.

While play-giving, as of several years ago, languishes, almost everything to which novelty attaches seems to have a chance, at least. Consequently everybody has lately tried to devise some new "gag" to catch the public fancy. The odder and more intimate the theatre the more it appears to capture. Dependable show presentations can meanwhile be reinstated only with the most valiant efforts to make them worth-while.

Those who know the past in this locality realize that more time and money must go to making plays interesting and successful. There is practically no place today for the shoestring production. Audiences are thoroughly disillusioned, and shun the ordinary almost habitually. However, they always have the money to pay for the distinguished undertaking. No finer proof of this could be afforded than by "Ah, Wilderness!" which is the noble memory of the past year. Of course, it is practically impossible to imagine any star as being more popular than Will Rogers.

And what an idea it was to put him in one of Eugene O'Neill's most human plays, and a character that fitted him perfectly! This was real showmanship, and more of that is needed hereabouts. It might also be noted that "Men in White" was excellently done, and enjoyed.

It is probable that next season will see a spreading of theatrical activities. Conditions are gradually becoming better on the Coast in a general way. The recovery has been slower than in the East, but promises to mature rather rapidly this coming fall and winter. With that improvement will come greater possibilities for the play in just the ordinary course of things.

Motion picture competition is not so severe today as it was when the talkies first started. That rivalry has somewhat adjusted itself, and the theatre is again finding its rightful place.

MARY OF SCOTLAND

A Drama in Three Acts

BY MAXWELL ANDERSON

IT was in late November that Maxwell Anderson's "Mary of Scotland" came trumpeting into the theatre lists, the second production of the Theatre Guild's season. We, the playgoers, professional and lay, had already been tremendously heartened by the success of O'Neill's "Ah, Wilderness!" and Kingsley's "Men in White," not to mention several plays of lesser worth but equal playing facility. "Mary of Scotland" heaped the new season's bowl and there was general rejoicing.

It seemed a fairly long way from the bold and profane "What Price Glory?" which was the first success that Anderson had shared (with Laurence Stallings as his collaborator) to "Mary of Scotland," the most eloquent historical romance drama of our time to date. And yet the grade had been taken in the vigorous stride of a playwright who is both gentle poet and rugged realist. Anderson had come honestly enough by this new success and accepted it as modestly as he did last season's Pulitzer award for "Both Your Houses."

"Mary of Scotland" was definitely popular from its first performance, with strings of superlatives trailing the performances of Helen Hayes as a small but splendidly regal queen and Philip Merivale as such a Bothwell as histories may fail to confirm but playgoers rush to adore. It ran the season through without trouble and goes into the Guild's record of major triumphs.

It is the summer of 1561 when Mr. Anderson picks up the history of Mary Stuart and begins weaving it into narrative form. The opening scene is a half-sheltered corner of the pier at Leith. "It is a sleety, windy night and the tall piles of the background and the planks underfoot shine black and icy with their coating of freezing rain."

Two iron-capped guards are trying to while away the time with a game of cards that is far from the liking of one, the loser, and is shortly discouraged further by the appearance of a tall, bearded, heavily muffled figure given to mumbling imprecations against the "papistical uses of the flesh," of which dicing and gaming, cards and drinking are a few.

Now a third guard, in considerable excitement, has come from the end of the pier to announce the arrival of the Queen's ship, but his fellows will have none of that.

"The Queen's ship, you goik!" they answer him in good soldier Scotch. "How could it be the Queen's ship? She's to come in a galley, and she's none due this month yet!"

It *is* the Queen's ship, as it shortly turns out. The muffled figure still lurking in the shadows confirms that fact, though there may have been no herald of it, nor anyone told—

"I have ways of knowing," says he. "And, hearing of it, I came myself to see this white face they speak of, and these taking graces, and to tell her to that white face of hers and despite her enchantments that we want and will have none of her here. For whatever beauty she may possess, or whatever winning airs, they are given her of the devil to cozen us, they are born solely of the concupiscence of hell and set upon her like a sign. They say when she speaks she drips honey and she smells sweet with boughten perfumes, but I say the man who tastes of her or the people who trust in her will chew on dry ashes in the last day and find no remedy for that thirst! I say she comes with a milk-white body and a tongue of music, but beware her, for she will be to you a walking curse and a walking death!"

The Earl of Bothwell has appeared on the pier. A stalwart, roughly handsome, upstanding figure of a man given to quick commands and the expectation of prompt response. He would have a chair brought by the guards. "The Queen of Scotland's stepping out of a boat in velvet shoes," says he. Let them be quick about the chair if they would not feel the weight of his fist.

The guards have scampered for the Inn of Leith and Bothwell turns to the muffled figure. This would be Master John Knox, and his presence there is a surprise to Bothwell.

"It seems some here heard of her coming, though not perhaps those she'd have chosen," he says. "You're not here, by chance, to greet the daughter of Mary of Guise?"

"If I have aught to say to her it will be for her own ears," tartly answers Knox.

"No doubt, no doubt. And I have a little observe to make to you about that, too, sir. Whatever it is you have to say to her you won't say it."

"And why not? Are the Papists muzzling the ministers of God?"

"I'm no Papist, as ye're aware, Master Knox, and if I were

I'm no such fool as to try to muzzle a minister, nevertheless, whatever it was you were going to say, you won't say it, that's my observe to you—"

"I shall say what I have come to say."

From the pier end voices are heard. The conversation is in French. And soon Mary Stuart and the Duc de Chatelherault, followed by four Marys-in-Waiting come upon the dock. This Mary is a little Queen, of gentle speech and stately bearing. Chatelherault is a fuming gallant of the courtier type. Their speech has changed to English now and is concerned principally with the distressing state of the weather. Chatelherault finds it heathenish. Mary would be loyal, even to the weather of her native Scotland. She remembers other and cheerier summers here. She recalls the bright thorn-apples of other Augusts.

"They are sweeter here than in France, as I recall," she says. "And all fruits are sweeter here, of those that grow—and the summer's sweeter—"

"And when they come they will bring excellent devices of masks and ornaments to deceive the eye, and soft words and stenches to cumber the senses of mankind," interrupts Master Knox, without further introduction. *"Adulterers, jig-masters* and the like will come in authority, and their counsel will be whoring and carousing, the flowers and fruits of evil, of that great sin, that sin that eats at the heart of the world, the church of abominations, the church of Rome."

Mary has turned to look back at this Old Man. She has been long away, she observes to Chatelherault, and the speech of her country falls strangely on her ears. Can such talk as she has heard be usual among her people?

"Yet is there a place reserved for them," continues Knox thunderously, "where the fire is unending and abates not, even as their desires abate not, where their tender flesh shall be torn from them with white-hot pincers, nor shall rank or station avail them, whether they be queens or kings or the lemans of queens and kings—"

Mary (*walking toward the intruder*)—Surely this is some jest, sir. Surely this is not said in welcome to me.

The Old Man—And what other welcome shall we give the whore of Babylon—the leprous and cankerous evangel of the Beast!

Bothwell (*entering*)—Your Majesty, they are preparing a room at the inn, and the chair will be here at once. If you would deign to take my cloak for your shoulders—

MARY—No, thank you. I wish to speak to this gentleman—

BOTHWELL—This is Master John Knox, of whom your Grace may have heard.

MARY (*crossing a little nearer* KNOX)—Nay, then I have heard of him, and I wish to speak to him. Master Knox, it is true that I am Mary Stuart, and your Queen, and I have come back from France after many years away, to take up my rule in this country. It is true, too, that I am sad to leave the south and the sun, and I come here knowing that I shall meet with difficulties that would daunt many older and wiser than I am—for I am young and inexperienced and perhaps none too adept in statecraft. Yet this is my native place, Master Knox, and I loved it as a child and still love it—and whatever I may lack in experience, whatever I may have too much of youth, I shall try to make up for if my people will help me, in tolerance, and mercy, and a quick eye for wrongs and a quick hand to right them—

THE OLD MAN—Aye, they told me you spoke honey—

MARY—And cannot you also—you and your people and those you know—cannot you too be tolerant toward me a little space while I find my way? For it will be hard enough at the friendliest.

THE OLD MAN—Woman, I remember whose daughter and whose voice you are—

MARY—If I were your daughter, Master Knox, and this task before me, would you think it fitting to lay such hard terms on me, beast and whore and I know not what? For I am not a whore, I can say truly, but the daughter of a prince, softly nurtured and loving honor and truth. Neither is my body corrupt, nor my mind. Nay, I am near to tears that you should think so, and I was not far from tears before, finding myself unexpected on this coast, and no preparation to receive me. What you have said comes as very cold comfort now when I need greeting and reassurance.

BOTHWELL—Your Majesty, if the old goat has said anything that needs retracting—

MARY (*facing* BOTHWELL)—Nay. He shall retract nothing in fear! I would have all men my friends in Scotland!

BOTHWELL—I'm afraid that's past praying for.

MARY (*facing* KNOX)—Sir. Can we not be friends?

THE OLD MAN—I fear not, madam.

MARY—I strongly desire it. I have no wish for any enemy of mine except that he become my friend. You most of all, for I have met you first, and it is an augury.

THE OLD MAN—Your Majesty, I have said what I came to say.

MARY—But you no longer mean it! See—I give you my hand, Master Knox—it is a queen's hand, and fair—and I look at you out of honest eyes—and I mean well and fairly—you cannot refuse me! Do you still hesitate? It is clean. (*She smiles. He bows stiffly over her hand.*) And will you come to see me at Holyroodhouse, and give me counsel? For God knows I shall need counsel—and I shall listen, that I promise.

THE OLD MAN—Your Majesty, I should be untrue to myself and my calling if I refused counsel where it is asked.

MARY—You will come?

THE OLD MAN—I will come.

MARY—I will send for you, and soon. (*Her words are a kindly dismissal.*)

THE OLD MAN—Good night, Your Majesty—

MARY—Good night, Master Knox.

And so it is left, with Mary wondering whether now Knox will hate her more or less, as she turns to Bothwell, remembering now that she has not heard his name. He is James Hepburn, Earl of Bothwell, the Duc de Chatelherault explains. It is the name of a friend, Mary recalls; the name of one who had fought ably for her mother. She is pleased to take his hand and his welcome.

"Tell me, my Lord of Bothwell, have I done well so far?" she queries. "Shall I make this Scotland mine?"

"Madame, it is a cold, dour, sour, bastardly villainous country, and the folk on it are a cold, dour, sour, bastardly lot of close-shaving psalm-retching villains, and I can only hope no harm will come here to that bonny face of yours, and no misery to the spirit you bring."

"Now here's a new kind of courtesy," smiles Mary.

"You'll hear far and wide I'm no courtier, madame," he answers, "but I have eyes, and I can see that the new sovereign is a sonsie lass and a keen one, and I was for her from the first I saw her face—but from my heart I could wish her a better country to rule over—"

"Now, will no one speak well of this poor Scotland of mine—?"

"Your Majesty, shall I praise it for you—as high as it deserves—?"

"Say whatever good you can!"

"Then this is Scotland, my lady: To the north a few beggarly thousands of Highland Catholics who have not yet learned the trick of wearing britches, and to the south a few beggarly thousands of Lowland Protestants whose britches have no pockets to them— Their pleasures are drinking and fighting, both of which they do badly, and what they fight about is that half of them are willing to sell their souls for a florin, whereas the other half have no expectation of getting so much. What business they have is buying cheap and selling dear, but since none of them will sell cheap and none will pay dear, the upshot is there's no business done."

"Enough! Enough! . . ."

Bothwell is still filled with apprehension and dire prophecies. This Master Knox has divided the country against her, by yelling nonsense into "the lugs of these poor, benighted, superstitious savages." There'll be bloodshed yet.

If Mary thought that, she would be of a mind to turn and bid the mariners hoist sail and put back for France.

"I shall win," she says confidently, "but I shall win in a woman's way—not by the sword!"

The chair has come and Mary has gone with Bothwell to enter it. The guards are wide-eyed with wonder. Surely this is a witch of a woman to be able to subdue Master Knox so completely. "She fair wenched him," says one. "The old man doddert a bit and then bent over like a popinjay!"

"She's that kind then?" queries another, interestedly.

"Aye. She's tha' kind," replies the first as the curtains falls.

The scene is in England. It is early morning. The sun is not yet up. At a table set in a corner of Queen Elizabeth's study at Whitehall the queen and Lord Burghley are in conference. Elizabeth is young and still beautiful, "with a crafty face." Burghley, the typical courtier, a man of positive statement but less decisive action. His papers are strewn upon the table in front of him. The light is from tall candles in a sconce behind the table.

Elizabeth would know more of the memoranda on Mary Stuart that Burghley has collected. This he has reduced to statements covering several major points. First, that Mary has crossed from France to Scotland against Elizabeth's advice, which may be accepted as a slight. Second, that Mary has been crowned Queen of Scotland, also against the wishes and in defiance of Elizabeth's policy. This can be construed as a breach of friendship, or it may be overlooked. Third, Mary is a Catholic, related by blood to the most powerful Catholic house in France, which constitutes her a danger to Protestant England. Fourth, she is next heir, after Elizabeth, to the throne of England, and already held by Catholic Europe to be the rightful Queen of England. Fifth, Elizabeth is held by Catholic Europe to be a pretender, the illegitimate daughter of Henry VIII and Anne Boleyn.

"Sixth, these things being true," Lord Burghley sums up, "Your Majesty must not allow Marie Stuart to succeed as Queen of Scotland. For insofar as she is secure in Scotland you are insecure in England. Your Majesty will forgive my bad habit of setting down in writing what is so obvious, but it is only by looking hard at these premises that I am able to discover what must be done!"

Marie Stuart, in Burghley's opinion, must be defeated. England must pick a quarrel and send an army into Scotland. Excuse can be found for a declaration of war.

So much Elizabeth admits. But let them not move too hastily. There must be a better way. It is difficult for Elizabeth to believe that in all those voluminous notes of Burghley's he has set down no other method of accomplishing their aims save by warfare—"the last resort, the most difficult, costly and hazardous of all."

"It is the only sure method, and you cannot afford to fail," persists Burghley.

"My dear Burghley, in any project which affects England and our own person so nearly we have no intention of failing," answers Her Majesty. "But you have overlooked in your summary two considerations which simplify the problem. One is the internal dissension. In Scotland, half Protestant, half Catholic, and divided in a mortal enmity—"

"Overlook it! Madame, it is the main argument for an immediate declaration of war— Edinburgh would rally to your arms overnight. This is our opportunity to unite England and Scotland!"

"A war would unite Scotland against us—unite Scotland under Mary. No—it is necessary first to undermine her with her own subjects."

"And how would that be accomplished?"

"This brings me to the second consideration which you overlook—the conduct and reputation of Mary herself."

To refresh her memory Elizabeth has Burghley read over the report of Mary's character in Randolph's latest budget of news, which includes these statements and conclusions: That Marie is, in truth, a Queen "of high carriage, beautiful in a grave way." That she is "somewhat gamesome and given to lightness of manner." That she is "addicted to mirth and dancing." That she has been seen much in the company of certain men, including the Earl of Bothwell, and has conducted herself in such a manner "as to give scandal to the stricter sort." That "she is not scanting to lend her eyes or hands or tongue to a kind of nimble and facile exchange of smiles and greetings which might better become the hostess of an ale-house, seeking to win custom."

It is a report which convinces Elizabeth that Marie is plainly a Stuart.

"Nevertheless she is liked," concludes Milord Burghley, "and greatly liked, by those on whom she hath smiled closely, they being won not as a wise sovereign wins subjects, but as a woman wins men. And in addition she hath borne her power thus far with so discreet and tolerant a justness, impartial to north and south, to Catholic and Protestant alike, that if she persevere in this fashion she is like to reconcile the factions and establish herself firmly on the throne of Scotland. For vast numbers who thought to curse her now remain her fast friends."

To Elizabeth what should be done is plain. To Burghley war is still the only solution. There will be war, says he, whether they make it or not. The quicker they act the less effort will be needed.

ELIZABETH—My lord, my lord, it is not easy to thrust a queen from her throne, but suppose a queen were led to destroy herself, led carefully from one step to another in a long descent until at last she stood condemned among her own subjects, barren of royalty, stripped of force, and the people of Scotland were to deal with her for us?

BURGHLEY—She would crush a rebellion.

ELIZABETH—She would now, but wait. She is a Catholic, and for that half her people distrust her. She has a name for coquetry and easy smiling, and we shall build that up into a name for wantonness and loose behavior. She is seen to have French manners; we shall make it appear that these manners indicate a false heart and hollow faith.

BURGHLEY—Can this be done?

ELIZABETH—She is a woman, remember, and open to attack as a woman. We shall set tongues wagging about her. And since it may be true that she is of a keen and noble mind, let us take care of that too. Let us marry her to a weakling and a fool. A woman's mind and spirit are no better than those of the man she lies under in the night.

BURGHLEY—She will hardly marry to our convenience,

madame.

ELIZABETH—Not if she were aware of it. But she is next heir to my throne; she will hope for children to sit on it, and she will therefore wish to marry a man acceptable as the father of kings. We can make use of that.

BURGHLEY—Only perhaps.

ELIZABETH—No, certainly. She is a woman and already jealous for the children she may bear. To my mind the man she marries must be of good appearance, in order that she may want him, but a fool, in order that he may ruin her, and a Catholic, in order to set half her people against her.

BURGHLEY—We know that she is seen much with Bothwell.

ELIZABETH—And he is a Protestant.

BURGHLEY—He is a Protestant. Now suddenly it occurs to me. If she were to marry a Protestant and turn Protestant herself, would she not make an acceptable ally?

ELIZABETH—I do not wish her for an ally! Have you not yet understood? I wish her a Catholic and an enemy, that I may see her blood run at my feet, lest mine run at hers! Suppose one lad with a knife in his heart—a Romish lad who planted that knife between my shoulders—my kingdom, my throne, are hers! It is too easy. Since Bothwell is a Protestant, the more reason for dangling some handsome youngster instantly in the north, as if by accident, nay, as if against my will; some youngster with courtly manners, lacking in brain, a Catholic, and of a blood-strain that would strengthen pretensions to the throne of England.

It has occurred to Elizabeth, too, that Darnley is the man. True, after Marie, Darnley is next heir to the English throne, but Elizabeth has discounted that. Darnley is handsome and of good bearing, a fool and a Catholic.

"If I give out that I am determined against it"—Elizabeth's smile is crafty—"she will marry him and he will drag her down, awaken her senses to become his slave, turn her people against her, make her a fool in council, curb this pretty strumpetry that gains her friends, haul her by the hair for jealousy, get her big with child, too, and spoil her beauty. I tell you, Burghley, a queen who marries is no queen, a woman who marries is a puppet—and she will marry—she must marry to staunch that Stuart blood."

So subtle a conspiracy will take time, Burghley is convinced. It may take years, Elizabeth is agreed, but she can wait. Nor will he find her lacking in devices by which to further the conspiracy. They must have constant knowledge of Mary of Scotland, "and agents about her continually, so that her acts and sayings may be misconstrued and a net of half-lies woven about her, yes, till her people believe her a voluptuary, a scavenger of dirty loves, a bedder with grooms. Aye, till she herself think ill of herself and question her loves, lying awake in torment in the dark.—There is a man called Knox who can be used in this."

"But that—to accomplish that—"

ELIZABETH—We live in a world of shadows, my lord; we are not what we are, but what is said of us and what we read in others' eyes. More especially is this true of queens and kings. It will grow up about her in whispers that she is tainted in blood, given over to lechery and infamous pleasures. She will be known as double-tongued, a demon with an angel's face, insatiable in desire, an emissary of Rome, a prophetess of evil addicted to lascivious rites and poisonous revenges. And before all this her own mind will pause in doubt and terror of what she may be that these things should be said of her—she will lie awake in torment in the dark—and she will lie broken, nerveless there in the dark. Her own people will rise and take her scepter from her.

BURGHLEY (*rising*)—But, Your Majesty—you—

ELIZABETH—However, I am not to appear in this. Always, and above all, I am to seem her friend.—You would say that I am in myself more nearly what will be said of her.

BURGHLEY—No, no—

ELIZABETH—Why, perhaps. But that is not what is said of me. Whatever I may be, it shall be said only that I am the queen of England, and that I rule well.

The curtain falls.

In the great hall of Mary Stuart's apartment at Holyroodhouse, a rectangular room with wide fireplaces glowing at either end, three of the Marys attending the queen, Mary Beaton, Mary Seton and Mary Livingstone, are engaged in hanging the royal arms of Scotland above the queen's chair.

Lords Darnley and Gordon, warming themselves at one of the fires, are given to chaffing the young women and getting as good as they send. Particularly Darnley, who comes off a slow second best in a joust of bawdy wit with Beaton.

Darnley is there to see the queen, to press his wooing by his own confession, but Mary is closeted with her secretary, Rizzio, and the most hopeful message that Mary Fleming brings him is that he is to remain within call.

Now Lord Bothwell has come boldly through the door and requested with confidence that his presence be announced. Let them tell the sweet queen that Lord Bothwell would see her alone. Nor will milord be put off by their report of the great pressure of state affairs that is taking all Her Majesty's time. It may be the Ambassador from England is to arrive, and that there must be a conclave of lords before his audience; it may be her ladies have been warned not to disturb Her Majesty and that even Rizzio himself suggests tomorrow as a better time, Bothwell still demands his audience—

". . . Now, before Christ, I've argued
Enough with women and women-faced men! A room's a room
And a door's a door! Shall I enter without warning
Or will you announce me to her? Great pressure on
Our time! *Our* time, he says! My fine Italian—"

Before Bothwell can say more Mary Stuart has appeared in the doorway. The sudden quiet is punctuated with her announcement.

"I will speak with my lord alone," she says.

Bothwell is still storming when Mary would know his reasons for this insistence. Since early morning he tells her, he has been standing with the crows at the cliff's edge waiting for the smoke to rise from her breakfast chimney. Four full hours—and he never has shown such patience for a woman before.

There were other times, Mary can recall, when there was no such patience shown on Bothwell's part—the time he wrecked an inn and left mine host lying in the road with a broken head and lay with his daughter. The time he had besieged a governor's house with his border knaves and roused all Edinburgh.

". . . Are you a man or a storm at sea, not to be brought indoors?" Mary would know.

"When I would see my girl, why I must see her, or I am a storm, and indoors, too," Bothwell answers.

MARY—
Your girl? Give me leave,
Since I am a queen, with a kingdom to reign over,
To queen it once in a while.

BOTHWELL—
I tell you truly

I've the manners of a rook, for we're all crows here,
And that's what's understood in this town, but I could
Be tame and split my tongue with courtly speeches
If I could be sure of you—if I could know from one day
To another what to make of your ways. You shut yourself up
With secretaries and ministers, harking for weeks
On end to their truffle—while I perch me on the rocks
And look my eyes out.

MARY—
When I was but thirteen
A pretty lad fell in love with me; he'd come,
Oh, afternoons, late midnight, early dawn
Sopping with dew-fall; he'd stand there, waiting for a glance—
I've never had such tribute.

BOTHWELL—
This is no boy.
This is a man comes beating your door in now.
It may be you're too young to know the difference,
But it's time you learned.

MARY—
You've had your way, my lord;
We've spoken together, though I had no time to give,
And now, with your pardon—

BOTHWELL—
You'll go about the business
Of marrying someone else. That's what this mangy
Meeting of councilors means, and that's what portends
From Elizabeth's ambassador! I warn you,
Make no decisions without me!

MARY—
I cannot marry you.
I beg you, ask it not; speak not of it. Our day
Has come between us. Let me go now.

BOTHWELL—
My lady,
I will speak softly. Have no fear of me
Or what I intend. But there have been days I remember
When you had less care what hostages you gave
The world. I think you showed more royally then
Than now, for you loved then and spoke your love, and I
Moved more than mortal for that while. Oh, girl,
If we would be as the high gods, we must live
From within outward! Let the heavens rain fire
Or the earth mud. This is a muddy race

That breeds around us. Will you walk in fear of mud-slingers,
Or walk proudly, and take my hand?

Mary—

I am a queen.

Bothwell—

They've made a slave of you,
This bastard half-brother of yours, this fox of a Maitland,
This doddering Chatelherault! They frighten you
With consequences. They're afraid of men's tongues
And they've made you afraid. But what they truly fear
Is that you'll win the country, be queen here truly
And they'll be out of it. What they'd like best of all
Is to wreck you, break you completely, rule the country themselves,
And why they fear me is because I'm your man alone,
And man enough to stop them.

Mary—

Yes. You are man enough.
It's dangerous to be honest with you, my Bothwell,
But honest I'll be. Since I've been woman grown
There's been no man save you but I could take
His hand steadily in mine, and look in his eyes
Steadily, too, and feel in myself more power
Than I felt in him. All but yourself. There is aching
Fire between us, fire that could take deep hold
And burn down all the marches of the west
And make us great or slay us. Yet it's not to be trusted.
Our minds are not the same. If I gave my hand
To you, I should be pledged to rule by wrath
And violence, to take without denial,
And mount on others' ruin. That's your way
And it's not mine.

Mary believes there is a way. As Queen of France—a child queen and foolish, perhaps—she had learned that to rule gently was to rule wisely. "The knives you turn on your people you must sometimes take in your breast," she warns. And later she adds, "For each enemy you kill you make ten thousand, for each one you spare you make one friend."

She knows of Bothwell's loyalty and his love. She would cling to both. But first she will be queen, nor permit her heart to betray her.

"Be staunch to me," she pleads. "You have been staunchest of all. Let me not lose your arm. No, nor your love—you know how much you have of mine. I'm here alone, made queen in a set, hard, bitter time. Aid me, and not hinder."

"So it shall be," he answers.

"And give me the help I'd have."

"That I can't promise. I'll help thee and defend thee. Lady dear, do you use guile on me?"

"No, sweet, I love thee. And I could love thee well." She has gone to him. He kisses her hand and then her lips. "Go now, and leave me. We've been seen too much together."

"You must lay this hand in no one's else. It's mine."

"I have but lease on it myself. It's not my own. But it would be yours if it were mine to give."

Mary Livingstone has come in to announce the assembling of the Lords of the Council. Mary goes to her chair of state as they file in. James Stuart, Earl of Mornay; Maitland of Lethington, the Duc de Chatelherault, Huntley, Morton and Erskine.

The Earl of Bothwell, being of the Council, has been asked to stay, which is somewhat embarrassing to Maitland. There is reason to believe that the earl's name may come up and it would be as well were he not present. Still Bothwell will remain. It is his intent and the queen's wish.

The subject uppermost in the minds of the Council is the marriage of their queen. Mary is aware of the importance of the question, but would await her own time. This, Maitland believes, would not be wise. The thrones of all the world are shaken. The throne on which Her Majesty sits is shaken too. A marriage, if the right one, would seat her more firmly and put an end to many questions.

"That's all we wish," says Maitland; "to see you safe on your throne that we may be safe in our houses."

To choose the man, however, has not been easy. Maitland admits as much. Any prince who has offered or been suggested would commit Scotland to some alliance of church or state that she'd find embarrassing. If the choice were to fall on a Scottish earl, as Bothwell suggests it might, those houses that were passed over would take it ill. Civil war might follow.

Mary admits that she cannot give herself out as a Virgin Queen, as her cousin Elizabeth has done. Yet she wonders if it were necessary that she marry at all? Lord Morton answers—

MORTON—

Your Majesty,
We have not yet said what we came to say,

And it needs saying bluntly. The people of Scotland
Are given to morals almost as much as to drink.
I'll not say they're moral themselves, but they'll insist
On morals in high places. And they've got in their heads
That you're a light woman.
(MARY *rises.*)
I don't know how it got there,
And I daresay it's not true—

MARY—
Thank you. For your daresay.

MAITLAND—
I could have wished to speak more delicately
Of this, but it's before us, and can't be denied.
Your Majesty, when you came to us from France
And I saw you first, I said to myself in my heart,
All will be well with Scotland. What I thought then
I can say now, for you are wiser even
Than I had supposed, and you have dealt more justly
Than any could have hoped, yet still it's true
Some spreading evil has gone out against you,
A crawling fog of whispers.

These whispers have stemmed partly from John Knox's preaching. More than that they have sprung from "a much more seeded, intentional crop of lyings," planted, Lord Huntley is convinced, by Elizabeth herself.

"You've lent them some color for it, Your Majesty," ventures Huntley. "You've been no statue."

"No, nor wish to be," answers Mary, quickly. "My Lord of Lethington, what you have said of me, how I was when you saw me, how I seem to you now, I swear to you, you were not wrong. I have not betrayed myself as woman or queen."

"I would swear that, too," admits the friendly Maitland.

"And since I know that is true, I have thought very little of whispers. For there is judgment somehow in the air; what I am will be known, what's false will wash out in the rains."

Still the Council's belief that a marriage would end such rumors persists and attention again is turned to the selection of a consort. The quicker the better is Lord Morton's somewhat fiery conclusion. There has been too much coupling of the queen's name with those of Bothwell and of Rizzio—

"I've thought often, Morton, one of us would die before the other," snaps Bothwell, hand on sword. "Now I'm sure of it.

And soon."

Mary would quickly put an end to this quarrel. She is quite capable of defending her own honor, if necessary. Is she accused with Bothwell, or Rizzio, or both, she would know of Lord Morton.

She, being a queen, is not accused, Morton answers. But if wife of his were seen abroad as she is, and half so free of contact with young or old, he would not answer for what was said about her. To which Mary answers:

MARY—
I will answer these things; as for Rizzio,
He is my secretary; if I spend time
In private with him, that is the reason. If I
Had not liked him, he would not be my secretary.
As for Lord Bothwell, he has put more strength
Behind what I wished to do than any among you,
And at times when I had despaired. He is my good friend.
We were here alone before this conference
And we differed in opinion. To wipe that out
I went to him of myself and kissed his lips.
We had kissed but once before, may not kiss again,
But that's at my option, not yours.

HUNTLEY—
Lassie, ye've been
Too honest for your own good.

MARY—
Why, if so much weight
Is placed on a kiss in Scotland, come now, each one
And take your kiss—or if that's no recompense
Come to me then in private, and you shall have,
Each one, one kiss.

MORTON—
And after that, there are kisses
Elsewhere—and when you've finished, whether you'll marry
Or not may not be the question, but whether we can find
A prince who'll have you.

MARY (*rising and taking a step down*)—
And having heard that word—
My lords—when you wish to talk with me again
As civilized men, and not barbarians,
You shall have audience. This Scottish kirk of yours
Has misled you as to the meaning of kisses. I am

Unsullied and young, and have my own faith to plight
And more to think of than these maunderings
Over pantry gossip. I shall not marry till
I find it wise, nor until I have made quite sure
What effect it will have on my inheritance
Of the throne of England. You come here in high conclave
And spend three farthings' worth of wit to chaffer
Over a kiss in my audience-chamber! The question
Is not to save my name, I hope, nor my throne,
But how best to meet the destiny that has made me
Full heir to all this island.—Scotland is mine,
And England will come to me or to the child
I hope to have. It's this that makes my marriage
A matter of moment.—And this—with your good pardon—
Will be the last for today.

Bothwell and Morton have gone when Mary Livingstone announces the arrival of Lord Throgmorton from England. He comes with messages from Elizabeth. One of these he would pass on to Lord James Stuart while Mary is still in her study. It is, whispers Throgmorton, Elizabeth's determination that James shall reign in Scotland, either again as regent or as king. Furthermore, James is not to be disturbed if Elizabeth's policy should seem at variance with her mind.

"It's a wide arc of intrigue," says Throgmorton, "but she carries these schemes in her head like a gambit, and she means to play it to the end. Your sister Mary is not acceptable to her."

Now Mary has come to receive Lord Throgmorton. Thus she hears that Queen Elizabeth sends her love to her cousin of Scotland; that she would have had briars of discord swept away; that Mary, being next heir to the throne of England, being Catholic, and this being a danger to both England and Scotland, Elizabeth would have her turn Protestant, even as Elizabeth herself had done for political reasons. With Mary Protestant, Elizabeth would at once recognize her as next heir to the succession.

"I should think she might," snaps Mary. "Since I am next heir." Mary cannot see that one's faith should be touched by politics. But, presses Throgmorton, why should one take so childish a thing as the rituals of one's youth so gravely now, when war or peace hangs on them.

"There are Catholics in England still," Throgmorton reminds her. "They still plot against our queen. Were she struck down by one of them you'd take her throne and rule us. It follows that your faith is a challenge to her—yes, if your Grace will pardon the word—a defiance."

"You were bid to say this to me?"

"Madame, it was said so smoothly by my queen there was no offense in it, but I have no gift of language. I must say things out."

Now Mary, thoroughly aroused by Throgmorton's insinuating manner, has threatened to have him thrown into the courtyard. Nor is she quick to forgive when he would frankly admit his error and phrase his words more tactfully. Frankly, then, there was no real hope that Mary would change her faith. There is, however, some hope that when she shall elect to choose a consort she will not do so to bolster up her claim to the English crown, which is strong enough already, but would, say, marry a Protestant lord. That would indicate she meant no harm to Elizabeth. What, for instance, would Mary think of the Earl of Leicester?

Mary does not think much of Leicester. "I hope her ears burn now," she snaps. "Leicester? Her cast-off—her favorite—the one she's dangled? This is an affront—"

Leicester was named, Throgmorton is quick to explain, only to give Mary some idea of what Elizabeth had in mind. Elizabeth had had a fear, Throgmorton reports, of young Lord Darnley, who had come north against her will. It is Darnley who "combines to exactness what Elizabeth dreads" in the way of Mary's choice.

"After you he's next to her throne, and he's Catholic," says Throgmorton. "Should you marry Lord Darnley and call up Catholic Europe to your back— Well, we'd be ringed in steel."

Even if there were no quarrel and Mary should marry Darnley and have a son by him, he'd be heir to England. "And I think the plain fact is that Elizabeth would rather choose her own heir."

Mary—
Now, God forgive me!—
I am heir to the throne of England, and after me
Whatever children I have—unless by some chance
The virgin queen should bear sons! Is it part of her love
To cut me off from my right?

Throgmorton—
It must be remembered
That England is Protestant, and it might come hard
To accept a Romish sovereign. In brief, my queen
Has wished that you might choose Bothwell, or perhaps some other

Of Protestant persuasion.

MARY—

And that's the message.
We're down to it at last. My lord Throgmorton,
I marry where I please—whether now or later,
And I abate not one jot of my good blood's lien
On the English throne. Nay, knowing now the gist
Of Elizabeth's polity toward that claim, I shall rather
Strengthen it if I can. The least worthy sovereign
Has a duty toward his blood, not to weaken it
Nor let it decline in place.

THROGMORTON—

This will hardly please.

MARY—

I could hardly expect it would. But I too am a power,
And it matters what pleases me. This was all?

THROGMORTON—

This was all
I'm commissioned with.

MARY—

I shall see to your safe-conduct.

Throgmorton has gone. Mary calls Rizzio. To him she retells the message of Elizabeth, and bids him send for Lord Darnley. Now she knows what it is she must do.

Before Darnley can be summoned Lord Bothwell is back and eager for news of Throgmorton's message. Suspicious, too, of what he hears. Let Mary believe none of it.

"Between the two—this cormorant brother of yours, and that English harpy, they'll have the heart out of you and share it," warns Bothwell. "Trust not one word they say to you, trust not even the anger their words rouse in you. They calculate effects."

Now Mary would know of Lord Morton, and is disturbed when Bothwell is reluctant to report that Morton has suffered a sudden indisposition. Had she not forbidden his fighting? Was he not bound to keep the peace?

It may be he was bound to keep the peace, Bothwell admits, but not when his lady's slandered.

"I'll teach them to hold their peace where you're concerned or find their sweet peace in heaven," storms his lordship.

MARY—

Would God I'd been born

Deep somewhere in the Highlands, and there met you—
A maid in your path, and you but a Highland bowman
Who needed me.

BOTHWELL—

Why, if you love me, Marie,
You're my maid and I your soldier.

MARY—

And it won't be.

BOTHWELL—

Aye, it will be.

MARY—

For, hear me, my lord of Bothwell.
I too have a will—a will as strong as your own,
And enemies of my own, and my long revenges
To carry through. I will have my way in my time
Though it burn my heart out and yours. The gods set us tasks,
My lord, what we must do.

BOTHWELL—

Let me understand you.
The gods, supposing there are such, have thrown us together
Somewhat, of late.

MARY—

Look, Bothwell, I am a sovereign,
And you obey no one. Were I married to you I'd be
Your woman to sleep with. You'd be king here in Edinburgh,
And I'd have no mind to your ruling.

BOTHWELL—

They'll beat you alone.
Together we could cope them.

MARY—

Love you I may—
Love you I have—but not now, and no more. It's for me
To rule, not you. I'll deliver up no land
To such a hot-head. If you'd been born to the blood
I'd say, aye, take it, the heavens had a meaning in this,
But the royal blood's in me.—It's to me they turn
To keep the peace, patch up old quarrels, bring home
Old exiles, make a truce to anarchy. Escape it I cannot.
Delegate it I cannot. The blame's my own
For whatever's done in my name.—I will have no master.

(BOTHWELL *is silent when she pauses.*)

Nay, I am jealous of this my Stuart blood.
Jealous of what it has meant in Scotland, jealous

Of what it may mean. They've attacked that blood, and I'm angry.
They'll meet more anger than they know.

Still angered, Mary tells Bothwell of Elizabeth's fear that she will marry a Catholic and further endanger the throne of England. Admits her plan to thwart this suggestion by marrying Darnley. And now she is facing a man both angered and disgusted.

"Aye, lady, would you stoop so low to choose a weapon?" he demands. "This is not worthy of the girl I've known. Am I to be ousted by a papejay who drinks in the morning and cannot carry his drink? An end of moldy string? You take too much on yourself of the future."

But Mary will not change her plan nor alter her decision. What's a little love to be set beside the name one will wear forever, or one's son will wear? She resents, too, Bothwell's belittling of Darnley and all his threats to be hard on Darnley. It may yet be necessary to teach Lord Bothwell that this is not his palace but hers. Lord Darnley being announced, Bothwell would leave abruptly. Mary calls imperiously that she has given no leave for departure.

"I need no leave nor leave-taking," storms Bothwell. "You see no more of me." And he is gone.

Darnley has been sent for, Mary tells him, to be informed that his suit has prospered; that his request for her hand in marriage has been granted.

Darnley is quite overcome. This is fortune such as he had hardly dared hope for. He would take Mary in his arms, but Mary is not prepared for that, though she would not mind if he would care to kiss her.

Thus favored, Darnley would seal the bargain with some enthusiasm, but now Mary has noticed that he is a little unsteady. His morning cup has betrayed him. There's a frown on Her Majesty's face as she draws away from him. She will hold to the bargain, but they will let the kissing go until the bond's sealed.

They are standing looking appraisingly at each other as

THE CURTAIN FALLS

ACT II

In a hall of the palace Mary and her ladies are sitting before the fire listening to Rizzio as he sings to his lute. It is a love song that Rizzio has written, and one verse of it interests Mary—

"My heart's in the north
And my life's in the south,
False I've pledged with my hand,
False I've kissed with my mouth."

So much is true. Yet it's past time for crying with Mary. She would warn Mary Beaton, though, that where she loves that is where she should marry, even though her love would have no more than a penny a day for their living.

Mary is unhappy. The fault she knows is her own. Darnley, in Rizzio's phrase, has proved their weakness and not their strength, but none could have known that. She will not permit them to talk of Bothwell, and what Bothwell might have done. When her child is born Mary may be happier, even though it will be Darnley's child as well.

Now Rizzio has put forward a plea that he be permitted to return to the Italy for which he is growing lonely. Mary would deny the plea. She knows why he would leave. She will not have her friends driven from her because of the petty jealousies of the king. The king being brainsick is jealous of everyone.

Lord Maitland of Lethington and Master John Knox have called and are admitted. Knox has come to voice the old protest, and he will not come close to the party at the fire. He will have his say from where he stands.

"You are a Catholic Queen in a Protestant land, Your Majesty," he thunders. "You have taken a Catholic husband and set him on the throne beside you, giving him what is called in the courts of this world the crown matrimonial. You have also set up an altar in this your palace, where the mass and other idolatrous rites are said for you. In these ways you encourage Lord Huntley and the Highland Catholics of the north in their heathenish practices, and in so doing bring grave dissension among your people. I come to warn you."

The forms and appurtenances of the Romish faith must go, says Knox. The celebration of the mass must cease. These things shall not be, even at the cost of a civil war and the slaughter of brother by brother. . . .

"Your Majesty, I have brought Master Knox here only because I am convinced that he voices an attitude which must be seriously considered," explains Maitland in part apology.

MARY—But I try to take him seriously and he speaks in parables. I ask him to define his words and he talks of a great fire. To him a priest is a priest of Baal, an idolator is the same as an adulterer, and those who come from France run especial danger of damnation. What can one say to such a man? Master Knox, I believe you mean well, but can you not see that I also mean well, and that there might be more than one opinion concerning the worship of Our Lord?

KNOX—There will be but one opinion held in that last day—when he comes with his armies, and driveth before him those who are not his children!

MARY—Look, what can one say to him? You ask him a question—and he threatens you with the Last Judgment! You see, Master Knox, you are not the judge who will sit over us in the Last Judgment! You are instead an elderly gentleman of provincial learning and fanatical beliefs, lately married to a niece of your own some forty years your junior, and one who conducts his conversations almost exclusively in quotations from the Old Testament. If you will talk sensibly with me I shall talk sensibly with you, but if you come here to frighten me I shall regard you as a most ridiculous antediluvian figure, and find you very funny. Which shall it be?

KNOX—Well I know you hold the Lord God as a jest and a mockery!

MARY—Do not confuse yourself with Lord God again! There's a difference!

KNOX—I am His spokesman.

MARY—Indeed. Will you show me your commission?

KNOX—I call ruin to fall on this house, the shelter of the great beast—!

MARY—And there again! Maitland, can you, by any stretch of the imagination, look upon me as the great beast?

Lord Huntley has come. There is no reason, thinks Mary, why Huntley and Knox should not meet. One being Catholic and the other Protestant and bound to live in the same small kingdom, it would be well if they understood each other.

But there is neither sympathy nor understanding between these two. It is Huntley's opinion that they probably understand each other too well as it is. As for Knox he quickly finds the air of the house offensive to his nostrils. He would call ruin upon it and leave.

". . . Yea, if there are any here who would avoid the wrath, let them turn now, for it is upon you and your servants!"

"Well—it would seem there's little to be done about that," answers Mary. "You are dismissed if you wish to go."

"Yes, those who breed and take their ease in the places of the anointed, turn, turn now, before the ax fall quickly and be followed by silence! For now it is not too late, but no man knows when he cometh, nor on the wings of what morning!"

Maitland and Knox are gone. The group by the fire is joined by Lord Huntley. The situation worries him. John Knox will yet make trouble for Mary. Huntley has his Highlanders, who are Catholic and loyal, but the rest are all against them—every noble and man of note. It is Huntley's idea that the one sound defensive move would be for Mary to strike first. John Knox should be put in Edinburgh castle, and some twenty others who are of his mind with him.

"Then you can go to work," he adds. "You're not safe here and I'm not safe here while a sect of Protestant lords divide your dominion with you. You rule by sufferance only."

Mary—They are here by my sufferance, Huntley.

Huntley—You have heard of the sheep nursed the wolf-pups till they tore her to pieces.

Mary—But we're not sheep and wolves, my lord. There's room for all of us here, and for whatever faiths we may choose to have.

Huntley—Never think it, my bird, never believe it! It's never yet happened that a state survived with two religions in it. Never. Elizabeth knows that. She's behind this Knox. He'd never dare be so bold if she weren't behind him.

Mary—But it's my thought that in Scotland, though it be the first time in the world, we shall all believe as we please and worship as we list. And Elizabeth may take it as she sees fit.

Huntley—She uses it against you, my dear, and uses John Knox against you. Ladybird, I'm willing to beg it of you, take heed of me now or we're both done!

Mary—Rizzio?

Rizzio—You know my mind. I'm with Lord Huntley in this.

Mary—But how can I bring myself to imprison men for no wrong they've done, on suspicion only, imprison them for their faith—?

HUNTLEY—It's more than faith. It's works. You heard John Knox!

MARY—It cuts athwart every right instinct I have, my lord! Every fiber I have that's royal shrinks at such penny-wise petty doings! And John Knox—a doddering imbecile, drooling prophecy!

HUNTLEY—He threatened you, lady.

MARY—No, no, I can't. Even if it were wisdom to do it, and it's not.

The door has opened and Darnley stands for a moment before coming unsteadily into the room. The domestic picture he sees amuses him. He thinks he may have arrived a thought too early. He would thank Lord Huntley for watching over his wife while he (Darnley) has been away. She is a good wife, so he's been told. And she sleeps alone—so far as he knows.

"A pretty wife," smiles Darnley. "These women—they get with child—you never know how—and then they won't sleep with you."

Lord Huntley has bowed and withdrawn. That surprises Darnley, too. An old married man like Huntley! He should know these things.

"You're tired, my lord," suggests Mary. "Will you wish some service, something to eat and drink?"

"She sends me off to bed, you note," protests Darnley. "You note it, Rizzio? There's a service she could do me, but I doubt she'll offer it. And I'm a king, by God, a king, and you're a clark by office!"

"My lord, I hoped you'd have some other word for me when you returned," pleads Mary.

"My pink, if I gave you the word you've earned the room would smell. I've been at the hunting. We had something to drink. Alban! Alban! Allons!"

The right hand door has opened. Lord Ruthven stands there in full armor. It is not, thinks Mary, a place for armor. She will see Lord Ruthven another time. She had heard that he was ill and had thought to go to him.

Douglas has followed Ruthven in. Mary would have them all leave. Darnley grows hysterical again. Now he is centering his attack upon the cowering Rizzio—"that grig, with that kinked hair there! He with the lady's hands and feet! Where does he sleep nights?"

Mary has stepped in front of Rizzio and bidden him go to her study. Lord Morton is next in the room; a threatening Morton who would run a drawn dagger in Mary Beaton's bodice when she tries to bar his way.

Rizzio has got to the study door, but as he opens it he faces a guard with a drawn claymore in his hand. Now Mary Fleming has rushed in to report other guards in Her Majesty's rooms. The women move backward toward the study, shielding Rizzio. Suddenly the Italian springs from them and back of the heavy drapes shielding the window. In a second Morton, Douglas and Ruthven have followed him, Douglas with dagger raised. A second's pause, and then the fall of a body back of the curtain.

"You've murdered him! You pack of filthy cowards!" cries Mary.

"Yea, and done well," coldly answers Ruthven.

There is nothing the women can do to help Rizzio now. Mary would speak from the hurt she feels of the gentleman these boors and swine have murdered, though he had never hurt them. Nor had she been guilty, as they would believe. Now none will believe that. "You've branded me deep with this murder and you've killed a guiltless man!" she says.

Ruthven, himself a dying man, would feel regret if he thought that were true. Morton has done defiantly what his king had commanded him to do. Darnley would defend himself by recalling the long time past that he had been denied entrance to Her Majesty's chamber, while Rizzio was always there.

"Never again while I live will you see me alone," declares Mary. "I bear your child in me or you'd answer for this! . . . I would that I knew in what strange dark chamber of your oafish brain you found reasons for Rizzio's death. If I saw you seldom remember how often you drank yourself imbecile before you came to me. You've slain your last friend, sir. It was Rizzio's counsel put you where you are and kept you there. These are not your friends, these three, nor Moray. They wanted Rizzio out of the way, and they wanted to drag you down, and drag me down, and you play into their hands. I've never been unfaithful to you, but we're at an end, we two. From this time forward if I touch your hand may God blight me and my child!"

"I wanted you! You kept away from me and it drove me mad!"

"You won't mend it now. Look, young Rizzio's dead, you've blackened me, blackened yourself, thrown a black doubt on the child who'll be your heir. The lords look on and smile, knowing they've trapped you. You'll never climb from the pit where you've fallen, and I may fall with you. Lord Moray weaves his web round us. You've helped him."

The lords have gone. The women are alone with the body of Rizzio, which they would lay somewhere, but are afraid in the presence of death. All but Mary. She would have them carry Rizzio's body to her room, and go herself with Beaton for the night.

"This will bring more blood after," she muses. "Now I see it. Before I reign here clearly there will be many men lie so for me slain in needless quarrel. Slain, and each one with blood to spill but once, like his. And yet one steps on into it—steps from life to life till there are thousands dead, and goes on still till the heart faints and sickens, and still goes on and must go on. (*An iron gate clangs outside.* BEATON *parts the curtains to look out.*) I tell you, Fleming, my soul is aghast at this blood spilled for me, and yet it hardens me, too. These are their manners, this the way they go to work. I shall work on them and not too lightly. They think of me as a girl, afraid of them. They shall see.—And yet my mind believes nothing of what I say; I'm weak as grief, stripped and wept out before them. They press me close, and I have no one to send."

There is a rattling of staves in the courtyard below. A moment later Beaton has reported the arrival of a gentleman from France who sends a crow's feather to Her Majesty in lieu of his name.

"Tell my Lord Bothwell I have no wish to see him, now or later," says Mary.

Then Bothwell is seen standing in the doorway. He has come from France to make an offer to his queen that he had made before. He would be her soldier. She should not, thinks Bothwell, turn away her friends, having now so few. He would, if she will permit him to, lay poor Rizzio away for them. And then, if she wishes it, he will go.

Mary has turned, determined to preserve the anger that should be hers, and would go to her study, when Bothwell is back. Again she would leave him, but may not. She weeps, but it is not now for Rizzio dead. "It's for all I wanted my life to be, and is not," she explains.

"Majesty, you have a fortunate star. It will come well yet."

MARY—

If I have a star at all

It's an evil one. To violate my room,
Kill my servant before my eyes— How I must be hated!

BOTHWELL—
They'll pay for that.

MARY—
Perhaps.

BOTHWELL—
I've taken an oath
They'll pay for it. Your Majesty, I wearied
Of France and exile, wearied of sun and wine,
And looked north over the water, longing for fog
And heather and my own country. Further, the news
Was none too happy from Scotland. They want your throne
And plan to have it. But I mean to live in this land
And mean you to be queen of it. The Earl of Bothwell
Is home, and spoiling for a fight. Before
Day dawns they'll hear from me.

MARY—
My lord, I thank you—

BOTHWELL—
Give me no thanks. I like a fight too well
To pretend it's a virtue. Moreover, if I'm to live here
I'd rather you were my liege than Moray. I'm none
So fond of your half-brother. This night's work
Should show you he's what I knew him, half-bred, half-faced.
And double-tongued.

MARY—
You have no army.

BOTHWELL—
I have
My border men. Lord Huntley's joined with me
With his Highland kilties. If you'd call your clans
We could drive them to the wall.

MARY—
It's a war then.

BOTHWELL—
It's war,
Already. They've turned your Darnley against you.
They'll use him
As long as they need his seal. Once they've got you out
They'll set Moray up as regent. They fear one chance:
That you and I should league together and balk them.
I've come back in time, not too soon.

MARY—

I think you have.
My lord, I had no heart to face you. The fault
Was mine when we parted.

BOTHWELL—

It's not too late. I've come
Only just in time, but in time.

MARY—

It is too late—
For you and me. These faults we commit have lives
Of their own, and bind us to them.

Bothwell is still enthused. Rizzio's killing was Darnley's work and Darnley has but little time to live. Not that Bothwell would see to that, as Mary fears, and against which her orders are positive, but because the lords, having used him as a pawn, will be rid of him when he is of no further use to them.

While Darnley lives Mary is his wife and bears his child, she would have him know. She cannot alter that. She may name Bothwell her officer, but only on the promise that no harm shall come to Darnley through him.

To that Bothwell will not give pledge. He has no project against Darnley, but will not be blocked should one arise.

"You have never yet learned how to take an order," sighs Mary.

"And never will," answers Bothwell, spiritedly; "from man or woman living, sovereign or knave, judge or vicegerent. I have not been conquered and will not be. But I offer you my fealty, and it's worth the more for that."

MARY—

You must make your own terms—
I'm but a beggar here.

BOTHWELL—

Nay, nay, it's I
That sue, a beggar for what's impossible,
With this Darnley standing between us.

MARY—

You shall be
My Lord Admiral, and act for me. Yes, and to that
Let me add how my breath caught when I knew you here,
Hoping I know not what, things not to be,
Hopes I must strangle down. Oh, Bothwell, Bothwell!

I was wrong! I loved you all the time, and denied you!
Forgive me—even too late!

BOTHWELL—
I tell you we
Shall be happy yet.

MARY—
No, for I think I've been
At the top of what I'll have, and all the rest
Is going down. It's as if a queen should stand
High up, at the head of a stair—I see this now
As in a dream—and she in her dream should step
From level to level downward, all this while knowing
She should mount and not descend—till at last she walks
An outcast in the courtyard—bayed at by dogs
That were her hunters—walks there in harsh morning
And the dream's done.

BOTHWELL (*stepping toward her*)—
You're weary. You've borne too much.
They shall pay for this.

MARY—
Come no nearer, my lord. It's not ours
To have. Go now.

BOTHWELL—
Yes, Your Majesty.
(*He turns.*)
Yet
I tell you we shall be happy. And there will be nothing
Not ours to have.
(*He goes out as the curtain falls.*)

In Elizabeth's study at Whitehall, London, Elizabeth and Lord Burghley are again in conference when Lord Throgmorton finds his way in. Throgmorton is just back from Scotland, having ridden all night with the news that Darnley's been murdered. Kirk o' Field, where he lay, has been blown up. The castle is in ruins, but there was murder in it, for Darnley had also been strangled.

It is Throgmorton's belief that probably the lords—Moray and Morton—perhaps Maitland, knew something of the crime. But not Bothwell, though Elizabeth suggests that Bothwell might have had a hand in it.

As for Mary, she, thinks Elizabeth, will probably weep and wear black, seeing it becomes her. Twice widowed and once a mother—Mary should herself begin to wear a little.

Throgmorton cannot confirm these views. Mary and Bothwell are good friends again, and Mary charms as she always has. Bothwell and Mary would likely marry were not Moray against it, and the earls behind him.

"Now in my day and time I have known fools and blockheads," protests Elizabeth, "but never, I swear, in such numbers as among these Scotch earls."

Why should Moray oppose Mary's marriage to Bothwell? Times have changed. This is a great love. A queen's love. A madness almost, Throgmorton agrees.

ELIZABETH—

Yes, yes,—and it's well sometimes
To be mad with love, and let the world burn down
In your own white flame. One reads this in romances—
Such a love smokes with incense; oh, and it's grateful
In the nostrils of the gods! Now who would part them
For considerations of earth? Let them have this love
This little while—let them bed and board together—
Drink it deep, be happy—aye—

She pays no heed to Burghley's fears of Bothwell as king. She would have Throgmorton turn and ride back to Scotland as fast as he came and advise Moray that if he would keep a friend in Elizabeth he should let his sister marry Bothwell, even hurry the match. Then Throgmorton should go as quickly, but with greater discretion, to John Knox and give him evidence that Bothwell slew Darnley with Mary's connivance and that now they bed together in blood. Then who will deny that Bothwell murdered Darnley, or credit Bothwell's denial?

"Go and do these things—" she orders Throgmorton. "They are to marry—we sanction it—let none oppose it— She refused him before when he could have saved her. She'll take him now when it's fatal. Let her have this love. This little while—we grant her that—then raise the winds against them—rouse the clans, cry vengeance on their guilty sleep and love— I say within this year at the very farthest, there's no more queen than king in Scotland!"

The lights are fading as the curtain falls.

Sentinels are guarding a hall in Dunbar castle, when Jamie, a messenger, arrives. It is sad news he brings. The queen has been taken prisoner. Her army is gone. Bothwell, happily, is still free and able to fight. They are to put the castle in posture of defense.

Now Lord Huntley has come to confirm the defeat. The battle's over and there is to be a parley at the castle. This is Moray's kingdom now, Huntley sadly reports to Beaton, come anxiously to hear of the queen.

"The queen's a prisoner, lass. My men have deserted, her own men turned against her. This was John Knox's battle, lady. The auld limmer took a stance on a hill some half-mile to windward and there he stood haranguing like the angel Gabriel, swearing Bothwell killed Darnley to have the queen. And the queen's men listened to him, the psalm-singing red-beards, and then turned and made her prisoner and delivered her up to Lord Moray."

Now the guard has been set and Lord Bothwell has arrived. They are not through yet, if Huntley will stand by, which Huntley is ready to do if it's any use.

"One can rally an army flying," admits Huntley. "But one that flies toward the enemy and makes friends—"

"Who spoke of rallying?" answers Bothwell. "They won by treachery and we'll treat them to some of the same." He has given orders for the disposal of the ninety men guarding the castle. "I'll talk with these lords, and if they listen to reason they may keep their mangy lives, but if they refuse to release the queen and give her back her kingdom then hell's their home! Watch my arm, and hark for my sword on steel. They're outnumbered three to one in this court."

"Kill them?"

"Cut their throats, if you like that better."

If that be plain murder, contends Bothwell, the lord's have earned it. And what if he and Huntley fall too? If the queen's deposed they both have lived long enough.

There is a trumpet call outside. The lords have arrived, Morton and Moray, with Maitland, Erskine, Gordon and Douglas following. Moray is first to speak. They have little to gain from this parley, he insists. The battle is theirs, the queen is taken prisoner. But to spare further bloodshed they have granted this respite and ask that Bothwell surrender without conditions.

To this Bothwell will not agree. Nor will he argue further with Moray. Lord Maitland takes up the statement. The lords have made war on the queen and on Bothwell because they were married and because Mary had planned to make Bothwell king.

"You made war on us," replies Bothwell, "like the pack of

lying hounds you are, by swearing in public and in court that we killed Darnley so that we might marry! You know where that guilt lies."

Bothwell wanted Darnley dead. He is willing to grant that. But he did not kill him, as they know, and may their mouths rot with the lie they told of it.

The terms that Maitland states are that Bothwell should leave Scotland and that Mary should delegate all her powers to the council, binding herself to act only with the consent of the lords present.

"Then here are my conditions," answers Bothwell. "I will leave and trouble you no more, if you pledge your word that the queen's to keep her throne and her power intact, without prejudice to her rights. But if you dare encroach one inch on her sovereignty, guard your gates, for I'll be at them!"

"And you make your terms!" sneers Morton.

"Aye, I make mine; defeated, I still make mine—and you'll do well to heed them," snaps Bothwell.

Maitland would be satisfied with this arrangement, but Morton and Moray will have none of it. Bothwell is willing to throw in his earldom. Moray has always wanted that. Let him take it. "I'll disband my army and threaten you no more," adds Bothwell. "But on condition the queen reigns here as before."

Still Moray is obdurate. Why fight and win a war and then throw the spoils away? Maitland and Erskine urge him to accept. It were wisdom to banish Bothwell, Erskine points out, but the queen's a queen and it would be dangerous to touch her. Even Morton is convinced that it were better to accept and send Bothwell away, if he leave his earldom. And so it is agreed.

"I give my pledge, Lord Bothwell, for all here present," says Maitland. "We have not rebelled against the queen and will not, if you are banished."

The lords have gone to the courtyard and given Bothwell leave to speak a moment with the queen. Mary has come to the door, a soldier either side of her. The guards retire and Mary is in Bothwell's arms.

Now Bothwell tells her of the bargain made, which he thinks the lords will keep, seeing Maitland gave his word. But it is not a bargain that pleases Mary. There can be no exile for one without the other. "I'm your wife and I love you, Bothwell," she says. Better that they should call in the men of the guard, cut their way through and make a ride for it, she thinks, than that they be separated.

"They'll never head us! We can rouse the north, ask help from France and England, return with an army they dare not meet!"

"You'd raise no army, Marie," he answers, sadly. "You forget what a drag I am on you. The north is sullen as the south toward you and me. What's left we must do apart."

MARY—
What if we lost?
At the worst we'd have each other.
BOTHWELL—
And do you vision the end of that?
A woman who was a queen, a man who was
The earl, her husband, but fugitives, put to it
To ask for food and lodging, enemies
On every road; they weary, heartsick, turning
At last on each other with reproaches, she saying:
I was a queen, I would be one now but for you,
And he, I have lost my earldom.
MARY—
I betrayed you once
And betrayed my love, but I learned by that; I swear
Though it cost my kingdom, not again!
BOTHWELL—
If you wish
To thrive, break that oath, betray me, betray your love,
Give me up forever—for you know as I know
We lose together. God knows what we'll ever win apart.
MARY—
Nothing. Oh, Bothwell, the earth goes empty.
What worse could happen than parting?
BOTHWELL—
Can I stay?
This once for the last I can save you from yourself,
And me. There's something wills it. I go alone.
This is your kingdom. Rule it.
MARY—
You must not surrender.
They'd serve you as they served Darnley.
BOTHWELL—
I'll not surrender.
I'll see to my own banishment, find my guard,
Force my way out, and go.
MARY—
We must say good-by?

BOTHWELL—

Aye, girl, we've spent what time we had,
And I know not when I'll see you. Let's have no pretense
Unworthy of us. It's likely we'll not meet again
On this same star.

MARY—

God help me and all women
Here in this world, and all men. Fair fall all chances
The heart can long for—and let all women and men
Drink deep while they can their happiness. It goes fast
And never comes again. Mine goes with you,
Youth, and the fund of dreams, and to lie a while
Trusted, in arms you trust. We're alone, alone,
Alone—even while we lie there we're alone,
For it's false. It will end. Each one dies alone.

BOTHWELL—

I'll come
If I can. We've loved well, lass, could love better.
We've had but the broken fragment of a year
And whenever I've touched you, something that broods above us
Has made that touch disaster. This is not my choice.
Lest I bring you utter ruin we must wait,
Wait better times and luck. I'll come again
If I can.

MARY—

Yes, if you can. Aye, among all tides
And driftings of air and water it may be
Some dust that once was mine will touch again
Dust that was yours. I'll not bear it! Oh, God, I'll not bear it!
Take me with you! Let us be slaves and pick
Our keep from kitchen middens and leavings! Let us
Quarrel over clouts and fragments, but not apart—
Bothwell, that much we could have!

BOTHWELL—

Is there refuge in this world for you
And me together? Go far as we could, is there one
Turfed roof where we'd not be reminded of good days
And end in bitterness? Face these lords like a queen
And rule like a queen. I'd help you if I could
But I'm no help. You must meet them now.

Huntley has been called. Together he and Bothwell make their way to the courtyard. There is a cry of "It's Bothwell" outside. Shouted orders are heard and a great stirring in pursuit. Two of the lords, Gordon and Douglas, rush into the room and would continue on through the door, but Mary blocks the way. Let them go the long way round, she orders. Nor will she step aside for Morton or Moray when they come. The lords are angered by the escape of Bothwell, but he's away now. Their plans for her are stated. She is to be lodged for the time in Holyroodhouse.

MARY—
I am to be lodged—
And your faith? You pledged your faith and word,—all of you—
To leave my power untouched, leave me my throne
If Bothwell and I were parted.

MAITLAND—
We'll keep it
When Lord Bothwell's surrendered to us.

MARY—
Go out and take him!
Take him if you can! But for your queen,
I warn you, never since there were kings and queens
In Scotland, has a liegeman laid his hand
On my line without regret!

MORTON—
We'll take care of that.

MARY—
My lords, if I go with you, expect no pardon,
No clemency; I have friends, this farce will end.
Once more, then, leave me in peace.
I have used you royally. Use me so.

MAITLAND—
What you need,
Gather it quickly.

MARY—
This is betrayal at once
Of your word and sovereign.

MORTON—
We know that.
(*A pause.*)

MARY—
I need nothing.
I am a prisoner, Beaton. Come after me
To Holyroodhouse. I may have my own rooms there, perhaps?

MAITLAND—
Yes, Madame.
MAITLAND—
You show great courtesy. For a liar and traitor.
You lied to us, a black and level lie!
Blackest and craftiest! It was you we believed!
MORAY—
Aye, sister. It was that we counted on.
MARY—
Aye, brother.

Mary turns from Maitland to Moray, then walks to the archway and goes out as

THE CURTAIN FALLS

ACT III

In a room in Carlisle Castle in England Mary of Scotland is sitting in the deep embrasure of a window, leaning her head against the bars. Two of her ladies, Beaton and Fleming, are with her, leaning over a map unrolled on a table in the center of the almost bare room. They would retrace the way they may have come to get there.

For a month now they have been prisoners. But prisoners of whom? Occasionally news comes from Scotland. Beaton's Jamie is expected even now. And there are friendly guards in the castle. But still they are prisoners. And who rules Scotland? Moray has no right to it, and the only one who can give him a right is Mary. Moray, Mary thinks, will soon come begging.

It is quite beyond Mary, this imprisonment. What could Elizabeth mean? "She is my friend—over and over she writes she is my friend, I am her dear cousin, her sister sovereign, that she suffers when I suffer, that she would confine me on no pretext if it were not to secure me against my own enemies! Enemies! What enemies have I in her kingdom? What right has she to imprison a sovereign who takes sanctuary in England?"

"Has anyone ever known Elizabeth's mind on any subject?" asks Fleming.

"Writes, too, that she will come to see me, writes again to put it off, writes to say she cannot bear the week to pass without reassuring me of her good love."

"And yet," ventures Beaton, "I believe if all else fails Elizabeth will be found a friend and a good one at the end. If only for her own interest."

"It may still be that she goes, in her own muddled and devious way, about the business of aiding me. It still may be."

The expected Jamie has arrived. His news is ill. Bothwell is taken in Scotland, after the battle of Little Minch. But Kirkaldy of Grange has come over to Her Majesty's side, and says that Bothwell shall be freed. There's a little comfort in that. Jamie, warned by a knocking at the door, is gone.

"It's this that drives one mad, Beaton," muses Mary. "To know that on one certain day, at a certain hour, if one had but chosen well, he'd have stood beside me in a land all mine and his. Choosing wrong, I bring him to fight a long war for me, and lose, bow his shoulders to a castle keep."

There is hope in the thought that Bothwell will be a hard man to hold. Mary has seen him before when his enemies thought him trapped. So long as they both live they'll not jail them apart, thinks Mary. There will be others to follow Kirkaldy to her side.

Young Ruthven has also come from Scotland. Things are not as they should be at home, he reports, nor can be until some approach is made between Mary and her brother. With Ruthven, is Moray himself, and with Moray are Morton, Maitland and Douglas waiting outside. All but John Knox, as Mary notes. Even Lord Throgmorton is now of the group.

It is Maitland who states the nature of their errand. They have come to offer their queen a speedy release. A pleasant suggestion to Mary, though she doubts not that their lordships come to ask for much and give little for it, as ever.

"Will Your Majesty give me leave to rehearse a brief history that may weary you, since you know it?" asks Maitland, and being given leave, continues:

"Your Majesty broke from prison in Scotland and fled to England. This action was tantamount to abandoning your throne."

"Indeed it was not. I came here for aid against you," sharply answers Mary.

That, decides Maitland, is a point that may be passed. The fact remains that Mary was taken prisoner in England; that her realm is governed only by makeshift, and that it is the plan of the lords to make her son, Prince James, king. Her absence makes this necessary.

"My absence is not permanent, I hope," answers Mary. "I am queen of Scotland and have not abdicated, nor do I intend to abdicate."

"Will you tell us what you think to find, should you return?" asks Morton.

MARY—

If I return
As I intend, I shall not find you there,
Lord Morton, if you're wise. The country's fickle
For you, as it was for me. Now they've pushed their queen
Aside, they begin to wonder if they were not wrong.
And wonder too if they profit by the exchange,
And give you side-long looks.

MAITLAND—

If it's still in your mind
That you might win your throne back, ponder on this:
The lord of the isles has given you up, the north
Is solidly with us, Bothwell has broken faith—

MARY—

Aye?

MAITLAND—

For the good of the kingdom, to secure your son
His right to the throne, we ask you tonight to sign
Your abdication, let us take it back with us.

MARY—

Yes,
But I catch you in two lies. Kirkaldy of Grange
Has come over to me; you have taken Bothwell prisoner,
But before he fights on your side you'll rot in the damp
Under Edinburgh castle, and he'll see you do it!

MAITLAND—

Madame,
You've been misinformed.

MARY—

I've been lied to and by you
Specifically! Let me rehearse for you
A history you may recall, you that stand before me:
It was you killed Rizzio, and made capital of it
To throw discredit on me. It was you
Killed Darnley, and then threw the weight of that
On Bothwell, saying through John Knox that I lived
With my husband's murderer. It was you that promised
To give me fealty if Bothwell and I were parted,
And then cast me into prison! I escaped,
As the truth will escape about you, and when it's known

My people will drive you out. What you ask of me
I refuse it, finally! I will not abdicate,
Not to this off-scum that's boiled up around
My throne to dirty me! Not now and not ever!

The lords have filed out. A moment later a guard pushes back the door through which they have left and Elizabeth stands there facing Mary. For a moment these two look appraisingly one upon the other. Then, at Elizabeth's suggestion, Mary dismisses her maids.

She has come, doubtfully and tardily, Elizabeth announces, because she has thought that if they were to see each other near, and they were to talk as sisters "over these poor realms of ours, some light might break that we'd never see apart."

"Have I been so much a problem?" asks Mary.

"Have you not?" queries Elizabeth. "When the winds blow down the houses and there is a running and arming of men, and a great cry of praise and blame, and the center of all this storm's a queen, she beautiful—as I see you are—aye, with the Stuart mouth and the high forehead and French ways and thoughts—well, we must look to it. Not since that Helen we read of in dead Troy, has a woman's face stirred such a confluence of air and waters to beat against the bastions. I'd thought you taller, but truly, since that Helen, I think there's been no queen so fair to look on."

This is not flattery, insists Elizabeth. Envy, rather. Which bids Mary hope that Elizabeth has come as a friend and not as an enemy, and that what she (Mary) was wont to believe of those things she had heard through others, were not true. She may have found a friend. If that is so it is a friendship that will embrace an enduring loyalty.

Elizabeth would not have so strong a pledge. In these uncertain times it will be slippery going for all of them. "If you'd keep your place on this rolling ball let the mountains slide and slip into the valleys," warns Elizabeth. "Put no hand to them or they'll pull you after."

"But does this mean you can lend no hand to me, or I'll pull you down?" asks Mary.

Elizabeth—
I say it
Recalling how I came to my throne as you did,
Some five or six years before, beset as you were

With angry factions—and came there young, loving truth,
As you did. This was many centuries since,
Or seems so to me, I'm so old by now
In shuffling tricks and the huckstering of souls
For lands and pensions. I learned to play it young,
Must learn it or die.—It's thus if you would rule;
Give up good faith, the word that goes with the heart,
The heart that clings where it loves. Give these up, and love
Where your interest lies, and should your interest change
Let your love follow it quickly. This is a queen's porridge,
And however little stomach she has for it
A queen must eat it.

MARY—
I, too, Elizabeth,
Have read my Machiavelli. His is a text-book
Much studied in the French court. Are you serious
To rede me this lesson?

ELIZABETH—
You have too loving a heart,
I fear, and too bright a face to be a queen.

MARY—
That's not what's charged against me. When I've lost
So far it's been because my people believed
I was more crafty than I am. I've been
Traduced as a murderess and adulteress
And nothing I could have said, and nothing done
Would have warded the blow. What I seek now is only
My freedom, so that I may return and prove
In open court, and before my witnesses,
That I am guiltless. You are the queen of England,
And I am held prisoner in England. Why am I held,
And who is it holds me?

ELIZABETH—
It was to my interest, child,
To protect you, lest violence be offered to a princess
And set a precedent. Is there anyone in England
Who could hold you against my will?

MARY—
Then I ask as a sovereign,
Speaking to you as an equal, that I be allowed
To go, and fight my own battles.

ELIZABETH—
It would be madness.

MARY—
May I not judge of that?

ELIZABETH—
See, here is our love!

MARY—
If you wish my love and good-will you shall have it freely
When I am free.

ELIZABETH—
You will never govern, Mary. If I let you go
There will be long broils again in Scotland, dangers,
And ripe ones, to my peace at home. To be fair
To my own people, this must not be.

MARY—
Now speak once
What your will is, and what behind it! You wish me here,
You wish me in prison—have we come to that?

ELIZABETH—
It's safer.

Elizabeth would not bar the Stuart line in Scotland. But it were better for both their kingdoms that Mary should remain her guest—until the world is quieter. And who should reign in Mary's place? It could be arranged that her son would be crowned king and her brother made regent, a consummation repulsive to Mary.

Again Mary would beg her freedom of Elizabeth, that she may return to one she loves in the north. ". . . My life's there, my throne's there—my name to be defended—and I must lie here darkened from news and from the sun—lie here impaled on a brain's agony. . . . As you are a woman and I am—and our brightness falls soon enough at best—let me go, let me have my life once more—and my dear health of mind again—for I rot away here in my mind—in what I think of myself—some death-tinge falls over one in prisons—"

"It will grow worse, not better," coldly answers Elizabeth. "I've known strong men shut up alone for years—it's not their hair turns white only; they sicken within and scourge themselves. If you would think like a queen this is no place for you. The brain taints here till all desires are alike. Be advised and sign the abdication."

MARY—
Stay now a moment. I begin to glimpse

Behind this basilisk mask of yours. It was this
You've wanted from the first.

ELIZABETH—

This that I wanted?

MARY—

It was you sent Lord Throgmorton long ago
When first I'd have married Bothwell. All this while
Some evil's touched my life at every turn.
To cripple what I'd do. And now—why now—
Looking on you—I see it incarnate before me—
It was your hand that touched me. Reaching out
In little ways—here a word, there an action—this
Was what you wanted. I thought perhaps a star—
Wildly I thought it—perhaps a star might ride
Astray—or a crone that burned an image down
In wax—filling the air with curses on me
And slander; the murder of Rizzio, Moray in that
And you behind Moray—the murder of Darnley, Throgmorton
Behind that too, you with them—and that winged scandal
You threw at us when we were married. Proof I have none
But I've felt it—would know it anywhere—in your eyes—
There—before me.

ELIZABETH—

What may become a queen
Is to rule her kingdom. Had you ruled yours I'd say
She has her ways, I mine. Live and let live
And a merry world for those who have it. But now
I must think this over—sadness has touched your brain.
I'm no witch to charm you, make no incantations;
You came here by your own road.

It is hard now for Mary, tracing back each sign and happening, to realize how she could have been so mistaken in Elizabeth for so much as an instant. But, corrects Elizabeth, Mary was not mistaken. "I am all women I must be," is her admission. "One's a young girl—young and harrowed as you are—one who could weep to see you here—and one's a bitterness at what I have lost and can never have, and one's the basilisk you saw. This last stands guard and I obey it."

Mary had come to Scotland a fixed and subtle enemy, more dangerous to Elizabeth than she had ever known. "I set myself to cull you out and down, and down you are," she says. And adds:

It was you
Or I. Do you know that? The one of us must win
And I must always win. Suppose one lad
With a knife in his hand, a Romish lad who planted
That knife between my shoulders—my kingdom was yours.
It was too easy. You might not have wished it.
But you'd take it if it came.

MARY—
And you'd take my life
And love to avoid this threat?

ELIZABETH—
Nay, keep your life.
And your love too. The lords have brought a parchment
For you to sign. Sign it and live.

Even though she abdicate Mary is not to be given freedom. With freedom, Elizabeth fears, she would go back to Bothwell and between them they would be too much for Moray. No, Mary would live on in London with Elizabeth. The court were better than a cell.

"And if I will not sign this abdication?"

"You've tasted prison. Try a diet of it."

"And so I will," says Mary.

"I can wait," smiles Elizabeth.

Mary can wait, too. Wait until Bothwell has fought free again, and Kirkaldy and others spring up to join him. Each week will she be stronger and Moray weaker. "This trespass against God's right will be known," she says. "The nations will know it. Mine and yours. They will see you as I see you and pull you down."

Elizabeth is not impressed. Each year she will send the abdication to be signed, and, not signing, Mary will step from one cell to another, each step lower—

"Till you reach the last, forgotten, forgotten of men,
Forgotten among causes, a wraith that cries
To fallen gods in another generation
That's lost your name. . . ."

MARY—
And suppose indeed you won

Within our lifetime, still looking down from the heavens
And up from men around us, God's spies that watch
The fall of great and little, they will find you out—
I will wait for that, wait longer than a life,
Till men and the times unscroll you, study the tricks
You play, and laugh, as I shall laugh, being known
Your better, haunted by your demon, driven
To death or exile by you, unjustly. Why,
When all's done, it's my name I care for, my name and heart,
To keep them clean. Win now, take your triumph now,
For I'll win men's hearts in the end—though the sifting takes
This hundred years—or a thousand.

ELIZABETH—

Child, child, are you gulled
By what men write in histories, this or that,
And never true? I am careful of my name
As you are, for this day and longer. It's not what happens
That matters, no, not even what happens that's true,
But what men believed to have happened. They will believe
The worst of you, the best of me, and that
Will be true of you and me. I have seen to this.
What will be said about us in after-years
By men to come, I control that, being who I am.
It will be said of me that I governed well,
And wisely, but of you, cousin, that your life,
Shot through with ill-loves, battened on lechery, made you
An ensign of evil, that men tore down and trampled.
Shall I call for the lord's parchment?

MARY—

This will be said—?
But who will say it? It's a lie—will be known as a lie!

ELIZABETH—

You lived with Bothwell before Darnley died,
You and Bothwell murdered Darnley.

MARY—

And that's a lie!

ELIZABETH—

Your letters, my dear. Your letters to Bothwell prove it.
We have those letters.

MARY—

Then they're forged and false!
For I never wrote them!

ELIZABETH—
It may be they were forged.
But will that matter, Mary, if they're believed?
All history is forged.

MARY—
You would do this?

ELIZABETH—
It is already done.

MARY—
And still I win.
A demon has no children, and you have none,
Will have done, can have none, perhaps. This crooked track
You've drawn me on, cover it, let it not be believed
That a woman was a fiend. Yes, cover it deep,
And heap my infamy over it, lest men peer
And catch sight of you as you were and are. In myself
I know you to be an eater of dust. Leave me here
And set me lower this year by year, as you promise,
Till the last is an oubliette, and my name inscribed
On the four winds. Still, *still* I win! I have been
A woman, and I have loved as a woman loves,
Lost as a woman loses, I have borne a son,
And he will rule Scotland—and England. You have no heir!
A devil has no children.

ELIZABETH—
By God, you shall suffer
For this, but slowly.

MARY—
And that I can do. A woman
Can do that. Come turn the key. I have a hell
For you in mind, where you will burn and feel it,
Live where you like, and softly.

ELIZABETH—
Once more I ask you,
And patiently. Give up your throne.

MARY—
No, devil.
My pride is stronger than yours, and my heart beats blood
Such as yours has never known. And in this dungeon,
I win here, alone.

ELIZABETH—
Good night, then.

MARY—

Aye, good night.

Elizabeth goes to the door, which opens before her. She goes out slowly. As the door begins to close upon her Mary calls "Beaton!"

ELIZABETH—

You will not see your maids again,
I think. It's said they bring you news from the north.

MARY—

I thank you for all kindness.

"Elizabeth goes out. Mary stands for a moment in thought, then walks to the wall and lays her hand against the stone, pushing outward. The stone is cold, and she shudders. Going to the window she sits again in her old place. She is staring out into the darkness."

THE CURTAIN FALLS

MEN IN WHITE

A Drama in Three Acts

BY SIDNEY KINGSLEY

HONORS fell thickly about the production of Sidney Kingsley's "Men in White" early in the season. It was, for one thing, the first outstanding dramatic hit of the year. It was, for another, the first real success achieved by the Group Theatre, Inc., an organization of earnest stage students who have for three years worked harder and more earnestly to achieve success in the theatre than any similar group has worked within the memory of this editor. Finally, it achieved the signal honor of being nominated by its reviewers as the one production of recent years that made the best and most complete use of all the practical resources of the living theatre.

The Group Theatre, which had in previous seasons won a *succès d'estime* with Paul Green's "The House of Connelly" and the Siftons' "1931," was the fifth purchaser of Mr. Kingsley's drama. Four times he had collected advance royalties on the script and four times had it turned back to him. The depression was a factor. So was a natural reluctance on the part of those who had been thrilled by the play to risk its production, it being a somewhat depressing atmosphere and theme, at a time when cheerful plays seemed much more in demand.

Once having made up its collective mind, however, the Group moved into the country in the spring of 1933 and for three months rehearsed and polished and pointed up the dramatic scenes of the drama. When they exposed it to its first audience, the night of September 26, at the Broadhurst Theatre, they were in such complete command of every feature of the production that the audience, including the critics, was ready to stand in the aisles and cheer. And did.

"Men in White" achieves that perfect realism in detail and atmosphere that, you may recall, characterized the production of "Journey's End." It is definitely theatrical without ever permitting its audience to become aware of that fact. It is both artfully and painstakingly detailed down to the last roll of gauze used in the operating room of a modern hospital, but never offensive in its realism. Which accounts for its having been classed as a minor masterpiece among the melodramas of a decade.

The library of St. George's Hospital, in which the first scene of "Men in White" is played, "is a large, comfortable room flanked on the left by tall windows, on the right by ceiling-high bookcases crammed with heavy tomes."

There is a long table, strewn with medical magazines. There are comfortable red leather club chairs. There is a bulletin board, containing notices of hospital activities, and at the back a series of telephone stalls. "Niched high in the wall is a marble bust of Hippocrates, father of medicine, his kindly, brooding spirit looking down upon the scene. At the base of the bust is engraved a quotation from his Precepts: 'Where the love of man is, there also is the love of the art of healing.' "

A hospital corridor at back is glimpsed through glass-paneled doors. This passage "is alive with its steady cavalcade of nurses, internes, etc. . . . The quick activity of the hospital outside contrasts noticeably with the classical repose of the library."

There are several groups of young internes in the library, "easily recognizable by their white, short-sleeved summer uniforms." Some are smoking and chatting. Some are listening intently to older men in civilian clothes. These would be attending physicians and they are doing most of the talking.

A loud speaker at one side of the room has been calling raucously for "Dr. Ramsey! Dr. Ramsey!" There has been a series of insistent telephone calls answered by the assembled internes. Then Dr. Hochberg enters the room and the attention is for the moment attracted to him.

Hochberg is "a short, vital man, whose large head is crowned by a shock of graying hair. He carries himself with quiet, simple dignity. There is strength in the set of his jaw, but the predominating quality expressed in his face is a sweet compassion, a simple goodness."

Dr. Hochberg as the attending chief of the surgical staff, is an important person at St. George's. Someone is always in search of him. Now Dr. Gordon, a middle-aged member of the staff, would have him look at a patient. Young Dr. Vitale would like to have the Hochberg opinion of the case he had sent to his clinic the day before, and is pleased that the chief thinks the Vitale treatment is all right and should be continued.

Dr. Hochberg finds time for a word with Dr. McCabe, grown old in medicine, who is still seeking library books to help him keep up with the advancement of his profession. McCabe can't understand how the young men ever find time to read half of what is written today.

"There's so much," the older man protests. "We've gone so far since I was a boy! In those days appendicitis was a fatal disease. Today it's nothing. These youngsters take all that for granted. They don't know the men who dreamed and sweated—to give them anæsthesia and sterilization and surgery, and X-ray. All in my lifetime. I worked with Spencer Wells in London, and Murphy at Mercy Hospital. Great men. None of these youngsters will equal them. They can't. There's too much! I'm afraid it will all end in confusion."

"Where the sciences *in general* are going to end, with their mass of detail, nobody knows," answers Hochberg. "But good men in medicine . . . we'll always have. Don't worry, Dr. McCabe . . . one or two of these boys may surprise you yet, and turn out another Murphy or another Spencer Wells."

Interne George Ferguson, for whom Dr. Hochberg has been looking, comes down the corridor and into the library. Young Ferguson "is about twenty-eight, handsome in an angular, manly fashion, tall, wiry, broad-shouldered, slightly stooped from bending over books and patients; a fine sensitive face, a bit tightened by strain, eager eyes, an engaging earnestness and a ready boyish grin."

Ferguson has been working with Dr. Hochberg on the preparation of a paper that is of mutual interest and the older man is pleased with the younger man's progress. He is pleased, too, at the reports Ferguson has to make on the various hospital cases directly under his care.

"Good boy," he mutters to Gordon, as Ferguson is called to the telephone. "Lots of ability! We're going to be proud of him some day!"

A lean shabby man has entered the library. He carries a large envelope of the type used for X-ray pictures. "He is a fairly young man, but worry has lined his forehead and prematurely grayed his hair."

A moment later Dr. Hochberg has recognized the newcomer. He is Dr. Levine, almost a stranger. It has been six years since Levine was on the staff, and six years is a long time when men are growing old. There is a bond of affection between these two. Hochberg would know all about the Levine fortunes, and the Levine wife, Katherine.

It is about Mrs. Levine that the doctor has called, and brought the X-rays. She has not been well. There is a slight, persistent cough. He produces the plates. He wants Dr. Hochberg's advice. Dr. Ferguson, returning from the phone, also has a look at the plates over Hochberg's shoulder.

"That shadow there! The right apex—" notes Ferguson.

"Yes," admits Levine, a little sadly; "I was afraid of—"

"Now, don't be an alarmist," quickly cautions Hochberg.

Let them first have an examination of the sputum specimen Dr. Levine has brought. Dr. Ferguson will attend to that. The laboratory report will be ready that evening. Dr. Levine can call for it in Dr. Ferguson's room, No. 106.

A nostalgic smile flits across Dr. Levine's face; 106, as it happens, was his old room.

FERGUSON—You interned here? Are you the— Oh, of course. Bellevue, aren't you?

LEVINE (*nodding*)—'23.

FERGUSON—Professor Dury mentions you quite often.

LEVINE—Dury? (*To* HOCHBERG.) He still remembers me. . . .

FERGUSON—He thinks a great deal of you.

HOCHBERG—George, here, is one of his prize pupils, too.

LEVINE—And does he want you to study abroad?

FERGUSON—Yes. I planned to go with Sauerbruch, but he has been forced to leave Germany. So, instead of that, I'm going to study under von Eiselsberg in Vienna.

HOCHBERG—Hm! I remember when I was a student in Berlin, one of my classmates came to an examination in military uniform . . . saber and all. Virchow looked at him, and said, "You! What are you doing here in that monkey suit? Your business is with death! Ours is with life!" Virchow was a man of science. He knew. (*He shakes his head.*) I wonder what he would say to our beloved Germany today.

LEVINE—Yes. . . .

FERGUSON (*to* HOCHBERG)—Well, Laura prefers Vienna, anyway, so . . . (*To* LEVINE.) I'm going on my honeymoon too, you see.

LEVINE—You'll find it difficult mixing the two. I know von Eiselsberg.

HOCHBERG—It's going to be very difficult. You don't know Laura.

FERGUSON—After a year in Vienna I'm working with Dr. Hochberg. So the real labor won't begin till I come back from Europe.

Hochberg—Oh, I'll drive you, George! With a whip, eh?

Levine—Lucky! (*Retrospectively.*) Yes. . . . I once looked forward to all that. (*He sighs.*)

Hochberg and Levine have gone to the laboratory. Ferguson turns to the other internes gathered around the tables—Michaelson, "Shorty" Otis, "Pete" Bradley. Pete is just back from an operation. Worried a little, too, about the insulin they have given the patient. Forty units. Twenty units would have been enough, says Ferguson, and Pete admits as much. But Dr. Cunningham ordered it—

"You should have told me before you gave it to her," insists Ferguson, with some asperity. "I'm not going to have any patients go into shock on the operating table! Understand?" He is slapping Pete good-naturedly on the back as he adds: "If this happens again, Pete, you get your behind kicked in—and not by Cunningham!"

Ferguson's order is o.k. with Pete, who is an amiable person, but determined. He is determined at the moment that he will not lend Shorty his white tux vest for the evening, not even in exchange for a date with a red-head. Ferguson, in love, should have the date, Pete thinks. It would do him good. The trouble with love, suggests Shorty, is that it kills a fellow's sex life.

Pete, like Ferguson, was in love once, but when it began to interfere with his appetite— "Hell, no woman's worth that!"

Dr. Gordon is in to report that 401 is a mighty sick boy. It may be he will need another transfusion. And if that should happen tonight Dr. Gordon wants Dr. Ferguson there to do it.

"This is my night out," protests Ferguson, lightly. "My fiancée has made arrangements. . . . So, I'm afraid I won't be here."

"I'm sorry, Ferguson. When the House needs you—"

Ferguson—I'd like to, Doctor, but the same thing happened last week. I can't disappoint my fiancée again . . . or—(*He smiles.*) . . . I won't have any.

Michaelson—Er—Dr. Gordon, couldn't I do that transfusion?

Gordon—I'm afraid not—the superficial veins are all thrombosed. Ferguson has followed the case from the start; he knows the veins we've used.

Ferguson—Laidlaw knows the veins. . . .

Gordon—Frankly, I don't trust any of the other men on this

case. I know I'm imposing, but I want this boy to have every possible chance. . . . He's a sick boy, Ferguson. What do you say?

FERGUSON—All right! I'll stay.

GORDON—Thanks! And if your sweetheart kicks up a fuss send her around to me. I'll tell her about my wife. Up at four-thirty this morning to answer the phone. Somebody had a belly-ache. . . . (*He laughs, nods and goes.*)

FERGUSON (*dejected*)—Damn it! I wanted to be with Laura, tonight.

MICHAELSON—That's tough, George. I'm sorry I couldn't help you out. (*The loud speaker starts calling—"Dr. Manning! Dr. Manning!"*)

FERGUSON—Laura's going to be hurt. You'd think they'd have a little . . .

NURSE (*coming in breathless*)—Dr. Ferguson? Dr. Ferguson, a woman just came in on emergency with a lacerated throat. She's bleeding terribly! Dr. Crane told me to tell you he can't stop it.

FERGUSON—Get her up to the operating-room. (*He snaps his fingers.*) Stat. (*She hurries off. He turns to* MAC.) Drop that, Mac, and order the O.R.! Come on! (MAC *goes to a phone. To* MICHAELSON.) Call an anæsthetist, will you? And locate Dr. Hochberg! Try the X-ray room!

MICHAELSON—Right! (*He jumps to a phone.*)

MAC (*on phone*)—Operating-room! . . . Emergency B! . . . Quick! . . . O.R.? . . . Set up the O.R. right away! Lacerated throat! Dr. Ferguson! Yes!

MICHAELSON (*on phone*)—Find Dr. Hochberg! Right away! Emergency! . . . (*The loud speaker, which has been calling "Dr. Manning!" changes to a louder and more persistent, "Dr. Hochberg! Dr. Hochberg! Dr. Hochberg!"*) Well, try the X-ray room! . . . And locate the staff anæsthetist! (*In the back corridor we catch a glimpse of an orderly hurriedly pushing a rolling-stretcher on which the emergency patient is lying, crying hysterically. An interne on one side, and the nurse at the other are holding pads to her throat and trying to calm her.*)

The lights fade out.

In the largest and most expensive private room in St. George's Hospital John Hudson, "a large man, haunched, paunched and jowled," is sitting on a lounge being shaved by the hospital barber. At the same time he is carrying on an animated conversation with a Mr. Mooney, one of his business associates, "a smaller, nattier, less impressive and, at the moment, highly nervous edition of Hudson."

Sputtering through the lather on his face Mr. Hudson is outlining to Mr. Mooney how it will be possible for them to break a Clinton street boom in order that they may possess themselves of all the property in that section they will need.

First they will get in touch with the real estate editors and tell them of certain changed plans. Then they will buy options on property in another district and sell several pieces of their own Clinton street property to dummy corporations, and sell it low. When the Clinton street owners are properly discouraged the dummy corporations will step in and buy their land for nickels and the Hudson company will be excavating by spring.

Mr. Hudson has lighted a cigar to help him think. Dr. Hochberg, coming upon the conference and also the cigar, brings the one to a close and throws the other away. Dr. Hochberg happens to know that Dr. Whitman, the attending physician, has forbidden cigars. Whether Mr. Hudson likes it or not, the Whitman orders are to be carried out.

"I don't understand people like you, John," protests Dr. Hochberg. "Whitman is the best cardiac man in the country, but he can't give you a new heart! Don't you know that? Are you such a fool?"

Before he can answer the door opens to admit Laura Hudson, "a spirited, chic young lady; lithe, fresh, quick, modern, a trifle spoiled perhaps, but withal eminently warm, lovable and human."

Laura kisses her dad and greets Dr. Hochberg with a cheery "Hocky, wie gehts!" She agrees with the doctor perfectly that there should be no cigars. Further than that, she is convinced that her father should not only do as the doctors tell him, but should give up his office entirely for a time and forget his business.

"What good is your money, damn it! if you can't enjoy it?" demands Laura, with spirit.

"Well, it can still buy my little girl a honeymoon," Hudson answers.

"I could spend my honeymoon right here! And have a swell time. As long as it is with George." Which reminds her. "Where is that man?" she demands of Hochberg.

"Upstairs,—busy!"

There had been a party the night before, but Laura had not enjoyed it very much. George could not be there.

"I spent most of my time upstairs with Doris' baby," she tells them. "It woke and wanted some attention. Babies are awfully human that way, aren't they? Do you know that Doris was going to let him cry himself to sleep? Can you imagine? . . . Believe me, when I have my baby, it's going to get all the care and love and attention it can use."

"You have the right instincts, Laura," smiles Hochberg.

Now Laura is more insistent about seeing George. She has not, she insists, had a real kiss in days. She would call him on the phone, but Hochberg advises against that. George is in the operating-room.

"God, they make a slave of that boy," protests Hudson. "And he doesn't get a dime! I can't see it!"

"He is not here for the money," gently answers Dr. Hochberg, smiling. "He's here to learn. The harder he works the more he learns. If he wanted to make money he wouldn't have chosen medicine in the first place. You know, when he comes with me, his pay is only going to be $20 a week, but there's a chance to work. The man who's there with me now works from 16 to 18 hours a day. He even has a cot rigged up in one of the laboratories, where he sleeps sometimes."

"For $20 a week?"

"Yes, yes. . . . (*To* LAURA.) George is a fine boy with great promise. The next five years are crucial years in that boy's life. They're going to tell whether he becomes an important man or not."

"George is an important man right now, Hocky, to me."

Laura has turned to her father and is making plans for taking him home when George Ferguson arrives. Her meeting with George is enthusiastic, for all he admits her new hat looks a little like a sailboat to him.

The talk turns to the wedding plans. Mr. Hudson suggests that George had better be getting in his list so the Hudson secretary can send out the invitations.

"You know—I still can't believe it's going to happen! I mean just happen!" George admits to Laura.

"Neither can I," says she.

"Vienna's going to be lots of fun!"

"Fun? You don't know. Wait till you've seen the Prater. It's Coney Island with a lift! Lights all over . . . and those lovely people all laughing and happy . . . and the whole place just tinkling with music."

"I've always had a yen to hear Strauss on his home grounds."

"When I visited von Eiselsberg," inserts Dr. Hochberg, "his

students spent all their time working—with an occasional glass of beer for relaxation. That's what George's Vienna is going to be, Laura."

George and Laura do not take very kindly to that suggestion. Before they can put their feelings into words the nurse is there to take Mr. Hudson for his sunbath, which she does over his protest.

Now Dr. Hochberg, lightly prodded by his young friends, has left them alone and they are deep in each other's arms as soon as the door is closed.

"You're lovely. . . . Lovely, Laura," George mutters as he crushes her in a big hug.

"If you knew how I've been aching for this," she answers, clinging to him. "Three months!" She is sighing now. "I don't know how I can live till then."

And now she has drawn George over to a huge easy chair and pushed him into it, curling up in his lap and taking his head in her hands the better to scrutinize his face.

"Let me look at you," she says, and shakes her head. "You're getting thin, young man. And your eyes are tired."

FERGUSON—I didn't have much sleep last night. It was a pretty sick house.

LAURA—You're overworked. . . . (*Pulls his head over on her shoulder.*) And I don't like it one bit. . . . You know, you've spoiled everything for me. I was thinking last night, all the music and noise and fun . . . didn't mean a thing without you. I don't seem to get a kick out of life any more, unless you're around. (*She pauses.*) And that's not very often, is it?

FERGUSON—Darling, we'll make up for it all . . . later on. Honestly.

LAURA—I don't know if we can, George. Last night, for instance. If you had been there—perfect! Now it's—gone. You see, dearest, the way I feel, if I had you every minute from now on, it wouldn't be enough. (FERGUSON *starts to speak, she puts her hands over his lips.*) I wish I'd lived all my life with you. I wish I'd been born in the same room with you, and played in the same streets.

FERGUSON (*smiles*)—I'm glad you missed them. They were ordinary and gloomy. They might have touched you . . . changed you. . . . (*He cups her face in his hands and looks at her.*) About seven months ago there was a boy here who'd been blind from birth. We operated on him—successfully. One night I showed him the stars—for the first time. He looked at them a moment and began to cry like a baby, because, he said, they were so lovely, and—he might never have seen them. When I look at you, Laura, I get something of that feeling. I . . . I can't tell you how large a part of me you've become, Laura! You're . . . (*The loud speaker is heard calling, "Dr. Ferguson! Dr. Ferguson . . ."*) Oh, damn it! . . .

LAURA—Don't move! (*She clutches him tightly.*)

FERGUSON—It's no use, Laura! That's my call! Let me up!

LAURA—No!

FERGUSON—Come on! (*He rises, lifting her in his arms, kisses her, sets her on her feet.*)

LAURA—Oh! You spoiled it.

FERGUSON (*at phone*)—Dr. Ferguson! . . . Yes! . . . Oh! Yes, sir! . . . Yes, doctor! I'll be ready. . . . I'll tend to all that. Right! (*He hangs up—turns to* LAURA.)

LAURA—All right, go on—go to work!

FERGUSON—I won't be needed for half an hour yet.

LAURA—Well, I have to go to my hairdresser's and make myself beautiful for tonight.

FERGUSON—Laura, dear, I . . .

LAURA—And what a night we're going to have! Doris asked us over there, but I want you to myself. I want to go to that cute little road house where the food and music were so good—then a long drive up the Hudson—and, darling, there's a full moon, tonight!

FERGUSON—Laura, I've some bad news. You won't be upset, will you?

LAURA—Why?

FERGUSON—I can't make it tonight. I have to stay in . . .

LAURA (*almost in tears*)—Again?

FERGUSON—I'm so sorry, dear. I tried to duck out of it, but I couldn't. There's a transfusion I have to do.

LAURA—What time? I'll wait.

FERGUSON—Better not! It depends on the patient. I've just got to be around and ready!

LAURA—Are you the only one here who can do that transfusion?

FERGUSON—Dr. Gordon seems to think so!

LAURA—George! They're overworking you. It's not fair. . . .

FERGUSON—I don't mind it so much for myself . . . only . . .

LAURA (*dully*)—No? Well, I do.

When Laura speaks again her voice has gone suddenly hoarse. She had been planning so much on this night. Of course it is not George's fault. She doesn't imagine he wants to stay at the hospital. But what is their life going to be like? It isn't just tonight. It is all nights.

"George, I know this is important to you," she says, in answer to his explanations; "and if it is going to help you . . . I can go on like this for another three months . . . for another year and three months; but when we come back to New York, let's arrange our lives like human beings. You can open up an office and have regular hours . . . specialize!"

FERGUSON—If I work with Hochberg, darling, I won't have the time to go into practice.

LAURA—That's just it. I know Hocky. I'll never see you then, George.

FERGUSON—But, Laura. . . . (*He laughs nervously.*) I've plugged all my life just in the hope that some day I'd have a chance to work with a man like Hochberg. . . . Why . . .

LAURA—I couldn't go on this way. I just couldn't. . . . I'd rather break off now, and try to forget you. . . .

FERGUSON—Laura! Don't ever say a thing like that!

LAURA—I mean it—it would kill me. But I'd rather die quickly than by slow torture. I can't . . . (*The loud speaker is calling him.* FERGUSON *and* LAURA *stand there both in anguish.*) They're calling you.

FERGUSON—I know. (*He hesitates a moment . . . goes to the phone.*) Dr. Ferguson! Yes . . . who? South 218 . . . yes? . . . well, call Dr. Cunningham. It's his case . . . let him. (*Suddenly his voice becomes brittle.*) When? What's her temperature? . . . Pulse? . . . Is she pale? . . . Perspiring? . . . Did she ask for food before she became unconscious? . . . No! No more insulin! Absolutely. I'll be right down. (*He hangs up.*) I have to go now, Laura. And please—please don't worry. (*He bends down to kiss her. She turns her face away. He straightens up and regards her with a worried expression.*)

FERGUSON—As bad as that?

LAURA (*in a low voice*)—Yes.

FERGUSON (*forcing a smile*)—Things will straighten themselves out.

LAURA—No, they won't.

FERGUSON—I'll see you tomorrow night, dear? Right?

LAURA—Yes. (*She puts on her hat.*) Think it over, George! We'll have to come to some decision!

FERGUSON—Oh, Laura, will you please . . .

LAURA—I mean it! Absolutely!

FERGUSON (*pauses for a moment in the doorway*)—All right . . . all right!

Ferguson goes. Laura stands there a moment, the picture of frustration and woe, then she walks in a little circle, crying quietly.

The lights black out.

The children's ward at St. George's is separated from the corridor by an all-glass panel to permit the nurse on duty to keep a watchful eye on the ailing youngsters inside. At the moment there is a bed screened off from the rest of the ward.

In the bed "a little girl of ten is lying back, eyes closed, skin pale and clammy. Her father stands at the foot of the bed, gazing fearfully at his little daughter. He is wan and unkempt, his hair disheveled, his eyes sunken, his collar open, tie awry—the picture of despair. His wife is standing beside the child, weeping."

Barbara Dennin, student nurse, is at the phone calling excitedly for Dr. Ferguson. A moment later Dr. Cunningham, whose case this is, enters the room. Cunningham is "a dignified impressive-looking gentleman, immaculately attired, goatee, pince-nez, throaty voice—just a bit too much of the 'professional manner.' . . . Cunningham believes that nine patients out of ten will be cured by nature anyway, and the tenth will die no matter what the physician does for him. . . . The sad part of it is that Cunningham is a successful practitioner—successful, that is, in terms of bank account. . . . Although he is not a member of the staff his success and influence have gained him the 'courtesy' of the hospital—meaning that he may bring his patients here for hospitalization."

At sight of Cunningham the parents of the child are greatly relieved. The doctor immediately takes charge. His patient, Nurse Dennin tells him, had suffered a complete collapse about two minutes before he arrived.

Dr. Cunningham glances over the chart; finds the patient's pulse barely distinguishable; applies his stethoscope to the heart and decides the condition indicates diabetic coma. It will be necessary for the now hysterical parents to leave the room.

Nurse Dennin is to prepare forty units of insulin at once, with fifty grams of glucose—

"But, sir, Dr. Ferguson advised against insulin," timidly protests Barbara.

"Ferguson? You please take your orders from me—forty units! Quick!"

Dr. Ferguson has entered the room. A glance at the patient causes him to shake his head.

"I was afraid of shock," admits Ferguson.

"This isn't shock! It's diabetic coma," snaps Cunningham.

"Her temperature's subnormal?" persists Ferguson.

CUNNINGHAM (*impatiently*)—Yes! (*To* BARBARA.) Is that insulin ready yet?

FERGUSON—I beg your pardon, Doctor, but isn't insulin contraindicated here?

CUNNINGHAM—No. It's our last chance. (FERGUSON *bites his lips to restrain himself.* CUNNINGHAM *takes the hypo from* BARBARA *and presses out the air bubbles.*)

FERGUSON—Doctor, I mean no offense, but I've studied this case history, and it looks like shock . . . not coma!

CUNNINGHAM (*pauses—looks at the patient, shakes his head*) —No . . . no. . . .

FERGUSON—But the clinical picture is so clear-cut. . . . Look at the patient! She's pale, cold, clammy, temperature subnormal. She's complained of hunger! Sudden onset!

CUNNINGHAM (*angrily*)—Suppose you let me handle this case, young man. (*To* BARBARA). Prepare that arm! (BARBARA *swabs the arm.* CUNNINGHAM *leans over the patient.* FERGUSON *hesitates a moment, then goes to* CUNNINGHAM, *puts his hand on* CUNNINGHAM'S *arm.*)

FERGUSON—Please, doctor! Call in one of the other men! . . . Ask them. Anybody!

CUNNINGHAM—There's no time! Take your hand off!

FERGUSON—That insulin's going to prove fatal.

CUNNINGHAM (*wavers for a moment, uncertain, hesitant, then he turns on* FERGUSON)—Get out of here, will you? I don't want any interruption while I'm treating my patient! (*He shakes* FERGUSON'S *arm off . . . bends to administer the hypo, hesitates a moment, then straightens up . . . confused and worried.* FER-

GUSON, *with sudden resolve, takes the hypo from* CUNNINGHAM'S *fingers and squirts out the insulin.*) Here! What are you . . . Why did you do that, you fool?

FERGUSON (*ignores him, turns to* BARBARA, *his voice crisp and cool*)—Shock position! (BARBARA *goes to the foot of the bed, turns the ratchet that elevates the foot of the fed.* FERGUSON *dashes to the door, looks out, calls down the corridor.*) Nurse! Nurse!

NURSE (*from down the corridor*)—Yes, sir?

FERGUSON—Sterile glucose! Quick! And a thirty c.c. syringe.

BARBARA—Some glucose here, sir, all ready!

FERGUSON—How much?

BARBARA—Fifty grams!

FERGUSON—Good! Half of that will do! Apply a tourniquet . . . right arm!

BARBARA—Yes, sir!

FERGUSON (*calls down the corridor*)—Never mind the glucose—a hypo of adrenalin!

NURSE'S VOICE—Yes, sir.

FERGUSON (*turns up the corridor*)—Nurse, nurse! Some hot packs . . . and blankets! Quick . . . come on . . . hurry! (*He starts to return to the patient, but* DR. CUNNINGHAM, *who has sufficiently recovered from his shock, blocks* FERGUSON'S *path.*)

CUNNINGHAM—What do you think you're doing? I'll have you brought up before the medical board. . . . I'll have you thrown out of this hospital . . . you can't . . .

FERGUSON—All right! Have me thrown out! I don't give a damn! I don't care! I really don't. . . . Pardon me! (*He brushes* CUNNINGHAM *aside and hurries to patient.*)

CUNNINGHAM (*flustered and impotent*)—I never heard of such a thing . . . why . . .

FERGUSON—Ready?

BARBARA—Yes, sir!

FERGUSON (*quickly*)—Let's have that glucose. (BARBARA *gives it to him.*) Swab that arm! Never mind the iodine! Just the alcohol! (BARBARA *swabs the arm.*) Thank God! A good vein! (*He administers the hypo.*)

CUNNINGHAM—You'll pay for this, young man! . . . That patient's life is on your hands. . . .

The assisting nurses are in with blankets and hot packs and the hypo of adrenalin, which Dr. Ferguson administers. That, he mutters, as he straightens up, is all that they can do.

Cunningham has growled an order for Ferguson to report downstairs. For seconds, strained and tense, they stand watching the patient. There is no change in the child's condition. Then, after a long moment, her arm, which has been hanging limp over the side of the bed, moves slightly. A second more and she has raised her hand to her forehead. Now she opens her eyes and sees Dr. Ferguson.

"Dr. George . . ."

"Yes, baby!"

"I'm thirsty! I want a drink! . . ."

"You bet, sweetheart!"

Nurse Dennin has jumped for the water. With Ferguson's encouragement the little girl empties the glass. Then she asks for her mother.

Ferguson turns inquiringly to Cunningham.

"I ought to report you, of course," growls Cunningham. "You're a damned, meddling young puppy. . . . However . . . under the circumstances, I guess I can afford to be lenient . . . this time. But if you ever dare interfere again in any of my cases . . . !"

The parents have rushed in and would wildly embrace their daughter if Dr. Cunningham did not restrain them. It would be better, he says, if they would leave the little girl alone for a time. They are leaving, and Dr. Cunningham is going with them. "How can I ever thank you enough for this?" the mother is saying, as they pass out of the ward.

Now the patient, with Dr. George sitting obediently at the side of her bed as she requested, has fallen into a light sleep. Nurse Dennin and Dr. Ferguson are gazing admiringly down upon her.

"Pretty kid, isn't she?" says Ferguson. "She has hair like Laura's."

"I think it was wonderful of you to stand up against Dr. Cunningham that way," insists Barbara, a note of rapture in her voice.

"Better clean up that mess," answers Ferguson, annoyed.

A moment later Barbara has dropped the hypo from trembling fingers. Its splintering attracts Ferguson's attention. He turns to see what is wrong with her. "Her jet black hair and serious, large brown eyes are set off to pretty advantage by the blue-and-white student-nurse uniform. She has a simple, naïve quality that lends her an air of appealing wistfulness. He sees how genuinely nervous she is . . . and smiles to reassure her."

FERGUSON—Has Cunningham been treating you too?

BARBARA (*smiles*)—No, sir. This is my first case with a sick child and I got to like her an awful lot. I guess that was . . .

FERGUSON—I see. What's your name?

BARBARA—Barbara Dennin.

FERGUSON—You're going to be a swell nurse, Barbara!

BARBARA—Thanks!

FERGUSON—Now, take my advice! I know just how you feel —nerves all tied up in a knot . . . want to yell! Feel the same way myself. . . . You get as far away from here as you can, tonight. Have a good time! Relax! Forget hospital! Tomorrow you'll be all right.

BARBARA—I . . . I can't. I have an exam in Materia Medica tomorrow.

FERGUSON—Materia Medica? . . . Hm! . . . I think I have some notes that may help you. . . . I'll leave them with the orderly on the first floor, and you can get them on your way down.

BARBARA—Thanks.

FERGUSON—May help you a bit. You won't have to cram all night, anyway. (*The loud speaker is calling "Dr. Ferguson."* MARY, *another and much older nurse, enters with a basin, etc.*)

MARY—Your call, Dr. Ferguson?

FERGUSON (*listening*)—Yes. Are you on duty here now?

MARY—Yes, sir.

FERGUSON—If she wakes with any pain, give her an opium suppository! If her temperature goes below normal, call me! I'll be in.

MARY—Tonight, too?

FERGUSON (*almost savagely*)—Yes, tonight, too! (*His name is called louder, more insistently. He turns to the door, mutters to the loud speaker.*) All right! All right! I'm coming! (*He goes.* MARY *turns to stare after him, her eyebrows raised in surprise.*)

MARY—Gee! Ain't he snappy today? (BARBARA *simply stares after him.*)

The lights fade out.

Room 106, which is Dr. Ferguson's cubicle, is "somber, austere, cell-like, with hardly enough space for its simple furniture. . . .

On the bureau is a small radio—the one luxury in the room. . . . The room is untidy, as all interne's rooms are. . . . A moonlit night filters through a single square window."

Ferguson, with spectacles adjusted, is poring over a huge medical work when Shorty Otis barges into the room. Shorty is in his tux, and he has, as he declares proudly, got Pete's vest. Now he wants a tie, and wants it fixed into a bow. He could also do with a bar of chocolate, if Dr. Ferguson happens to have one handy.

Pete Bradley, joining the group, has two objects in calling, in addition to adding a few words of warning regarding the proper protection of a white vest. First he reports that the patient for whose care Dr. Ferguson is staying in, is dead. Second, he would like to have someone watch his floor while he goes out and gets a sandwich. His hospital dinner was lousy. . . .

With Shorty and Pete gone Dr. Ferguson gets Laura Hudson on the telephone. Tells her that he will be able to keep their engagement after all. He finds Laura unresponsive. She is still concerned about the future.

"Listen, Laura," he insists earnestly. "That chance to work with Hochberg is one of the best breaks I've ever had! You don't expect me to throw it over, like that, at a moment's notice, simply because you have some crazy idea that . . . No, no! I don't want to even talk about it tonight. I'm tired, Laura. It's been a hell of a day! Three operations and . . . I can't think! I can't make an important decision tonight . . . in a minute! Oh, Laura! What the hell are you doing? Punishing me? . . . All right, Laura. (*A knock at the door.*) All right. . . . I'll see you tomorrow night!"

It is Dr. Levine at the door. He has come for the report on the X-rays of Mrs. Levine. The room recalls the old days.

"Poor Katherine," he mutters. "She's had so much! Things were so different when I was here . . . before I married."

"Yes," Ferguson answers. "Professor Dury told me."

LEVINE—Dury? I know just what he says: Levine—the fool!—wealthy mother—chance to work with Hochberg—to be somebody. Threw it all away . . . for a pretty face. (*He laughs to himself, sadly.*) Hm . . . Dury!

FERGUSON—Your mother? Hasn't she . . . ? (DR. LEVINE *shakes his head.*) Not yet? . . . Well, she'll come around to your way.

LEVINE (*shakes his head again*)—No. When I married Katherine, a gentile, and my mother disowned me . . . it must have broken her heart. But still, she was doing the right thing from her point of view. . . . (*He sighs.*) Poor Katherine! I didn't count on that! East Side! Tenements! Fifty-cent patients! Poverty! Dirt! Struggle! (*He shakes his head.*) I don't know. Maybe it would have been better for her the other way . . . maybe. (*He smiles sadly at* FERGUSON.) Burnt offerings! Jehovah and Æsculapius! They both demand their human sacrifice. . . . (*Pauses.*) Medicine! Why do we kill ourselves for it?

FERGUSON—I don't know. I often wonder, myself, whether it was worth the grind of working my way through college and med school. . . .

LEVINE—Med school, too?

FERGUSON—Yes.

LEVINE—I don't see how you kept up with classes.

FERGUSON—I managed.

LEVINE—Terrific grind!

FERGUSON—It wasn't much fun . . . but, still . . . I guess it's the only thing I really want to do. . . . (*Pause.*) My dad used to say, "Above all is humanity!" He was a fine man—my dad. A small town physician—upstate. When I was about thirteen, he came to my room one night and apologized because he was going to die. His heart had gone bad on him. He knew if he gave up medicine and took it easy he could live for twenty years. But he wanted to go right on, wanted to die in harness. . . . And he did. (*Pause.*) Above all else is humanity—that's a big thought. So big that alongside of it you and I don't really matter very much. That's why we do it, I guess.

LEVINE—You're right, of course! Ah . . . it's not good—too much suffering! Kills things in you. . . . A doctor shouldn't have to worry about money! That's one disease he's not trained to fight. It either corrupts him . . . or it destroys him. (*He sighs.*) Well . . . maybe some day the State will take over Medicine. . . .

FERGUSON—Before we let the State control medicine, we'd have to put every politician on the operating table, and cut out his acquisitive instincts.

LEVINE (*laughs*)—That, I'm afraid, would be a major operation!

FERGUSON (*smiles*)—Yes. . . . (*Then he becomes serious again, working himself up, thinking of Laura.*) But, it *is* a danger! We can't allow outside forces, or things . . . or people to interfere with us. . . . We can't! And, if they do, we've got to bar them out . . . even if we have to tear out our hearts to do it.

A puzzled look spreads over Levine's face. Ferguson realizes that his thoughts have taken a decidedly personal turn and stops suddenly. "I guess that's a bit off the track," he says.

There is a knock at the door. An orderly has brought the laboratory report on the X-rays. Dr. Ferguson looks at them and suddenly stiffens. The next second he is on the phone demanding confirmation of the laboratory doctor. Dr. Levine has sensed what has happened. He had expected it.

"Tuberculosis!" he mutters, sinking weakly into a chair. "Oh, my poor Katherine. What are we going to do now?"

Ferguson, dragging himself up from his first shock, is tenderly sympathetic. There is always a chance in a drier climate. If Dr. Levine were to try that. But, as Levine points out, that means starting all over again. "We're not young any longer," he sighs.

Levine has gone. Ferguson has thrown himself disconsolately on his bed when a timid knock at the door is followed by the entrance of Barbara Dennin, "breathless with the adventure." The little student nurse has come for the notes on Materia Medica that Dr. Ferguson had promised her, and she's hoping nobody has seen her.

Dr. Ferguson finds the notes, contributes a few words of explanation and dismisses the incident from his mind. But Barbara, at the door, discovers the head-nurse pacing the corridor. She will have to wait.

While she is waiting they go over the notes together. Barbara is very sympathetic. She has an idea that Dr. Ferguson is working too hard. If she thought Dr. Cunningham meant Dr. Ferguson any harm she would go right down and tell them all exactly what happened. But it is not Cunningham that is worrying Dr. Ferguson. He is just not quite himself tonight.

They have put the book of notes on the desk and are going over them together now. Their heads are close together. Barbara is puzzled by some of the Ferguson writing. He has passed her the book to explain and as his hand touches hers she clings to it.

"You know, when I thought Dot was going to die," she murmurs excitedly, "I got the feeling like I . . . I . . . God! . . .

I can't put it into words!"

"I know. I know that feeling," he says.

BARBARA—You, too?

FERGUSON—Me, too? (*Clutching his throat.*) Up to here, Barbara! Right now! Christ! I'm tired of work, and blood and sweat and pain! And the chap in 341 is dead! And Levine's wife is going to die. . . . And one begins to wonder where in Heaven's God, and what in Hell's it all about, and why on earth does anything make any difference.

BARBARA (*clutches his arm with her hand*)—Yes, that's the feeling . . . and you get so lonely . . . and you feel . . . tomorrow it's me . . . and the only thing that matters is just being alive . . . just being alive. Now! . . . Isn't it? (*She is very close to George now, clutching his arm with her hand.*)

FERGUSON (*looks at her sympathetically*)—You kids have a pretty tough time of it, don't you? Grind all day and lights out at ten o'clock.

BARBARA—And only one night out till twelve-thirty . . . and I haven't taken mine in two months. There's just nobody . . . (*They are very close now. She almost whispers the last words to him.*)

FERGUSON—You're a sweet girl, Barbara. (*Suddenly he takes her in his arms and kisses her. She clings to him for a moment. Then they separate. He is confused and upset.*) I'm sorry, Barbara . . . I . . . (*He goes to the notes, opens them—after a pause.*) These diagrams here go with this page. Aside from that, I guess they'll be pretty clear. (*He gives the book to her . . . grips her shoulder.*) Please don't feel that I . . . just . . .

BARBARA—Oh! No! No!

FERGUSON—Thanks. (*Goes to the door . . . opens it . . . looks out.*) I'm going up to Ward C, to look around for a few seconds. The coast is clear—you'd better go now. (*Exits.*)

"Barbara takes up the notes . . . walks slowly to the door . . . hesitates there a moment . . . is about to go out, suddenly stops . . . decides to stay. For a moment she leans against the door, breathless, then she goes back into the room, slowly drops the notes on the table, goes to the bed, sits down, takes off her cap, throws it on the bed and sits there . . . waiting."

THE CURTAIN FALLS

ACT II

It is three months later. In the board-room of St. George's Hospital, "a rich board-room of the same general conspiratorial appearance as the board-room of a railroad, a steel, oil, banking or other big business institution," three laymen and four doctors are gathered together.

Mr. Houghton, the economist member of the board, has just informed his associates that the institution's deficit at the moment amounts to one hundred and sixty-three thousand dollars and that there will have to be further cuts in operating costs.

The fact, Dr. Wren adds, that everything has already been cut to the bone, is not enough. Mr. Houghton feels that perhaps the personnel of the laboratories might be reduced, but this brings a quick denial from Dr. Hochberg. Without the laboratories there would be no St. George's.

Leaving finances for the moment the report of the medical board is considered. Seven new internes are recommended for two-year service on the basis of competitive examinations. The fact that a young man named Ten Eyck, son of Senator Ten Eyck, is not mentioned among them is accounted for by the further fact that young Mr. Ten Eyck had finished fourth from the end in a list of three hundred men examined. Buttressed by the report of Dr. Wren, who had given him his oral in medicine, Dr. Wren is convinced that young Ten Eyck's an ignoramus. Still Mr. Spencer is not sure that, the Ten Eyck's connections being what they are, some special consideration should not be given his case.

Which leads to the matter for which this particular meeting has been called.

"Two of our trustees are very shaky, and may not be able to meet their usual subscriptions at all," solemnly reports Mr. Spencer. "They've already spoken to me about resigning." The doctors consider this very bad news indeed. "And so, I've been looking around carefully for a new Trustee—and believe me, Doctors, it was a mighty hard search. But, finally— (*He smiles.*) I found someone to underwrite our deficit. (*Sighs of relief and approval from the doctors.*) A man well known for his philanthropies, his generous soul, his civic and social services —John Hudson—the real estate Hudson. (HOCHBERG *grunts.*) A friend of yours, I believe, Doctor!"

DR. HOCHBERG—Yes. But I didn't recognize him by the description. (MR. SPENCER *laughs.*) He'll be useful. The only real estate man I heard of who's made money the last few years. Good business head. He'll put St. George's on a paying basis.

MR. SPENCER (*laughs*)—If he can do that, he's a wizard. Mr. Houghton will resign in favor of him tomorrow.

MR. HOUGHTON—With pleasure.

MR. SPENCER—I've talked the matter over with him, and he's definitely interested. (*Chorus of approval from the Committee.*)

MR. HOUGHTON—If we can get him to subscribe for . . .

MR. SPENCER—Mr. Houghton! Please!

MR. HOUGHTON—Sorry!

MR. SPENCER—Now, it happens that one of our internes is marrying John Hudson's daughter—in a few weeks, I believe. Of course, Doctors, appointments lie completely in your hands, but we feel here is an opportunity. We suggest the medical-board offer Dr. Ferguson an associateship. . . .

DR. HOCHBERG—What? Impossible!

MR. SPENCER—Impossible? A serious student, capable, going to study a year abroad under a well-known man—why impossible?

DR. HOCHBERG—He won't be *ready* for the job!

MR. SPENCER—Have you any personal prejudice against the boy?

DR. HOCHBERG (*annoyed*)—No . . . no! (*He rises.*) As a matter of fact I'm very fond of that boy. I think he has promise of becoming a good surgeon, some day. But not over night. He has years of intensive study ahead of him. I don't care what strength of character is native to a man—he will not work for something he can get for nothing—and Ferguson's no exception. An associateship here now simply means he'll go into practice and drop his studies.

DR. LARROW—And why shouldn't he? He's marrying well. . . . With his wife's connections, he ought to . . . er . . . do very nicely.

DR. HOCHBERG—If he doesn't continue his studies, he'll never be worth a damn as far as medicine goes.

MR. SPENCER—After all, Dr. Hochberg, that's his concern, not ours.

DR. LARROW—Oh! (*Dubiously.*) He's all right. . . . But (*with conviction*) he's no infant Cushing by any means.

MR. SPENCER—We must think of the hospital, Doctors! That's our job.

DR. HOCHBERG (*losing his temper. To* DR. LARROW)—You're wrong, Doctor. That boy has *unusual* ability. Yes, yes—another Cushing, perhaps! (*Controls himself. To* MR. SPENCER *quietly.*) Exactly, Mr. Spencer! The hospital! Do you realize the responsibility in precious human life that lies in an associate's hands? Ferguson doesn't know enough, yet; he's apt to make mistakes that will hurt not only himself, but the integrity of St. George's Hospital.

MR. SPENCER—Oh, come now, Dr. Hochberg!

There is a considerable explosion of temper inspired by Dr. Hochberg's attitude. The laymen are convinced it is foolish. Even Dr. Wren thinks it possible that Ferguson could be given the appointment and then covered by an older man. Dr. Gordon feels that facts have to be faced, and that unless something is done it may easily become necessary to close down St. George's. This, of course, means closing up all the charity wards, which happen to be full at the moment. To Dr. Larrow it is quite plain that they stand greatly in need of Mr. Hudson.

"We do," admits Hochberg, spiritedly. "And till hospitals are subsidized by the community and run by men in medicine, we'll continue to need our wealthy friends. I realize that. I say by all means make Hudson a Trustee. Take all the help he can give. And promise Ferguson an associateship as soon as he's *ready* to go into practice."

"And that'll be when?"

"In five or six years."

"Oh, for Christ's sake!" explodes Mr. Houghton. "You're dealing with a business man there, not a child!"

Finally, it is the sense of the meeting that young Ferguson be appointed to the associateship and that Mr. Hudson be so notified. Incidentally, Dr. Gordon thinks, it might also be a good time to suggest to Mr. Hudson that it would be a fine thing if the hospital could extend its X-ray therapy, too.

Dr. Hochberg is ready to throw up his hands. But before he does so he would advise them not to count their chickens too soon. They cannot be at all sure that Ferguson will accept the appointment.

"I know the boy," declares Hochberg, with feeling. "He's too honest, too wise, to sacrifice his career for a nice office and an easy practice. Besides he won't have the time. He's going to work with me! And . . . er . . . well . . ." He laughs. "It was perhaps a bit foolish to waste so much energy arguing the matter." He starts for the door.

"As a matter of fact I had dinner last night at the Hudsons' and I spoke to Ferguson about the appointment," laughs Spencer.

"He's delighted with the idea. . . ."

"He said that?" demands Hochberg.

"Certainly! And why not? It's a fine opportunity for him!"

The meeting is adjourned. All except Hochberg move toward the door. "He stands there, stock still, palpably hit," as the lights fade out.

In the library of St. George's the venerable Dr. McCabe is trying to concentrate over a book. The fact that several of the internes loafing about are interested in a variety of other subjects and want to talk about them does not help him.

Once or twice Dr. McCabe frowns in protest. Once he shushes the internes vigorously. That is when they are laughing at Pete Bradley's story of a smart alec in 310 who had invited him to share a special lunch with him. Pete, liking his food, had accepted with alacrity, only to learn that 310 was in the hospital for rectal feeding.

Finally Dr. McCabe can stand no more. Fixing his eye upon Shorty Otis he demands: "Young man! How would you treat the different forms of pancreatitis?"

"Er . . . acute pancrea . . . mm . . . Why, the same way, I'd—"

"Wrong!" thunders McCabe, tossing a pamphlet toward the embarrassed interne. "Read that, and find out something about pancreatitis!"

Through the glass-paned door Dr. Ferguson and Laura Hudson are seen in the corridor. Ferguson is in civilian clothes and they are very happy, laughing and joking together. Arrived at the library Ferguson hesitates about bringing Laura in, but the others insist and soon she is gayly relating the terrifying experience she and George have just been through at a wedding ceremony rehearsal. Every step was like a major operation, Ferguson reports. Shorty starts the wedding march as a funeral dirge—and Dr. McCabe, with a snort and a bang of his book, recovers his hat and cane and stamps out of the room.

"Don't mind old Dr. McCabe," Pete reassures Laura. "He thinks the world ended in 1917 when he retired."

"Retired?" marvels Laura.

"Yes, but he still comes around to talk, read and watch operations," explains George. "Gives us hell for not knowing anything. Medicine's not just his profession—it's his life." (*He shakes his head admiringly.*) "Great guy! If I live to be eighty that's the way I want to grow old!"

"Not I," protests Laura, with conviction. "When I'm too old to enjoy life first hand I want to lie down, and say, 'Laura, it was good while it lasted. Now, fini!'"

"My idea exactly," agrees Shorty. "Why sit around and listen to your arteries hardening?"

There isn't much chance of any of them living very long, Pete suggests. Most doctors begin to weaken around forty-five. Heart goes bad. Which isn't altogether a cheerful thought.

Now Ferguson steps back into the routine. What calls have there been for him? Several, it appears. Mostly from Dr. Cunningham who has been quite impatient. Cunningham is still something of an irritation, but George decides he can stand it for another four days and then he'll be through—through and headed for Vienna!

The library is empty now, save for Dr. Ferguson and Laura. She thinks she will smoke a cigarette, if he thinks it would be all right. She is quite thrilled with everything when he lights one for her.

LAURA—Darling! You're marvelous this way. I've never seen you so high.

FERGUSON—I've never been so high! You know, dear, I love this old place, and yet, my God, I can't wait to get out of here.

LAURA—I was worried last night, after Mr. Spencer spoke to you—you looked so glum. I was afraid you might change your mind.

FERGUSON—Not a chance!

LAURA—Not bothered about that appointment?

FERGUSON—No. That'll be all right—if I get it.

LAURA—You'll get it.

FERGUSON—What do you know about it?

LAURA—I know you, you fish!

FERGUSON (*grins, then suddenly becomes serious*)—I wonder if . . . Mr. Spencer spoke to the committee, yet?

LAURA—If he did, it's quick work.

FERGUSON—I hope he hasn't yet.

LAURA—Why?

FERGUSON—Well, I want to talk to Dr. Hochberg first.

LAURA (*laughs*)—Why are you so afraid of Hocky? He won't bite you! Or, do you think by delaying it, you can change my mind—and work with Hocky when we come back?

FERGUSON—No, that's not it.

LAURA—Because if you do, I'm warning you! I'll just drop

out of the picture, George. Even if we're married—you'll come home one day, and I just won't be there.

FERGUSON (*takes her in his arms. Tenderly*)—Shut up, will you? It's just that I don't want to seem ungrateful.

LAURA—Oh, he'll probably find somebody else.

FERGUSON—Of course he will. (*Smiles, somewhat wistfully.*) There isn't a man I know who wouldn't give a right eye for the chance to work with Dr. Hochberg. You don't realize it, dear, he's an important man. He . . .

LAURA (*impatiently*)—The important man, George, is the man who knows how to live. I love Hocky, I think an awful lot of him. But, he's like my father. They have no outside interests at all. They're flat—they're colorless. They're not men—they're caricatures! Oh, don't become like them, George! Don't be an important man and crack up at forty-five. I want our lives together to be full and rich and beautiful! I want it so much.

FERGUSON (*fervently*)—Oh, my dear, so do I. . . . And believe me, that's the way it's going to be. (*He looks at her fondly.*) And I once thought I could live without you.

LAURA—What? When?

FERGUSON—Never!

Laura is in his arms and he is kissing her passionately when Nurse Jamison enters a little embarrassedly. She has come to report to Dr. Ferguson that Mrs. D'Andrea, mother of a boy brought in that morning from an automobile accident, is outside and demanding to see him.

Now Mrs. D'Andrea has forced her way past the nurse and is demanding excitedly to know whether or not her son is all right. Nor will she be put off by Dr. Ferguson's repeated assertion that nothing positive will be known until another twenty-four hours have passed. Gently they try to get her out into the corridor.

"Oh, lady, heeza my boy," she wails. "Heeza my boy! Heeza besta boy I got! Heeza besta boy in the world. If he's gonna die I'm gonna die, too."

She is mumbling her prayers as they lead her through the door. Dr. Hochberg passes them coming in. He, too, is interested in the Italian boy's case and a bit anxious when he learns that, because Dr. Ferguson had been in a hurry to keep his appointment with Laura he had turned the case over to Dr. Michaelson. It brings up indirectly the whole matter of Dr. Ferguson's future.

"George . . . I heard something this morning—I didn't know quite what to make of it," says Dr. Hochberg, speaking deliberately. "You still want to accomplish something in medicine?"

"Certainly."

"You love George, don't you, Laura?" asks Dr. Hochberg, turning to Miss Hudson.

"You know I do," she answers.

DR. HOCHBERG—Of course you do and you want to help him—but that's not the way, Laura. Believe me, nobody can help George but himself—and hard work! He cannot buy this; he must earn it. (*To* FERGUSON.) That appointment they talked to you about, George . . . you won't be ready for it. . . .

FERGUSON—After a year with von Eiselsberg, I thought . . .

HOCHBERG—One year? (*He shakes his head.*)

FERGUSON—It's not as if I were going to drop my studies. I intend to keep on. (HOCHBERG *shakes his head.*)

LAURA—I don't see why not!

HOCHBERG (*to* LAURA)—My dear child . . .

LAURA—After all, George has worked so terribly hard till now, Hocky. If it's going to make things easier . . .

HOCHBERG—There are no easy roads in medicine.

FERGUSON—I didn't expect it to be easy. I counted on work. Hard work!

DR. HOCHBERG—Ten years of it! Then . . . yes.

LAURA—I can't see how it's going to hurt George.

DR. HOCHBERG—There are a great many things you can't see, Laura.

LAURA—If he goes into practice, we'll have some time for ourselves, Hocky.

DR. HOCHBERG—Time? How? There are only twenty-four hours in a day. He's working with me and if— (*He suddenly stops short as the truth strikes him.*) Or is he—? (*To* FERGUSON.) Are you?

FERGUSON—Doctor Hochberg, I haven't loafed yet, and I don't intend to start now. But Laura and I are young. We love each other. I want a little *more* out of life than just my work. I don't think that's asking too much.

DR. HOCHBERG—I see. I see. (*Pause.*) So, you've decided not to come with me next year. (*There's a long silence. Finally* LAURA *answers apologetically.*)

LAURA—After all, Hocky, we feel that we'll be happier that way—and . . .

DR. HOCHBERG—Of course, Laura. It's George's life and yours. You've a right to decide for yourselves—what you're going to do with it. I didn't mean to meddle. . . .

LAURA—Oh, Hocky, you know we don't feel that way about you.

DR. HOCHBERG—I'm glad you don't. . . .

To hide his hurt Dr. Hochberg suddenly changes the subject. He would know how Laura's father is getting along. Still sneaking smokes, is he? Now he is reminded of an operation that will have to be performed probably within the hour. It is that of one of their own nurses—little Barbara Dennin. Such a nice little girl, too. But—here she is, suffering from a septic abortion!

Dr. Ferguson starts under the impact of this news and its possible significance. Before he can make further inquiry Dr. Michaelson has burst in to report that the boy injured in the automobile accident has lapsed into unconsciousness. There also appears to be something the matter with his lower jaw. Might be tetanus.

"No," corrects Hochberg. "Not so soon! Anyway you gave him anti-toxin, didn't you?"

"Why—er— No!"

"What? Don't you know that T.A.T. is routine in this hospital?"

MICHAELSON—Yes, sir. . . . But I thought— (*To* FERGUSON.) You didn't tell me. I thought you gave it!

DR. HOCHBERG (*to* FERGUSON)—Doctor Ferguson!

FERGUSON—I intended to . . . mention it to him. I guess—I—forgot . . .

DR. HOCHBERG—Forgot? Is that a thing to forget? You should have given the anti-toxin yourself!

LAURA—It's my fault, Hocky, I dragged him away—we were late.

DR. HOCHBERG—That's no excuse. He's not supposed to leave the house at all! And a very sick house, too. You know that, Dr. Ferguson!

FERGUSON—Yes, sir.

LAURA—Oh, Hocky—it was important! Terribly important! It was a rehearsal of our wedding.

DR. HOCHBERG—A rehearsal? Yes, Laura, that's nice. A rehearsal of your wedding. But, do you realize, upstairs, there is a boy all smashed to bits. There'll be no wedding for him, if he develops tetanus. (*To* FERGUSON.) Doctor Ferguson! Inject that anti-toxin at once!

FERGUSON—Yes, sir. (*He goes.*)

DR. HOCHBERG (*turns to* LAURA, *looks at her a moment, then shakes his head and says slowly*)—Laura, you deserve to be spanked! (LAURA'S *face becomes angry and defiant. Her jaw tightens, but she says nothing.*) Don't you realize what that boy's work means?

LAURA—Of course I do, Hocky.

DR. HOCHBERG (*softly*)—No . . . no, you don't! (*Louder.*) Would you like to see perhaps?

LAURA—Yes . . . why not? . . .

DR. HOCHBERG (*calling*)—Doctor Michaelson! (MICHAELSON *enters.*) Take Miss Hudson here upstairs, see that she gets a cap and gown, and have her in the operating room in about—(*With a sharp jerk of his arm he bares his wrist watch and looks at it.*) twenty minutes!

Without so much as another glance at Laura, he marches briskly out of the library as the lights fade out.

In a corner, at the end of the corridor, the night desk and a medicine cabinet stand. At the moment Nurse Mary Ryan is in charge here. Near the desk is the door to room 401. It is Barbara Dennin's room. Near by are the elevator doors. There is considerable activity in the corridor, with visitors arriving and departing, attendants and doctors proceeding from task to task.

Soon Dr. Ferguson arrives. He is plainly agitated. The report of Nurse Ryan that Barbara's temperature is 106 and that in her delirium she has called repeatedly for him does not serve to calm his jumpy nerves.

"God! I never dreamed this would happen," mutters Ferguson.

"Men don't—usually," answers Mary, coldly.

FERGUSON—Why didn't she come to me? Why didn't she tell me? Why did she keep away?

MARY—I guess that was my fault. Long time ago I saw she was falling for you. I told her you were in love with someone else, and engaged to be married—and to keep away from you. I didn't know then that she already . . .

FERGUSON—I see! I see! That's why she— I thought after that night . . . she'd just realized how crazy we'd both been. . . . Crazy! I thought she at least knew how to take care of herself. But when this happened . . . she should have told me!

You should have told me! Why did you let her do this?

MARY—I didn't know . . . till last night. It was . . . too late, then! She was just a green kid! Didn't realize what it was all about!

FERGUSON—God! I wouldn't have let this happen! I wouldn't have let this happen. . . .

MARY—I suppose you'd have helped her—

FERGUSON—Yes! Yes! Yes . . . rather than this . . .

DR. HOCHBERG (*pokes his head out of the door of 401*)—Where's that hypo?

MARY—In a second, Doctor!

HOCHBERG (*to* FERGUSON)—Did you tend to D'Andrea?

FERGUSON—Yes, sir! Gave him the T.A.T. He's conscious, now.

HOCHBERG—That business with his jaw—?

FERGUSON (*mechanically*)—Slight dislocation. Put it back into place. Bandaged it! No further evidence of internal injury. . . . Although there may be a slight fracture of the tibia or the fibula of the left leg. I'll have some X-ray pictures taken this afternoon!

HOCHBERG—Uh, huh! Pain?

FERGUSON—Complained of slight pain . . . general.

HOCHBERG—Did you give him some morphine?

FERGUSON—No, sir. . . .

HOCHBERG—Why not?

FERGUSON—Accident case! Didn't want to mask any possible internal injuries.

HOCHBERG—Ah! Yes. Very good, very good.

In Barbara Dennin's case Dr. Hochberg thinks her relatives or friends should be notified. So far as Nurse Ryan knows there is no one but a stepfather. Dr. Hochberg, having seen Barbara, has decided an immediate operation is necessary. Ferguson had better order the operating room.

"Don't you think operation is contra-indicated?" ventures Dr. Ferguson.

"Not in this case," replies the older man, sharply.

"If we put her in Fowler's position and . . ."

"You see, the infection is localized in the uterus . . . and it's been my experience in cases like this . . . the only way to save the patient is to remove the focus of infection. Otherwise she hasn't a chance. . . ."

"The girl was up in the children's ward. She asked to be put there, because she loves them. It seems a terrible shame to deprive her of the chance of ever having any of her own."

"It is. It is a terrible shame—yes. But, it's future life or her life. We'll save hers . . . if we can. Order the operating-room!"

Dr. Hochberg is of the opinion that the man responsible should be notified, if anyone knows who he is. Dr. Ferguson seems stunned by that suggestion. It is the sharpness of Dr. Hochberg's commands that brings him out of it.

Now the hospital routine is taken up with spirit. The operating room is ordered made ready for a hysterectomy. Orders are issued to have the patient prepared. Nurse Ryan is to give her the hypo. Orders are phoned for the rolling stretcher. Dr. Wren volunteers to give the anæsthesia. It will have to be a spinal anæsthesia, Hochberg decides.

The whining of the elevator indicates the approach of the orderly with the stretcher. Dr. Ferguson starts for the operating room to begin his "scrubbing up." The lights fade.

The first sight of the operating room inspires "a feeling of sharp, white gleaming cleanliness." At the back of the room hangs a huge kettledrum lamp which, "with its hundreds of reflecting mirrors, throws a brilliant, shadowless light on the chromium operating table."

"There is one sterile nurse, wearing cap and gown, mask and long rubber gloves; there are two unsterile nurses, similarly clothed but wearing no gloves. They move to and fro like so many pistons, efficiently, quickly, quietly—ghost-like automata."

There is a row of faucets at the side of the room, with a shelf above them littered with sterile brushes, pans of liquid soap, etc. There are two basins in a portable white enamel stand, one containing blue bichloride and the other alcohol. There is a long glove table with sterilized gloves wrapped in canvas books.

A nurse has come from the sterilizing room with a steaming tray of instruments which she places on the instrument table at the foot of the operating table. The sterile nurse sees to their proper arrangement.

Dr. Wren is washing hands and arms at the bichloride table, holding his hands up so the antiseptic rolls down the forearm and off the elbow back into the basin. He repeats this washing twice at the alcohol basin.

"A sterile nurse gives him a sterile towel. He dries his hands, using the separate sides and ends of the towel for each hand, then he tosses the towel to the floor, and crosses to the glove table." There he powders his hands, gingerly picks out a glove, handling it by the cuff, and slips it on. Other doctors follow him at the basins, employing the same technique. Some turn to the glove table. Others to the "gown drum," from which the sterile nurse deftly extricates the gowns.

["Behind the fascinating ritual of this 'sterile' or 'aseptic' technique, which has the beat and rhythm of some mechanical dance composition," footnotes the author, "lies the whole story of modern surgery and, indeed, the modern hospital. Less than eighty years ago, hospitals were festering death-houses. It was far safer to be operated on in a private home than in a hospital, where the slightest surgical cases almost inevitably developed infection. So high was the fatality that surgeons began to discuss seriously the demolition of all hospitals. Medicine pondered, 'Where did infection spring from; and, how to combat it?' Dr. Oliver Wendell Holmes, appalled at the devastating mortality in child-birth, was one of the first to suggest that the physician himself might be the carrier of infection. Semmelweis, a Hungarian doctor, cleaned up his assistants' hands, and lo!—he transformed a Viennese delivery ward from a chamber of almost certain death to one of birth and hope. Then the Frenchman, Pasteur, looked through a microscope, and the whole course of medicine was changed. After Pasteur there was Lister, the British surgeon, 'who took the torch from Pasteur and led surgery out of darkness into light.' "]

An unsterile nurse has helped Laura Hudson into a cap and gown and brought her into the room. A moment later Dr. Hochberg and Dr. Ferguson follow. Both are in operating pajamas and are putting on their masks. They are scrubbing up when Hochberg first notices Laura and calls George's attention to her. She would go to George, but Hochberg motions her away.

"Stand over there—in the corner!" he orders. "Don't come near us! We're getting clean. You're full of contamination. . . . You can look around, but keep out of the way. Don't touch anything! Put your hands behind your back!"

For a long moment only the rasping sound of scrubbing brushes vigorously applied breaks the stillness of the room. Hochberg and Ferguson follow the same routine at the antiseptic basins as the others, and get into gown and gloves with the same routine.

Now Dr. Wren has called to the orderly to bring the patient in. Barbara Dennin is wheeled in. Dr. Wren is leaning over her when Dr. Ferguson approaches the table.

"How is she, Doctor?" he asks, softly.

"George!" calls Barbara, at sound of his voice.

"Yes?"

"What are they going to do to me?"

"There is nothing to be afraid of, Barbara!"

"You won't let them hurt me?"

"No, of course not."

"Will you be there? George, darling, please be there!"

"I'll be there."

"Thanks, dear. . . . I loved you. . . . I don't care. . . ."

Almost defiantly Barbara has thrown her head back on the stretcher. Wren, with a startled look at Ferguson, has ordered the orderly forward. They are transferring Barbara to the operating table as Laura asks—

"What was that all about?"

"Laura, I'm sorry as hell," George answers; "I wish I . . ."

Impulsively she has reached out and clutched his arm. With a cry he recoils from the touch. Now he is throwing gown and gloves to the floor. One nurse picks them up. Another brings him a sterile gown as he again washes his hands and arms at the bichloride-alcohol basins.

Laura has been standing staring at him, listening vaguely to his mumbled apology that they have to be very careful. When the nurses have helped him into fresh gown and gloves she faces him again.

"Did you. . . . Did you have an affair with that girl, or what?" she demands.

"Yes . . ." Ferguson's voice is hardly audible.

"Oh!" gasps Laura, and then, with a bitter little laugh, she adds: "That's a funny one!"

Dr. Hochberg, standing on a footstool, has called sharply for Dr. Ferguson. Other doctors repeat the call. A nurse takes it up—

"Dr. Ferguson! The patient is draped and ready," she reports.

"All right! I'm coming!" he says, and starts for the operating table.

"If you want to watch—you'd better go over," says the nurse to Laura. "I'll get a stool for you—mask!"

"No, thanks," answers Laura, sharply. "I've had enough . . . ! I've had enough!"

Now she has torn off the cap and gown and started for the

door. She will accept no help from the nurses. "I'm fine!" she calls and begins to sob.

1st Nurse—Med-student?

2nd Nurse—Of course! First time! What else?

1st Nurse—She's got a long way to go, yet! (*They laugh. Nurse and Doctors about the table turn and say, "Sh! Sh!" The nurses immediately hush.*)

Hochberg—Ready, Dr. Wren?

Wren—All set!

Hochberg—Ready, Dr. Ferguson?

Ferguson—Ready!

Hochberg (*reaching out his hand, without looking up*)—Scalpel!

"The operating nurse hands over the scalpel, cutting a gleaming arc through the air, then she clumps it into Dr. Hochberg's hand. He bends over the patient. There is a sudden burst of activity and gleam of clamps about the table.

"The unsterile nurses, hands behind their backs, stand on tiptoes, and crane their necks to see over the shoulders of the assistant.

"All lights dim down, except the operating light, which bathes the tableau in a fierce, merciless, white brilliance."

THE CURTAIN FALLS

ACT III

Next morning the curtain is still drawn in Dr. Ferguson's room when Dr. Hochberg knocks on the door. Ferguson is sitting on the bed, his head in his hands. His clothes are wrinkled, his eyes are red, his hair is mussed.

Hochberg puts up the shade and the sunlight floods in. George had no idea it was so late. He had, as Dr. Hochberg has heard, been watching Barbara Dennin all night. Barbara's temperature, Hochberg is glad to announce, is down this morning.

"You must think it was pretty low of me," ventures Ferguson, refusing to permit Hochberg to divert his mind to other things. ". . . I didn't know anything about it till yesterday. I wouldn't have let her. . . . I swear I wouldn't have. . . ."

"It was a bad job!"

"Oh, that poor kid. God, I ought to be shot!"

"Did you force her to have an affair with you; or did she come to you of her own free will? Then why do you blame yourself so?"

"That has nothing to do with it."

"That has everything to do with it."

When the subject of Laura comes into the conversation Ferguson is equally inconsolable. All day he had tried to phone Laura. She would not talk with him. She is through with him, he knows that. He has made up his mind to one thing—he is going to marry Barbara Dennin. He will go into practice to support her. The fact that this may be sheer Mid-Victorian idealism does not dissuade him. Nor Hochberg's reminder of what happened to Levine. These things have nothing to do with him, Ferguson insists.

"I won't answer for Levine," replies Hochberg . . . "at least he loved Katherine. But you don't love this girl. It was an accident—and for that you want to ruin yourself—the rest of your life—destroy your ambition, your ideals—fill yourself with bitterness, live day and night with a woman who will grow to despise you. . . ."

"Dr. Hochberg. Please—it's no use. I've thought of all that! It doesn't make any difference. There's only one decent thing to do—and I'm going to do it."

Laura has arrived downstairs and is asking for Dr. Hochberg. He asks that she be sent from his office to Ferguson's room. George does not feel that he can see Laura now. He would apologize to Dr. Hochberg for everything and go.

"Yesterday . . . I must have seemed very ungrateful," he says. "But it's just because there are so many other things that I thought I wanted."

"I know. It's our instinct to live, to enjoy ourselves. All of us."

"I love Laura so much. She's so full of life and fun, and all the things I've missed for so many years. I just didn't have the guts to give them up. I kidded myself that I could have that, and still go on. And last night, I realized I kidded myself out of the most important thing that ever happened to me, a chance to work with you. . . ."

"Do you still want to? You can, if you do."

"No, not now."

"But why? If you realize now what you really want . . ."

"I'm going into practice, I told you."

"Now, George, calm down. Give yourself a chance to think

it over."

"I've thought it over."

"I warn you, George. You'll be sorry."

"I can't just ignore this!"

"In that case, you're through—you're finished—you're . . ."

"All right, then I am! Why not? What good's a profession that can't give you bread and butter after you've sweated out ten years of your life on it? And if I can't make a go of practice, I'll find a job at something else—and to hell with medicine! I won't starve. I'll always make a living. . . ."

Laura is at the door. As she enters the room she speaks deliberately to Dr. Hochberg, ignoring George. She has come to see Hocky alone, and she has little time. She would explain why she had disappeared from the operating room, but Hochberg has heard all about that. He knows how she was hurt and he did not intend it so.

Suddenly, a little limp, Laura slips into a chair. Sleep? Of course she had slept. Why not? Nervously she lights a cigarette. She is, she says, washed up with the whole business—

"I'm sorry you feel so bitter about it, Laura," interjects Ferguson . . . "I don't blame you. I . . ."

"There is no excuse for a thing like that. You know it, Hocky —none at all. . . ."

"I know nothing—except the human body, a little. And I haven't met the wise man or woman, Laura, whom impulse couldn't make a fool of. . . ."

Ferguson would leave them, but there is no reason why he should, Laura insists. She must go. She still has some packing to do. She is sailing on the *Olympic* at midnight.

There is a phone call for Dr. Hochberg. A few quick orders over the phone and he is gone. Laura, too, would follow, but Ferguson calls her back. He would not have her go feeling as she does. Whether she will believe it or not he loves her. He is holding her by the arms to impress the fact upon her, but she forces him to release her. He sinks despondently onto the bed.

She has turned again. "I don't quite understand," she says. "I didn't sleep a wink last night, George. I was trying to figure this out. But it doesn't make sense . . . except that . . . I don't know. If you cared for me how could you do that?"

FERGUSON—I don't know myself, Laura. Everything had gone wrong that day. Six long operations. I had a battle with Cunningham, I lost a patient. . . . Things sort of kept piling up till

I thought I'd bust . . . this kid came to my room for some notes . . . she was sympathetic and lonely herself, and . . . well. . . . But after that I didn't see her around, and . . . I just forgot about it. You'd think she'd come to me when this happened. But, she didn't. I know I should have looked her up. I know I was pretty small and rotten. I thought . . . I thought it didn't mean very much to her. But it did, Laura! Now she's up against it, and . . .

LAURA—If we meant anything at all to each other, you'd have come to me. I don't give a damn about ceremony! But the point is you didn't really care about me, George. Not for a minute.

FERGUSON—I wanted you more than anything else in the world that night, Laura. But we'd quarreled and—you wouldn't even go out with me.

LAURA—It was that night?

FERGUSON—Yes.

LAURA—Oh!

FERGUSON—I didn't want to give up Hocky . . . and I didn't want to give you up . . . and I was fighting you . . . and . . .

LAURA—Through her?

FERGUSON—Yes . . .

LAURA (*laughs bitterly*)—And you say you loved me!

FERGUSON—If I hadn't, I'd have called quits then and there, Laura. I'd have gone to Vienna and worked my way through. That's what I was planning to do . . . before I met you. Alone in Vienna. I'd really accomplish something. . . .

LAURA—Well, why don't you go on? Go on and do it, now. If it's so important to you. I won't be around to distract you! Go on! . . . But you're not, you see. You're going to marry a girl you say you don't care for. You're going to let a casual incident rob you of all the things you say are important.

FERGUSON—It's not a casual incident, any more, Laura.

LAURA—All right, make your beautiful gestures. Marry her!

FERGUSON—I'm going to.

LAURA—Go ahead! And inside of a year you'll be hating the sight of each other.

FERGUSON—That's a chance I'll have to take.

LAURA—You think you're being brave and strong, I suppose. But you're not. You're a coward. You're doing it because it's the easiest way out. Because you're afraid people'll say things about you! You have no backbone.

FERGUSON—Yes, Laura. You're right. I had no backbone when I let myself be talked out of a chance to work with Hocky.

And maybe to do something fine some day. But right now I have no choice. I'm not doing this because I give a good God damn what anybody says or thinks; I'm doing it because that girl's life is smashed, and I'm responsible, and I want to try and help her pick up the pieces and put them together again. (*He stops short.* LAURA *is weeping quietly.*) Oh, Laura . . . Don't!

LAURA—I knew how you felt about Hocky and I shouldn't have . . . insisted. I've been selfish, but it was only because I loved you so much. And . . . I still do. That's the way I am, George. I can't help it. I . . .

Dr. Hochberg comes slowly into the room. His face is drawn. There is "something tragic written on it."

"What is it, Doctor?" George demands, anxiously.

"Miss Dennin died," Hochberg answers. "There's nothing you can do, George," he adds, as Ferguson starts wildly for the door. "Embolism! Went into collapse! Died instantly!"

Ferguson has dropped weakly on his bed. Both Hochberg and Laura would comfort him. The thought that only a few hours ago that little nurse was pleading for a chance to live is torture to him. She was so young. She did not want to die. . . .

Laura would have him stop torturing himself. Hochberg is at pains to explain that everything known to medical science that could be done was done—"caffeine intravenously; adrenalin directly into the heart. Useless! That little blood clot in the lung . . . and we're helpless. Forty years I've spent in medicine, and I couldn't help her," sighs Hochberg.

"Then what's the use?" shouts Ferguson. "What good is it all? Why go on? It takes everything from you and when you need it most it leaves you helpless. We don't know anything. . . . We're only guessing."

HOCHBERG—We've been doing a little work on embolism . . . getting some results. It's slow, though . . . slow. Maybe, some day, George . . .

FERGUSON—Some day . . . ?

HOCHBERG—There isn't a man in medicine who hasn't said what you've said and meant it for a minute—all of us, George. And you're right. We are groping. We are guessing. But, at least our guesses today are closer than they were twenty years ago. And twenty years from now, they'll be still closer. That's what we're here for. Mm . . . There's so much to be done. And so little time in which to do it . . . that one life is never long enough. . . . (*He sighs.*) It's not easy for any of us. But in the end our reward is something richer than simply living. Maybe it's a kind of success that world out there can't measure . . . maybe it's a kind of glory, George. (*Pause.*) Yes, question as much as we will—when the test comes we know—don't we, George?

FERGUSON—Yes . . .

HOCHBERG (*goes to the door slowly, pauses there*)—Er . . . we'll reduce that fracture at ten. Schedule the appendix at three . . . the gastric-ulcer immediately afterwards.

FERGUSON—Yes, sir. (HOCHBERG *goes.* LAURA *turns to* FERGUSON.)

LAURA—Oh, darling! I'm so sorry! (*Pause.*) George, let's get away from here. Let's go some place where we can talk this thing over quietly and sanely.

FERGUSON—No, Laura. This is where I belong!

LAURA—Yes. . . . (*Pause.*)

FERGUSON—You see . . .

LAURA—I understand. . . . (*Pause.*) Well . . . when you come back from Vienna, if Hocky'll let you off for a night give me a ring! I'll be around. And, maybe some day we'll get together, anyway. (*The loud speaker is heard calling: "Dr. Ferguson." She smiles wryly.*) They're calling you.

FERGUSON—Yes.

LAURA—Work hard.

FERGUSON—So long, Laura. (LAURA *tears herself away and hurries out.* FERGUSON *stares after her till she disappears. The loud speaker calls him back. He goes to the phone, slowly, a bit stunned. He picks up the phone.*) Yes? Dr. Ferguson! . . . Who? . . . Oh, Mrs. D'Andrea? Sure! Your boy's all right! Yes. Now, you mustn't cry, Mother! You mustn't! He's all right! (*With his free hand he is brushing the tears from his own eyes and nose, for he is beginning to weep himself. But you could never tell it by his voice, which is strong with professional reassurance.*) We'll fix his leg this morning, and he'll be home in a week. Yes . . . he's going *to live* . . . don't cry!

He is still reassuring her as

THE CURTAIN FALLS

DODSWORTH *

A Comedy in Three Acts

BY SIDNEY HOWARD

(From the novel of the same title by Sinclair Lewis)

THIS unusual theatre season had been pretty well humanized before "Dodsworth" was offered the last of February. Playgoers had grown accustomed to acknowledging their more spontaneous emotional reactions. They had cheered "Men in White," "Ah, Wilderness!" and "Mary of Scotland," and these were frankly theatre pieces. They had openly reveled in such light domestic comedies as "Her Master's Voice" and "The Pursuit of Happiness." And they had gone unashamedly sentimental in their acceptance of "The Wind and the Rain," "Wednesday's Child" and "The Shining Hour."

"Dodsworth" crystallized the season's prevailing sentiment. It combined the homeliness of subject and the vigorous character honesty of the best plays of the year. It, too, was cheered. Cheered a little more vigorously than any of the others. Both for its well-nigh perfect characterizations by Walter Huston, playing the retired automobile manufacturer, and Fay Bainter who was the irritating but excessively human Mrs. Dodsworth, and for the frank theatricalism Sidney Howard had employed in his craftsmanlike adaptation of the Sinclair Lewis story.

As the run continued the play's popularity grew. It doubtless could have continued through the summer, but Mr. Huston had agreed to play Othello at the Colorado drama festival in July, which necessitated a temporary break in the engagement.

As the play opens in the office of the President of the Revelation Motor company in Zenith, which is a mid-Western American city of some size, Samuel Dodsworth, president, is bidding good-by to his employees. It is a January day and late in the afternoon. The men file in through one door marked "President," shake hands

* The complete text of the play version of "Dodsworth" is to be issued this fall by Harcourt, Brace & Co., and will include introductions by both Sidney Howard and Sinclair Lewis on "The Art of Dramatization."

with "the chief," and file out a second door marked "Private." The vice president of Revelation Motors, Mr. Harry E. Hazzard, is directing the party.

We of the audience can see only the Dodsworth back, which twitches occasionally with the repressed emotion of the moment. He shakes each hand extended to him, accepts with a friendly smile the greetings of his workmen and his office force, but finds his emotions too deep for speech.

"Good-by, sir!" . . . "Good-by, Chief!" . . . "Sure wish you luck!" . . . "Been a long time since we started in together, Sam!" . . . "Me too, Chief. But I'd do every day of it over again!"

They are mostly shop employees, this division. Then come the sales manager and his crew; the publicity man, and the Dodsworth secretary.

"Never sell for any boss like I did for you, Chief!" . . . "Pretty rough on my publicity sometimes, sir, but you were always right! Yes, sir, always right!"

Only the secretary seems in immediate danger of breaking down. She must express her feelings through sobs she strives vainly to suppress.

"I'd like to go on being your secretary forever," she sobs. "I'm going to feel just lost without you. Excuse me, sir, I can't help it!"

This is the last of the line. Now Hazzard adds his pumphandle shake to the others, also with deep feeling. He will be at the station to see Dodsworth off. Meantime he would have Sam know that wherever he may get in Europe old Harry Hazzard will be serving as nothing but his mouthpiece in Zenith, waiting to turn the Presidential office right back to him.—

"Because you know, Sam, that you're the greatest automobile man on earth to me."

Hazzard has worked the pumphandle again, gulped and made his way through the door.

"Dodsworth stands motionless for a moment. Then he turns for the first time to take a long last look at his office. When he has looked his full, he goes to the desk and stands over it; laying his hands upon it as though it were the cradle of a dead child."

He has opened the empty drawers of his huge desk and slammed them shut with the metallic clang peculiar to modern office furniture. He stops at the window and looks out over the roofs of the plant to the skyscrapers of Zenith. He has jammed on his hat and is leaving quickly as the curtain falls.

In the library of Dodsworth's house in Zenith, "a warm room with deep chairs, heavy hangings, thick carpets, low lights and an open log fire in operation," Fran Dodsworth, an attractive woman some years younger than Dodsworth, smartly dressed for traveling, is checking over a list with Mary, a maid.

There are a few books selected by Mr. Dodsworth that still have to go in his suitcases; there are the dresses to be sent to the Thrift Shop; there are the magazines that are to be sent to the Salvation Army (all except *Fortune*); there are messages to be left for Miss Emily and Mr. McKee when they get back from their honeymoon, and—

Dodsworth has come through the door. Mary is dismissed and the Dodsworths are in each other's arms.

"Is everything settled?" anxiously inquires Fran.

"The Revelation Motor Company, Samuel Dodsworth, President and founder, became the property of United Motors a little over an hour ago," Dodsworth answers, with an additional hug.

FRAN—How do you feel?

DODSWORTH—How would any man feel who's just sold twenty-five years of his life?

FRAN—I suppose you feel kind of lost.

DODSWORTH—I knew what I was doing when I sold, Fran. I know what I'm after from now on. (*He sits in a chair by the fireplace.*)

FRAN—You want a drink, Sam. Let me mix you one. (*She goes to the table to make a whiskey and soda; his eyes following her.*) You mustn't feel lost, though. I mean, that will wear off. Life isn't going to be empty from now on. It's going to be fuller than ever! And richer! For both of us, Sam! Think! You're free! After twenty years of doing what was expected of us, *we're* free! (*She has brought the drink to him where he is sitting by the fire.*) Don't look so mournful about it, darling! Is that the wrong thing for me to say? I'm sorry! It all seems so exciting to me!

DODSWORTH—I'm just as keen on this trip as you are, Fran; I'm rarin' to go! I've always wanted to see London and Paris!

FRAN—Oh, but I want much more than a trip out of this, Sam! I want a new life all over from the beginning! A perfectly glorious, free, adventurous life! And it's coming to both of us,

Sam! Haven't we earned it?

DODSWORTH—What's to prevent?

FRAN (*gayly*)—Nothing if we start off on a free foot! Why, I'd—I'd almost sell this house so we wouldn't have anything to tie us down!

DODSWORTH—Good Lord, Fran! It's our home! We've built ourselves into it!

FRAN—What I want is to get us some new selves now!

DODSWORTH (*amused*)—Me?

FRAN—Yes, you! Give yourself a chance to enjoy your leisure and you'll see! Why, you might get to be an ambassador, Sam!

DODSWORTH (*impressed*)—Me?

FRAN—Yes, you might, easily! Why, if we weren't tied to this deadly, half-baked Middle Western town!

DODSWORTH (*rising*)—Now, Fran, don't start knocking Zenith!

FRAN—I'm not knocking Zenith, Sam! But I can't help wanting. . . . I'm thinking of my freedom, too! And I want the lovely things I've got a right to! In Europe a woman of my age is just getting to where men take a serious interest in her! And I just won't be put on the shelf by my daughter when I can still dance better and longer than she can! I've got brains and, thank God, I've still got looks! And no one ever takes me for more than thirty-five or thirty even! I'm begging for life, Sam! No, I'm not! I'm demanding it!

DODSWORTH—Well, if that's how you feel . . . (*He takes her in his arms.*) I'll enjoy life if it kills me! And it probably will!

FRAN—I'll love you much more when you're not just an old horse in a treadmill!

The Tubby Pearsons are in. He is high-spirited and garrulous. She, called "Matey," is "a generously proportioned lady in her forties." They are both excited over the leave-taking and, incidentally, amused at finding the Dodsworths still clinging to each other, "carrying on," as Mr. Pearson suggests, "like Anthony and Cleopatra."

The Pearsons were not satisfied with just going to the station. They must have a little private leave-taking of their own. Now Matey has followed Fran upstairs to help with the last of the packing and Tubby has moved over to the whiskey table to have a drink with Sam.

Tubby has really come over to give Sam hell. The United people have been consulting Tubby, as a banker, and have asked him to use his influence with Dodsworth.

"Sweet jumping Jesus, man," explodes Tubby, "what are you up to? They tell me they offered to make you first vice president of their whole outfit in charge of production of all their cars, and . . ."

"They offered me a hundred thousand the first year in addition to my stock, which would come to . . ."

"And you turned it down! But Americans like you and me can't quit work, Sam! We're meant to keep on working till we die in harness!" Tubby is quite indignant.

"I'm out to make a new life for myself, Tubby," smiles Dodsworth. "I'm out to learn how to enjoy my leisure now that I've retired. Been doing what people expected of me always. Want to sit under a linden tree, now, and not worry about anything more important than the temperature of the beer. If there is anything more important."

"If you think I can see my oldest and closest friend turned into an expatriate parlor snake because Zenith isn't good enough for his wife . . ."

"Easy now, Tubby!"

"Ever since college I've yessed you and looked up to you! You're pretty God-damn near everything that I'm not and ought to be! But you're the rear end of a horse about your wife!"

"The hell I am! You don't know what you're talking about! I'm not through! I'm going on doing plenty more before I . . ."

There is a loud cry of "Dad!" from the hall. A second later the Emily Dodsworth that was, the Emily McKee that is, has burst into the library and has hurled herself on her father and is enfolded in his arms.

The McKees, realizing suddenly that they would have only time for lunch with the travelers in New York, decided to fly back to Zenith for a farewell dinner.

Dodsworth isn't sure he likes the idea of Emily flying around in airplanes, and he is a little worried about their breaking off the honeymoon just for a visit with the old folks. But Emily is content.

"I don't think so much of sending a girl off on a trip with a husband she doesn't know yet," says she. And Harry McKee is of the opinion that so long as the Dodsworths are turning the old house over to them to live in, the least they could do was to come on and accept it formally.

Now Fran and Matey have come down to the big surprise. Fran is very happy at finding Emily. Everybody is happy, in fact, and entirely agreed with Dodsworth when he declares this to be an occasion calling for champagne.

"How do you get champagne cold in a hurry?" he asks, joyfully.

"You might try putting it on ice!" suggests Tubby.

HARRY—What's this about the sale of the company, sir? The New York afternoon papers were full of it!

DODSWORTH—All good things have to come to an end some time, Harry.

FRAN—So that even better things can have a beginning.

TUBBY—Not better for Sam Dodsworth! Sam's going to regret this to the end of his life!

MATEY—Now, Tubby.

FRAN—Tubby's famous for his own peculiar brand of humor!

TUBBY—Now that's all right, Fran. But Sam knows as well as I do that . . .

DODSWORTH (*tolerant—good-humor*)—No, I don't, Tubby! All I know is I'm out to see some of the world I haven't seen and get a perspective on the U. S. A. Might get to know myself at the same time. (*He goes, smiling, to* FRAN.) Might even get to know my wife. (FRAN *smiles back at him. He touches her.*) Did I remember to tell you today that I adore you?

The lights fade.

The scene changes to the S.S. "Ultima." It is the evening of the Captain's dinner. In the smoke room, "trimmed in cork and chromium which belong to the more recent aspects of modernistic decorative taste," the corner devoted to the bar is fairly busy.

From the salon adjoining the strains of seductive dance music float in. At one table Clyde Lockert, "attractive, fortyish, tropic-bronzed, British, dinner-coat," is smoking a cigarette and drinking brandy and soda. At another table a young American couple are just finishing their drinks, and at another two American ladies are trying to figure out what they should tip. "They belong to the far-flung matronly type which travels with the pince-nez and the large handbag." At the bar two Jewish gentlemen are comparing the respective virtues of brandies as represented by Hennessy and Martel.

The American wife is trying to convince the American husband that the Crion is the place to go, even if it does cost a little more. And will he remember she has hidden his American cigarettes in his pockets.

The first Jewish gentleman favors trying a different boat for each crossing and the second Jewish gentleman prefers to stick to one boat and get service. They decide to take a turn around the deck for the air and would take Mr. Lockert with them, but he is waiting for Mrs. Dodsworth.

The first American lady takes another draw at the straw in her crème de menthe and remembers that the smoke room was ever so gay the night before when Mr. Dodsworth auctioned off the pool. Tonight she thinks she will sit and watch the dancing.

"Have you taken many books out of the library?" inquires her companion.

"Just the 'Châteaux of Old Touraine' and 'The Well of Loneliness.' "

"Then a dollar's plenty for the library steward," agrees the first.

A slightly intoxicated American, still wearing his paper hat, is in to order a flock of champagne cocktails, but his wife, who follows quickly after, would change hers to a gin fizz.

The bar corner is comparatively empty when Fran Dodsworth arrives from the deck. "She is charmingly dressed, a most sumptuous evening wrap bundled about her."

"I left him outside to cool off," she explains, as she sits down at Lockert's table. "Four martinis, most of a quart of champagne and three cognacs do leave a glow behind them. The fresh air won't hurt him. He thinks he sees a lighthouse or something."

Fran would have Lockert finish his drink and dance again with her. She is not sorry the voyage is over. Thanks to Major Lockert and his British friends she has not been bored, but she is even more eager than Sam to set foot on British soil. And when she does . . .

"You'll try your wings?"

"That's very pretty, Major. I hope I don't fall."

"You won't. You'll soar out of sight. I shall be there with my telescope watching you."

Mrs. Cortright has come in from the salon, smiled and spoken pleasantly as she passed the Lockert table. "She is not much older than Fran, but she has not made Fran's effort to disguise her years. She is dressed with supreme distinction."

"I've been laying out things for us to do in London," Lockert confides to Fran, as Mrs. Cortright passes on to another table.

"For us to do?" Fran smiles skeptically. "No. I know all about these steamship intimacies."

The two American ladies, having paid their check and gathered their bags, are leaving. Mrs. Cortright is at the window peering out.

"Look at those two women!" says Fran, a thinly disguised disgust in her voice. "Can't you see them in Venice with their Baedeckers? Why is the traveling American always so dreadful?"

"Why are you Americans all so hard on each other?"

"You enjoy talking me down, don't you?"

"Only know two peoples who run down their own race. Americans and Jews."

"That's idiotic! Is it snobbish to want to see something besides one's fellow citizens abroad? Or to want to know more of life than one's always known? (*Her tense restlessness again comes over her.*) I was thinking of that story you told Sam this afternoon. About the snakes you find on your plantation veranda, down in Cuba or wherever it is!"

"Guinea!"

"I've never found anything but the morning paper on mine! You don't know what one misses living a safe and sane American life. I may be a snob, but I know what I want, you see! Please finish your drink! I want to dance now."

Mrs. Cortright has returned to her table and ordered coffee and cognac and a pack of cards when Sam Dodsworth comes bursting in from the deck.

"Fran! It *was* land!" he cries.

"Was it, Sammy, dear?"

"Bishop's Light, they call it. If I had a motor boat I could be ashore in half an hour! Ashore in England! I can't believe we've done it!"

"If you keep on across the ocean in a straight line, Sammy, you're bound to strike land sooner or later."

"But England!"

"That's the most natural part of it," puts in Major Lockert. "If it were Africa now, where England ought to be. . . ."

"My first sight of England isn't funny to me!" Dodsworth answers, sharply.

"I don't know what I'm going to do about Sam's Anglomania," protests Fran.

She will not go see the light with him. It's cold on deck and, besides, she wants to dance with Major Lockert. Dodsworth is still calling after Fran as she and Lockert continue on their way toward the music. A moment later he is asking the Steward's advice about something that will quiet his nerves.

"Why don't you try stout?" speaks up Mrs. Cortright from

her solitaire game at the table.

It seems a good suggestion, though a bit surprising to Dodsworth, and he orders stout—a double stout.

"And what was it you just called that light? I saw it, too," continues Mrs. Cortright.

"Bishop's Light!" Dodsworth tells her, moving over to the table. "Never been across before. Got excited. Took one look at that light and all the things I've ever read about England came to life. The town behind it, with those flat-faced brick houses and a cart crawling up a hill between high hedges! And Jane Austen and Oliver Twist and Robin Hood! England! Mother England! Home!"

MRS. CORTRIGHT (*struck by his eloquence*)—Have you always felt that way about England?

DODSWORTH—I don't know! It just now struck me, but I guess I must have. Most Americans would, you know, if it weren't taught out of 'em. Why, all my people came from England! Why . . .

MRS. CORTRIGHT (*slightly alarmed*)—Sit down, Mr. Dodsworth, and drink your stout. You do need soothing.

DODSWORTH (*obeying*)—Been having such a good time on this trip! Everybody's so nice.

MRS. CORTRIGHT—Oh, there's nothing like a first trip to Europe!

DODSWORTH—Especially when you're old enough to know what you're after.

MRS. CORTRIGHT—What you're after? What *are* you after?

DODSWORTH—My wife. . . . Of course she's been over before . . . she wants me to learn how to enjoy my leisure now I've retired. What it boils down to: been doing things myself for a long time now. Thought I'd give things a chance to do something for me.

MRS. CORTRIGHT—The education of an American!

DODSWORTH—You might call it that!

MRS. CORTRIGHT—How long have you given yourself?

DODSWORTH—Six months.

MRS. CORTRIGHT—To get all that done?

DODSWORTH—I'll be homesick by then. (*Pauses.*)

MRS. CORTRIGHT—Yes; I was homesick the first year I came over.

DODSWORTH—Came over? Where from?

MRS. CORTRIGHT—Michigan.

DODSWORTH—Are you an American?

MRS. CORTRIGHT—I don't know what I am. (*She smiles.*) I used to be a British subject by marriage. I don't know that one can be a British subject by divorce. I expect I'm just a woman who lives in Italy.

There are thousands such as she living in Italy, Mrs. Cortright explains. It's cheap. Dodsworth's interest grows. He wonders that he has not met Mrs. Cortright before. Fran had told him she seemed to prefer being by herself. That, explains Mrs. Cortright, depends largely on how she is feeling. She feels much better tonight than she has before.

In further exchange of confidences Dodsworth admits that he feels a man without a job and a wife who wants a fling can do worse things than travel. But for a steady thing he thinks America is the best place, especially for Americans. Fran will find that out, too.

Mrs. Cortright, it appears, is not playing solitaire, as Dodsworth assumes. She is telling her fortune.

"The cards told me to speak to you," she smiles, turning to her game. "Look, there it is again! The black king and the red queen after him." She smiles at this slip of the tongue. "Well, I don't know that I should take that too seriously," she adds. "There should be an obstacle. Odd I don't seem to find—"

The other passengers are coming back from the salon, variously interested in more drinks before the bar closes.

"I wanted to ask you to join us the other night," confesses Dodsworth. "Fran said you wouldn't like it. I claim anything friendly goes on shipboard."

"Bar's just closing!" calls the barman.

"Bar closing?" echoes Dodsworth, in some excitement. "Hey! Wait a minute! Bring us a bottle of champagne and two glasses. No, make it four."

He turns again to Mrs. Cortright.

"I was almost forgetting I had a wife. I must see that you and Fran get acquainted before it's too late," he says. The lights fade.

The Dodsworths are in their sitting room in the London Ritz. "The familiar chilly French taste has employed the familiar plaster moldings to divide the walls into 'paneled effects.' The familiar boule cabinets, escritoire, gilt sofa and empire table are all present."

From the window Dodsworth can see Piccadilly Circus. There's a thrill in that. Fran is fixing flowers that have come from sweet old Lady Enderly.

"She says she cut these herself in her own garden in Enderly Castle," reports Fran. "She wants us to dine with her in town next Wednesday. Now London's really beginning!"

"Remember the first time I asked you to marry me and said we'd come here together?" sentimentalizes Dodsworth.

"And here we are!"

"God, I love you more than ever, now I've got time for it!"

"I love you, Sammy!"

A knock on the door announces the arrival of Major Lockert. He is used to sneaking about the Ritz without having himself announced, though he feels a little strange there without an American passport.

While Sam is busy with a shaker of dry Martinis Major Lockert has a chance to compliment Fran on the smartness of her gown. Suggests to him that she would look fine on a horse. He hopes the Dodsworths will come for a week-end at his uncle's, Lord Herndon's. Fran is excited about that.

"The real English, Sam!" chirrups Fran. "And it isn't four weeks yet since we left Zenith! Thank you, Clyde! Thank you for all you've done for us here."

"Fran, dear!"

Dodsworth is at the telephone. A friend named Hurd is announced, and told to come up. Fran had particularly asked Sam not to ask Hurd.

"I will not be the ex-president's lucky little woman to that back-slapping salesman!" announces Fran.

"You're both going out!" protests Dodsworth. "He's taking me out! It won't hurt you to give him a minute."

Hurd is a busy, "round-faced, horn-spectacled, heavy-voiced man." He bursts in with great exuberance. This is a great occasion for him, introducing Samuel Dodsworth to the British Empire!

"By Jove, the way my chest was sticking out down in the lobby they must have guessed I had something up my sleeve," beams Hurd. "How are you, Mrs. Dodsworth? You look well, and not a year older! Well, if seeing you doesn't take me right back to Zenith. And I hope you don't hold it against me for taking your husband out on a bit of a bender, as we say over here?"

"Not at all, Mr. Hurd. Don't think about me."

"Guess it would be pretty hard not to think about you, Mrs. Dodsworth," answers the gallant Hurd.

Now he has met Major Lockert and recalled that he knows the Major's uncle, General Herndon.

"General Lord Herndon of the Italian drive," Fran adds.

"Want to get the Major to take you out to the General's place in Kent, Mrs. Dodsworth," Hurd rattles on. "Have a barrel of fun every time I go out. . . . How's she making out in London, Chief? Guess she finds our English customs kind of strange. (*To* FRAN.) You've got to come out to dinner with me some night soon. (*To* DODSWORTH.) Got to give the lady wife a break, too, Chief? (*To* FRAN.) Eh, Mrs. Dodsworth? (*Patting her arm.*) I'll take you to the Savoy Grill, Mrs. Dodsworth, where you can get real American grub. Guess that'll taste pretty good to you on foreign soil! Real American grub! And we'll take in a show. You folks ought to enjoy the London stage. Real gentleman actors who know how to speak the language like . . . as I've learned . . . how to do. And you've got to come out to Mrs. Hurd and I in the country. . . ."

That is about all Fran can stand. She manages finally to attract and hold Major Lockert's attention, but not until he has taxed her patience further by stopping for a short discussion of the merits of American whiskies and the native ability to distinguish between rye and Bourbon. "It's Bourbon for juleps and rye for Old Fashioneds," explains the increasingly expansive Hurd. And that is all anyone needs to know.

The men have had a drink from a bottle of pre-war Old Crow which Hurd has brought as a present to Sam and the party is ready to move.

"I hope you enjoy your dinner, Sam," Fran calls from the door. "I hope it brings back all the charms of Zenith! Don't drink too much, will you? Good night, Mr. Hurd."

"Good night," calls Hurd, looking after Fran in all sincere admiration. "She's a lovely woman, Mrs. Dodsworth! A lovely woman!" he assures Sam.

Dodsworth has put his Old Crow away and found his hat and coat as the lights fade.

It is after 12 when Sam Dodsworth opens the hall door slowly and lets himself and Hurd in that night. They are both wearing their coats and hats and both have had something to drink. Dodsworth does not show the effects of his celebration particularly, but Hurd is of a mind to continue with his singing.

"My name is Yon Yonson, I come from Wisconsin . . ." is the tune of his choice.

"You'd be surprised, Chief, the music there is in men like me that never comes out except at stag dinners," explains Hurd.

"My wife always says she's got nothing against stag dinners except the fellows I bring home with me afterwards," answers Dodsworth.

Hurd is not to be easily turned aside from his thirst for what he calls "a wee deoch in doris," but Dodsworth is determined to serve no more drinks in the room. They will get one downstairs. Dodsworth has just swept Hurd out through the bedroom when the hall door again opens to let in Fran Dodsworth and Major Lockert.

There had been some talk of their going on to a night club, but they are both now agreed that night clubs are foul places. Fran does not know exactly how long her husband will be. That will depend upon the amount he may have had to drink. But she is rather in hopes that Major Lockert will not mind amusing her until Sam does come home.

The Major is perfectly agreeable. He might worry a bit if he thought Dodsworth was likely to come home roaring and shoot when he found him there. Men have done such things.

"Sam has all the old-fashioned virtues except jealousy," Fran explains reassuringly.

"Call it a virtue, do you?"

"Well, when a wife who isn't exactly plain seems attractive to other men and doesn't mind—when they show her they are attracted . . ."

"Oh, quite! Yes, I see what you mean. . . ."

They are sitting on the sofa now. Major Lockert admits that he is not feeling particularly amusing. He had rather hold Fran's hand, if she doesn't mind.

Fran doesn't mind, particularly, though "this has not happened to Fran for a long time and she has to swallow a bit to summon up her worldliness."

"The great thing is never to hold a woman's hand too lightly," explains the Major.

"You're holding mine as though it were a sacred relic," smiles Fran.

LOCKERT—Like to hear me take a sacred oath on it?

FRAN—Sounds flattering. What is it?

LOCKERT—To settle down and do something with my life.

FRAN—Surely you don't need my hand for that!

LOCKERT (*just the required note of burlesque*)—You've given me the courage to look squarely at myself and to turn about, my dear Fran. And you've made turning about seem worth while. And not too late!

FRAN—I've read that in books, but it's nice of you to say it!

LOCKERT—Don't go trekking over the Continent. Stay here! You belong here! We need you and love you here! I need you and love you!

FRAN (*really bewildered by this direct attack and unable to control her nervousness*)—You don't mean that! And I don't want you to mean it!

LOCKERT—You're so wrong, Fran, dear! There's so much of you that's never been given a chance!

FRAN—Well, I shouldn't be human if I didn't love hearing that! But if you don't change the subject, Clyde . . . (LOCKERT *bends over suddenly and kisses her on the lips. She is startled.*) That was a very silly thing to do, Clyde. And I didn't like it! (*Then, further to support her worldly poise, she finds herself a cigarette.*)

LOCKERT (*on his feet to light a cigarette for her*)—Do you mind my saying that there's something about you at the moment that I'm finding astoundingly attractive?

FRAN—Don't you think we're seeing too much of each other, Clyde?

LOCKERT—My dear Fran, dismiss that idea from your mind at once and come to tea at my place tomorrow!

FRAN (*rising*)—I shall not come to your place tomorrow and I shall say good night now.

LOCKERT—Can't you think of something cheerier to say than just "Good night"? I mean, "Good night, Clyde," or even "Good night, Clyde dear," would . . .

FRAN—"Good night's" all I'm inclined to say to you!

LOCKERT—You know, you're taking a wickedly unfair advantage of me, trying to make me feel you resented my . . .

FRAN—Did you think I wouldn't resent it?

LOCKERT—May I ask what reason you've given me to think you would? (*This somewhat jars the pleasure in the thrill.*)

FRAN—I haven't given you the slightest excuse!

LOCKERT—I thought I was doing what was expected of me.

FRAN—What I expected of you?

LOCKERT—Not you alone, Fran. There's a tradition about this sort of thing.

FRAN (*her worldliest*)—I thought civilized people knew where an innocent flirtation stops!

LOCKERT—For a civilized woman who's been married as long as you have, you're making a great deal of a small matter. (*He intends this to anger* FRAN, *and it does.*)

FRAN—It isn't a small matter to me! Will you go without saying any more, please?

LOCKERT—I'll go, of course! (*He rises.*) And I offer you my most abject apologies. (*Smiles.*) If I may also offer you one bit of advice, give up undertaking things you aren't prepared to finish. It's evident they only lead you out of your depth.

FRAN (*outraged*)—Out of my depth!

LOCKERT—. . . which is not all it should be.

It is Major Lockert's further opinion that Fran is acting a good deal less intelligently than a modern school girl would have done and that her "most charming and childish misconception" about herself as a woman of the world is not only all wrong, but not likely soon to be corrected.

Fran is mad enough to call the hotel servants and have Major Lockert put out, but just then Dodsworth comes back. He is jovial and friendly, glad to report a pleasant evening at the dinner, with more good talk than he has heard the whole three weeks he has been in England.

Now Major Lockert is going. His good nights are friendly, but formal. He would make sure that Mrs. Dodsworth is positive she is not free for tea the next day—which she is. That, declares the Major, seems a pity. "You'd have enjoyed that tea," says he.

"He's not so bad," agrees Dodsworth, when the Major has gone. "He's fresh, but he's not so bad."

Fran has dropped into a chair and burst into hysterical sobs. Sobs inspired by anger. Lockert's a rotter, she tells her husband.

He has insulted her and when she had tried to put him in his place he had humiliated her. . . . The sobs are redoubled and hysteria threatens.

"I suppose it's up to me to go out and shoot him," ventures Dodsworth, a little hesitantly.

"Don't joke, Sam!"

"I would feel like a fool!" admits Dodsworth. "You and I aren't up to this kind of thing. Makes us look like the hicks we are."

"Sam!"

"Well, it does. And it's your own fault for leading him on!"

"So I'm to blame?"

"He must have had some excuse for making a pass. You have been flirting with him! And you've got such a sweet way of bawling me out in front of him, he'd naturally conclude . . ."

"I've never said anything to embarrass you! I'm always loyal to you! Oh, you'll be sorry! You'll be sorry!"

Dodsworth is tired. He'll smoke a cigarette and turn in. But Fran is not finished.

"We never used to scrap so much at home," she says, looking up at him pathetically.

"Guess we haven't got enough else to do over here."

FRAN—Don't say that! (*He looks at her. She stops.*) It's England! England's such a strain! I want to go over to France, tomorrow, Sam!

DODSWORTH (*protesting*)—But I like it here!

FRAN—I don't!

DODSWORTH—I'm just beginning to get on to London. I've got a date to look at some aeroplane factories here!

FRAN—I don't care if you have!

DODSWORTH—France'll be so foreign!

FRAN (*going to him, pleading passionately*)—I want it to be! I want to start all over! I'm so ashamed about this Lockert business. Ashamed way down inside me! And I can't stay in this country with that man laughing at me and saying . . .

DODSWORTH (*taking her tenderly in his arms*)—What? That you kicked him out?

FRAN—That isn't what he'll say! You've got to take me away! (*Pressing her face against his chest.*) You've got to look after me! You really have, Sam! I don't trust myself! I'm afraid of myself.

DODSWORTH—Afraid, sweetheart?

FRAN (*nodding*)—Yes, I am! (*Clinging to him, she looks away as though fearing that some specter might walk through the door.*) I'm just a woolly American like you, after all. If you ever catch me trying to be anything else will you beat me?

DODSWORTH (*tender but wary*)—Will I have to beat you very long at a time?

She nestles against him as

THE CURTAIN FALLS

ACT II

A month later the Dodsworths are in Paris. Their salon at the Ritz so closely resembles the salon they had in the London Ritz it is difficult to tell one from the other. "To be sure, the curtains and carpets have changed to another pastel shade and the arrangement of the furniture is slightly different, but the same spirit of cheerless *bon goût* prevails."

"Fran, Mrs. Cortright and Mme. de Penable are drinking their after dinner coffee. Fran is dressed exquisitely, Mrs. Cortright with her usual simple distinction and Mme. de Penable to suit her Gallic and well-preserved hatchet face."

"Aren't the French too divine?" Fran is asking. "Everything done so perfectly, with such taste and ease! That salon next door turned into a salle-à-manger at a moment's notice! Sam wanted this little dinner chez soi, you know. He was so particular when he heard I'd got you. I've never been more flattered than at your staying in Paris just to dine with us. . . ."

Mme. de Penable is eager that Fran shall not forget to sign a lease before the men come back. It is a lease of the Duchesse de Quatrefleurs' villa at Montreaux on Lake Geneva which, according to Fran, and the pictures she has of it, is indescribably lovely.

Mrs. Cortright is a little surprised. She had thought the Dodsworths were sailing for home in June, and she had heard Mr. Dodsworth getting estimates on renting a car from both the American Express and Cook's.

"I remember so well the talk I had with your husband the last night on the boat about what he was after in Europe," Mrs. Cortright says to Fran. "You're evidently after something quite different." She looks up quite coolly.

"I hope so!" says Fran.

Now the men are in. With Dodsworth are Arnold Israel, "the perfect international Jew" and Kurt von Obersdorf, "a thoroughly attractive young Austrian who speaks English with an agreeable Viennese accent."

Dodsworth is leading the conversation, holding forth with some enthusiasm about his sight-seeing experiences. He has got as far as the room in which Napoleon was crowned, and where Sam Dodsworth of Zenith looked through the rose window and caught a glimpse of things of which he had never dreamed before. Dodsworth likes sight-seeing.

The talk turns to the reaction of those present to Paris. Von

Obersdorf detests it. "For me it is a motion picture made by lunatics," says he, scornfully. "Even Berlin I like better! But Vienna!"

"There are so many Parises," protests Israel. "The Paris Mrs. Dodsworth has found and come to love in the month she has been here is really an American city. It's the most agreeable of all American cities."

"I have listened while an American automobile magnate, an Austrian travel agent and an international banker have explained Paris to me, a Parisienne," adds Mme. de Penable. "Now I go home."

The party breaks up with many graceful compliments.

"May your second month in Paris be happier than your first," wishes Kurt, kissing Fran's hand, "and may you then move on to gladden the eyes of Berlin and Vienna." He is most grateful to them both, and he will call Fran next day.

Arnold Israel stays on while Dodsworth is putting Kurt and Mme. de Penable in a taxi. He, too, is grateful for a charming evening. He would have the Dodsworths for dinner soon.

"Where do you call your home, Mr. Israel?" asks Fran.

"I was born in Cracow, I grew up here. I keep a residence in New York, a flat in London, a *pied-à-terre* beside the Seine, and a villa at Antibes."

"What an ideal existence."

"I believe in freedom and variety," smiles Israel.

"So do I!" agrees Fran.

"That should cement our friendship," says he.

Fran withdraws her hand a little nervously as Israel is kissing it, just as Mrs. Cortright comes from an inner room with her wraps.

"I stole a bit of your letter paper to write my Italian addresses on," she says, as she says good-by to Sam.

"Fine! We'll make use of them when we're down your way," he answers.

"You like that woman, don't you?" demands Fran after Mrs. Cortright and Mr. Israel have left.

"You thought she was the most distinguished woman on the boat," Sam answers.

"She seems a frump in Paris," says Fran. "Though you know I'm always glad to see any friends of yours, Sam. Even the not particularly amusing ones. I thought it went off well enough for a quiet evening. I like good talk, too. Though that did get a bit heavy towards the end."

The Dodsworths are undressing. Fran has disappeared in the bedroom to get into a dressing gown. Sam is pulling off coat, vest and trousers where he is. The running conversation concerns the advisability of making plans about going back home. Sam has seen about enough of Europe. A couple of months of the Mediterranean and Germany and he will be ready for a June sailing. He has business to attend to at home. And his class reunion—his thirtieth—is this summer.

But there is a lot more of Europe that Fran wants to see. Why, she wonders audibly, doesn't Sam go home alone? Let him go back without her, get himself a new lease on life, then come back and join her.

"But I wouldn't want to go home without you, Fran!" protests Dodsworth.

"Well, I can see you aren't enjoying Paris," Fran goes on, continuing the massaging of her face with cold cream. "I'm only thinking of your pleasure. If you thought of mine you wouldn't ask me to leave here just as we've got to know some really nice people!"

DODSWORTH—I don't think they're so nice. . . .

FRAN (*wearily*)—We needn't go into that again.

DODSWORTH (*the tact that made the bulldog famous*)—But I don't. And I'm damned if I see what you see in 'em! This Israel may be all he says he is internationally and financially, but he certainly is no Barney Baruch. Mrs. Penable may be all right but I hate to think who pays the bill when that young Austrian takes *you* out!

FRAN (*grinding it out*)—Arnold Israel happens to be one of the most distinguished living financiers as well as an art collector and his business is mostly secret missions for governments so it's not surprising he doesn't talk about it!

DODSWORTH (*disgustedly*)—Ah! (*Rises.*)

FRAN—Renée—it's Madame de Penable not Mrs. Penable—Renée's a true woman of the great world here! As for Kurt, he may be poor, but he holds one of the oldest titles in Austria. And they all belong to the most amusing and exclusive crowd in Paris!

DODSWORTH—Fran! Do you think the real thing in Paris would hang out with a couple of hicks like us? (FRAN'S *eyes blaze.*) What else are we? I'm an ordinary American business man, and I married the daughter of a Zenith brewer who seems to be flying pretty high thcsc days!

FRAN (*icily, wiping the cold cream from her face*)—I suppose you know what you mean by that!

DODSWORTH—Why won't you sit at a sidewalk café with me?

FRAN—Because smart people don't!

DODSWORTH—I'm not smart.

FRAN—I am!

DODSWORTH—Then you ought to be smart enough not to care what people think!

FRAN—It's a matter of principle! Like the Englishman dressing for dinner in a jungle!

DODSWORTH—I read about him! He probably never did it!

FRAN—Oh, you simply won't understand!

DODSWORTH—I can't! And if I like men to be something more than waiters . . .

FRAN (*rising*)—I've heard my friends insulted enough!

DODSWORTH—A lot of gigolos!

FRAN—I do think you might use something beside that word gigolo which I taught you!

DODSWORTH—You did not!

FRAN—You never learned it at Yale! They didn't know about such things at Yale!

DODSWORTH—Will you stop sneering?

FRAN (*letting him have it*)—Now let's have the one about the great motor magnate and all he's done for the automobile industry! You may be the most impressive man in Zenith, but you're not in Zenith now! You're in Paris now. And I'm sick and tired of apologizing to my friends for the way you . . .

Their voices have mounted with their anger. Now the telephone interrupts them with a seemingly furious ringing. The call is from the office. Someone has complained of the noise. A most humiliating experience to Fran.

Their voices are lowered but the discussion continues. "If you had the mistiest notion of civilization here," Fran is saying.

"Maybe I don't think so much of it," retorts Dodsworth, his spirits ruffled, his voice muffled. "Maybe clean hospitals and concrete high roads and no soldiers along the Canadian border come nearer my idea of the real thing! My God! There are twenty million cars at home in America and I've contributed something to every one of them out of my own personal civilization! And if that isn't more than just knowing how to order a dinner, which your friend the madam . . ."

"Don't call her the madam, either!" snaps Fran. "You don't want to learn. I could teach you. I belong here!"

DODSWORTH (*his face set*)—I'm going to get out of this town and back to doing something and take you along.

FRAN (*rising—almost afraid to say it*)—I'm not going, Sam!

DODSWORTH—Oh, yes, you are!

FRAN—I think we need a vacation from each other.

DODSWORTH—I don't feel that way. I think I've been weak with you long enough!

FRAN (*a swallow, then*)—I've taken a villa for the summer with Renée de Penable in Switzerland. At Montreux on Lake Geneva. (*He gasps, she faces him unflinchingly.*) I've signed the lease. (*A pause.*)

DODSWORTH—I think you might have told me.

FRAN—I've got my own money.

DODSWORTH (*unable to believe his ears*)—Fran!

FRAN—What?

DODSWORTH (*a step towards her*)—Oh, Fran, my darling! You're not drifting away from me?

FRAN—I hope not.

DODSWORTH—You and I, Fran! After twenty years! (*Quick decision.*) I won't go home. I'll give it up. I'll . . .

FRAN (*suddenly completely hysterical*)—You've got to go! You've simply got to go! I can't stand being torn this way any longer! I'm suffocating! I'm sorry for everything mean I've said! But if we're going on together, I've really got to be left alone this summer! Don't look so hurt and please don't be angry—or do be angry, if it will make you any happier. (*She flings herself on the couch.*) Remember that I did make a real home for you! And I'll do it again! But you've just got to let me have my fling now! Because you're just simply rushing at old age, Sam, and *I'm not* ready for that yet! (*A long pause. He turns away from her, aimlessly looking about for something. He finds it on the boule cabinet. It is the* Paris Herald.) What is it, Sam?

DODSWORTH—Just thought I'd see the first boat I could catch. (*She starts violently as he opens the paper.*)

The scene fades out.

In the offices of the Revelation Motor Company back in Zenith President Henry E. Hazzard is dictating dynamically to the same blonde secretary who previously served Sam Dodsworth.

A sheaf of letters and notes is the result of his morning's work.

President Hazzard, a busy man, is also a constant victim of interruptions, members of the staff who must see him; appointments made for him he must keep. He is perspiring rather freely this warm morning, and beginning to feel the need of an electric fan.

There is a knocking on the door marked Private, but President Hazzard refuses to pay any attention to that. Let whoever it is go 'round the regular way. Hazzard has turned to his publicity man and is saying, with an automobile executive's confidence—

"Can't sell a cheap car on a cheap catalogue, Joe! She is a pretty job, though. Prettier than anything Sam Dodsworth ever turned out. Just leave these here, Joe, where I can look at 'em and get after those printers. Got to keep moving, Joe. Got to keep . . . (*Again a knock on the door, this time louder.*) Well, for God's sake! (*The publicity man has risen to open.*) No, you go along! I'll attend to that boy! I may be busy but I always take time out to give a piece of my mind to anyone who thinks he's important enough to use the boss's private door."

He opens the door with an angry flourish and faces Sam Dodsworth standing on the threshold.

"This used to be my way, so I thought I'd just surprise you privately," explains Dodsworth, smiling.

He had arrived the night before, the ex-president explains. Came on to visit Emily. He's taking Tubby Pearson to their thirtieth reunion at New Haven. After that—

Hazzard is full of the activities of Revelation Motors. They are dropping the price to eleven fifty for the five-passenger sedan, and that is going to give Buick and Chevrolet something to think about. It won't be the same car they used to put out, Hazzard admits, but—

Now the morning appointments are pressing. Dodsworth thinks he will just sit quietly in the corner while Hazzard rids himself of them. They might go to lunch together at the club. But Hazzard doesn't go out to lunch. Just a sandwich and a glass of milk at his desk—

It must be great to be free, Henry thinks. Great to be out of it, like Sam.

"Aren't you glad to be?" he demands. "Don't we all look forward to the day when we can get out from under? Take things easy? Look around a bit? I envy you, Sam! By God, I do!"

"Yeah, it's great! You're free! You enjoy your leisure!" Dodsworth almost hisses through his teeth.

HAZZARD—That's what Mrs. Hazzard's always saying to me!

DODSWORTH—Yeah?

HAZZARD—Yeah. . . . I don't know though. . . . (*Then with a brisk handshake he returns to his executive manner.*) Come to dinner, Sam! I'll get the wife to arrange a date! Certainly has been great to see you!

TUBBY (*bursting in*)—Sam!

DODSWORTH—Well, you fat little runt! (*More pump-handling—but* HAZZARD *watches it all very gravely.*)

TUBBY—You big stiff! So they couldn't stand you in Europe any more, eh? So you had to sneak back here, did you, you big bum!

DODSWORTH—I didn't sneak!

TUBBY—Bring me home any of that swell French wine?

DODSWORTH—Sure, I've got a whole case in my collar-box!

TUBBY—Why didn't you bring Fran home with you?

DODSWORTH—She's taken a villa for the summer in Switzerland.

TUBBY—Pretty swell!

DODSWORTH—Yeah! Come out to lunch?

TUBBY—Sure I'll come out to lunch!

DODSWORTH—Well, thank God! I've been trying all morning to get someone to eat lunch with!

TUBBY—You got me, Sambo! (*To the secretary.*) Can I trouble you to call Billings at my bank, and tell him I can't eat lunch with him today? Tell him it's all right for golf after lunch though. Tell him I'll get away by two-thirty. (*To* DODSWORTH—*as he takes his arm.*) Do they still whoop it up all night long in Paris? Did you pick up a little cutie on the side?

DODSWORTH—Did you say cutie or cootie?

TUBBY—I said cutie!

DODSWORTH—Nope! I'm still the same old respectable . . . They have gone out. Hazzard shakes his head. Then business as usual and the scene blacks out.

On the terrace of the Villa Doree at Montreux, Fran Dodsworth, Kurt Obersdorf and Arnold Israel have gathered after a trip across the lake. It has been a jolly day, and now they have come to the end of it with a wager that none of them can quote a line from "The Prisoner of Chillon," which Byron may have written in that very house.

Kurt wins the wager and no one cares greatly. Except Mme. de Penable, who has waited dinner an hour for them and then eaten by herself. She might have known—when Fran had both men quite to herself!

It is Kurt's last night at the Villa. His vacation is over. To-morrow he must be on his way back to Berlin to become a mere travel agent again.

Kurt has gone into the house and found his violin. With Renée de Penable to accompany him he plays very well.

On the terrace Fran and Arnold Israel drift into an intimate conversation inspired largely by a letter from Sam Dodsworth that has come for Fran.

It is Israel's idea that Fran should read her letter. Not to him, but to herself. It is quite likely to clarify her mind on certain matters in which Israel admittedly has a personal interest.

It is a typical Dodsworth letter, Fran finds, containing practically all the news of Zenith.

"My daughter's well . . . Tubby and Matey are well . . . they're great friends of Sam's . . . His golf's gone off . . . He misses me . . . His friends seem to have grown much older . . . You don't know how old men *can* grow until you've seen Sam's classmate friends . . ."

She has crumpled the letter in her hand following the summary and is pacing the terrace nervously.

"What will your life be like when your husband comes back?" calmly asks Israel.

"Why did you have to make me read that letter?" demands Fran, almost hysterically. "I've been having such fun today! That letter's spoiled everything! Switzerland! The lake! This house! All of it's just so much Zenith now!"

"Presently he'll be taking you back to Zenith! . . ."

"What are you doing? Trying to torture me?"

"Torture you? No, I'm making love to you!"

It is Israel's idea that Fran should not run away from life; that she should escape the whole way, now, this night; that she should not try to deny the attraction that he and she feel for each other; one's first obligation is to one's self. . . .

There is heat in Fran's reply. She is confident of Sam's love, and she knows that Israel would never have married her nor have remained faithful to her if he had. At least she can trust Sam.

"My attitude may be more normal than yours *or* his," answers

Israel, slowly and with a smile. "When I want a woman who obviously wants me, I expect her to bow with me before the inevitable power of that fact, and to give herself to me as completely as I'm prepared to give myself to her. With the understanding that she and I will remain morbidly faithful to one another. As long as the thing may last, and no longer!"

"Well, that's putting it pretty clearly!"

"I'm leaving in a few days, Fran!"

Israel has moved over close to her. In her nervous hands Fran has twisted Dodsworth's letter into a long rope. From the villa come the sounds of Kurt's violin. For the moment Fran wishes neither Kurt nor Renée was there. No, she is not afraid. . . . Yet, she would not like to do anything that might hurt Sam. . . .

"If I come to your room to say good night, that needn't hurt your husband," suggests Israel. "Live in the present tonight, Fran. That letter's the past."

"It's the future, too, Arnold. At least, for me!"

"Then let's get rid of both past and future."

He has produced his cigarette lighter significantly. The idea reaches Fran. She smiles weakly back at him as he holds the lighter toward her, then thrusts Sam's letter into the flame. As it blazes she lets it fall into a dish of water lilies. The lights fade.

The Dodsworth library in Zenith "has been submitted to minor alterations under Emily's occupancy." The colors are gayer, there is less of the "whiskey-periodical-tobacco table" atmosphere than there was. The display now is more on the Vanity, Vogue, New Yorker order. A jig-saw puzzle has also crept in. Emily and Matey Pearson are working on it.

Voices in the hall indicate the return of Dodsworth and Tubby Pearson from the reunion and in not very pleasant mood. They are snapping at each other when they enter the room, and the presence of the women is no deterrent. Matey doesn't know whether it is the heat wave or a hangover.

Dodsworth's principal irritation is the absence of a cablegram which he is expecting. There should have been a cable. If there had been a cable, and Fran had been there, it would have been laid out for him on the table, with his mail and his whiskey. The fact that there has not been any mail, or any cable, doesn't explain everything. Where's the whiskey?

And where are the cigars? What has become of that humidor? That very nice, quite expensive humidor? Emily has planted flowers in that, has she! And this jig-saw puzzle! What childish— Get it out—

"That thing would never have been in here in your mother's day," explodes Dodsworth. "Your mother had some respect for a man's library! No mail, no cigars, no cable, no drink . . ."

The arrival of Harry McKee is a help. The drinks, at least, are soon on the way.

"Father, I'm sorry things aren't the way they used to be, but Harry and I are living in this house now. And I wish you'd stop speaking of Mother as though she were dead!"

"I'm not speaking of your mother as though she were . . ." And then, noting a challenging look in Matey's eyes, he adds: "Her mother's coming home!"

There is excitement over this announcement and much questioning as to when Fran will arrive. Dodsworth doesn't know that. That is the cable he is expecting. . . .

"Would you believe it, Father, when Mother didn't come home with you and you seemed so worried and unlike yourself, I was afraid there might be some kind of trouble between you."

"Between your mother and me? Not a chance!" answers Dodsworth, with considerable conviction.

Now the drinks have arrived. And soon after the drinks the expected cable has been discovered in Harry's pocket. Dodsworth opens it a little hesitantly while Harry is fixing the drinks. He doesn't move for a second. Then he crushes the cable in his hand. It isn't the one he expected, he says. It's not from Fran. But Matey and Tubby know better.

The McKees have gone to a cocktail party and the Pearsons are about to go. They try to be as consoling as possible. Tubby allows that Sam is an old horse thief and Matey adds as her opinion that he is an old darling. Which impels Sam to confess that Fran is not coming.

"God, I'm so lonely for her!" he says.

"What's she say?" asks Matey.

"'Want few more months Europe; hope you having good time at home,'" Dodsworth reads.

"Well, if she's enjoying herself, Sam . . ." begins Matey.

"I asked her to come back. She doesn't even speak of me going over."

"She's thoughtless!"

"No, she's not. She's scared!"

"Fran scared? What of?"

"Of growing old."

"That's very smart of you, Sam," declares Matey. "She's a child and that's all she wants to be."

Sam has brought out a letter from Fran that he wants Matey to read. Sounds to Matey as though Fran was having a pretty good time.

"Know these friends of hers?" Matey asks.

"Oh, yes, sure."

MATEY—Like 'em?

DODSWORTH—Oh, they're all right. Not my style. They're very clever people.

MATEY—I see. (*She returns the letter.*)

DODSWORTH—Well?

MATEY (*blandly*)—Nothing.

DODSWORTH—You're an old friend, Matey. I don't know what to think.

MATEY (*absently*)—Who's Arnold Israel?

DODSWORTH—He's one of those custom-built internationals you see in the rotogravure section every Sunday.

MATEY—Oh! (*Then.*) Give us a kiss now. (*He does.* TUBBY *enters.*)

TUBBY—I thought . . . (*Then.*) Will you lay off those European liberties with my wife! (MATEY *takes* TUBBY *by the arm and turns him. They go.* DODSWORTH *stands quite still until the door slams off stage. Then he moves suddenly to telephone.*)

DODSWORTH (*into telephone*)—Western Union? . . . Western Union . . . Samuel Dodsworth speaking. Take a cable. Going to Mrs. Dodsworth. Same address as my last, yes. Ready? "Sailing 'Aquitania' Wednesday meet me Ritz, Paris. Love, Sam." And take another. To A. B. Hurd, cable address, Revelation London. "Sailing 'Aquitania' Wednesday stop using utmost discretion ascertain day to day address Arnold Israel of Paris keep me informed wireless stop signed Dodsworth." Send 'em both straight. Repeat that—

The lights fade out as he ends the message.

The Dodsworths are back in their suite at the Paris Ritz. Sam has just arrived. Fran has also taken the room in which they had held her birthday party on their last visit. With the weather what it is she is sure Sam would not mind separate rooms.

Fran has been in Biarritz. Her letter explaining why had evidently crossed Sam coming over.

"You don't know that Renée de Penable and I had rather a row," explains Fran, a little nervously. "Oh, you were so right about her, Sam! She's everything you said she was. She said things to me I couldn't possibly forgive! So I just chucked the whole thing at Montreux and did some traveling on my own! I always wanted to see Biarritz. Of course I was alone there, but— (*She is suddenly conscious of the fixity of* DODSWORTH'S *stare.*) What are you looking at?"

"Did I remember to write you that I adore you?"

"Why, no! I don't believe you did! Do you? That's very nice and comforting, Sam, darling! Let's go out to a cool place in the Bois and get something to drink."

Sam must wait for a man he has asked to meet him there. Yes, it is someone Fran knows. No, it is no one from Zenith. Everybody in Zenith is fine. And Emily—Emily's marriage is working out all right.

The caller has arrived. It is Arnold Israel. His appearance is a complete surprise to Fran. She feels that she has been badly used in not being told. Israel had tried to reach her by phone, but Dodsworth had no thought of telling her.

"I wanted to see you two face to face," Dodsworth explains calmly. "Fran alone would have wasted time acting. I knew you'd been in Biarritz together. (FRAN *gasps.*) I'm sorry, Fran. I don't like undercover work myself. But I wouldn't have got where I have in the world if it hadn't been in me to be a bit ruthless on occasion. You know, I wouldn't do this at all if I didn't love you so much and want to protect you."

FRAN (*rising excitedly*)—I've never heard anything so outrageous in my life! What if Arnold *was* in Biarritz . . .

ISRAEL—Won't you let me handle my part, Fran?

FRAN—Don't get him angry.

ISRAEL—Let me remind you, Dodsworth, that Shakespeare's "Othello" ends badly for the hero.

DODSWORTH (*not to be angered*)—I'm not Othello. This isn't the Middle Ages. We none of us talk blank verse. Not even you!

FRAN—Are you implying that there's been anything wrong between Arnold and me? Isn't it absurd, Arnold, to hear one's self using an old cant phrase like—like "anything wrong"? (*Then back to* DODSWORTH.) Do you know how insulting you are?

DODSWORTH—You don't know how insulting I'm going to be if you don't quit this damn play-acting.

FRAN—Play-acting! If Arnold and I take . . .

ISRAEL—You *are* rather jumping at conclusions, you know!

DODSWORTH—Have you never noticed how transparent people are when you really look at 'em? (*Back to* FRAN.) I want to know if you're coming back to me as my wife or keeping him on as your lover? (FRAN *gasps.*)

ISRAEL—You wouldn't put matters so bluntly if you understood . . .

DODSWORTH—I understand. I'm sure you've given her things she wanted and needed and never got from me. But I'm interested in what I want and need too. And that happens to be peace of mind.

ISRAEL—But if you can bring yourself to see matters reasonably . . .

DODSWORTH—My God, I've crossed the Atlantic Ocean to be reasonable! (*He turns to* FRAN.) I've loved you and been married to you for twenty years, and I'd like to hang on to you if I can. (*Then to both.*) Do you want to marry each other? (*Pause; then as* ISRAEL *says nothing.*)

FRAN—I won't let you throw me at Arnold's head! I'll answer for both of us! No, we don't!

DODSWORTH—Do you want to divorce me then?

ISRAEL—I can tell you she doesn't. On the contrary she's repeatedly . . .

DODSWORTH—Is that true, Fran?

FRAN—Why should I want to divorce you? You're my husband!

DODSWORTH—You couldn't very well divorce me if I weren't!

FRAN (*hysterically*)—You can laugh!

DODSWORTH—I could do worse than that!

ISRAEL—That much being cleared up, what have you to suggest?

DODSWORTH—That Fran and I forget what's happened. Start out on a long hike tomorrow. The Tyrol, Italy, any place. Then sail back home in October.

FRAN (*after a pause*)—No, Sam. No. Oh, I can see how fine you're trying to be, but, no, I mean you've got to look at this as I see it too. And I . . . I can't come back to you, as your wife. Not just yet.

DODSWORTH—Then you'll have to divorce me and use your own judgment about him. Or I'll divorce you for adultery.

Such action, Dodsworth agrees with Israel, would be brutal. But peace of mind, he contends, is worth any amputation. Fran can treat him badly once, but she can hardly expect him to go on. . . .

Fran is hysterical with anger. Her husband is trying to take her youth away from her; trying to deny her happiness, the only romantic happiness she has ever known—

"He's made me feel like a bride as you never did!" she cries, finally. "Not even in the beginning!"

"Good God, Fran!" protests the sincerely shocked Israel. "That was unnecessary."

"I didn't call you in to defend me!" interrupts Dodsworth. The situation is distasteful to Israel and ridiculous to Dodsworth. It is the old, old husband, wife and lover stuff. They all look like damn fools to Sam.

Now, with a passing hope that Dodsworth will achieve his peace of mind, Israel has left. Dodsworth stands with his back to the door after he has seen him out.

"I'm going to see this through, Fran, if it can be done," he says, quietly. "And I'm ready to wipe the slate clean if you are!"

FRAN—When do we start? Where do we go?

DODSWORTH—Wherever you like. Till we go home in October.

FRAN—Home in October. Zenith in October!

DODSWORTH—You'll be wanting to go home in October. (*A step or so towards her, then he plays his trump.*) Emily's having a baby in October. (*The scene becomes quick with* FRAN's *astonishment.*)

FRAN—Emily! A baby! She didn't tell me! (*She rises.*)

DODSWORTH—She left it to me to tell you. I was saving it up to . . .

FRAN—How is she? Is she well?

DODSWORTH—She's fine!

FRAN—I must send her a cable! Couldn't I telephone her? (*She makes for the telephone.*) Think of Emily having a . . .

DODSWORTH—You see we damn well got to behave ourselves

when we'll be a couple of old grand-parents in October.

Fran starts towards the phone as

THE CURTAIN FALLS

ACT III

The Dodsworths are in Berlin. Their sitting room at the Adlon "differs from their sitting rooms in the Ritzes of London and Paris. It belongs to a more mature school of hotel decoration, a Germanic and more serious school, a somehow tragic school."

It is an evening in October. Fran, dressed for the evening, is standing at the window, enraptured by the lights shining through the trees Unter den Linden. Dodsworth is fascinated by her enthusiasm for Berlin and his reawakened love for her. He has at last won her back as his wife.

"Shall I tell you how?" Fran asks, tenderly, feeling his arms about her. "By not being a Tartar husband. By understanding. By letting me have fun with nice little Kurt and not thinking that I'm a hussy. By helping me to forget Arnold Israel. By forgetting him yourself. That's how you've won me back, my noble, big Sam!"

He has turned away. There is nothing he can think of to say. Probably, he thinks, because he is self-conscious. All reconciled couples must feel self-conscious with each other after . . .

Kurt Obersdorf is coming to take them out to dinner. Sam doesn't feel much like dressing. He would like to telephone Emily again; like to hear how the baby got through its first day.

"I know how thrilled you are over this baby," says Fran, quickly. "But you mustn't tell Kurt, Sam. . . . Oh, I don't mean just Kurt alone! I mean all of our friends here in Berlin! Because they think of me as young! And I am! Oh, I am! . . . Please! Please! I was such a kid when you married me! It isn't fair! Not that I'm not utterly happy for Emily, but . . . Kurt mustn't know that I'm a . . ."

Kurt has arrived, and in high spirits. He is dressed for the evening and eager to go. He is taking them to the smartest restaurant in Berlin. . . .

But Sam is irritated rather than pleased. What fun do they think it is sitting up all night watching them dance? Let him stay where he is. He has just had some pretty important news from home. He would like to sit by himself and think it over.

Fran understands. She think perhaps it would be better to

leave Sam by himself. He can get a very decent dinner in the hotel, and he likes the orchestra. . . .

Fran has kissed Sam, snatched up her gloves and compact. Kurt follows her into the hall. The lights fade out as Dodsworth stands staring gloomily after them.

The lights come up as Fran puts her key in the lock and opens the door. It is after midnight. Kurt stands in the door back of her until she insists upon his coming in. She is too excited, for all her weariness, to go to bed this night. Certainly they have given Sam no reason to mind, and Sam is dead to the world. But they mustn't talk loud.

Kurt has returned the change from the bills she had given him. It worries Fran that he should let such dull, ugly things come up on such a night. . . .

"If you knew, Kurt, how they reach out and catch at me! The dull, dreary, ugly things! No! I won't ask you to be sorry for me! I want you to remember me as I was tonight! So don't spoil things! Just let poor little Fran have her fun while she can!"

"Ach, darling! Darling! You know I love you, Fran! You know that!"

"Kurt, you must stop this kind of talk!"

KURT—Is it so wicked? Have you not been happy with me here in Berlin?

FRAN—Happy? Oh, yes, I've been terribly happy! I've loved it, Kurt! You know I have!

KURT—I think that you could love me, Fran! I think you could!

FRAN—But there's no good talking about that!

KURT—Why not?

FRAN—That ends so badly.

KURT—Yes, I know, Fran. (*She looks up, surprised.*) I knew already in Montreux. I left Montreux without saying good-by. Don't you remember? (FRAN *is distressed. He presses on, however.*) But my last night in Paris I telephoned you. I loved you so! I had to hear your voice!

FRAN (*low*)—You telephoned, yes.

KURT—And you must like me at least a little, Fran. Because you promised that night to come here in October to see me! And you have come!

FRAN—You must go home now, Kurt!

KURT—Will it always be like this? Will I go always like this, without you, Fran? (FRAN *nods mournfully.*)

FRAN—And I'll have to let you go. I'll have to. There's nothing we can do about it, is there?

KURT—No. That is true. My hands are tied. You are married to Sam. To my friend. I cannot ask you to be my wife!

FRAN—Kurt! (*She goes to him. Then incredulous.*) You want to marry me, Kurt?

KURT—Does that surprise you? (*Then, desperately.*) Oh, why are you not free? (FRAN *looks at him intently for a moment, then moves again to* DODSWORTH'S *door, again to listen. This time she comes away in a deeper mood, her eyes on the ground.*)

FRAN—If I *were* free, Kurt—

KURT—Oh, Fran, if you were free! (*An inarticulate sound from him as he takes her in his arms.*)

FRAN—Don't. Please, don't.

KURT—Forgive me!

FRAN—Oh, I'm not angry, oh, my dear . . .

KURT—Will you not say a more kind word, Fran?

FRAN—Some other time.

KURT—Will you let me kiss you good night? (*She looks up for the first time. He kisses her passionately. Then they separate.*)

FRAN—Good night, Kurt.

KURT—Good night, Fran.

Kurt has gone. Fran is alone for a moment. "Her lungs fill. Her eyes blaze. The world and all the promise of youth are hers once more. There may even be some gesture of wild triumph. Then she goes quickly into her room, slamming the door."

A moment later Dodsworth comes into the room. His hair is tousled; he is in his pajamas; the light sets him blinking. He finds Fran's wrap on a chair and is pleased. He turns smilingly toward her door, but hesitates. He knocks diffidently. Fran opens the door and stands facing him. Her face is set.

Sam had thought, he admits, to come into her room. It seemed wrong that she was not with him. But Fran has no such ideas. She suggests that he go back to his room. She is too tired to talk tonight.

"If things have got this bad, Fran, they've got to stop altogether," he says, firmly.

"Yes? Well, we can talk in the morning," she answers.

DODSWORTH—Listen, dear! This is serious! I'm willing to do everything I can to make you happy. I love you. You know that. Only, if we're going on together, as you said to me back in Paris—*I'm* saying it now! If we *are* going on together, we've got to cut out this homeless stuff and beat it right back where we belong!

FRAN—Is that your idea of making me happy?

DODSWORTH—It's October and Emily's had her baby without us, though we agreed . . .

FRAN—I never agreed!

DODSWORTH—Yes, you did, Fran! And we've got to have things clear, or . . .

FRAN—They're clear enough to me!

DODSWORTH—Will you be good, then, and let me grab off the first sailing? (FRAN *shakes her head.*) I'm taking no chances on another Arnold Israel! I know this friendship for Kurt's harmless enough. But you might get fascinated and . . .

FRAN (*looking up for the first time*)—You think I might? You really think I might? (*She lets him have it with swiftly increasing intensity.*) I love Kurt and Kurt loves me, and I'm going to marry him. He asked me tonight. I've only just decided it now, this minute. Since I found you here, hiding behind doors! The great Dodsworth! Great prowling elephant!

DODSWORTH (*open-mouthed*)—Fran. . . .

FRAN (*rapidly rising hysteria*)—I'm sorry Kurt didn't stay to punch your head for spying on us!

DODSWORTH—I wasn't spying! I didn't hear . . .

FRAN—You can't play the injured innocent with me! You've never known me! You've never known anything about me! Not what I had on, nor what I thought, nor the sacrifices I've made, nor . . .

DODSWORTH (*his tone hardening*)—Look out now!

FRAN (*wildly*)—I'll be happy with Kurt! I'm fighting for life! You can't drag me back!

DODSWORTH—Fran! . . . God! I'd respect you more if you'd stuck to Israel. (*He goes to fireplace.*) Can you . . . can you get your divorce here?

FRAN—What?

DODSWORTH—Your divorce?

FRAN—Oh, yes, I think so!

DODSWORTH—I wish you'd wait a few months.

FRAN—Why?

DODSWORTH—I'd like you to feel absolutely sure about him.

FRAN—It's my funeral now, isn't it?

DODSWORTH—I'll have to get used to that idea. I guess I can!

The lights fade out.

Two months later, in the Naples branch of the American Express Company, the room is filled "with bright Neapolitan sunlight and weary American customers."

There is the usual assortment of tourists, going through the usual tourist forms of cashing checks, inquiring about trains, keeping dates, planning excursions and worrying about the non-arrival of an expected letter from Nettie.

Sam Dodsworth stops in for his mail. There is nothing for him. He thinks perhaps he had better wait around a few days longer. Meanwhile he might go sight-seeing. The clerk suggests Herculaneum and Pompeii. Dodsworth's been there. He has also taken the drive around Amalfi and Sorrento and seen Capri.

"How would you like Pæstum, sir?" inquires the clerk, submitting a folder.

"What's Pæstum?"

"Greek temples, sir. In excellent preservation."

"That's more than I am," admits Dodsworth. "But I'll take a chance. Get me a car."

Mrs. Cortright, very smartly dressed, has entered the office and gone to the cashier's cage. As she turns away and looks up from her mail she recognizes Dodsworth.

Now she has spoken to him, reminding him of their steamer meeting, and discovered that he has been traveling alone for two months. He has seen so many museums and American Express offices they all look alike now. He has given up getting an education, too. Found he was learning things he didn't want to learn.

The clerk is back to tell Mr. Dodsworth that his car is ready, and Mrs. Cortright hopes he will find it possible to have lunch with her soon. Today, if he will.

"Mrs. Cortright, even if it weren't you, if it were damn near anybody, I'd be so glad to have someone to talk to!" Dodsworth is fairly spilling over at the moment. "Listen! There's a couple at my hotel. They sit at the next table to me every night. They never say a word to each other at dinner. After dinner they sit in the lounge till ten. Then, at ten, the husband says: 'Mary, it's getting late.' Just those four words. And except to waiters and taxi drivers—and they don't count—that's four words more than I've said any night for the past three weeks!"

"I don't want to intrude or be impertinent, but . . . Well, I'm sorry," says Mrs. Cortright, leaning toward him with ready sympathy.

He has taken the spectacles with which he was reading the Pæstum circular off his nose. As he does so he smiles up at her. "Never wore these things before," he says. "Never needed 'em till lately." He snaps the case shut and adds, quickly, "Guess it's a pretty ordinary story. My wife's younger than I am, and livelier." His own words startle him a little. "Oughtn't to be undressing in public like this," he adds. "Never did that before, either."

MRS. CORTRIGHT—You haven't said anything you shouldn't have said. (*She rises, gathering up her letters.*) Will you keep on traveling now?

DODSWORTH—Got to stay over and be on hand for the divorce.

MRS. CORTRIGHT—Where?

DODSWORTH—Berlin.

MRS. CORTRIGHT—I see! Come along now. And we'll use your car to help me do my marketing. I don't often have the luxury of a car and some healthy marketing will do you more good than ruined temples.

DODSWORTH (*rising*)—No argument there! (*He picks up some letters she has let fall.*)

MRS. CORTRIGHT—What would you like for lunch?

DODSWORTH—Couldn't we fix up some American dish? Could we have clam chowder? Say! Get me the clams and I'll make you the chowder!

MRS. CORTRIGHT—Are you a cook, too?

DODSWORTH—Dress me up in my camp clothes and I'm a chef! Want to hire me? First-class cook and mechanic and a hell of a fisherman!

MRS. CORTRIGHT—Could you let yourself enjoy life for a while?

DODSWORTH—Show me how!

MRS. CORTRIGHT—I wonder if you could!

DODSWORTH—None of this that's happened to me was my idea!

MRS. CORTRIGHT—Well, then, why don't you break away from

your hotels, forget about Berlin, and move out to me? (*This stops him.*)

DODSWORTH—Out to you?

MRS. CORTRIGHT—Out where I live at Posilipo. It may be straining our slight acquaintance and I can't make you as comfortable as your hotel does. . . . When you want a bath you'll have to choose between the tin tub and the Mediterranean! But if you like swimming and fishing and a willing listener . . .

DODSWORTH (*overwhelmed*)—Well, that's awfully kind of you, Mrs. Cortright, and mighty friendly, but I don't see how I could!

MRS. CORTRIGHT—Why not?

DODSWORTH—What would your neighbors say?

MRS. CORTRIGHT—Being Italians they'd say you were my lover!

DODSWORTH—Exactly!

MRS. CORTRIGHT—That doesn't mean you'd have to be or that I'd have you if you wanted to be! (*She turns and is going out.*) No, Mr. Dodsworth, I like you and I think we might bolster each other up. And I'm certain you need a little peace of mind.

He has followed her out as the lights fade.

Back at the Adlon in January, Fran Dodsworth, "charmingly and very simply dressed," is holding the door to admit the Baroness von Obersdorf, "a small, impoverished, but notably distinguished old lady from Vienna."

Kurt von Obersdorf follows his mother in. "The atmosphere exceeds the usual strain of such occasions." Fran is very gracious, the Baroness gravely seriously over the introductions.

It is decided that they shall speak English. Fran is working at her German preparing herself to meet Kurt's friends and to be a good housekeeper for him after they are married. But she does not yet understand the language well. . . .

"I should have come to you in Vienna," Fran is saying, "but Kurt couldn't get away and I was too shy to face you without him! But I feel so honored that you've come here to see me! Such a long journey just to see little me!"

"It was more suitable for me to come to you."

"Really? You see, I don't understand foreign customs. I'm only just beginning to be a European. Sit down, Kurt. You look so strained! I'm the one who should look strained. But I don't feel it! Not one bit! I love your mother! I hope she's going to love me!"

"I would not find it difficult to become most fond of you, my dear. And I sympathize with all my son's feeling for you."

Quite gently but firmly the Baroness admits that her son has asked her permission to marry Fran and that she is sorry to have been obliged to refuse it. It is not that Kurt is not a free agent, but this is the way such things are arranged in old families.

"I wanted her to see you, Fran! I knew when she saw you she would think differently," hurriedly explains Kurt.

"She doesn't seem to," answers Fran. Then, turning to the Baroness she says: "Since you've got so far, won't you tell me what you've got against me? I love your son and I'm really rather a nice person."

BARONESS—But we are Catholics, my dear.

FRAN—I'm going to become a Catholic. I'll do it before we're married if you like. So that part's all right.

BARONESS—Your husband is living, Mrs. Dodsworth. You will be divorced. No priest would marry you.

FRAN—Well, that isn't so serious, is it?

BARONESS—It is most serious to us.

FRAN (*with a pathetic and hurried eagerness*)—Well, believe me, I've every respect for your feelings! But with Kurt's happiness at stake and yours, too, Baroness! Perhaps it isn't quite my place to bring this up, but it's an argument and you must let me use it! I'm a woman of considerable means, in my own right. Enough for all three of us in Vienna. And in addition—because I shouldn't like Kurt to feel dependent on me—I'm already pulling wires. . . . I hadn't told Kurt about this yet! . . . but I'm already pulling wires with a big New York firm. So you see, Baroness. . . .

BARONESS—Oh, yes, indeed, I see. I do not deny that we are poor since the war. And your influence and money would be most helpful. But even if there were not the religious question . . .

FRAN—What else is there?

BARONESS—Will you leave us, Kurt? (KURT *goes into the hall.*) There is the question of children, too.

FRAN (*frightened*)—Of children?

BARONESS—Rich or poor, Kurt should have children to carry on the name. Could you give them to him?

FRAN—What makes you think I couldn't?

BARONESS—I am so much older than you, my dear! You will forgive me if I observe that you are older than Kurt.

FRAN (*through her teeth*)—Children or no children, Kurt loves me and I love him, Baroness! So why shouldn't we do without your permission and marry anyway and take our happiness!

BARONESS (*after a pause*)—I do not know what power you have over Kurt. I should think of my own happiness, if I were you.

FRAN—I am thinking of that!

BARONESS—Have you thought of how little happiness there can be for the old wife of a young husband? (FRAN *looks at the* BARONESS *in such tragic terror that the older woman, for all her poise, cannot conceal her embarrassment. Then suddenly* FRAN *rises and going to the door calls out.*)

FRAN—Kurt! (KURT *returns.* FRAN *just manages self-control.*) Your mother's going.

Kurt is plainly distressed at the outcome of the meeting. He would talk later with Fran about it. He is sure they still can be married. But, of course, he must consider his mother—

Fran has broken down as Kurt disappears through the door. "It isn't fair! It isn't fair!" she weeps. "I haven't done anything to deserve this!"

For a moment she continues to weep wretchedly. Then she totters to the desk and finds a letter. Through her tears she makes out an address she is looking for. Her hand is trembling as she takes the telephone.

"I want to put in a long distance call to Naples," she says. "Naples. In Italy. I want the Villa Cortright at Posilipo. I want to speak to Mr. Samuel Dodsworth!"

The lights fade.

That same afternoon, at the Villa Cortright, Edith Cortright is standing outside the living room windows. Behind her is the Bay of Naples, and beyond the cone of Vesuvius.

The telephone has been ringing furiously. Now when a maid answers she can get nothing but confused answers from the call.

Sam Dodsworth has appeared from the direction in which Mrs. Cortright has been looking. He is in his shirtsleeves, is wearing flannel trousers and is in the best of health and spirits. A reel of deep-sea fishing tackle is occupying his attention at the moment. Mrs. Cortright, seeing him, "gives such evidence of a warm heart that only Dodsworth could be unperceiving."

The tackle is being made ready for a fishing trip with Pietro a little later. Dodsworth is anxious to show that young man a few Florida tricks, and Pietro is eager for new ideas.

"You weren't expecting a long distance call, were you?" Mrs. Cortright asks, as the telephone rings again.

"Here? Good God, no! Why?"

"That telephone hasn't stopped ringing since lunch and makes absolutely no sense when it's answered and Teresa thought . . ."

The put-put of a motor comes from the bay. Dodsworth looks a little guilty. He has put a motor in Pietro's beautiful sailboat and Mrs. Cortright is distressed.

"Don't be hard on me, Edith," he pleads. "Setting up that motor is the first real fun I've had since I quit business. And it's got me rarin' to go again for the first time."

"To go?" The brightness goes out of Mrs. Cortright's face.

"Damn right!"

"Away from here?"

"Any place where I can get back in harness!"

"Well, fishing and swimming have done their work faster than I expected."

"Yeah!"

He will get into something new, thinks Dodsworth. Aviation, perhaps. The idea of a Moscow to Seattle air line has already appealed to him, and the Soviet people seem agreeable.

"I know what we'll do! We'll make a little preliminary survey," he says, with some excitement.

"We?"

DODSWORTH—Got my pilot all staked out! You ought to see what those Germans are up to at Friedrichshafen! I'll buy my own plane, and—(*The maid enters to answer the telephone*)—the day after this divorce comes through we'll hop off and go straight across . . .

MAID (*at the same time*)—Si! Pronto!

MRS. CORTRIGHT—We, Sam? We?

DODSWORTH—Where the hell is that map! (*He finds it on the console.*)

MAID—Scusa, Signora! E dalla Germania!

MRS. CORTRIGHT—From Ger— (*On her feet, white.*) Momento! (*A quick decision to the maid.*) Say there's nobody home! (*She corrects herself.*) Dica che non c'e nessuno!

MAID (*surprised*)—Si, Signora. (*Into the telephone.*) Non c'e nessuno! Non chiamare piu! (*She rings off.*)

MRS. CORTRIGHT (*a sigh of relief*)—Bene. (*The* MAID *goes wondering.* MRS. CORTRIGHT *turns nervously back to* DODSWORTH.) You were just hopping off. Across what?

DODSWORTH—Siberia! Lay out a route! Pick out landing fields! (*He is walking to and fro in his excitement.*) No end of ramifications! Branch line from Irkutsh to Tashkent or Samarkland! Swell name, Samarkland! By God, if those Soviet boys'll let me! (*He pauses to consider her.*) Tough going for you, though. Only one little suitcase! Cold as blazes! Think you could stand it?

MRS. CORTRIGHT (*breathless*)—Are you taking me with you?

DODSWORTH—Don't you want to go?

MRS. CORTRIGHT (*rises to it*)—Sam, all my life I've been waiting for something exciting to happen! I'll fly across Siberia with you on one suitcase! I'll go through life with you on one suitcase if you'll give me the chance! (*A pause. He goes to her to take her hands.*)

DODSWORTH—I've spent one short month here in this house with you and I can't imagine ever living without you again.

MRS. CORTRIGHT (*the most simple candor*)—I can't imagine living without you either. I think I must love you a great deal, Sam.

DODSWORTH—Thank God for that, Edith.

The telephone is ringing again. From the bay comes the put-put of the motor boat. Suddenly Mrs. Cortright decides to join the fishing party. She wants to get out of the house. She wants to get out on the water where no one can get at them. She would hurry Dodsworth. But he must wait until he gets his tackle together.

Now the maid has understood the telephone message. It is from Berlino—and the call is for Signor Dodsworth.

Dodsworth has taken the phone. Mrs. Cortright, flushed and tense, misses nothing.

"Hello! . . . Yes, Fran. This is Sam! . . . I'm sorry to hear that. . . . When are you sailing? . . . Guess I'll have to. . . . No, it's all right. . . . Get the tickets. . . . Good-by."

He has rung off. "He stands heavily by the telephone for a minute. When he looks up he is an old man again."

"Her lover's chucked her," he explains. "She's dropping the divorce. She's going home on the 'Ultima' day after tomorrow. I've got to go with her."

"I won't let you go," she says, moving swiftly to his side. "I won't let you go back to her."

"Please, Edith. I know this is a jolt! It's a jolt to me!"

"I won't see you killed by her damned selfishness!"

"You don't understand. It's pretty tough on her with all the talk there'll be!"

"I love you and she doesn't! You're content with me! You're miserable with her!"

All that Mrs. Cortright says is true. Dodsworth admits that. But he must go back. Fran's in a hole. She needs him.

MRS. CORTRIGHT—I won't make you choose just between two women! Think of Moscow and Seattle and Samark . . .

DODSWORTH—I know, Edith! I know every bit of it!

MRS. CORTRIGHT—One word from her and you trot back.

DODSWORTH—You've just got to be patient with me!

MRS. CORTRIGHT—What *is* this hold she's got over you!

DODSWORTH—I've got to take care of her. A man's habits get pretty strong in twenty years! (*Pause, then.*) I'll go back now.

MRS. CORTRIGHT—I'll send Teresa in to help you.

DODSWORTH—If you could get me a taxi somehow. You might call the American Express.

MRS. CORTRIGHT—Back to the American Express already! (*He comes directly back to her, takes her in his arms and kisses her passionately.*)

DODSWORTH—It's giving you up that's the hell of it!

The lights fade.

The smoke room of the "Ultima" is filling with tourists a little excited about getting aboard on time, and a little peeved because the steward insists no drinks can be served until after the ship has sailed. We recognize the two Jewish gentlemen who crossed with the Dodsworths going over. They are still arguing the merits of the different fleets.

Fran and Dodsworth come through the door from the deck, "she exquisitely turned out; he just as he left Naples, and his mood even more somber."

"It is nice to be going somewhere again after all those weeks I was so bored in Berlin," Fran is saying as they find a table. "And you were so right about Kurt, Sam dear! I can't think how you guessed it, because you aren't usually so awfully good at judging character! Except in the case of business men, of course! But, you were right that time. His family may be as old as the Coliseum, but when I saw his mother! My dear; the most awful old country frump!"

"Don't!" He has involuntarily crushed her hand to stop her.

"Sammy! Please! Don't get ardent yet! Remember, I've still got to get used to—"

"I'm not ardent. I meant don't ride Kurt and his mother that way, that's all." . . .

The arriving passengers amuse Fran. The things they wear, the way they look. Sam should see some of the things she has bought.

He sits staring at her. It is not her clothes that interest him. She is suddenly conscious of that.

"I don't seem able to strike the congenial note," she admits. "I do think you might meet me half way. As I look back, though, I don't blame myself. I can't, really! You were a good deal at fault, too. There are sins of omission, Sam!"

Dodsworth has risen suddenly, called the steward, given him a check and told him to go to Suite 7 and fetch the suitcase the check calls for. There is a warning blast of the steamer's whistle.

"What's the idea, Sam?" demands Fran, a little stunned.

DODSWORTH—I'm not sailing with you.

FRAN—You're not sailing!

DODSWORTH—No, I'm not.

FRAN—Sam, what are you—

DODSWORTH—No use trying to put it tactfully.

FRAN—Sam!

DODSWORTH—We just can't make a go of things any longer.

FRAN—And this is the man I've loved for twenty years!

DODSWORTH—Oh, no! It's the man who's loved you.

FRAN (*aghast*)—You haven't learned a thing! Not one single thing out of all our sorrows. And I've been flattering myself you really wanted to come back to me.

DODSWORTH—I tried, didn't I?

FRAN—I might have known you'd be just the same! I did know it. And yet I gave you another chance.

The warning gong for "Visitors Ashore" roars through the ship. There is more confusion among the passengers. Above the noise Dodsworth's voice rises firmly.

"I'm not taking another chance!" he is saying. "Because I'm through! Finished! That's flat!"

"But what is going to become of me?"

"I don't know. You'll have to stop getting younger some day."

"Oh! You can hurt!" Fran's hand covers her face.

"Sorry! Good-by!" he answers, starting for the door. There is another blast of the whistle.

"Are you going back to that washed-out expatriate in Naples?"

"Yes! And when *I've* got my divorce I'm going to marry her! And she and I are going on doing things!"

"Do you think you'll ever get me out of your blood?"

"Maybe not. But love's got to stop somewhere short of suicide."

He has gone into the crowd and disappeared. The steward is fearful lest the gentleman will miss the boat.

"He's gone ashore!" explains Fran, ruefully. And then she repeats the statement, screaming above the din: "He's gone ashore! He's gone ashore!"

The passengers are milling about. They do not hear. Nobody hears.

THE CURTAIN FALLS

AH, WILDERNESS!

A Comedy in Three Acts

By Eugene O'Neill

ONE of those fascinating stories of the theatre concerned with the history of a popular play came to notice with the production of "Ah, Wilderness!" This comedy, Eugene O'Neill reported, when he turned the script over to the Theatre Guild, was literally "a dream walking."

The playwright had been working unusually hard on his "Days Without End." When he had finished the third draft he determined to put that drama aside and rest for a week. He awoke next morning with the story, characters, plot scheme and practically all the details of "Ah, Wilderness!" in his mind clamoring to be put down on paper.

O'Neill went back to work and within a month had completed a first draft of "Ah, Wilderness!" Then he went on with "Days Without End." When this much more difficult drama was finally ready to be delivered to the Guild O'Neill took out the first draft of "Ah, Wilderness!" and was startled to find that, so far as he could judge, the first draft was quite as good as he could make it. He brought the play with him to New York and submitted it to the Guild directorate. They not only bought it on sight, but put it into rehearsal within a week, scoring one of the outstanding hits of Theatre Guild history with its production. "Days Without End," for which they had been waiting, was not produced for three months and when it was produced was pretty generally blasted by a divided press.

"Ah, Wilderness!" is homely stuff, quite foreign in content and spirit to anything the playwrighting O'Neill has previously contributed to the theatre. There is nothing like it in any of his short sea stories, his stabbing social satires or those experiments with spoken thoughts and character masks that have made him America's outstanding dramatist.

It goes back in the American theatre scene to such homely old hits as "The Old Homestead" and "Shore Acres," and was inspired by much the same desire to translate to the stage truthfully and pleasantly a comedy of American home life peopled by recognizable native characters.

The dedication of "Ah, Wilderness!" is to Mr. O'Neill's friend, George Jean Nathan, "who also, once upon a time, in peg-top trousers went the pace that kills along the road to ruin."

It is the morning of July 4, 1906, that we first meet the Nat Millers in the sitting room of their home "in a large small-town in Connecticut." The room is of good size, "homely looking and cheerful in the morning sunlight, furnished with scrupulous, medium-priced tastelessness of the period."

There is a sofa with silk and satin cushions; a bookcase, with glass doors, filled with cheap sets; portières hung in the double doors leading into the back parlor. A large comfortable center table holds a green-shaded reading lamp, with a cord reaching to the electric light socket above. Four or five chairs are grouped around the table, mostly rockers.

There is a buzz of conversation in the off-stage dining room, where the family is just finishing breakfast. Mrs. Miller's voice can be heard above the others admonishing her son Tommy, who has just appeared in the doorway, to come back and finish his milk. Tommy, "a chubby, sun-burnt boy of eleven, with dark eyes, blond hair wetted and plastered down in a part," is "bursting with bottled-up energy and longing to get started on his Fourth." Tommy's stomach is already full, he has said "excuse me," and he can't see—

His father's voice settles the argument. Tommy is allowed to go, but he had better be careful to set his firecrackers off away from the house, or there is likely to be trouble. Tommy is through the screen door letting onto the porch like a shot—and, of course, the door is left open.

Now the family filters in. First there are Mildred and Arthur. "Mildred is fifteen, with big, irregular features, resembling her father to the complete effacing of any pretense at prettiness." Arthur is nineteen, "tall, heavy, barrel-chested and muscular, the type of football linesman of that period. . . . His manner is solemnly collegiate; he is dressed in the latest college fashion of that day with padded shoulders, pants half pegged at the top, and so small at their wide-cuffed bottoms that they cannot be taken off with shoes on."

A moment later Mildred and Arthur are followed by their mother and their Aunt Lily, their father's sister. "Mrs. Miller is around fifty, a short stout woman with fading light-brown hair sprinkled with gray. . . . She has big brown eyes, soft and maternal—a bustling, mother-of-a-family manner." Lily Miller is forty-two, tall, dark and thin. "She conforms outwardly to the conventional type of old-maid schoolteacher, even to wearing glasses. But behind the glasses her gray eyes are gentle and tired, and her whole atmosphere is one of shy kindliness."

The fact that Tommy has left the screen door open, and the conviction that the house will soon be alive with flies, is enough to set Mrs. Miller off on her day's disturbances.

Nat Miller and Sid Davis, Mrs. Miller's brother, drift in from the dining room, both smoking cigars and interested in their exchange of personal conclusions. Nat Miller is in his late fifties "a little stoop-shouldered, more than a little bald, dressed with an awkward attempt at sober respectability imposed on an innate heedlessness of clothes. . . . He has fine, shrewd, humorous gray eyes." Sid "is forty-five, short and fat, bald-headed, with the Puckish face of a Peck's Bad Boy who has never grown up."

Family gossip has about run out at table. Now Nat Miller would like to know "what's on the tappee" for the day. Sid and he, of course, will go to the Sachem Club's picnic. Neither Mrs. Miller nor Lily is entirely pleased with that decision. Knowing the men folks as they do they also know what can happen at Sachem Club picnics. Even Nat's statement that Sid is practically a reformed character these days is not altogether reassuring. Still, they are resigned—and can only hope for the best.

Arthur and his friend Bert Taylor are taking the Rand girls canoeing and are to have a picnic lunch on Strawberry Island. Mildred is going to the beach with Anne Culver. It is of little or no importance to her whether Johnny Dodd is going there or not, she adds, in answer to her brother's teasing. Johnny, insists Mildred, is not the only pebble on the beach.

As for mother and Lily, they have made no plans. They probably will just sit around and talk. Nat thinks an automobile ride might help.

"I'll get out the Buick and we'll drive around town and out to the lighthouse and back," says he. "Then Sid and I'll let you off here or anywhere you say, and we'll go on to the picnic."

That suits everybody. In the evening Sid would like to take Lily to see the fireworks, if she'll go. Lily, "flustered and grateful" for the invitation, would like to go with Sid very much—only, there is still the thought of what may happen at the picnic!

"Evil-minded, I'm afraid, Nat," the embarrassed and humiliated Sid calls it. "I hate to say it of your sister."

They are all laughing at that when Arthur tries to ease the situation further by threatening to call a policeman if he should come upon Lily and Sid spooning on a bench at the beach. But only Mildred giggles at this.

Suddenly Mrs. Miller is reminded of another son, Richard. Where's Richard? They have been forgetting all about Richard.

Richard, it appears, has been putting in most of his vacation time writing poetry to Muriel McComber, according to Mildred, and reading books, according to Arthur. Which is a silly way to spend a vacation.

"He read his schoolbooks, too, strange as that may seem to you," caustically inserts Nat. "That's why he came out top of his class. I'm hoping before you leave New Haven they'll find time to teach you reading is a good habit."

Which reminds Richard's mother that Richard has been reading some pretty awful books. He should have a good talking to from his father. Mother had found several of the offending volumes hidden on the shelf in Richard's wardrobe and will go right now and fetch them.

"Seems to me she might wait till the Fourth's over before bringing up—" Nat Miller grins as Mrs. Miller disappears. "I know there's nothing to it, anyway. When I think of the books I used to sneak off and read when I was a kid!"

"Me, too," adds Sid. "I suppose Dick is deep in Nick Carter or Old Cap Collier."

"No, he passed that period long ago. Poetry's his red meat nowadays, I think—love poetry—and socialism, too, I suspect, from some dire declarations he's made. (*Then briskly.*) Well, might as well get him on the carpet."

It takes a good deal of shouting to rouse Richard. Once he gets his nose in a book he is in another world. But he comes finally. He "is going on seventeen, just out of high school. In appearance he is a perfect blend of father and mother, so much so that each is convinced he is the image of the other. . . . But he is definitely different from both of his parents, too. There is something of extreme sensitiveness added—a restless, apprehensive, defiant, shy, dreamy, self-conscious intelligence about him. In manner he is alternately plain simple boy and a posey actor solemnly playing a rôle. He is dressed in prep. school reflection of the college style of Arthur."

Richard is apologetic. He had not heard his father call. He is angered, too, when Arthur and Mildred would tease him. But he quiets down when his father speaks sharply and would know what Richard is planning to do with the holiday.

For one thing Richard is not planning to go to any silly old skirt party at the beach. He thought perhaps he would stay home —all morning anyway.

"Help Tommy set off firecrackers, eh?" suggests Miller.

"I should say not," explodes Richard, drawing himself up with dignity. "I don't believe in this silly celebrating the Fourth of July—all this lying talk about liberty—when there is no liberty!"

"Hmmmm!" hmmms Nat.

RICHARD (*getting warmed up*)—The land of the free and the home of the brave! Home of the slave is what they ought to call it—the wage slave ground under the heel of the capitalist class, starving, crying for bread for his children, and all he gets is a stone! The Fourth of July is a stupid farce!

MILLER (*putting a hand to his mouth to conceal a grin*)—Hmm. Them are mighty strong words. You'd better not repeat such sentiments outside the bosom of the family or they'll have you in jail.

SID—And throw away the key.

RICHARD (*darkly*)—Let them put me in jail. But how about the freedom of speech in the Constitution, then? That must be a farce, too. (*Then he adds grimly.*) No, you can celebrate your Fourth of July. I'll celebrate the day the people bring out the guillotine again and I see Pierpont Morgan being driven by in a tumbril! (*His father and* SID *are greatly amused;* LILY *is shocked but, taking her cue from them, smiles.* MILDRED *stares at him in puzzled wonderment, never having heard this particular line before. Only* ARTHUR *betrays the outraged reaction of a patriot.*)

ARTHUR—Aw say, you fresh kid, tie that bull outside! You ought to get a punch in the nose for talking that way on the Fourth!

MILLER (*solemnly*)—Son, if I didn't know it was you talking, I'd think we had Emma Goldman with us.

ARTHUR—Never mind, Pa. Wait till we get him down to Yale. We'll take that out of him!

RICHARD (*with high scorn*)—Oh, Yale! You think there's nothing in the world besides Yale. After all, what is Yale?

ARTHUR—You'll find out what!

SID (*provocatively*)—Don't let them scare you, Dick. Give 'em hell!

LILY (*shocked*)—Sid! You shouldn't swear before—

RICHARD—What do you think I am, Aunt Lily—a baby? I've heard worse than anything Uncle Sid says.

MILDRED—And said worse himself, I bet!

MILLER (*with a comic air of resignation*)—Well, Richard, I've always found I've had to listen to at least one stump speech every Fourth. I only hope getting your extra strong one right after breakfast will let me off for the rest of the day. (*They all laugh now, taking this as a cue.*)

RICHARD (*somberly*)—That's right, laugh! After you, the deluge, you think! But look out! Supposing it comes before? Why shouldn't the workers of the world unite and rise? They have nothing to lose but their chains! (*He recites threateningly.*) "The days grow hot, O Babylon! 'Tis cool beneath thy willow trees!"

MILLER—Hmm. That's good. But where's the connection, exactly? Something from that book you're reading?

RICHARD (*superior*)—No. That's poetry. This is prose.

MILLER—I've heard there was a difference between 'em. What is the book?

RICHARD (*importantly*)—Carlyle's French Revolution.

MILLER—Hmm. So that's where you drove the tumbril from and piled poor old Pierpont in it. (*Then seriously.*) Glad you're reading it, Richard. It's a darn fine book.

RICHARD (*with unflattering astonishment*)—What, have you read it?

MILLER—Well, you see, even a newspaper owner can't get out of reading a book every now and again.

RICHARD (*abashed*)—I—I didn't mean—I know you— (*Then enthusiastically.*) Say, isn't it a great book, though—that part about Mirabeau—and about Marat and Robespierre—

There is no chance for Richard to finish. Mrs. Miller has appeared with a rush from upstairs. She has not been able to locate the tainted literature Richard has evidently hidden a second time and demands that he go at once and bring it to his father.

Nat objects to this plan. They can waste the whole morning over Richard and his books. What books are they, anyway? Before Richard can answer, his mother has announced that there are at least two by that awful Oscar Wilde who "they put in jail for heaven knows what wickedness."

"He committed bigamy," declares Arthur, with solemn authority. ". . . A fellow at college told me. His father was in England when this Wilde was pinched—and he said he remembers once his mother asked his father about it and he told her he'd committed bigamy."

"I wouldn't put it past him, nor anything else," agrees Mrs. Miller.

There was also "The Picture of Dorian Gray" among Richard's books. "One of the greatest novels ever written," insists Richard. And "The Ballade of Reading Gaol." "One of the greatest poems ever written," announces Richard, pronouncing gaol as in goalposts. And two books by Bernard Shaw, who had, mother remembers, written a play so vile they would not let them play it even in New York. And a book called "The Quintessence of Ibsenism," which would be about Ibsen, "the greatest playwright since Shakespeare," according to Richard. And another, "Poems and Ballads by Swinburne," "the greatest poet since Shelley," contributes Richard. "He tells the truth about real love!"

Finally there was "The Rubaiyat of Omar Khayyam," and that, according to Richard, was the best of all. Nat had read that. Had a copy at the office. Sid had read it, too, and considered it a pippin. Especially the verse beginning—"Thou who didst with pitfall and gin beset the path I was to wander in—"

"You would pick out the ones with liquor in them," tartly protests Mrs. Miller. She is quite startled to discover that Lily, too, has a favorite verse from the Rubaiyat—

> "The Moving Finger writes, and having writ,
> Moves on: nor all your Piety nor Wit
> Shall lure it back to cancel half a Line,
> Nor all your Tears wash out a Word of it."

Richard's favorite, however, is

> "A Book of Verses underneath the Bough,
> A Jug of Wine, A Loaf of Bread—and Thou
> Beside me singing in the Wilderness—"

There can be no more of poetry quoting for the moment. Arthur at the window has caught sight of old man McComber on his way up the walk, and the announcement is rather disturbing. McComber, to judge from Nat's reaction, is something of a darned old fool. Nat will have to stay and talk to him and get rid of him as soon as he can, hurriedly decides Mrs. Miller.

Nat can't imagine what it is brings McComber. But it's to complain about something, he knows that. "I only wish," he says, "I didn't have to be pleasant with the old buzzard—but he's about the most valuable advertiser I've got."

"I know. But tell him to go to hell, anyway," sympathetically suggests Sid. "He needs that ad more than you."

David McComber "is a thin, dried-up little man with a head too large for his body perched on a scrawny neck, and a long solemn horse face with deep-set little black eyes, a blunt formless nose and a tiny slit of a mouth. He is about the same age as Miller but is entirely bald, and looks ten years older."

The thing that has brought him there, Mr. McComber confesses, is something disagreeable, though disgraceful would be a better word for it, and it concerns Richard.

"Let's get down to brass tacks," sharply interrupts Nat. "Just what is it you're charging him with?"

"With being dissolute and blasphemous—with deliberately attempting to corrupt the morals of my young daughter, Muriel."

"Then," answers Nat, calmly, "I'm afraid I will have to call you a liar, Dave!"

McComber (*without taking offense*)—I thought you'd get around to that, so I brought some of the proofs with me. I've a lot more of 'em at home. (*He takes a wallet from his inside coat pocket, selects five or six slips of paper, and holds them out to* Miller.) These are good samples of the rest. My wife discovered them in one of Muriel's bureau drawers hidden under the underwear. They're all in his handwriting, you can't deny it. Anyway, Muriel's confessed to me he wrote them. You read them and then say I'm a liar. (Miller *has taken the slips and is reading them frowningly.* McComber *talks on.*) Evidently you've been too busy to take the right care about Richard's bringing up or what he's allowed to read—though I can't see why his mother failed in her duty. But that's your misfortune, and none of my business. But Muriel is my business and I can't and I won't have her innocence exposed to the contamination of a young man whose mind, judging from his choice of reading matter, is as foul—

Miller (*making a tremendous effort to control his temper*)—Why, you damned old fool! Can't you see Richard's only a fool kid who's just at the stage when he's out to rebel against all authority, and so he grabs at everything radical to read and wants to pass it on to his elders and his girl and boy friends to show off what a young hellion he is! Why, at heart you'd find Richard just as innocent and as big a kid as Muriel is! (*He pushes the slips of paper across the table contemptuously.*) This stuff doesn't mean anything to me—that is, nothing of what you think it means. If you believe this would corrupt Muriel, then you must believe she's easily corrupted! But I'll bet you'd find she knows a lot more about life than you give her credit for—and can guess a stork didn't bring her down your chimney!

McComber—Now you're insulting my daughter. I won't forget that.

Miller—I'm not insulting her. I think Muriel is a darn nice girl. That's why I'm giving her credit for ordinary good sense. I'd say the same about my own Mildred, who's the same age.

McComber—I know nothing about your Mildred except that she's known all over as a flirt. (*Then more sharply.*) Well, I knew you'd prove obstinate, but I certainly never dreamed you'd have the impudence, after reading those papers, to claim your son was innocent of all wrongdoing!

Miller—And what did you dream I'd do?

McComber—Do what it's your plain duty to do as a citizen to protect other people's children! Take and give him a hiding he'd remember to the last day of his life! You'd ought to do it for his sake, if you had any sense—unless you want him to end up in jail!

Miller (*his fists clenched, leans across the table*)—Dave, I've stood all I can stand from you! You get out! And get out quick, if you don't want a kick in the rear to help you!

McComber (*again in his flat brittle voice, slowly getting to his feet*)—You needn't lose your temper. I'm only demanding you do your duty by your own as I've already done by mine. I'm punishing Muriel. She's not to be allowed out of the house for a month and she's to be in bed every night by eight sharp. And yet's she's blameless, compared to that—

Miller—I said I'd had enough out of you, Dave! (*He makes a threatening movement.*)

McComber—You needn't lay hands on me. I'm going.

There is, however, one more thing. Mr. McComber has brought a letter from Muriel to Richard which, according to her father, tells Richard how she has come to feel toward him. After reading that if Richard should not heed its implications, and should ever show himself again at the McCombers', he's liable to arrest. More than that Mr. McComber has decided to take his ad out of Nat Miller's paper and not put it back again until Nat publicly apologizes—

"I'll see you in hell first," announces Nat, with some vehemence. In addition to which it is now his declared intention to refuse to print the McComber ad, even if it is sent in. More than that he will start a campaign to encourage outside capital to start a new dry goods store that shall completely expose the McComber business as the swindle that it is.

"When I get through there won't be a person in town will buy a dishrag in your place!" shouts Nat, shaking with anger.

"That's all bluff! You wouldn't dare—" answers McComber, paling a bit and moving toward the door, his eyes shifting furtively. . . .

McComber has gone. Sid has heard a part of the scrap from the yard and is delighted. But the anger has drained from Nat's face, leaving him "looking a bit sick and disgusted."

"He knows it was all talk," he says, dully. "Anyone who knows me knows I wouldn't use my paper for a dirty, spiteful trick like that—no matter what he did to me."

The "samples of the new freedom" that McComber has left with Nat are disturbing to a father. Nat feels that he will have to do something to curb the young anarchist who is his son, but just what he doesn't know.

"Putting the curb bit on would make him worse," he tells Sid. "Then he'd have a harsh tyrant to defy. He'd love that, darn him!"

Sid has been going over the excerpts from Richard's letters. Some of them are certainly warm lulus—

"My life is bitter with thy love; thine eyes
Blind me, thy tresses burn me, thy sharp sighs
Divide my flesh and spirit with soft sound—"

That, thinks Nat, would be Mr. Swinburne. "I've never read him," he admits, "but I've heard something like that was the matter with him." Sid reads another:

"That I could drink thy veins as wine, and eat
Thy breasts like honey, that from face to feet
Thy body were abolished and consumed,
And in my flesh thy very flesh entombed!"

"Hell and hallelujah!" shouts Nat, boyishly. "Just picture old Dave digesting that for the first time! Gosh, I'd give a lot to have seen his face!"

But Nat is worried. Richard's passion is more serious than he thought, and that's no kind of stuff for him to be sending a decent girl.

"I thought he was really stuck on her—as one gets stuck on a decent girl at his age—all moonshine and holding hands and a kiss now and again," says Nat. "But this looks—I wonder if he is hanging around her to see what he can get? (*Angrily.*) By God, if that's true, he deserves that licking McComber says it's my duty to give him! I've got to draw the line somewhere!"

All he can do, he thinks, is to put it to Richard straight. He's never known the boy to lie to him. With Sid gone to hurry up the women Nat has his chance. Richard has come in, evidently nervous about McComber's call. Now Nat has walked over to him and put both his hands on the boy's shoulders.

"Look here, Son," he says. "I'm going to ask you a question, and I want an honest answer. I warn you beforehand if the answer is 'yes' I'm going to punish you and punish you hard because you'll have done something no boy of mine ought to do. But you've never lied to me before, I know, and I don't believe, even to save yourself punishment, you'd lie to me now, would you?"

"I won't lie, Pa," answers Richard, drawing himself up a little.

MILLER—Have you been trying to have something to do with Muriel—something you shouldn't—you know what I mean.

RICHARD (*stares at him for a moment, as if he couldn't comprehend—then, as he does, a look of shocked indignation comes over his face*)—No! What do you think I am, Pa? I never would! She's not that kind! Why, I—I love her! I'm going to marry her—after I get out of college! She's said she would! We're engaged!

MILLER (*with great relief*)—All right. That's all I wanted to know. We won't talk any more about it. (*He gives him an approving pat on the back.*)

RICHARD—I don't see how you could think— Did that old idiot McComber say that about me?

MILLER (*joking now*)—Shouldn't call your future father-in-law names, should you? 'Tain't respectful. (*Then after a glance at* RICHARD'S *indignant face—points to the slips of paper on the table.*) Well, you can't exactly blame old Dave, can you, when you read through that literature you wished on his innocent daughter?

RICHARD (*sees the slips for the first time and is overcome by embarrassment, which he immediately tries to cover up with a superior carelessness*)—Oh, so that's why. He found those, did he? I told her to be careful— Well, it'll do him good to read the truth about life for once and get rid of his old-fogy ideas.

MILLER—I'm afraid I've got to agree with him, though, that they're hardly fit reading for a young girl. (*Then with subtle flattery.*) They're all well enough, in their way, for you who're a man, but— Think it over, and see if you don't agree with me.

RICHARD (*embarrassedly*)—Aw, I only did it because I liked them—and I wanted her to face life as it is. She's so darned afraid of life—afraid of her Old Man—afraid of people saying this or that about her—afraid of being in love—afraid of everything. She's even afraid to let me kiss her. I thought, maybe, reading those things—they're beautiful, aren't they, Pa?—I thought they would give her the spunk to lead her own life, and not be—always thinking of being afraid.

MILLER—I see. Well, I'm afraid she's still afraid. (*He takes the letter from the table.*) Here's a letter from her he said to give you. (RICHARD *takes the letter from him uncertainly, his expression changing to one of apprehension.* MILLER *adds with a kindly smile.*) You better be prepared for a bit of a blow. But never mind. There's lots of other fish in the sea. (RICHARD *is not listening to him, but staring at the letter with a sort of fascinated dread.* MILLER *looks into his son's face a second, then turns away, troubled and embarrassed.*) Darn it! I better go upstairs and get rigged out or I never will get to that picnic. (*He moves awkwardly and self-consciously off through the front parlor.*)

Richard has finished Muriel's letter, and continues to stare at it. "His face grows more and more wounded and tragic, until at the end his mouth draws down at the corners, as if he were about to break into tears."

"The little coward!" Richard suddenly mutters to himself. "I hate her! She can't treat me like that! I'll show her!"

The family is coming now. Richard quickly crushes the letter into his pocket. He would appear calm and indifferent and has a try at whistling "Waiting at the Church." The whistle peters out miserably.

The family is ready for the automobile ride "dressed in all the elaborate paraphernalia of motoring at that period—linen dusters, veils, goggles, Sid in a snappy cap."

MRS. MILLER—Well, we're about ready to start at last, thank goodness! Let's hope no more callers are on the way. What did that McComber want, Richard, do you know? Sid couldn't tell us.

RICHARD—You can search me. Ask Pa.

MRS. MILLER (*immediately sensing something "down" in his manner—going to him worriedly*)—Why, whatever's the matter with you, Richard? You sound as if you'd lost your last friend! What is it?

RICHARD (*desperately*)—I—I don't feel so well—my stomach's sick.

MRS. MILLER (*immediately all sympathy—smoothing his hair back from his forehead*)—You poor boy! What a shame—on the Fourth, too, of all days! (*Turning to the others.*) Maybe I better stay home with him, if he's sick.

LILY—Yes, I'll stay, too.

RICHARD (*more desperately*)—No! You go, Ma! I'm not really sick. I'll be all right. You go. I want to be alone! (*Then, as a louder bang comes from in back as* TOMMY *sets off a cannon cracker, he jumps to his feet.*) Darn Tommy and his darned firecrackers! You can't get any peace in this house with that darned kid around! Darn the Fourth of July, anyway! I wish we still belonged to England! (*He strides off in an indignant fury of misery through the front parlor.*)

MRS. MILLER (*stares after him worriedly—then sighs philosophically*)—Well, I guess he can't be so very sick—after that. (*She shakes her head.*) He's a queer boy. Sometimes I can't make head or tail of him.

MILLER (*calls from the front door beyond the back parlor*)—Come along, folks. Let's get started.

SID—We're coming, Nat.

He and the two women move off through the front parlor as

THE CURTAIN FALLS

ACT II

A little after six that evening Mrs. Miller and Norah are setting the table in the Millers' dining room. "The room is much too small for the medium-priced, formidable dining-room set, especially now when all the leaves of the table are in." A rather dismal room, too, with a dark rug and somber brown wall paper carrying a dark red design. Norah, the second girl, is "a clumsy, heavy-handed, heavy-footed, long-jawed, beamingly good-natured young Irish girl—a 'greenhorn.' " She is as awkward as a greenhorn might be expected to be, and has great difficulty understanding Mrs. Miller's instructions.

It is Lily Miller who finally helps with the finishing touches, and gets the table right. Lily likes to help. Makes her feel a little less conscious of "sponging," as she terms it. True, she pays something, but she knows that Nat and Essie let her do that only to save her feelings.

The talk turns to Sid Davis. Remembering the invitation to the fireworks, Lily has spruced up a bit, which adds something to Mrs. Miller's worry.

"You mustn't mind if Sid comes home feeling a bit gay," warns Essie, trying to be casual. "I expect Nat to, and we'll have to listen to all those old stories of his about when he was a boy. You know what those picnics are, and Sid'd be running into all his old friends."

"I don't think he will—this time—not after his promise," says Lily, agitatedly.

"I know. But men are weak. (*Then quickly.*) That was a good notion of Nat's getting Sid the job on the Waterbury *Standard.* All he ever needed was to get away from the rut he was in here. He's the kind that's the victim of his friends. He's easily led—but there's no real harm in him, you know that. (Lily *keeps silent, her eyes downcast.* Mrs. Miller *goes on meaningly.*) He's making good money in Waterbury, too—thirty-five a week. He's in a better position to get married than he ever was."

"Well, I hope he finds a woman who's willing—though after he's through with his betting on horse races, and dice, and playing Kelly pool, there won't be much left for a wife—even if there was nothing else he spent his money on."

"Oh, he'd give up all that—for the right woman. (*Suddenly she comes directly to the point.*) Lily, why don't you change your mind and marry Sid and reform him? You love him and always have—"

"I can't love a man who drinks," says Lily, stiffly.

Mrs. Miller is not to be fooled. She knows Lily loves Sid and always has. And Sid loves her. But Lily is not to be convinced. It has been sixteen years, and even if she could forgive Sid for a lot of things she'd always remember the cause of that last quarrel—his taking up with bad women. Even if he had sworn he got raked into that party and never had anything to do with those harlots, Lily doesn't believe him.

"You know how much I like Sid in spite of everything," she says. "I know he was just born to be what he is—irresponsible, never meaning tc harm but harming in spite of himself. But don't talk to me about marrying him—because I never could."

Lily finds some outlet for her hunger for a home and children in the home Nat and Essie have made for her. And in the children she teaches at school.

"I like to feel I'm a sort of second mother to them and helping them to grow up to be good men and women. So I don't feel such a useless old maid after all."

"You're a good woman, Lily," says Essie, kissing her sister-in-law impulsively. "Too good for the rest of us."

Now everything is about ready, excepting a warning for Tommy. There is to be bluefish and Nat has always insisted he cannot eat bluefish. It contains a certain oil that invariably poisons him. So, every time they have bluefish Essie tells Nat it is weakfish, and he eats it contentedly. But she must warn Tommy to keep his face straight.

Richard, "beginning to take a masochistic satisfaction in his great sorrow, especially in the concern which it arouses in the family circle," walks aimlessly through the room. His face is bitter and when his Aunt Lily tries to sympathize with him he will have none of it. He wasn't even thinking of Muriel McComber. Anyway, life's a joke, and nothing ever comes out right.

"You can have your silly optimism, if you like, Aunt Lily. But don't ask me to be so blind. I'm a pessimist! (*Then with an air of cruel cynicism.*) As for Muriel, that's all dead and past. I was only kidding her anyway, just to have a little fun, and she took it seriously, like a fool. (*He forces a cruel smile to his lips.*) You know what they say about women and trolley cars, Aunt Lily: there's always another one along in a minute."

"I don't like you when you say such horrible, cynical things. It isn't nice."

"Nice! That's all you women think of! I'm proud to be a cynic. It's the only thing you can be when you really face life. I suppose you think I ought to be heart-broken about Muriel—a little coward that's afraid to say her soul's her own, and keeps tied to her father's apron strings! Well, not for mine! There's plenty of other fish in the sea!"

Mrs. Miller still has no patience with her son, especially for sending a nice girl all those things he got out of indecent books. She is, she admits to Lily when Richard has gone "out into the night," as he has tragically announced, "when it isn't even dark yet," she is actually grateful to old man McComber for putting an end to his nonsense with Muriel. Richard is not old enough for such silliness.

Mrs. Miller and Lily have gone into the sitting room when Richard comes back. He is still serious. "They do not know the secret in the poet's heart," he quotes, standing in the doorway as he surveys the table. The sight of food disgusts him a little, but he does reach for a couple of olives.

A moment later there is a ya-hoo from the yard and Wint Selby is in looking for Arthur. Wint is nineteen, "a typical, good-looking college boy of the period, not the athletic, but the hell-raising sport type. He is tall, blond, dressed in extreme collegiate cut."

Arthur not being there sort of gums things up for Wint. He doesn't mind confessing to Richard, if Richard will keep his mouth shut, that he (Wint) has just met a couple of "swift babies from New Haven" and dated them up. Now it is too late to get anyone else and Wint is practically broke.

Richard thinks he might help some. He's got eleven dollars saved up. Wint, of course, wouldn't think of taking the money—*but,* if Richard hasn't got anything on for the night he might like to come along.

"I'm not trying to lead you astray, you understand," protests Wint. "But it'll be a help if you would just sit around with Belle and feed her a few drinks while I'm off with Edith. (*He winks.*) See what I mean? You don't have to do anything, not even take a glass of beer—unless you want to."

"Aw, what do you think I am—a rube?" demands Richard, boastfully.

"Ever been out with any girls—I mean, real swift ones that there's something doing with, not these dead Janes around here?"

"Aw, what do you think? Sure I have!"

"Ever drink anything besides sodas?"

"Sure. Lots of times. Beer and sloe-gin fizz—and Manhattans."

"Hell, you know more than I thought," concludes Wint, properly impressed.

It is arranged that Richard, who is to keep his mouth shut to everyone, including Art, is to be at the Pleasant Beach Hotel at nine-thirty and come to the back room. Incidentally he is to grab some cloves to take the booze off his breath. Wint will introduce him as a Harvard freshman. He wouldn't want them to think he is traveling around with a high-school kid.

With Wint gone Richard stands for a moment, "a look of bitter, defiant rebellion coming over his face, and mutters to himself."

"I'll show her she can't treat me the way she's done!" he mutters. "I'll show them all!"

Tommy has rushed in to report the approach of his father and Uncle Sid. He giggles a little as he thinks of the fish and is eager to get at his dinner. A moment later from the yard Sid's voice is heard. He is singing "Poor John" a little uncertainly.

"Mmm! Mmm! Lily I'm afraid—" says Essie. But she smiles as she says it.

"Yes, I might have known," answers Lily bitterly.

They are all trying not to laugh, or even smile, and to appear quite casual. But Tommy knows what's going on. "Uncle Sid's soused again," says Tommy.

They have all found their places at table when Nat Miller's voice is heard jovially announcing his and Sid's arrival as he comes in from the back parlor. "He isn't drunk by any means. He is just mellow and benignly ripened. His face is one large, smiling, happy beam of utter appreciation of life. All's right with the world, so satisfyingly right that he becomes sentimentally moved even to think of it."

"Here we are, Essie! Right on the dot! Here we are!"

He has pulled his wife to him and given her a smacking kiss—on the ear, it happens, as she pulls away from him. And when she would chide him pleasantly "he slaps her jovially on her fat buttocks." Tommy and Mildred roar with glee. Even Norah, coming in with the soup, explodes with laughter and nearly drops the soup.

"Nat! Aren't you ashamed!" protests the scandalized Essie.

"Couldn't resist it," chuckles Nat. "Just simply couldn't resist it!"

The dinner started, Norah manages to serve the soup with some little difficulty, what with Mr. Miller inclined to be increasingly jovial. Now he would tell them all of the day's adventure.

"We did have the darndest fun today," he beams. "And Sid was the life of that picnic! You ought to have heard him! Honestly, he had that crowd just rolling on the ground and splitting their sides! He ought to be on the stage!"

"He ought to be at this table eating something to sober him up, that's what he ought to be!" answers Essie, tartly.

Sid, Nat reports, is a little embarrassed about coming to table. Let everybody pretend not to notice. Especially Lily. Sid's scared of Lily.

"All right, Sid! The coast's clear!" calls Nat, beginning to absorb his soup ravenously.

When Sid comes from the back parlor "he is in a condition that can best be described as blurry. His movements have a hazy uncertainty about them. His shiny fat face is one broad, blurred, Puckish, naughty-boy grin; his eyes have a blurred, wondering vagueness."

Sid's effort to appear cold sober is strained and exaggerated. "Good evening!" he calls cheerfully. "Beautiful evening. I never remember seeing—more beautiful sunset—" Of course he would bump into Lily's chair trying to reach his own. He is deeply sorry for that. By the time he is firmly seated he has decided that a sunset is, after all, really none of his business. Let 'er set!

Discovering the soup Sid is pleasantly surprised, but discovering the location of his mouth is not so easy. Not with a spoon. He thinks it much simpler to drink the soup as a toast to all. The family, trying as it has to remain casual, is sniggering freely into its plates and young Tommy is in stitches. Nor will Sid stop drinking his soup, even at Mrs. Miller's request. Soup is a liquid and liquids should be drunk.

"Oh, no, Essie," Sid protests firmly, "if I ever so far forget myself as to drink a leg of lamb, then you might have some—excuse for— Just think of waste effort eating soup with spoons—fifty grueling lifts per plate—billions of soup-eaters on globe—why, it's simply staggering! (*Then darkly to himself.*) No more spoons for me! If I want develop my biceps, I'll buy Sandow Exerciser!"

They have finished the soup and Norah brings in the fish. Sid would also pass a friendly word or two with Norah, if Essie did not scare the urge out of him. The children find this passage highly diverting, and when Norah side-wipes their father's head with the fish platter in her excitement they are convulsed.

"This isn't by any chance bluefish, is it, my dear?" calmly inquires Nat.

"Of course not," answers Essie, with a quick look at Tommy. "You know we never have bluefish, on account of you."

"Yes," Nat explains to the company, "I regret to say there is a certain peculiar oil in bluefish that invariably poisons me."

That is too much for Tommy. He explodes in laughter. Soon the whole family has joined in and Nat's dignity is noticeably ruffled. He can't see that there is anything so darned funny about being poisoned. Nor can Sid. The fish looks exceedingly blue to Sid, even despondent and desperate. He points an accusing finger at the confused Essie.

"See how guilty she looks—a ver-veritable 'Lucretia Georgia!' Can it be this woman has been slowly poisoning you all these years? And how well—you've stood it! What iron constitution! Even now, when you are invariably at death's door, I can't believe—"

The whole table is now convulsed, with the exception of Nat. Nor does he feel much better after Essie has confessed the joke. Come to think of it, Nat now recalls, he has felt upset every time they have had fish.

But by the time the fish is finished, and Norah is bringing in the lobster, he has recovered his temper. Now, apropos Mildred's day at the beach, Nat would tell the story of what a good swimmer he used to be as a boy. A regular water rat.

"You know, speaking of swimming, I never go down to that beach but what it calls to mind the day I and Red Sisk went in swimming there and I saved his life."

Again the family indulges in a general snigger. They all know what is coming. But Nat is not to be easily discouraged, either by the family's lack of attention or Sid's frequent interruptions. They may give him pause, but they cannot stop him until he has, by recital and vocal demonstrations, told how he heard the gurgle in Red Sisk's voice when they were in the water racing for the pile and he turned to see his opponent struggling with a cramp in his leg. With that Nat had turned about, grabbed Red, and started for the pile still two hundred feet away. It was, according to Sid, two hundred and fifty feet away the last time Nat told it.

"I've taken down the distance every time you've saved Red's life for thirty years, and the mean average to that pile is two hundred and fifty feet!" insists Sid, to the vast amusement of the family. "Why didn't you let that Red drown anyway, Nat? I never knew him, but I know I'd never have liked him."

It is Essie who comes to Nat's rescue. The swimming story is a perfectly good story, she insists, and Nat shall tell it whenever he wants to. And if Sid were in any responsible state she'd give him a piece of her mind.

"Getting old, I guess, Mother—getting to repeat myself," smiles Nat, a little sadly. "Someone ought to stop me."

"No such thing. You're as young as you ever were."

Essie would further repress the irrepressible Sid, but has little success. Her brother is no more than half through his lobster before he is reminded of a story. In fact Sid, as he tells Tommy, is the man who invented the lobster. It was while he was building the Pyramids—he just took a day off and dashed off a lobster.

"He was bigger'n older than me and he had the darndest reddest crop of hair but I dashed him off just the same!"

Essie finally gets Sid to agree to take a nap. He is, he admits, in a delicate condition, in spite of which Nat had kept plying him with chowder all day—even though he knew full well that there is a certain peculiar oil in chowder that invariably—

Sid has arrived at the back of Lily's chair on his way to bed when he pauses for the performance of a daily duty. He must ask Lily to marry him. Lily will not—ever. Which, allows Sid, is probably just as well. Among the precepts he had been taught at his mother's dying knee was never to marry a woman who drinks.

Sid is pretending to be a Salvation Army parade, raising his voice in the old Army hymn, "In the Sweet Bye and Bye," and alternating as a bass drum as he disappears. The family is roaring with laughter and Lily is giggling hysterically. Now, as Essie would excuse them all for laughing so at Sid, Lily becomes suddenly rigid, her face jerking convulsively as she stands and faces them.

"That's just it—you shouldn't—even I laughed—it does encourage—that's been his downfall—everyone always laughing, everyone always saying what a card he is, what a case, what a caution, so funny—and he's gone on—and we're all responsible—making it easy for him—we're all to blame—and all we do is laugh!"

They would all comfort Lily if they could, but Lily is so thoroughly disturbed she thinks she had better go and lie down for a little while. It is probably her disappointment about the fireworks, Essie explains. Nat is willing to substitute for Sid, but Essie knows wild horses couldn't drag Lily to the fireworks after what has happened.

MILLER—Hmm. I thought she'd got completely over her foolishness about him long ago.

MRS. MILLER—She never will.

MILLER—She'd better. He's got fired out of that Waterbury job—told me at the picnic after he'd got enough Dutch courage in him.

MRS. MILLER—Oh, dear! Isn't he the fool!

MILLER—I knew something was wrong when he came home.

Well, I'll find a place for him on my paper again, of course. He always was the best news-getter this town ever had. But I'll tell him he's got to stop his damn nonsense.

MRS. MILLER (*doubtfully*)—Yes.

MILLER—Well, no use sitting here mourning over spilt milk. (*He gets up and* RICHARD, MILDRED, TOMMY *and* MRS. MILLER *follow his example, the children quiet and a bit awed.*) You kids go out in the yard and try to keep quiet for a while, so's your Uncle Sid'll get to sleep and your Aunt Lily can rest.

TOMMY (*mournfully*)—Ain't we going to set off the sky rockets and Roman candles, Pa?

MILLER—Later, Son, later. It isn't dark enough for them yet anyway.

MILDRED—Come on, Tommy. I'll see he keeps quiet, Pa.

MILLER—That's a good girl. (MILDRED *and* TOMMY *go out through the screen door.* RICHARD *remains standing, sunk in bitter, gloomy thoughts.* MILLER *glances at him—then irritably:*) Well, Melancholy Dane, what are you doing?

RICHARD (*darkly*)—I'm going out—for a while. (*Then suddenly.*) Do you know what I think? It's Aunt Lily's fault, Uncle Sid's going to ruin. It's all because he loves her, and she keeps him dangling after her, and eggs him on and ruins his life—like all women love to ruin men's lives! I don't blame him for drinking himself to death! What does he care if he dies, after the way she's treated him! I'd do the same thing myself if I were in his boots!

MRS. MILLER (*indignantly*)—Richard! You stop that talk!

RICHARD (*quotes bitterly*)—

"Drink! for you know not whence you come nor why.
Drink! for you know not why you go nor where!"

MILLER (*losing his temper—harshly*)—Listen here, young man! I've had about all I can stand of your nonsense for one day! You're growing a lot too big for your size, seems to me! You keep that damn fool talk to yourself, you hear me—or you're going to regret it! Mind, now! (*He strides angrily away through the back parlor.*)

MRS. MILLER (*still indignant*)—Richard, I'm ashamed of you, that's what I am. (*She follows her husband.* RICHARD *stands for a second, bitter, humiliated, wronged, even his father turned enemy, his face growing more and more rebellious. Then he forces a scornful smile to his lips.*)

RICHARD—Aw, what the hell do I care? I'll show them! (*He turns and goes out the screen door.*)

THE CURTAIN FALLS

ACT III

Ten o'clock that evening Richard Miller and a girl named Belle are sitting in the rear room of an obscure hotel. It is a small, dingy room, "dimly lighted by two fly-specked globes in a fly-specked gilt chandelier suspended from the middle of the ceiling."

There are three round tables, with four chairs and a brass cuspidor by the side of each table. A nickel-in-the-slot player-piano stands against the wall. The wall paper is a forbidding saffron and the floor is littered with cigar and cigarette butts.

Belle is twenty, "a rather pretty peroxide blonde, a typical college 'tart' of the period, and of the cheaper variety, dressed with tawdry flashiness. But she is a fairly recent recruit to the ranks, and is still a bit remorseful behind her make-up and defiantly careless manner."

Belle has been drinking gin-rickeys. Richard has a half-empty glass of beer in front of him. "He looks horribly timid, embarrassed and guilty, but at the same time thrilled and proud of at last mingling with the pace that kills."

The piano-player is grinding out "Bedelia." The bartender, "a stocky young Irishman with a foxily cunning, stupid face," has moved inside the bar entrance in the cause of encouraging business.

Belle is a little disgusted with Richard. He is not at all her idea of a hot sport. Also she is thirsty. In answer to her heckling Richard gulps down the rest of his beer "as if it were some nasty-tasting medicine," and orders another. Also one for the bartender, who prefers a cigar.

Belle is puzzled. Surely things can't be as slow up at Harvard as Richard would indicate. Filling up on beer! Why can't he take a man's drink!

Just for that Richard orders a sloe-gin fizz and, with a wink from Belle, the bartender promises to make it a real one.

"Christ, what a dump!" suddenly ejaculates Belle. Richard recoils from the shock of the curse. "If this isn't the deadest burg I ever struck! Bet they take the sidewalks in after nine o'clock. Say, honestly, kid, does your mother know you're out?"

"Aw, cut it out, why don't you—trying to kid me!" answers

Richard, defensively.

"All right. I didn't mean to, Dearie. Please don't get sore at me."

"I'm not sore!"

"You see, it's this way with me," Belle explains, seductively. "I think you're one of the sweetest kids I've ever met—and I could like you such a lot if you'd give me half a chance—instead of acting so cold and indifferent."

"I'm not cold and indifferent," protests Richard, his tone solemnly tragic. "It's only that I've got a weight on my mind."

"Well, get it off your mind and give something else a chance to work."

The bartender has brought the drinks, greatly pleased with the one with which he has taken special pains for Richard. When he has gone back to the bar Belle takes a new interest in the party. Stealthily, to Richard's shocked amazement, she has lifted her skirts and taken a package of cheap cigarettes from her stocking. Girls aren't allowed to smoke except in rooms upstairs, she explains, but she will steal a puff or two. Does Richard smoke?

Oh, yes—Richard has been smoking for the last two years. In another year Richard will be allowed pipes and cigars. But he doesn't inhale. Inhaling is bad, especially for girls.

"Gee, kid, you're a scream!" laughs Belle. "You'll grow up to be a minister yet. Well, here's how! Bottoms up, now! Show me you really know how to drink. It'll take that load off your mind."

They have drained their glasses. Impatiently Belle is waiting for Richard to take a new interest in everything. She's afraid he doesn't like her. If he does, why doesn't he show it? Does he want her to come and sit on his lap? Richard does—but—Which is invitation enough for Belle.

"She comes and sits on his lap. He looks desperately uncomfortable, but the gin is rising to his head and he feels proud of himself and devilish, too."

BELLE—Why don't you put your arm around me? (*He does so awkwardly.*) No, not that dead way. Hold me tight. You needn't be afraid of hurting me. I like to be held tight, don't you?

RICHARD—Sure I do.

BELLE—'Specially when it's by a nice handsome kid like you. (*Ruffling his hair.*) Gee, you've got pretty hair, do you know it? Honest, I'm awfully strong for you! Why can't you be about me? I'm not so awfully ugly, am I?

RICHARD—No, you're—you're pretty.

BELLE—You don't say it as if you meant it.

RICHARD—I do mean it—honest.

BELLE—Then why don't you kiss me? (*She bends down her lips toward his. He hesitates, then kisses her and at once shrinks back.*) Call that kissing? Here. (*She holds his head and fastens her lips on his and holds them there. He starts and struggles. She laughs.*) What's the matter, Honey Boy? Haven't you ever kissed like that before?

RICHARD—Sure. Lots of times.

BELLE—Then why did you jump as if I'd bitten you? (*Squirming around on his lap.*) Gee, I'm getting just crazy about you! What shall we do about it, eh? Tell me.

RICHARD—I—don't know. (*Then boldly.*) I—I'm crazy about you, too.

BELLE (*kissing him again*)—Just think of the wonderful time Edith and your friend, Wint, are having upstairs—while we sit down here like two dead ones. A room only costs two dollars. And, seeing I like you so much, I'd only take five dollars—from you. I'd do it for nothing—for you—only I've got to live and I owe my room rent in New Haven—and you know how it is. I get ten dollars from everyone else. Honest! (*She kisses him again, then gets up from his lap—briskly.*) Come on. Go out and tell the bartender you want a room. And hurry. Honest, I'm so strong for you I can hardly wait to get you upstairs!

RICHARD (*starts automatically for the door to the bar—then hesitates, a great struggle going on in his mind—timidity, disgust at the money element, shocked modesty, and the guilty thought of* MURIEL, *fighting it out with the growing tipsiness that makes him want to be a hell of a fellow and go in for all forbidden fruit, and makes this tart a romantic, evil vampire in his eyes. Finally, he stops and mutters in confusion*)—I can't.

BELLE—What, are you too bashful to ask for a room? Let me do it, then. (*She starts for the door.*)

RICHARD (*desperately*)—No—I don't want you to—I don't want to.

BELLE (*surveying him, anger coming into her eyes*)—Well, if you aren't the lousiest cheap skate!

RICHARD—I'm not a cheap skate!

BELLE—Keep me around here all night fooling with you when I might be out with some real live one—if there is such a thing in this burg!—and now you quit on me! Don't be such a piker!

You've got five dollars! I seen it when you paid for the drinks, so don't hand me any lies!

RICHARD—I—Who said I hadn't? And I'm not a piker. If you need the five dollars so bad—for your room rent—you can have it without—I mean, I'll be glad to give— (*He has been fumbling in his pocket and pulls out his nine-dollar roll and holds out the five to her.*)

BELLE (*hardly able to believe her eyes, almost snatches it from his hand—then laughs and immediately becomes sentimentally grateful*)—Thanks, Kid. Gee—oh, thanks— Gee, forgive me for losing my temper and bawling you out, will you? Gee, you're a regular peach! You're the nicest kid I've ever met! (*She kisses him and he grins proudly, a hero to himself now on many counts.*) Gee, you're a peach! Thanks again.

RICHARD (*grandly—and quite tipsily*)—It's—nothing—only too glad. (*Then boldly.*) Here—give me another kiss, and that'll pay me back.

Being in funds, Belle would buy a drink, too, and Richard thinks that's darned nice of her. She's a nice girl, really, when you get to know her. But there's a reason why he did not want to go upstairs with her. Richard has sworn off. Took an oath he'd be faithful. He won't tell Belle who the girl is, but he would, after another drink, reason with her about the life she is leading. She really ought to reform.

Belle suggests rather tartly that Richard mind his own business. And let him be not too sure about that girl of his. She is probably out with some other fellow this minute giving him everything he wants. Why should he be a sucker?

Richard is ready to fight at this. He is becoming perceptibly more intoxicated. The bartender is back, bringing a salesman with him, "a stout, jowly-faced man in his late thirties, dressed with cheap nattiness, with the professional breeziness and jocular, kid-'em-along manner of his kind."

The salesman, highball in hand, would edge into the party. He is tired standing at the bar. So far as Belle is concerned he is more than welcome. Richard, having reached the poetry-reciting stage, is of a mind to object without knowing just how.

"But I wouldn't do such, 'cause I loved her too much,
But I learned about women from her."

Richard has intoned the lines sentimentally and then given some sign of passing out. Belle is ready to move over to the salesman's table if Richard will let her up. The desertion is a blow to Richard. Reminds him of—

"Yet each man kills the thing he loves,
By each let this be heard—
Some do it with a bitter look,
Some with a flattering word,
The coward does it with a kiss,
The brave man with a sword!"

The salesman is encouraging, but Belle is all for canning both Richard and the bunk.

"And then—at ten o'clock, Eilert Lovborg will come—with vine leaves in his hair," prophesies Richard.

"And bats in his belfry, if he's you!" adds Belle.

Now Richard would rise to protect Belle from the intentions of this interloper who has come among them. He would give the salesman a good poke in the snoot, that is what Richard would do. But the bartender is back. The salesman suggests that perhaps it might be wise if he were to get Richard out and into some other gin mill. Obviously the boy is under age, and that might spell trouble.

With this suggestion the bartender lays hands on Richard, at the collar of his coat and the seat of his trousers, and marches him ignominiously out of the room and through the swinging doors of the barroom.

"Poor kid! I hope he makes home all right," says Belle. "I liked him before he got soused."

SALESMAN—Who is he?

BELLE—The boy who's upstairs with my friend told me, but I didn't pay much attention. Name's Miller. His old man runs a paper in this one-horse burg, I think he said.

SALESMAN (*with a whistle*)—Phew! He must be Nat Miller's kid, then.

BARTENDER (*coming back from the bar*)—Well, he's on his way—with a good boot in the tail to help him!

SALESMAN (*with a malicious chuckle*)—Yes? Well, maybe that boot will cost you a job, Brother. Know Nat Miller who runs the *Globe?* That's his kid.

BARTENDER (*his face falling*)—The hell he is! Who said so?

SALESMAN—This baby doll. (*Getting up.*) Say, I'll go keep cases on him—see he gets on the trolley all right, anyway. Nat

Miller's a good scout. (*He hurries out.*)

BARTENDER (*viciously*)—God damn the luck! If he ever finds out I served his kid, he'll run me out of town. (*He turns on* BELLE *furiously.*) Why didn't you put me wise, you lousy tramp, you!

BELLE—Hey! I don't stand for that kind of talk—not from no hick beer-squirter like you, see!

BARTENDER (*furiously*)—You don't, don't you! Who was it but you told me to hand him dynamite in that fizz? (*He gives her chair a push that almost throws her to the floor.*) Beat it, you—and beat it quick—or I'll call Sullivan from the corner and have you run in for street-walking! (*He gives her a push that lands her against the family-entrance door.*) Get the hell out of here—and no long waits!

BELLE (*opens the door and goes out—turns and calls back viciously*)—I'll fix you for this, you thick Mick, if I have to go to jail for it. (*She goes out and slams the door.*)

BARTENDER (*looks after her worriedly for a second—then shrugs his shoulders*)—That's only her bull. (*Then with a sigh as he returns to the bar.*) Them lousy tramps is always getting this dump in dutch!

The curtain falls.

The Miller family has been spending the evening in the living room of the Miller home. Now, about eleven o'clock, Richard is still out and both the parent Millers are beginning to worry.

Nat, having discarded collar and tie and brought out his old dressing gown and disreputable-looking carpet slippers, has difficulty keeping his mind on the paper he is pretending to read. Essie Miller, trying to concentrate on a doily she is hemming, has been asking the time every five minutes as her nervous uneasiness has mounted.

Lily is trying to read. Mildred is practicing on a new signature for herself that will feature a new set of flourishes, and young Tommy, on the sofa, is devoting all his attention to keeping awake. His eyes blink frequently, but the second he feels anyone looking at him he "goads himself into a bright-eyed wakefulness."

Why doesn't Richard come? Where could he have gone? What could have happened? Again and again the worried voice of Richard's mother is raised in query. Nor can all the assurance of all the family satisfy her.

Finally Lily suggests that probably Richard went to see the

fireworks and, because he could not get a seat in the trolley, is walking home. Which would account for a considerable lapse of time. It is excuse enough to satisfy Richard's mother until she can get Tommy to bed. But no longer.

Now Arthur Miller has come home from his evening at the Rands'. He hasn't seen or heard anything of Richard, but it is his opinion that Richard sneaked off to the fireworks and failed to say anything about it because of the way he had talked in the morning—"bawling out the Fourth like an anarchist" and all that. "He wouldn't want to renege on that to you—but he'd want to see the old fireworks just the same," says Arthur, complacently. "I know. He's at the foolish age."

"Well, Arthur, by gosh, you make me feel as if I owed you an apology when you talk horse sense like that," agrees Nat, greatly relieved. "Arthur's hit the nail right on the head, I think, Essie. That was what I couldn't figure out—why he—but now it's clear as day."

With a little help from the wig-wag system Nat has suggested to Arthur that he should sing for his family to take up the tension. Word has come from the Rands' and other places that Arthur has a good voice, but the family never hears it. With this urging Arthur and Mildred go into the front parlor.

They are at the piano when Sid appears. "All the effervesence of his jag has worn off and he is now suffering from a bad case of hangover—nervous, sick, a prey to gloomy remorse and bitter feelings of self-loathing and self-pity."

Sid has forced a smile and flattened himself against the edge of the bookcase, "miserably self-conscious and ill-at-ease there but nervously afraid to move anywhere else."

In the parlor Arthur has started "Then You'll Remember Me." "Miller gazes before him with a ruminating melancholy, his face seeming to become gently sorrowful and old. Mrs. Miller stares before her, her expression becoming more and more doleful. Lily forgets to pretend to read her book but looks over it, her face growing tragically sad. As for Sid, he is moved to his remorseful, guilt-stricken depths. His mouth pulls down at the corners and he seems about to cry."

Now Sid would apologize to everybody for coming home the way he did. Everybody would save him the humiliation by assuring him that everything is all right, and forgotten. Even Lily has forgotten missing the fireworks. But by the time Arthur has got through "Dearie" Sid is in tears, his voice choked "in a passion of self-denunciation."

"You're right, Lily!—right not to forgive me!—I'm no good and never will be!—I'm a no-good drunken bum!—you shouldn't even wipe your feet on me!—I'm a dirty, rotten drunk!—no good to myself or anybody else!—if I had any guts I'd kill myself, and good riddance!—but I haven't!—I'm yellow, too!—a yellow drunken bum!" (*He hides his face in his hands and begins to sob like a sick little boy. This is too much for* LILY. *All her bitter hurt and steely resolve to ignore and punish him vanish in a flash, swamped by a pitying love for him. She runs and puts her arm around him—even kisses him tenderly and impulsively on his bald head, and soothes him as if he were a little boy.* MRS. MILLER, *almost equally moved, has half risen to go to her brother, too, but* MILLER *winks and shakes his head vigorously and motions her to sit down.*)

"There! Don't cry, Sid! I can't bear it! Of course I forgive you," says Lily. "Haven't I always forgiven you? I know you're not to blame— So don't, Sid!"

At their father's suggestion Arthur and Mildred have found something more cheerful in "Waiting at the Church." By the time they reach "Can't get away to marry you today, my wife won't let me!" Sid has joined in. They're laughing now—all except Mrs. Miller. She has suddenly become conscious of the time again, and her worries have taken new hold upon her. Nobody knows what might have happened to Richard. Every day there are stories in the papers about young boys getting run over by automobiles. Tonight everybody who owns one is out and a lot of drivers are drunk! Or he might have gone down to the beach dock and fallen overboard—

MRS. MILLER—Oh, I know something dreadful's happened! And you can sit there listening to songs and laughing as if— Why don't you do something? Why don't you go out and find him? (*She bursts into tears.*)

LILY (*comes to her quickly and puts her arm around her*)—Essie, you mustn't worry so! You'll make yourself sick! Richard's all right. I've got a feeling in my bones he's all right.

MILDRED (*comes hurrying in from the front parlor*)—What's the trouble? (ARTHUR *appears in the doorway beside her. She goes to her mother and also puts an arm around her.*) Ah, don't cry, Ma! Dick'll turn up in a minute or two, wait and see!

ARTHUR—Sure, he will!

MILLER (*has gotten to his feet, frowning—soberly*)—I was going out to look—if he wasn't back by twelve sharp. That'd be the time it'd take him to walk from the beach if he left after the last car. But I'll go now, if it'll ease your mind. I'll take the auto and drive out the beach road—and likely pick him up on the way. (*He has taken his collar and tie from where they hang from one corner of the bookcase, and is starting to put them on.*) You better come with me, Arthur.

ARTHUR—Sure thing, Pa. (*Suddenly he listens and says:*) Ssshh! There's someone on the piazza now—coming around to this door, too. That must be him. No one else would—

MRS. MILLER—Oh, thank God, thank God!

MILLER (*with a sheepish smile*)—Darn him! I've a notion to give him hell for worrying us all like this. (*The screen door is pushed violently open and* RICHARD *lurches in and stands swaying a little, blinking his eyes in the light. His face is a pasty pallor, shining with perspiration, and his eyes are glassy. The knees of his trousers are dirty, one of them torn from the sprawl on the sidewalk he had taken, following the bartender's kick. They all gape at him, too paralyzed for a moment to say anything.*)

MRS. MILLER—Oh, God, what's happened to him! He's gone crazy! Richard!

SID (*the first to regain presence of mind—with a grin*)—Crazy, nothing. He's only soused!

ARTHUR—He's drunk, that's what! (*Then shocked and condemning.*) You've got your nerve! You fresh kid! We'll take that out of you when we get you down to Yale!

RICHARD (*with a wild gesture of defiance—maudlinly dramatic*)—

> "Yesterday this Day's Madness did prepare
> Tomorrow's Silence, Triumph, or Despair.
> Drink! for—"

MILLER (*his face grown stern and angry, takes a threatening step toward him*)—Richard! How dare—!

MRS. MILLER (*hysterically*)—Don't you strike him, Nat! Don't you—!

SID (*grabbing his arm*)—Steady, Nat! Keep your temper! No good bawling him out now! He don't know what he's doing!

MILLER (*controlling himself and looking a bit ashamed*)—All right—you're right, Sid.

RICHARD (*drunkenly glorying in the sensation he is creating—recites with dramatic emphasis*)—"And then—I will come—with vine leaves in my hair!" (*He laughs with a double-dyed sardoni-*

cism.)

MRS. MILLER (*staring at him as if she couldn't believe her eyes*)—Richard! You're intoxicated!—you bad, wicked boy, you!

RICHARD (*forces a wicked leer to his lips and quotes with ponderous mockery*)—"Fancy that, Hedda! (*Then suddenly his whole expression changes, his pallor takes on a greenish, sea-sick tinge, his eyes seem to be turned inward uneasily—and, all pose gone, he calls to his mother appealingly, like a sick little boy.*) Ma! I feel—rotten! (MRS. MILLER *gives a cry and starts to go to him, but* SID *steps in her way.*)

SID—You let me take care of him, Essie. I know this game backwards.

MILLER (*putting his arm around his wife*)—Yes, you leave him to Sid.

SID (*his arm around* RICHARD—*leading him off through the front parlor*)—Come on, Old Sport! Upstairs we go! Your old Uncle Sid'll fix you up. He's the kid that wrote the book!

MRS. MILLER (*staring after them—still aghast*)—Oh, it's too terrible! Imagine our Richard! And did you hear him talking about some Hedda? Oh, I know he's been with one of those bad women, I know he has—my Richard! (*She hides her face on* MILLER'S *shoulder and sobs heartbrokenly.*)

MILLER (*a tired, harassed, deeply worried look on his face—soothing her*)—Now, now, you mustn't get to imagining such things! You mustn't, Essie! (LILY *and* MILDRED *and* ARTHUR *are standing about awkwardly with awed, shocked faces.*)

The curtain falls.

It is one o'clock the following day. The Millers have had their mid-day dinner, for which Nat has come home on the special pleading of Essie that he must say something to Richard. Nat knows he must say something to Richard and it makes him very cross because, as he confesses to Sid, he doesn't know what to say. It had been easier to talk to the other boys. Someway Richard is different.

The situation is also a bit complicated by the fact that evidently Richard had been the victim of others' schemes. A note has been left at the *Evening Globe* office by a woman that indicates something of the kind.

"Your son got the booze he drank last night at the Pleasant Beach House," it reads. "The bartender there knew he was under age but served him just the same. He thought it was a good joke to get him soused. If you have any guts you will run that bastard out of town!"

Unsigned, but definitely feminine, the note is quite evidently from a lady who would like to be even with a bartender, as Sid sees it. Under the circumstances it will not do to be too hard on Richard.

Essie has been to call Richard so his father can talk to him, but she just didn't have the heart to call him when she found him sleeping so peacefully. He certainly needs rest after what he has gone through and, anyway, Nat can see him when he comes home to supper.

His father gone, Richard is not long in putting in an appearance. "His expression is one of hang-dog guilt mingled with a defensive defiance." Richard is not sorry for what he has done. He will never do it again, because it wasn't any fun. But—

"I'm not sorry I tried it once," insists Richard; "—curing the soul by means of the senses, as Oscar Wilde says. But what does it matter what I do or don't do? Life is all a stupid farce! I'm through with it. It's lucky there aren't any of General Gabler's pistols around—or you'd see if I'd stand it much longer!"

A few moments later all those suicide thoughts are swept from Richard's mind by sister Mildred's admission that she has a letter for him from Muriel. Now Richard has grabbed the letter and read it feverishly.

"Gee, Mid, do you know what she says—that she didn't mean a word in that other letter," Richard explodes, his eyes shining. "Her old man made her write it. And she loves me and only me and always will, no matter how they punish her."

More than that Muriel is going to try to sneak out that night and meet Richard.

"Ha! I knew darned well she couldn't hold out," exults Richard, feeling his enthusiasm before Mildred might have struck a wrong note. " 'Women never know when the curtain has fallen. They always want another act!' " he quotes, cynically.

"But what'll you do till nighttime? It's ages to wait."

"What do I care how long I wait! I'll think of her and dream! I'd wait a million years and never mind it—for her! The trouble with you is you don't understand what love means."

Richard is disappearing into the back parlor as the curtain falls.

On a strip of beach along the harbor Richard Miller is sitting sideways on the gunwale of a rowboat that has been drawn up, "its bow about touching the bank, the painter trailing up the bank, evidently made fast to the trunk of a willow."

The crescent of the new moon "casts a soft, mysterious, caressing light over everything. . . . In the distance the orchestra of a summer hotel can be heard very faintly at intervals."

Richard "is in a great state of anxious expectancy, squirming about uncomfortably on the narrow gunwale, kicking at the sand restlessly, twirling his straw hat, with a bright-colored band in stripes, around on his finger."

Richard is also thinking aloud—thinking it must be nearly nine o'clock; thinking his mother probably had a fit when she discovered that he sneaked out; thinking he will catch hell when he goes back, but feeling that it will be worth it, if only Muriel appears.

He takes a note from Muriel from his pocket, reads it again and sheepishly kisses it as he puts it back. He tries to think of something else to make the time pass faster, and his thoughts go back to the experience of the night before; back to Belle and the Pleasant Beach House, and— But he doesn't want to think of anything like that, now that Muriel's coming.

"That's a fine time to think of—!" he mutters, restlessly pacing up and down. "But you hugged and kissed her . . . not until I was drunk, I didn't . . . and then it was all showing off . . . darned fool! . . . and I didn't go upstairs with her . . . even if she was pretty . . . aw, she wasn't pretty . . . she was all painted up . . . she was just a whore . . . she was everything dirty . . . Muriel's a million times prettier anyway . . . Muriel and I will go upstairs . . . when we're married . . . but that will be beautiful . . . but I oughtn't even to think of that yet . . . it's not right . . . I'd never—now . . . and she'd never . . . she's a decent girl . . . I couldn't love her if she wasn't . . . but after we're married . . . (*He gives a little shiver of passionate longing—then resolutely turns his mind away from these improper, almost desecrating thoughts.*) That damned barkeep kicking me. . . . I'll bet you if I hadn't been drunk I'd have given him one good punch in the nose, even if he could have licked me after! . . . (*Then with a shiver of shamefaced revulsion and self-disgust.*) Aw, you deserved a kick in the pants . . . making such a darned slob of yourself . . . reciting the Ballad of Reading Gaol to those lowbrows! . . . you must have been a fine sight when you got home! . . . having to be put to bed and getting sick! . . . Phaw! . . . (*He squirms dis-*

gustedly.) Think of something else, can't you? . . . recite something . . . see if you remember . . .

"'Nay, let us walk from fire unto fire
From passionate pain to deadlier delight
I am too young to live without desire,
Too young art thou to waste this summernight—'

. . . gee, that's a peach! . . . I'll have to memorize the rest and recite it to Muriel the next time. . . . I wish I could write poetry . . . about her and me. . . ."

Again he becomes conscious of the beauty of the night, of the world, of all that's in it. Then nine o'clock arrives, struck faintly on the distant bells, and Richard's anxiety increases. Perhaps Muriel isn't coming; perhaps she got caught; perhaps she's just late, like all women—and then he sees her far down the path. He must not seem too pleased, however. "If women are too sure of you, they treat you like slaves," declares Richard; "let her suffer for a change!" . . .

Muriel McComber "is fifteen going on sixteen. She is a pretty girl with a plump, graceful little figure, fluffy, light brown hair, big, naïve, wondering, dark eyes, a round, dimpled face, a melting drawly voice. Just now she is in a great thrilled state of timid adventurousness."

Muriel calls to Richard, but he resolutely goes on whistling with his back turned. When he answers it is with the utmost casualness. He had no idea it could be nine o'clock so soon. He had not forgotten Muriel was coming, he says, but he had been thinking about life.

MURIEL—You might think of me for a change, after all the risk I've run to see you! (*Hesitating timidly on the edge of the shadow.*) Dick! You come here to me. I'm afraid to go out in that bright moonlight where anyone might see me.

RICHARD (*coming toward her—scornfully*)—Aw, there you go again—always scared of life!

MURIEL (*indignantly*)—Dick Miller, I do think you've got an awful nerve to say that after all the risks I've run making this date and then sneaking out! You didn't take the trouble to sneak any letter to me, I notice!

RICHARD—No, because after your first letter, I thought everything was dead and past between us.

MURIEL—And I'll bet you didn't care one little bit! (*On the *verge of humiliated tears.*) Oh, I was a fool ever to come here! I've got a good notion to go right home and never speak to you again! (*She half turns back toward the path.*)

RICHARD (*frightened—immediately becomes terribly sincere—grabbing her hand*)—Aw, don't go, Muriel! Please! I didn't mean anything like that, honest I didn't! Gee, if you knew how broken-hearted I was by that first letter, and how darned happy your second letter made me!

MURIEL (*happily relieved—but appreciates she has the upper hand now and doesn't relent at once*)—I don't believe you.

RICHARD—You ask Mid how happy I was. She can prove it.

MURIEL—She'd say anything you told her to. I don't care anything about what she'd say. It's you. You've got to swear to me—

RICHARD—I swear!

MURIEL (*demurely*)—Well, then, all right, I'll believe you.

RICHARD (*his eyes on her face lovingly—genuine adoration in his voice*)—Gosh, you're pretty tonight, Muriel! It seems ages since we've been together! If you knew how I've suffered—!

MURIEL—I did, too.

RICHARD (*unable to resist falling into his tragic literary pose for a moment*)—The despair in my soul— (*He recites dramatically.*) "Something was dead in each of us, And what was dead was Hope!" That was me! My hope of happiness was dead! (*Then with sincere boyish fervor.*) Gosh, Muriel, it sure is wonderful to be with you again! (*He puts a timid arm around her awkwardly.*)

MURIEL (*shyly*)—I'm glad—it makes you happy. I'm happy, too.

RICHARD—Can't I—won't you let me kiss you—now? Please! (*He bends his face toward hers.*)

MURIEL (*ducking her head away—timidly*)—No. You mustn't. Don't—

RICHARD—Aw, why can't I?

MURIEL—Because—I'm afraid.

RICHARD (*discomfited—taking his arm from around her—a bit sulky and impatient with her*)—Aw, that's what you always say! You're always so afraid! Aren't you ever going to let me?

MURIEL—I will—sometime.

RICHARD—When?

MURIEL—Soon, maybe.

RICHARD—Tonight, will you?

MURIEL (*coyly*)—I'll see.

RICHARD—Promise?

MURIEL—I promise—maybe.

RICHARD—All right. You remember you've promised.

Richard would have Muriel come over and sit in the boat, but Muriel thinks it much too light there. She gives in after a time, though she thinks she really should be getting right back home. She must be back in bed pretending to sleep by ten. She had had the most exciting time getting out. She had gone to bed at eight, which is part of her punishment, and her mother had come up to see that she really was undressed and everything. Then she got up and dressed in a terrible hurry. Richard has no idea what Muriel has gone through for his sake.

As for that Richard has also been through quite a lot. Muriel can't have any idea of what her letter made him do. But that is too long a story to be repeated. "Let the dead past bury its dead," says Richard.

Muriel is insistent, and soon Richard is going through most of the terrible details. "Hell is the only word that can describe it," says Richard. After he had read her letter he didn't want to live any more. "Life seemed like a tragic farce" to him then. He had sat and brooded about death. He had wanted to kill himself, beautifully, like Hedda Gabler, but he didn't have a pistol. And, anyway, if Muriel had meant what she said in the letter she wouldn't be worth dying for.

"So I said to myself, I'm through with women; they're all alike," confesses Richard.

"I'm not," protests Muriel.

RICHARD—And I thought, what difference does it make what I do now? I might as well forget her and lead the pace that kills, and drown my sorrows! You know I had eleven dollars saved up to buy you something for your birthday, but I thought, she's dead to me now and why shouldn't I throw it away? (*Then hastily.*) I've still got almost five left, Muriel, and I can get you something nice with that.

MURIEL (*excitedly*)—What do I care about your old presents? You tell me what you did!

RICHARD (*darkly again*)—After it was dark, I sneaked out and went to a low dive I know about.

MURIEL—Dick Miller, I don't believe you ever!

RICHARD—You ask them at the Pleasant Beach House if I didn't! They won't forget me in a hurry!

MURIEL (*impressed and horrified*)—You went there? Why, that's a terrible place! Pa says it ought to be closed by the police!

RICHARD (*darkly*)—I said it was a dive, didn't I? It's a "secret house of shame." And they let me into a secret room behind the barroom. There wasn't anyone there but a Princeton Senior I know—he belongs to Tiger Inn and he's fullback on the football team—and he had two chorus girls from New York with him, and they were all drinking champagne.

MURIEL (*disturbed by the entrance of the chorus girls*)—Dick Miller! I hope you didn't notice—

RICHARD (*carelessly*)—I had a highball by myself and then I noticed one of the girls—the one that wasn't with the fullback—looking at me. She had strange-looking eyes. And then she asked me if I wouldn't drink champagne with them and come and sit with her.

MURIEL—She must have been a nice thing! (*Then a bit falteringly.*) And did—you?

RICHARD (*with tragic bitterness*)—Why shouldn't I, when you'd told me in that letter you'd never see me again?

MURIEL (*almost tearfully*)—But you ought to have known Pa made me—

RICHARD—I didn't know that then. (*Then rubbing it in.*) Her name was Belle. She had yellow hair—the kind that burns and stings you!

MURIEL—I'll bet it was dyed!

RICHARD—She kept smoking one cigarette after another—but that's nothing for a chorus girl.

MURIEL (*indignantly*)—She was low and bad, that's what she was or she couldn't be a chorus girl, and her smoking cigarettes proves it! (*Then faltering again.*) And then what happened?

RICHARD (*carelessly*)—Oh, we just kept drinking champagne—I bought a round—and then I had a fight with the barkeep and knocked him down because he'd insulted her. He was a great big thug but—

MURIEL (*huffily*)—I don't see how he could—insult that kind! And why did you fight for her? Why didn't the Princeton fullback who'd brought them there? He must have been bigger than you.

RICHARD (*stopped for a moment—then quickly*)—He was too drunk by that time.

MURIEL—And were you drunk?

RICHARD—Only a little then. I was worse later. (*Proudly.*)

You ought to have seen me when I got home! I was on the verge of delirium tremens!

Muriel does not think she could have stood that. She hates people who get drunk. Richard, by his recount, keeps right on drinking champagne. Now, as he tells it, Belle has fallen in love with him and is sitting on his lap kissing him. But he didn't kiss her. He just said good night finally and went home.

Muriel doesn't believe that. Tearfully she recalls how she was lying in bed crying her eyes out while all these awful things were going on.

"I hate you," she cries out, suddenly jumping to her feet in a tearful fury; "I wish you were dead! I'm going home this very minute! I never want to lay eyes on you again! And this time I mean it!"

"Muriel! Wait! Listen!"

"I don't want to listen! Let me go! If you don't I'll bite your hand!"

"I won't let you go! You've got to let me explain! I never—Ouch!"

The marks of Muriel's teeth are on Richard's hand, but Muriel is free and running down the beach.

Still rubbing his hand, Richard is of a mind to let Muriel go, and she, seeing he is not coming after her, stops at the foot of the path. But she is not coming back. Let him go back to Belle, if that is the kind of a girl he likes. He's owned up he kissed her—

"I did not," shouts Richard. "She kissed me."

Sounds fishy to Muriel. How does he know, anyway, what he did if he drank all that champagne? If she could be sure he didn't love that girl— And was never going to see her again—And that it really was her letter—the letter her father had made her write, standing right over her and telling her each word to put down. She just had to write that letter or she never would have had a chance to see Richard again. Still, she can see how he might think she was to blame. So, if he'll swear that he never even thought of loving that—

"I didn't! I swear, Muriel! I couldn't! I love you!"

"Well, then—I still love you!"

She has come back to the boat now, and cuddled up to him a little when he puts his arm timidly around her. "I'm sorry I hurt your hand," she says.

"That was nothing—it felt wonderful—even to have you bite!" he assures her.

MURIEL (*impulsively takes his hand and kisses it*)—There! That'll cure it. (*She is overcome by confusion at her boldness.*)

RICHARD—You shouldn't—waste that—on my hand. (*Then tremblingly.*) You said—you'd let me—

MURIEL—I said, maybe.

RICHARD—Please, Muriel. You know—I want it so!

MURIEL—Will it wash off—her kisses—make you forget her ever—for always?

RICHARD—I should say so! I'd never remember—anything but it—never want anything but it—ever again.

MURIEL (*shyly lifting her lips*)—Then—all right—Dick. (*He kisses her tremblingly and for a moment their lips remain together. Then she lets her head sink on his shoulder and sighs softly.*) The moon *is* beautiful, isn't it?

RICHARD (*kissing her hair*)—Not as beautiful as you! Nothing is! (*Then after a pause.*) Won't it be wonderful when we're married?

MURIEL—Yes—but it's so long to wait.

RICHARD—Perhaps I needn't go to Yale. Perhaps Pa will give me a job. Then I'd soon be making enough to—

MURIEL—You better do what your pa thinks best—and I'd like you to be at Yale. (*Then patting his face.*) Poor you! Do you think he'll punish you awful?

RICHARD (*intensely*)—I don't know and I don't care! Nothing would have kept me from seeing you tonight—not if I'd had to crawl over red-hot coals! (*Then falling back on Swinburne—but with passionate sincerity.*) You have my being between the hands of you! You are "my love, mine own soul's heart, more dear than mine own soul, more beautiful than God!"

MURIEL (*shocked and delighted*)—Ssshh! It's wrong to say that.

RICHARD (*adoringly*)—Gosh, but I love you! Gosh, I love you—Darling!

MURIEL—I love you, too—Sweetheart! (*They kiss. Then she lets her head sink on his shoulder again and they both sit in a rapt trance, staring at the moon. After a pause—dreamily.*) Where'll we go on our honeymoon, Dick? To Niagara Falls?

RICHARD (*scornfully*)—That dump where all the silly fools go? I should say not! (*With passionate romanticism.*) No, we'll go to some far-off wonderful place! (*He calls on Kipling to help *him.*) Somewhere out on the Long Trail—the trail that is always new—on the road to Mandalay! We'll watch the dawn come up like thunder out of China!

MURIEL (*hazily but happily*)—That'll be wonderful, won't it?

The curtain falls.

By ten o'clock that night peace had settled over the Miller sitting room. Nat Miller, having drawn a rocker up to the center table, is reading a book. Essie Miller, her face wearing an expression of unworried content, is again working on a doily, with her sewing basket in her lap.

The book that Nat is reading is one of those confiscated from Richard's collection. One of Shaw's. Shaw, Nat has discovered, is a comical cuss, even if his ideas are crazy. And Swinburne's got a fine swing to his poetry, if he'd only write about something beside loose women. The "Rubaiyat of Omar Khayyam," too—Nat has got a lot from that, at least from those parts that aren't all about boozing.

The talk turns to Richard. They are glad they know where he is tonight, but that, insists Nat, does not clear him of what he did the night before. Richard still will have to be punished for that.

Mrs. Miller is convinced that Richard has been punished enough as it is. He has told her he is sorry and that he is never going to touch liquor again.

"It didn't make him feel happy like Sid," explains Richard's mother, "but only sad and sick, so he didn't see anything in it for him."

"Well, if he's really got that view of it driven into his skull, I don't know but I'm glad it all happened," says Nat. "That'll protect him more than a thousand lectures—just horse sense about himself."

Still, Nat feels that something's got to be done about the question of family discipline. He thinks he will tell Richard that he cannot go to Yale—

Essie will have none of that. Every man of Nat's means in the town is sending his boys to college. The other Miller boys have had their chance and if Richard wants to go he's going. Richard's got an exceptional brain. His mother is sure of that. And he has proved it by the books he likes to read.

"But I thought you—" interjects the amused Nat.

"You thought I what?"

"Never mind."

"You mark my words, that boy's going to turn out to be a great lawyer, or a great doctor, or a great writer, or—"

"You agree he's going to be great, anyway."

"Yes, I most certainly have a lot of faith in Richard."

"Well, so have I, as far as that goes," says Nat.

When the subject of Richard's interest in Muriel McComber comes up Mrs. Miller is inclined to favor it. True, she had said once that she thought Muriel stupid. But, Essie's mother had not thought Nat so very bright when Essie was first interested in him. And Nat turned out all right. Muriel's a cute-looking girl, and she might be good for Richard.

"You don't mean to tell me you're actually taking this Muriel crush of Richard's seriously, do you?" demands Nat. "I know it's a good thing to encourage right now but—pshaw. Why, Richard'll probably forget all about her before he's away six months, and she'll have forgotten him."

"Don't be cynical," says Essie.

Peace again settles upon the Miller household. Sid and Lily have gone to the beach to listen to the band. Arthur is at the Rands'. Mildred is out walking with her latest. So far as Nat can see the Millers are completely surrounded by love. Even the excited McComber has become pacified. Nat had met him on the street and he was as meek as pie. All in all it has been a good day.

Then Richard comes. "He walks like one in a trance, his eyes shining with a dreamy happiness, his spirit still too exalted to be conscious of his surroundings, or to remember the threatened punishment."

For a moment Essie is apprehensive. Has Richard taken to liquor again? "It's love, not liquor, this time," says Nat reassuringly.

Nat thinks perhaps it would be better if Essie were to leave them alone. With his father Richard is drawn into a confessional mood. He knows he acted like a darned fool.

MILLER (*thinking it well to rub in this aspect—disgustedly*)—You sure were—not only a fool but a downright, stupid, disgusting fool! (RICHARD *squirms, his head still lower.*) It was bad enough for you to let me and Arthur see you, but to appear like that before your mother and Mildred—! And I wonder if Muriel would think you were so fine if she ever saw you as you looked and acted then. I think she'd give you your walking papers for keeps. And you couldn't blame her. No nice girl wants to give her love to a stupid drunk!

RICHARD (*writhing*)—I know, Pa.

MILLER (*after a pause—quietly*)—All right. Then that settles—the booze end of it. (*He sizes* RICHARD *up searchingly—then suddenly speaks sharply.*) But there is another thing that's more serious. How about that tart you went to bed with at the Pleasant Beach House?

RICHARD (*flabbergasted—stammers*)—You know—? But I didn't! If they've told you about her down there, they must have told you I didn't! She wanted me to—but I wouldn't. I gave her the five dollars just so she'd let me out of it. Honest, Pa, I didn't! She made everything seem rotten and dirty—and—I didn't want to do a thing like that to Muriel—no matter how bad I thought she'd treated me—even after I felt drunk, I didn't. Honest!

MILLER—How'd you happen to meet this lady, anyway?

RICHARD—I can't tell that, Pa. I'd have to snitch on someone—and you wouldn't want me to do that.

MILLER (*a bit taken aback*)—No. I suppose I wouldn't. Hmm. Well, I believe you—and I guess that settles that. (*Then, after a quick, furtive glance at* RICHARD, *he nerves himself for the ordeal and begins with a shame-faced self-conscious solemnity.*) But listen here, Richard, it's about time you and I had a serious talk about—hmm—certain matters pertaining to—and now that the subject's come up of its own accord, it's a good time—I mean, there's no use in procrastinating further—so, here goes. (*But it doesn't go smoothly and as he goes on he becomes more and more guiltily embarrassed and self-conscious and his expressions more stilted. Richard sedulously avoids even glancing at him, his own embarrassment made tenfold more painful by his father's.*) Richard, you have now come to the age when—Well, you're a fully developed man, in a way, and it's only natural for you to have certain desires of the flesh, to put it that way—I mean, pertaining to the opposite sex—certain natural feelings and temptations—that'll want to be gratified—and you'll want to gratify them. Hmm—well, human society being organized as it is, there's only one outlet for—unless you're a scoundrel and go around ruining decent girls—which you're not, of course. Well, there are a certain class of women—always have been and always will be as long as human nature is what it is— It's wrong, maybe, but what can you do about it? I mean, girls like that one you—girls there's something doing with—and lots of 'em are pretty, and it's human nature if you— But that doesn't mean to ever get mixed up with them seriously! You just have what you want and pay 'em and forget it. I know that sounds hard and unfeeling, but we're talking facts and— But don't think I'm encouraging you to— If you can stay away from 'em, all the better—but if—why—hmm— Here's what I'm driving at, Richard. They're apt to be whited sepulchers— I mean, your whole life might be ruined if—so, darn it, you've got to know how to— I mean, there are ways and means— (*Suddenly he can go no farther and winds up helplessly.*) But, hell, I suppose you boys talk all this over among yourselves and you know more about it than I do. I'll admit I'm no authority. I never had anything to do with such women, and it'll be a hell of a lot better for you if you never do!

RICHARD (*without looking at him*)—I'm never going to, Pa. (*Then shocked indignation coming into his voice.*) I don't see how you could think I could—now—when you know I love Muriel and am going to marry her. I'd die before I'd—!

MILLER (*immensely relieved—enthusiastically*)—That's the talk! By God, I'm proud of you when you talk like that! (*Then hastily.*) And now that's all of that. There's nothing more to say and we'll forget it, eh?

There is still the question of punishment, but Nat is ready to forget that, too. He had thought of not letting Richard go to Yale, but when he finds that nothing would please Richard better than that, he decides to hold to Yale.

They call Mother. Essie comes in from the yard. It's a beautiful night, she reports. Perhaps the most beautiful night she has ever seen. Nat, too, can remember only a few nights as beautiful as this—and they were long ago.

"Yes, I'll bet those must have been wonderful nights, too. You sort of forget the moon was the same way back then—and everything," says Richard, looking quickly at his father and mother, "as if he'd never seen them before."

"You're all right, Richard," says Nat, getting up and blowing his nose.

"You're a good boy, Richard," adds Essie, fondly.

It's bed time, they all agree. But Richard is sure he couldn't sleep. He thinks he'll go out and sit on the piazza until the moon sets.

He has kissed his mother good night and turned to his father. Nat a little awkwardly puts his arm around the boy and gives him a hug. "Good night, Richard," he says. Impulsively Richard kisses his father and hurries out the screen door.

"First time he's done that in years," mutters Nat. "I don't believe in kissing between fathers and sons after a certain age—seems mushy and silly—but that meant something! And I don't think we'll ever have to worry about his being safe—from himself—again. And I guess no matter what life will do to him, he can take care of it now. (*He sighs with satisfaction and, sitting down in his chair, begins to unlace his shoes.*) My darned feet are giving me fits."

MRS. MILLER (*laughing*)—Why do you bother unlacing your shoes now, you big goose—when we're going right up to bed?

MILLER (*as if he hadn't thought of that before, stops*)—Guess you're right. (*Then getting to his feet—with a grin.*) Mind if I don't say my prayers tonight, Essie? I'm certain God knows I'm too darned tired.

MRS. MILLER—Don't talk that way. It's real sinful. (*She gets up—then laughing fondly.*) If that isn't you all over! Always looking for an excuse to— You're worse than Tommy! But all right. I suppose tonight you needn't. You've had a hard day. (*She puts her hand on the reading-lamp switch.*) I'm going to turn out the light. All ready?

MILLER—Yep. Let her go, Gallagher. (*She turns out the lamp. In the ensuing darkness the faint moonlight shines full in through the screen door. Walking together toward the front parlor they stand full in it for a moment, looking out.* MILLER *puts his arm around her. He says in a low voice:*) There he is—like a statue of Love's Young Dream. (*Then he sighs and speaks with a gentle nostalgic melancholy.*) What's it that Rubaiyat says:

> "Yet Ah, that Spring should vanish with the Rose!
> That Youth's sweet-scented manuscript should close!"

(*Then throwing off his melancholy, with a loving smile at her.*) Well, Spring isn't everything, is it, Essie? There's a lot to be said for Autumn. That's got beauty, too. And Winter—if you're together.

MRS. MILLER (*simply*)—Yes, Nat. (*She kisses him and they move quietly out of the moonlight, back into the darkness of the front parlor.*)

THE CURTAIN FALLS

THEY SHALL NOT DIE

A Drama in Three Acts

By John Wexley

THE propaganda drama has taken an important place in the theatre of this troubled world. It represents the viewpoint of a class, a dramatic expression of that type of radicalism that must have an outlet to escape internal combustion.

During this particular theatre season there were three propaganda dramas produced in New York. The first was George Sklar's and Albert Maltz's protest against war called "Peace on Earth." The second was John Wexley's dramatic brief for the nine colored boys twice convicted of the crime of rape in Scottsboro, Alabama (though the author is at pains to insist that his characters and story are fictional), and the third was George Sklar's and Paul Peter's exposé of a dock laborers' strike in New Orleans called "Stevedore."

Of the three I have selected "They Shall Not Die" as the most pertinently representative, in story, in timeliness and as a cohesive and moving dramatic entertainment.

Like most propaganda plays "They Shall Not Die" suffers from the effect of overstatement. John Wexley, remembered for his death house drama, "The Last Mile," is not one to temper or restrain an impulse. He is utterly partisan and would have the world know it. But the very earnestness with which he supports his prejudices makes for exciting drama.

"They Shall Not Die," beginning with a prelude of exposition that is passionately devoted to an unadulterated and brutalized realism, moves steadily forward with the development of the colored protagonists' defense to one of those electrifying trial scenes such as has frequently made theatregoing an exciting adventure ever since Shakespeare made Antonio of Venice a sacrificial hero and Shylock the humbled victim of a smart lawyer's trick.

The county jail in Cookesville, in a Southern state, is divided into three sections as we of the audience see it in "They Shall Not Die." At one side is what is known as a "run-around" and a cage for white prisoners. In the center is the office of the jail with a door at the back leading to a stairway landing. The stairs lead to the street below. At the other side is a "pen," a large steel cell for "niggers."

In the white prisoners' cage is an inner steel mesh inclosure. There are straw mattresses on the floor. Three white prisoners of the hobo type are variously disposed. They are Red, Blackie and the St. Louis Kid.

In the office two deputy sheriffs, rough, nondescript citizens named Willie Cooley and Henderson, are leaning back lazily in their chairs, moving forward occasionally to spit at a bespattered cuspidor standing in front of a battered roll-top desk. To the back wall an old Red Cross cabinet is fastened and beneath it a dilapidated, badly chipped white hospital table.

Cooley and Henderson are carrying on a desultory conversation concerned with local gossip, including the quality of certain batches of home-brew and an approaching fair day that is likely to bring crowds to town.

As the Cooley-Henderson conversation lags the hobos in the mesh cage can be heard. Their conversation, too, is scattered and unimportant, concerned principally with their various attempts to escape from chain gangs they have known and the unhappy results of being caught and returned for increased sentences.

Cooley and Henderson have got around to national politics, the general calamity that has followed the death of President Wilson and the taking over of affairs by the Republicans, headed by "that Yankee fish-face Coolidge," when the telephone rings violently.

Someone wants to get in touch with Sheriff Trent. There is trouble on the way. Cooley agrees to send over to the billiard hall for the Sheriff right away.

"That was the Stebbinsville law," he explains excitedly to Henderson as he hangs up the receiver. "Seems like a half a dozen white kid hoboes was thrown off the freight from Chattanoogie by some *niggers* . . . and they're stoppin' the train at Rocky Point fo' 'em. But I gotta git Sheriff Trent . . . or we lose our badges. . . ."

Before Cooley can call the Sheriff there is a second phone call, more exciting than the first. Up the line they have stopped the freight train and taken off a gang of niggers. They are being brought over to the Cookesville jail. Henderson better get the guns out of the cabinet and load 'em—

Now Cooley has Louise, the telephone girl, on the wire and wants her to find Sheriff Trent in a hurry—

"No, Louise . . . I cain't tell you nothin'. . . . It's agin the law," Cooley explains excitedly over the wire. "Well . . . there's been a hull to-do on the freight. . . . Hello, Sheriff Trent? Well, all hell's done gone and bust loose on the through freight from Chattanoogie! Big fight, 'bout fifty or a hunerd niggers . . . no, half dozen white kids got themselves throwed off this side o' Stebbinsville. . . . They're bein' sent on heah right now by truck. . . . Then I'm jest 'bout to call yuh when the Rocky Point law calls up . . . an' they done stop the train at Rocky Point . . . huh? Sho' . . . they got 'em all . . . and listen, Mist' Trent, they found two white gals on the train dressed like boys, with overalls. . . . Well, they musta crossed the line if they come from Tennessee . . . they all comin' on heah to Cookesville. . . . Sho', I'm gittin' ready now . . . huh? . . . No, they didn't say whut the niggers done to 'em. . . . Mebbe they did an' mebbe they didn't . . . huh?" (*To Henderson.*) He hung up. . . . (*Hangs up.*)

Cooley has been sent down to the gun room to get rifles ready for Mist' Trent. Hillary and Kenneth and Smith will have to be rounded up, too, to be deputized. The white boys, sensing the excitement, have scrambled up the side of their cage trying to get a view of what is happening outside a window letting into their cell.

There is a rumble of voices outside. A voice reports the appearance of a Rocky Point truck coming down the road. Sheriff Trent is on his way across the street with Bob Smith. Out of the mumblings of the gathering crowd snatches of excited conversation can be heard—

"Where're the niggers, Fred?" . . . "They'll be along!" . . . "I'm gittin' my gun!" . . . "Where're them gals?" . . . "Whut's up, Jeff?" . . . "They musta near killed 'em." . . . "Theah's be'n a rape." . . . "A rape?" . . . "A rape!" . . . "A rape!"

Sheriff Trent barges into the office. He is large, red-faced, a square, brutal jaw, obviously the sadist type. The crowd's voices come through again—

"We wanna git fust chance at 'em black bastards!" . . . "Women ain't safe no mo' !" . . . "Gittin' worse an' worse wid 'em niggers!"

The deputies are getting their rifles and pushing the crowd back. The truck has arrived with six white boys and a couple of armed deputies. The white boys are put in the cage with the hoboes. Trent has fastened his revolver belt and holster around his thick waist.

Cooley has called up Solicitor Mason's house and told Mrs. Mason to waken the solicitor and get him over to the jail. "Somethin' excitin's happenin'," he explains.

The crowd below stairs is growing in size and aggressiveness. A string of automobiles has followed the truck in. There's likely to be trouble when the other truck, with the niggers, arrives.

Trent is shouting orders and defiance. The girls have arrived and are being pushed through the crowd and up the stairs. Trent talks to the crowd over their heads—

"Hi, theah, Jackson, pass out those rifles. . . . Whut's the matter with *you?* Lemme know when the niggers come. Lemme know when yuh see 'em down the road. I don't want no trouble. (*The crowd rumbles ominously.*) Remember, folks. . . . I'm the law heah in Cookesville . . . an' I'll 'rest anyone of yuh who tries somethin' smart—"

The two girls are pushed into the room. One is blonde and defiant, a rough, washed-out factory girl type, probably in her early twenties. The other is dark and small, a frightened, white-faced, timid person sticking as close as she can to her companion.

Sheriff Trent would begin questioning them at once, but first he must answer a telephone call. His wife is on the phone and demands to know things—

"Now, listen here, Emma . . . whut fo' yuh callin' up . . . when I'm so busy? . . . Huh? No . . . I ain't gittin' fresh. . . . Huh? Well, you tell her she's gaffy. No niggers chewed nobody's breasts off. . . . No. Good-by. No, don't wait—"

He turns again to the girls. He has got out a ledger and provided himself with a pencil. The blonde one (Virginia Ross) does the talking.

"Whut were yuh doin' on that train?" demands Trent.

"We was jest tryin' tuh git back tuh Humbolt from Chattanoogie . . . where we went. . . ."

"What fo'?"

"To look fo' a job . . . an' after we . . ."

"Jest hold on. It 'pears to me that these heah niggers musta fooled 'round with you gals. . . ."

"We never done nuthin' like that. . . ."

"We'll find that out soon 'nuff."

Trent is ready to go on with the examination when Solicitor Mason, a small-town lawyer, arrives.

"Well . . . you're certainly needed heah," Trent greets him. "Have yuh heard whut's up?"

"Well . . . I heard quite a few things while I was dressing," grins Mason. "Mrs. Jenkins called my wife, then Mrs. Cooley called and as I was leaving Mrs. Henderson called."

TRENT—These are the gals they tuk off the train at Rocky Point.

MASON—That so? (*Crosses to them. Professionally.*) What's your name? Your right name?

VIRGINIA—Virginia Ross.

MASON—And yours?

LUCY—Lucy Wells.

MASON—Where you from?

VIRGINIA—We're from Humbolt.

MASON—What do you do there for a living?

VIRGINIA—We work in the Henrietta mills, spinnin' cotton.

MASON—And what else?

VIRGINIA (*snapping right back*)—Nuthin' else if I know whut yuh mean.

MASON—You know what I mean. . . . Now what were you doing on that train?

VIRGINIA—Jest ridin'.

MASON—What for? Where?

VIRGINIA—Well, we went to Chattanoogie to visit some friends an' we didn't have no money tuh come on back with. . . .

TRENT—I thought you said you went lookin' fo' *work*.

VIRGINIA—Well . . . I said that too. . . .

TRENT—I'll bet I know whut so't of work yuh looked fo'.

VIRGINIA—Now . . . don't yuh go insinuatin' . . .

MASON—Whom did you girls leave Humbolt with?

LUCY—We went with . . .

VIRGINIA (*quickly*)—We didn't go with nobody. . . .

MASON (*after a slight pause*)—Well, girls . . . you know that I can arrest you for being traveling prostitutes?

VIRGINIA (*innocently*)—What's that?

TRENT (*snapping*)—A whore. That's what.

VIRGINIA (*indignantly*)—Well . . . I ain't that. . . .

MASON—Then what were you doing on that train with those boys and crossin' a state line?

VIRGINIA—I never crossed no line.

MASON—You came from Tennessee into this State in violation of the law.

VIRGINIA—That don't give you the right tuh call me a whore.

MASON—It gives me the right to arrest you for being one.

Now . . . I can prosecute you under the law . . . you and your boy friends. Understand?

VIRGINIA (*somewhat frightened*)—Yes, suh, but we weren't doin' nothin' atall. We were jest . . .

TRENT (*crosses to her*)—Shut up! 'Cose everythin' yuh say will be held against yuh. (*Turns to* COOLEY.) Willie, take them gals into the run-around. I'll call yuh if I need yuh.

COOLEY (*taking* VIRGINIA'S *arm*)—Come along, gal. (*They exit.*)

VIRGINIA (*haughtily*)—Tryin' to call us indecent . . . the low-down son-of-a . . .

Trent has his case shaped up for Solicitor Mason, and his anger mounts as he states it. Them niggers had seen them gals, got themselves together and throwed the kids off the train and then attacked the gals! His impatience is violent when Mason dares question the logic of his conclusions. To Mason the girls neither look nor act as though they had been assaulted. If that had happened they would most likely have been crying all over the place and their clothes would have been torn. Whatever happened the girls were probably party to the arrangement for whatever they could get.

"I don't keer if they are whores," shouts Trent, in a rage; "they're white women! You think I'm gonna let them stinkin' nigger lice get away from me? Like hell I am! They're gonna git whut's comin' to 'em long as I'm the law round heah. . . . (*He is at the height of his temper and his feelings run away with him.*) What the hell will folks heah say of us . . . ? Why, they'll spit on us if we don't git them niggers when we got the chance. . . . The hull county, the hull State, the hull South'll be down on our haids. . . ."

"Trent, I want to get these girls examined by a doctor as soon as possible," says Mason.

"You . . . you ain't figgerin' on jest a plain, ordinary charge, Luther. . . ."

"What are you figgerin' on, Sheriff?"

"What I'm figgerin'? Them black bastards had them white gals and theah's only one charge fo' that . . . RAPE!"

The Sheriff has called Cooley and started the girls for the doctor and an examination. Virginia Ross does the talking for both of them. She would know what she and Lucy are to be examined for and when she is told of the assault and rape charge she is frankly puzzled. No nigger ever done nothin' like that to them.

She doesn't want them callin' her Miss Ross, either. She's a married woman; she's a Mrs.

They are pushing the girls through the crowd when the "nigger truck" is reported up the road. There is some trouble opening up a way in front of the jail in all the excitement and frequent clashes between Trent's deputies and the angered citizens.

"Stand back, folks!" Trent can be heard shouting. "Git back there! Hi there, Jackson! Hold 'em back, boys! I don't want no trouble at all!"

The temper of the crowd is evident from the expressions that rise above the mob noises: "Are the wimmin hurt bad, Sheriff?" . . . "We oughta git the Klan together" . . . "Theah them nigger rapers, goddam 'em" . . . "Jest thirty cents o' rope. . . ."

There is more trouble making a way for the colored boys through the crowd, which continues to shout its threats and curses. Now the nine young negroes, tied together with ropes, are pushed through the door into the office, Sheriff Trent, Deputy Jackson and two Rocky Point deputies holding the crowd back as they herd the prisoners in.

There is further trouble when it is discovered that Willie Cooley has gone away with the key to the nigger pen. There is some thought of putting the black boys in the run-around with the white hoboes, but there is an awful yell from Red at that. He'll complain to the Governor if they try putting the niggers in with them.

They have taken the rope off the boys and herded them into one end of the office. Mason begins a temporary investigation and Trent takes part whenever the chance offers. The girls, according to Allen, one of the Rocky Point men, were in an open gravel car and the seven white boys in a car nearby. The Negroes were scattered all over the train, according to Allen. One of them, Roberts, they found in a cattle car, groanin'. Said he was sick. Roberts is the one Trent decides to see. Wants him to tell where they threw the white boys off the train.

"I never see'd 'em, please, suh," groans Roberts. "I was good and sick in that cow car . . . all the way from Chattanoogie. . . . I never see'd . . ."

"Shet up!" shouts Trent, giving the boy a hard punch in the stomach which doubles him up with pain. "Think it over now careful."

Trent has sent Allen down with the others and turned again to the ledger to get on with the examinations. Happily for him Jackson has a flask with him. Trent takes a drink and keeps the flask. Then he turns to the boys.

"Whut's yo' name, nigger?" he asks the first.

"Ozie Purcell!"

TRENT (*writing*)—How old are yuh?

PURCELL—Sixteen, please suh.

TRENT—Where from?

PURCELL—Atlanta, Georgia . . . please suh. But I ain't done nothin'.

TRENT—I didn't ask yuh that. . . . (*Kicks him on the shins fiercely.* PURCELL *screams and falls. The boys in the cage crowd up front to see better.*) Don't talk 'til I ask yuh somethin'. (*Addresses another negro.*) Whut's yo' name?

MOORE—Olen Moore, please suh.

TRENT—How old?

MOORE—Seventeen, please suh.

TRENT—Where from?

MOORE—Monroe, Georgia, suh.

TRENT—Whut's the matter with yo' eye?

MOORE—I cain't see outa this un, suh . . . an' I'm goin' slow blin' on the other one. . . .

TRENT—Whut were yuh doin' on that freight?

MOORE—I was tryin' to git tuh Memphis where they's got a colored hospital fo' eyes. . . .

TRENT—Never mind with that. . . . (*To another negro.*) Whut's your name?

WALTERS—Gene Walters.

TRENT—How old?

WALTERS—Thirteen yeahs.

TRENT (*looks up from ledger, then writes*)—Yuh mean sixteen.

WALTERS (*puzzled*)—Thirteen, please suh. . . .

TRENT (*slaps his face hard*)—Sixteen! Doan't yuh understand English . . . you dumb nigger mule . . . ?

WALTERS (*finally understanding*)—Yassuh. Sixteen yeahs.

TRENT—Where're you from?

WALTERS (*holding his injured face*)—Chattanoogie. Tennessee, suh.

SMITH (*enters with keys*)—Heah yuh are, Sheriff. . . .

TRENT—Open up this heah door fo' the niggers. . . . (SMITH *proceeds to do so. At this moment much noise is heard from outside.*) That mob still yellin' . . . ?

SMITH—I speck they done heerd the news the gals be'n raped, Sheriff. (*Searches for proper cell-key. At this point* ALLEN *and*

KILLIAN *enter rear door with* OLIVER TULLEY *between them.*)

TRENT (*rather confused*)—Hullo! Who's this?

ALLEN—This is that theah other hobo kid who stayed on the train.

TRENT—Set him down theah. Stay with him. (TULLEY *sits.* ALLEN *stands next to him.* SMITH *is opening the cell doors.*) Hurry up, Smith.

MASON (*in the interim*)—What's your name?

PARSONS (*one of the negroes*)—Heywood Parsons, please suh.

SMITH (*calls to* TRENT *as he opens the cell*)—Okay, Sheriff. (*Enters corridor.*)

TRENT (*crosses to crowd of negroes*)—Come on . . . git in theah! (KILLIAN *and* SMITH *begin to herd the negroes into the cell.*)

PARSONS (*as* KILLIAN *pushes him into cell*)—What fo' . . . what fo' we 'rested . . . please suh? We ain't done nuthin'. . . .

TRENT (*strides over to him*)—Git in theah yuh black bastard . . . befo' I kick yo' teeth down yo' throat. . . . Git. . . .

Trent and the deputies have shoved and mauled the prisoners into the pen. With the door locked Trent turns to the hobo Tulley just brought in. Tulley is one who stayed on the train. He tried to jump, but one of the colored fellows pulled him back, not to fight him, just to save his life. Tulley didn't know anything about jumpin' off trains and was doin' it all wrong. Yes, Tulley had seen the girls in the gravel car. He had winked and hollered at 'em, but he'd never gone over to 'em. He might of, but he was skeered about climbin' along the train.

"Did yuh see any of them niggers together with the girls?" asks Mason.

"No, I didn't see that," answers Tulley.

"Now, don't you try to lie to us . . . yuh little . . ." injects the angry Trent.

"I ain't lyin'."

"We'll see 'bout that soon 'nuff. Maybe you'll change yo' mind after a couple of days or so . . . on the chain-gang. . . ." He has opened the door and pushed the boy into the run-around. "And maybe longer'n that, too."

The crowd below stairs has grown to considerable size. Trent is attracted by the noise, punctuated by occasional shouts and threats.

"Jest listen tuh that bunch, Luther," Trent mutters. "They know all 'bout it now."

The mob sounds become articulate. Voices can be heard. "We want tuh talk tuh Sheriff Trent." . . . "I'd like to cut off their . . ." "We gotta keep 'em in their place. . . ."

"You sure you have enough men . . . Sheriff?" Mason inquires, anxiously.

"Sho'," answers Trent, reassuringly.

Trent would have the examination of the negroes continued at once. Mason had rather wait until he has the doctor's report. Outside the crowd grows increasingly restless. The shouts are heard again: "Save the county money, Trent!" . . . "Jest a coil of rope!" . . . "We got guns!" . . . "An' we kin use 'em, too!" . . . "Come on out, Sheriff, an' talk it over!"

"Cain't yuh heah them?" asks Deputy Allen. "They're talkin' of stringin' up these heah niggers tonight. They feel mighty bitter 'bout this heah rape an' . . ."

"You're certain you can take care of your prisoners, Trent?" Mason again demands.

"I sho' can . . . if I want tuh . . . Luther. But maybe it wouldn't be such a bad idea to let the boys . . ."

"No, don't you try that, Trent," Mason is quick to answer, "or I'll drop the whole business. This county has got a bad lynch reputation plenty . . . and I don't want anything like that held against me. What we want . . . is just a nice speedy trial. That's all."

"So yo' kin play yo'self up . . . eh?"

"Well . . . it certainly won't play you up as a sheriff . . . if you let that mob take out your prisoners from your jail."

It is Mason's idea that Trent should call up the Governor and ask for troops. That would be the smartest thing they could do. Then whatever happens the whole state will hear about it. It'll be in the papers in Birmingham and Atlanta and Chattanooga—their names will be in the papers. The home folks are only interested in a quick conviction. . . .

The door at the head of the stairs is pushed slowly open by six or seven men at the head of the crowd. They want the prisoners. They don't want to cause Trent any trouble, but they want those blacks. They're goin' to get some of the Klan over from Gideon and Williamstown. . . .

Trent is able to shove them out and get the door shut. He sends Allen then to round up all the town boys he can find and tell them to get their own guns and be sworn in.

Then he thinks it would probably be a good thing to call the Governor. He had rather Mason would do the talking. Mason talks better.

"I'm sure you're doing the wisest thing, Trent," insists Mason. "And if you get an appointment as Federal Marshal . . . you can thank this idea of mine."

A marshal's salary would certainly be a help with Mrs. Trent's needed tumor operation, Trent agrees, not to mention—

Mason at the telephone reports that the Governor is tied up with a committee, but the Lieutenant-Governor will handle the Cookesville matter. At the Capitol they already have had some word of the trouble.

"That's fine," Solicitor Mason is saying over the phone. "I don't know if you remember me. . . . I had the privilege of being introduced to your excellency in New Orleans, last Mardi Gras. . . . Well, you understand, sir . . . that these nine negroes that the Sheriff at Rocky Point took off the freight . . . well, we have since discovered . . . (*Glances up at* TRENT *significantly.*) . . . sufficient evidence to indict them for rape and assault on two white girls. Yes . . . we have them all here now. . . . Well, that's just it, your excellency. The town is all up in the air . . . in fact the whole county. . . . Yes, it's absolutely necessary, sir. I would appreciate it, sir. Captain Kennedy? . . . That'll be just fine. Yes, sir. Yes, your excellency."

The official okay having been delivered by an excited Sheriff Trent, Louise, the telephone girl, is given permission to call up a few of the women and spread the news. Troops will be there in five minutes—well, an hour, anyway.

Willie Cooley is back with Dr. Thomas, a small, timid little medic, and the two girls. The Doctor thought best to come himself, though he is in pretty much of a rush on account of Mrs. Summerset's expected baby. The girls, reports Dr. Thomas, have been examined by him and he is convinced that they both have consorted with a man. He turns to Lucy Wells for confirmation, but Lucy doesn't know what he means. She is crying when she denies vehemently that any negro had anything to do with her—

The evidence is sufficient, thinks Mason, to indicate that both Lucy and Virginia have been raped. Dr. Thomas is not at all positive as to the rape. Lucy is quietly sobbing, but Virginia is alert and trying hard to understand. Once or twice she would protest, but decides to wait.

Mason, his legal manner becoming more pronounced, would force the doctor to an admission that an assault has been committed; that it is possible five of the negroes attacked Virginia and four of them Lucy—

"We never done that at all," protests Virginia, hotly.

"Shut up! I'll deal with you later . . ." shouts Mason.

Again admitting the possibility of assault Dr. Thomas, with some show of spirit, would protest that, after all, he is a physician and has his ethical—

"I only asked you if it were possible, Dr. Thomas," insists Mason smoothly. "That's all I'm interested in. The evidence is present. The circumstances and motivation are our concern. You needn't worry, you won't lose your license." (*He says this last with a bit of a sneer.*)

"Very well. But that's all I said. Possible."

The doctor has gone to Mrs. Summerset's. Mason and Trent take up the examination of Virginia Ross. She should know that they want to protect her. What will people think if they learn that she did not want to prosecute those black fiends, those savage brutes? What would the proprietor of the Henrietta mills say if he were to learn that he had an employee who let niggers get away with a crime like that? He certainly wouldn't want a girl like that workin' in his mill.

Virginia persists in denying the assault. She never has slept with no man outside of her husband. She's divorced from him. Then, what about the doctor's report, Mason demands.

Virginia is floundering now. She is willing to tell Mr. Mason anything he wants her to, but she wishes they would do something for Lucy. Lucy has been weeping again and is frightened. Mason and Trent agree that she needs a rest and take her to an inside cell to lie down. Virginia promises to be with her in a minute.

Mason has become more friendly in his examination of Virginia now. "You understand, Virginia," he says, "we just can't let these niggers get away with such things because of the bad effect on other niggers."

"Well, I guess you're right," admits Virginia, grateful to be treated like an equal.

Mason (*as* Trent *comes back*)—After all, if we let 'em git away with this once, a white lady wouldn't be safe any more.

Virginia—Yeah . . . they git uppity mo' an' mo'. . . .

Trent. Sho'. All kin' o' fool notions nowdays . . . some even talk of votin' an' down in the Birmingham steel . . . they're havin' all sorts o' trouble with 'em . . . and down 'round Tallapoosa I heerd they're formin' a share-croppers' union. . . .

Did you know that, Luther?

MASON (*ignoring the question*)—I know how you feel, Mrs. Ross. I know you're ashamed. It's not pleasant to have everybody know of such a disgrace. I know too well how you must have suffered. But you must realize too what a splendid brave thing you'll be doing for our kind of people. . . . And have no fear, this state and Hatchachubbe County will not soon forget your sacrifice. . . . In fact the whole South. . . .

VIRGINIA (*impressed but cautious*)—Well . . . I don't keer to git in no trouble. . . .

MASON—You're certainly headed for plenty of that if you let folks get the idea you took on those niggers of your own free will. . . .

VIRGINIA (*mechanically denying*)—I never tuk none of 'em niggers on. . . .

MASON (*meaningfully*)—But you heard the doctor tell what he found in you. . . . Yes . . . it means a great inner struggle but you are only the victim of a cruel fate . . . no one will blame you for telling the truth. For having the courage to tell the truth. The newspapers, the Governor, every man, woman and child will thank you and praise you. The whole state will have your name on its lips. Your picture will be in every newspaper. . . .

TRENT—Sho' . . . instead of sayin' . . . what a low trash. She wouldn't even help the law and admit what the niggers done tuh her. . . .

MASON—And then losing your job too. . . .

VIRGINIA—Yuh sho' I wouldn't lose my job if I tell. . . .

MASON—You can hold me personally responsible, Mrs. Ross. Sheriff Trent's a witness.

VIRGINIA (*shrewd, smiling*)—Well, couldn't I have a new dress fo' tuh take them newspaper pictures in? This don't look so good. . . .

MASON (*smiles*)—Why, certainly, we can arrange that. Most of the women here would be proud to help out.

VIRGINIA—I would 'preciate it . . . Lucy too . . . I'm sho'. An' . . . er . . . maybe a lil change too? Jest a coupla dollars fo' the time I have tuh stay heah. Yuh see I have an old sick maw who I support. . . .

TRENT (*becoming annoyed*)—Now looka heah, gal . . .

MASON (*stopping* TRENT)—Why, certainly. Besides you'll get three dollars a day as witness. Your friend too. . . .

VIRGINIA (*tremendously impressed*)—Three dollars every day?

(MASON *nods smilingly.*) Fo' a coupla days?

MASON—Why, certainly . . . and maybe a little contribution from the citizens of the town heah. . . .

VIRGINIA—Kin I bet on that?

MASON—My word as a gentleman.

VIRGINIA—And the snap-shots too?

MASON—Why, certainly. . . .

VIRGINIA (*a slight pause . . . then quite matter-of-fact*)—Well, what do yuh want tuh know . . . ?

MASON—Only the truth . . . that you and your friend were attacked by these niggers. . . .

VIRGINIA (*a slight pause*)—I guess they did do that to us. They absolutely did. . . . (*Smiles.*) Is that all?

MASON—No . . . but I want you to talk first to your little friend. Can you take care of her?

VIRGINIA (*smiles*)—Well, I guess so. I've been her best friend sence she was fourteen and she always listens tuh me. . . .

MASON—Fine and dandy. All right, then you go and talk to her and I'll see you later. . . . (*Extends his hand to her.*)

VIRGINIA (*wipes her palm on her dress and then shakes with him*)—Thank you. And please . . . yuh won't be forgittin' them pictures?

MASON—Certainly not. . . . (*Laughs gayly.*)

TRENT (*leads her to run-around*)—This way, Mrs. Ross.

VIRGINIA (*crosses*)—Say, couldn't I jest have a dip o' snuff fo' chewin' while we're waitin'? (*Winks at* TRENT *and rubs up against him.*)

TRENT—Sho'. Sho'. (*As they exit.*) You're one hot gal, ain't yuh?

VIRGINIA (*throwing her head back proudly*)—I sho' am. Hottest in Chattanoogie.

They have brought in Lewis Collins, one of the white boys thrown off the train by the negroes. Collins begs a cigarette and then tells them that he didn't see a thing. When he got to his feet on the roadbed the train was a mile away. He doesn't believe the niggers done anything. But Trent's threat of ninety days on the chain gang ain't goin' to give Collins eyes to see whut didn't happen.

"Now, looka heah, you," shouts Mason. "You can make a nice bit o' money for yourself as state's witness if you're willing to do what's right."

"Well, then, I guess I'm goin' tuh have some money, 'cause

I aim tuh do jest what is right. (*Suddenly.*) But my idea of right and yourn is two different things. . . ."

They take Collins back to the run-around still protesting that he doesn't intend to swear away the lives of nigger kids for their benefit. And if they try any tricks on him he'll talk his head off.

Mason and Trent get in Deputy Hillary with his typewriter to take the affidavits of the colored boys, Mason dictating the form.

"Write . . . I . . . leave a space for the name . . . hereby swear and confess that I attacked and raped the woman, Virginia Ross and committed this assault against her will and desire on the eighteenth day of March, in the year of our Lord . . . (*Phone rings.*) Hello . . . Who? . . . Oh, how are you Mr. McNary? Yes, pretty near finished now. Of course . . . and in a planned cold-blooded way. . . ."

As Hillary writes the affidavit snatches of conversation can be heard from the cell blocks.

"Now, yuh listen tuh me, Lucy," Virginia is saying. And a moment later a part of Lucy's answer comes floating in. ". . . but I am the baddest talker . . . I jest cain't tell no story. . . ."

Trent has herded a small negro in from the pen, cursing and cuffing him as he comes. The boy is Willie Roberts. His voice is husky. His throat is parched. He begs a drink of water and Mason would give it to him. Trent, however, would let Roberts wait until after he talks.

"Now, yuh tell us quick how yuh attacked those gals," shouts Trent.

"Attacked?" queries Roberts.

TRENT—Yes . . . don't play dumb. . . .

MASON—How you jumped on them in the train and forced them . . .

ROBERTS—I never done that, please suh. I tol' yuh how I was so sick with misery, I couldn't move myself. . . .

TRENT—Shet up! What yuh gonna say to the jedge in court? (*Slaps his face.*)

ROBERTS (*wetting his lips, swallowing*)—I dunno, please suh.

TRENT—What do yuh mean yuh don't know? (*Punches him hard. The negro sprawls on the floor and lies still.* HILLARY *at this moment finishes his typing.*) Hillary, throw some water on him. He asked fo' it befo'. (HILLARY *does so.* TRENT *kicks him.* ROBERTS *gets up to his knees.*)

VIRGINIA (*as* HILLARY *throws the water on* ROBERTS)—Doan't yuh see, Lucy, they kin sen' us tuh jail fo' yeahs an' yeahs. . . . Crossin' the state line with men. . . .

MASON (*to* ROBERTS, *now on his knees*)—Come on now, did you do it . . . did you?

ROBERTS—I never done nuthin', please suh.

TRENT—Yuh want some mo'? (*Bangs* ROBERTS *around a few times.*) Did yuh do it?

ROBERTS—Yassuh. I done it. I done it.

TRENT—Tuk yuh too long a time. . . . And don't fo'git tuh say the same thing in court . . . yuh black bitch . . . or I'll pump yuh full o' holes right theah in court. . . . Right theah on the witness chair. Understand? (ROBERTS *nods exhausted and staggers to his feet.*) Okay. Now git in theah, and don't yuh fo'git what I said 'bout that shootin'. (TRENT *unlocks the door,* ROBERTS *crosses to threshold.*)

ROBERTS—Yassuh. (*As he crosses into cell* TRENT *gives him a hard shove and he falls to his face with a thud.*)

TRENT—You theah. . . . (*Points to* ROY WOOD.) Git in heah. . . . (ROY *rises and enters.*) We ain't got yo' name yet . . . huh?

ROY—No, suh, please suh. (TRENT *bolts the door.*)

MASON—Write this down, Hillary. What's your name?

ROY—Roy Wood, please suh.

MASON—How old?

ROY—Fourteen, please suh.

MASON—You mean sixteen.

ROY (*nods understandingly*)—Yassuh. Sixteen, please suh.

MASON—Where from?

ROY—Chattanoogie, Tennessee.

MASON (*suddenly*)—What the hell are you bumming around for, so young?

ROY—I was lookin' fo' tuh work with my brudder, Andy. . . . Please suh.

TRENT—Yuh helped yo' brother rape those white gals, didn't yuh?

ROY—Rapded? Please . . . I dunno know that word. . . . (*Wags his head not understanding.*)

TRENT—Yuh don't? (*Slaps his face hard.*) Well, it means jumped on, tore off their clothes . . . tuk 'em by force. That's what it means. Understand?

ROY (*stares at* TRENT *blankly. Nods eagerly*)—Yassuh, yassuh.

TRENT—Didn't yuh help him do that? Didn't yuh try it

yo'self too?

MASON (*somewhat guiltily. Waves* TRENT *aside*)—Looka heah, boy. I know you're a youngster, but just because of that, you deserve the worst. If a youngster can be so bad, so plumb wicked, then how will you be when you grow up?

ROY—I ain't done nuthin', please suh.

MASON—Now listen . . .

TRENT (*at the same time*)—Nobody asked yuh that. (*Slaps his face a few times, very hard. The boy staggers up against the desk and bursts out crying like a child.*)

MASON (*gestures to* TRENT *to desist*)—Now listen to me. We're goin' to let you get away with plenty because you're so young. You don't have to say you did anything . . . but you do confess that you saw the rest do it. You did see them do it, didn't you?

ROY (*crying*)—I done see nuthin'. An' Andy didn't done nuthin' too. . . .

MASON—Do you want to get shot? Show him that gun, Sheriff. Show him what it means to lie.

TRENT (*pushes boy's chin up with gun*)—This heah can blow yo' goddam head off right back to Chattanooga, yuh lil black son-of-a . . .

ROY (*fearful, almost in a frenzy*)—I'll talk, please suh. I'll talk anything yuh want me tuh. . . .

Virginia's treble in argument with Lucy punctuates the moment's silence. "Don't you see, Lucy, they kin sen' us tuh jail fo' yeahs an' yeahs. . . . Crossin' the state line with men. . . . Dresses an' cash; three dollars a day. . . ."

Trent has thrown Roberts back into the cell and pulled out a boy named Herbert Parsons. Parsons appears a cut above the others in intelligence. "He is sullen and his voice has a rebellious quality that enrages the Sheriff."

"Which of them gals did you attack?" shouts Trent.

"I done attacked nobody," protests Parsons.

Trent's huge fist flies out, catching the boy's jaw. His head rolls back. "Yuh better think that ovah, nigger," Trent advises.

"No, suh, I done did nothin'," repeats Parsons, shaking his head slowly to clear it.

"Stubborn, huh? Didn't yuh jump that blonde-haired gal?"

"I never seen her. . . ."

Trent has leaped upon the boy, punching him in the head and stomach, kicking him as he falls against the desk, swearing he'll kill him if he doesn't 'fess up.

"I was never near them gals all the time," stubbornly repeats Parsons.

"Backward as an army mule," says Mason. "You'll never get that buck to confess, Sheriff."

TRENT (*storming, breathless with unsuppressed fury. He drags out a drawer from the desk and snatches from within a short thick crop*)—I'd like tuh see the nigger I cain't make do that. (*To* PARSONS, *cracking the crop.*) Goin' tuh tell the truth . . . ?

PARSONS (*hunched up, his arms up ready to defend himself from blows*)—I'm tellin' yuh the truth, white man. So help me Jesus.

TRENT (*strikes him with the crop*)—Git yo' damn hands down! I'll chop 'em off. Talk! Talk! (*Strikes him again. In the negro cell, the occupants stare at each other with white, horrified eyes. In the cage, the white prisoners hearing the crop cracking, bunch up against the mesh to hear better. The girls frightened, move down the run-around to the extreme right.* LUCY *is trembling with fear.*) Don't yuh know theah's a mob of Klu Kluxers outside ready tuh hang yuh and burn yuh inch by inch . . . and I'm pertectin' yuh? Do yuh want me tuh hand yuh ovah tuh 'em? Tuh lynch yuh? Tonight? Right tonight?

PARSONS (*exhausted—panting*)—Please suh, lemme 'lone. Let this po' nigger be. I never done no harm to nobody in the world. Mary, mother of Jesus, kin tell yuh that. . . .

TRENT (*losing all control, proceeds with* HILLARY'S *help to beat the negro into unconsciousness*)—I'll fix yuh, yuh lousy, low-down . . . (*The crop cracks mercilessly.* PARSONS *cringes, tries to crawl away under the desk but* HILLARY *drags him out.*) I'll fix yuh, takin' the name of Gawd . . . I'll kill yuh . . . I'll cut yuh tuh shreds. . . .

LUCY (*crying, frightened*)—Oh . . . Virginia . . . they'll kill them nigger boys yet. . . .

VIRGINIA—Ssssshh. Hush yo' mouth. . . . Don't yuh talk like that. . . .

MASON (*to* TRENT)—Listen, Sheriff . . . listen . . . Sheriff Trent. You'll be killin' him. . . .

TRENT (*unheeding*)—Drag him out . . . the yaller-livered black bastard. . . . Hillary! Make him suffer like he made them po'r white gals suffer. . . . (PARSONS *is now completely out and lies on the floor, senseless. In the negro cells,* MOORE *suddenly screams, terrified.*)

MOORE—Lo'd . . . Jesus Christ. . . . (*The other negroes suddenly begin to scream and moan and wail almost like wild beasts. One whimpers like a dog. Another howls.* HILLARY *unbolts the door and rushes in to quiet them.*)

TRENT—Git up . . . git up. . . . (*Kicks the unconscious* PARSONS.)

MASON—But . . . listen here . . . Sheriff Trent . . . you . . .

The door opens and Captain Kennedy of the militia, followed by a Sergeant, comes into the office. A detachment of soldiers can be seen outside trying to push their way through the door. The Cookesville case has spread all over the county, Captain Kennedy reports. The roads are choked with machines and even a few mule wagons are headed that way.

The captain has brought a temporary company of seventy-five men and two machine guns. There are sixty more men coming over from Mount Crawford, with tear gas. Kennedy will post his men around the jail, with one machine gun at the head of the stairs and another at the entrance below. Two men are detailed to the corridor outside the negroes' cell.

"I want you boys to take good care of 'em niggers," orders the captain. "You all know what they done. . . . They're a purty mean bunch o' niggers."

"Yes, suh. I catch on," answers the Sergeant with a grin.

A moment later the soldiers are jabbing the negro boys between the bars with their bayonets. The boys are pleading to be let alone. In the run-around Virginia can be heard again promising Lucy that she is to have new dresses. Trent is basking expansively in the excitement.

"Hell, I won't be gittin' any sleep with sech crowds around every night . . . and Mrs. Trent wouldn't be catchin' much sleep either. (*Phone rings.* TRENT *answers.*) Hullo . . . who? . . . what? (*To* KENNEDY.) Will yuh ask yo' men to quiet down with them niggers, please? I reckon they got enough with the present. . . . (KENNEDY *crosses to men. There he stops their bayonet practice.*) Hello . . . yes? How you, Bill? Sho', Mabel's fine . . . yes. . . . I'll tell her. (*Throughout phone conversation there is heard the whimpering of one of the younger negro boys.*) Who? . . . Yeah . . . he jest loves that academy down in Mobile. . . . Yeah, he's a fine boy, stands all of six foot now, writes his daddy every day. . . . No, they didn't kill the gals, jest raped 'em . . . yes. . . . Huh?"

". . . will they take my pictures too, 'Ginia?" Lucy's plaintive plea comes through the confusion.

"Sho'. We kin take 'em together," answers Virginia.

"And they'll really put them in the papers?"

Trent is at the telephone. "Sho', we got the soldiers, but we don't want no cuttin' up," he is saying. "Sho' . . . we got 'em tuh talk. . . . O' course the niggers're natchurly stubborn. . . . Huh? . . . Sho'. We jest gotta keep them black bastards in their place. . . . Sho'. . . ."

As Trent waits to hear what the other party is saying . . .

THE CURTAIN FALLS

ACT II

Three weeks later, in the home of Lucy Wells in "Nigger Town," at the edge of Humbolt, Lucy's mother, Nora Wells, is finishing an ironing. It is a small, dirty cottage of three rooms. Outside a bit of the late afternoon sun filters in. Three negro children are playing on the porch.

Presently a door at the right side of the room is opened and a young white man enters. A little sheepishly he crosses the living room, passing the time of day with Mrs. Wells and continuing on through the street door. He is followed a moment later by Lucy. She is adjusting the belt to her dress.

"How much did he give yuh, Lucy?" queries the mother.

"Same as allus," answers Lucy, sinking into a chair. "It's in my room on the bed."

Lucy won't go fetch the money. She doesn't want to tech it. It's dirty money. Lucy, according to Mrs. Wells, is gettin' mighty high hat since she got that fo'teen dollars from the trial. An' she only done whut's right. Decent people would look down on 'em if Lucy hadn't done whut she done. But Lucy is not convinced.

"They still look down at us," she protests. "They promised me all so'ts of things. They promised me steady work at the mill . . . an' heah they haven't given me mo' than seven or eight days in all the weeks sence the trial. . . ."

Virginia Ross, on the other hand, is gittin' everything, according to Lucy. Lots of work. And struttin' around town telling how smart she is, how she showed up at Cookesville and how dumb Lucy is.

Lucy don't appreciate her luck. Mother Wells insists. She has no cause to be glum. She ain't never had no kids and a rum-hound husband. She doesn't know whut it is to starve. Lucy doesn't know—

Lucy is moved by her mother's recital. She finds a dollar in her pocket. She will give that to her mother. A stranger had given it to her the night before.

"I was jest lucky," she explains, accounting for the dollar. "We were standin' around the drug-sto', me an' that Brooks gal an' this feller come alongside in his car. It was one of 'em new Chevvies. An' he begun tuh gab with me. Edna Brooks had a date an' so I druve off alone with him. (*With a smile as she reminisces.*) He was awful nice. He's a sales-feller. He sells dresses an' aprons tuh sto's like Frederick's an' . . . Greenstein's. . . ."

"He musta been a Yankee tuh give yuh a dollar," concludes Mrs. Wells.

The stranger is from Oklahoma, explains Lucy. He may be comin' back to say good-by. He said he might. Lucy thinks she'll fix herself up a bit thinkin' he might come. . . .

Lucy has gone to her room when the young man arrives. He is Russell Evans. Hails from Fairchild, Oklahoma, he tells Mrs. Wells, though he was born in Vicksburg, Mississippi. Vicksburg —"owned by the Jews, run by the Catholics, for the benefit of the niggers," says Evans. Mrs. Wells remembers that Vicksburg.

Mrs. Wells has retired to the kitchen when Lucy comes in. Lucy is glad to see Mr. Evans. A little embarrassed about callin' him by his first name, as he suggests. Surprised and delighted when he gives her a present he has brought her. A couple of print dresses. Jest about the prettiest she has ever seen. She would cry a little about the dresses. But she doesn't want to try them on now. She'd rather talk to him.

"I'll bet . . . you forgot all about me soon as you got home last night," ventures Evans. "Didn't you?"

LUCY (*looking at him with shining eyes*)—No, I didn't fo'git about yuh at all, Mist' Russell.

EVANS—Aw, sure you did. You've got a sweetie somewhere . . . and I don't count at all.

LUCY—No . . . I ain't got no boy-friend. If I had, well . . . I wouldn't be havin' no dates with anyone else. . . .

EVANS—Then you're sorry about having had a date with me?

LUCY—No, I ain't sorry.

EVANS—Well, you don't seem very glad. . . .

LUCY (*her eyes fastened on him in admiration*)—Yes . . .

I'm glad, Mist' Russell. . . .

EVANS (*another short pause*)—You know, Lucy . . . I was thinking about it last night after I left you. . . .

LUCY—'Bout what?

EVANS—Oh, well . . . 'bout that money . . . I gave you. . . . (*Her eyes drop. Her features take on an expression of fear.*) Wait, don't get me wrong. No . . . I don't want you to feel bad. . . . You see . . . I figured that you think because I'm a traveling salesman that I'm just like the rest of them. Now don't make no mistake. . . . I'm not what you would call an angel but you see . . . I took you first . . . well . . . for just one of those country girls . . . and when you said something about . . . about money . . . well . . . I was sort of surprised and I couldn't understand. . . . I was kind of disappointed and the like . . . I thought . . . Well,—just another of these— Well, you know how a feller thinks. . . .

LUCY (*depressed*)—Yes. . . . I know how they think. . . .

EVANS—. . . But when I got back to my hotel I gave it some real thinking and that's why I come over today. . . . (LUCY *looks up again, hope in her eyes.*) . . . I wanted to talk it over with you and . . . You see when I asked you for your address, well, I was doin' that—sort of out of habit . . . didn't really mean I was coming . . . but then . . . later I made up my mind I would come and have a talk with you about it, if you . . . wanted to. . . .

LUCY (*almost happy again*)—Well, what do yuh want tuh know, Mist' Russell. I'll tell yuh anything yuh like to know. . . .

EVANS—Well . . . you see . . . I mean . . . you needn't tell me if you don't want to. It's none of my business. . . .

LUCY (*assuringly*)—Yuh kin ask me, Russell. . . .

EVANS—Well . . . I mean . . . do you have to go on these dates all the time? I mean . . . do you have to . . . with anybody . . . for a living . . . ?

LUCY (*rises. A slight pause*)—Somethin' like that. . . .

EVANS—But you told me you worked in the spinning mills here . . . ?

LUCY—Jest now and then. That ain't much.

EVANS—Why, don't that pay enough . . . ?

LUCY—No mo'. When times was good . . . we could make three, fo' dollars a week, but now . . . I cain't make mo' 'n' a dollar at that . . . (EVANS *is silent. He looks at her, his expression is one of extreme compassion.*) Yuh think . . . I ain't so good . . . don't yuh, Mist' Russell?

EVANS (*firmly. Crosses to her, places his hand on her shoul-*

der)—No, I don't, Lucy. You bet I don't. I don't blame you. It's just a damn shame! (*She looks up at him with worship in her expression.*) But when did you begin having these dates? I mean . . . can't you try to start a sort of new life and jest fo'get your past—'cause you . . . well, it sho' is a shame fo' you to ruin you' life thisaway. . . . I mean . . . Oh, I guess I must sound like a lawyer or something. I don't know why I ask you all those personal things. . . . I guess it's just curiosity and that killed a cat. . . . We can talk about something else. . . .

LUCY—I don't mind tellin' yuh, Mist' Russell. . . .

EVANS (*boyishly*)—You see, Lucy . . . I guess . . . I sort of . . . well, I guess I do like you and every man wants to know all about somebody he likes. . . . (*She nods, her eyes shining again.*) But . . . if you don't want to talk about it . . . just say . . . it's none of your durn business, Russell Evans. And I'll deserve that.

LUCY—Well, I'll tell yuh. . . . I don't mind tellin' yuh. . . . I jest don't know where to haid in . . . but after I fust come tuh work in the Henrietta mill, I met a gal theah . . . and though she was much older'n me . . . she tuk a likin' tuh me an' began tuh carry me 'round tuh places an' parties and automobile rides an' all that. Well, I was jest achin' fo' a lil fun, workin' all day in the mill . . . an' when Virginia would ask me tuh go tuh a homebrew party . . . why, I jest natchurly went along. Well, one time I got all drunk up an' theah was a boy theah . . . he was drunk too . . . an' Virginia, she said . . . go right ahaid, Lucy . . . go on, be a sport . . . an' I . . . I jest lost my haid . . . yuh see, Virginia Ross was my only an' best friend then an' I jest natchurly did everythin' together with her. . . .

The mention of Virginia Ross has reminded Evans that Lucy must be that girl of the nigger trial up at Cookesville. He had read a lot about it. It must have been pretty terrible for Lucy and her friend Virginia.

Lucy would like to talk about something else, if Russell doesn't mind. He doesn't mind, but the longer he stares at her the more embarrassed he becomes. Suddenly he decides it is about time he is going. There will be customers to see in Birmingham.

"I sure was glad to meet you, Lucy," says Evans, taking her hand.

"Were you?"

EVANS—And maybe, sometime, we'll meet again. Huh?

LUCY—I sho' hope we will, Mist' Russell. . . . (*He takes a step toward the door.*) I want tuh thank yuh fo' yo' bounty . . . if yuh're sho' yuh don't need 'em. (*Gestures toward the parcel. He waves his hand.*)

EVANS—No. . . . I don't need them. . . . I hope you'll like them.

LUCY—I know I will. . . . (*Her lip trembling.*)

EVANS—Well . . . s'long. (*Crosses to door.*)

LUCY—Good-by, Mist' Russell. . . . (*Biting her lips to keep from crying.*)

EVANS (*stops at the door. Feels guilty. Hesitates an instant, then*)—Er—would yuh like me to kiss yuh good-by?

LUCY (*wistfully*)—I sho' would. . . .

EVANS (*crosses to her quickly and kisses her. She stands there motionless. A slight pause*)—Well . . . s'long.

LUCY (*trying to find her voice. A bit breathlessly*)—Kin I . . . kin I ask yuh a favor, Mist' Russell?

EVANS—You bet.

LUCY—Will . . . will yuh let me write tuh yuh sometime?

EVANS—You bet. Sure. You write care of my firm . . . Wilcox Cotton Goods Company . . . no . . . you better make it . . . General Delivery, Tulsa . . . Oklahoma. . . .

LUCY (*looks at him, repeats mechanically*)—Tulsa, Oklahoma. . . . General Delivery . . . Russell Evans. . . .

EVANS—That's it . . . well s'long, Lucy. . . . See you again.

Evans "crosses to door and exits. Lucy remains still for a moment staring at the place Evans stood in. Then she turns and notices the parcel and the dresses. She bites her lip to keep from bursting into tears and slowly looks about the room with a peculiar, wide-eyed, terrified expression. . . ."

The curtain falls.

The negro death-cells in Pembroke prison are modern and new. There are four barred windows through which the sun is shining out of a deep blue sky. The cells are high, steel-barred and covered with mesh work. The only attendant is a guard seated at one end of the row, smoking a corn cob pipe.

Four of the cells hold two prisoners each. Heywood Parsons is by himself. They are variously disposed at the moment, some standing at the doors of their cells, others lying on the cots within, two or three whispering together. One of them, Morris, would recite a dream he has had the night before. Does recite a part of it, even over the opposition of the others who object strenuously that Morris's dreams are all quite awful.

Before this dream can be made properly impressive visitors have arrived, the Principal Keeper bringing in Jackson, a colored preacher, a Mr. Lowery and William Treadwell, a mulatto. Lowery and Treadwell are attorneys. They represent the American Society for the Progress of Colored People and, as Treadwell explains with some enthusiasm, the society has secured the services of Mr. Lowery, who comes from Birmingham, to join with Attorney Brady, who defended the boys in Cookesville, in an appeal for a new trial.

"An appeal," explains Treadwell, fearing the boys do not understand, "is a chance for a new trial and we can only get that from the Supreme Court of this state. (*To* PARSONS.) Do you understand that?"

"Sho', I understand yuh," answers Parsons. "But how yuh goin' tuh git it?"

"Well, you just leave that to Mr. Lowery. He's the attorney. But I would like to prepare you in case we don't get it . . . do not become discouraged. We still have another resort and that is the Governor."

"Whut he goin' tuh do?"

"Well, he can do a great deal for you. He can have mercy on you and commute your sentences from death to life imprisonment."

"He kin do that?"

"Yes, that's in his power. But he won't do it unless he feels you deserve it. Unless he feels that you're innocent."

"Well, if he feels we is innocent then why should we be gittin' life?"

Now Mr. Lowery takes a hand and shuts Parsons up. What they are there for is to get the boys' signatures to an order for their attorneys to take the case to the Supreme Court. The paper is ready and all the boys have to do is to sign it.

Again Parsons would say something if they will let him speak. That Brady they had in the other trial wasn't any good, says Parsons. They were never quite sure which side he was workin' for until someone told them after the trial. The other boys are quick to agree to this. Treadwell tries to stop them.

"Now, you listen to me, boys," he shouts. "We've helped many a colored person out of many a difficulty. And we've been fortunate enough to find that there are white gentlemen like Mr. Lowery and Mr. Brady who are willing to go to all sorts of trouble to help you. . . ."

"But theah was a white man heah day befo' yistidy from the No'th who asked tuh help us out," speaks up Parsons. "He said he was from the . . . He wrote it down on a piece of paper. . . . Hi . . . You got it theah, Andy . . ."

"The National Labor Defense," reads Treadwell from the slip Andy hands him. "The N.L.D."

The Principal Keeper confirms the Treadwell suspicions. The young Yankee representing the N.L.D. has been to see the boys again and he's been promised another chance to talk to them today. He's bringing papers for the boys to sign, too.

Before they do anything else Treadwell thinks it is time for Preacher Jackson, who has come all the way from Chattanoogie to console them, to say a few words. Being asked, Preacher Jackson takes out his prayerbook, clears his throat and begins speaking. Soon he is chanting rhythmically, as in prayer.

"My chillun! I want tuh put the Lo'd in yuh. I want yuh tuh feel that the Lo'd Almighty is in us an' is in the great A.S.P.C.P. An' wherever the Lo'd is, don't yuh feah tuh tread. This N.L.D. is a contraption of the devil's and Satan. He sent them tuh make trouble an' bring down hate an' prejudice on God's colored chillun. An' I want yuh tuh know that Mist' Brady who fo't fo' yuh up theah in Cookesville, helped yuh an' fo't fo' yuh 'cause we ministers come tuh him in Chattanoogie an' made him see that the Lo'd would reward him with Heavenly love an' Christian spirit if he would help yo' po' nigger boys. An' he did! An' he labored fo' yuh up theah in Cookesville an' he didn't lose, my chillun. No! 'Cause if yuh all is 'lectrocuted an' dies yuh'll all go tuh Heaven sho' as yuh're born if yuh're sho' yuh ain't had a hand in this terrible crime. That's my lesson tuh yuh. An' Mist' Lowery heah who has come tuh help yuh fo' a small amount, 'cause he feels the Lo'd in him too . . . he is gonna work hard fo' yuh like yo' own mudders an' fadders would. An' so I bless yuh and warn yuh tuh fergit that N.L.D. devil's bunch an' sign up with the blessed A.S.P.C.P. O Lo'd, looka down on these po' misguided nigra chillun an' lead 'em safe an' holy tuh yo' kin'ly light. Amen, O Lo'd. Amen."

After the prayer Attorney Lowery would have the boys sign the paper and let the help begin. The boys are hesitant. One, Walters, asks if it wouldn't be possible for him to see his mother. None of the boys has seen his folks since he was arrested.

Attorney Lowery doesn't think that would be possible. It isn't likely the jedge would issue any such order. It would only increase the anger and feeling against them.

They pass the paper into the first cell. The prisoner Roberts signs it, despite the significant nudging of his cellmate, Ozie Purcell. Purcell thinks he will wait until he hears what the other feller has to say. Parsons, too, thinks there is still plenty of time. The others, despite the pressing attitude of attorneys and keepers, are still hesitating when other visitors are announced. A moment later the Warden has shown in and introduced Attorney-General Cheney, a Mist' Rokoff of the N.L.D. from New York City and Frank Travers.

Attorney Treadwell is not pleased with the interruption. He would protest to the Warden, but the matter of the attorneys is outside the Warden's jurisdiction. The Warden has, however, promised Mist' Rokoff a chance to speak to the boys. He also permits the keepers to open the cells so the boys can stand in front of them and Rokoff can see their faces.

"Open up the doors, Ira," orders the Warden. "And keep yo' hands on yo' guns. . . . Listen, niggers . . . jest step outside o' yo' cells 'bout two feet and stay still in front of them and *don't move*. . . . Go 'haid, Mist' Rokoff, but please make it quick-like."

"I will, Warden. Thank you very much. You've been very kind. . . . What's your name, boy?" He has crossed to one of the prisoners and shaken his hand.

"Andy Wood, please suh."

"And is this your brother?"

Attorney-General Cheney is moved to protest quietly, after an exchange of significant glances with the others. He whispers something in the Rokoff ear. The attorney of the N.L.D. excuses himself for a lack of understanding of the customs and returns to the prisoners, without again greeting them individually.

ROKOFF—Well, boys . . . my name is Joe Rokoff and I'm chief attorney for the National Labor Defense, the N.L.D., the same thing that Mr. Travers spoke to you about. (*Turns to* WARDEN.) Do you mind if I smoke, Warden?

WARDEN—'Course not. Go right ahaid. I'm about tuh smoke myself. (*Lights a cigar.*)

ROKOFF (*nods his thanks and takes a cigarette from a package and lights it. He observes* WARNER *looking at the package with an intense expression of desire*)—Would you like to have these?

WARNER—Please suh . . .

ROKOFF—Here you are. (*Extends the package.* WARNER

timidly extends his hand.) Go on, take 'em all. (WARNER *takes them and pushes them into his shirt-pocket quickly.*) Now, boys, you can choose to represent you anybody *you* like. That's your right and privilege. But before you do that, let me tell you who we are, what we stand for and what we want to do for you. (*He notices some disturbance between* WARNER *and* MORRIS.) What is it, fellers? What's the trouble? Don't you understand me?

WARNER—Sho'. We understand yuh, suh . . . but this nigger heah done axes me for some of them cigarettes an' yuh gave 'em tuh me. . . .

ROKOFF—Well, what of it? Give him some. He's your friend, isn't he? He likes to smoke, same as you. . . . (WARNER *quickly gives* MORRIS *a few cigarettes.* ROKOFF *continues. From now on there are no serious interruptions and the prisoners all listen attentively and become absorbed. The speaker increases his tone and temper as he goes on until he quite loses himself and everyone on the stage including the* WARDEN *and* CHENEY *are quite absorbed by the power of his speech.*) Now, you boys are in a jam but there are a lot of other fellers, black and white, all over this country and they're in jams, too. And we're an organization that tries to get these fellers out and free. Now you just saw how this boy here . . . (*Points to* WARNER.) . . . refused to give his buddy any of those cigarettes I gave him. You've got to understand right away that that's the wrong idea to have. Men should stick together. Now, I'd like to show you what I mean and how we work. Just suppose there are two men on this side of me . . . (*He demonstrates with gestures his meaning.*) fighting against a certain thing and they're being licked. And on this other side, are three men fighting against almost the same kind of thing and they're being beaten, too. But if these two fellers and these three fellers would get together . . . (*He holds up two fingers on one hand and three on the other.*) . . . then there would be five . . . and nobody could lick 'em! That's what we work for. You see, up North and out West and here in the South there are white workers fighting for liberty and justice and a right to live happy. And down here in the South you black workers are fighting for the same thing. But you're all fighting apart. Now, if you will fight for the white workers in the North and the South and the East and West then they'd get together and fight for you black fellers down here. Now, you know as well as I do that it's going to be very hard for you boys to get a fair trial down here. I don't have to tell you that. I can't fool you with promises and fine words. You know you didn't get a fair trial in Cookesville.

PARSONS (*with some feeling*)—No, we didn't. . . .

TREADWELL (*somewhat excited, unable to contain himself*)—Listen to me, boys! I'm one of you and God-willing, I'd like to be darker than I am if that would help my people. And therefore I want to warn you against this dangerous N.L.D., this radical organization which only wants to use you boys as a cat's-paw to pull their chestnuts out of the fire. You poor children are too young to know it but they are the worst, insidious group of traitors to this country. . . . They not only want to spread rebellion and revolt through your case but they also want to destroy and ruin the great, benevolent A.S.P.C.P.

WARDEN (*to* LOWERY, *in a low voice*)—That high yaller ain't sech a bad talker.

PARSONS—Well, whut do yuh want tuh do fo' us?

TREADWELL—We have only one object. *One object.* And that is to get you boys a fair trial. We have no ideas of overthrowing the government as they have.

PARSONS—How . . . how yuh gonna git this fair trial?

TREADWELL (*annoyed*)—We . . . we will not spare any effort to protect you from the death penalty. . . .

ANDY—Well. . . . We don't want no lip-talk.

ROKOFF—And I'm not going to give you any lip-talk. I'm not going to say you're going to get that fair trial that these high-sounding organizations will try to get. And you know why you can't get it. You can't get it because the South wants you to burn. They want to teach you blacks a lesson, they want to frighten you blacks with the burned-up bodies of nine negro boys. They want to make you shut up and keep quiet. They want to keep the nigger in his place . . . that's why . . . And so . . . the only thing fair that you'll ever get will be a fair amount of electric juice to burn you alive on the chair in there. . . . (*Points to door leading to electrocution chamber.*)

LOWERY (*striding forward, angrily*)—Now, don't you pay attention to this talk. You better be white man's niggers, or . . .

ROKOFF—I object to these interruptions, Warden Jeffries.

The Warden is not quite sure what his decision should be, but when Rokoff reminds him of the boasted Southern courtesy he lets him go on. Rokoff finishes his talk to the boys in a burst of eloquence. The N.L.D. will force the South, and those in the South who are trying to murder them, to free these boys.

"They'll be afraid to keep you, afraid to kill you . . . they'll be afraid of fifteen million black workers who will stand shoulder to shoulder with fifty million white workers who will roar. . . .

Don't you touch those boys! Don't you dare touch those black children workers!"

The Warden cannot stand any more of that. No man is going to stir up niggers in his jail! And Rokoff has stopped, apologizing for having lost control of himself for the moment.

Now the boys have been put back in their cells and their kin-folk have been brought in. Cheney and Rokoff have an order from the Cookesville judge permitting the visit. The relatives are to be given two minutes, but they are to be careful not to get too close to the cells.

The two minutes are up about as quickly as they are begun and the unhappy kin-folk are herded back from the cells.

"Good-by, Heywood, an' God bless yuh," calls Mrs. Parsons, backing away. "Don't give up yo' hope, an' keep a-lookin' at the Lo'd. . . ."

"Don't worry, my chillun . . . we got the N.L.D. wid us," cries Mrs. Wood.

"Don't fo'git tuh pray, Ozie," calls Mrs. Purcell.

Now Rokoff, with the Warden's permission, has presented the paper for the boys to sign if they want to. Even if they don't sign it the N.L.D. will continue to be their friend and will bring their folks to see their children, he assures them. He would have the boys do whatever they think is right. If they want to work with the Treadwell organization that is their privilege.

The boys think they would like to talk it over. Lowery and Treadwell are opposed to wasting any more time, but Rokoff would give them all the time they want.

The lawyers have gone and the boys undertake to make up their minds. Morris believes he was right in signing for Treadwell and the preacher. Andy never would trust a preacher too far. Parsons remembers that no preachers ever come to see them when they were in Cookesville. Andy ain't feeling very trustin' toward that high-yaller, that Treadwell, either.

Parsons is unreservedly for the Yankee lawyer, but he's suspicious of the Brady person who helped them in Cookesville. Everybody knows that Brady was in the crazy-house twicet.

Morris and Roberts are still for the colored lawyers and the preacher. Walters and Gene lean that way too. Moore, he's on the top of the fence, willin' to go with the majority. Then Parsons takes the floor.

Parsons (*in a low voice with suppressed feeling*)—Listen tuh me, you niggers! When we asked that high-yaller if we could see our kin-folk, he said, we couldn't. But this man . . . from the No'th, he didn't wait to be asked. No, suh! He knowed we wanted tuh see our mudders and fadders an' he didn't wait a bittie. He jest brought 'em 'long wid himself. An' listen tuh me, you niggers! Yuh all purty dumb. Maybe yuh don't understan' his talk. But it 'peared tuh me he was talkin' our own language an' I understood ev'ry word he say. An' he say a-plenty! He ain't no yaller-belly tuh sell us out. Lo'd A'mighty . . . when he talked I felt jest as strong as a bull. I felt I could bust open these heah bars. An' I'm tellin' yuh all dat I don't keer if Gawd or the debbil or the N.L.D. saves me, I wanna be saved. An' this heah man kin do dat. . . . Yes, right down heah in the South. So I say tuh yuh all . . . Sign up! Sign up, niggers, befo' he gits angry an' changes his min' wid us dumb bastards.

ANDY—Yeah. We sign. We sign wid the N.L.D. . . .

ROY—Me too. . . .

WARNER—Right. The N.L.D. Sign up, niggers. . . .

MORRIS—Count me too, Heywood. . . .

ALL (*together*)—We sign. The N.L.D. Sign up. Right. Sho'. Sign, sign, sign. . . .

WARNER (*with fervor*)—The Lo'd be wid us an' the N.L.D. Come on, Olen. Sing us somethin' fo' the Lo'd tuh heah us. . . .

MORRIS—Sing dat Gabriel's trumpet, Olen. . . .

WARNER—Yeah . . . throw us down that trumpet, Gabriel . . . !

ANDY—Go on, Olen. It do my heavy heart good. . . .

MOORE (*sings*)—

"Oh, han' me down, throw me down. . . .
Han' me down a silver trumpet, Gabriel.
Oh, han' me down, throw me down. . . .
Anyway yuh git it down. . . .
Han' me down a silver trumpet, Gabriel.
If religion was a thing money could buy,
Han' me down a silver trumpet, Gabriel.
Oh, the rich would live an' the po' would die.
Han' me down a silver trumpet, Gabriel.

So, han' me down, throw me down. . . .
Han' me . . .

PARSONS (*his hands gripping the bars; with intense feelings*)—Dat's it! You heerd dat, niggers. If religion was a thing money could buy . . . (*Singing continues.*) . . . You heerd dat? . . .

Well, it do. It do. . . . It do buy it. . . . (*Singing continues.*) . . . the po'r would die. . . . (*Singing.*) . . . NO . . . No, niggers! We ain't gonna die. No. No. . . . NO. . . . NO.

The singing continues as the curtain falls.

Several months later, in the home of the Wells, which has taken on a little additional dirt and dilapidation for each month passed, Lucy Wells is lying on the couch, a shawl about her shoulders, an old coat over her feet. She is quite evidently recovering from an illness.

Mrs. Wells is finishing her lunch at the table and urging her daughter to eat. There's no sense feelin' and actin' the way Lucy is, talkin' about wantin' to die and all. No gal of eighteen should talk that-a-way. If Lucy was as miserable as her mother's been a lot of times that would be different.

Mrs. Wells is also concerned about a report from Tommy that Lucy has been having a nigger boy in the house and giving him a letter. Who was that letter for?

It was a letter for that Mist' Evans, Lucy confesses. Mist' Evans is at the hotel in town, and Lucy was afraid if she posted a letter to him it wouldn't be delivered in time. Besides Lucy doesn't trust the postoffice man and she didn't have any money to buy a stamp if she did. After she sent the letter by the boy Lucy sat up till mawnin' thinkin' Mist' Evans might come, but he didn't.

"I reckon yuh sort of stuck on that boy . . . huh, Lucy?" ventures Mrs. Wells.

"Uh, huh." Lucy's eyes have filled with tears.

MRS. WELLS—Well . . . he must have fo'gotten all about yuh. It's sech a long time . . . ain't it?

LUCY—I wrote tuh him twice. . . .

MRS. WELLS—Well . . . ?

LUCY—Nuthin'.

MRS. WELLS (*she looks at her daughter, with pity*)—Now, don't yuh take on, honey. All men are like that.

LUCY (*staring ahead, dully*)—No, it were my own fault. I tol' him about that Cookesville thing an' that cooled him off, I guess. . . .

MRS. WELLS (*impatient*)—Well, whut did yuh go an' do that fo'?

LUCY (*wearily*)—Oh, he'd 'a' found out by himself, anyway. . . . (*Suddenly cries.*) I sho' made a mess of my life. . . .

MRS. WELLS (*sits by her and caresses her*)—It ain't yo' fault, Lucy. You couldn't help that train thing happenin'. . . .

LUCY (*turns suddenly. With feeling*)—But I could have helped it, Maw. I could. That damn rotten Virginia Ross put me up tuh it. . . .

MRS. WELLS—Huh? Whut yuh sayin'?

LUCY (*she speaks as if what she has to say could not be held back a moment longer. It pours out of her*)—I . . . I cain't sleep nights. That's why I got so sick. I'm all run down with thinkin' of it. Thinkin' of them po' nigger kids, goin' tuh burn any day on that 'lectric chair. I dream. . . . I dream of them screamin' an' yellin' in pain. . . . I see myself, always lightin' fires an' helpin' tuh burn them. . . . (*She sobs bitterly.*)

MRS. WELLS (*frightened*)—When is they set tuh die, anyway?

LUCY—I dunno. I'm skeered tuh read the papers any mo'. I shy 'way from them. (*Breaking out again.*) Every time . . . every time I see one of 'em black boys on the street, I think I'm back in the Cookesville co't house agin . . . an' how them po' kids looked theah . . . skeered like a treed rabbit . . . all full of swellin's an' bruises from the beatin's they give 'em in the jail. . . .

MRS. WELLS—How do yuh know they beat 'em?

LUCY—How do I know? I heard them. I still hear 'em screamin' fo' pain. . . .

MRS. WELLS—But it weren't yo' fault . . . my baby. . . . Yuh couldn't do nuthin'. . . .

LUCY—I could. . . . (*She is literally trembling with emotional stress. She is almost hysterical.*) I didn't have tuh listen tuh that bitch of a Virginia Ross . . . an' she's still workin' steady at the mill. . . .

There is a knock at the door. A Mr. Nelson and a constable are calling. They would like to see Lucy alone. It ain't nuthin' serious or important, so Mrs. Wells needn't feel she has to wait outside, as she suggests.

Nelson has come to ask Lucy about a letter he and his men have taken away from a nigger they caught in a crap game. The nigger said it was fo' a Mist' Evans at the hotel. Nelson had called at the hotel and found Mist' Evans was drummin' up business in Fullerton. They left word for Mist' Evans to call them. Then they called up Mist' Luther Mason, state solicitor in Cookesville, and read Lucy's letter to him ovah long distance. Solicitor Mason was sorry to heah that letter.

"He said if yuh was goin' tuh write letters like that, with this new trial comin' up soon . . . yuh would git things all balled up fo' him," says Nelson.

"Whut do I keer fo' him?" answers Lucy, sullenly.

NELSON—Now, Lucy . . . I want tuh tell yuh, 'cause I know yuh as a kid, yet, that yuh are puttin' yo'self in fo' a lot of grief, if yuh keep on writin' sech kin' of talk. Why, you might be 'rested fo' perjury.

LUCY—Whut's that?

NELSON—Perjury? That's when yuh sweared at that Cookesville trial tuh tell the truth an' now you're writin' somethin' different. . . . (LUCY *is silent.*) Now, this Luther Mason ain't sech a bad sport. He realizes yuh must have ben drunk or somethin' when yuh wrote this letter. . . .

LUCY—I weren't drunk. I ben sick fo' two weeks in bed.

NELSON—Well . . . that's fine. That's still better. Yuh ben in fever an' didn't know whut yuh were doin'. . . .

LUCY (*heatedly*)—I did, too. . . .

NELSON—Now, hol' on. Don't lose yo'self. Lemme finish whut I got tuh say. Mist' Mason dictated over the phone tuh me an affidavit fo' yuh tuh sign. . . . (*He takes a paper from his pocket.*) As saying how yuh didn't know yo' own min' when yuh wrote that letter an' how it ain't true whut yuh wrote theah. An' he asked me tuh have yuh sign this right away. He's comin' 'long down heah tuh Humbolt by the evenin' train tuh see yuh himself an' talk tuh yuh 'bout it.

LUCY (*on the point of tears*)—I won't sign nuthin'. An' I don't want tuh talk tuh that Mason man.

NELSON—Lucy. Yuh don't keer tuh be 'rested, do yuh?

LUCY—Who's goin' tuh do that?

NELSON—I'll have tuh do that, I'm afraid. . . .

LUCY—But I'm still ailin', Mist' Nelson. . . .

NELSON—I'm mighty sorry, but them's my orders. (*She is silent, sullen. He thinks of a new tactic.*) Yuh know very well, Lucy . . . that I never said anything all the while I see yuh on the street an' in front of the hotel . . . yuh know I allus turn my haid. . . . (*She nods, slowly.*) Well, you'll not look fo' trouble an' sign this heah paper, like a smart gal. Huh?

LUCY (*a slight pause, then wearily*)—I guess so. . . .

NELSON—That's a smart gal. . . . (*Crosses to table and prepares the paper and pen. She crosses phlegmatically to it.*)

LUCY (*looks at paper*)—Right heah?

NELSON—Yeah. Wheah the lil cross is, yeah . . . right theah. . . . (*Bends over her. She signs.*) That's fine. (*Takes up the paper, waves it slowly.*) That shows yuh as a smart gal, Lucy. Well, we'll be runnin' long now. (*Folds up and puts away the paper.*) An' I'd keep a tight lip on this if I were you. . . . (*She nods, slowly.*) Well, good-by. Hope you're on yo' two feet right soon. . . .

Lucy stares after them as they close the door. Suddenly she bursts into tears, sobbing convulsively. Her young brother Tommy rushes in through the door, into the kitchen and out again, pausing long enough to ask what the trouble is and to announce that he doesn't care anyway.

A moment later there is another knock on the door. To Lucy's invitation to come in the door opens and Russell Evans steps over the threshold. Lucy is both surprised and confused and Evans is plainly embarrassed, but they manage to explain themselves finally. Lucy has been sick-like and Russell has just heard that the Sheriff was lookin' for him to tell him somethin' about a letter Lucy is supposed to have written. He had come over to find out about it, whut was in the letter and all—

Lucy is reluctant to tell what she wrote. First she would know why Russell had not answered the other letters she sent to Tulsa. He did not answer those letters, Russell confesses guiltily, because he was still thinkin' a good deal about that Cookesville thing.

"But what was it you wrote me last night?" he asks again. "Don't yuh want to tell me?"

"Yes, I'll tell yuh," she says, after finding it difficult to begin. "I wrote yuh that . . . that them nigger boys didn't do that at all, whut I said they did at the trial. . . . I wrote yuh that the police skeered me . . . and I made up that story on them boys. . . ."

"You wrote me that?" demands Evans, amazed.

"Yes, I did."

EVANS—Well, why did you want to write me, that?

LUCY—I wrote it tuh you, 'cause my heart was hurtin' me . . . and I wanted tuh tell it tuh someone . . . 'cause I hated myself fo' it, ever sence that trial an' couldn't sleep at night an' was 'shamed of myself an' got sick fer worryin'. . . .

EVANS (*becoming a little warmer to her*)—Well, why didn't you write it to me before in your other letters?

LUCY—I would 'ave . . . if you'd 'a' answered one. I ben tryin' tuh write it tuh yuh an' jest couldn't . . . 'cause yuh didn't write back an' I was skeered of the law, but last evenin' when I learned yuh was back in town, I made up my mind to write yuh the whole truth. . . .

EVANS—Uh, huh. (*He looks at her, sympathetically, for the first time since he entered the room.*) But how did you know I was in town?

LUCY—Well, I asked the hotel man, after I didn't git no answer from yuh, to please let me know when yuh did get tuh town . . . an' he sent around his boy yest'day an' that's how I learned it.

EVANS (*slowly*)—You mean . . . even after I kept quiet to your letters, you still wanted to see me . . . ?

LUCY—Sho'. I wanted tuh see yuh. I jest hoped yuh would come back, an' I talked tuh Mist' Fredericks an' asked him if yuh would be 'round sellin' agin, an' he said . . . yuh might . . . an' so I didn't give up hopin' tuh see yuh jest once mo'.

EVANS (*with his desire to know, he loses what little veneer of worldliness he does possess and is very much the boy*)—Why . . . why, Lucy?

LUCY—Well, 'cause you're 'bout the only one in the world that I ever keered fo'. . . .

EVANS (*the boy looks at her, he is almost embarrassed by her simplicity and sincerity; then slowly*)—You mean . . . that you're in love with me . . . ?

LUCY (*smiles wistfully, hoping for him to understand her*)—Well, I don't know 'bout love, Mist' Russell, but I do know I never keered fo' nobody else but you in my hull life. . . .

EVANS (*pretending not to believe her. He delights in hearing this*)—You don't mean that with all those fellers you've been out with, you never liked one of them more than me . . . ?

LUCY (*simply*)—No . . . I never liked none of them at all. Not like I do you. . . .

EVANS—Well . . . (*Smiles helplessly.*) . . . if you're sure you mean it. . . . (*He looks at her. Then suddenly takes her by the shoulders and embraces her. He kisses her.*) I like you, too, Lucy. And I'm happy to know that all that Cookesville mess isn't true about you. It isn't, is it?

LUCY (*almost breathless*)—No . . . they never touched us at all.

EVANS—I hope you're not just saying this for me. . . .

LUCY—It's Gawd's own truth, Mist' Russell. . . .

EVANS—Would you swear to it if . . . ?

LUCY (*quickly*)—Yuh know I wouldn't lie tuh yuh. . . . I'll swear it by the Lo'd A'mighty an' I don't keer if the law do git me fo' it . . . or what people say of me. . . .

EVANS (*a slight pause, admiringly*)—I believe you, Lucy. . . .

Russell's sympathy is aroused now as he looks admiringly into Lucy's swimming eyes. People around there probably been talkin' a lot—the poor kid! He is sure now he likes Lucy. He has a feeling that he wants to take care of her and protect her. Suddenly he would know if she will go away with him—to Tulsa, to St. Louis, to anywhere he goes. Would she?

Lucy will go anywhere at all with Mr. Russell, but she'd be awfully skeered. There was that Constable and the letter she wrote to Russell.

"They wanted me to swear that I was drunk an' didn't know what I was doin' when I wrote it," she reports.

"Did you sign it?"

"Yes, I did. I was feelin' so tired then, and gived up hope you was comin'. . . . But if I'd 'a' knowed you was comin' . . . I woulda died 'fo' I signed anythin'."

She tells him of Nelson's talk with the solicitor in Cookesville, and of the solicitor's coming tonight to talk with her. She is afraid they might 'rest her if she tried to leave town.

"He will like hell!" declares Russell. "He'll have a fine chance tryin' to do that. Now, look here, Lucy. I want you to leave this damn place with me. I'll take care of you from now on. You won't have to fear nothing, no more. . . . Don't you forget that. . . ." (*He holds her tightly to him.*)

"I won't fo'git it, Mist' Russell. . . ."

EVANS—Now, you cut out the Mister. I'm just Russ . . . I'm your Russ. Do you understand that? (*She nods, holding tightly to him.*) And no law, no solicitor is goin' to trouble you from now on. Now, do you feel strong enough to do some traveling by automobile?

LUCY—What, now?

EVANS—Sure. Right now. This minute.

LUCY—I feel strong with you, Russell. . . . (*She is all excited and can hardly speak.*)

EVANS (*with determination*)—Then get your things packed.

LUCY (*moves toward her room*)—I haven't but a coupla old dresses. . . .

EVANS—Then leave them here. We'll get you some new ones. Take your coat, though. It'll be cold, going fast. . . . This it? (*Points to her coat on the couch that she used to keep her warm. She nods quickly. He crosses to it and hurrying back, helps her into it.*) Come on, let's go. My grip is in the car, and that's right around the corner. Think you can make it?

LUCY—I sho' can, Russ.

EVANS—Well, let's go, Lucy. (*His arm about her, they take a few steps toward the door. Suddenly he stops.*) Don't you . . . maybe you'd like to say good-by, huh? Maybe I have no right to drag you off like this . . . ?

LUCY (*a short pause. She turns and looks about the room, slowly, almost with an air of abstraction, then turns back to* EVANS.) No, Russ. . . . I got nuthin' tuh say good-by tuh. . . . (*With* EVANS'S *arm about her, they exit rapidly.*)

THE CURTAIN FALLS

ACT III

The New York office of Nathan G. Rubin, attorney, overlooks the skyscraper towers circling the Battery. A stocky man of the Anglicized Jewish type is Rubin. He is sitting now at a large desk in front of tall windows at the back of his private office. With him in the office are Vicky Salvatini, a New York racketeer type, and Johnny, who has been the Rubin secretary for many years. Johnny is mixing drinks at a bar that ordinarily is concealed in one of the bookcases with which the room is lined.

The drinks ready, the Salvatini business is continued. It is a question of raising "twenty grand" to pay Rubin for grabbing a pal of Salvatini's named Freddie away from the "hot seat" with which he is threatened up the river. Rubin is confident of his ability to save Freddie, having a record of having grabbed no fewer than eighty-two from that same hot seat in his time. But he wants the twenty grand first and he wants it in cash.

Salvatini finally is convinced and promises to have the money before the end of the month. Rubin is going South and will need it.

The next Rubin callers are Joe Rokoff and Harrison, a colored attorney of the N.L.D. They have come for the Rubin decision in respect to the Cookesville case. He had agreed to come into it on two conditions: First, that he be convinced the boys were innocent and, second, that he could win the case.

Rubin, after going over all the testimony of the first trial, is convinced the boys are innocent. But— He is not so confident that he can get a complete acquittal.

"The state's entire case as it stands is the word of two white girls against the word of nine negro boys. About the state's other witnesses, I'm not worried. We can show them up easy enough. These affidavits you've gotten together are swell. But the state statute says simply that if the woman swears to a rape then she's been raped and that's all. And if the jury believes her, then it's just too bad. . . ."

"Yes . . . ?"

"So our job is to make the jury believe she's a liar. . . ."

"Certainly."

"Not so certainly," protests Rubin, quickly. "True enough, you've got some swell affidavits showing these girls and especially this Virginia Ross to be of low character . . . still, we've got no real, concrete evidence that will conflict with her story. And that is the only but chief technical weakness. . . ."

Harrison has been doing some work along that line and has a wire from Attorney-General Cheney disproving that any such person as Cary Richy ever existed in Chattanooga. The people living at the address given had been there for fifteen years and had never heard of her. That bit of evidence, thinks Rubin, is something to work on, the first crack in the cement.

"Well, then, Mr. Rubin," smiles Rokoff, "does this give you the certainty you require?"

"I guess you don't know me, Rokoff," smiles Rubin. "If I had to wait for 100 per cent fool-proof cases every time then I'd have to begin doing divorce actions. No. I feel and I know that these boys are innocent and if I didn't know that . . . we wouldn't be sitting here together now. But I don't want no five or ten or twenty year verdicts. . . . I'm going down there to get a full acquittal. I'm going down there to bring those boys home with me and . . . and it's evidence like this . . . (*Shakes the telegram form.*) that'll give us that full acquittal. Get me?"

As to further details, there is one other point Rubin wants cleared up before he agrees to take the case. Are they or are they not Communists?

Rokoff explains that he is not a member of the party, but he does agree with a great many things they advocate. One, that the best legal defense is the best political defense.

"Have you ever been down South?" he asks Rubin.

"Sure, Washington, D. C."

ROKOFF—I mean the real South. Mississippi, Georgia, Alabama. (RUBIN *shakes his head.*) Well, I've been in these places and I've fought for dozens of negro and white workers in Southern courts. I fought that strike case in South Carolina in 1928. . . .

RUBIN—Yeah. I remember. A swell job. . . .

ROKOFF—Thanks. So, I think I know what I'm talking about when I warn you that if you expect to get an unprejudiced jury or an impartial judge or anything resembling a fair trial, you're mighty mistaken, Mr. Rubin. . . .

RUBIN—Well, you leave that to me.

ROKOFF—We intend to. That's our policy. A two-fisted one. (*He clenches both his fists and holds them up.*) With the right fist . . . the finest legal analytic defense in the country, Nathan G. Rubin . . . and with the left fist . . . the greatest, widest mass protest action on a national and international scale. . . . Two-fisted. . . .

RUBIN—That's just it. A lot of people have been saying that if it hadn't been for this south-paw, left fist policy of you reds . . . I mean your organization . . . those boys would have been free. . . .

HARRISON—If that were so, Mr. Rubin, why weren't they freed in Cookesville two years ago, when there was no mass action, when the boys had only Southern lawyers and when the N.L.D. was a thousand miles away?

RUBIN (*puffing his pipe, thoughtfully*)—That sounds logical enough. But I wouldn't want to be hampered in any way. . . .

HARRISON—We don't intend to hamper you. Last summer we engaged as you know one of the finest Constitutional attorneys in the United States to plead the case in the Supreme Court in Washington and we didn't hamper him any. But we do attribute to a great extent the decision for this new trial, to the demands of thousands of workers all over the world and not to any generosity on the part of the courts. . . .

RUBIN—That's fine. As long as you keep out Communism from the courtroom I don't care what you do outside. . . .

ROKOFF—We agree to that. You see, all I wanted to do was to show you the various underlying reasons for this case, economical and sociological. . . . This is not merely a rape case . . . it's bigger than that. It's the Southern ruling class on trial . . .

it's . . .

RUBIN (*laughing good-naturedly*)—Sure, sure! But I'm only interested in this case. You do what you like on the outside.

When it comes to a question of money, Rokoff is sorry to report that there is no Moscow gold around them; every penny they have had has been donated by nickels and dimes from the workers all over the country. They are tremendously grateful that Rubin is not asking any fee at all, but he will have to go even farther than that and lay out his own expenses. It is embarrassing, but—

"Well, I figured on bringing my assistant along," admits Rubin. "That'll run up, hotels, fares . . . Well, I don't know. . . . Hey, John! Get in touch with Salvatini. Tell him I want that dough by Monday." (*He turns back to* ROKOFF.) "Okay, Joe. We'll put the expenses on the ice, too. (*They shake hands with enthusiasm.*) But don't you fellers make me any revolution in the courtroom. And no bombs whatsoever. . . . (*They laugh.*) You know . . . I may joke about it but you've got me pretty worried with this mass action and protest meetings. Maybe . . ."

A moment later the telephone has announced the arrival in the outer office of Frank Travers and Lewis Collins. Travers is the Rokoff assistant, Collins one of the white boys who jumped off the train.

Collins, as he relates it, has been bummin' around the country evah since the Cookesville frame-up—

"Frame-up!" shouts Rubin, at first mention of the word.

"Sho'. That's whut it were," quietly answers Collins. "A frame-up. I seen it all. They tried tuh make me tell stories too. But, I wouldn't do it. Not fo' them bastards. Hell, no!"

It was in a Kansas City paper that Collins read of the new trial being granted the Cookesville boys and he decided then and there to get to New York. He thought first he would go to the Yankee Governor in Albany and tell him. The governor was busy and his assistant advised Collins to see the attorneys for the defense. He went back to reading papers and found Mist' Rokoff's name. He got the office address from the directory and they had shipped him down heah right quick an' in a *taxi.*

"That's fine. That's swell," declares the excited Rubin. "But what makes you think these boys are innocent?"

COLLINS—Well . . . (*He takes another drink, and smiles with satisfaction.*) This heah is better'n Coca-cola. Huh? Well . . . (*Wipes his lips with the back of his hand.*) It's this-a-way. I read as how that Virginia Ross woman tol' how she went tuh Chattanoogie with Lucy Wells tuh look fo' work in the mills theah an' how she spent the night with a lady called Mrs. Cary Richy. . . .

RUBIN—That's right. That's her story.

COLLINS—Yeah, but it's all one big, damn lie. She never went theah tuh look fo' a job. She went theah with me an' Lucy to go bummin'.

RUBIN—Wha-at?

COLLINS—Sho'. Virginia an' Lucy never spent that night with no Cary Richy whoever she is . . . they spent the hull night with me an' Oliver Tulley in a hobo jungle. . . .

RUBIN—What did you do there . . . in the jungle?

COLLINS—Oh, we talked an' ate some sandwiches that we bummed an' . . .

RUBIN—What else?

COLLINS—Well, we had some fun. . . .

RUBIN—What do you mean, fun? With whom? With this Ross woman?

COLLINS—No, I wouldn't tech that Ross gal. She's poison. I was with Lucy. . . . Lucy Wells.

RUBIN (*all are quite tense*)—You mean you slept with her there in the jungle?

COLLINS—Well, we didn't sleep much. . . .

RUBIN—You mean . . . you . . . ?

COLLINS (*smiling*)—I sho' did.

RUBIN—That's all. (*He says this as if he had just finished the examination of a witness in court. He is terribly elated and gives almost full vent to his voice.*) Joe! We got 'em. This'll knock their medical evidence for a loop. Jeez. We'll go down there and we'll batter their brains out. (*All chatter noisily with unsuppressed glee.*) Yeah . . . and this little boy from New York is gonna bring those nine kids home and dump 'em into your lap. . . .

The curtain falls.

It is nearing the end of the first week of the trial of Heywood Parsons in the courthouse at Dexter. A hot sun beats through yellow blinds at the windows. The room is crowded with an audience made up mainly of whites. There is a small section given over to negro spectators.

The witness chair is placed directly in front of the judicial dais. Both face the jury, separated from the court crowd by a wooden railing. There are brass railings on which the jurors rest their feet as they tip back their chairs. And brass cuspidors between each pair of jurors that are frequently and expertly used.

At the defense table are Rokoff, Rubin, Cheney and the defendant, Parsons. At a similar table to the left of the judge sit Slade, the circuit solicitor; Mason, the Cookesville solicitor, and Dade, the Attorney-General.

"The judge, ironically enough, resembles Abraham Lincoln without the beard. He speaks in a soft drawl." There is a reporters' table at which are about ten busy scribblers.

"Placed in strategic positions about the courtroom are many soldiers carrying rifles with bayonets and in full uniform. A captain is in charge of them."

Attorney Rubin is conducting the examination of an elderly, good-looking negro. He is Dr. Theodore Henry Watson, a graduate of Tuskegee who had his master's degree from the University of Illinois. But the doctor has never been called for jury service nor examined on his qualifications to serve.

This fact is a matter for sly mirth on the part of Attorney-General Slade, when the witness is turned over to him. "You don't mean to say that you consider yourself eligible to sit on a jury with white men!" sneers Slade, and the crowd guffaws loudly.

"If it please the court," protests Rubin as the laughter ceases, "for twenty-five years the officials of this county have illegally and systematically excluded negroes of this community who are more than qualified to serve on juries. I have proven that, your honor. No witness, white or black that has been on this stand this past week can remember or ever heard of a negro juryman."

"Hell, no!" shouts a spectator and the laughter is renewed.

The state calls the Commissioner of Juries to prove that there has never been any systematic exclusion of negroes from jury service. It is merely a matter of selection. Negroes, testifies the Commissioner, "durn't have no sound jedgement and they durn't understand no law an' no justice."

"I move for dismissal on the grounds that negroes are being denied their rights as guaranteed them in the thirteenth, fourteenth and fifteenth amendments to the Constitution of the United States," moves Attorney Rubin.

"The counsel for defense has established a prima facie case of systematic exclusion on racial grounds in violation of the fourteenth amendment but this court has decided to hear no further testimony on this question. The motion is denied," rules the judge.

There is much whispering and a quick writing of statements at the reporters' table. Rubin takes an exception and the trial proceeds. The judge is hopeful, speaking to the jury, that nothing will be allowed to stand in the way of justice.

"We in the South have always tried to be fair and just," announces his honor, gravely. "Let us continue that noble record. So far as the law is concerned, it knows neither Jew nor Gentile, black nor white. We must do our duty and if we are true to ourselves then we cannot, no, we cannot be false to any man. (*Turns to* DADE.) Will the state kin'ly continue to call its witnesses."

Virginia Ross is the first witness. Interrogated by Solicitor Mason she repeats her Cookesville evidence: She is a housewife; she was on a train from Chattanooga; she was attacked and ravished by five negroes; she can identify Heywood Parsons as one of the five.

Taking the witness Attorney Rubin seeks to show, by affidavit and proof, that Mrs. Ross has been arrested, convicted and served sentence for offenses of lewdness and drunkenness; he is ready to prove that she also has consorted with negroes. But these are violations of city ordinances, rules the judge, and inadmissible as evidence.

"You testified at the Cookesville trial that you and Lucy Wells slept in the home of a Mrs. Cary Richy on the night before the train ride," says Rubin. "Is that right?"

"We did sleep theah."

RUBIN—Where does Mrs. Richy live?

VIRGINIA—In Chattanoogie.

RUBIN—What street? What number?

VIRGINIA—I don't remember no number. It was the third house from the corner.

RUBIN—What street?

VIRGINIA (*simulating exasperation*)—I don't exac'ly remember. . . .

RUBIN—As a matter of fact, Mrs. Ross, isn't it true that you got this name Cary Richy from a character in the *Saturday Evening Post* stories by Octavius Roy Cohen—sis Cary—that you got this name there? (*Offers copy of magazine to clerk.*)

DADE—Objection. I don't care what she did, the only thing we're interested in is whether she was raped.

RUBIN (*heatedly*)—I'm testing her credibility.

DADE—You know that is no proposition of law.

RUBIN—Address your remarks to the court!

DADE—You make it necessary to address them to you.

RUBIN—I have been a gentleman but I can be otherwise, too.

JUDGE—Wait, gentlemen. Don't either of you say anything. I won't have another word between you. Ask the question and the court will pass on it. General Dade's objection is sustained. Proceed, please.

RUBIN—Didn't you spend the night in a hobo jungle with Lucy Wells, Lewis Collins and Oliver Tulley?

VIRGINIA (*defiantly*)—No, I never done that.

RUBIN—Do you deny you know Lewis Collins?

VIRGINIA—I never heard of him or seen him in my life.

RUBIN—Didn't you make up this whole tissue of lies about those negroes attacking you, and didn't you force Lucy Wells to swear to your lies because you were afraid of being arrested yourself for prostitution?

VIRGINIA (*rising, screams*)—I'll have you know . . .

DADE (*simultaneously*)—I object.

RUBIN—This is perfectly relevant, your Honor.

JUDGE—Well, suppose you reword it, Mr. Rubin.

RUBIN (*after a sigh*)—Did you not make up this story for that reason?

VIRGINIA (*very angrily, in a shrill voice*)—You bet' not talk tuh me in that so't of talk, Mister. I'm a decent lady an' I'll have yuh know . . .

RUBIN—Answer the question, please.

VIRGINIA—I never done made up no story . . . you . . .

VOICE—Let's get that goddam Jew bastard, boys.

There is a great tumult in the courtroom. The pounding of the judge's gavel punctuates the barking of the soldiers as they push the crowd back into its seats. The judge finally orders the removal of the offending spectator.

Rubin restates his possession of proof of Virginia Ross's concocting her story to save her own skin, proof that he only needs the presence of Lucy Wells to corroborate. But there is no Lucy Wells, Dade shouts triumphantly. What has become of that state's witness? Who has done away with Lucy Wells?

Rubin goes on with his examination. Virginia repeats that she had taken the freight train home because she was broke; that there was the fight with the white boys; that after the negroes had thrown them off the train the ravishing began; that Heywood Parsons was the first of the ravishers to attack her; that, throwing her on the stones on the floor of the car, he made her back bleed; that he hit her over the head with a gun and her head bled, too; that he swore after that he was goin' tuh take her up no'th and make her his woman—

"Yes, an' he said he was goin' tuh cut my neck open if I didn't let him . . ." Virginia shrills.

Rubin would know why it is that Mrs. Ross, a white woman, was held in jail at Cookesville. What happened in that jail before the grand jury met to indict the negro boys? No one in all the history of the state ever heard of a white woman being held in jail when she is the complaining witness against a negro! Before he is through, promises Rubin, he will show that this witness is an out-and-out perjurer.

Dr. Thomas, the physician who examined the two girls in Cookesville, is called. He repeats his belief that the women had had commerce with men, but his evidence cannot be said to prove that five men had attacked Virginia Ross. Probably there should have been more evidence than there was. No, Dr. Thomas had not found Virginia bleeding from either back or head. What marks her body bore could easily be accounted for by her jumping on and off trains and sleeping in the open. Neither was Mrs. Ross hysterical or excited when she came into his office. Her pulse was normal. The same was true of Lucy Wells.

Benson Allen is called by the state. He had helped put the girls in the automobile at Rocky Point. They were, he says, highly hysterical. They were cryin' and complainin' of bein' attacked. Mrs. Ross was also bleedin' turrible-like. It is testimony that greatly pleases Dade and his associates.

Allen had also searched Heywood Parsons, he reports when he is turned over to Rubin. He found no gun on him, but he found a knife. Parsons said he stole it from Mrs. Ross.

Again Dade is highly gratified. His actions stir Rubin to move for a mistrial. The judge denies the motion and again admonishes the prosecutors.

The state calls Seth Robbins, a farmer, dressed roughly in overalls and boots. Mr. Robbins testifies that he was standing on a hay wagon in his field and had witnessed what happened on the train; saw the negroes throw the white boys off; saw Parsons grab and attack Virginia Ross.

Rubin produces a map that shows the Robbins farm to be a half mile from the railroad and contends that it would be impossible for the farmer to have seen anything happening on a fast-moving train at that distance. Furthermore, if Robbins had seen this outrage why did he not report it to the sheriff of Stebbinsville? It just slipped Robbins's mind. Neither had he ever told anybody anything about it, which makes it difficult for the attorney to understand why he had been called as a witness.

The defense now calls the defendant, Heywood Parsons. There is a boiling up of anger in the crowd. Epithets are passed as Parsons takes the stand. The judge is obliged to make an announcement. There have been rumors of meetings at which mob spirit was ready to determine the guilt or innocence of the defendant, he says. Men attending such meetings should be ashamed of themselves—

"And if any group is thinking of engaging in anything that would cause the death of this defendant . . . then that to me is murder, cowardly murder . . . and I hereby order these deputies and soldiers to defend with their lives and to . . . kill any man who attempts such an action."

Parsons' testimony is a complete denial of the charges against him. He was on the train with Eugene Walters, Andy Wood and Roy Wood; he had never seen the girls; he had never met the other boys until they were roped together at Rocky Point.

Dade takes the witness and tries to lead him into a confession in keeping with his Cookesville testimony. Parsons is firm in his denials. His story could have been corroborated by the boy Tulley, whom he had pulled back on the train to save his life, but Tulley was never called to testify.

"You confessed in Cookesville that you saw these other negras attack the girls," hisses Dade. "Didn't you confess to this?"

"Yessuh, I done dat, but—"

"You did it! That's all!"

"Why did you make that confession?" asks Rubin, taking the witness.

"They made me tuh do it, please, suh," answers Parsons. "They beat me up awful theah. An' woulda killed me if I hadn't done it. I held out but I jest couldn't no mo'. . . ."

"Then it is not true that you saw your friends attack the girls?"

"No, suh, it ain't true at all, please, suh."

Dr. Oswald Morton, state gynecologist is called by the defense. He is inclined to support the implied doubt of Dr. Thomas that Virginia Ross could have been attacked by five men on the evidence deduced from the examination of the girls two hours later. He admits that the condition discovered might be explained if it were proved that the girls had spent the two previous nights in the intimate company of two white boys—

Lewis Collins is called to tell of his own and the Tulley boy's adventure with Virginia Ross and Lucy Wells on a bummin' trip. He had met Virginia Ross when she was in jail with a Jim Arthur, with whom she had been arrested in Humbolt for lewdness. It was then Virginia had first brought Lucy Wells with her, when she came to see Jim Arthur and bring him tobaccy.

After they got out of jail the four of them planned the bummin' trip while they were in a place just outside of town havin' fun. They met the Tulley boy after they got to Chattanoogie, and all of them spent the night in the hobo jungle. Parsons saw them. A Chile parlor man where Parsons had bummed sandwiches saw them.

"And you expect the jury to believe this cock-and-bull story?" shouts the disgusted Dade, dismissing the witness.

"Did you testify at any of the trials at Cookesville?" asks Rubin.

"No, suh."

"Why not?"

"They jest didn't want me tuh."

"That's all."

Collins repeats for the state's benefit his reluctance to have anything more to do with the case after he got away until he read of the new trial and felt that he must tell whut he knew.

Dade is calling the attention of the court to the fact that Lucy Wells, whose name has again been mentioned by the defense attorney, has not been produced after having been spirited away three weeks before by parties interested in keeping her testimony out of the courtroom, when there is a sudden upheaval of emotion in the courtroom. Reporters and court attachés are in a fever of excitement. "It almost seems as if the slow, slumbering volcano suddenly blew up. Everything now belies the amenities and niceties that were observed before." Dade is shouting a demand for an explanation.

"Are you implying that we kidnaped Lucy Wells?" Rubin shouts back.

"I imply nothing," answers Dade. "I only repeat that Lucy Wells has either been killed or hidden away by interested parties."

Suddenly Frank Travers has appeared in the courtroom and hurried to Rokoff. Rokoff in turn whispers excitedly to Rubin. Rubin petitions the court for a fifteen minute recess. The court cannot grant it. Nor ten minutes. Nor five—

Travers has rushed in again. There is more whispering.

"If the court please, I shall call my next witness," says Rubin, turning and pointing his finger dramatically to the rear of the room. "Lucy Wells!"

Lucy Wells walks in and down the aisle. She is modestly but becomingly dressed. Russell Evans is with her, but remains in the back of the room.

"I ask that she be sworn," continues Rubin, as Lucy takes the stand.

Two or three newspaper photographers start forward but are sent back by the Judge.

"Lucy Wells, have you ever seen me before in your life?" asks Rubin in a slow, tense voice.

"No, I never did."

Lucy confirms the story of Lewis Collins that she had spent the night with Collins, Jim Arthur and Virginia Ross in the hobo jungle; that they had gone bummin' to Chattanoogie; that the second night the Tulley boy joined them. Lewis Collins is brought in and identified. Virginia Ross is brought in and identified.

"She's her, right sho'. Tho' she's fleshened up some," says Lucy, as Virginia faces her.

"Now, you listen heah, yuh slutty!" shrieks Virginia, before Dade can reach her. "Yuh bet' stop yo' lyin', Lucy Wells, an' tell whut yuh oughta. . . ."

A man has stood up to shout that that Collins boy and Lucy Wells ain't fit tuh belong to the white race and oughta be strung up. There is much noise and confusion, punctuated by Rubin's demand that the court be cleared and the judge's effort to restore order.

Lucy continues her testimony with a denial that she was attacked. She was with Virginia all the time and saw no colored boy come near her.

"You swore at Cookesville that these five negras raped you. Didn't you?" demands Dade.

"I did. But I tol' that story 'cose Virginia frightened me. She said we'd be 'rested fo' crossin' the state line with men an' have to lay out a sentence in jail."

When she disappeared on February 21, Lucy testifies, she had gone to Chattanooga with a young feller she liked and who liked her; he wasn't any N.L.D.; she made up her mind to come and tell the truth because her heart was achin' for them negra kids; she bought the clothes she wears herself up No'th; a Christian minister had given her the money to come back and testify.

"You told the truth at Cookesville, and now you've decided for certain reasons . . . to come heah and lie and betray your own kin," shouts Dade.

"I lied theah in Cookesville 'cose I didn't know what it all meant. If I would've knowed them black boys was going tuh burn fo' my lies, I never woulda done it . . . but Virginia Ross, she . . ."

"Are you trying to say Mrs. Ross threatened you?"

"She frightened me, suh . . . an' she said, 'What do we keer 'bout niggers, Lucy, we don't keer if they put all niggers in jail.' She said that."

"I didn't ask you what she said."

"I thought yuh wanted to know, suh. . . ."

There is excitement now at the reporters' table, the newsmen scribbling frantically and sending out their messages. As Dade goes back to his table he is handed a bunch of telegrams. He reads a few and tears them up in anger. With a restatement of Lucy's denials the defense rests.

In the presentation of arguments Slade is to lead for the state, followed by Dade. General Cheney will lead off for the defense and Rubin will close.

The Slade statement is florid and impassioned, largely an attack upon the interference of the Jews from the North—this Collinsky with his New York clothes. In another week Rokoff would have had him peddlin' goods with a pack on his back. It was the N.L.D. who brought in Lucy Wells and bought her soul. This Lucy Wells couldn't tell all that happened in New York because part of it was in the Jew language. And why did the Supreme Co't reverse the decision? Because these Communists threatened the jedges' lives with bombs an' poison!

"Gentlemen of the jury, don't you know that these defense witnesses are all bo't and paid fo'? Oh, my friends, may the Lo'd have mercy on the soul of Lucy Wells."

The uproar in the courtroom impels Rubin again to move a mistrial on the ground that the solicitor has made open appeals to "religious prejudice, bigotry and local sectionalism." The motion is denied. Slade continues to his peroration:

"Gentlemen of the jury, tell 'em, tell 'em that Southern justice cannot be bought an' sold with Jew money from New York!"

The court rules out the statement about Jew money, but again denies the motion for a mistrial.

General Cheney's plea is from one Southerner to another for fair play for the negra boy on trial. "Gentlemen, I am a Baptist and a Democrat and as the Lo'd is above me I am certain this heah boy is innocent," says the General.

Rubin would put off his summation until the next day, with the Judge's permission, but the request is denied. The county cannot afford unnecessary delays.

Slowly and quietly Rubin begins his plea. It shall be to the reason of the jury as logical, intelligent humans to give "this poor scrap of colored humanity a square deal." The appeal of the prosecution was in effect an appeal to the jury to come on and whip this Jew from New York. A hangman's speech. There had been no talk of that kind when the country needed soldiers, and Jew and Gentile alike braved Flanders Fields.

There have been threats and warnings against this Jew from New York, but he is not frightened. Let the mobs take him if they will. "Life is only an incident in the Creator's scheme of things and if I can contribute my little bit to see that justice is served, then my humble usefulness will be fulfilled," the attorney says.

He reviews the evidence of Virginia Ross and its contradictions and evidences of perjury. It is all a contemptible, lying frame-up on its face. Lucy Wells had told the truth because her child's heart could no longer bear the awful thought of sending an innocent boy to the chair.

"No, Lucy Wells didn't betray you people of the South. She wants to save you from committing a legal lynching," warns Rubin.

How silly is the talk of clothes and money. No jury could believe that for a ten-dollar suit or a five-dollar dress these brave young people could be induced to risk shame and possible injury to testify as they had. He appeals to the jury's sympathy for the mother of Heywood Parsons, who stands tragically in the back of the room. Her skin is black, but she is a mother. Are they going to tear out her heart? Are they going to strap her son into the electric chair and fry him, scorch him, burn him alive, "then cut out his insides in an autopsy and finally throw back his charred and mutilated corpse into his mother's waiting arms on the sole, lying miserable testimony of a *whore?"*

"Gentlemen of the jury," concludes Attorney Rubin, as a stillness comes upon the restless crowd; "you have been chosen as intelligent, reasoning men. You cannot have any prejudices, any hates, any preconceived ideas on this case. You are to judge it only on its merits and on the evidence. Consider carefully and well, before you take on your souls and consciences, the awful crime of convicting an innocent man. An innocent boy though his skin is black. Remember that when we, in times of need and doubt, call upon our Maker to help us, we do not call in vain. The Almighty God above us does not ask if we are praying to a black man's God or to a Jewish God. No. He listens to all his children with the same compassion and generosity, and so I ask you to join with me in common prayer. . . . (*Lifts up his arms, and with trembling tired voice.*) "Our Father, which art in Heaven, hallowed be Thy name, Thy Kingdom come. Thy will be done on earth as it is in Heaven. Give us this day our daily bread and forgive us our trespasses, even as we forgive those who trespass against us. And lead us not into temptation, but deliver us from evil. Amen."

Rubin has nodded to the jury and the Judge and returned to his seat, exhausted.

Dade, nervous, tense and rather shrill, takes his place before the jury. He, too, wants a verdict on the merits of the case and not on racial prejudice. A verdict of death in the electric chair for the rape of Virginia Ross.

Dade is no murderer. He does not have to have people come down theah to tell him the right thing to do. If he thought these negras were innocent he would dismiss all the indictments. If his daddy, sittin' on the bench of the Supreme Co't of the state had thought them innocent he would not have written the majority opinion against a new trial.

"Two thousand yeahs ago our Lo'd was sold out by Judas fo' a few dirty pieces of silver," shouts Dade, with waving arms, "but Lucy Wells did it fo' a gray coat. And who bought Lewis Collins's clothes? Who paid his way heah? To lie and swear falsely? Who? I leave it to your own imaginations, gentlemen. Remember this, that we cannot, we must not permit this fiendish criminal theah to go free. You yourselves know what that would mean. It would mean, *theah would be no holdin' 'em down anymo'*. Your wives', your sisters', your daughters' very lives and honor are at stake. And therefore, gentlemen, I ask, nay, I demand that this horrible fiend, this rapist die for his terrible crime he and his cronies committed on the white body of Virginia Ross. I demand the highest penalty—Death."

The Judge's charge is brief. Let the jury remember it is trying only one thing—"Whether or not this defendant forcibly ravished this woman. We, the white race, must be just to our colored brethren," he preaches.

"The charge is rape and the penalty must be fixed by yourselves. The minimum is ten years in prison and the maximum is death by electrocution. If the evidence shows you he is innocent, then you must acquit him. If guilty, you will fix a penalty."

The jury has passed into the jury room. The crowd is silently impressed. Suddenly, from the jury room, there is a sound of loud laughter, raucous and decisive. Rubin has turned, wonderingly. An expression of mixed astonishment and dismay crosses his face. He rises slowly to his feet and addresses the court—

RUBIN—If the court please . . . I have seen and heard of many strange and crazy things in my time, but I have never heard of anything like that . . . in there. (*He gestures toward jury room.*) But I'm not through yet. Let them laugh . . . let 'em laugh their heads off . . . this case isn't ended yet. . . .

ROKOFF (*rises and stands at* RUBIN'S *side*)—No . . . and our fight isn't ended either. . . .

JUDGE (*rapping his gavel*)—This . . . this is out of order. . . .

ROKOFF (*continuing over the interruption*)—You have the jurisdiction to stop us in this court . . . but there are hundreds of thousands of men and women meeting in a thousand cities of the world in mass protest against the oppression and ownership of man by man . . . and over them, you have no jurisdiction. . . .

RUBIN (*inspired and fired by* ROKOFF)—No . . . we're not finished. We're only beginning. I don't care how many times you try to kill this negro boy . . . I'll go with Joe Rokoff to the Supreme Court up in Washington and back here again, and Washington and back again . . . if I have to do it in a wheelchair . . . and if I do nothing else in my life, I'll make the fair name of this state stink to high heaven with its lynch justice . . . these boys, *they shall not die!* (*The laughter from the jury room dies down. Court and audience stare at him with eyes and mouths agape. . . .*)

THE CURTAIN FALLS

HER MASTER'S VOICE

A Comedy in Three Acts

By Clare Kummer

ADDED interest attached to the production of "Her Master's Voice" in late October. It was the second Clare Kummer comedy of the season and the first, a tenuous trifle called "Amourette," had not turned out well. What, demanded numerous experienced playgoers, had become of the Clare Kummer of other and brighter days? What had happened to the gifted author of "A Successful Calamity" and "Good Gracious Annabelle"?

This Miss Kummer, it transpired, had been so occupied with the second play she had paid little attention to the first, which was only a warmed-over vaudeville skit called "The Choir Singer" anyway. She came back with a flutter that was practically a rush with "Her Master's Voice" and found herself gleefully returned to those newspaper columns devoted to extolling the more popular playwrights.

"Her Master's Voice" also performed a second service for the theatre by bringing home from Hollywood three popular players who had been away a considerable time. These included Roland Young and Laura Hope Crews, the stars, and Elizabeth Patterson, specialist in flat-chested females. It was Mr. Young's first Broadway appearance since he had played in "The Queen's Husband" in 1929, and the first part Miss Crews had played in the East since "Olympia" was produced at the Empire with Fay Compton, the English actress, in the cast.

"Her Master's Voice" is written with many graceful twists of dialogue and many revealing bits of character observation. These are common virtues of the Kummer equipment when she is in her livelier and more inventive mood.

The Ned Farrar living room in Homewood, N. J., where the comedy begins, is "tastefully but inexpensively furnished." On this particular evening in September Queena Farrar is seated at a baby grand piano "which belonged to Queena before she married Ned" singing something from "La Bohème" in a "rather anxious voice." Queena "is an attractive, rather frail young creature with an air of daintiness, almost smartness. Over her dress she wears a pink rubber apron."

As Queena's light soprano reaches determinedly for a high note there is a slight crash of glass in the kitchen, bringing the aria temporarily to an end. Queena's mother, Mrs. Martin, frequently subject to sympathetic nerve attacks when her daughter practices, has dropped a glass. Fortunately, mother is able to report, it was cracked anyway.

Mrs. Martin, a thin, acidulous but well-meaning and generally kindly person, is induced finally to leave the dishes, of which there is still a great stack. The fact that soap flakes are ruining her hands, coupled with her daughter's suggestion, convinces her she should rest a bit.

The sight of Queena in a rubber apron is always distressing to Mrs. Martin. When she thinks of what Queena might have had! Literally everything! And to see her now wearing linoleum—

The Farrar children are at a neighbor's and are to stay the night. That also is a cause of concern to their grandmother. Also she is none too well pleased at a turn in the weather that has brought summer back again, and with it a flock of mosquitoes. It may be too late for mosquitoes, as Queena says, but if it is, insists Mrs. Martin, it is a pity the mosquitoes don't know it.

A radio is playing across the way. Playing a familiar song of the moment—"Only With You." Queena used to sing that. Queena is joining in the refrain now, singing softly as though to herself:

"Dreams that I know—fill my heart again—
Songs that were dear so long ago—"

"Go on, Queena," urges Mrs. Martin. "I haven't heard you sing that in years." And Queena goes on to finish the chorus—

"Long to be sung again—for love is young again—
For love is young again—only with you!"

"The first time I heard that was in Venice," muses Queena; "on a June night—in a gondola with Ned!"

"I just can't imagine Ned in a gondola," protests Mrs. Martin.

QUEENA—He was wonderful. That's how it all started, Mamma—evenings in a gondola with Ned. It seems funny to think I was ever there.

MRS. MARTIN—It must seem funny to Aunt Min, if she ever thinks of it. The money she spent on your voice—and then to have you settle down in this God-forsaken place—married to a man that can't even—

QUEENA (*bristling*)—Can't even what, Mamma?

MRS. MARTIN (*thinking better of it*)—Come home to dinner—on time.

QUEENA—Lots of men are too busy to come home to dinner on time. . . . And I don't see that this place is so much more God-forsaken than any other.

MRS. MARTIN—Perhaps not. Maybe He's forsaken them all.

QUEENA (*opening envelope*)—I had a letter from Aunt Min this morning.

MRS. MARTIN (*anxiously*)—Why didn't you tell me?

QUEENA—I didn't know you'd written to her—what did you say?

MRS. MARTIN (*troubled*)—What does she say I said?

QUEENA—Did you tell her I was unhappy with Ned?

MRS. MARTIN—No, I didn't. . . . I said you looked peaked and you do. . . . I thought it would be so nice if she asked you to come and make a little visit.

QUEENA—If she wanted me she'd have asked me, Mamma . . . without anyone's suggesting it.

MRS. MARTIN—What's that, Queena?

QUEENA—It's a bill from the Country Club.

MRS. MARTIN—Mercy, I don't see how you can afford to belong to a country club.

QUEENA—We can't. Ned thought we'd meet the nice people of Homewood there—but now he's met them he says he'd rather read a good book.

MRS. MARTIN—Probably hasn't paid his dues since he joined. Has he asked Mr. Pearsall for a raise yet?

QUEENA—I don't know. It isn't a very good time to ask for it.

MRS. MARTIN—It's just as good a time as there ever will be. Does he expect you to go on forever like this, without any servants, and not a stitch of clothing—a girl that had everything—and could have married a rich man and had more?

QUEENA—Oh, Mamma, please. . . .

MRS. MARTIN (*her indignation rising*)—He just doesn't seem to care. Doesn't he ever worry about the future? What does he think he's going to do for his children? Hasn't Eddie got to go to college . . . and Baby to a finishing school?

QUEENA—But we don't have to think about that now, Mamma.

MRS. MARTIN—Of course you do! Why, you have to apply to

Dr. Powys's School for Boys as soon as the child is born!

QUEENA—Then it's too late.

MRS. MARTIN—If Ned realized what his position is, and was real depressed for once, he might get somewhere.

QUEENA (*hearing footsteps*)—He *has,* Mamma, he's got *home* —so please—

Ned Farrar is carrying a large typewriter under one arm and a zipper bag filled with his office papers which he hastily sets down just inside the door. "He is somewhat exhausted, as he has carried these from the station." He is a smallish man with a normally serious, all but forbidding expression of preoccupation, through which an engaging smile breaks when urged.

It is nearly eight o'clock and Ned has had no dinner. The fact that he has brought his typewriter home does, even as Queena suspects, indicate that he has lost his job and he is not particularly happy about that.

Still, Ned has nothing to reproach himself for. He had followed family instructions and asked for a raise.

"I told Mr. Pearsall I thought I was worth more," Ned explains. "He said he did, too—and as he couldn't give it to me I'd better get it from someone else."

"Oh, Ned, won't he take you back—if you say you're not worth more—say you're not worth anything?"

"We'll never know. It wasn't a very good job anyway—I only made just enough for us not to get along on." On second thought he adds: "I can get something just as bad—maybe worse—"

The news is pretty hard on Queena. To have this happen on top of everything else. Ned doesn't seem to care, though he promises he will try to feel worse as soon as he feels a little better. Queena feels that everything lovely has gone out of her life—all the romance is gone. She has depended so long on faith and now even that has failed her.

Ned has an idea that being fired is going to help. Having had a bad job that took all his time he never had time to look for a good one. And he hopes Queena won't insist on telling her mother—not before morning anyway.

Mrs. Martin has brought some dinner for Ned and is a little surprised to find him with his arm about Queena, comforting her. "I haven't seen you with your arm around her since I came," protests Mrs. Martin.

"You have no idea what goes on when you're not looking, Mrs. Martin," replies Ned.

Mrs. Martin has noticed the typewriter and would know about that. She also decides the zipper bag is the one Aunt Min had given her, and before they know it she has zipped it open and found it stuffed with Ned's office trinkets including a bottle.

The bottle is a surprise, even to Ned. It is a bottle of champagne. Piper Heidseck 1914, no less.

"But, Ned, who could have put it there without your knowing it?" demands Queena.

"God!" promptly decides Ned. "Put it on ice!"

Now Ned has discovered the kitchen stacked with dirty dishes. The children, it appears, have had a party. It was young Ned's birthday and both his parents had forgotten it.

"And who remembered it?" asks Ned.

"Mamma," answers Queena. "I didn't have any presents for him, but I let him wash the Nellis's dog in the bathtub. He said he'd rather do that than anything."

Queena has gone into the kitchen to get a start on the dishes when Mrs. Martin finds a note in the straw wrapper of the champagne. Ned takes it from her and reads:

" 'Mr. Pearsall is a dirty s-k-u-n-ch . . . skunch.' . . . Must be a Russian word. . . . Oh, skunk! Of course, 'Mr. Pearsall is a dirty skunk. . . . Yours truly, Bert.' Well, bless her heart!"

The champagne, it transpires, is from a woman, which excites Mrs. Martin quite a bit. Ned does not know whether or not she is a pretty woman because he has never seen her dressed. Which excites Mrs. Martin a little more. "Bert" is the scrubwoman at the office. Her husband is a waiter and brings home a lot of champagne.

Queena thinks they will have to tell Mrs. Martin what has happened to Ned, but Mrs. Martin, having put two and two together, knows already. She is even a little resentful that Ned was trying to keep the bad news from her. After all whom should he tell, if not her and Queena?

In the excitement Ned is convinced that this is the time to celebrate. And with champagne. Even if it is warm champagne—they need it and they need it now.

Mrs. Martin is quick to find some jelly glasses. It is no time for small glasses. And because the wine is warm she thinks it would be just as well if they drank it right down.

"What shall we drink to?" asks Queena, smiling.

"My baby!" promptly answers mother.

"Why not drink to having another bottle sometime?" demands Ned, trying to avoid sentiment. . . . "Well, here's to better days, better nights, better jelly, better everything. . . . And now, as a ruined man I want to congratulate you both—you're behaving splendidly."

"Well, what's the matter with the way you're behaving?" demands Mrs. Martin.

"I don't know," admits Ned good-naturedly. "Something, I suppose, or it's most unusual."

It is Queena's suggestion that now that Ned has a free day or two they might get a motor car and take mother for a drive. Mother would like awfully to go, especially if she could be driven through the estate of a Mr. Twilling, for whom Ned formerly worked.

Ned is for the ride, but not through the Twilling estate. There had been certain misunderstandings when Ned quit Twilling to marry Queena. Those were the days—when Queena and Ned and Twilling were all in Europe, and Ned and Queena were dancing the nights away and being very much in love. They do quite a wild dance now, as a sample. And then suddenly remember that Ned has been fired and it is no time for such happy outbursts.

Something naturally will have to be done. Mrs. Martin is all for Queena's singing for Mr. Twilling, even if he doesn't like Ned. Mr. Twilling is the head of the whole Radio Realm thing—and Queena's voice is just as good as it ever was. To test that statement Queena sings "Only With You" again and breaks again on the high note.

The resulting discussion takes in Ned's alleged disapproval and discouragement of Queena's singing. He was, he admits, irritated at the familiar habits of some of her singing teachers in Europe. He never did approve of their pawing, even if they were merely giving Queena instructions in breath control. But he never wanted Queena to give up her singing. She gave it up because Aunt Min cut off the allowance that was paying for the $12 an hour lessons, and Ned thinks Aunt Min was pretty damned mean.

As for Mr. Twilling, Ned doesn't think that Twilling would like Queena's voice either. Twilling doesn't like good singing. He likes to hear himself sing. He even liked to hear Ned sing.

"Good-by my beautiful voice," sighs Queena.

"Queena, do you want to kill me?" plaintively inquires Mrs. Martin.

NED—No. I'm the one who wants to kill, because I'm responsible!

QUEENA—Oh, you're cruel! But no one is to blame. No one but—myself.

NED (*seizing* QUEENA *by the wrist*)—Now, you listen to me—

MRS. MARTIN—Ned, don't you touch Queena!

NED—And *you* listen to me,—for once I'm going to have the floor! (QUEENA *gives a quick pull at her wrist and it seems for a moment as though* NED *would be precipitated on the floor, but he recovers himself and keeps his hold on* QUEENA.)

MRS. MARTIN—Let go of my child, you're hurting her!

QUEENA—No, Mamma, he's not.

NED—Suppose I was to tell you that Twilling thought I had a beautiful voice—he wanted *me* to sing!

MRS. MARTIN—I don't believe it! (NED *plunges toward the piano.*)

QUEENA (*frightened*)—Don't, Ned—please don't! (NED *begins to play wildly on the piano and sing.*)

NED—

"Now on my tongue again—
Long to be sung again—
For Love is *young* again!"

MRS. MARTIN (*as* QUEENA *gives a wail of surprise and woe*)—Queena, come upstairs—come right up and leave him! (*They exit hurriedly up the stairs,* QUEENA *sobbing.*)

NED (*melodramatically*)—"For Love is young again!" (*Stops suddenly, crashes keys.*) Damn! (*Rises wearily; removes coat, goes to the pantry; he comes back wearing* QUEENA'S *apron. He brings in the garbage pail.* MRS. MARTIN *appears on the stairs. She comes down softly.*)

MRS. MARTIN—Ned!

NED—What is it?

MRS. MARTIN—I've given Queena a sleeping powder and I'm going to take one myself.

NED—Good! I hope you enjoy yourselves.

MRS. MARTIN (*looking at the pink apron*)—What are you doing in that apron?

NED—Dishes.

MRS. MARTIN—Don't, Ned. Leave them until morning. (*As he goes—softly.*) Ned—wait a minute. I want to speak to you. (*Confidentially.*) I wouldn't say this to Queena—but I think there is something in your voice, and I really believe, Ned, if Mr. Twilling feels the way you say he does you ought to see him.

NED—Mr. Twilling and I are not speaking.

MRS. MARTIN—Well, that wouldn't prevent your singing for him. Maybe you're a crooner without knowing it.

NED—A what?

MRS. MARTIN—I mean it—you may be a born "crooner"—You know what they get!

NED—I know what they ought to get.

MRS. MARTIN—Well, it was just an idea, Ned.

NED—Yes, don't have any more. . . .

MRS. MARTIN—Good night, Ned. . . . (*Starts off up the stairs.*) Oh! (*Turning again.*) Will you telephone the Nellises not to come?

NED—All right— (*She goes.* NED *goes to phone.*) Two-four-four.

There is a knock at the door. A moment later Craddock has entered. "He is an important-looking, stout chauffeur in uniform."

Craddock, whose manner is rather insolent, has been looking for the Farrars' number. He still hasn't seen it, but being told that this is it he promptly retires.

Ned has completed his phone message to John Nellis about the bridge being off, and has dived rather desperately into the job of cleaning the table. He has brought in the garbage pail and is dumping the remains of his dinner into it when Aunt Min appears in the doorway. "She sweeps in with all the authority of a rich relative—her eyes seem to take in the entire room at a glance, especially the garbage pail which Ned sets under the table, at once. Though she is older than Mrs. Martin she looks younger. Her face is fresh and attractive. Her manner is aggressive. Her motor coat and smart little hat of the latest fashion."

"Is Mrs. Farrar at home? I'm her aunt, Mrs. Stickney," says Aunt Min.

"Oh! Are you?" gasps Ned, a bit horrified.

AUNT MIN—I believe I'm expected. I sent a telegram yesterday saying I was coming.

NED—Did you? I'm sure they didn't get it—for Mrs. Farrar is out. And I'm sure she'd have been in if she'd known you were coming.

AUNT MIN—And where is Mrs. Martin? Is she out, too?

NED—Well, in a way she is. She's taken a sleeping powder and gone to bed.

AUNT MIN—I'm late, but if she had to take a sleeping powder she might have sat up for me, I should think.

NED—Oh, she would have—I'm sure she would.

AUNT MIN—I'm late because my chauffeur tried to turn around in the tunnel—it delayed us though no one was hurt.

NED—Excuse me, but why did he want to turn around in the tunnel?

AUNT MIN—He's nearly sixty. He decided it would be better to take the ferry. We passed a place in the village that said "Shore dinners and rooms to rent." A place called the Hummocks—do you think it's all right?

NED—For you?

AUNT MIN (*looking at him sharply*)—For him—I expected to stay here.

NED—Oh!

AUNT MIN—Is there a spare room?

NED—Yes—but Mrs. Martin has it.

AUNT MIN—Then there isn't a room for me.

NED—Well, there's the children's room.

AUNT MIN—I couldn't sleep with children!

NED—They're not in it.

AUNT MIN—Where are they?

NED—They're staying out all night. . . .

AUNT MIN—What?

NED—With friends across the street.

AUNT MIN—Is Mr. Farrar out with Mrs. Farrar?

NED—No . . . he's not . . . but he won't be home till late.

AUNT MIN (*suspiciously*)—I believe they did get my telegram. . . . It's just the welcome I might have expected in Mr. Farrar's house.

NED—I'm sure they didn't know you were coming. Only tonight I heard Mrs. Martin talking about you . . . Mrs. Farrar too. . . .

AUNT MIN—Talking about me—and what were they saying?

NED—Just how good you'd been to them . . . and what a pity it was you couldn't forgive Mrs. Farrar . . . for marrying . . . Mr. Farrar.

Craddock has brought in Aunt Min's suitcase and been sent with it to the children's room. Craddock has also been assigned to an inn for the night. And now Aunt Min thinks she could stand a little something to eat—a sandwich, or something—or she might take one of the meat cakes—

Ned has sliced a biscuit for Aunt Min and fixed her a sandwich. He has even got out the family's "hysterics" brandy and poured a little on some ice for her. Aunt Min is quite impressed.

"Sit down," she says. "You're tired, and I want to have a little talk with you. When people who work for us are kind and respectable we can take liberties for they won't be misunderstood. . . . There's no reason why you shouldn't sit down. . . ."

"Thank you." And he sits, a little uncomfortably, on the edge of a stool.

Aunt Min had heard someone singing as she drove by the house. If it were Ned (whom she addresses as George, having heard Craddock use that name) if it were Ned he has a really very nice voice. He might easily do something with his voice. And does Mrs. Farrar sing any at all now?

"George" can't really say as to that. He is never there in the daytime. He just gives the Farrars his evenings. He works days in the city, but he is thinking now of staying on in the country for awhile.

Have the Farrars a motor? Oh, no. Mr. Farrar walks to the train. At least he walks when he doesn't run. Tonight? Well, tonight "George" thinks Mr. Farrar is probably at a banquet. He had just lost his job and he was probably celebrating.

Aunt Min is not surprised. Farrar had had his chance, as everyone has, and he had not taken it.

"Sometimes I'm sorry for Mr. Farrar . . . because I know how he worries about Mrs. Farrar and the children," ventures Ned.

"He should have started worrying before he had things to worry about," snaps Aunt Min.

"Yes—but does anyone?"

AUNT MIN—Not usually . . . that's the trouble. . . . I don't suppose they'll be able to afford having you . . . if he's lost his position.

NED—Oh, well, I don't cost much. . . . I'll give them my evenings until I get a job. (*Smiling a little.*)

AUNT MIN (*who has taken an extraordinary liking to* GEORGE) —Well, I must say that's very nice of you. . . . Do you cut grass?

NED—Oh, yes.

AUNT MIN—And you're a good houseman?

NED—Well—I don't know how good I am!

AUNT MIN—I haven't a houseman at Dewellyn. . . . I think perhaps I'm making a mistake. . . . If I could find the right one

I would seriously consider it.

NED—Yes . . . it's a good idea to have a man in the house. . . . People think he might be strong or a good shot or something; even if he isn't.

AUNT MIN (*looking at him*)—Exactly. . . .

NED—Yes! . . . Will you have a little more brandy?

AUNT MIN (*firmly*)—No. Well, just a little bit. I don't think Mrs. Farrar will need it, and it isn't good for Mrs. Martin, her heart is too weak!

NED—Excuse me . . . but why won't Mrs. Farrar need it?

AUNT MIN—I'm going to take her away with me for a visit.

NED—Oh . . . does she know?

AUNT MIN—Not yet! (*Rising.*) Well, that was very nice and I feel much better! . . . I think I'll go to bed.

NED—Let me get some clean sheets and pillow cases. . . . (*Dashes into closet, returns with laundry in a paper package.*)

AUNT MIN—Just give them to me. . . . I'll take them up with me. . . . You must get on with your work here. (NED *extracts two sheets and two pillow cases from the package.*)

NED—Are you sure you can do it?

AUNT MIN—Make a bed? Certainly. I should hope so—good night—and I want you to take this— (*Opens her handbag.*)

NED—Oh, I couldn't really. . . .

AUNT MIN (*taking bill from her purse*)—Certainly you must—and I may not see you tomorrow—I'm leaving early in the morning—

NED (*embarrassed*)—No, really, I couldn't.

AUNT MIN—Nonsense! (*Presses the money into his hand.*) Good night!

NED—Do you think you can find it?

AUNT MIN—The bed? I should hope so. Good night.

NED—One dollar! . . . (*Comes down and picks up the brandy bottle, looks at it a moment. As he takes it to the sideboard and puts it in, starts to laugh and half sob with his head on the table.*)

The curtain falls.

Next morning, as Queena comes downstairs she is suddenly conscious of her mother staggering into the room laden with bundles. Discovering Aunt Min to be in the house Mrs. Martin has made a hurried trip to the village to get the things she knows Min will be asking for.

Queena can hardly believe her ears, but is much less excited than Mrs. Martin. It might be bad for Aunt Min to find Ned home and out of work. She thinks perhaps she can keep Ned in bed. Mrs. Martin is more distressed about the house than anything else. If she could only get the stairs vacuumed before Aunt Min sees them that would help. But the vacuum cleaner won't work and they have to call Ned after all.

Ned in his pajamas manages to fix the fuse that is blown out, but he is not much good at answering their questions about Aunt Min. There is nothing to tell. Aunt Min had come; he had told her they were both out (and so they were, with sleeping powders); he had given Aunt Min the children's room together with clean linen, and he had fed her meat cakes and brandy.

Aunt Min's contribution to the news, Ned reports, was that she was going to take Queena away with her for a long visit. With an excited cry of "She's forgiven us! Aunt Min's forgiven us!" Mrs. Martin is about to faint, probably would faint if Ned had not remembered that there wasn't enough brandy left for a faint. Queena manages finally to get her mother out on the porch and Ned takes up the vacuuming of the stairs. He is pretty mad about the excitement Aunt Min has stirred up and about the way Queena and her mother cringe before her.

"Now, Ned—please don't say anything against Aunt Min," Queena calls from her dusting. "She's been very good to us."

"Us?"

"Mamma and me."

NED (*going to* QUEENA)—Listen now, Queena, if you want to go with her, you go! Then I'll know a little better how I stand with you.

QUEENA—Oh, Ned, I haven't said I want to go—but it is wonderful to think Aunt Min wants me—maybe she really has—

NED—Really has what?

QUEENA—Forgiven us.

NED—Forgiven you for what?

QUEENA—For going against her judgment.

NED—For marrying me!

QUEENA—You must admit it hasn't turned out the way we thought it would— I was going on with my work— Well, I certainly have worked—but not at what I thought I was going to! Keeping house and having children. . . .

NED (*following her*)—Well, how did we know we were going to have children . . . we were a couple of kids ourselves . . . your mother ought to have taught you something.

QUEENA—How could she? Mamma doesn't know anything

herself. . . . (*Coaxingly.*) Now, Ned, please . . .

NED (*stiffly*)—Let me finish these stairs. . . . (*Goes to stairs.*) Is there anything else I can do?

QUEENA (*taking his tone*)—Could you put the laundry away? (*She goes into pantry.*)

NED (*angrily*)—Yes—I'll put it away! (*He gathers up laundry and throws it into the closet under the stairs. He starts the vacuum cleaner on the stairs. As he does so,* AUNT MIN *appears and he looks up and sees her. . . . She comes down the stairs.*)

AUNT MIN—Good morning. . . .

NED (*makes way for her to pass, apologetically*)—I'm awfully sorry. . . . The family know you came and they wanted to get a little cleaning done. I slept here last night and that's how it happens that I'm dressed like this. . . .

AUNT MIN—That's quite all right. . . . A very good way to dress when you're using that terrible thing.

NED—They didn't think you were coming down. . . . Wouldn't you rather have your breakfast in bed?

AUNT MIN—Mercy, no, I take a little walk before my breakfast.

NED—But you haven't had a bath— I mean there's plenty of hot water.

AUNT MIN—I don't have anything but a cold sponge in the morning. I was going to have a bath last night . . . but the tub was full of dog hairs.

NED—That's too bad. . . . Why didn't you tell me?

AUNT MIN—I thought you had enough to do!

NED—The children gave the dog across the street a bath. . . . They don't like to have their bathtub used. It's just a little white dog.

AUNT MIN—Well, the hairs in the tub weren't white.

NED—No. . . . The dog isn't white when he goes in, but he is when he comes out. . . . I . . . I do wish you'd go back to bed. . . . I mean I . . . wouldn't you rather have your breakfast upstairs?

AUNT MIN—Well, it will be less trouble if I have it down here. . . . Go right on with your work. . . . I'm not in any hurry. . . . I only want a cup of black coffee. . . . I'll have it when I come in. . . .

They have shooed Ned upstairs when Aunt Min comes back from her walk, and are prepared to greet her with family enthusiasm. Aunt Min is glad to see them too, and convinced, from the letter she had from her sister Ellie (Mrs. Martin) that it was about time she took a hand in straightening out whatever happens to need it. . . .

Queena has gone to fix breakfast for Aunt Min and Mrs. Martin is put through a stiff questioning by her sister. It is no use for Ellie to pretend that all is well with the Farrars, because it happens Aunt Min knows differently. She can see that Queena has lost all her color and she knows that Ned has lost his position. She had it all from the man who works for the Farrars.

There are several changes that should be instituted at once, Aunt Min feels. For one thing Ellie will have to stop drinking and taking sleeping powders. Then Min will take Queena with her to Dewellyn for a visit and a long rest cure before they even think of anything else. Ellie can stay on at the Farrars and look after the children. Aunt Min is prepared to help, although her obligations at the moment are fairly heavy. She is planning to drain the pond at Dewellyn and she has agreed to give a memorial window to the little church in Hagerstown where Grandpa was taken to church as a child.

"Grandpa didn't care for those things much," protests Mrs. Martin. "Don't you remember he said Henry Ellsworth's monument looked like a successful attempt to prevent resurrection?"

"Well, perhaps he feels differently about all those things now," answers Aunt Min.

Mrs. Martin has taken her breakfast upstairs and Aunt Min thinks perhaps she could eat a little something. When Queena has fixed a breakfast for her Aunt Min is ready to go forward with her other plans.

QUEENA—I've been wondering, Aunt Min, how you would feel about taking Mamma for a visit instead of me?

AUNT MIN—No, my dear. Your mother and I don't get on. It isn't that we dislike each other, really, but we do, almost when we're together.

QUEENA—Mamma is trying at times . . . but she doesn't mean to be.

AUNT MIN—I'm not so sure of that.

QUEENA—I'm awfully fond of her . . . more than I used to be, I think.

AUNT MIN—You're very affectionate, Queena, it's too bad. I suppose you're fond of your husband too.

QUEENA—Yes, I am.

AUNT MIN (*hopefully*)—But you're not happy. Only one piece of bacon, Queena. . . .

QUEENA—What makes you think I'm not happy?

AUNT MIN—Well, are you?

QUEENA—Well, I would be if—

AUNT MIN—You would be, if you were—exactly!!

QUEENA—No, I mean—if I weren't so worried about things.

AUNT MIN—But you won't be because while you're with me I'll make Ellie an allowance. It won't be large. Do you think two hundred dollars a month would do?

QUEENA—Two hundred dollars! It would be wonderful. . . . When would I have to decide, Aunt Min?

AUNT MIN—Right away. . . . I must leave by 11 o'clock.

QUEENA—Eleven! Oh, then I couldn't.

AUNT MIN—Why of course you could.

QUEENA—But the children. . . . I won't see them again . . . they've gone on a picnic.

AUNT MIN—Well, you don't want to say good-by to them; you couldn't do anything worse. . . . Now, I'll have my coffee. . . . This is your opportunity, Queena. Some people who make mistakes don't have another chance, remember that! I'll take it up and have it with your mother. (*She rises.*)

QUEENA (*rising*)—Oh, do you think you'd better? Mamma's so nervous this morning. (*Going to foot of stairs.*)

AUNT MIN (*on stairs*)—I have a great many things to say to her. She can wait and be nervous after I'm gone.

Ned has changed to trousers and sweater and is pretty worried when he talks with Queena again and finds her rather set on going with Aunt Min. He can't work up much enthusiasm about Queena's "renting" herself out for two hundred dollars a month that Aunt Min has agreed to settle on Mrs. Martin. And he cannot see how it is going to help to have Queena leave him just now, when he will probably be home for a few days, and will want someone to talk to. Of course there will be a lot of worrying to do, but they might set aside certain hours each day for that and still have time over to visit with each other and with the children.

Queena finds Ned quite hopeless. She is serious as she reminds him that Aunt Min has said she is going to have a second chance.

"A second chance to what?" Ned demands.

"To sing, I suppose."

"I wonder!"

QUEENA—Well, what do you think she meant?

NED—Perhaps she meant a second chance to get married!

QUEENA—Oh, no. . . . She wouldn't want me to do that again!

NED—Well, anyway, she wants to break up your family—your home.

QUEENA—Oh, no, she doesn't . . . it's much more likely to be broken up if I don't go. At least you can live on what Mamma will have while I'm gone.

NED—Who can? You don't suppose I'd touch a penny of it!

QUEENA—You won't have to touch it, but at least the rent will be paid and there will be something to eat in the house when you come home.

NED—Home from where?

QUEENA—From—from trying to get something to do.

NED—That's encouraging.

QUEENA (*going to him*)—Darling, I'm sorry if I said anything to hurt you . . . but you know it may be weeks before you find anything that you can do. . . . I mean that you want to do. . . .

NED—That's all right—you go—don't worry about me.

QUEENA—You're hard and bitter, because—you haven't had any breakfast!

NED—Yes, I have—I ate your mother's breakfast.

QUEENA—Oh, Ned!

NED—She didn't want it. . . . She said she couldn't eat after she got upstairs, thinking how damned mean Aunt Min has been to her. . . .

QUEENA—I don't believe she said that—it doesn't sound like Mamma.

NED—Well, it was what she meant, anyway. And your aunt did say a lot of mean things to her . . . and made her promise not to tell you.

QUEENA—What sort of things?

NED—Explaining why you couldn't expect anything from her . . . because she's spending her money on memorial windows and draining ponds.

QUEENA—Well, people have a right to spend their money on whatever they want to—I think!

NED—She never earned a cent in her life.

QUEENA—She married Mr. Stickney. He was a dreadful old man and she earned her money making him happy.

NED—So happy that he died! I suppose you think I'm the only thing standing in the way of your receiving the Stickney fortune—but I assure you she will leave it to the town pump anyway.

QUEENA (*indignantly*)—Ned—please . . .

NED—She'll take you abroad, I suppose. That will be the next thing. Back to Gaspani's—to be mauled and made into an opera singer.

QUEENA—Ned, listen . . . if I'd wanted to be an opera singer more than anything in the world I'd have stayed in Italy and studied—but I didn't—I married you.

NED—And now you're sorry, I suppose.

QUEENA—Yes, just this morning, I am!

NED (*startled*)—Sorry you married me?

QUEENA—Just this minute, Ned, because you're behaving very badly.

NED—Well, don't you want me to be behave badly? Do you want me to be pleased because you're leaving me?

QUEENA—I'm not leaving you.

NED—Then you're not going?

QUEENA—Yes—I am going! (*She starts for the stairs, runs quickly up and exits.*)

NED—Well, go then—damn it! I'll go too!

Ned has started for the stairs. At the foot of the stairs he runs into Aunt Min herself. She discourages his going in search of Mrs. Farrar. Mrs. Farrar is packing and should not be disturbed.

Aunt Min also has something more she would like to say to "George." It goes back to her suggestion that she could use a man at Dewellyn. Now that the Farrars are breaking up perhaps he would like to come to work for her and see how they get along.

"Well, I don't see how I could, exactly," Ned answers, nervously. ". . . I couldn't come anyway for—a few days—maybe a week. I have relatives."

"Too bad—but we all have," answers Aunt Min, confidently. "Just send me a wire—if you're coming. Send it collect."

Queena is a little doubtful when she is finally ready to go. She would back out now, if her mother were not there to urge her on.

She is in tears by the time Craddock comes for the bags, and they send them on without her. There is no doubt in Aunt Min's mind as to what Queena should do.

"She's doing the right thing for the first time in years!" says she.

"But, Min, after all it's a serious thing to separate husband and wife," protests Mrs. Martin, feeling a little doubtful herself.

"Don't be old-fashioned, Ellie. If she wants to come back she can. You have to get away from things to look at them—

don't you know that?"

"No, I don't know how you can see things if they are not there."

"There are things in the world that aren't material things, Ellie. I mean there are things in the world besides men—"

"Yes, but not much, Min."

Queena has come back with her eyes dried and they have maneuvered her out of the house before she can start a new protest. They can talk over her not going as they drive along, suggests Aunt Min.

"Good-by, Ellie," Min calls as they are leaving. "I hope you'll do the best you can . . . and try not to write for a week or two."

Ned is back from Nellises to find Queena really gone. He is plainly unhappy and he has got what Mrs. Martin discovers to be a queer look in his eye. In both eyes, in fact. It is a look, declares Ned, that means many things—"rage, determination, anxiety, hope, fear," and Mrs. Martin is a little frightened.

There is a knock at the door and the knocker, a moment later, is revealed to be none other than the frequently discussed Mr. Twilling—"a gentleman large, somewhat burly, dressed in flannels."

Mr. Twilling is there because he had heard Ned had called him up. Perhaps Ned wants to go back to work, now that his wife has left him and he has lost his job. Mr. Twilling had told Ned six years before what would happen. Now the news is all over town. Mr. Twilling had it indirectly from Mrs. Stickney's chauffeur, who had told the Twilling gardener during his stay at the Hummocks.

"So, Mrs. Stickney confides in her chauffeur," sneers Ned.

"All women confide in everybody, Ned, don't you know that?" answers Twilling. "They don't mean to, they don't even know they do. But as I said it's a good thing; your job wasn't worth holding down anyway. . . . You can't do anything like that. What a terrible secretary you were!"

"Oh, I thought you wanted me back."

TWILLING—I never found those papers you lost in Venice. Took them out in a gondola to look over, didn't you?

NED—A wind came up.

TWILLING—Of course it did. Ned, a wind will always come up. You must never have anything to do with papers. You don't belong in an office—you don't belong in a bank. Wherever you are you'll always be looking out the window. Why? . . .

Because you belong out the window—you belong outside the building— Well, how are you going to get out and make a living; and support your wife and three children?

NED—Two.

TWILLING—Two?

NED—I think so. Yes, of course!

TWILLING—Well, you'll probably make it three . . . and your wife to support in luxury . . . that's the only way to support them. Now, how are you going to do it?

NED—I sometimes wonder.

TWILLING (*smiling*)—How's your voice? (*Rising.*)

NED—Terrible!

TWILLING—Sing at all nowadays?

NED—No. No one asks me to, fortunately. But to get back to what we were saying?

TWILLING—What were we saying?

NED—I thought perhaps you could use me in some way. You think I'm a poor secretary—but at least I can keep your secrets. No one knew about your Radio Realm until you told them yourself—did they?

TWILLING—I'm not saying you haven't your good points. Let's talk about business later. (*Eyes twinkling.*) Ned, let's sing "Sweet and Low." (*Goes up to piano and strikes a key chord.*)

NED (*feebly*)—I couldn't, really!

TWILLING (*coming to* NED)—Come now, Ned. . . . (*He begins to sing the air of "Sweet and Low" in a husky but sweet voice:*)

"Sweet and Low—Sweet and Low—
Wind of the Western sea—
Blow, blow, breathe and blow—"

(*On "Blow, blow"* NED *reluctantly joins in.*)

NED—

"Blow, blow, breathe and blow—
Wind of the Western sea . . ."

(*As* NED *sings the air,* TWILLING'S *face takes on a beatific expression . . . he drops into the second part. Their voices harmonize as*

THE CURTAIN FALLS

ACT II

At Dewellyn, which is Aunt Min's country place in the Connecticut hills, the sleeping porch of Queena's room is screened and looks out upon a pretty country view. The furniture is wicker, the cushions attractive and there is a day bed and chaise longue for comfort.

Queena is occupying the day bed until she suddenly remembers that she has missed a part of her daily exercises. Then she jumps up in her dressing gown and begins a little violently to twist and turn and count.

Phœbe, Aunt Min's maid, "a comfortable, middle-aged maid, very tidy and sure of herself," breaks up the exercises by bringing in a tray of tea and biscuits. It is nearing sundown and Mrs. Stickney is still out riding with the new man, which is more or less irritating to Phœbe. Phœbe can't imagine what the neighbors will think. Especially as the new man is good-looking and evidently has "it."

Neither is Phœbe in favor of keeping Queena sleeping on the porch, now that the frosts have come. It may be all right to stay until her cure is finished, but not if she's likely to be finished first. But sleeping on the porch is Aunt Min's idea—and here's Aunt Min back from her ride, very smart and brisk in her riding suit and ever so enthusiastic about the gallop she has just had through the old Fogleby estate.

Aunt Min may be all warmed up from her ride, but Queena is still cold and thinks it would be better if she were to go into the house to sleep hereafter. She is not at all convinced that she has a nervous breakdown, whatever Aunt Min may think, and she knows the sleeping porch has become uncomfortably draughty.

With comparatively little urging Aunt Min would talk of the new man, whom Queena has not seen. "He peels an apple as I haven't had one peeled in years," Aunt Min admits. "You know I eat an apple every night before I go to bed and drink a glass of milk. . . . I think that's one reason why my skin keeps so fresh. Look at your mother— She's younger than I am and she looks ten years older."

"Poor mamma!" sighs Queena. "She's had a hard life, Aunt Min. . . . She hasn't been able to go to bed early with a man peeling apples for her. . . . She's sat up night after night with my babies."

Aunt Min—Well, that's her own fault. If she'd taken my advice and kept you in Italy you wouldn't have had any babies.

QUEENA—Why, they have more babies in Italy than we do.

AUNT MIN—Well, you wouldn't have had any, I hope, while I was paying for your singing lessons.

QUEENA—Aunt Min, I want to pay you back—every cent.

AUNT MIN—I wanted to develop what voice you had, Queena. I thought you'd be a good singer,—not a great one.

QUEENA—Oh, I had a lovely voice! Everyone said so.

AUNT MIN—Now, don't get excited, Queena. You had a very sweet voice; we all had sweet voices in the family—and I thought you might do something with yours. But you didn't . . . you had two babies instead . . . that was what you wanted.

QUEENA—I didn't. . . . I tried my best not to have them.

AUNT MIN—Well, we won't go into that. I don't see what you married for if you didn't want babies.

QUEENA—What have they to do with it? I married because I loved Ned. . . . I loved him, do you understand? *Loved* him!

AUNT MIN—Very well. I suppose you did. But that's all over now, and we won't talk about him. Because you know how I feel about a man who marries a woman he can't take care of.

QUEENA—He didn't know he couldn't take care of me. . . . He didn't know there were going to be four of me!

AUNT MIN—What do you mean—four of you?

QUEENA—Two babies and Mamma and me are four.

AUNT MIN—He thought Aunt Min would go right on supporting you . . . and he found he was mistaken.

QUEENA (*rising*)—Oh, he didn't! He didn't! Don't you know when people are in love they don't think? Merciful Heavens!

AUNT MIN—Well, they ought to. I don't know of any time when it's more important for them to think. In love! In foolishness!

QUEENA—Aunt Min, have you been in love, really in love?

AUNT MIN—Why, Queena, you talk as though I hadn't been married for years and years.

QUEENA—What has being married to do with being in love?

AUNT MIN—You've been reading French novels, Queena. . . . Mr. Stickney adored me! He built this house for me and showered me with fur coats up to the day he died!

QUEENA—But did you love him—when he was away did you long for him?

AUNT MIN—I didn't have to long for him. He was always here.

Queena is about convinced that she cannot stay with Aunt Min any longer. She is too homesick. But Aunt Min is sure she will feel differently as soon as she is feeling better. Then they will take up the matter of doing something with Queena's voice, even though Queena has not practiced in ages. One of the important men of WVY is in the village, and he has found some perfectly beautiful voices for radio that sound perfectly terrible.

Aunt Min has gone to the phone when suddenly a ladder appears at an opening where one of the screens has been left out. It is the new man coming up to fix the screen. Queena pops quickly back into bed, and sends Phœbe for Aunt Min's fur coat.

A moment later Ned Farrar has tossed a kit of tools into the porch and climbed in himself. Queena, completely amazed, is kneeling on the bed staring at him. It can't be that he is the new man Aunt Min has been talking about! But it seems that he is. He has come to fix the screen.

The whole thing started, Ned explains, the night he had given Aunt Min the meat cakes, and he doesn't propose stopping it now until he is ready. Aunt Min will not have the truth from him, nor will he let Queena tell. He is perfectly capable of handling Aunt Min.

How could he leave Mrs. Martin and the children? Well, there aren't any more children or Mrs. Martin. He has given them away. The Nellises, who had always wanted them, have taken the children, and Mr. Twilling has taken Mrs. Martin for his housekeeper.

"He didn't want a woman in the house—afraid he'd fall in love with her," explains Ned, tactfully; "but I talked to him a little about your mother and he decided she'd be just the thing."

Queena would go and see if it is Mrs. Martin who has telephoned, but Ned will not have that, either. Let Queena stay where she is. Mamma is all right, living at Castlecrest with Mr. Twilling. And the rest cure is evidently working for Queena or she would not have the strength now to be so perfectly frantic.

Queena explains again that she came only because of Ned's money problem, though she did think she might do something with her voice. As it has turned out the only thing she has got is a cold and she is miserably lonesome and uncomfortable sleeping out there on the porch. She nearly froze last night. And she doesn't think that more covers can completely remedy the situation.

"Aunt Min likes you," Queena reports, noting how handsome Ned looks in Craddock's riding clothes.

"I know it," admits Ned.

"Aunt Min's crazy about you, Ned."

"Is she?"

"The more she likes you the worse it will be when she finds out what you've done."

"Perhaps she won't find out until I've gone."

"Are you going? When?"

"Well, I have plans."

"What's going to happen to me?"

"I guess you'll have to choose between us."

"Can't you tell me what your plans are?"

"Not yet."

"You know, Ned, you don't seem to love me a bit."

"Well, I'll tell you about that—but not now."

Aunt Min has come back. It was Mrs. Martin on the phone and she is now in a station bus on her way over. As near as Aunt Min could understand the telephone conversation it seems that Mrs. Martin has been living with some man and is in a terrible state about it.

When Mrs. Martin arrives "looking amazingly well in a tailored traveling dress and becoming hat," she has a story to tell starting with the exciting information that Ned Farrar has disappeared. Before he went he had sent the children over to the Nellises and got her a position as Mr. Twilling's housekeeper. That experience was exciting. Mamma is practically breathless remembering all that has happened.

"Mamma, what is the matter?" demands Queena, apprehensively.

"Yes, Ellie, do come to the point," adds Aunt Min. "I never saw you looking better."

Mrs. Martin—That's partly what's the matter. This man is not the quiet, retiring old gentleman he seemed at all. . . . He's a sort of hypnotist I think. (*Sits on foot of bed.*) He sent for a dressmaker almost the first thing, and had her take my measure . . . said he liked a certain kind of house dress . . . but they weren't ordinary dresses at all. They were made of lovely taffeta—it must have cost three or four dollars a yard. Then he began to want me to have dinner with him. . . .

Aunt Min (*ominously*)—Hm—Hm!

Mrs. Martin—He sent to a shop in New York and had hats and suits sent out . . . this is one of them.

Aunt Min—Ellie, you're not wearing it!

Mrs. Martin—Yes, I am . . . this hat! And—(*takes off hat*) he had the barber come and bob my hair. . . .

QUEENA—Mamma!—Bobbed!

AUNT MIN—Go on, Ellie—get to the point, if there is any.

MRS. MARTIN—He took me to the movies nearly every night. You know he has a big car—like yours, Min—and last night, he asked me to marry him.

AUNT MIN—He must be crazy!

QUEENA—But, Mamma! You seem so changed! I suppose it's your hair.

AUNT MIN—Are you going to marry him, Ellie?

MRS. MARTIN—Why, of course not. . . . I wouldn't think of such a thing.

AUNT MIN—Well, what are you going to do? Here you sit in his clothes—I don't understand it.

MRS. MARTIN—I don't either. Of course he tells me all sorts of things to make it seem all right. He says his father knew Grandpa, Min, and cheated him out of a lot of money—so he really owes me much more than he'll ever be able to repay.

AUNT MIN—I don't believe it! No one could cheat Grandpa. He was a splendid business man. He could cheat anybody.

MRS. MARTIN—Then he laughs.

AUNT MIN—Weren't you afraid of him, Ellie?

MRS. MARTIN—Not exactly.

AUNT MIN—Well, you stay here tonight and we'll decide what's best to be done. You can sleep inside in Queena's room.

MRS. MARTIN—He's given me a lovely traveling case all fitted up with French enamel.

AUNT MIN—Did you bring it?

MRS. MARTIN—Yes.

AUNT MIN—But why did you take these things, Ellie?

MRS. MARTIN—I don't know. I seem to have lost all my ideas of—everything.

AUNT MIN—Well, you'd better get your ideas back at once, Ellie, I should say . . . if things haven't gone too far.

MRS. MARTIN—Well, of course, they've gone too far . . . why, I'm about the best dressed woman in town, and I certainly wasn't when I went to Castlecrest.

AUNT MIN—Castlecrest! What's that—a road house?

MRS. MARTIN—It's the Twilling estate—five hundred acres with bronze stags and artificial lakes all over it, Min.

AUNT MIN—Well, Ellie, I can't understand now why you accepted dresses and hats and bags from a man—

QUEENA—Why, they were pretty and she wanted them, Aunt Min.

AUNT MIN—But certainly a woman of your age, Ellie, isn't going to care enough about such things to be really tempted by them.

MRS. MARTIN—Well, I don't know—I don't feel as old as I did.

Aunt Min and Queena are not of the same mind regarding Mrs. Martin's adventure at Mr. Twilling's. Aunt Min is sure people must have talked. And they did. Mrs. Martin can vouch for that. The Nellises would not even speak to her until she had them over to dinner.

In Aunt Min's day girls were brought up not to accept presents from men, even if they did no more in return than keep house and cook an occasional flapjack for them. But, Queena points out, times have changed.

Mr. Twilling, Mrs. Martin reports further, is going to do something for Ned—if they can find him. At which moment Ned reappears at the head of the ladder and Mrs. Martin stands aghast on the verge of a faint.

"What's the matter, Ellie?" cries Aunt Min.

"Mamma's surprised to see George here," Queena hurriedly explains. "Mamma expected him to stay in Homewood with—with Ned. Didn't you, Mamma?" But Mamma has toppled over.

Ned takes charge of this situation. He knows what to do. Get the brandy. Mrs. Martin always needs it when she is like this.

Aunt Min hurries for the brandy. Ned explains quickly that he has been at Aunt Min's ever since he disappeared; that he took the job because of Queena; that he doesn't know whether or not Aunt Min is really sort of in love with him, as Queena charges, because he does not know how Aunt Min acts when she is in love.

"She rides with him—and he peels apples for her before she goes to bed," Queena reports to Mamma. "She says that's why she looks so much younger than you do. But she doesn't any more. . . . Ned, doesn't Mamma look sweet?"

"Yes, I guess so," Ned guesses. . . . "Have you left Mr. Twilling permanently?"

"Why, yes—that is, I think I have," Mrs. Martin admits, a little coyly. "He kept giving me things and last night he asked me to marry him—so I left the first thing this morning."

"I see."

"She couldn't stay after that—could she, Ned?"

"Why, I suppose not—unless she wanted to discuss it."

"Discuss what?"

"Marrying him."

Aunt Min is back with the brandy. Ellie is not sure she needs it now, but she takes a little to make sure. Then she takes Queena to see the new traveling case Mr. Twilling gave her with her initials on it. She couldn't send it back on account of the initials.

"George" has returned to his work on the broken screen. Aunt Min is greatly interested in his reactions to his job in general, and hopes that he likes whatever work it is he is doing outside.

"Thanks," says Ned. "It is awfully nice of you not to ask me what it is."

"Well, I suppose if you wanted to tell me you would."

NED—That's true. I appreciate your letting me use the old Buick.

AUNT MIN—How does it go?

NED—I don't know—but it does and I'm very grateful to you for letting me have so much time off.

AUNT MIN—I'm very glad to—if it turns out well.

NED (*thoughtfully*)—It may amount to a lot of money—if that means anything.

AUNT MIN (*seriously*)—It does, George—it's all very well to talk about money as though you despise it. I know a great many people do—but without it you can do nothing—you can't even buy a piece of soap. I suppose tramps don't mind that—but we do, don't we?

NED (*appearing to enter into the spirit of the conversation*)—You might not believe it, but if I don't have a shower in the morning I'm miserable for the whole day—for half an hour, anyway.

AUNT MIN (*interested*)—I don't take a shower myself. I like to sit comfortably in the bathtub—and I've always wondered if people taking a shower use soap.

NED—Not always.

AUNT MIN—Well, even water without soap is something.

NED—Yes, indeed. (*Looking at the screen.*) Well, I guess that's fixed. (*Rising.*)

AUNT MIN (*to detain him*)—Dr. Pounce is very much interested in you, George.

NED—Is he?

Aunt Min—He's very mysterious about it—but I think he has an idea—

Ned—He looked as though he was going to have one last time I saw him. (*A little restless.*)

Aunt Min—Did he tell you what it was?

Ned—No. He didn't have it while I was with him. (*Taking screen up to place it beside its proper place.*)

Aunt Min (*seeing he is about to go*)—You must be tired—sit down a minute. (Ned *sits on the stool of the chaise longue.*) That sunset was the finest I've ever seen on the pond, George.

Ned—Yes, it's a pretty pond. I think you're going to make a great mistake to drain it.

Aunt Min—Well, it's never been drained and I think it must need it. Then I'll have a nice grassy bank with benches on it that people can sit on.

Ned—It won't be nearly as pretty as the rushes. They're half the beauty of it. People sitting on benches won't turn such a nice color in the fall. (Aunt Min *looks at him a little mystified.* Ned *continues.*) And if you get a man with a dredge in that pond, you won't get him out very soon. I knew of a case—

Aunt Min—You did? What was it?

Ned—The man had a sort of little house on the dredge and he just lived on the pond for years. It's sort of like retiring, when a man gets a job like that.

Aunt Min—Mercy! I did think Mr. Bigelow was a little eager about doing it—and he's getting old.

Ned—It would certainly spoil the pond if he retired on it.

Aunt Min—Well, perhaps I'll have a bridle path made round it instead.

Ned (*rising*)—I think you'd get lots more out of it.

Queena has found Aunt Min's squirrel coat and is delighted to wear it. She is going to wear it even in bed. Unless Aunt Min will change with her. Aunt Min likes the porch. She always slept there until Queena needed the cure. Queena wishes she would sleep there again.

"I think it would do me good to be warm and comfortable inside, just for one night," pleads Queena.

Mrs. Martin—I don't think either of you ought to be out there. There's a chill in the air at night this time of year—and there's the pond, too.

Aunt Min—And what's the trouble with the pond, Ellie?

MRS. MARTIN—Well, I don't know, Min, aren't they supposed to give off a sort of damp something at night?

AUNT MIN—Miasma? No. Not a fresh, clean pond like this. The miasm depends on what's going on in the pond.

MRS. MARTIN—But how do you know what's going on there, Min?

AUNT MIN—The frogs and the fish take care of everything in this pond. They eat each other and that makes it nice for everybody.

QUEENA—The pond has nothing to do with it . . . it's just that the nights are cold—the crickets know it—they chirp so loud trying to pretend they don't—and I know it. . . .

AUNT MIN—Well, if you want to sleep in my room perhaps you'd better, Queena. I knew how it would be with your mother here. All my work to get you well will go for nothing, I suppose. For real appreciation and understanding we have to look outside our families, I guess! (*She goes.*)

MRS. MARTIN—What do you suppose she meant by that?

QUEENA—Ned!

The curtain lowers for a brief moment to indicate a lapse of time.

Midnight that night the sleeping porch is in darkness. Only the moon sends a ray of light across the bed. Aunt Min's fur coat is thrown over the chair in the corner. There is a sleeping figure in the bed.

Suddenly at the top of the ladder Ned appears. He quietly lets himself into the porch, moving tiptoe toward the bed as he takes off his overcoat. He is wearing pajamas. Softly turning down the covers he crawls in and confidently puts an arm around the sleeping woman in the bed.

"Darling—didn't you know I'd come to you," he whispers.

With a start Aunt Min sits bolt upright in bed. "George!!" is all she can say.

To which George, with a groan, replies helplessly: "Oh, my God!"

"Sh-h!" cautions Aunt Min. "George—you know I can't scream in my own house!"

"Oh, you don't have to," promises Ned, scrambling hurriedly out of bed.

"Sh-h!" repeats Aunt Min, pleadingly.

George is reaching for his coat, whispering that he will explain everything some other time, when he strikes a table and sends it crashing to the floor with a scattering of a china tray, several books and a basket of fruit. He ducks under the fur coat just as Mrs. Martin appears in the door in her night clothes.

"Min, what's the matter?" she demands.

"Nothing, Ellie. Go back to bed!" commands Aunt Min.

But Mrs. Martin will not go back to bed. She heard a sound like someone falling. She knows there must be a man somewhere around. She is sure she can see him even without her glasses crouching in the corner! She will turn on the light—

Aunt Min would stop that by reaching out and holding Mrs. Martin's hand, but the light is turned on. What Ellie sees in the corner is nothing but her fur coat, Aunt Min explains. She had thrown it on the chair herself. She had also tipped over the table herself when she got up to draw the curtain so the moonlight would not disturb her. She wishes Ellie would go back to bed! Which, with further protests, Ellie does.

"George, are you still there?" calls Aunt Min.

"I'm afraid so," answers Ned, coming out slowly from under the fur coat.

AUNT MIN—George, how did you get on the porch?

NED—Up the ladder.

AUNT MIN—Through the screen?

NED—Yes.

AUNT MIN—You left it—so you could get through?

NED—Yes. I think I'd better tell you everything.

AUNT MIN—No, just tell me one thing, George. Did you do this because of anything I said this afternoon?

NED—No—no—I came because you see—I thought—

AUNT MIN—Stop—don't tell me now—wait until tomorrow. I must be to blame in some way—I would rather think so.

NED—You don't understand—if you'll only let me—

AUNT MIN—Be careful going down the ladder—it wouldn't look well—

NED—For me to break my neck— I won't. (NED, *surprised, comes to her, seizes her hand with a little groan and kisses it. He goes.* AUNT MIN *sits looking after him, the moonlight shining on her face.*)

AUNT MIN—Go, George. Can you go quietly?

NED—Oh, God, I hope so.

The curtain falls.

Next morning Aunt Min is having her breakfast on the sleeping porch. Phœbe, finding the squirrel coat on the bed, is pleased to think her mistress had also found the porch a little cold during the night. Aunt Min would like to see George before he goes to the village, she tells Phœbe, and turns to greet Queena, who comes in, bright and fresh in a flannel suit.

In an exchange of morning pleasantries Queena reports having slept very well indeed inside. Aunt Min had slept very well outside, save that the moonlight had disturbed her a little. She got up in the night to pull the shades and tipped over the table—as Ellie has probably told Queena. It was too bad if Ellie's rest had been disturbed.

"Mamma has a way of going right back to sleep and forgetting everything that's happened in the morning," reports Queena.

"Really?" smiles Aunt Min. "Well, that's most encouraging. I mean, she can't be as nervous as she appears to be."

Ned has come in response to Aunt Min's summons. "His manner is very respectful and humble. He is pleased to see Queena, but he does not see her for long. Aunt Min would speak with George alone.

Aunt Min is puzzled about last night. She has gone over everything in her mind and still she cannot understand. Perhaps George had been drinking? George is sorry, but he really hadn't been drinking.

Aunt Min—You have seemed so trustworthy and reliable and superior—a man I could really take pleasure in being with. How could you have thought I would permit such a—such a—liberty?

Ned—I didn't think you would. I didn't think. I—

Aunt Min—I have been trying to remember what it was, George, that you said.

Ned—Please don't—

Aunt Min (*hesitating*)—You said, didn't I know you would come to me—

Ned—Did I?

Aunt Min (*courageously*)—I'm sure you did. You meant that you were under the impression that I expected—something of the kind.

Ned (*horrified*)—Oh, no! No! I'll tell you—I had been drinking. (*With assurance.*) I was very, very drunk—and that's why I did it. Then suddenly when you spoke, I realized where I was . . . and who you were . . . And what I was! What I really wasn't but what it looked as though I was. . . . I'm terribly, terribly sorry. I hope in time you can forget it—and me—and that it won't make you nervous about sleeping on porches for the rest of your life.

AUNT MIN (*after a moment*)—George, I can't believe you'd been drinking.

NED—I'm sorry. I was afraid you couldn't.

AUNT MIN—There has been, I won't deny, quite a little thrill to me in having you here.

NED—Thrill?

AUNT MIN—Yes. I didn't think about it, for I wouldn't encourage the feeling. I didn't think about it but I felt it. Now maybe you realized this and maybe you were deceived by it. You might have thought I did expect some—some—

NED—Insult? No—I didn't really.

AUNT MIN—But it wouldn't have been an insult to the kind of woman that perhaps you thought I was.

NED—No—I didn't think that—really.

AUNT MIN—Perhaps you didn't realize that you thought it. Perhaps you felt it without thinking—like my little thrill that I didn't allow myself to think about.

NED (*simply*)—You can be awfully sweet.

AUNT MIN (*almost weeping*)—I'm just trying to think of a way out.

NED—The door is the best way out for me. I'll—I'll write you.

Queena is back, surprised to find Ned still there. Surprised a moment later to hear him saying that he has a message from Mr. Farrar he would like to give her. Mr. Farrar wants Mrs. Farrar to know, reports Ned, that he had lost his position. He had been away from Homewood but he was going back and thought perhaps she might have some message for him.

Queena has no message for her husband, save that she will write him soon.

There is quite a chance, Ned quotes Mr. Farrar as saying, that he may be able to do much better than he had been doing and that it was possible Mrs. Farrar might go abroad and study if she wanted to, and have the children back, and her mother, and him.

"He's really thinking only of you," Ned tells Queena. "There is something quite heroic about what he is going to do."

"What's he going to do? Kill himself?" demands Aunt Min. "George, if you see Mrs. Farrar's husband I don't want you to encourage him about coming back . . . because I don't think she is going to."

"Excuse me," protests Ned, "but I don't understand exactly

what he's done to be deserted by everybody."

"He's failed in everything," declares Aunt Min, grasping for a thought and getting one, "and there just isn't time in the world to do that."

"That's right. That's why I have to go instantly," concludes Ned.

Aunt Min is very sorry to see George leave. He is, as she tells Queena, a man with as great a general knowledge of affairs as any she ever met. George, she is convinced, is pretty sure to amount to something.

"I've never asked him a question he couldn't answer," declares Aunt Min. "A remarkable man."

Mrs. Martin, making sure the situation is approachable, comes from a walk in the garden and is glad to have a word with Queena after Aunt Min has gone to answer a phone call.

Mrs. Martin, having made up her mind not to tell Queena, begins at the beginning with an account of the noise that awakened her in the night and the strange way Aunt Min's coat was acting—humped up and moving. There is only one person who could have been under that fur coat, and that was Ned.

A light breaks upon Queena. It was Ned! He had thought she was sleeping on the porch!

"Yes—but why didn't Aunt Min scream? That's what I want to know!" And Queena echoes: "Why didn't she?"

Aunt Min is back to report that Dr. Pounce has promised her a great surprise. It is just possible he has cured someone. The next thing to settle is what's to be done with Ellie. It probably would be best for her to take a furnished room. In Newark, perhaps. She could have her trunk sent on from Mr. Twilling's, and—

But Mrs. Martin doesn't want to take a room in Newark. She had rather go home and sit and wait until something happens. Which would probably mean going back to Mr. Twilling, as Aunt Min sees it.

"The damage is done, Ellie, it seems to me," says Aunt Min. "Now you must just realize that you can't do anything for yourself and adjust yourself to—circumstances."

QUEENA (*as* MRS. MARTIN *looks at her helplessly*)—I think she's done very well, Aunt Min. . . . After all, to have a man worth millions want to marry you . . .

AUNT MIN—Well, I don't know, Queena. But from all I can gather your mother has compromised herself with an old lunatic.

I don't see anything very desirable about that.

MRS. MARTIN—Compromised myself! I don't know what you mean, Min. There were no sleeping porches at Castlecrest—and no squirrel coats. . . .

QUEENA—Oh, Mamma!

AUNT MIN—What do you mean by that, Ellie?

MRS. MARTIN—You know perfectly well what I mean, Min.

AUNT MIN—Do you know what your mother means, Queena?

QUEENA (*anxiously*)—She doesn't mean anything, Aunt Min.

AUNT MIN—But you can't make remarks like that about porches and squirrel coats without some explanation.

MRS. MARTIN—Do you want me to explain?

AUNT MIN—I certainly do.

MRS. MARTIN—Very well, then, Min. . . . I'm talking about last night . . . about the man under the squirrel coat. . . . Mr. Twilling never got under a squirrel coat or anything of the sort.

AUNT MIN—Ellie, do you think I had a rendezvous with the man who was on the porch last night?

MRS. MARTIN—I don't know what you had, Min, but I can't understand why you didn't scream.

AUNT MIN—I had a reason, Ellie. He explained how he happened to be there, in a way—perfectly satisfactory to me, this morning.

MRS. MARTIN—This morning! My goodness, Min—you don't mean he waited until this morning to explain?

AUNT MIN (*severely*)—I don't mean that he "waited" at all, Ellie. But at least I don't have to explain anything in my own house, I should *hope*.

A telegram has come for Mrs. Martin. It is from Mr. Twilling and it reads: "Ellie, I want you to come home."

"It's from him—Murgatroyd!" Mrs. Martin is quite excited. "I just think I'll go, too," she adds.

In that case, Aunt Min decides, Ellie and Murgatroyd will have to be married, and married at Dewellyn. There is dignity at Dewellyn and Mrs. Martin should think of her position and her family, thinks Aunt Min.

The question is still being debated when Mr. Twilling himself arrives in the Dusenberg and is waiting outside to see if he can help Ellie down with her luggage. Aunt Min would send word by Phœbe that Mrs. Martin is having a nervous breakdown on the upper porch and cannot come down, but Mrs. Martin stops that.

"Tell him nothing of the kind, Phœbe," she snaps. "I haven't time to have a nervous breakdown. We're going through the White Mountains in the Dusenberg—to see the trees—on our honeymoon."

"Why, Ellie, you're shaking like a leaf . . . Ellie." Aunt Min is worried. "I'm afraid taking care of Grandpa was too much for you. You don't act like yourself."

"How do you know I don't? Maybe I'm acting like myself for the first time in years."

"Well, I hope not. Ellie—I always thought the women of our family could control their feelings—where men were concerned."

"Well, I've always thought we'd scream when the time came for it, Min, but I found I was wrong."

Queena has been talking with Mr. Twilling and is also quite excited. Twilling is not far behind her. He has come up for Ellie, fearing she might not come down if he didn't. Twilling has great news. It is about Mrs. Stickney's hired man, George. It seems Mr. Twilling had also hired George about the same time Mrs. Stickney did. Mr. Twilling hired George to sing and he is on the radio now, if they would like to hear him.

With trembling fingers Queena turns on the radio and Ned sings "Only With You" for them.

"You have been listening to Sylvester Silverton," intones the announcer as the song is finished. "Beginning next Friday at seven-thirty, Eastern Standard Time, this new popular singer will be heard over the network of Radio Realm, in a nation-wide broadcast, sponsored by the Sleepwell Mattress Company."

Aunt Min is not surprised at George's success. She knew he had it in him. And Mr. Twilling is not to be credited with all the discovery either. As for Mr. Twilling and Ellie, Aunt Min feels she should ask Mr. Twilling a few questions regarding both the seriousness of his intentions and his antecedents. Questions which Mr. Twilling is perfectly willing to answer. His mother was a direct descendant of John Quincy Adams and his father was a farmer in Suffolk.

"I've always hoped I was descended from an old English sheep-dog, but I don't know," says Twilling, as he goes quickly to Queena and pulls her up from her chair by the radio. "Good-by, my dear—and you're going to sing, if you want to. We'll fix that. You can sing in the Metropolitan—if it's there when you're ready—or Radio Realm—anywhere you like—if you'll just let me have Sylvester Silverton. (*He gives* QUEENA *a bear-like hug, both laughing, she almost crying.*) Good-by, Mrs. Stickney.

(*To* Mrs. Martin.) I'll give you five minutes, Ellie—then if you're not down, I'll be up again!" (*He goes.*)

They are back to George now. To think he has a fortune in his voice and Queena never suspected it. Aunt Min can't understand that.

"I didn't—but his voice was one of the things I loved about him," mutters Queena, dreamily. She stops suddenly, realizing what she has said at Aunt Min's startled exclamation. So, that's it! Queena is in love with George! It was Queena he had crawled through the screen to see! Queena has been having an affair with him!

Queena cannot explain. George will have to do that. But, she insists, it is not nearly so terrible as Aunt Min may think. And there is nothing that need be done about it.

Queena has hurried away to see Mrs. Martin to the Twilling car when Ned comes back. He hesitates in the doorway, seeing Mrs. Stickney, but she is eager to talk with him. She knows his secret now. Mr. Twilling has told them. And he is going to make a fortune. He should be very happy about it.

"I always wanted not to sing," Ned explains, a little shamefacedly. But he thought Aunt Min might have been referring to another secret.

"I know about that, too," admits Aunt Min. "She told me."

Ned—Then you understand about last night—that I came because—

Aunt Min—Yes, I know.

Ned—I thought she was cold.

Aunt Min—And you took this position—because of her?

Ned—Oh, yes. . . .

Aunt Min—And I can't blame Queena—seeing you and comparing you with her husband it was unavoidable.

Ned (*surprised*)—Oh, then you *don't* know.

Aunt Min—Is there anything more?

Ned—Oh, yes—much more—you only know the end. There was a beginning.

Aunt Min—Mercy!

Ned—There always is.

Aunt Min (*alarmed*)—Mercy! What is it, George?

Ned—My name isn't George. Now you must just be brave about it. (*Patting her shoulder.*) I'm Ned Farrar!

Aunt Min (*she swallows—then drinks*)—I don't believe it. Does Queena know it? I mean, it's not possible!

Ned—Oh, yes.

AUNT MIN—You can't be.

NED—Oh, yes—I have been all the time.

AUNT MIN (*breathless*)—That night when I came—and you were washing the dishes—

NED—Yes, that night, too.

AUNT MIN (*rather severely*)—I don't know how I feel about it.

NED—Of course not—and the worst of it is that now I've gotten awfully fond of you. (*Sound of departing motor is heard.*)

AUNT MIN—There goes Ellie!

NED—And Queena?

AUNT MIN—No, Queena wouldn't go without saying good-by to me. I don't think she'd go anyway now that she knows you're her husband—I mean, now that we both know it!

NED—I want to make sure of that. (QUEENA *enters leaving the door open.*) Oh, you didn't go!

QUEENA—No, I couldn't! Mamma's so happy she doesn't need me.

AUNT MIN—You'll be happy too. We'll all be happy, won't we?

QUEENA—Ned, you're what I always wanted to be—a singer.

NED—Well, we'll just have to bear it the best we can.

AUNT MIN—Don't you have to sing again this morning, Ned?

NED—Why, yes—I'm afraid so. . . .

AUNT MIN—Then you and Queena must stay tonight. I'll have Phœbe make up the room inside.

NED—The porch will be all right. (*As* AUNT MIN *smiles a little tremulously.*) I can kiss you now we're related. I wanted to last night.

AUNT MIN—And I wanted you to!

QUEENA (*coming down*)—Oh, Ned! What really happened last night?

NED (*coming to* QUEENA)—Why, I thought you were here, and I came up and got in bed with Aunt Min!

QUEENA (*shocked*)—Ned—you didn't! Good heavens! What did she do?

NED—Well, it was terrible—but she forgave me—she knows now I thought it was you! . . .

QUEENA—She didn't forgive you before she knew, did she?

NED (*smiling*)—Are you jealous of Aunt Min, Baby?

QUEENA—Ned, why haven't you called me that for so long.

NED—I was too poor! (*His arms around her.*)

THE CURTAIN FALLS

NO MORE LADIES

A Comedy in Three Acts

By A. E. Thomas

AFTER the theatre season's brilliant opening with a quartet of what are known professionally as "smash hits" there was a natural reaction. For a month or more successes were scattered and through the early weeks of the new year the new plays proved rather definitely commonplace.

A bright spot in the January contributions, however, was this comedy by A. E. Thomas. Like all better comedies it is backed by a fairly purposeful and meaningful theme. By the author's admission he did not intend it should be accepted as entertainment and nothing more.

"I believe it says something worth saying about the problem of marriage as it confronts the present younger generation," he has written. "Is success in marriage worth a struggle, or, if it is not at once successful, should one discard it as if it were an unbecoming hat, and casually provide one's self with another? One point of view shows character, I think. The other has lamentable effects upon human souls."

Though the plot structure of "No More Ladies" is not in any sense original, the characterization is definitely human, the dialogue touched with both wit and wisdom and the action agreeably natural.

The living room of the Townsends' apartment on Park Avenue, New York, to which we are first introduced, is richly and tastefully furnished. A distinguishing feature is an illuminated fish bowl over the fireplace, rather generously stocked with sea plants and tropical fish. There is a large window at back through which moonlight is streaming. It is about 11.30 in the evening and Fanny Townsend is still up. An item worthy of note only because Fanny is the Townsend grandmother, a bright and well-preserved lady of sixty-odd who has accepted her grandchildren's generation as a lot of fun rather than as a menace. However, she admits to Oliver Dickens, who has called to see her son, Anderson, that the only way anyone can expect to keep tabs on this generation is to check up on their nocturnal activities. Therefore Fanny is usually the last member of the household to go to bed.

The Anderson Townsends are at the opera. Marcia Townsend, their daughter, is out somewhere and there is no telling when she will be back. If Marcia were a painter, thinks Fanny, she would probably specialize in sunrises, she sees so many of them.

Fanny is knitting, and without her glasses. As far back as the year the *Maine* was blown up an oculist had told her she should wear glasses and she had told the oculist to go chase himself. Whether he did or not, Fanny is not wearing glasses.

"It's a woman's business to look attractive," says she. "She must interest the beholder—by hook or by crook—or else she's sunk."

"Well, there's one thing about you, Mrs. Townsend," admits Oliver, gallantly, "you certainly look the way a man wants his grandmother to look."

"There's art in it, young man," confesses Fanny, pausing just long enough to tell the butler to bring her a Scotch highball, man's size; "I don't know many old ladies. I don't cultivate 'em— Don't like 'em—much. But I see a lot of 'em as I go around this town, and most of 'em give me a swift pain. Bobbed hair—well—that's all right—neat, anyhow—but beauty parlors, rouge and calcimine and the airs and graces of youth—to me they are asinine." . . . "I saw all these things coming along—all my contemporaries growing to look more and more like a lot of superannuated ballet dancers. And I saw I had to make up my mind about it and I did. Even when skirts were short mine never were."

OLIVER—I congratulate you on the result!

FANNY—I suppose, really, it was my legs!

OLIVER—I beg your pardon!

FANNY—I never liked 'em much. But that's not all. The fact is, when I go out, as I do a great deal, people notice me. I look like something out of the Mauve Decade. People smile and nudge each other and I can hear them whisper: "Oh, look, isn't she quaint?"

OLIVER—Anyhow, you have dignity!

FANNY—I don't care a damn about that. The fact is: I stand out. And I admit I like it.

OLIVER—You still enjoy life, don't you?

FANNY—I do. It's a great show, and I've got an aisle seat in the front row. Maybe it wouldn't be so nice if I had to sit in the top gallery.

OLIVER—What do you mean?

FANNY—Change your mind?

OLIVER—No, thanks.

FANNY—Well, cheerio! (*She drinks.*) I mean I'm independent. I've my own apartment, my own maid, my own car and chauffeur. And I do as I damn well please. I go out when I like, and come home when I'm ready. I shall go to Palm Beach in February, and to Paris in June; and the fact that I've quite a bit of money that unfortunately I can't be able to take with me when I shuffle off confers on me a pleasant if slightly spurious popularity with my friends and relatives.

OLIVER—Nonsense, Mrs. Townsend. Everybody'd like you just as much if you hadn't a dollar.

FANNY—Mm! Perhaps. But if I'm a dependent, I'd have to take orders disguised of course, as suggestion. Oh, yes, but a rotten egg, my dear young man, is a rotten egg, no matter how you cook it!

Fanny has her ideas about Oliver. He won't drink with her. He doesn't smoke. He hardly notices Jacquette, a chic French maid who would put Fanny to bed if she could, and he thinks he wants to marry Marcia.

"You and Marcia! Splendid! Why not Mary Garden and Bishop Manning?" explodes Fanny, amusedly.

Oliver considers the comparison most inept. He is fond of Marcia, that's true. And he is convinced that she stands in a fair way of throwing her life away on a certain individual.

That would be Sherry Warren, Fanny concludes. Fanny rather likes Sherry. He may have been something of a lady killer, and he may have broken up a few marriages. But any marriage that can be broken up ought to be, as Fanny sees it.

"The only marriage that's entitled to persist is one that is built on an indestructible foundation," declares Fanny.

"Don't you approve of marriage," queries the wide-eyed Oliver.

FANNY—No. It's a dreadful thing. Marriage is a mirage. When you get to it it's never what it looked like from a distance.

OLIVER—Well, really, now—

FANNY—But it's necessary, and do you know why? Because somebody hundreds of years ago invented a hideous word.

OLIVER—What word?

FANNY—The word is *bastard!* (OLIVER *gasps.*) Don't faint! Have a drink!

OLIVER (*rises up to fireplace*)—Really, Mrs. Townsend, well—we'll pass that! But I honestly don't see how you can defend a man like Sheridan Warren. He's—he's—no better than a libertine.

FANNY—There's a good deal to be said for libertines. They're a much abused lot. The accepted idea of a libertine is a man endowed with a high degree of low cunning and a low opinion of high principles, who deliberately sets about the business of seducing innocent young women for the sheer joy he gets from spoiling their lives. As a matter of fact, a libertine is usually as much his own victim as any of his victims. He's almost always uncommonly sensitive to beauty and responsive to it; he can tell a lark from a buzzard. He reacts to the subtiles of life and human relations. Monotony repels him. Ugliness enrages him. Beauty enthralls him. Fragrance delights him. He's a wild bird lost and whirling in a storm until he dashes his life out against some lighthouse of beauty. So there! As for libertines, that's what they call the low-down.

OLIVER—Is this a defense of Sheridan Warren?

FANNY—Lord, no! Sherry's no libertine. He's just a highly civilized, uncommonly sophisticated young man with a sense of humor and too much money.

Fanny doesn't think she would like to see Marcia married to Sherry Warren, but she does not feel that she has to worry about that. Sherry has too much sense.

Now the Anderson Townsends are back from the opera. They don't know where Marcia is, either. Nor do they ever know, according to Fanny. They neither know where she is nor what she is doing. Marcia may be married right now for all her parents know.

Anderson and Oliver have retired to the library to talk company reports. Fanny is still going on to Helen Townsend, about Oliver, who's a prig, and wants to marry Marcia, who's a hussy. Yes, repeats Fanny, to the horror of Helen, Marcia is a perfect hussy—

Sheridan Warren is announced. He is a personable young man, probably in his late twenties, possibly early thirties; handsome, smartly groomed and carries an air of sophistication not too consciously.

Sheridan has just dropped in looking for Marcia. Somehow Sherry has mislaid Marcia. They were dancing at the Moscow when along came a friend who introduced Ronald Harcourt, the picture star.

"He seemed a nice chap," reports Sherry. "Bit fond of double negatives. But fairly sober. He asked Marcia to dance and off they went. After an hour and no Marcia, it was borne in upon me that I had been left holding the baby—"

About that time, Louis, "the bandit who runs the dive," according to Fanny, told Sherry that the place was to be raided. He had been letting people drink standing up instead of sitting down, which was the law of the day. Sherry went out to get his car only to find that Marcia and the picture boy had taken it and disappeared.

Helen is worried. She has an idea something should be done. But Fanny isn't worried. Marcia, likely as not, will turn up dragging her prey with her. Didn't she bring home a prize-fighter the week before?

Helen Townsend has gone to bed, leaving the night again to Fanny and Sheridan. They have fresh drinks now and take up the subject of Oliver, who wants to marry Marcia and doesn't think so much of Sherry. Sherry is sorry, but not interested. He has no intention of marrying Marcia, either. As for that, says Fanny, Sherry will have very little to say about it, and if he is wise the quicker he arranges a graceful exit the better it will be for him.

"She's an attractive baggage; needs checking," observes Fanny, wisely. "It's a lucky thing for you it's no longer possible to compromise a lady."

SHERRY—Probably because there are no longer any ladies.

FANNY—Or gentlemen?

SHERRY—Damn few, my good woman!

FANNY—Call yourself one?

SHERRY—Good God, no!

FANNY—What do you call yourself?

SHERRY—Nothing at all. Lots of other people attend to that.

FANNY—You know what I call you?

SHERRY—We shall be ravished to hear.

FANNY—Casabianca.

SHERRY—Oh, standing on the burning deck, am I?

FANNY—In my opinion, you are!

SHERRY—My dear Fanny, you alarm me! I don't smell any

smoke.

FANNY—I want to alarm you.

SHERRY—If it was anybody else I should laugh at it. But take it all in all, you're not so cuckoo!

FANNY—Take it on the word of a brother Elk—look around and choose your nearest exit.

SHERRY (*rising*)—You may be right.

FANNY—Don't walk—run!

SHERRY—The *Aquitania* sails at 1 A.M. (*Back to* FANNY.) I could just make it!

FANNY—Got a passport?

SHERRY—Never without one.

FANNY—I might have known it. Any crook worthy of the name always arranges his getaway.

SHERRY—Very good, me gal. Can I do anything for you on the Riviera?

FANNY—Yes. Put 2,000 francs on the single—0, hundred at a time.

SHERRY—It's done.

FANNY—After that, get thee to a Monastery—go!

Marcia is home. A tall handsome girl, probably twenty-five. Walks with a healthy stride and generally commands the situation conversationally. Her greeting is pleasantly casual, though she does take time to apologize to Sherry.

As for the "handsome picture man," Marcia imagines that if no taxi has come along he is walking home.

"I had to throw him out somewhere in Central Park," she reports.

"My dear!" Fanny is anxious.

"Oh, don't fret yourself. All in a night's work!"

"My dear, you really ought to spare yourself more," protests Fanny. "'All work and no play,' you know—"

"Some fun! I have hopes he's got a black eye," says Marcia.

Sherry will not permit Marcia to thank him for coming to see if she were all right. He had really come to see about getting his car back. No one worries about the self-reliant type of woman any more, only about the clinging vines, and they went out with the Florodora sextette.

"You're a pair of brutes!" declares Marcia, who would prefer to be worried about a bit. "You have no decent feelings at all!"

"I like that!" answers Fanny, with spirit. "You leave this poor innocent boy flat in a honky-tonk, dash off with a cheap picture actor you never met before; get what's coming to you, and now you expect us to wipe away your tears and say: 'There, there, little girl, don't cry!' That's swell! I'll be seeing you!"

Fanny has left them. They have freshened their drinks and settled to explanations. Marcia is really sorry. Sherry is really worried. She thinks she may be all wrong. Sherry thinks perhaps a job would help. Marcia might get married. She might have children. Which is a worrisome thought to Marcia. Her children might take after their mother. Or Sherry. Or even their father!

A father, insists Sherry, should be selected with some care and not on the eeny-meeny-miney-mo plan—

"Men, men, how I detest them—all of 'em!" protests Marcia, spiritedly.

"Good night, Miss Townsend, and thank you for a pleasant evening."

"Oh, Sherry, I do think you might be a little decent to me."

"Well, with a little more encouragement—"

"Oh, sit down, and shut up!"

"Damned unhappy, aren't you?"

"A little."

"Too bad."

"Yes, I'm sure your heart's breaking."

"As a matter of fact—"

Then Oliver comes. In reply to their casual inquiries, he is glad to assure them that his health is perfect, that everything is uncertain in Wall Street, and would Marcia go to the Philadelphia orchestra with him Tuesday week?

Marcia is sorry her taste in music isn't quite up to Stokowski. Oliver thinks, in that case, he probably had better be going and finally manages it.

Speaking of marriage, as they shortly are again, Marcia would like to know why Sherry shouldn't get married. Nor is she satisfied with his explanation that he is already provided with a good cook and a hot water bottle.

How he has managed to escape all those women Marcia is at a loss to understand. Particularly that blue-eyed one, that Diana Salston? It is a good thing Lord Moulton turned up in the nick of time or Diana would have married Sherry in spite of himself.

The Lord Moulton feature of the conspiracy was Sherry's own idea. "Diana was always mad about titles," Sherry explains.

"His Lordship was a widower and stony broke. A drowning Lord will grasp at an heiress. So I introduced him. Well, I mean to say—fusion instant and inevitable."

Marcia thinks she will take a bromide and go to bed. Sherry would stop her for a moment. They haven't found a father for her children yet—

"Please go," pleads Marcia, suddenly tired. "I don't feel comic tonight."

"Nor I—"

Marcia—I feel like hell. And I'm sick of it. I want to be alone. For a long, long time. Sherry, please go and don't come back.

Sherry—You mean—never?

Marcia—Yes.

Sherry—Sorry. I rather thought you liked having me around, more or less.

Marcia—So I would—

Sherry—Would you like me to be around more or less?

Marcia—One or the other, old man. Either a great deal more—or a whole lot less. So now you've got it. Think it over.

Sherry—No, don't think I will. Every time I think a thing over I make a mess of it. Everything I've ever done that was any good I've done on impulse.

Marcia—Come, come, my bromide is waiting.

Sherry—I have an impulse to make it a great deal more.

Marcia—Shall you obey that impulse?

Sherry—With your permission.

Marcia—Won't you sit down, Mr. Warren?

Sherry (*takes her chin in his hand*)—You know, my Juliet, the damn thing isn't as simple as it sounds.

Marcia—Little Boy Blue, it isn't simple at all. Getting married is as easy as bon jour. It's making it work, that's the catch.

Sherry—Yeh. The rock-bound coast is strewn with wrecks.

Marcia—And the more sophisticated the people the heavier the odds against them. Now take a truck driver and a waitress from Childs. They'll marry, raise a family of from four to eight kids, quarrel happily for half a century and pass out from hardening of the arteries, still husband and wife . . . but . . .

Sherry—You're quite right. We expect too much of marriage, and when we don't get it, we sulk.

Marcia—Do we expect too much?

SHERRY—We expect a Paradise on earth and what we usually get is a kick in the pants.

They have tried to think of their happily married friends and have to compromise on those who are happily divorced. It's not that people expect too much of marriage, insists Marcia, but that they expect too little.

"If they really expect a Paradise on earth, they're going to give everything they've got to make it come true, if only to save their self-respect. Most of them are disillusioned about marriage before they marry. A fat chance they have."

"Horse breaks down at the post, what?"

"Precisely. But he runs all the same."

"Also runs, is the phrase."

"So that's that! We seem to be entirely agreed. Marriage is no good. The odds against success are tremendous. Experience proves it. Only the blind can fail to see it. Am I right?"

"Absolutely, old girl!"

"So, what?"

"So let's get married."

"What!"

SHERRY—Well, of course, at least a hundred times I've sworn I'd never ask you to marry me.

MARCIA—Are you doing it now?

SHERRY—Incredible as it seems.

MARCIA—Isn't nature wonderful?

SHERRY—It's one of those believe it or not things.

MARCIA—Makes you look pretty silly, doesn't it?

SHERRY—Not at all. At last I've succeeded in getting the better of my will power.

MARCIA—I suppose you've no doubt about my answer.

SHERRY—Not much.

MARCIA—What do you think I'll say?

SHERRY—You'll say yes, damn it!

MARCIA—Well, damn it, you're right!

SHERRY—Tough—what?

MARCIA—Foul.

SHERRY (*kneels beside her chair*)—Anyhow, you can stick one feather in your cap, you'll be the only one of 'em I ever married—or wished to.

MARCIA—The champion of champions, that's me.

SHERRY—Mind you I make no promises—except one—I swear

never to call you darling; unless I mean it.

MARCIA—Fair enough.

SHERRY—And so, my darling, they were married and lived unhappily ever after.

MARCIA (SHERRY *kisses her hand*)—I'll tell you one thing, it's going to be the most marvelous party in the world; or it's going to be hell. So watch out!

SHERRY—I've always wondered if there was really a hell!

MARCIA—Well, my lad, you'll have a sporting chance to find out.

SHERRY (*pulls her up*)—Well, we're off.

MARCIA—Just a moment, my good man. Let's get this straight.

SHERRY—Right-ho!

MARCIA—We're a pair of fools.

SHERRY—Imbeciles.

MARCIA—We haven't a chance.

SHERRY—Not an earthly!

MARCIA—It's bound to be the most heart-rending flop.

SHERRY—Hideous!

MARCIA—We can't miss—

SHERRY—Horse breaks down at the post.

MARCIA—So we bet on him just the same.

SHERRY—Every dollar we've got.

MARCIA—Well then. Let's go! (*They embrace.* FANNY *enters.*)

FANNY—My God! The ship's afire!

THE CURTAIN FALLS

ACT II

The summer following Sherry and Marcia have their own apartment in Southampton, L. I. "It is an airy, beautiful and comfortable room. The appointments, of course, are perfect."

It is late afternoon of a lovely summer day. Marcia and her mother are having tea. Mother's car has been ordered. Fanny Townsend is with them. Sherry isn't home and hasn't been for three days. Helen is not surprised. It happens that she had seen Sherry at the Ritz in town a day or so before. He was with a pleasant-faced blonde girl, a Miss German.

That would be Teresa German who plays a banjo in a night club in Fifty-fourth Street, decides Fanny. She knows about Teresa through the tabloid columnists.

"She is supposed to be from the élite of Milwaukee—or is it Minneapolis?"

"You mean she was the co-respondent in the James's divorce?" queries Helen.

"O-kay Park Avenue!" answers Fanny.

It is time that Marcia called a halt, thinks Helen. "We all know the kind of life Sherry led before he married you—that affair of Jim Salston's wife—not to mention others—and if he's going back to that sort of thing, I think—"

"That's my business, Mother," answers Marcia, quickly. "I'll attend to it in my own way, if you please."

"Have you said anything to him?"

"That, Mother, is NOT my way."

Helen has gone. She is, allows Fanny, an old-fashioned piece. "Belongs to the 'where-were-you-last-night' school of wives." Then Fanny asks Dickens to bring her a dry Martini. She has had enough tea.

Marcia is not surprised, she confesses to Fanny, at what her mother has reported about Sherry. She has her own plans for handling the situation and Fanny is going to help, but what the plans are she refuses to reveal at the moment. She is not, however the sort of ass that would be thinking about alimony at this time.

"I told Sherry he'd be a fool to marry you, and you'd be a bigger one to marry him," snaps Fanny. "I'm sorry to see that I'm right."

"You're not. You're wrong," replies Marcia. "We've had a marvelous time. It's been grand. And if the bloom's a bit worn off for him—maybe that's my fault. But if it's worn off for him it's the same for me. So it'll be God speed ye, my lad, and on your way!"

Fanny thinks perhaps she had better clear out, but Marcia will not listen to that. There is not going to be any shooting, and there is lots of room. Marcia has invited a few guests for the week-end.

"You were in on this thing at the start," she tells Fanny. "So you'd better stick for the finish. Then you can say: I told you so!"

Sherry is home and as quick with bantering answers as they are with their accusations. He had attended a meeting of the stewards of the Jockey Club—gone to dinner and then to the Follies—anyway that would be his story if he had not met his mother-in-law at the Ritz.

Marcia has gone to the piano, Fanny to the garden. Sherry follows Marcia.

"Sorry, darling!" he says.

"It's all right."

SHERRY—Rotten of me to stay away so long.

MARCIA—No—no—this house is no jail!

SHERRY—But I do get so damn restless!

MARCIA—I know. But haven't I any attractive friends? Why a banjo player?

SHERRY—Oh, Teresa, I suppose? Well, if you don't mind my saying so most of your friends—

MARCIA—Bore you? That's just too bad.

SHERRY—One wearies of the eternally flippant.

MARCIA—And Teresa is a serious-minded thinker?

SHERRY—At all events she makes no pretenses; she's frankly what she is—ordinary I suppose you'd say. Perhaps that's why I like her. One meets so few ordinary people.

MARCIA—I see. Still fleeing from monotony.

SHERRY—The trouble with monotony is that it sounds so much like monogamy.

MARCIA—So naturally you occasionally confuse the two.

SHERRY—Why—er—

MARCIA—Don't apologize. Quite a natural error—tell me more about the fascinator.

SHERRY—Well, let me see—Teresa is a graduate of the old speak-easies. (MARCIA *stops playing.*)

MARCIA—Tell me, grandpa! Why did they call 'em speak-easies?

SHERRY—I'll tell ye, gal! When the talkies came along none of the old stars in the silent pictures could talk. They had to teach 'em, and the speak-easies are where they did it!

MARCIA—I see. So Teresa's a kind of college president?

SHERRY—Emeritus!

MARCIA—Thought your college days were over.

SHERRY—I'm—er—taking a post-graduate course.

MARCIA—Sherry: look here. Straight between the eyes. Have you been unfaithful to me?

SHERRY—No lies, you understand. Never have been any, never will be any. Now, shall I answer you?

MARCIA—Please!

SHERRY—The answer is yes! I'd have told you anyhow. Came home on purpose to do it.

MARCIA—I should have known it anyhow.

SHERRY—Maybe that's why I told you.

MARCIA—No, it isn't. You're a bad, bad husband. But in other ways you're fairly decent.

SHERRY—By God! Marcia, you're amazing!

MARCIA—Are you under the impression I'm forgiving you?

SHERRY—I didn't mean that!

MARCIA—I haven't a forgiving nature.

SHERRY—I meant your self-control!

MARCIA—Expect me to throw the fire irons at you?

SHERRY—No.

MARCIA—I might, you know. But there would be no speeches.

SHERRY—May I say I'm sorry?

MARCIA—You may—but you're not.

SHERRY—I am, and I'm not. Anyway it doesn't prevent me from being mad about you, very! (*Kisses her hand.*)

MARCIA—Doesn't it?

SHERRY—Kiss me?

Marcia does not accept the invitation. Instead she slaps Sherry's face soundly. And immediately apologizes, though her anger mounts. She would hear more of this banjo woman who has proved so irresistible. There is a sting in her queries.

"Now, listen, please, never mind the sarcasm," Sherry finally protests. "You can't make me feel any worse than I do. I've been an ass, and I'm sorry as hell! And that's all there is to it. Now you can either kick me out or give me another chance. It's perfectly simple—"

It is not as simple as that for Marcia. Suddenly she feels as though, after all, there must be something in the broken heart idea. She never before has felt as though her heart were being torn in red hot pieces.

Sherry would renew his pleas for a less painful understanding. The arrival of Jim Salston, first of the dinner guests, interrupts. Jim, an attractive young idler, is awfully glad to have been asked. Sherry might think it damned decent of him to come, considering everything. But Jim doesn't feel that way. Jim is really very grateful to Sherry for having broken up his unhappy home.

"Oh, I know you didn't look at it like that," Jim is quick to explain. "You saw yourself as a dashing love bandit stealing beautiful, misunderstood wife from stodgy, unappreciative husband."

But didn't Jim laugh when he saw Sherry had discovered his

mistake! "You went about looking as though you were afraid you had swallowed a bad oyster," says Jim, merrily. "And then, just in the nick of time, along blows this besotted bird with the title—what's his name?"

"Lord Moulton."

"Moulton—that's the sap! What a rotten time he must be having! And what a sap he must be."

Sherry would soften Jim's criticism of Diana's new husband. After all there is the question of international good feeling and all that. Besides, Jim should remember that Diana has her points.

She has, admits Jim. Decimal points. If he had to choose between Diana and the national debt of England he would take the debt and be grateful.

"Do you know she used to call me Jimsey Boysie?" says Jim.

"Hard to bear," admits Sherry.

"What sort of tag did she tie on you?"

"That's a secret that shall die with me," answers Sherry.

Fanny is back from the garden and properly surprised to find Jim Salston talking amiably with Sherry. "Old pals reunited, old wounds healed—and all that," reports Jim.

Now Lord and Lady Moulton have arrived, Diana gushing volubly over the delight Marcia's place is giving her. Sherry has come forward smartly to meet Diana and her "Ducky." A moment later he has called Jim. There's a surprise for Diana. Fancy meeting Jimsey there! And finding him having a reunion with Sherry! Still, if the lion and the lamb can lie down together, why not?

Lord Moulton is also glad to know Salston. His lordship has heard so much of Jim as a perfect husband.

"I must have improved in retrospect," suggests Jim.

"Blessings brighten as they take their flight," quotes Fanny.

Lord Moulton is all for family harmony. He means to call Jim, Salston, and expects Jim to call him Moulton. After all it should be a jolly week-end.

"Here's old Salston happily divorced and here's me happily married and here's Warren, er— . . ."

"Well, he's married!" admits Fanny.

"Sherry, wasn't it too, too precious, our meeting Marcia at the Beach Club! We're over for the polo, you know!" chimes in Diana.

"Does his lordship play?" Fanny would know.

"Ducky? Lord, no! He'd ruin a truck horse. He just sold

'em some ponies. If he had Jimsey's figure now—you still play, Jimsey?"

"Well, I still knock 'em about a bit!"

Marcia has joined them, looking, according to Diana, "just too fearfully, frightfully marvelous," and a few moments later they have organized a contract bridge game, the cut for partners putting Diana and Jim together against Sherry and Lord Moulton.

"Well, here we are—husband, wife, ex-husband and er—jolly old middleman," laughs his lordship. "Are we playing for love?"

They are playing for a penny a point, at Jim's suggestion, and are soon deep in the game. Diana must first know if Jimsey-Boysie does anything different from what he used to, and that being settled bids two hearts. Jim leaves Diana in, much to her disgust, and excuses himself on the plea that he happened to be thinking of something else—of a certain New Year's party they once gave and, after everyone was gone, found Chick Johnson asleep in Diana's bed wearing Sherry's pyjamas! That was a night—

It now appears that Diana's pet name for Sherry was Petty Wetty, which, to Marcia, sounds like publishing their memoirs.

"Well, here's Jimsey Boysie, Ducky Wucky and Petty Wetty," notes Lord Moulton. "I say, Mrs. Warren, mustn't leave you out. Suppose you call me Cuffy Wuffy? And I think I'll call you—er—Queenie Weenie."

"Queenie Weenie, my God!"

"What say?"

"Please yourself, Cuffy Wuffy."

"Now everything's all nice and matey."

"My name's Fanny Wanny, Cuffy Wuffy!" prompts Fanny, refusing to be ignored.

"Right-ho! Fanny Wanny it is!"

Presently Jim and Diana are having an old-time row. Diana has bid three hearts when all they need is two, and that's just plain damned silly to Jim.

However, the play goes on. Marcia is at the piano, idly strumming over "In the Gloaming." When Jim is dummy again he wanders over. It is Sherry's idea that if Marcia must play something he would like it better if she were to switch to chess. Jim, on the other hand, would be willing to play any game of Marcia's choosing.

"Where have you been all my life?" smiles Marcia.

"Wasting my time. But maybe it's not too late— Think is it?"

"Who knows?"

Another guest has arrived. A young woman is at the door asking for Mrs. Townsend. Fanny is at a loss to understand, but Marcia knows. Fanny must have invited someone, says Marcia, else they would not be asking for her. A moment later the butler has announced Miss German. She is blonde and pretty, a superior night club entertainer type.

"How do you do, Miss German?" inquires Fanny, rising to the occasion.

"Pleased to meet you," admits Teresa, as Marcia swings into the breach.

"Oh, Miss German, how good of you to come," says Marcia, and then to the others, including the somewhat flustered Sherry, she adds: "Isn't it nice? Miss German's to sing for us at dinner tonight. Meantime she's our guest."

"Oh, I say, didn't I see you at the Club Monaco one night last spring?" Lord Moulton has adjusted his monocle inquiringly.

"Very likely—I sing there," answers Teresa.

MOULTON—Teresa with the banjo! What?

TERESA—So they call me.

FANNY—Such a pretty name.

MARCIA—You don't know any of us—except Mrs. Townsend—but I shan't bother to introduce you. We'll get acquainted easily enough.

TERESA—I shouldn't be surprised. I'm easy to know.

MARCIA—So I have heard. Perhaps you would like to go to your room and tidy up a bit.

TERESA—Thank you, I think I would. (STAFFORD *enters, followed by* DICKENS *with two grips.*)

SHERRY—How do you do, Miss German?

TERESA—Oh, hello, Sherry, fancy meeting you here.

SHERRY—Nice to see you here. Let me present you to Mrs. Warren.

TERESA—Oh, yes?

MARCIA—Delighted! (*There is a tense pause broken by* DIANA'S *cough.*)

MOULTON—I say, Miss German, what are you going to sing for us tonight?

TERESA—I don't know exactly—anything you wish, if I know it. That is why I am here.

FANNY—So sweet of you to come.

DIANA—Charming.

TERESA—Thank you.

JIM—Er—don't you sing a thing called—oh, yes—"What's Gone Wrong with the Man I Love?" (SHERRY *drops bottle at portable bar.*)

TERESA—Oh, yes.

MARCIA—Why, of course. You must sing that, Miss German.

TERESA—Certainly, if you wish.

MARCIA—Splendid. And now, if you like, Stafford will take you to your room.

TERESA—Thank you so much. (*Exits with* STAFFORD.)

FANNY—As the Governor of South Carolina *used* to say to the Governor of North Carolina—

MARCIA—Jim, you're a good bartender, shake up some cocktails, will you?

JIM—Right-ho! (*Goes to bar.*)

MOULTON—How do we stand?

DIANA—I'm just finding out.

MARCIA—Have you finished your rubber?

SHERRY—Yes, we've finished our game. And now I suppose, we are to play yours?

THE CURTAIN FALLS

ACT III

The next morning discovers Sherry pacing the Warrens' living room in a troubled state of mind. It is about 11.30. He has had no breakfast, wants no breakfast, though he agrees finally to allow Stafford to bring him a cup of black coffee.

Sherry is still pacing up and down when Fanny comes back from the ocean. She has enjoyed her morning's bath and carries a large rubber zebra with which she has been cavorting in the water.

Fanny would know where Marcia is. So would Sherry. It appears that Marcia and Jim Salston had started for the club in Salston's car just about as the party broke up at 3 in the morning, and neither of them has so far returned.

"Let's hope there's been an accident," submits Fanny.

"I don't think it's any accident," growls Sherry.

A moment later laughter is heard coming from the yard, caused by the high spirits of Marcia and Jim. They are still in full evening dress and happy as can be. They've had such fun. They hope no one sat up for them. Especially Sherry. And they are both fairly starved. They will want a lot of breakfast, quickly,

Marcia tells Stafford. While breakfast is being prepared they will go and change into something less scandalous. It would be quite terrible if they were to start gossip.

"Well," admits Fanny as Marcia and Jim disappear, "the guilty couple kept a stiff upper lip. Casabianca, the ship has blown up."

"What?"

FANNY—The boy? Oh! Where was he? Answer! In the gumbo!

SHERRY—Somebody's in the gumbo. But it's not me!

FANNY—Oh, isn't it?

SHERRY—Not much—if she thinks I'll take this sitting down.

FANNY—Hoity-toity-tut-tut-tut and fol-de-rol-rol-rol!

SHERRY—Well, I won't. That's all.

FANNY—Oh, no, that's not all—not by a damn sight! Fido, you're all wet. Now you charge and listen to this ancient and repulsive hag. In an ideal state we should all be a lot of wild horses—nothing to do but make love and roam the prairies. Unfortunately we are supposed to be civilized. We aren't, but we have to pretend. In the society in which we live there is love to be made but there is also work to be done. You and Marcia are a pair of two-year-olds, being broken to double harness. Can't be done in a minute. Bound to be a lot of kicking and a runaway or two. But a fine team is the very best thing in the world. Never forget it. . . . Are you listening to me?

SHERRY—Certainly.

FANNY—What did I say?

SHERRY—Er—something about horses.

FANNY—Oh, my God!

SHERRY—Fanny, there are things you can't stand for!

FANNY—The hell there are!

SHERRY—Mean to say you approve of—

FANNY—I mean to say I'm begging you not to be an ass. You can't bear the feeling of harness. Neither can she. You kicked over the traces. So did she. Let it go at that.

SHERRY—Can't be done.

FANNY—Of course, if you're no longer in love—

SHERRY—Now don't you be an ass.

FANNY—And she's no longer in love with you—

SHERRY—How could she care anything about me and do what she did last night?

FANNY—What did she do last night?

SHERRY—I don't know.

FANNY—Well, find out.

SHERRY—By God, I'm going to.

Of course, Fanny would further remind Sherry, whatever Marcia has done she did because he had done whatever it was that he did. He knows that if Jim Salston were to shoot him today everybody would say that it served him damn well right.

"I have the misfortune to be fond of you two idiots," admits Fanny. "And if you go and bust up the finest team I know just because you're a trifle saddle sore, why, by heaven, I'll punish you in the only way I can—I'll cut you out of my will. And it's some will!" . . . "If you're going to let your marriage go to smash as if it were nothing more than a bad guess in the stock market, why then I will say to you that you are nothing more than a regrettable incident in the sex life of your parents."

Diana Moulton is down, followed by Lord Moulton. His lordship is amused. He has seen Marcia and Jim Salston drive in in all their pretty party frocks and he wonders what Diana would do if she knew that her Ducky had stayed out all night with another woman. Diana fails to answer. Instead she goes looking for Sherry. She wants to show Petty Wetty her new bathing suit.

Fanny and Lord Moulton are not in complete agreement as to what happened the night before. Fanny was convinced, when she saw his lordship sneaking up the beach with the banjo player, that he was a bit light-hearted, and Moulton, who can see nothing improper about being entertained by an entertainer, is also sure Fanny herself had a bit of a list to starboard.

Fanny would hotly resent the accusation. She was home and in bed by two-thirty and had asked Stafford to call her early. Stafford is pleased to confirm this statement. Mrs. Townsend had distinctly requested that he should wake and call her early, because she was going to be Queen of the May.

Jim Salston is back, normally dressed and still bright and merry. If, as Lord Moulton charges, he has made a night of it, why not? "What's the poet say: 'For the night was made for loving and the day returns too soon.' "

"The day may have returned too soon, but you didn't," retorts Moulton, significantly.

It has struck Jim that Sherry isn't very gay this morning. He thinks perhaps something should be done about it. "All of us such old pals, you know," he reminds Diana and Moulton. "Been through so much together and all that. We should strive to promote his happiness."

When Sherry arrives his attitude confirms their suspicions, but when they would know the trouble Sherry is elaborately evasive. He is really worried about Europe, and the debt, and Hitler; Hitler, who according to Moulton, "is all swelled up and no place to burst."

They think perhaps if they were to play games it might distract Sherry, but the only game Sherry feels like playing is murder. Jim isn't interested in murder. It is his idea that they should write a play and act it. He (Jim) will play the husband, Sherry can be the great lover, and Moulton—

"Wait, there's a nice part for you," Jim tells Moulton. "This is the eternal quadrangle. Now here's the idea, Sherry. I'm fed up with Diana. She's fed up with me, along you come. You're bored. So you steal her from me. Something to pass the time away. At least you think you're stealing her, but we have a great laugh behind your back. (DIANA *laughs;* JIM *laughs;* MOULTON *laughs.*) All in good part, you understand. Then of course, you get bored again—you always get bored. You're just the type—and that's where he comes in—but you're not interested."

"No— Sorry, but I keep thinking about Europe," protests Sherry. "It's all so sad. I just don't see how you all can go on being so light-hearted, laughing and playing games with all the suffering going on in the world—I really—"

"I say, old chap—"

"I'm sorry. I didn't mean to make a scene. I—I must go and compose myself. Thanks for your sympathy, dear friends, thanks —and NUTS to you!!"

Sherry is gone when Teresa comes down dressed for her trip back to town. She accepts their congratulations on her evening's performance smilingly and invites them all to come and see her at her club. They have left her and she has started for her taxi when Sherry appears. He, too, is grateful to Teresa for being such a good sport.

"I didn't know I was coming to your house," says Teresa. "Why didn't you tell me?"

"Very simple. I didn't know it. . . . Is it likely I'd ask you to come to my own house to meet my wife?"

"Not good enough?"

"Oh, have some sense."

"Well, you're right. I'm not good enough, and neither are you."

Marcia knows what they have been to each other, Sherry confesses. He has told her. And now, Teresa supposes, there will be a cute little divorce suit. The more she tries to keep out of trouble the more she gets into.

There will be a divorce suit, admits Sherry, but Teresa will not be in it. It will be a suit that he will bring himself.

"Well, you certainly have some quaint ideas," Teresa admits. "You've been cheating. She caught you and so you sue her for divorce. Tell me, Mr. Warren, you can trust your old doctor. Do you hear strange voices calling you? How's your knee-jerk? (*Flecks it.*) It's all right."

"I'm not joking."

"Is that all you're going to tell me?"

"See the daily papers for details."

Marcia comes in before Teresa leaves and adds her thanks to those of the others for the entertainment. Marcia makes sure that Teresa has her check and it would be nice if sometime when she is in the neighborhood she would drop in on them—

"And don't mind if I'm not here. Make yourself quite at home. It would be a God-send to Sherry. The poor boy gets so bored."

Marcia also insists that Sherry shall take Miss German to the station. Nor will she accept any excuses. . . .

Fanny finds Marcia a moment later and tries to reason with her. She hopes Marcia will not talk with Sherry until she has cooled off. But Marcia knows exactly what she's going to do.

"Very well," snaps Fanny. "Burn down the house and get rid of the rats!"

"Would you have me stand Sherry's immorality?"

"Would you have Sherry stand yours?"

"Who says I've been immoral?"

"I don't know anything about you. You're a damn fool. I wash my hands of you."

"All right, Mrs. Pilate. Get 'em good and clean."

Sherry is back and wants to talk with Marcia. Fanny is perfectly willing to leave them, but before she does she has something to say and says it:

"I thought you were a couple of thoroughbreds," she says; "but now I apologize to all horses—you're nothing but a pair of mules—and mules, as you recall, are creatures with no pride of ancestry and no hope of posterity!!!"

As soon as Fanny leaves them Sherry would know what Marcia meant by filling the house up with bores. She knew he'd hate it. And as if that weren't enough she stays out all night with that impudent skunk of a Salston! Where was she?

"It's a new side of your character," says Sherry, angrily. "By God, I'd never have believed you had it in you to be deliberately malicious."

"Oh, Sherry, you're a scream," lightly answers Marcia.

SHERRY—You think it's funny, do you?

MARCIA—I think you are.

SHERRY (*crosses to her*)—Come, come, little girl. . . . Tell me where you were last night, and what you did.

MARCIA—Must I?

SHERRY—You must or else—

MARCIA—Or else what?

SHERRY—Or else—it's all off.

MARCIA—Why not?

SHERRY—Marcia, tell me, have you been unfaithful to me?

MARCIA—No lies, you understand; never have been, and—never will be!

SHERRY—I repeat. Have you been unfaithful to me?

MARCIA—What do you think?

SHERRY—Answer me!

MARCIA—That's my answer.

SHERRY—You won't tell me?

MARCIA—No.

SHERRY—You don't deny it?

MARCIA—No. And I don't affirm it either. After all, why should I tell you the truth?

SHERRY—I told you the truth.

MARCIA—And don't you wish you hadn't?

SHERRY—Marcia, can't you see I'm in hell; don't you care at all?

MARCIA—And I? What about me? I should put on mourning—parade in sack-cloth and ashes! Not at all. I—do the best I can. That's all.

Diana, Jim and Moulton are back from the beach. Diana is just too, too disgusted because her bathing suit split just as she was going into the water. And "irrevocably and importantly—right across the vaccination mark," Lord Moulton adds. She must go in the pool to finish her swim and Marcia goes with her to find another suit.

Sherry takes advantage of the opportunity to talk with Jim. He would like to know what Jim means by staying out all night with Marcia. Jim doesn't think he has to mean anything. Certainly there would be no point in staying out all night alone. Besides, why doesn't Sherry ask Marcia?

Sherry would like to have Jim leave his house, but there again Jim refuses to stir without word from his hostess. Even if Sherry were to throw him out it would do little good. He would only stand outside and throw pebbles at the window and call to Marcia to come out, too. Which, in her present frame of mind, she probably would do.

It occurs to Jim that Sherry cuts rather a ridiculous figure playing the jealous husband. Once Jim had bought a revolver on Sherry's account. Sold it next day, however, and lost fifty cents on the transaction. Sherry promptly offers to reimburse him and Jim smilingly takes the money. Now their account is closed—unless Sherry chooses to reopen it.

Sherry is content. Jim has gone to the pool and Sherry has ordered his hat and coat and the car. He is at the desk writing a note when Marcia comes back. He is checking out, he tells her. Going to town. For the present his club will serve as an address to which she may send such letters and bills as come for him. He is at the door when Marcia calls to him.

"Since this is likely to be the last intimate talk you and I are ever likely to have together," she says earnestly, "I'd like to try and find out what the hell it's all about."

"Don't you know?"

MARCIA—You're not the best-looking man in the world, and certainly you haven't the sweetest temper; you can be rude—you can be cruel—why, then, is it that without you, everything's a washout? Why is it that you feel the same about me, for no matter how stupid you've been I know damn well you do.

SHERRY—Ah, if you really did know.

MARCIA—I do know, I tell you. But why? That's what sticks me.

SHERRY—Simple enough. It's chemistry.

MARCIA—Chemistry?

SHERRY—Two elements continually seeking each other, object union.

MARCIA—I see. I'm X3 NO4, and you're N20. So it's all chemistry—just a natural law. We've nothing to do with it.

SHERRY—Devilish little.

MARCIA—Then, when these two elements have found each other, why not contentment? Why hell instead of heaven?

SHERRY—Speaking as N20, damned if I know.

MARCIA—Why should I be able both to adore you and hate

you—so poisonously that I could gayly see you in agony. You said just now that you were in hell, and I didn't care. You were right. I was glad of it. I'm glad of it.

SHERRY—I can't blame you for that.

MARCIA—I'm ashamed of it but it's true. What's gone wrong, Sherry? Have you taken things too much for granted? Have I? Should I have played the coquette?—from the beginning? Being sure of you was one of the finest things about it. To have to threaten you with other men—so as to hold you—too foul. Of course what I did was rotten—

SHERRY—What do you mean?

MARCIA—This business of Jim Salston—only I did it not to hold you, but to hurt you.

SHERRY—Felicitations on your success.

MARCIA—So you see, I'm worse than you, because whatever you did, it wasn't done to hurt me.

SHERRY—True enough that is.

MARCIA—Why was it done?

SHERRY—Once an ass—always dumb I suppose.

MARCIA—Do you remember once I told you, Mr. Pitcher, not to go too often to the well? Do you still find the water sweet? So now you bad, delightful boy, saddle your horse and get the hell out of what's left of my life.

Sherry would go, but he would have Marcia know, first, that he had never dreamed what he did would hurt her as it did. It may be too late to be sorry, but he would like to have her believe that. And there is one other thought he is urged to release. It is not an original thought—but—if there had been a child—

"I know," admits Marcia. "This is the age of speed, but after all we've only been married seven months. Be reasonable."

"Marcia! Do you mean to say you're—"

"Nothing of the kind. I never had any intentions of having a child until I could be perfectly sure there'd be a father for that child, more or less regularly around the house. Imagine a baby voice saying: 'Where's my daddy?' and me having to answer: 'My little precious, I don't know, and for heaven's sake let's talk about the N.R.A.' "

"No, not so good."

MARCIA—No, I have no intentions of playing matron to a collection of semi-orphans.

SHERRY—You're right.

MARCIA—I suppose there must be thousands of people in exactly this situation at the present moment.

SHERRY—Undoubtedly. . . .

MARCIA—And most of them will do as we are doing—let it all go to smash—as if it weren't worth the battle—and if they're good for anything at all, their spirits will go—like ours—crippled and scarred to the grave.

SHERRY—I'm afraid you're right!

MARCIA—I had hoped that when it came my time to go I'd be able to take your hand in mine for the last time and say, "Thank you for a perfectly swell party."

SHERRY—It all comes down to this, doesn't it? How much are two people willing to hurt each other?

MARCIA—And what sacrifices are they willing to make to prevent those hurts precisely?

SHERRY—Have you thought of this? Once a man has seen a woman he loves suffer on his account it might be that he couldn't bear the thought of doing it again. Purely selfish, of course it would mean that he would suffer too.

MARCIA—Oh, yes, for a time—but he'd get bored again—

SHERRY—I suppose so.

MARCIA—And restless.

SHERRY—Oh, yes!

MARCIA—The polygamous male would stir again within him, there would be times when that slight difference between monogamy and monotony would reach the vanishing point, no woman can thrill a man 24 hours a day seven days a week.

SHERRY—No, hardly—but there would be thrills.

MARCIA—Oh, yes!

SHERRY (*kneeling by her*)—Marcia! Marcia! My darling! I—I cannot hurt you any more. Never again—you must believe that, do you, my darling?

MARCIA—Almost.

SHERRY—Then—is there any more to say?

MARCIA—Do you still wish to know what happened last night?

SHERRY—As you like.

MARCIA—Then I'll tell you—

SHERRY—Wait—I'm not sure, I—I—

MARCIA—Don't worry, I'll tell you on our Golden Wedding Day!

Sherry has taken Marcia in his arms as

THE CURTAIN FALLS

WEDNESDAY'S CHILD

A Drama in Two Acts

By Leopold Atlas

THEATREGOING having again become one of the more popular of New York's winter sports, mid-season developed a perverseness that resulted in a series of rather distinguished failures.

Among these was the expectantly-awaited Eugene O'Neill drama, "Days Without End." A little later came Clemence Dane's poetic and beautifully played Chatterton drama, "Come of Age."

George Abbott, one of the theatre's saner judges of plays and a master in the staging of them, missed it completely with an English playwright's serious attempt to dramatize the life of our martyred "John Brown." And finally Arthur Hopkins, taking over the play Philip Barry had carefully fashioned for Maude Adams's return to the stage, called "The Joyous Season," suffered a two-week failure with Lillian Gish in the chief part.

It was during these dolorous weeks that a light domestic drama called "Wednesday's Child," written by Leopold Atlas, a young man of Brooklyn previously unknown in the Broadway theatre, was hopefully produced at the Longacre.

The story, which is that of a "divorced kid," the child of parents who separate and can find no place, comfortably, in either of their new homes for their son of ten years, rests pretty heavily upon the shoulders of the lad engaged to play the boy. Fortunately for the producers of "Wednesday's Child" there was a talented young man available in Frank M. Thomas, Jr., the ten-year-old son of Mona Bruns, actress, and Frank M. Thomas, who has played juveniles for many years.

The comedy's reception was enthusiastic in some quarters and less than that in others. The tragedies of childhood have a peculiar appeal to a definite section of the playgoing public, and the specific tragedy of the children of divorced parents is particularly poignant in this divorce-ridden land. But there is also a divorce-conscious public that does not care to be reminded of its failures and a considerable public of playgoers that is frankly opposed to child actors, however talented.

As the play begins in the dining room of the Phillipses, which is "the typical dining room found in 'developed' districts," Ray, Kathryn and Bobby Phillips are finishing their dinner.

"Ray is thirty-five, dark-complexioned and medium sized." Kathryn is a pretty blonde of about twenty-nine or thirty. A vivacious person, normally, but one whose natural vivacity "has been dulled by control and boredom." "Bobby is a normally built boy of about ten," resembling his mother more than his father, his head of tawny hair hanging in unrestrained locks over his forehead, his eyes "black, clear, luminous and wide with childhood."

Ray Phillips, it appears, has arrived home unexpectedly from a trip and dressed himself up for a celebration. Came on from Baltimore two weeks ahead of his schedule just to surprise his wife and son. Ray thought it would be fun, but Kathryn is plainly put out. It frightened her to come into the house and suddenly hear someone, she didn't know who, walking around upstairs.

"You got so frightened and slammed the icebox door and right off you said: 'That's Ray!'" reports Bobby.

Kathryn can't remember that.

Ray has brought good news from Baltimore. He has landed a sizable contract. With it goes a chance that they may be able to move out of the suburbs and live in town, as Kathryn has always wanted to do. But now Kathryn receives the news with no more than an exclamation of surprise. Ray can't understand that.

"Here I come in two weeks ahead of time with good news and all I get is 'Oh!'" he pouts.

"Why, no—it's marvelous," Katbryn quickly protests. "Congratulations!"

"I came home and wanted to change into a fresh suit and this was the first one that caught my eye," Ray goes on; "so I put it on thinking—well—I thought I'd dress up to sort of celebrate my first dinner home in a month—and that contract—but I guess it wasn't a very good idea—"

Ray has gone to the kitchen to serve the dessert and Bobby has been sent to see if he can find his mother's cigarette holder when Kathryn tries a little excitedly to dial a number on the telephone. She manages to keep in touch with Ray by calling instructions to him while she waits for an answer to her call, but Bobby is more difficult. He is back at the head of the stairs just a little too soon and the phone has to be suddenly abandoned.

Ray would introduce a little comedy as a waiter with the dessert, but his audience is not responsive. Kathryn is preoccupied and Bobby has gone suddenly silent. His father would twit him about this. What trouble is he in? Report card all right? What boy in the neighborhood has got a black eye? If everything is all right, let Bobby drink his milk and eat his cakes.

Now, then, what has Kathryn been doing that's interesting, while her husband has been away?

"Interesting. . . . Here?" demands Kathryn, with a trace of a sneer.

"Well, I know this place can be awfully dull," admits Ray. "Sometimes I'm sorry we bought this house. But at the time I thought it would be great. You did, too. (KATHRYN *is silent.*) Well—if this new contract will land me the New York territory, then—well, there's a chance. . . . But in the meantime you ought to go out somewhere—meet people."

KATHRYN (*with a smile*)—Well, perhaps I have— (BOBBY *stops eating cake and stares at* KATHRYN.)

RAY—Who?

KATHRYN—Well—

RAY—Keeping something from me?

KATHRYN—Why, Ray!

RAY—Been hobnobbing, huh? (*To* BOBBY.) Your mother been hobnobbing, son? (BOBBY *still stares at* KATHRYN *silently.*) Hey—what *is* this?

KATHRYN (*quickly*)—Nonsense. I've stayed at home and home and home. And as for things of interest—there's plenty to do in this house—without a maid—visitors—

RAY—Visitors?

KATHRYN—Well, Mrs. Williams was here on Monday for tea and on Wednesday—well, as for going out, I've taken a stroll or two on the boardwalk with Bobby. (*She half turns to* BOBBY *and as she does is attracted by his stare. She frowns.*) Why are you staring at Mother like that?

BOBBY (*shifting his eyes*)—I'm not staring.

KATHRYN—You mustn't stare at anyone, dear. It isn't good manners.

BOBBY (*to* RAY)—I wasn't staring at her. I was just watching her talk.

RAY (*easily*)—Well, he shows good taste, anyhow. (*Hall clock strikes eight.*)

Kathryn (*startled*)—Is it eight o'clock already? (*She rises and goes to arch door.*)

Ray—Sounds like it. Where are you going?

Kathryn (*stopping in door*)—Oh, I—I'm going upstairs. (*Playfully.*) Now don't ask me why; I'll be back in a minute.

Ray (*complacently*)—Very well—why?

Kathryn—I guess I may as well tell you—I'm going to put on an evening dress.

Ray—We're not going out this late?

Kathryn (*reassuringly*)—No. . . . We're staying home to-night.

Ray—Then why the evening dress?

Kathryn—Why the tuxedo?

Ray—Oh, I see.

Kathryn—I must rise to the occasion.

Kathryn has gone upstairs to change. Bobby and his father are clearing the table and stacking the dishes on a tea wagon. They can be washed tomorrow. Suddenly it occurs to Ray that Bobby's mother is all right. Nice of her to want to dress up that way. Why shouldn't they telephone the florist—

But when he would call the florist Ray finds Kathryn trying to talk on the extension from upstairs. She wanted to order some ginger ale, she explains.

Again Ray would find out what it is that is keeping Bobby so quiet. What's wrong? Has he broken any windows? What is it?

Bobby is ready to cross his heart that he hasn't done anything. Isn't in any trouble. Hasn't eaten too much candy. He's all right.

They are on the floor trying to work out a jig-saw puzzle that Ray has brought Bobby when Kathryn comes down. She is looking very beautiful in an evening dress now. Beautiful enough to be kissed, thinks her husband, suiting the action to the thought.

"I shouldn't have to travel so much," Ray decides, finding contentment in an easy chair with a cigar. "Traveling men shouldn't marry pretty wives," he adds, smiling at Kathryn. "But—oh, what's the difference; it all comes out in the wash. Miss me?"

"Of course!"

"How much?"

"Oh, Ray!"

"Oh, come on. That's not missing me very much."

She has tried to kiss him as he expected to be kissed when Bobby suddenly jumps up from the floor with a hurt cry.

"Don't do that!" he shouts.

It must be Bobby's jealous, laughs Ray, and his father doesn't blame him. Kathryn thinks it is because it is after Bobby's bedtime that he is acting so. He often acts that way at bedtime.

Now Bobby has gone to bed. Not upstairs. On the sun porch. Kathryn has had his bed moved down there, she explains, since the weather has turned nice.

Kathryn, still restless, would have Ray tell her something of his experiences on the road, as they settle down for a talk.

"Tell me—when you're on the road do you—" She is trying a little desperately to frame the thought in her mind. "Well, I know you have to go out and entertain your customers, but I mean—"

RAY—Don't worry, old girl. I don't stay in any town any longer than I can help it.

KATHRYN—I know.—But—Ray—have you ever wanted to—well, have you ever wished you weren't married, sometimes on the road?

RAY—Not me. Any time a pretty telephone gal gives me the eye I say, "Nothin' doin', dearie—I'm a married man." Hey, not jealous, are you?

KATHRYN—Why, no. I only meant—well, I wondered—if sometimes you wished you weren't a married man.

RAY—Jealous as sure as I'm born. Well, rest easy. I'm perfectly satisfied the way I am.

KATHRYN—You're—perfectly satisfied the way you are.

RAY—Say—what's got into you?

KATHRYN—Ray—I— Well, if I only could make you—

RAY (*he moves over and puts his arm around her*)—Ah, cheer up! I'm *here*. And I'm liable to be here this trip for two months. There now. Aw, I know how you feel— (*With sincerity.*) Well, I feel that way, too. What'd you think I clipped two weeks off my route for—eh? (*Kisses her.*) Hey! (*Rises.*) How about that ginger ale? (*Slyly imitating speak-easy man when someone is watching; out of the corner of his mouth.*) What'll you have—scotch or rye?

KATHRYN—Whatever you say.

RAY (*goes to kitchen*)—Rye it is.

KATHRYN (*a slight pause; looking straight front*)—I'll help you if you want me to.

RAY (*off*)—No, sir—this is a man's job.

Kathryn's eyes are slowly drawn to the telephone. Now she has dialed a number quickly and left the receiver while she crosses to the kitchen door to assure herself that Ray is still busy. Back at the phone she gets the connection.

"Hello—Howard—He's back!—Yes!"

She hangs up quickly and has returned to the center of the room when Bobby walks in. He has come, he explains a little surlily, to get the present his father had given him.

Bobby gathers his jig-saw puzzle together and goes back to the porch doors. He turns there and looks hard and accusingly at his mother. She is staring back at him as the lights fade.

In the corner of a fence surrounding an abandoned suburban building project the boys of the neighborhood have started building a fort. In one corner there are stacks of old boxes, piles of stones, brick and tile. Back of the fort is a brick wall and presently Bobby is heard to warn a noisy crowd the other side of the fence that the last one over will be a yeller-belly. As a result of the threat five heads suddenly appear at the top of the wall and a second later five excited boys have dropped inside the yard. The wrangling for the next several minutes concerns the fairness of a contest in which Alfred, just now getting over the wall, was tripped up.

Now the fort building goes forward with fair success, until Bobby tries to send Joie and Alfred into the woods as scouts to watch for a band of woppies who might attack at any moment. Joie and Alfred have no fear of the enemy, but neither have they any liking for ghosts, of which Lenny's sister has intimated the woods are full. On second thought it is decided to let Joie and Alfred stay close to the fort and pile up the smaller stones.

There is further progress until Joie and Alfred get into an argument that interferes seriously with their getting of ammunition. Joie, it appears, has insisted that a bastard is a kid that is born in a basket.

"Hey," yells one called Herbie, approaching the disputants menacingly; "don't you say that word or I'll tell mamma on you. It's a dirty word."

"I didn't say it," Alfred yells back. "Some kid in school did and Joie says it's a baby that was born in a basket and left near a hospital door."

"Sure it is. I saw it in the movies," shrills Joie. "How a

mother leaves a baby and rings a doorbell."

"Aw, you're nuts!"

"All right, you tell them what you think it is if you're so smart."

"It's a kid without a father or mother."

"That's an orphan," laughs Georgie.

"Well, ain't orphans bastards?" demands Alfred.

"Hey!" warns Herbie.

"I'm just saying it because he made a bet," pleads Alfred.

"There can't be any kids without mothers," soberly announces Bobby, climbing to the top of the boxes. "There can be without fathers, but not mothers."

The work goes on. Also the discussion. Georgie now comes forward with the real explanation. A bastard, insists Georgie, is a kid who doesn't know who his father is. If that's right, argues Alfred, he wins the argument, because he came closest when he said it was a kid without a father or mother. But it is Georgie's decision that the two of them are cock-eyed, so the argument is dropped.

Now most of the army admits being tired. It's getting dark, and anyway they've done enough. Ain't they got all summer to finish it? Bobby is the only one eager for work. He wants to see a regular castle with turrets and towers and a moat. It can be done, if they do a little every day.

There is not great interest in the future of the castle, but it's important what a fella is going to be. Georgie is going to be a cop, like his father. Lenny is going to take up fishing and go fishing every Sunday, like his father. Herbie is going to be an automobile racer. Bobby has them all beat—he's going to be an engineer. That beats a cop. An engineer travels all over the world.

". . . I spoke to my father, and he said an engineer was one of the best things to be," concludes Bobby, with a suggestion that the discussion is closed.

"Which man is your father," inquires Lenny.

"You know my father," answers Bobby, sharply, after he has stood for a second as though a thunderbolt had struck him.

"Is it that man we saw you walking with last night?" persists Lenny.

"Yeah."

Georgie—We never saw him before.

Bobby—He was away on a long trip. He came back last week. He went away this morning again.

LENNY—I thought that man we saw in an automobile with your mother about two weeks ago was your father. (*As* BOBBY *hesitates.*) Remember that time we took a hike.

BOBBY (*confused*)—I don't remember.

GEORGIE—You do so. Remember, we saw a woman with a man in an automobile that was parked and we sneaked up and saw it was your mother.

BOBBY—Maybe it wasn't my mother.

LENNY (*boyishly malicious*)—What are you lyin' for? You reco'nized her. Don't you remember you were going to go to her when she kissed the man?

BOBBY (*cornered*)—She didn't kiss him!

LENNY—Yes, she did.

BOBBY (*angrily*)—She was only talking to him.

GEORGIE—She kissed him. Boy, for about a half hour! (*He smacks his lips.*) What a kiss!

LENNY—Herbert saw it too, didn't you, Herbert?

BOBBY (*at his wit's end*)—Well, that man was my father.

LENNY—Wow, did you ever see such a dumb kid. You just said the other man was your father.

BOBBY—They're both the same man.

LENNY—The man in the automobile was blond and the man you walked with had black hair. (*Triumphantly.*) He doesn't even know who his own father is.

BOBBY—I do so.

LENNY—Who is he then? The blond one or the other man?

BOBBY (*white with rage*)—Shut up, you dirty little sneak.

LENNY—It's better to be a dirty little sneak than be a bastard.

BOBBY (*rushing at him with both fists flying*)—You take that back!

There is a scramble for positions from which to view the fight, accompanied by much yelling. Georgie takes the fight off Lenny's hands, seeing he's nearer Bobby's size. Now Georgie and Bobby are wrestling and Georgie trips Bobby. As Bobby falls Georgie runs over and gets back of the fort. The others run for the wall and scramble over.

"You don't know who your father is! You don't know who your father is! You don't know who your father is!" The chorus floats back.

Bobby is after Georgie, who ducks below the fort. Now he climbs after Alfred, who ducks back of the wall.

"You don't know who your father is! You don't know who

your father is!" The chorus swells and continues persistently.

"You take that back. You take that back too. You take that back."

Bobby has grabbed a handful of rocks. Georgie has climbed out of the fort and is on the wall.

"Come on, Herbert. It's getting darker. We'll leave the bastard alone!" calls Georgie, scrambling over.

"I'll show you!" yells Bobby, hurling a stone. "You're on my side, aren't you, Herbie?"

"No, I'm not," shouts Herbert. "My mother says your mother's a wild woman."

The five are over the fence and have swung into a kind of chant as they return the rock fire and gradually move away.

"Bobby is a bastard!" . . . "Your mother kissed a feller down 'n the cellar!" . . . "Who's your father?—Who's your father?" "I don't know."

"I'll show you!" shouts Bobby, throwing another stone over the fence. "I'll show you! I don't need you skunks to help me. It's my fort!" . . . "Run, run, you bunch of yeller-bellies. Wait until I get you alone. I'll make you eat dirt!" . . . "Wait until I grow up. I'll show you. You'll come begging on your knees to me!" . . . "My mother didn't kiss that man. Even if she did, you didn't see her. I'll show you!"

Bobby is down on his knees now, starting to work again on the castle. Suddenly his emotions get the better of him and he leans heavily against the wall, raising a choking voice in prayer.

"Please make my mother love only my father, God," he prays, his shoulders shaking. "I've only got one father. You know who he is. Kill the other man, God, kill him and I'll always love you and do anything you want me to do, anything in the world. And please don't let anyone find out what my mother did. Please, God."

It is quite dark. Slowly Bobby conquers his sobs and gets to his feet. There are many shadows about him and they are a little frightening. Now he climbs hurriedly up the boxes and disappears over the wall as the lights fade.

Bobby is asleep in his bed, which has been placed at one side of the sun porch. The moonlight, coming through a window back of the bed, falls on his head. Just now it is a restless Bobby tossing about a good deal. Faintly, as from a great distance, the chorus of yelling boys can be heard: "You don't know who your father is!" . . . "Bobby's a bastard!" . . .

Through the long glass panels of the French door leading into the Phillips' hall the shadows of Ray and Kathryn are thrown into strong silhouette when Ray turns on the light in the living room. Kathryn evidently has just come home. Ray is facing her accusingly, demanding a report of the Ladies' Club meeting she is supposed to have attended.

Ray's questioning is direct. Kathryn's explanation is evasive. His anger flares as he announces that he knows she has not been to a club meeting and that he knows damn well what she has been doing. Kathryn is greatly relieved that he does. But it is not the way he thinks—

"You've been making a fool out of me for God knows how long, and it's not the way I think," he sneers.

"I want to—God knows I want to—tell you everything—but if you won't let me—" she protests.

Bobby has begun to stir in his bed. Now he wakens and raises himself on one elbow. The pacing shadows on the door fascinate him.

"Who is he? What's his name?" Ray's voice has risen above its first guarded tones.

"What difference does it make?"

"Not a damn bit of difference."

"Ray, please—"

Bobby is out of bed, standing, listening. The voices in the other room have risen to a muffled shouting. The shadows on the door move restlessly about, now growing to menacing proportions, now dwindling to doll shapes.

"I'm just as miserable as you are about the whole thing," Kathryn is saying.

"I marry you—I buy you a decent home—well, it's not a mansion—but it is a home—I minded my own business—never looked at another woman—and look—look what happens."

Bobby has moved away from the bed closer to the door.

"I was young, Ray. I shouldn't have married so soon. We should have waited—taken more time to realize more about—us."

"Yeah. I guess we shouldn't have got married at all."

"And as for Bobby—and Frankie—well, it was just unfortunate that I had them so soon."

Bobby backs away until he sits on the side of the bed, his face a study in childish horror.

"Unfortunate? You mean—you didn't want them?" Ray demands.

"That's not the point. We shouldn't have had them. We weren't ready for them."

"You shouldn't have been bothered! Children get in the way of women who want to play around!"

The quarrel goes on. Charge and counter-charge. Ray has never understood, Kathryn protests. The way he is acting now is proof that he never understood. He is at least partly to blame.

"Ray, all I ever meant to you was someone to come home to, a housekeeper. I tried to tell you over and over, but I never could make you understand. . . . I stayed with you for ten years hoping for things to get better. They didn't. I didn't mean to fall in love—I didn't want to—"

The confession continues. Kathryn has known the man with whom she is in love for seven months. She has hated sneaking in and out and wondering what was going to happen next.

That is a question that has to be settled, realizes Ray. What are they to do? Perhaps there can be a settlement of some sort. Perhaps—if she will stop seeing this fellow—

"No, Ray," Kathryn answers firmly. "It's gone further than that. . . . We've got to break it up. I'm going to leave you!"

Bobby starts toward the door, as though in protest. He is stopped as the shadowed figures come closer to the window.

"Oh, that's the way it is!" Ray is shouting. "All right—go ahead—leave me. Go back to your *boy friend.* I know a little about these guys who play around with married women."

"He's not that kind. . . . He loves me."

"He loves you. Ha! Ha! That's rich." He is laughing bitterly. The shadows on the wall have grown until Bobby cowers a little before them.

"Stop laughing!" shouts Kathryn, hysterically.

RAY—He's just using you for what he can get.

KATHRYN—That's not true.

RAY—You're just a nice little—

KATHRYN—Ray. If you don't stop saying these things I'll—

RAY—What does he give you for his little fun?

KATHRYN—Stop it.

RAY—Jewelry? Money?

KATHRYN—Oh! ! (*She slaps him. He backs up and then raising his arm advances.*)

RAY—Why, you rotten little—

KATHRYN—Ray, don't you dare—

There is the sound of a resounding slap, followed by the noise of falling chairs and crashing pottery. Bobby has started forward, excitedly—

"Stop! Stop! Please don't, Mother, Dad! Please don't—"

The figures are swaying back and forth. There are cries of defiance and threats. Bobby stands silhouetted against the door. They have not heard his calls.

"Let me go! Let me go! I want to get out of here!" shouts Kathryn.

"Get out! I don't ever want to see you again!" roars Ray.

"Don't worry. You won't! This is the end of everything!"

She has broken from Ray and run toward the door, the shadow on the screen rapidly diminishing. There is a slam of a door.

"Good! That's fine! I'm through!" shouts Ray.

Bobby is still calling. He runs to where his clothes have been left on a chair. He is starting feverishly to put them on as the lights fade.

A half hour later Kathryn is sitting on a bench on a boardwalk overlooking the sea. There is a railing at the edge of the walk, and other benches are placed against it.

Kathryn has evidently been waiting for some time. The approach of a man walking hurriedly toward her brings her quickly to her feet. As she recognizes the man she goes to him with a sigh of relief.

Howard Benton is a man of about thirty-two, "tall, lean, and dressed in a summer suit." A calm and collected young man, surprised to find Kathryn trembling, worried until he has heard what has happened. He is glad that Kathryn has broken with her husband completely. He has wanted her to take that step for weeks, as she knows, though he had rather they had talked it over with her husband before the move was made.

Kathryn's report of the quarrel and that Ray had struck her makes a difference. Howard is incensed at that. Now she must get her divorce at once.

"One thing I'll never understand," says Howard, taking Kathryn in his arms and kissing her ardently, "is why you married him without having waited first for me."

"I'll never understand it myself," Kathryn answers happily.

"It doesn't matter now, dear, does it? We have a long time before us to make up for it."

Kathryn's arms are about Howard when a movement down the walk attracts her. She stares off into the dark, and recognizes Bobby. His father must have sent him, she thinks. She doesn't want Bobby to see them together yet.

Howard has gone on down the walk. A moment later Bobby

calling "Mom!" excitedly, has come in. He has been running. "Several buttons of his pajama shirt are unbuttoned. His shoes are unlaced. He wears no stockings and his hair is disordered." Kathryn takes him in her arms. Her suspicion grows.

KATHRYN—He sent you to follow me, didn't he? To see what I'd do.

BOBBY—No!

KATHRYN—Well, you ought to be proud of him, getting you out of bed to find me.

BOBBY (*protesting*)—No—no. He didn't send me.

KATHRYN—He didn't tell you to lie too, did he?

BOBBY—I'm not lying.

KATHRYN—No?

BOBBY (*pleading*)—Come on home. It's cold here and—and— What do you want to stay here for? Come on home.

KATHRYN—Home. (BOBBY *starts.*) Go back to where he's waiting for you and tell him that if he's changed his mind—I haven't. (BOBBY *doesn't move, but stands before her, his head lowered. She moves toward him.*) What's the matter with you? Are you crying? Oh, don't cry, Bobby. There's nothing to cry over. All this can't be helped. That's the way things are. (*Then she becomes angry at the thought of* RAY.) But he should never have sent *you.* He should have known better than that.

BOBBY (*blurting out in defense of his father*)—He didn't send me. He's home.

KATHRYN (*puzzled*)—He's home?

BOBBY (*nods, rubbing his eyes*)—I came myself. He didn't even see me.

KATHRYN (*astonished, her eyes wide with awe*)—Bobby— Did you hear your father and me quarrel? (BOBBY *nods.*) Oh!

BOBBY—I looked all over for you. I couldn't find you and then I suddenly thought you might be here.

KATHRYN (*quickly; searchingly*)—You thought I might be here?— Why? (BOBBY *squirms, refusing to answer. A horrible suspicion enters her mind.*) Have you ever seen me here before?

BOBBY—No.

KATHRYN—Then what made you think you'd find me *here?*

BOBBY—I don't know. I just thought so.

KATHRYN—Why?

BOBBY (*hesitantly*)—Because—because—it's near the water.

KATHRYN (*astonished, uncomprehending*)—Near the water? What has that to do with my being here? (BOBBY *doesn't an-*

swer.) Well?

BOBBY (*blurting out in a mixture of plaintive appeal, horror and earnestness*)—You didn't come here to throw yourself in the water—did you?

KATHRYN (*completely astonished*)—Throw myself in the water?

BOBBY—When father—hit you—you screamed out he'd never see you again—you were going to end everything—and I got afraid—because that means—

KATHRYN—And—and you thought I was going to— (*Suddenly she cries out and hugs him.*) Oh, no, no. Mother isn't going to drown herself. Oh, Bobby, you should never have thought that. When one drowns oneself, one dies, and mother doesn't want to die. She wants to live. She wants to live now no matter— (*She stops. There is a silence. She dabs her eyes, and then laughs caressingly at* BOBBY.) Look how you're dressed. You didn't even lace your shoes. No, let mother do that for you this time. Come, let's sit on the bench. And you mustn't ever go out like this again, Bobby, or you'll catch a cold. Look at you without stockings. Aren't you cold now? (BOBBY *shakes his head.*) Now your other foot. You button your shirt; it's open. There you are, all tight and snug.

BOBBY—Thanks.

Kathryn would have Bobby run back home, now. She can't explain to him just why she doesn't want to come with him. He wouldn't understand. Some day, when he is grown up, if he should want to know she will tell him.

Bobby thinks if she is staying away because his father hit her, she must remember she hit him first. She called him (Bobby) a bad name, too. She called him an unfortunate—and that means a bastard.

Kathryn is sure she couldn't have done that, even if she was excited. Again she insists he shall go home and when she has arranged several things she will come and get him and take him to her new home.

"Are you waiting for someone?" Bobby demands.

"No. Mother only wants to sit here and think," she says. "Now, Bobby. . . . Do run along, and mother'll come to see you soon. And take care of you. She promises that."

Bobby has started off angrily. He is not anxious to come back and be kissed. He knows now that she does not love his father any more and he knows why. It is all her fault too. Hers and that other man's.

"You came here to meet that man. . . . That's him—standing there—waiting for you—he's going to take you away. . . . I hate him . . . and I hate you, too."

"Bobby!"

"I know. You don't want to come back because you want to go away with that man. . . . I know more. . . . I know a lot more. . . . I wouldn't tell anybody in the world—but you—I'll tell you. . . . I'll tell you now. . . . I don't care, about anything, any more."

Bobby's voice is shaken as he rushes on with his charge. He knows what has happened. He has followed them. He knows where that man lives and he knows she has been in his house. He saw her.

His voice still shaking with his sobs Bobby has rushed off toward his home. Kathryn sinks weakly on a bench. Suddenly the force of Bobby's tragedy has come home to her. For a moment it is overwhelming.

The returning Howard is reassuring, but she does not tell him all that Bobby has said.

"I heard him shouting and saw him run off," Howard says. "He seemed kind of upset."

"He—wants me—to come back—with him," Kathryn answers, slowly. "He'd been awakened from his sleep—by our quarreling —and when I left he tried to find me."

HOWARD (*moving closer*)—Oh. It's a shame he had to hear you quarrel . . . unfortunate.

KATHRYN (*alarmed, turning quickly to him*)—Howard! Let's get away from here. Take me with you.

HOWARD (*quietly*)—Yes, you must be pretty well fagged out. (*He puts his arm around her.*) You've had enough excitement for one evening. I'll drive you to a hotel.

KATHRYN—Not your apartment?

HOWARD—We don't want to jeopardize your chances for a divorce, do we?

KATHRYN—No—we mustn't.

HOWARD—Things are a little different now. Come on.

KATHRYN (*after looking after* BOBBY *she turns quickly to* HOWARD *and grabs him tight*)—Howard—the boy—Bobby. . . . We'll take him with us, won't we?

HOWARD (*quietly, smilingly, comfortingly*)—Why, of course,

dear. He's your son. That goes with me.

They start off as the lights fade.

Some time later, nearing the conclusion of the divorce trial of Phillips vs. Phillips, it is the contention of the attorney for Mr. Phillips that the attorney for Mrs. Phillips has failed to produce corroborative evidence that the "mild discolorations of the skin commonly called bruises" suffered by Mrs. Phillips were caused by her husband.

The attorney for Mrs. Phillips thereupon insists that he has a corroborative witness to the beating, but he has hesitated to call him in view of his tender years.

"Your Honor, to my pleas let me add the proper indignation of Mrs. Phillips, the boy's mother, against the introduction of her child as a witness. Her mother feeling naturally revolts against the subjection of her boy to examination in his parents' divorce action, as counsel insists—"

"I do more firmly insist on his being called now," answers the attorney for Mr. Phillips. "I cannot permit counsel to pose as the savior of innocence. The court will recall that it was he and not I, who suggested him as a witness in the first place, and I will not allow him to evade his responsibility in calling the boy to the stand."

As a result of the arguments Bobby is finally called. He comes into court a trifle timid, but determined not to show it and assures the Judge, who has a quiet talk with him, that he doesn't know exactly what a gentleman is, but he knows gentlemen do not tell lies.

"And do you know what happens to people when they do tell lies?" asks the Judge.

"I—I think they're punished," answers Bobby.

"They are—they're punished by God. Do you know who God is?"

"Yes."

"Who is He?"

"I—I can't describe Him to you, but I've seen Him several times."

The Judge is forced to suppress the ripple of merriment that follows.

"You've seen Him?"

"I—I think so."

"When did you see Him?"

"Well, just after I close my eyes to go to sleep I look into someone else's eyes. He has a long beard. That's all; I look into someone else's eyes and fall asleep."

Bobby's testimony covers his going to sleep at half-past eight on the night of September 11; of his sleeping in the sun parlor, which is next to the living room; of his being wakened. He tries to get out of saying his father and mother were quarreling.

"Were they just quarreling or were they fighting like kids in the street?" demands Mrs. Phillips' attorney. When Bobby does not answer the attorney adds: "Did you see your father strike your mother?"

"I won't tell."

"Why won't you tell?"

"Because I don't want to."

"Did your mother scream when your father struck her?"

"Yes, she said—" Bobby catches himself. "I told you, didn't I, that I won't tell—"

"You don't have to tell us any more," triumphantly concludes the attorney.

Bobby is not any happier in the hands of his father's counsel. He would know if Bobby had ever wakened in the night to see his mother entertaining another man in the house; if it were not true that he was moved to the sun porch from upstairs so his mother could entertain a visitor, a man, upstairs; and if he ever had seen his mother walking and driving with a strange man.

To these interrogations Bobby cries a vigorous "No." And when his mother's attorney presses him for a statement as to whether or not he ever saw his mother kiss a strange man, or his father kiss a strange woman, he cries out in protest:

"Why don't you all leave me alone? . . . I want to go home!"

JUDGE—Gentlemen, I don't think the boy is in a position to testify as to the fidelities or infidelities of his parents. Unless you have any further point to make I would suggest that you discontinue the examination of the boy.

KEYES (*standing*)—There is no need for further questioning, Your Honor, since the boy has corroborated his mother's statement that Mr. Phillips struck her.

PROCTOR (*jumping up*)—Your Honor, I'm only trying to examine the boy to show—

RAY (*grabbing* PROCTOR'S *arm and stopping him*)—Never mind. Let it ride.

PROCTOR (*in half whisper to* RAY)—Mr. Phillips, don't you see—

JUDGE (*turning to* BOBBY)—All right, Bobby, we won't ask you any more questions. You may go now.

The attorneys have made their motions for dismissal of the action. The Judge has reserved decision. The lights fade.

A few hours later the jury has returned a verdict which is handed to the Judge. The parties to the action are called into court. Bobby is also summoned.

JUDGE—The jury having brought in a verdict for the plaintiff, I hereby award to the plaintiff a decree of divorce and in view of the facts shown, it is the opinion of this court that the mother shall have custody of the child. However, it is not the court's desire to deprive the child of the care of either of his parents. A boy in his growing years requires the supervision and guidance of the father as well as the mother, and there will therefore be incorporated into the decree, a provision, that the child shall be with the father during the months from June to September, inclusive, and the rest of the year with his mother, until the child has reached his majority. (*After a pause he turns to* BOBBY.) Now come here, Bobby, and I'll explain it to you. Do you understand what I have just said to your parents?

BOBBY (*with a nod of assent*)—Yes. Mamma and papa aren't married any more. (*Turning to* RAY *with a slight smile.*) I'm to be with my father from June to September— (*Then turning to* KATHRYN *accusingly.*) and the rest of the year with my mother.

THE CURTAIN FALLS

ACT II

Eight months later, in the home of his mother and stepfather, Bobby is hard at work finishing a box. A strong box that he can, if he wants to, send by express, he tells Carrie, the maid. It's a better box than he ever made in manual training class, even if there is a little hole in it. He left that purposely so air could get in.

Bobby is a funny kid, Carrie insists. He has been packing his things for days, as though he were going away for ten years. After all he is only going to his father for the summer. But Bobby is sure he needs the box. He can put all his things in it so they can be sent to him.

Carrie thinks the room had better be cleaned up. Mr. and Mrs.

Benton are coming. And Carrie has an idea they are bringing a surprise for him.

Bobby has carried some of the box scraps out of the house when Kathryn arrives. A minute later she has signaled to Benton, who rolls in a new bicycle.

"This ought to make him sit up and take notice," smiles Howard. "He can ride it here today and Monday I'll have it sent over to his father and—"

"You're really glad he's going, aren't you?" ventures Kathryn.

Howard insists he isn't glad. He doesn't like Kathryn to say such things. Soon she will be believing them. As for the bicycle, he thinks it would be better if Kathryn were to tell Bobby it is a present from her. She has been neglecting Bobby lately, and— But Kathryn would rather it would be a present from both of them.

The Bentons are standing together, with their arms about each other when Bobby comes. He stops short as he sees them. Then he sees the bicycle. His face lights up at sight of the wheel. He thanks Howard first, and then Kathryn, when they explain that it is a joint gift. His happiness is noticeably increased when they tell him he can take the bicycle with him to his father's and he pushes the wheel joyously before him as he goes to show it to Carrie and to take his first ride. He does not ask them to watch him ride it. That worries Howard.

HOWARD—Kathryn, there's no getting away from the fact that he's not happy here. Has it ever occurred to you that if he could be with his father all of the time—

KATHRYN—Howard!

HOWARD—Let's not deceive ourselves any longer. Let's admit what we've both been thinking.

KATHRYN—I know. You want his father to have him for good.

HOWARD—That's not the point. I like Bobby. I want him to be happy. But he isn't. It's what he's doing to you that worries me.

KATHRYN—I can't give him to his father entirely.

HOWARD—I want him to be with us just as much as you do. I like him. But if his being here is going to make you miserable —and him unhappy—and me—

KATHRYN—I can't give him up yet.

HOWARD—Good Lord, Kathryn, maybe he'd rather be with his father. You mustn't torture yourself like this. It's not your fault.

KATHRYN—It's both our faults.

HOWARD—How? I've done everything I can—I've gone out of my way to be nice to him—and so have you. We've given him everything he wants—

KATHRYN—It isn't giving him things that—

HOWARD—It's natural for him to feel strangely— He has a right to be bewildered—but he's doing more than that. He's making you feel as if you had committed a crime because you left his father and married me. Why, I've begun to feel that way myself. Every time I've kissed you, it's as if we'd been doing something nasty.

KATHRYN—I know.

HOWARD—But we're not doing anything nasty. We have a right to be happy. Why should he make us feel guilty and ashamed? It's the way he walks around, saying nothing, always by himself. It's enough to get on anyone's nerves.

KATHRYN—You don't understand what he's going through.

HOWARD—Of course I do. But that's no reason why he should go out of his way to make us all miserable.

KATHRYN—He's not—

HOWARD—Then why should he feel that way? What's he got against us? (KATHRYN *doesn't answer.*) Everywhere I turn I'm made to feel that I've hurt someone. I haven't. There's no reason for his taking it out on us this way.

KATHRYN—There is a reason. It's my living with you that he resents.

Kathryn thinks that, perhaps, if Howard were willing to let her be with Bobby alone for a time it would help. It isn't that Bobby doesn't like Howard. It is their living together. She will never have any self-respect, she feels, until she can get Bobby to respect her.

Howard is not pleased, but willing to make the sacrifice. Let Kathryn tell Bobby that when he comes back he can live alone with his mother. They can try it for awhile, anyway.

"I wish for your sake I could just—let him go and forget everything," confesses Kathryn, going to Howard's arms. "But—I couldn't live. I guess I'm just—"

Bobby is back. Howard has left. A little desperately Kathryn tries to talk with Bobby. He is restless and plainly embarrassed. He thinks he will go out and take another ride. Kathryn draws him back with a suggestion that they—just the two of them—take the car and have a picnic. They could roast marshmallows—and potatoes— And when he comes back from his father's—Bobby hadn't thought of coming back—

"You haven't been very happy here, have you, Bobby?" Kathryn finally asks.

"Well—"

KATHRYN—You haven't. Your bags have been packed for two days now. You packed them yourself. Do you want to get away from here—from me—so badly? (BOBBY *doesn't answer.*) You think you'll be happier with your father? (*Then with almost a cry.*) Oh, Bobby, why don't you forget what you're holding against me? If I could only make you understand. You must forget what you're holding against me. You must forget what's happened before. You mustn't remember everything. There are some things— (BOBBY *tries to get up but* KATHRYN *holds him. Her face grows desperately determined.*) All right, Bobby. I told you once I'd explain everything when you grew older, do you remember? You're not much older now. I don't know if I should but I'm going to try. It's time. Now, please, Bobby, try to understand— Listen— (*She gropes for words, a beginning, but cannot find it. But she continues nevertheless.*) If I still lived with your father as you want me to, you wouldn't be happy at all. Even if I went back to him now and we lived together without caring for each other— (*Seeing his adamant expression, she falters.*) No, that isn't what I wanted to say—I want to say this— Oh, why can't I—

BOBBY—Please, may I go out now?

KATHRYN (*anxiously pleading, she holds on to him*)—No, you must hear me. You *must* listen. You owe at least that much to me. You don't like my living with Howard. Now that isn't right, Bobby. Howard and I are married and we love each other. We've loved each other for a long time and anything we did a long time ago, or after, wasn't wrong, because when two people love each other there is nothing wrong, no matter what they do. Do understand! What's happened can't be helped or changed now. Oh, Bobby! You must learn to accept things. You mustn't bear resentment against me. You're spoiling your life and mine, too.

BOBBY—I have to go to my room.

KATHRYN (*frantically*)—You can't—you've got to listen! Because your mother's going to tell you something now that will make you very happy.

BOBBY—No.

KATHRYN—Look, Bobby! If I left Howard—I mean if you didn't see Howard any more . . . I'd go away from here and get another house—

BOBBY (*struggling hard to get away from her*)—No.

KATHRYN—And then you could come and live with me and I'd take care of you—

BOBBY—No.

KATHRYN—And we'd be together—

BOBBY (*with a sudden cry*)—Why can't I be with my father? Let me go. I want to go away from here! (*He finally breaks away and runs out.*)

KATHRYN (*following him to the door*)—Bobby! (*Leaning back against the door, giving up.*) All right. Go—go away.

The lights fade.

Two days later Ray Phillips and Bobby are just getting back to the Phillips home. The room is not greatly changed. The window drapes and portières are done up in white cloth bags and the center of the room is occupied by a large and a small packing case.

The room looks about the same to Bobby. Anyway, it looks O.K. Being men together and this being sort of a bachelor party, they decide to take off their coats.

The house has been pretty lonesome without anybody in it Ray confesses. He is glad to hear that Bobby's mother is all right, though Bobby's report of his mother has been indicated by nods rather than statements. However, if she is happy, and Bobby's happy, why everybody's happy, and that's fine and dandy.

Bobby is pretty close to tears with all this reminiscence, but men don't cry. It's probably an eyelash that got in his eye. Ray finally manages to find an eyelash, and that's all right.

They talk of the fine vacation they are going to have. They will go up to Maine for a couple of weeks, suggests Ray, and fish. Hunt, probably, too. They'll get a cabin and there'll only be the two of them and Ray'll cook a lot of steaks. He is a little worried about Bobby. He looks thin. Bobby isn't worried about that. Indians are thin, too, but they're strong, he points out. Bobby's all ready to start on that fishin' and huntin' trip right now. He wants to get into those big woods, where the Indians used to live. Once he had read a book about an Indian boy and a white boy—

Suddenly Ray thinks of something. Perhaps, after all, it would be better if Bobby were to go to a camp. Then he (Ray) could come up week ends— But Bobby wouldn't like it in a camp if his father couldn't be with him.

BOBBY (*insistently*)—But you said before—WE.

RAY—I know and I meant it. I hate to disappoint you this way. Well, maybe I'll be able to manage somehow. But what would you do while I was working? You'd be alone all day.

BOBBY—I won't mind that.

RAY—Yes, but I will.

BOBBY—Can't we do *this*, Dad? Can't we go for two weeks together and then you send me to camp?

RAY—But— (*He stops and smiles at the boy.*) Well, we'll see.

BOBBY—I don't want to be in your way—if you can't manage it—

RAY—Be in my way?

BOBBY—If you've got business—

RAY—No, I'll arrange it. Just us two, huh?

BOBBY—You'll fix it all up?

RAY—I sure will—you just leave that to dad.

BOBBY—Boy! (*Impulsively he kisses his father.*)

RAY (*slightly taken aback*)—Hey! . . . Say—we ought to celebrate this in some way. Reunion of father and son.

BOBBY—How'll we celebrate?

RAY—Well—there was a carnival here last week but that's not much good now—and we've had dinner—want to go to a movie?

BOBBY—I'd rather go to a movie when I can't be with you.

RAY—Movies aren't my idea of celebration either. You ought to be a couple of years older—then we'd—

BOBBY—We'd play Governor of North Carolina and Governor of South Carolina, then, wouldn't we?

RAY—Hey, where did you pick that up?

BOBBY—I don't know—

RAY (*grinning*)—Taking after the old man, eh?

BOBBY—Sure!

RAY—All right. We'll play that game of governor.

BOBBY—I want to be Governor of North Carolina.

RAY—Right. You'll drink ginger-ale and I'll drink ginger-ale and— (*He winks.*) Okay?

BOBBY—We'll get drunk and—

RAY—Bobby, your father is a gentleman.

BOBBY—We won't really get drunk, will we?

RAY (*laughing*)—Nope. You leave that to dad. Now if you'll set the glasses on the table I'll get the ginger-ale.

BOBBY (*all activity*)—The glasses are in the kitchen.

RAY (*pointing to tall glasses on buffet*)—No—use the tall ones —there. (*He goes into the kitchen.*)

BOBBY (*going to the glasses*)—I see.

RAY (*from the kitchen*)—Okay?

BOBBY (*placing the glasses on the table*)—Okay. (BOBBY *goes back to the sideboard and gets a table luncheon cloth from the drawer in sideboard. He spreads it on the table, putting the glasses on so one is at the left and the other at the right. Then he puts an ash tray in the center. He takes a chair and places it at the table. Then he goes up to the kitchen door and calls:*) Ready.

Ray can't find any ginger-ale in the kitchen. Just empty bottles. He thinks he had better run down to Huber's and get some. He can't telephone. The phone has been disconnected. But he'll be back in a jiffy.

Bobby is having a great time setting the table. Suddenly in an exuberance of spirit he leaps over the packing cases. Then he decides to turn a somersault, laughing when it isn't a very successful somersault. He finds candles and ceremoniously puts them on the table and lights them.

The door slams. Bobby sits up, scared. A woman is standing in the doorway. "She is pretty and neatly dressed. About twenty-six years of age. She smiles charmingly at Bobby." Bobby stares back at her.

"You're Ray's boy, Bobby, aren't you?" she says.

"Yes."

"Well—"

She turns to the room, amused at the table decorations. "All lit up with candles. Been playing house? My name's Louise. I know your father very well."

Bobby explains that his father's there, but he's gone out. Then he dceides he had better put the candles out. If she is going to wait for his father he may not be back for a long time. He's going to be awful busy when he does come.

Louise doesn't mind. She takes off her hat and gloves. She'll wait, and while she waits she wants to know more about Bobby. About his school and what he likes best. Bobby still thinks he'd better blow out the candles.

There is a call from the kitchen. A moment later Ray has come into the room, his arms full of stuff for the party. He is pleased to find Louise there, but a little embarrassed, too. Now he wants Bobby to know her. She's Miss Norman. Even so, Bobby is not greatly impressed.

Louise rather takes charge of the party, going through Ray's purchases with enthusiastic exclamations of approval. There's two kinds of ice cream and macaroons. Bobby shall have an extra large helping of both kinds, Louise agrees, just to show that she likes him.

They have drawn up to the table when Louise suddenly remembers some snapshots she has brought to show Ray. Pictures taken on a jolly party at the beach. Pictures showing all members of the party caught off guard and in the most outlandish poses. Pictures of Louise wearing sailor pants, which please Ray. One of Ray is so terrible he insists on tearing it up, even though Louise thinks it cute and wants to keep it.

For the moment they have forgotten Bobby. They remember him later. At least Ray does. It is when Louise is reporting with enthusiasm that she has arranged to have her vacation the same two weeks Ray has his, which she considers a perfectly marvelous thing to have happened. Bobby gets up from the table. He doesn't think he'll have any ice cream. He thinks he will go to bed, and starts for the sun porch. His bed is still there, but his father suggests that so long as there are two beds in his room Bobby should take one of those. Which is all right with Bobby. Ray is a little worried when he finds Bobby's head seems hot, but that may be nothing but excitement.

"He's nice, Ray," admits Louise, as Bobby disappears up the stairs. "Now that I've seen him I don't blame you for boasting the way you do." Ray has come back to the table. "Now I'll tell you what I came here for tonight," Louise continues with enthusiasm. "I was thinking—if we got married before our vacations, we could use those two weeks as a sort of honeymoon."

"Sure," answers Ray, absent-mindedly.

Louise—I have to be back by the fifteenth—and you have to be back by the sixteenth—so why not— (*There's a noise upstairs of someone falling.*)

Ray—Hey, what's that? Did you hear something?

Louise—Yes.

Ray (*listening for a moment. Then with slight concern, but without moving, he calls*)—Bobby! (*There is no answer. He listens again, then he calls more loudly:*) Bobby!! (*Still no answer. He crosses to the foot of the stairs and listens. Then shouting:*) Bobby!!!

Receiving no answer he dashes up the stairs as the lights dim and fade.

About a week later Bobby is in bed on the sun porch. At the moment he's asleep. Miss Chapman, a trained nurse, moves quietly about the room. Soon Ray comes to make the usual parental inquiry, hopefully assuming that Bobby is a lot better. Bobby's mother, too, has been coming over every day.

Ray is sitting at the head of the bed watching Bobby when Kathryn arrives. She is glad to feel the worst is over. It will, agrees Ray, be nice to get some sleep again. They have both been pretty worried.

Bobby will probably be up and around in a week, they think, and then great care will have to be taken with his diet. He will have to be built up. He was pretty thin when he came to Ray—

He may have been thin, but he has always had the best of food and the best of care with her, Kathryn retorts. If Ray is trying to suggest subtly that she hasn't taken good care of Bobby, and is hoping to get the boy away from her for that reason, he is going about it very clumsily.

It isn't that he doubts Kathryn's ability to take care of Bobby that worries Ray. He is just trying to figure out some plan that would be best for the boy. Things are becoming a bit complicated with Ray. The fact that he is planning to get married next month doesn't help to clear them.

"So . . . as long as he'd be better off with you . . . than with me," Ray stammers, uncertainly, "I'd be willing . . . for his sake . . . and as long as you want him anyway . . . You do want him, don't you?"

KATHRYN—Of course I want him.

RAY (*after a pause*)—Well?

KATHRYN—Oh, if it were only as easy as my merely wanting him.

RAY—Huh?

KATHRYN (*now in her turn, uneasily*)—You see—Ray . . . Well, it's no use hiding it. . . . You see—Bobby wasn't happy with us.

RAY—Didn't Benton treat him right?

KATHRYN—He did everything he could to make friends with

him. But he couldn't. And that made us all wretched.

RAY (*going to* KATHRYN)—But I thought you told me you did everything you could.

KATHRYN—We did, Ray. Believe me. But it didn't work and I was hoping that when he came to you—

RAY (*suddenly realizing the situation*)—Oh!

KATHRYN—Perhaps it will be different with you. If you're to be married, you'll have your home— (*Suddenly conscious of what she's doing.*) Good Lord. Look at us.

RAY (*worriedly*)—It wouldn't be fair to her—to tie her down with a child so soon—especially a grown one— (*Turning directly to her.*) You once taught me that lesson. . . . I still remember it.

KATHRYN (*ironically*)—Isn't it lovely how we've adjusted our lives.

RAY (*hopelessly, after a pause*)—I'll speak to Louise again . . . maybe we can work something out— But how can I be sure the kid won't feel the same about Louise as he does about Benton?

A ring at the doorbell announces Dr. Stirling. A cheerful physician of the small town type, he is pleased with the reading of the nurse's chart and convinced that Bobby is doing so well physically that they will be safe in cutting out the capsules and starting a tonic treatment. All Bobby will need for the next few weeks will be rest, and then—

The doctor dismisses the nurse that he may talk more intimately to the parents.

"Now, . . . what are you going to do about this boy?" he asks, looking from one to the other.

"Everything we can, Doctor," Ray answers. "He's got to get well and strong."

"Yes, of course. That's understood. . . . Now, we'll have him on his feet in a week or so . . . and then—I would suggest a change of scene and air. That's always good. . . . But—well—I don't like to talk about these matters—but the child's in an unfortunate position. . . . This business of uprooting a child every six months or so and transplanting him isn't healthy. That isn't the change of scene and air I advise. . . . Now—with a child—or a very old person for that matter—but especially with a child, the great thing is permanence. It's waking up in the morning day after day in the same bed—in the same room—knowing that the same things are right where you can find them.

It gives him a sense of confidence. . . . I'd like to suggest—that he remain with one of you permanently for the next few years."

Neither Ray nor Kathryn answers the implied query. Finally Ray asks, hesitantly, which of them the doctor would suggest. That, Dr. Stirling tells them, is for them to decide. He knows all about the court having awarded Bobby to his father for four months and to his mother for eight months a year. He can fix that. The only problem they have to settle is that of which of them is willing to give Bobby up to the other.

"I know both of you would like to have him—but I would suggest, if possible, one of you might be unselfish enough to make the sacrifice."

"I see what you mean, Doctor, but—" begins Kathryn.

"It's a little more complicated than you imagine, Doctor," says Ray.

"I see. You both want him, isn't that it?" They are both silent, and the doctor goes on. "Of course that's up to you to decide. Outside of the usual alternative it is the best thing I can suggest for the boy."

The usual alternative, Dr. Stirling explains, would be that of a good school, off in the hills somewhere, where Bobby would meet boys of his own age and make friends he can hang on to. It would mean, of course, that they would both have to give Bobby up. If they did, it might work. Bobby would probably like it. Most boys do. In fact the doctor has a nephew at such a school. A military school. There are a lot of them. Both Kathryn and Ray think Bobby would like a military school, with uniforms and parades and all that.

Dr. Stirling has gathered his kit together and has left them to talk the situation over. He will be looking in tomorrow and they can tell him their decision. Cautiously they return to the subject.

RAY—Well—what do you think?

KATHRYN—I don't know—

RAY (*venturing*)—Might be the very thing. Fine places, most of them.

KATHRYN (*dropping some of her caution*)—Yes.

RAY—I don't think there'd be any difficulty finding the right one.

KATHRYN (*with growing enthusiasm*)—We could get a list from the magazines—and write to the better ones. . . .

RAY—Sure.

KATHRYN—It would have to be one of the better ones. I wouldn't want him to go to just *any* school.

RAY—The best. Expense won't matter.

KATHRYN—Of course not. We'll share it.

RAY—I suggest that we go to the schools ourselves and see that we enter him in just the right one.

KATHRYN—We can visit him from time to time.

RAY—Sure. See that he's well taken care of.

KATHRYN—The doctor says it'll be good for him.

RAY—That's so.

KATHRYN (*happy in the feeling that she will now be able to take care of* BOBBY, *goes to his bed*)—Ray, let's tell him about it the moment he wakes up.

RAY—Yes!

KATHRYN (*as she sees* BOBBY *asleep her enthusiasm vanishes in sense of betrayal*)—Oh, Ray! He's sweet, isn't he?

RAY—Yeah. Swell kid.

The lights dim and fade.

In the Freemont Military Academy the room assigned Robert Phillips and Charles Nevins is square, comfortable, plainly furnished and rather austere. A closet door stands open most of the time, revealing towels and linen neatly piled on a high shelf, uniforms neatly hung below and a row of shoes on the floor.

At the moment, it being Sunday, Nevins, a somewhat taller and slightly older boy than Bobby, is lying prone on his cot, his head hanging down and his gaze fixed on the floor. It is, according to Chic, all there is to do on Sunday.

Bobby, with his uniform dress trousers on, is sitting on the edge of his bed polishing a shoe. This also is against custom, if not the regulations, Chic informs Bobby. Shoes are to be shined on Saturday. The fact that Bobby had stepped in mud is grudgingly accepted as a reasonable explanation.

This getting dressed up, as Bobby appears to be doing, also distresses his roommate. He must be expecting visitors, which Bobby admits to be the case.

"Old man or old lady?" Chic would know.

"He was supposed to come last week, but he couldn't make it. And yesterday I got a letter from her," Bobby explains.

"I used to get visits this early in the term from my four parents," admits Chic.

"Four parents—you got four parents?"

"I started out with two—but I sort of picked up two more on

the way. *You* got four parents; your father 'n' mother got married again, didn't they?"

"Yeah."

"Then you got four parents."

Bobby is in full regalia now, his dress coat adjusted. His belt's crooked, Chic tells him, barking like a hard-boiled sergeant on inspection.

"Suck up your guts!" . . . "Wipe that smile off your face!" . . . "Pin back your ears! . . . Chest out! . . . Shoulders back! . . . Heels together!" Bobby takes it seriously, but there is a shadow of a smile on his face.

There is a knock at the door. It's Ray. He starts in breezily and affectionately, but meets a good deal of disconcerting attention from Chic and a straight-arm formal handshake from Bobby. Even after Chic has ceremoniously withdrawn Bobby is still embarrassedly distant.

He has been doing all right, he explains; he has put on his dress uniform because his mother is coming, too; no, they don't call him general, or colonel, or anything like that; they call him "runt," and they don't have any generals at that school.

"You know . . . I got rid of the old house," Ray is saying. Bobby is slightly upset, but immediately gains control. "That's why I couldn't come up last week. Got a good price for it, though. . . . I may move down to Wilmington, Delaware. . . . You see, Louise has all her relatives down there. And she's been—well, they own a big department store.—They want me to go into the business with them. (*Changing his tone in an attempt at jocularity.*) How'd you like to be the son and heir of a big department store owner? Come in any time—take anything you like. How'd you like that?

"Wilmington's pretty far away, isn't it?"

Ray—Not so very. Oh. It's quite a trip—but I can make it up here easy in oh—six or eight hours—whenever I get off. Want you to visit us first vacation you get. (*Remembering.*) Oh, that's right, you're supposed to go to your mother for Christmas. Well, Easter. That's better. I'll be settled by then. That's an invitation, now.

Bobby—Some of the fellows have to stay here for Easter.

Ray—Oh—well—we'll see. (*Then as if trying to placate his conscience.*) Oh, I'm going to deposit an extra fifty dollars for you with the Academy Quartermaster in case you want to go on a spree.

BOBBY—We're only allowed to draw twenty-five cents a week.

RAY—I know. But you may want something special and I may be tied up. Otherwise you have everything you need, don't you?

BOBBY (*slowly*)—Yes.

RAY—Louise wanted to come up too, you know, but she wasn't feeling well so I made her stay at home. But she sends you her love.

BOBBY (*formally*)—Send her mine, please.

This time the knock at the door reveals Kathryn. She, too, would rush in and embrace Bobby, but she finds him standing looking intently in Ray's direction, and discovers they are not alone.

The second meeting is formal and pleasant. Kathryn would congratulate Ray on his recent marriage. When he turns the subject quickly to Bobby she shares with him pride in the boy's fine appearance. Then Ray thinks he will get out and wait for Bobby below. Ray will be hanging around until five, which will give them time for a visit.

Kathryn has brought Bobby a pair of hockey skates. Howard thought of those. She didn't know what to get. They're the best kind. But she does hope Bobby will be careful to go skating only with one of the older boys or the instructors. . . . It's nice Bobby has such a lovely room, so orderly and everything. And such a pretty uniform, too. But she does hope they won't make him shoot guns and everything!

KATHRYN—It's too bad your father and I happened to come the same day. I mean—he must have wanted to see you very much and then I walked in—look, Bobby—I wonder—oh—Howard's downstairs waiting to see you. He knows one of your instructors—a Mr. Temple.

BOBBY—He teaches chemistry.

KATHRYN—Well—I thought—to make things easier— Your father is only staying until five—you see we're going to be here for dinner anyway—and I could be with you for the whole evening after that—and your father could be with you until dinner. . . . I wouldn't mind giving you up for a little while—it isn't quite fair to him after he's come all this way. You wouldn't mind it either, would you—and while you're away from me I could talk to Mr. Temple about you—and find out how you're getting along.

BOBBY—I'm not in any of Mr. Temple's classes.

KATHRYN—Well— (*Rising.*) perhaps he knows about you anyway. So I'll go now and you run along to your father, and then I'll see you the rest of the evening. That way both your father and I can have you to ourselves.

BOBBY—Yes, ma'am.

KATHRYN—Then I'll say good-by for a little while— (*She goes to the door and turns back.*) Or—would you rather come down with me?

BOBBY—No—I'll go down a little later.

KATHRYN—Perhaps that would be better. (*Opens door.*) See you soon.

Bobby stands staring at the door a minute. He tries to interest himself in the skates. He goes listlessly to the mirror "and looks at himself to see what has changed in him to make his parents so abrupt with him." Suddenly he has thrown himself on his cot and is sobbing bitterly. A second later Chic has opened the door and found him so.

CHIC (*almost irritably*)—Hey! What you doing? Cryin'? What are you cryin' for? (*He turns around and looks at* BOBBY. *He pulls* BOBBY's *legs.* BOBBY *jerks away.*) Hey, runt. Cut that out. Do you think I want a cry baby for a roommate? What are you crying about anyway?

BOBBY (*sitting up, his sobbing has become a slight snivel*)—Not cryin'.

CHIC—You were too. I saw you. What'll my friends think of me if they knew you was a cry baby?

BOBBY (*swallowing hard*)—I'm sorry.

CHIC—I saw your father talking to some lady downstairs. Was that your mother?

BOBBY—Guess so.

CHIC—They goin' home so soon?

BOBBY—Nope. . . . I'm gonna see my father until five and then my mother until eight.

CHIC—What'd they bring you?

BOBBY—Money and skates. My mother brought the skates.

CHIC (*he runs over to skates and looks at them*)—Boy—they're swell. Did you try 'em on?

BOBBY—Not yet—

CHIC—Well, try them on. What's the matter with you? You don't want to let your old man and your old lady get your goat like that. They only come once in a while. And after a few times they won't come so often. They'll start writing instead. And pretty soon they won't bother you at all, except Christmas or Easter and that's not so bad because you spend Christmas with one and Easter with the other—and you get presents. Gee—I get twice as many presents now as I did before the split-up—don't you?

BOBBY—Uh-huh.

CHIC—Unloosen the laces first. Anyway, you won't see her for a while now that she's gonna have a baby.

BOBBY (*incredulously*)—Huh?

CHIC—That's what Cullen told me. He says he can tell. Didn't your mother say anything?

BOBBY (*a bit broken*)—No—she didn't tell me anything.

CHIC (*his smile slightly bitter*)—Well, what do you care—you got something—those Blue Streaks are nutsy.

The skates don't fit, but that's no reason Bobby should give 'em to another fellow. Let him make his mother exchange 'em, the way she'd have to do at home. That's what Chic did with the catcher's mitt his mother gave him. She forgot he caught lefty and gave him a righty.

"Get all you can out of them—it's the only way," advises Chic. "You'll find out. You ain't the only divorced kid in this school. There's others. Gwan—put your shoes on!"

"Well—whatta you do?" asks Bobby, helplessly.

"I get over it," boasts Chic, defiantly. "You'll get over it, too. Everybody gets over it. You just gotta learn to take care of yourself, I guess—"

"Yeah, you do, I guess."

The school ain't so bad, Chic points out. Someways it's even better. "Nobody cryin' about you or askin' what you're doin' all the time—or makin' you kiss Aunt Minne!"

A boy named Spotsie has stuck his head in the door. "Hey, runt! Did they bring you anything?" he yells. They brought him skates, Bobby answers. "Nothin' to eat?" "No!" "So long!" And Spotsie has slammed the door.

"Look at Spotsie," says Chic, being reminded. "He gets letters from his old man in Yokohama and his mother in Switzerland. And he's got a big brother in London. And he's got some stamp collection, too. (*Sees* BOBBY *is still disconsolate.*) We can have loads of fun if you wanna. In a couple of weeks they're going to call for the hockey team. You come out with me and maybe you'll make the runt squad."

"I don't know if I can play good enough."

"I'll show you how to play good enough."

"Will ya?"

"Sure." He is sitting on the cot beside Bobby now. "Maybe I'll teach you how to play checkers too. Then in a year or so you might even beat me."

"Aw, you're the house champ."

"That's nuthin'. The old champ taught me. That's how I learnt. And I beat him too."

"Did ya?"

"Yeah!"

They are smiling at each other now, and starting to laugh, when the campus chimes begin to play "Goin' Home." That puts them in a serious mood again. They do play the dumbest pieces at that school, Chic admits, and that "Goin' Home" is one of the dumbest. Bobby kinda likes it.

CHIC—So did I at first— Maybe they play it just to break ya in or kind of harden ya up. (*He sits for a moment just staring. Then not being able to stand it any longer he rises and stares defiantly out the window.*) Let 'em play it. I don't care.

BOBBY (*echoing* CHIC)—I don't care either.

CHIC (*turning to* BOBBY)—Let 'em forget us! We don't need them!

BOBBY—No—we don't need 'em. (*He breaks a little.*) And—they'll be—sorry.

CHIC (*softly and thoughtfully*)—Yeah. (*He turns and looks out of the window again silently for a while. Then he goes back to* BOBBY.) You goin' to college?

BOBBY (*deep in his own thoughts*)—Guess so.

CHIC—Me too. . . . And then I'm going to be a lawyer, or a doctor—

BOBBY (*speaking slowly and thoughtfully*)—I'm goin' to build forts—and bridges—and—

CHIC (*turning to* BOBBY *with determination but no rancor*)—If they don't think about us—we don't need to think about them, do we? (*With a half smile.*) I guess we can get along.

BOBBY (*admiringly*)—I guess you can get along.

CHIC—Sure I can.

BOBBY—So can I—too—

CHIC—Sure.

BOBBY—And then— (*With growing enthusiasm at the pros-*

pect.) When we grow up, we can have our own place.

CHIC (*pleased at the prospect*)—And nobody can take it away from you.

BOBBY—Yeah.

CHIC (*after a pause*)—I'm goin' to have a place.

BOBBY—Me too.

CHIC (*with happy anticipation tempered by the thought*)—We just gotta—wait.

BOBBY (*likewise*)—Yeah . . . wait.

The chimes continue as

THE CURTAIN FALLS

THE SHINING HOUR

A Drama in Three Acts

By Keith Winter

IN mid-season a series of fairly pretentious English plays made their appearance on Broadway. These proved stimulating to playgoers and exciting to native actors. The presence of so many "alien" players in the city rallied the radicals to the support of a bill in congress which would allow only such actors of foreign citizenship as were absolutely essential to a proper performance of the dramas in which they performed to appear on the American stage.

The three most successful English plays were Keith Winter's "The Shining Hour," Gordon Daviot's (Alice MacIntosh's) "Richard of Bordeaux," which proved a trifle too robustious as historical drama to attract the larger crowd, and Merton Hodges' "The Wind and the Rain," a sentimental school-boy romance which lingered a considerable time, but never was more than moderately popular.

Young Mr. Winter's "The Shining Hour" was brought to this country by Max Gordon before it was produced in London. It was taken directly to Canada with an all-English cast headed by Gladys Cooper. For a quarter of a century Miss Cooper had been a popular leading woman in London but had not previously acted in America. Associated with her was Raymond Massey, who played here a year ago in a Norman-Bel Geddes version of "Hamlet" and Adrianne Allen, Mr. Massey's wife, who had previously appeared here as the shop-girl heroine of "Cynara" and in several pictures.

The play's reception in Canada was marked by a typically restrained enthusiasm. The greater success in New York came as something of a pleasant surprise to all those interested in the play.

In "The Shining Hour" Mr. Winter makes conventional use of the familiar story of two women who love the same man with something more than a conventional degree of force and originality. They are all essentially decent folk forced by chance into a tragically dramatic situation. They extricate themselves with few false pretensions and with such courage as they are able to muster.

It is early June in Yorkshire when the play opens. An early evening sun, streaming through the windows of Windsend, the Elizabethan farmhouse of the Lindens, reveals furniture of a heavy variety. "But the brightness of the chair covers, the gayety of the chintz curtains and the extreme cleanliness of the whole contrive to give the room a pleasant and almost light-hearted appearance."

There is a stairway at the rear of the room, and a gallery across the back leading to the bedrooms. There are two mullioned windows. Through one a pear tree shows, and near the other, inside the room, is a baby-grand piano. The piano does not seem quite in keeping with the rest of the house. "It wears an air of mild surprise."

Judy Linden is sitting at the center table working on a jig-saw puzzle. Judy is twenty-two. "Her hair is short, nondescript brown and very tidy. Her face is clear-cut, intelligent and rather boyish. She is wearing an inexpensive dress, attractive in its simplicity."

At a writing desk nearby Hannah Linden is going over accounts. Hannah "is a woman of about forty-five, gray-haired and neatly built. Her face is sharp-featured, alert and rather acidulated. There is a 'no-nonsense-about-me' look in her eyes, but they are not unkind."

The talk is desultory. With Judy it concerns the curious shapes and amusing fitting of the pieces of her puzzle. With Hannah it clings rather closely to the affairs of the house—the fact that the hens, who have not been doing very well, are likely to be greatly surprised when they get a bit of the spice Hannah is feeding them. Also the fact suddenly discovered, that it is six o'clock and the table has not yet been laid for tea.

Setting the places at the tea table reminds Hannah and Judy that their brother Henry is back with them. Henry is forty-eight but, according to Judy, he has "worn well." He has been a long time in the East, it appears. Having made as much money as he wants, he has come home to retire, bringing with him a second wife.

"If I'd married a woman who drank like a fish and ran off with my groom I'd know better the second time," allows Hannah.

"Everybody isn't lucky enough to meet the right person the first time," Judy answers. "I think she's attractive. There's something rather witch-like about her."

"That should make her useful about the house," mutters Hannah.

Mariella is the name of Henry's new wife. Henry is building a house across the valley which likely will not be ready for six months and Judy has asked him and Mariella to stay with her and David, her husband, until the house is finished.

Now Henry Linden has joined Judy and Hannah. He "is a tall, well-made man of forty-eight. Like Hannah, the kindliness of his eyes belie the slight bitterness of his mouth. . . . He is the most polished of the Lindens."

Henry is a little anxious about the family's feeling regarding his return. Anxious, too, to know how they are going to take to Mariella. Judy, he thinks, likes Mariella. Probably Hannah doesn't. But she will when she knows her.

"I expect she'll find you all a little odd at first," ventures Henry.

"I suppose that means that she'll behave as if she were on a visit to the Zoo," says Hannah. "Well, just let her try prodding me through the bars."

"Hannah, you're going to be nice to her, aren't you?"

"What do you think I'm going to do? Eat her?"

"I wouldn't put it past you," says Henry.

Judy has brought the tea things in and Hannah has gone to the kitchen to see about Milly, the maid. Being pregnant Milly is a bit uncertain at the moment. Cries a good deal. The fact that the father of her expected offspring is congenital does not help the situation particularly.

Micky Linden is the next family member to arrive. "Micky is twenty. His figure is slim but strong. His dark face will probably coarsen with the years, but at the moment he is undoubtedly extremely handsome. Easy assurance can, in some people, be an attractive quality. In Micky we feel it is somehow misplaced."

Micky has won what Judy describes as another egg-cup at a meeting over by York. Micky could have won a better prize, he feels, if David had given him a horse to ride. His mount of the day was much more like a cow, and not the cow that jumped over the moon, either.

When Mariella Linden joins them she is discovered to be "tall, fair and unusually beautiful. In a curious way she seems to combine the nervousness of a child with the assurance of a woman. There is something wild about her, but there is also something very still. All this makes it difficult to determine her age. She is probably about thirty."

Mariella has been for quite a walk, through a field presided over by what she modestly assumed to be a cow, but which turned out to be a bull, and into a woods apparently in command of a rather furious-looking man with a gun.

It happens the woods are private and that the keeper usually shoots on sight, but Mariella didn't suspect that until Micky tells her. She had gone on from the woods to the village, and there what appeared to be the whole population turned out and stared at her with dull loathing.

"They'll have got used to you in a couple of years, dear," encourages Henry.

"I expect your bare legs startled them a bit, too," ventures Judy.

"But I always have bare legs," protests Mariella.

Micky has gone to tidy up a bit, having suddenly acquired a new interest in tea. Judy is called to the kitchen to help Hannah. It is the first time Henry and Mariella have been alone.

Mariella senses how she stands with the Lindens up to now. She likes Judy and Micky and feels they like her. But not Hannah. It will take time, as Henry says, for Hannah to get used to her. Mariella also thinks she will have a drink of whiskey, however strange the custom may be to the house, and however Hannah may frown upon it.

With her drink in her hand Mariella stands looking out the window. She likes England. Thinks she might grow fond of it—it is so very green and quiet. She wonders what David Linden is like. Is he, too, very sure of himself? Nearly everyone she has met in England has given her the impression of never having had a single doubt about anything.

"Do you object to people being sure of themselves?" asks Henry.

"Not in the least," Mariella answers. "I was only wondering what exactly they were sure of."

"Well, what about you? You're extremely sure of yourself."

"Do you think so, Henry?"

Mariella has started for the stairs. She thinks she will change for tea.

"Oh, Mariella, you're in England for the first time and I'm with you—it's all so perfect," blurts Henry.

And Mariella, coming back to take his head between her hands and kiss him upon the cheek, admits that he is very sweet.

Hannah, bringing in the boiled eggs and ham, is not pleased

to hold tea while Mariella changes her dress. After all it's only boiled eggs and ham—nothing to wear diamonds for. Still, Mariella thinks she will change.

Now Hannah, moving toward the tea table, has found Mariella's whiskey glass, and that gives her a new thought.

"Mariella drink much?" she asks Henry.

"Rather! She gets roaring drunk every night."

"Perhaps next time she gives a party she'll ask us," snaps Hannah. "I suppose she feels she can't face the family without being half-soused."

"I see her point entirely," protests Judy.

"Now, don't you encourage her to be grand, because she doesn't need any encouragement," says Hannah. "I tell you, Judy, that I scent trouble."

At which moment David Linden comes through the door from the yard. "David is about twenty-five. Like all the Lindens he is tall and well-made. He is not nearly as good-looking as Micky but his face has an infinitely greater variety of expression. He lacks Henry's poise but he possesses a simple charm which is very appealing. His nose and chin are nondescript, his hands are quite exceptionally beautiful. The large mouth is sensitive and mobile, the eyes puzzled but not unhappy. It is an interesting face and like most interesting faces a curious mixture of the weak and the strong."

David accepts the family's congratulations on his winning another cup at York with modest insistence that there wasn't much competition. He is interested in hearing that Henry and Mariella have arrived and a little startled by Hannah's report that Mariella, after having drunk quantities of his whiskey, has probably gone to lie down.

David prefers Judy's report that Mariella is really quite charming and extremely beautiful. That's good. David thinks that probably he will fall in love with Mariella—but Judy puts a damper on that idea. And cements it with a kiss. She is stroking her husband's head affectionately and telling him that she really is his nurse when Micky arrives, all fixed up spruce and clean.

Henry is in from the kitchen still laughing at something Milly has said. By the time he is at table his laughter, become infectious, has attacked the family. David, leaving the table, has thought to rush upstairs for a quick wash and is half way up when he meets Mariella, coming as quickly down.

For a second they stand, face to face, staring at each other in slight embarrassment.

"You're David," says Mariella.

"Yes. How do you do?"

"Oh, Mariella, this is David," calls Henry from the table.

"Yes, we've just met," answers Mariella, and with a smile for David she continues to her place at table while he goes on to his room.

"Shouldn't pass on the stairs. Very unlucky," murmurs Micky.

"I'm not superstitious," answers Mariella.

It is a jolly table scene that David comes back to, with all the Lindens trying to make Mariella feel quite at home with their banter and family pleasantries. Soon he, too, is devoting himself to Mariella, urging her to eat more of this and that; inquiring with polite earnestness of her reactions to England; interested to learn that she is really only half English, her father having been Dutch.

David is pleased to know that Mariella rides, and rides extremely well, according to Henry. They will organize a family point-to-point contest the next day and give Hannah the milk horse with a handicap of a couple hundred yards.

Now Micky has caught sight of a fox out of the window, and the Lindens are pretty excited about it while it remains in sight. David is the first to come back from the window. He finds Mariella still at table "with a very curious expression on her face."

"There's nothing to be frightened of, really, you know," says David, reassuringly, and Mariella is smiling again.

After tea Henry is for a run in the car. He would take them all to see the sunset at Blue Ridge. But Mariella feels suddenly tired and thinks she will lie down. Judy will go but not David. He is no more than half finished with his tea. Micky has an engagement at 8. This leaves a place for Hannah, who isn't interested in sunsets, having seen several. But she goes.

Mariella has gone to her room. First Judy would know what David thinks of her. David thinks she is all right. Certainly no fool. Then Micky would know David's opinion of Mariella. David repeats. Mariella is all right.

"Yes, old Henry has picked a peach in my opinion," declares Micky, with enthusiasm. "How he did it is nobody's business."

"No, it isn't."

"Shouldn't think she's any gilded lily, either. What do you think?"

"I hadn't thought."

"Oh, you make me sick!" blurts Micky, hurrying through the door.

David has taken a lemon curd tart and strolled over to the piano. He is eating the tart from his left hand and playing the piano idly with his right, until he puts the tart down and begins to play in earnest, breaking finally into Rachmaninoff's concerto in C Minor. David plays extremely well.

Shortly Mariella appears at the head of the stairs and stands there until David, conscious of her presence, stops playing suddenly.

"Oh, so it's you," smiles Mariella.

"Yes."

MARIELLA—I'd no idea that you had any tricks of this kind.

DAVID—Does it astonish you so much?

MARIELLA—Yes, it does rather.

DAVID—Yes, I gathered you thought that you'd walked into a family of imbeciles.

MARIELLA—That's rather unkind.

DAVID—I'm sorry.

MARIELLA—Will you go on playing?

DAVID—Yes, if you like. Are you fond of music?

MARIELLA—Yes.

DAVID—Well, what shall I play to you?

MARIELLA—Anything you like. (*He begins to strum.*) I'm afraid I must have appeared rather superior at tea.

DAVID—I didn't think so.

MARIELLA—Weren't you playing Rachmaninoff's concerto when I came in?

DAVID—Yes, I was.

MARIELLA—Will you play it again?

DAVID—What is it that you like about it?

MARIELLA—I think it's the happiest music I've ever heard.

DAVID—All right. (*He begins to play—at first a little self-consciously, then with increasing ease.* MARIELLA *sits down on the stairs. She smiles at him. He smiles back. He looks very happy. He goes on playing.*)

THE CURTAIN FALLS

ACT II

One afternoon a week later Henry is teaching Judy to play bezique. It is, thinks she, a perfectly idiotic game, but it does fill in the time.

David and Mariella are riding, and a rain storm is threatening. Judy hopes David will not let Mariella get drenched. But Henry isn't worried. Mariella is quite used to taking care of herself in all kinds of weather.

Now the rain is coming down in sheets. Mariella comes dashing out of it with David's coat thrown over her shoulders. He would not let her cross the yard without the coat, Mariella reports, David being one of those chivalrous men.

Mariella is in a gay mood after her ride. She and David had ridden over the site of the house. David thinks they might do another round next day and Mariella is keen for that.

Now Mariella has gone to her room and David back to the barn. The game of bezique languishes. Henry pauses to remark that it is very decent of David to show Mariella so much attention, but Judy is sure David does not find the task at all irksome.

Hannah breaks up the game finally by warning Henry that it is getting late if he is planning to go into town to see his architect.

After Henry has left Hannah takes advantage of the moment to speak to Judy about David and Mariella.

"Do you think it wise, Judy?" she asks, quite seriously.

"Do I think what is wise?" demands Judy, quickly.

Hannah—To let David go about with her so much.

Judy—What do you expect me to do? Can you see David's face if I said: "David, I don't want you to go about with Mariella so much."

Hannah—Yes, but—

Judy—Do you think it wise of Mariella to let Henry play cards with me all afternoon?

Hannah—That's rather different.

Judy—Is it? I find Henry extremely attractive.

Hannah—Really, Judy!

Judy—And do you think it wise of Henry to let Mariella spend so much time with David?

Hannah—No, quite honestly, I don't!

Judy—Have you noticed any signs of David and Mariella

falling madly in love?

HANNAH—No, of course not.

JUDY—I haven't seen any marked symptoms either. So in the meantime Henry and I aren't spending any sleepless nights. Henry presumably understands Mariella, and I, oddly enough, understand David. I shouldn't agitate myself unduly, Hannah.

HANNAH—I won't.

JUDY—Well? I'm going along to the dairy for a few minutes. If David and Mariella display any adulterous tendencies in my absence, perhaps you'll drop in and let me know?

HANNAH—I'm sorry, Judy. My intentions were good.

JUDY (*coming back*)—I know. Silly! (*She kisses her.*)

HANNAH—I was born with a strong sense of interference and I expect I shall die with one.

Micky is in from what he considers a hard day's work in Long Field, a little anxious to find out where everybody is—particularly Mariella,—which amuses Hannah.

"Mariella's in her room and as far as I know she's staying there," says Hannah. "So you might as well leave your card and call another day."

But Mariella has just appeared at the head of the stairs, greeting Micky graciously as she comes down. Micky is hoping the rain will clear so he and Mariella can have their ride after all—Mariella had forgotten completely about having told Micky she would ride with him, and she is just back from a ride with David. She is awfully sorry. Micky is plainly hurt. He slams the door behind him as he goes out.

"Micky's still very young," explains Hannah.

"I should have thought he was old enough to have acquired a few manners," retorts Mariella.

HANNAH—His manners have never been very tidy.

MARIELLA—All the same it was silly of me to forget.

HANNAH—I shouldn't worry. Perhaps he'll do some work instead.

MARIELLA—Do you think I want to prevent him from working?

HANNAH—No.

MARIELLA—Then why do you bother to make remarks like that?

HANNAH—Of course, if you choose to take it that way. . . .

MARIELLA—You meant me to take it that way.

HANNAH—Well, perhaps you know best.

MARIELLA—Why are you so determined to find fault with everything I do and everything I don't do?

HANNAH—It isn't a question of finding fault.

MARIELLA—When I dusted the drawing-room this morning. . . .

HANNAH—I thanked you, didn't I?

MARIELLA—Yes, and you managed to make even that sound offensive.

HANNAH—I'm sorry. I had no intention of being offensive.

MARIELLA—But that just isn't true. You see, Hannah, like so many of your type, your much boasted honesty isn't honesty at all. It's just rudeness.

HANNAH—Well, that's one point of view.

MARIELLA—It seems to me that it's the obvious point of view. You want to be offensive but at the same time you haven't the courage to commit yourself completely. And so when you'r challenged all you can do is to mutter that you "didn't mean it that way," and take refuge in a rather feeble kind of humor.

HANNAH—Very well, Mariella, shall we say that you don't understand me and I don't understand you, and leave it at that?

MARIELLA—No, we will not!

HANNAH—Then what do you propose to do about it?

MARIELLA—Well, in the first place, perhaps you'll tell me what it is about me that you resent so much?

HANNAH—Well, oddly enough, I don't resent you personally. . . .

MARIELLA—I see nothing very odd in that. But go on.

HANNAH—Haven't you ever had a fixed instinct about a person?

MARIELLA—Yes.

HANNAH—I had one about you the moment I saw you. I felt that you didn't fit in here. I still feel it . . . you're a disturbing influence about the house.

MARIELLA—I never wanted to come here. That was Henry's idea entirely. As far as I can see you're the only person I appear to have disturbed and that doesn't upset me very much because I think someone should have done it long ago.

HANNAH—Aren't you being "just rude" now?

MARIELLA—Yes, I am—and with intention. I've tried to be reasonable, and that hasn't worked. I've tried to be pleasant and that's made you all the more offensive. I've endured your petty persecutions for a week but now I'm tired of them. So in future if you're rude to me, I shall be infinitely ruder to you.

The general embarrassment will be considerable. (HANNAH *is silent.*) And now perhaps we do understand each other rather better.

Hannah is surprised to find that she and Mariella are so much alike but Mariella is not at all convinced of that. Furthermore Mariella thinks if Hannah persists in being frightened of her and of what she may do to the family it is quite likely to put ideas in her head.

Hannah has gone to see what may be done about the separator, which Judy reports out of order, and Judy has taken her place at exchanging confidences and opinions with Mariella. Judy knows what is wrong between Hannah and Mariella. They have different senses of honesty.

"Hannah is as honest as her imagination and instinct allow her to be," explains Judy. "But you've got a much bigger imagination and a far deeper instinct."

They are working on one of Judy's jig-saw puzzles and Mariella notices that Judy's hand is trembling. Mariella's hand is trembling, too.

"Funny that we should make each other so nervous when . . . when we like each other so much," says Judy. "We do like each other, don't we?"

"I like you very much indeed, Judy," Mariella answers.

"I like you, too."

Mariella thinks it would be better if she and Henry were to go somewhere else until the house is ready, but Judy would not think of letting that happen. Nothing would be simplified by their going away.

"Why did you marry Henry?" Judy asks suddenly.

"You mean why did I marry him when I wasn't in love with him?"

"Yes."

"Because I liked him very much, because I was very lonely, and because . . . well, because I just wanted to get married."

JUDY—That would shock Hannah terribly.

MARIELLA—But not you?

JUDY—No. I should have done the same. (*After a slight pause.*) I have done the same.

MARIELLA—You haven't!

JUDY—Oh, yes, I have. You married a man you didn't love, and I persuaded David to marry me, but he was never in love with me, you know. Never.

MARIELLA—Did he think he was?

JUDY—Oh, yes, he thought he was, and I took care not to enlighten him. Did you ever tell Henry that you loved him?

MARIELLA—No. Never.

JUDY—I told David that he loved me. So you see, you made the more honest bargain.

MARIELLA—Then why did you marry him?

JUDY—Because I couldn't help myself, and because I thought second best was better than nothing. And it is too—while the going's good.

David has come in with a stirrup strap he is trying to fix. Judy quickly remembers something she has to do in the dairy, nor will she listen to Mariella's protest that she stay and help with the puzzle.

With Judy gone David draws nearer to the puzzle and Mariella. He would be chatty, and interested, but there is not much response from Mariella. It is quite evident to David that Mariella is troubled about something. Evidently she would rather he would leave her, which is quite unlike her mood when they were on the Ridge.

"On the Ridge I was feeling a little mad," admits Mariella.

"But you're not feeling mad any more?"

"Not in the least."

David has put the stirrup down and drawn a chair up beside the puzzle. Mariella is agitated by the contact. She wishes David would let her work out the puzzle alone. It is much more fun alone.

David, retired to the piano, is determined to play Mariella into a better mood. She continues to avoid the responses he had hoped for. Now he is playing the Rachmaninoff concerto again and she is trying to ignore it. Suddenly she is sick of the concerto. She would leave him and go back to her room.

"Why are you suddenly so angry with me, Mariella?" David demands.

"I'm not angry with you," she answers from halfway up the stairs.

He has left the piano and joined her, pleading that she stay with him.

"I think I'm feeling lonely this afternoon," he says, taking her hand.

"Please, let me go!"

"Your eyes are full of tears!"

"They're not!"

"Mariella!"

David has taken Mariella in his arms and kissed her warmly. For an instant they stand apart facing each other, a little frightened.

"And what do you think happens next?" asks Mariella.

"I don't know."

"I suppose you hadn't thought."

"No."

"You should have done, David," she says, going up the stairs.

"Listen, Mariella!"

Mariella has disappeared in her room. David, agitated and uncertain, comes down the stairs. Judy is back from the dairy. David looks intently at her.

"You're looking very nice this afternoon, Judy," he says, earnestly.

"Am I, dear? Where's Mariella?"

DAVID—She's gone upstairs.

JUDY—Has she? (*Going to table.*) She hasn't got very far with this.

DAVID—No, I don't think she's very good at puzzles.

JUDY—Is she coming down again?

DAVID—She didn't say!

JUDY—Oh! (*She goes on with the puzzle.*)

DAVID (*comes and stands behind her*)—You're a talented little creature, aren't you?

JUDY—Yes.

DAVID—Oh, Judy!

JUDY—What?

DAVID—Nothing. Just "Oh, Judy"!

JUDY—Oh, is that all? (*He puts his hand on her head. His face is turned to the stairs. He seems to be standing in a dream.* JUDY *turns around.*) Have you seen a ghost or something?

DAVID (*covering her eyes with his hand*)—No, dear. (*She removes his hand. The inevitable has happened and she knows it. The whole of life is slipping away and she can do nothing to prevent it. She makes a tremendous effort to control her face.*) Mariella said you were one of the finest people she'd ever met.

JUDY—Did she? That was nice of her.

DAVID (*touching the back of her neck with his lips*)—Dear Judy! Dear Judy!

Judy (*the agony almost more than she can bear. She picks up a piece of the puzzle.*) I think this goes here.

The curtain falls.

It is after supper a week later. Henry, at the window, is happy to report to Mariella progress on their house. The foundations are finished. It is going to be a grand house when it is done, thinks Henry.

Mariella is not interested, save in what might happen if, after the house is done, Henry should not like it. One can never tell about houses. They can be like dress patterns. Fine when they are selected, but not at all appealing when finished.

"Well, you'll like this all right," insists Henry. "I'll see to that. Why, I'd rather live there than anywhere else in the world. A good house, perfect position, and the best country in England. Nice and near the family, too."

"Yes, it's near the family. Henry, you don't think it's too near the family?"

"Good Heavens, no! It's nearly half a mile away. Just the right distance!"

"Half a mile isn't very far," says Mariella.

Henry is puzzled. He thought Mariella liked the family. He knows she likes David. And Judy. He is not surprised if she does not like Hannah. Hannah takes a lot of knowing. And he can understand her when she says she neither likes nor dislikes Micky.

"I don't think I like any family as a family," explains Mariella. "They suffocate me. They suffocate each other, too, but I suppose that's their business."

Mariella repeats a request that she had made some days before. She wants to get away. It isn't, she assures Henry, a childish whim. Henry has known her for ten years and they have been married for a year. Never before has she asked anything unusual of him. What she is asking him now she has a reason for asking. Let them leave the Linden place.

Henry is finally convinced. He will take Mariella away—for ten days. It is weak of him to give in, but he'll do it.

"I know exactly what's wrong with you, my dear. Liver. You've spent the best part of this week moping about your bedroom. Why don't you get about more? Why have you given up riding with David?"

"I don't want to interfere with his work."

"Nonsense! You get out and take some exercise. Your inside

is thoroughly out of order—that's all that's worrying you . . . Can't breathe indeed!"

"Oh, what blind idiots men are!" cries Mariella. "I won't stay here, Henry. I won't! I won't! I won't!"

"You'll stay exactly where I tell you, see!" thunders Henry. "Now stop being a hysterical little fool."

Micky is in to report the successful birth of a foal. David follows, equally excited. But Mariella isn't interested. Only Henry goes back to the barn with David.

Micky lingers in the house. He wants to talk to Mariella. The new colt is his. He had thought of naming her Mariella. Micky is a real farmer. David isn't. David, says Micky, is too sensitive to see little pigs killed. David likes to stay indoors and play the piano. Frequently he plays Bach. And certainly that is nothing for a farmer to be doing. Micky much prefers jazz. Micky, by his own admission, is quite virile.

Micky is wandering about the room when he stops suddenly in front of Mariella. Isn't it true that she was having a bit of a "dust up" with Henry? A row? A shindy? Isn't it true that she has found life with the Lindens rather dull? Wouldn't Mariella like to have someone to talk to—someone like Micky, for instance? Why did she ever marry Henry? Micky has a feeling that Mariella likes him. And he likes Mariella.

Suddenly, "with a kind of crude ferocity," Micky kisses Mariella.

MICKY—I've been wanting to do this from the moment I saw you. (*She stares at him in amazement.*) Well, don't look so startled. You must have known it was coming.

MARIELLA—No, this is too much. (*Rising.*) Either you're drunk or mad or both. Please get out.

MICKY—What's the fuss about? There's no harm done, is there?

MARIELLA—There will be if you don't go immediately.

MICKY—So that's all the thanks I get for trying to brighten up a dull evening.

MARIELLA—You're insufferable!

MICKY—Well, I'm not all that impressed. Because I've heard this kind of talk before. I wasn't born yesterday, you know.

MARIELLA—Then it was certainly the day before. Are you going or must I . . . ?

MICKY—Now what's the point of getting grand? You don't mind a bit of fun, do you?

MARIELLA—Fun?

MICKY—Certainly.

MARIELLA—I don't think you've been remotely funny, Micky. Just imbecile—and a little nauseating. (*Moves toward the stairs.*)

MICKY (*standing in her way*)—I'm crazy about you, Mariella!

MARIELLA—Will you please get out of my way?

MICKY—No.

MARIELLA—Oh, please don't stand there breathing like a bull! I wish you could see yourself. You look perfectly grotesque.

MICKY—Well, what are you going to do about it? Tell Henry?

MARIELLA—I don't think Henry is interested in the antics of little boys.

MICKY—And you're not either?

MARIELLA—No.

MICKY—Prefer something older? I suppose that's why you didn't waste any time setting your cap for David. (*She strikes him across the face.*) I see that went home! (*With sudden fury.*) Well, you might as well sample the whole family while you're about it! (*He pulls her into his arms.*)

MARIELLA—Let me go!

MICKY—Give me a kiss then!

David has come through the door. Micky releases Mariella and stands defiantly facing David, who is ready to break his younger brother's damned neck if he doesn't clear out immediately.

Micky, too, is belligerent. They are rushing toward each other when Hannah comes in. She stops them. "I thought you and Micky had given up these rough games some time ago," she says to David.

If Micky had tried to get fresh with Mariella, as David says, Hannah would tell Henry, but Mariella doesn't want Henry to know anything about what happened. Hannah can't understand that. Nor can she understand why Mariella doesn't go away. David answers that.

"Listen to me, Hannah," he says. "If I have any more trouble from Micky I'm going to kick him out of the house. And if you can't prevent yourself being offensive to Mariella you can pack your bags and go with him."

"Very well, David," Hannah answers, calmly, as she leaves the room.

David and Mariella find themselves alone. Mariella is disturbed. Only a fortnight has passed since she came into that house. They were happy before she came. It may be a little late for regrets, as David suggests, but it isn't too late for common sense.

MARIELLA—You were happy before I came. You'll be happy when I've gone away.

DAVID—Do you believe that? (*She does not answer.*) I wasn't happy before you came. I was content.

MARIELLA—Then be content again.

DAVID—I shall never be content again.

MARIELLA—Yes, you will.

DAVID—Never.

MARIELLA—How can you say that?

DAVID—Because I love you. I love you with all my heart. I shall love you for ever.

MARIELLA (*after a long pause*)—Yes, I know you will.

DAVID—You feel the same about me.

MARIELLA—Yes.

DAVID—Could you ever be content again?

MARIELLA—No.

DAVID—Then . . .

MARIELLA—No, there isn't any "then" about it.

DAVID—Why not?

MARIELLA—You remember that first evening when you played to me?

DAVID—Of course.

MARIELLA—People don't seem to think like this these days, but I've always believed somehow that if only I waited, if only I could be patient enough, I would one day meet a man who for me would be perfect . . . for ever. You see, it may sound very young and silly, but I believed in deathless romance. . . .

DAVID—I do believe in it.

MARIELLA—Well, I waited and waited—and then I couldn't wait any longer. Did you ever think like that, David?

DAVID—I don't think I ever really thought until you came. Here we just seem to grow up and get married, and it's all in the day's work.

MARIELLA—Then that evening when you were playing, quite suddenly I knew, I didn't think—I just knew . . .

DAVID—And I knew too. Everything was . . . was kind of shining.

MARIELLA—Well, that was the moment, David. That was when we should have walked out.

DAVID—Or is it now?

MARIELLA—No.

DAVID—I'll go with you, Mariella. Anywhere you like.

MARIELLA—Would you, David?

DAVID—This moment if you're ready.

MARIELLA—No. Too much has happened.

DAVID—But nothing has happened.

MARIELLA—I've got to know Judy. That's what's happened.

DAVID—Judy's terribly nice.

MARIELLA—She's very nearly a saint. I'm going to bed now.

DAVID—I noticed you haven't mentioned Henry.

MARIELLA—No.

DAVID—Would you come away if there were only Henry to consider?

MARIELLA—Yes. Henry is very fond of me. But Judy loves you. Just as I love you. That makes a big difference.

DAVID—There are two of us.

MARIELLA—But together we don't amount to her. (*After a pause.*) I'm going to get Henry to take me right away from here. I've tried once and I'm going to try again.

DAVID—Supposing he won't?

MARIELLA—Then I shall go alone.

DAVID—How can you love me and say these things?

MARIELLA—I don't know. But I do love you, and I do say these things.

DAVID—Everything that matters is slipping away, and you can just stand by and watch.

MARIELLA—David! (*She is about to go to him and comfort him, but suddenly she turns away.*) Good night!

Judy has come in from the yard. She has been for a walk to the Ridge. She is strangely composed. "There is about her a power almost embarrassing in its certainty." She doesn't want them to leave her and go to bed. She wants to talk.

They have some difficulty making conversation. Both Mariella and David look strange to Judy. "Anyone would think that something had died," she says. She has gone to David and brushed something off his coat. She wishes he would learn to look after himself a little better. Then she kisses him awkwardly. When David leaves them a little sob escapes Judy. She tries to hide it with a laugh.

A sort of revelation has come to Judy. "As I was looking across the valley I had a rather strange sensation," she tells

Mariella. "I felt suddenly that I knew everything. . . . Well, no. I didn't know everything. But I knew for certain that *everything* I did *know* was right. Absolutely right."

Among the reëstablished truths that Judy has come upon is the old saying that there are occasionally people who were "made for each other." It may happen very seldom, but it does happen. Mariella must believe that, too. Mariella does.

"And when it does happen," persists Judy, "it's more important than people being hurt, more important than anything, isn't it?"

"I suppose so. It depends."

"No, it doesn't. It doesn't depend on anything. You're quite wrong. . . . Listen, Mariella, you know that I like you and admire you enormously. . . . No one knows why they like anyone. But I know why I admire you. I admire you because you are clear-cut and logical and—and 'right.' You're a terribly 'right' person."

"I'm not at all 'right,' " protests Mariella, thoroughly unhappy.

"Yes, you are," persists Judy, relentlessly. "You know you are. It would be an awful pity if you were ever to stop being logical . . . if you were ever to become blurred and messy-minded. It would disappoint me, Mariella, more than I can say. Do you understand?"

Mariella has turned suddenly toward the stairs, but before she can go far Judy has stopped her.

"There's something I want you to do, Mariella," she says, excitedly.

"What?" demands Mariella.

"Go away with David! At once!" Judy says, earnestly.

"You're mad!"

"I'm brilliantly sane!"

"Please let me go!"

"Why do you want to go?"

"I'm going to get out of this house and I'm going to get out now."

"And then, I suppose, David and I will settle down to a happy ever after?"

"In time. . . ."

"Liar," coolly answers Judy, still holding Mariella. "No, Mariella, you're going to do what I tell you—you're going to do what I would do!"

"I know what I'm going to do, and you can't stop me!"

Mariella has broken away from Judy and rushed a little wildly up the stairs. Judy's power has gone, too. "She is an ordinary, very frightened girl who has no idea what to do next."

Outside a red glow that neither Mariella nor Judy has seen has deepened perceptibly. Suddenly there is a shout from Micky as he comes running down the stairs.

"The little barn's caught fire!" he calls. And then, to Judy: "For God's sake, don't stand there staring!" At the window he turns. "God! the roof will be down in a moment! Come on, Judy!"

Micky has rushed from the room. Judy, with a little cry of "David!" on her lips, has followed him. Henry, all excitement, comes rushing in to get Mariella. She'll miss it if she doesn't hurry. And there's no need of her looking so tragic, he says, when Mariella does appear at the head of the stairs. The barn is quite adequately insured.

Mariella goes back to her room. She has no time for fires. Henry has rushed into the yard.

Hannah comes running from her room, an overcoat over her night things. It may not be much of a fire, as Henry intimates, admits Hannah. But if a few sparks would come flying over in that direction there would be plenty to worry about.

Suddenly Hannah is brought up with a start. She has heard something. Mariella, rushing from her room, has heard something, too. A second later Micky has come through the door below, calling to Hannah hysterically. There is a confused turmoil outside.

"The roof fell in! She's dead!" sobs Micky, hysterically. "Judy's dead! She's dead, I tell you!"

With a frightened cry for David Hannah has run into the yard.

"It wasn't an accident, Mariella—she stepped forward!" Micky's sobs control him. "You and David didn't manage things very carefully, did you?" he cries, falling on the sofa.

"It isn't true, is it, Mariella?" demands Henry.

Mariella doesn't hear him. "Her face is suddenly old." When she speaks her voice is almost a whisper. "Judy, how could you . . . how could you!" she says.

Micky's sobs shake the sofa as

THE CURTAIN FALLS

ACT III

It is tea time again, about a week later. Hannah, in black, is laying the table when Henry wanders in. There are only four places on the table. Hannah didn't know until Henry tells her that Mariella is coming down. Henry is awfully in hopes Hannah will let it be an easy meal.

Hannah is willing enough. Conversation and wit should flow, she suggests, with a slight curl of her expressive lips, and they might have a few songs afterward.

"Hannah, must you be so . . . so . . . fanatical?" pleads Henry.

"Yes. I'm afraid I must."

"It doesn't help much."

"I know. But I hate her."

"Don't poison yourself like this, Hannah. It's horrible."

"The whole place is poisoned," retorts Hannah. And Henry agrees to that.

The workmen have been making progress on Henry's house. He wonders if Hannah will like him and Mariella as neighbors. Hannah has a feeling that while Henry may live in the house some day, it will not be with Mariella. She does not think Mariella is in danger of dying, but doubts that she will be with Henry long. In fact Hannah doesn't see why Henry doesn't get a divorce.

In addition to the fact that there are no grounds for divorce, Henry feels that when a man takes on an obligation he should go through with it. Anyway, he doesn't feel about Mariella as the rest of them do.

"She's not scheming, or anything like that," says Henry. "She hasn't committed a crime. To me it's just something that's happened."

"Yes, it's happened," admits Hannah, with finality.

HENRY—I think I'm probably being unjust in feeling towards her as I do, but I can't help it. I can't even like her any more. I've tried but I just can't! There's something about her that horrifies me.

HANNAH—She's always horrified me!

HENRY—I suppose I've never really understood her.

HANNAH—You never have understood women.

HENRY—All these last few days when she's been ill . . . when she was just turning over and over in her bed . . . calling Judy's name, I felt sorry for her. But this morning when she woke up it was as if nothing had ever happened. She was almost gay. And I couldn't feel even sorry for her any more.

HANNAH—Yes, she's made a quick recovery.

HENRY—God! I know one can't go on grieving forever, but somehow . . .

HANNAH—Yes, I know.

HENRY—And then David . . .

HANNAH—Try not to be too hard on him, Henry. He wasn't used to people like Mariella.

HENRY—I've tried to speak to him—but I can't think of anything to say.

HANNAH—I'm frightened about David.

HENRY—Frightened?

HANNAH—He hasn't woken up one morning feeling suddenly gay. He's been so strange lately that I wonder sometimes . . .

HENRY—I don't know! I've lived forty-eight years and at the end of it, it seems that I know nothing!

Mariella is back from her walk. With not so much as a nod in response to her cheerful greeting Hannah picks up the breakfast try and leaves the room.

For a moment Henry tries to make conversation, but Mariella quickly sees through that. He has a strange feeling, Henry admits, that he is meeting Mariella for the first time. To him she seems to be behaving in "a callous and disgusting manner." She is of a mind to make light of their going away to Scotland and the good shooting they may find there.

Mariella resents the implication, but she cannot pretend to a sense of sin when she feels none.

"Listen, Henry," says Mariella, earnestly. "I didn't know Judy for very long but I knew her better than you or Hannah or David ever knew her. And—though you may find it hard to believe—I was very, very fond of her. Now she's dead. And I am responsible for her death. If you were to fall down and hit your head on that chair and die, that chair would be responsible for your death. No one in their right senses would blame the chair."

"Are you human, Mariella?"

MARIELLA—Human? I'm never quite sure what it means. These last few days when I've been in bed—ill and hysterical—I suppose I have been what you would call "human." Judy would have called it blurred and messy-minded. But this morning when I woke up everything became suddenly quite clear and I, too, realized that everything I knew was right.

HENRY—I should hate to contradict you!

MARIELLA—You see, Henry, Judy hadn't got a life of her own. Her life was David. When David fell in love with me there was nothing left for her at all. If I'd gone away, if I'd died—it wouldn't have made the slightest difference. Her life was finished.

HENRY—I see your point entirely. She's much better dead.

MARIELLA—Henry. . . .

HENRY—If you could bring her back to life, would you do it?

MARIELLA—No. It would be the most cruel thing I could do.

HENRY—I find it difficult to understand you, Mariella. You've reached a higher plane. It seems a pity that someone should have had to die in the process.

MARIELLA—I understand you, Henry. I understand your bitterness—and I sympathize with it. Won't you just for a moment try to understand what I'm saying?

HENRY—I know you're not really wicked, Mariella, only . . . only . . .

MARIELLA—Only you'll never like me again.

HENRY—I'll try! I will try! But now it's so . . . so difficult.

MARIELLA—I don't want you to try because I know somehow that you'll never succeed.

HENRY—What do you think of me now?

MARIELLA—I like you tremendously. As I've always done.

HENRY—Then is there something wrong with me that I can't . . . I can't . . . ?

MARIELLA—Nothing, Henry dear. You have a different honesty, that's all.

David comes from the yard. "There is a wretched, hunted look about him." He is plainly at a loss just what to say or do. He is pleased to see that Mariella has come down. For a moment Mariella stares at him with a sort of fascinated horror. Then, at Henry's suggestion, both she and Henry leave him.

David wanders nervously about the room, fussing with the window curtain, adjusting the piano stool, stopping to read the inscription on one of his cups. He starts up the stairs and then comes down again. He starts violently when Micky comes into the room.

With Micky David tries to discuss the affairs of the farm casually, but the strain on his nerves is apparent. He is glad Micky is coming in to tea. It will be nice to see all the old faces around the board again. Is Micky speaking to everybody? Micky is speaking to everybody who speaks to him, which convinces David that everything should go with a swing.

Micky is worried about David. Thinks he should go away for a holiday. He will have a nervous breakdown or something if he doesn't. Micky is also fearfully sorry for what had happened that night.

"I've always been ungrateful and rotten about you," admits Micky.

"Not rotten. Just young," corrects David, with a trace of a friendly smile. "I can't sleep, you know, Micky. That's the trouble. I can't sleep at all."

"Well, you must take something."

"I've tried—taking something."

"Hadn't you better see a doctor, then?"

"No."

David is at the piano. Idly he strums a few chords of the concerto, then turns to something else. "He'd probably think I was going dotty," David continues, shaking his head foolishly. "But people like me don't go dotty. I'm too dull to go dotty. I'm too dull to go dotty. I'm too dull to go dotty!" He is humming to the piano.

"Shut up!" commands the frightened Micky.

"How masterful you are, Micky! When you have a farm of your own I wonder if you'll be as good as you think you are?"

"Well, that remains to be seen, doesn't it?"

"I suppose so. How would you like to run this one?"

"Why?"

"Perhaps I might take your advice and go for a holiday. A long holiday."

"I think it would be a good idea, David."

"I hate every stone of this place. Oh, how I hate it!"

Hannah has brought in the food. The sight of her is exciting to David. Reminds him that he mustn't play the piano. Suggests to him that Hannah has gone crawling about the house like a death's-head. He is sorry a moment later. Hannah must know that he isn't quite his old self these days. It's because he can't sleep. He can't sleep and he hates this room. However can he live there alone? Can Hannah answer that? And he will be alone—quite alone.

Hannah would be encouraging. Things aren't going to be as they are always, she reminds him. He will get out of his hell one day. Judy would not want him to be as he is.

"Why did Judy die, Hannah?"

"Don't torment yourself, David."

"Why did Judy die?"

"I suppose she died because she didn't want to live any more."

"I wonder. . . ."

"She'll be happier now."

"You bet she will!"

David is shouting with startling savagery. He has gotten up from the piano and is pacing the room. His speech grows wilder and wilder.

"Oh, yes, I expect she's feeling as happy as a sandboy now! Sitting on a cloud, twanging her harp, and feeling as pleased as punch with her dirty trick! Well out of it, aren't you, Judy? (*Shouting.*) I hate her! Do you hear, Hannah? I hate her guts!"

"David!"

Then he is quiet again and sorry. "I don't know what I'm saying! Judy, I didn't mean it! I didn't mean it!" he cries fervently.

Now David is on the verge of tears as Hannah seeks to quiet him, to get him into the other room before the others come in for tea. He still is mumbling his apology to Judy.

"You've never been in love, have you, Hannah?" he asks.

"Have you, David?"

"Yes, Hannah!"

"Do you know the difference between love and infatuation?"

"Yes. I know the difference." There is a long pause. "I never knew Judy," David continues. "I know her better now she's dead. I know how good she was—how far too good for me. But I'll tell you something, Hannah—you cannot fall in love with someone just because they've died!"

Henry and Mariella have come back for tea. Micky is down from his room. David has gone back to the table. Again there is an effort at natural conversation. About the farm mostly. Micky has decided to name the new foal Daisy in place of Mariella. Mariella can understand. Daisy is much easier to say, anyway.

There is a reference to Henry's and Mariella's trip to Scotland. David remembers Scotland, too. He spent his honeymoon there. He is up from the table now, and at the window, looking at the sunset. All the buildings are quite red, he reports, nervously. It is taking the men a long time to clean up the mess around the barn.

Now David is back at table again, pressing more food on Mariella. Hannah doesn't like to see David act so. It is plain to her that Mariella does not want anything more. Henry has already suggested that they are through—

"Who the hell do you think you are? They're my guests, aren't they?" shouts David.

It is Henry now who protests that David should not carry on so. David, calmer a moment later, is again contrite. It is sleep he needs, as he was telling Micky. Mariella will understand. She hasn't slept much lately, either, has she? No, Mariella has not. At which admission Micky dashes out of the room.

"Fancy me being able to upset Micky," muses David. "However . . . Judy always slept like a log. Well, it's no use looking at me like that, Hannah. It's perfectly true. Judy—always—slept—like—a—log!"

Mariella is the only one who understands. She is sure David will sleep again. Mariella and Henry are going next day. David thinks perhaps another day—but Hannah protests the suggestion with a horrified "David!"

"Stop Daviding me, will you!" shouts David, turning upon Hannah furiously. "Minding other people's business! You haven't got enough of your own, that's what's wrong with you! Well, I'll give you some! (*Picking up a cup and smashing it on the floor.*) Get busy with that!"

"David!" (*Everyone has jumped to their feet.*)

"And that! And that! And that!" (*Tearing off the tablecloth.*) And that! (*He rushes up the stairs crying. . . .*) You'd like to stop me sleeping, wouldn't you, Hannah? And so would Judy! But you shan't, do you see? I will sleep! I will! I will!"

David has rushed up the stairs and into his room. Mariella would follow him, but Hannah is before her at the stairs, facing her menacingly.

"Let me go, damn you!" shouts Mariella.

"You're not going to kill him, too!" shrieks Hannah, pushing Mariella into a chair.

A second later David has reappeared on the stairs, carrying his coat and hat. He rushes down past them, announcing that he is going away. He is at the door when Mariella calls to him. She would have him come back that she may talk with him. Just for a minute. He can go then.

She turns to ask the others to leave them. Anything that she has to say to David she will tell Henry later. Hannah is obdurate. She will not stir a step. She would not have Henry listen to Mariella. But they both go finally.

When they are gone Mariella tries with fair success to speak calmly to David. He has, she tells him, a little chidingly, reduced them all to a fine state of nerves. Look at the mess he's made! David, like a chastened boy, would go now, but Mariella calls him back.

For a moment David hesitates. There are tears in his eyes, she can see that, when he stands before her. Suddenly he falls on his knees and buries his face in her lap.

"I'm not very brave, am I?" mutters David, controlling his sobs.

"Not many people are, David."

DAVID—Judy was!

MARIELLA—Yes, Judy was. . . .

DAVID—You do see why I can't bear to stay here, don't you?

MARIELLA—Of course I see.

DAVID—It's been getting more on my nerves every day until . . . until . . .

MARIELLA—I know. (*Stroking his head.*) Are you feeling a bit calmer now?

DAVID—Yes, thank you.

MARIELLA—Good.

DAVID—I think there must be something wicked about me, Mariella.

MARIELLA—Why do you say that?

DAVID—When I was crying just now . . . I wasn't crying about Judy.

MARIELLA—I know.

DAVID—When . . . when it happened, I tried to stop loving you, but I couldn't. And now I know that I shall never stop . . . Mariella.

MARIELLA—Why were you crying?

DAVID—Because now we can never . . . never . . .

MARIELLA—What makes you so certain of that?

DAVID—How can we after . . .

MARIELLA—After the way Judy died?

DAVID (*very quietly*)—Yes.

MARIELLA—David, do you know why Judy killed herself?

DAVID—Because she was so unhappy, I suppose.

MARIELLA—No.

DAVID—Why, then?

MARIELLA—Because she wanted you to be happy, David.

DAVID—What do you mean?

MARIELLA—Just before the fire Judy talked to me about "us." I didn't understand then exactly what she meant. But I understand now.

DAVID—What did she say?

MARIELLA—She said—"It would be an awful pity if you were to stop being logical—if you were to become blurred and messy-minded. It would disappoint me, Mariella, more than I can say."

DAVID—And then she killed herself?

MARIELLA—Yes. (DAVID *covers his face with his hands.*) Well, David, I won't disappoint her. (*After a pause.*) Will you?

DAVID—What do you mean?

MARIELLA—I mean that I'll come away with you now—if you'll take me.

DAVID—No! Oh, no!

MARIELLA—Then Judy died for nothing? And it's all waste and futility?

DAVID—I hadn't thought of it that way. I can't think of it that way all in a minute!

MARIELLA—Do you want me, David?

DAVID—You know I do.

MARIELLA—Then there's nothing more to be said.

DAVID—Yes, there is.

MARIELLA—What?

DAVID—You don't think it would be easy, do you?

MARIELLA—No. I know it wouldn't.

DAVID—You know what people would say?

MARIELLA—Yes.

DAVID—And you don't care?

MARIELLA—Yes, David, I do care. But not enough to make any difference.

DAVID—Do you think we'd be happy?

MARIELLA—Not always.

DAVID—What else can I say to stop you?

MARIELLA—Only one thing you could say would stop me—and you'll never say it.

DAVID (*after a long pause*)—No, I'll never say it. (*They embrace.*)

MARIELLA—You can tell them to come in now.

DAVID—Yes. . . . It isn't going to be pleasant. . . .

MARIELLA—No.

DAVID—Oh, Mariella, you *know,* and I don't! I don't know the difference between right and wrong. . . . I don't know anything. I haven't any faith except you!

MARIELLA—I shan't let you down.

DAVID—I'll call them in. (*He goes rather hesitatingly to the door. There he stands irresolute. She smiles at him. He smiles back.*) When I'm frightened . . . like I am now . . . will you always be there . . . behind me, making me braver?

MARIELLA—Always, David.

DAVID (*opening the door*)—Hannah, we're ready!

THE CURTAIN FALLS

THE GREEN BAY TREE

A Drama in Three Acts

By Mordaunt Shairp

IT was reported of "The Green Bay Tree" when it was produced in London that it was frankly played as a much more decadent drama than it was in New York. Which for once in a way reverses a familiar order. The London censor of plays has formerly been the outstanding bar to such Anglo-Saxon liberties of speech and action as the more liberal-minded playwrights of both England and America have demanded a right to indulge.

In the version of Mordaunt Shairp's play which Jed Harris staged in New York all suggestion of degeneracy is carefully minimized and the play becomes the taut and fascinating contest of a man and woman for the affections of a young man who is the foster son of one and the fiancé of the other.

It is in effect a revealing study of a certain social decadence, a habit of luxurious living, the tendency of which is to weaken the moral fiber and corrupt the souls of its practitioners. A normal opposition is represented by the religious fanaticism of the young man's Victorian parent and the wholesome affection a girl of clean and open mind feels for him.

"The Green Bay Tree" is one of those dramas that must make its appeal to a particular type of audience and not to audiences in general. Those audiences to which it will appeal as an intelligent discussion of a timely and adult theme are entitled to their representation in any year book of the drama that pretends to represent the theatre season truthfully and fairly.

On an evening in May we meet at Mr. Dulcimer's flat in London. The atmosphere of the room into which we are ushered "is one of luxury, fastidiousness and just a touch of the abnormal. The owner is an artist, obviously, in the sense that everything in the room has been chosen for its intrinsic value and given its absolutely right position in the general scheme of decoration. The walls are painted a delicate shade of bluey-green, the ceiling is also painted, likewise the furniture, which is all of the good modern type."

"To the outsider the room is artificial and a little bizarre, but it excites curiosity about the owner. To him it is a constant source of pleasure. It reflects his personality, his sensitiveness, and delicate appreciation of beauty."

There is a handsome radio-gramophone and, a little way from a high window, an embroidery frame with a high stool beside it. Going from the room to the roof garden outside the windows one would find two conventional trees of the cypress pattern "which stand out against a sky-blue screen that is fastened to and rises from a parapet. By means of skillful flood-lighting, the owner of the room is able to imagine at night and especially in the Summer that he is looking out onto an Italian landscape."

A grand piano, a writing table, a large Knowle couch covered with cushions, a round dining table with chairs, set for two, topped by four candlesticks with tall slender tapers in them add to the distinctive beauty of Mr. Dulcimer's quarters.

It is eight o'clock, by the chimes, when Trump, an immaculate butler, appears with the evening papers, arranging them precisely on the desk by the fireplace. Trump would steal a look at one of the papers, but a step in the hall is a warning to him to desist. He is puttering a little with the things on the dining table when Mr. Dulcimer comes in.

Mr. Dulcimer "is a man about forty-five, immaculately turned out, and wearing at present a double-breasted dinner jacket. He speaks exquisitely in a clear voice, and with now and then a slight drawl. He has a habit of looking at you from under his eyes, and though a complete dilettante, he has an alert, vibrating personality. A man who could fascinate, repel and alarm. Instantly we know that he is the one thing missing in the room, and he seems to know it, too, for he stands a moment inside the doors, almost as if he were 'taking a call' for having created it."

Mr. Dulcimer, surveying the room with a critical eye, has a feeling that it looks quite naked. The nakedness, he senses, is the absence of flowers. The flowers should have been done, as Trump knows. They must still be done, and Mr. Dulcimer certainly feels over-dressed for doing flowers. Still, he will do them, and without an apron. Mr. Dulcimer could not think of trusting Trump to do the flowers. Trump, we gather, is not a tulip type.

There are other minor irritations. Mr. Dulcimer finds one of the evening papers rumpled. He does hate sharing a paper. And Mr. Julian is not yet in, which means that Mr. Julian may be late for dinner again. Also, Trump had been so careless as to let Mr. Dulcimer go out without his cigarette case. Mr. Dulcimer had been obliged to smoke Lady Pelham's unfiltered brand, a brand, Mr. Dulcimer is convinced, Lady Pelham smokes for the coupons.

Trump has brought in a jug of flowers. There are tulips and irises. Mr. Dulcimer, with gloved hands, cuts their stems daintily and arranges them in vases, the irises for the piano, the tulips for the dinner table. He is still at it when Julian Dulcimer arrives.

Julian is "a handsome boy in the early twenties, charming and well-made, but self-assured and self-indulged. Like Mr. Dulcimer he is dressed perfectly."

Julian, with just a suspicion that he may be late, is ready with explanations. He has fallen in love with the new car and has been giving the new love a run in Richmond Park.

Mr. Dulcimer is pleased with Julian's enthusiasm, but is disappointed that he had been denied the young man's advice at the "heart-rending private view" which Julian had promised to attend with him, and had forgotten completely.

"You've been forgetting a good many things lately," chides Mr. Dulcimer. "Don't forget that we're going to the opera tomorrow night."

"Are we?"

DULCIMER—Yes. Edward Trammle has offered me his box. (*Looks up.*) Fortunately I was out when he brought it in. I only hope he won't come too. I shall never forget how he fidgeted through the whole of Götterdämmerung.

JULIAN—What is it tomorrow?

DULCIMER—Tristan!

JULIAN—That means early dinner.

DULCIMER—Not at all. I never arrive at Tristan till the second act.

JULIAN—Good! I shall be in the mood for Tristan tomorrow.

DULCIMER—It's the most exquisite love-story ever imagined. Quite perfect. I'll go through the score again with you in the morning.

JULIAN—Aren't these first Spring days marvelous?

DULCIMER—Don't use that dreadful word! (*He is all the time doing the flowers.*) "Marvelous" is the expletive of the ignorant and unimaginative. When you hear anyone describe an experience as "marvelous" you can be sure it has made no impression on them whatever.

JULIAN—I don't know how to describe what I felt this afternoon. (*Moving about the room.*)

DULCIMER—Don't try. Only poets can do justice to the Spring, "in a mist" that cruel terrifying time.

JULIAN—Terrifying?

DULCIMER—There is always something terrifying in the remorselessness of nature, something shattering in all this re-assertion of the principle of life. *Trump* has got it badly. He rumpled the *Evening Standard.*

JULIAN—I believe I've got it too.

DULCIMER—There is a distinctly bucolic look in your eye. In another moment you'll tell me you've been to the Westminster Baths.

JULIAN—I felt very like it.

DULCIMER—When the really warm days come, we'll go down to Silver Gates. You'll find the amber pool preferable to the sweaty transports of Westminster Baths. Yes. (*Reflectively.*) I think I shall have amethyst cushions this year in the seats round the edge of the pool. Tomorrow we'll go and choose (*He makes a lot of the word.*) the material together.

JULIAN—How you love the word "choose!"

DULCIMER—Choice is what separates the artist from the common herd. *Nobody* knows how to choose nowadays. I hope you will never forego your prerogative of choice. Never do anything that is ill-considered, or take what is second best.

JULIAN—But supposing one is carried away? There are moments when one just can't choose.

DULCIMER—Rise above those moments with a colossal assertion of your individuality. (*Pointing through the open window.*) Look at those colors down there in the Square. That is how *I* like to see nature, controlled and at my feet. Don't wallow in her—

JULIAN—I don't think I've quite got your detachment.

DULCIMER—Then you must learn to have it.

JULIAN—Not now, Dulcie. First I think I'll wallow a bit.

DULCIMER—What do you mean?

JULIAN—Don't get frightened. I'm only going to rush into a dinner jacket.

Julian has gone to dress. Trump has been summoned to extricate Mr. Dulcimer from the lager of tables in which he finds himself "looking like a wayside shrine." The sun has gone in and the shadows have brought out new beauties in the room. Now Mr. Dulcimer has drifted to the piano and played for a moment, and risen from the piano to help himself daintily to an olive and then to take a glass of sherry from the tray Trump has brought in.

To Trump it seems a propitious time to break a bit of bad news to Mr. Dulcimer. The drills are coming to the Square. The pneumatic drills. They are coming to take the road up and the news is a shock to Mr. Dulcimer. It will, he fears, prevent his eating a thing at dinner.

The news of the drills is less of a shock to Julian, but he finds it a little difficult to decide between Mr. Dulcimer's country estate, Silver Gates, and the place in Italy as a haven of retirement while the road is being remade. As a matter of fact Julian is of no mind to tear himself away from London at this particular time of the year, when London is at its best. Even the thought of "a Square full of men in tarpaulin huts" is not too discouraging to Julian.

Trump has removed the first course and served the second when Julian recovers a sufficient courage to tell Mr. Dulcimer of a surprise he has had in store for him for some time. It explains why he has a reason for wanting to stay in town. Julian has fallen in love. Not only with the new car. Julian has fallen in love with a lady and is quite earnest about it.

"I've known for some time that something was absorbing you," says Mr. Dulcimer, in tones entirely conciliatory, though he finds it a little difficult to be serious with Julian. "Haven't I been discretion itself in asking no questions?"

"I suppose I have been a bit secretive."

DULCIMER—Never mind if you have. I know. You wanted to wait until you were sure. Tell me about it. I must be slightly responsible for the good impression you have made.

JULIAN—I'm afraid you've had nothing to do with this!

DULCIMER—Perhaps not. Every lover likes to think that he is original.

JULIAN—I mean you might not quite understand what I feel. I don't think you've ever been in love. (MR. DULCIMER *winces, but* JULIAN *is not looking at him, and so does not see him.*) Her name is Leonora Yale. Her people are retired Army and live somewhere in the country. She's a veterinary surgeon. She's really a quite remarkable person. (*A moment's silence.*)

DULCIMER—I suppose Peter introduced you?

JULIAN—I suppose he did in the first place.

DULCIMER—Another argument against dogs. They create unsubstantial intimacies.

JULIAN—Why unsubstantial?

DULCIMER—Everything *seems* durable while it lasts. May I put this crude question? How long will your passion for Miss Yale last?

JULIAN—You are certainly crude. I thought you'd be a little out of your depth over this.

DULCIMER—Out of my depth! Because I ask the old question that has echoed down the ages. Very well then. I won't probe any further, but I must make my arrangements. You take your ecstasy to Silver Gates and I'll go to Margherita. That seems the best arrangement as you're both attached to animals.

JULIAN—I don't think you quite understand. (*Quietly.*) I want to *marry* Leo.

DULCIMER (*his face full of shadows but his voice controlled*)—You never mentioned the word "marry." (*Leaning forward.*) My dear boy, are you serious?

JULIAN—Perfectly.

DULCIMER—How long have you known her?

JULIAN—About three months.

DULCIMER—Why didn't you tell me before?

JULIAN—I kept quiet until I was sure.

DULCIMER—And when did you feel sure?

JULIAN—Last night.

DULCIMER—Julian?

JULIAN—Yes.

DULCIMER—You don't think you'd like to give it another three months and then open the question again?

JULIAN—Ten years won't make any difference. I've made up my mind. I've seen Leo nearly every day. I've been to her surgery, I've met her under a variety of circumstances, and always felt the same.

DULCIMER—In another moment you'll tell me that you were made for each other.

JULIAN—Perhaps we were. But nothing you can say will laugh me out of it. This isn't just a matter of "choosing." It's got to be. That's the part I don't expect you to understand.

The conversation has got back to Julian and Leonora Yale. Leonora, Julian explains, has made a great success of her Canine Infirmary at Notting Hill—she and her partner Ranulf. Julian realizes what his parting with Dulcie will mean to them both. His life has been wonderful. No one, not even his real father, could have given him a better life than Dulcie has given him.

But now he would get married. He has thought, too, that while Ranulf carried on the infirmary he and Leonora might go to Italy for their honeymoon, might stay there for several months. Then probably they would have to settle down somewhere. Leonora is hoping some day to have a better surgery in a more central place, and Julian has hoped that he might give it her. Leonora is also rather keen on Julian's getting a job, but he has not encouraged her greatly in that.

Mr. Dulcimer smiles craftily. He is ready to agree that Julian has handled the whole situation with tact and imagination. He will buy the trousseau and give Julian away at St. Paul's, Knightsbridge. And after St. Paul's—

"I did rather hope that you'd increase my allowance," ventures Julian. "You will, Dulcie, won't you?"

"I've always loved your ingenuousness, Julian," smiles Mr. Dulcimer. "It's one of your greatest charms. I shouldn't dream of increasing it. In fact, if you leave me, I don't propose to make you any allowance whatever."

Mr. Dulcimer does not feel that he is turning Julian adrift. Julian proposes to undertake to support a wife, which may sound rather dreary, but is an ugly middle-class term which Mr. Dulcimer is forced to use. It will be a novelty for Julian to earn his own living.

"Come and sit over here and let us try and understand one another," suggests Mr. Dulcimer, indicating the couch and taking Julian's arm to direct him toward it. "Julian, will you let me put the case from my point of view?"

JULIAN—Of course. But I don't quite understand your attitude about my allowance. Certainly you don't expect me to get along without money? Of course I'm not your son and I know I haven't got any rights but . . .

DULCIMER—What are rights? You've had privileges. You've been my constant companion. Have you ever appreciated the compliment?

JULIAN—Of course I have. You've given me everything I could possibly want.

DULCIMER—I did more than that. I created you. I've made you what you are, because I rescued you from a life of squalor. I chose you instinctively, just as I have chosen everything else in my life. It was a bold experiment, but I didn't make a mistake. You have always been a very delightful son and companion to me. But life with me and life with Leo are two very different things. You can't expect them to overlap.

JULIAN—I suppose I can earn my own living like anyone else?

DULCIMER (*craftily*)—What's to stop you? You're personable and accomplished. You've traveled. Above all, you've got my training and experience behind you. The blossoming time has come a little earlier than I expected. Never mind! All I ask is that in return for my careful nurture I may be allowed to watch you flower. That will interest me enormously, and I shall be very proud if you succeed. If you fail, I can always rescue you again.

JULIAN—I shan't fail!!

DULCIMER (*craftily*)—You'll be a poor advertisement for me if you do. My dear boy, people will be only too glad to get you!

JULIAN (*eagerly*)—Do you think they will?

DULCIMER—I'm sure of it. We must look out for an opening immediately.

JULIAN—You didn't mind my asking you?

DULCIMER—Of course I didn't.

JULIAN—I believe I can do anything I want to. Don't you think so, Dulcie?

DULCIMER—I have every confidence in you, my boy.

JULIAN—I know you have.

DULCIMER—I think I should be very wrong to smother your initiative with a few hundreds a year.

JULIAN—I see. I suppose I shall have to put off marrying Leo for a bit. She'll understand that. She's really awfully sound about things.

DULCIMER—Sound, Julian? Sound? Am I to understand that you have succumbed to the solid virtues?

JULIAN (*laughing*)—You shall see for yourself. She'll be here in a few minutes.

DULCIMER (*in his usual ecstasy of protestation*)—I do wish you wouldn't spring surprises on me. I'm as shy as an antelope when I'm surprised.

Leonora Yale, who arrives a moment later, is a beautiful girl, "clean-cut, charming, strong-willed, decisive, quite free from pose, does not take other people's opinions, or judge things on their face value. She is modern in the best sense of the word. She can wear clothes and knows how to wear them. As usual she makes an impression, and she makes it on Dulcimer. She is not quite what he expected. There is nothing middle-class about her. There is something about her of the thing well-done, well-turned out, that appeals to him. She speaks well and decisively."

The introductions are pleasantly informal. Mr. Dulcimer is delighted to meet Leonora, of whom he never even knew until this evening, and Leonora is pleased to know Mr. Dulcimer, of whose actual existence she has been long in doubt, thinking of him as a figment of somebody's imagination.

Leonora is impressed with Trump and with the beauty of Mr. Dulcimer's rooms. She agrees with Mr. Dulcimer that it is too sensitive a room for dogs to rampage about in, but she has a feeling that a dog that would keep very still, a decorative Borzoi, for instance, might add a touch, and Mr. Dulcimer is partly convinced she may be right.

With Julian gone to dress, Leonora and Mr. Dulcimer are free to exchange confidences. Dulcimer is interested in knowing whether or not Leonora would have taken him and Julian for father and son, had she not known of their relations. Leonora is inclined to believe she should, noting many mannerisms which they have in common. She is also interested in the sort of man Julian's own father may be. That, Dulcimer assures her, will be easy to learn. Julian's father is still running a dairy or a drapery or something in Camden Town. Julian has never seen him, nor ever will, with Mr. Dulcimer's permission, though he is reported to be a reformed character now.

"Have you ever known any reformed drunkards, Miss Yale?" inquires Mr. Dulcimer. "They're positively dangerous. Society really shouldn't permit it. It should compel its drunkards to keep on drinking. Of course, I haven't seen him since I adopted Julian."

"It was very decent of you to rescue him," laughs Leonora.

DULCIMER—I shall never forget the day I first heard him sing at an Eisteddfod in Wales.

LEONORA—You fell in love with his voice?

DULCIMER—If you like to put it that way. He had the most exquisite treble voice I've ever heard. I had some records made of it. Perhaps you'd like me to play one for you sometime.

LEONORA—That's very kind of you.

DULCIMER—I pursued that voice to a back alley in some unpronounceable Welsh town, and there I found Julian with a violent, drunken father and no mother. It would have been sacrilege to have left him there, but no one else had sensibility enough to see that.

LEONORA—You didn't send him to school, did you?

DULCIMER—I thought of doing so, but my interviews with Headmasters were scarcely encouraging.

LEONORA—I wish you had a record of them.

DULCIMER—He may not have had a Public School education, but Julian is as much at home in Paris or Rome as he is in London. He can paint. He knows something about music. He's cultured and charming, because I taught him to be so.

LEONORA—Yes, I see you've taken a lot of pains with him. (*She realizes what she's up against.*)

DULCIMER (*slowly*)—He's more than a son to me, and it will mean more to me to give him up. Perhaps that won't be necessary immediately?

LEONORA—Perhaps not quite immediately.

With Mr. Dulcimer gone to get into something comfortable for his lonely evening at home Julian tells Leonora of the beastly revelations of the evening. Not only has his guardian refused to increase his allowance, but he is expecting him, after he is married, to earn his own living.

"I never felt such a fool in my life," admits Julian.

"We'll have to wait a bit, that's all," is Leonora's reaction.

It is quite evident to Leonora that Julian's guardian doesn't want Julian to marry at all. As for earning his living, that, too, presents a problem. Nothing that Julian can do, such as paint a bit, play a bit, and declare a keen eye for color, is worth a sixpence in the workers' market, according to Leonora. Perhaps, on sober reflection, it would be better for them to call everything off.

"It seems so unfair to you," Leonora explains. "There's no earthly reason why you should suddenly become like everyone else. And slave and grind out a living."

"Look here, Leo, I haven't any illusions about myself," sharply answers Julian. "I know it's laughable at my age to be wondering what I'm going to be like a boy in the IVth form, but I do know I'm going to be something, so that I can marry you. I love you more than anything in the world. You ask me what I want to do. Well, anything that will make the time before we can get married as short as possible."

A declaration of mutual confidence in each other and in their love brings Julian and Leonora into each other's arms. Still they realize they must be sensible. It is Leonora's thought that Julian might learn to be a veterinary. He should not have much trouble with the exams, with her help, and after he had passed she and Ranulf could take him into the business. She and Julian could be married, perhaps, after the first exams, which would mean two or three months. But, first, Julian would have to break away absolutely from his present surroundings and live on his own. That, without any money to go on, is not going to be easy. Yet there would be no hope for him so long as he stayed with Dulcimer. He never would do a stroke of work.

It is agreed that Julian shall make the break and will take the matter up with Mr. Dulcimer at the earliest psychological moment that presents itself. Leonora is rewarding his expression of determination with a fond look when the thought of his other father suddenly recurs to her.

"Who are you?" she demands. "I mean, what's your real name? You've never told me."

"Didn't Dulcie?"

"No."

"My original name was Owen—David Owen."

"You're not even Julian?"

"No. I'm plain David."

"And very nice, too."

"But I'm patented, 'Julian Dulcimer,' or naturalized, or whatever it is."

"When we're married, shall I be Mrs. Owen or Mrs. Dulcimer?"

"Which would you like to be?"

"Mrs. Owen."

"I knew you'd say that. We'll have to see about it. I suppose I can be rendered down again, or something."

A moment later Mr. Dulcimer has discreetly coughed his way into the room to bid them good-by and invite them back later in the evening for a drink.

"There's a wonderful atmosphere about this room in the small hours of the morning," he promises.

"They mustn't be too small. I'm a working woman, Mr. Dulcimer," warns Leonora.

Mr. Dulcimer is standing in the middle of the room looking after them as they close the door.

The curtain falls.

It is a quarter to twelve the same evening. Mr. Dulcimer has been listening to a band playing dance music over the radio. Trump has brought in a plate of sandwiches, thinking Mr. Julian would like some when he comes, and Miss Yale, too.

As it happens Leonora does not come in with Julian. She is tired and has gone home. Julian is glad of the sandwiches and a drink. He would cheer Dulcie, too, with a spot of brandy, but Dulcie is in no need of stimulant. Julian would also be rid of Trump, who is swallowing yawns, that he may have a talk with Mr. Dulcimer.

Julian and Leonora did not go to the ballet, after all, it appears. They went instead to see Julian's father. The elder Owen was quite a surprise to Julian. Not a bit disreputable. Both Julian and Leo had liked him. They had found him sitting quietly at home reading the Bible.

"Good Heavens! Don't I read the Bible?" demands Mr. Dulcimer. "Haven't I told you that you can't form your style without it?"

"He's a preacher in some local chapel," explains Julian.

"I knew it. He should have kept on drinking."

"We told him some of our plans for the future, and he thought we were being very sensible. Leo and I have been mapping things out this evening. We decided that we can't be married till I've got a job, and so I'm going to become a vet."

Julian realizes that it is going to mean a lot of hard work. He thinks it will be possible for him to live with his father while he is learning. The college is quite close to his father's house.

Mr. Dulcimer is plainly disgusted. He considers Julian not only a little mad but rather uncouth.

"I can see it quite clearly," he says. "An impetuous boy, because he has fallen in love, wants to rush headlong out of my house at a moment's notice, without giving a thought to my wishes or plans."

Certainly Julian cannot believe that he will find living with his father congenial! Congenial or not, Julian expects to be too busy to think much about it.

"Dulcie, I don't want to offend you, but surely you must see that I couldn't work here."

DULCIMER—Why not? You can pore over diagrams of dogs' intestines to your heart's content.

JULIAN—You'd loathe it if I did. You know you would. (*Going to writing table.*) Look at this! (*He returns with a large quill pen, exquisitely feathered in jade green.*) That's your idea of a pen! I couldn't work with that!

DULCIMER—Pray remember, dear boy, that it was a Christmas gift—from you.

JULIAN—The point is that it's typical of everything here! I don't want to be uncouth or ungrateful, but I know that the only sensible thing to do is to get away on my own.

DULCIMER (*with a penetrating voice*)—On your own? Julian, are you hinting that I am the obstacle to your success?

JULIAN—We should get on each other's nerves a thousand times a day.

DULCIMER—Did Leonora make you think that?

JULIAN—No, not exactly. She agrees with me, though.

DULCIMER—You mean that you agree with her. (*As if thinking.*) I see, I see, she's determined to get you away from me, and she's not wasting any time about it.

JULIAN—Well, I think I shall go to bed now. I've got a lot of things to arrange tomorrow. Dulcie! We're going to be friends, aren't we? (DULCIMER *turns aside and refuses to take his hand.*) Oh, all right! But you're behaving very childishly!

DULCIMER (*turning round on him*)—You fool! You little, self-confident fool!

JULIAN—I'm not going to quarrel with you. You'll see things differently in the morning.

THE CURTAIN FALLS

ACT II

It is three months later. William Owen's sitting-room in Camden Town is small, neat and simply furnished. "On the mantelpiece there is a clock which belonged to Owen's mother, and on either side are photographs of the various members of his family. It is a comfortable room and contains good, solid furniture. Mr. Owen is proud of it; Julian detests it." There is a harmonium, "symbolic of a great deal of Mr. Owen's soul," and a writing table where Mr. Owen writes his sermons. "In the middle of the room is a solid, square dining table with a red velvet cloth and four upright chairs to match."

At the moment Julian is lolling in an armchair with his book, pretending to work. Leonora is nearby ready to help. Julian finds studying difficult, and no brain response whatever. He would make a new bargain with Leonora—that she will marry him even if he does not pass. Leonora is too smart to agree to that. It would mean no more study at all for Julian. Now she takes up the book and would help him through his troubles with Boyle's law. And with Dalton's law of Partial Pressures that follows.

Julian is not greatly interested in either Boyle or Dalton. He does like anatomy, however, and is willing to have a go at that. But soon he is mixed up with that, too, and Leonora decides that he has done enough for that day.

"Even Isaiah would admit that I've had a hell of a day," thinks Julian, after he has convinced Leonora that though for many years he had been living an amateur life he is not really an amateur lover, offering kisses in evidence. "I've had three hours with the crammer, taken down his damn notes, and read Boyle at home."

"You're beginning to feel that it is home?"

JULIAN—No. I can't quite say that. I haven't been trained to live with a minor prophet.

LEONORA—He is full of fervor, isn't he? Still, there is something very admirable about him.

JULIAN—I do wish he'd stop calling me Davy!

LEONORA—I imagine he thinks of you as David.

JULIAN—Yes, but Davy. It doesn't go with me at all. What's he up to this afternoon?

LEONORA—It's Thursday. He closes the shop early today.

JULIAN—And writes his sermon, and bellows it into us.

LEONORA—Let's try to keep off chapel for once. It always leads to trouble.

JULIAN—Chapel's like strong drink to him, isn't it?

LEONORA—Not a very fortunate remark.

JULIAN—You know, Leo, I think it would do him good to drink a bit. Really I do. It might make him more cheerful. He has such a marvelous capacity for violent feeling, it's a pity he should waste it all on chapel and on me. (*The front door bangs.*)

LEONORA—There he is now. Do be careful what you say. There's no need to hurt him.

JULIAN—Woe unto the ungodly. (OWEN *enters.*)

OWEN—Been studying hard, Davy? Hullo, Leo. Has he done well today?

JULIAN (*teasing him*)—Top in everything. The teachers were awfully pleased. At least this one was. (*Puts his arm around* LEONORA.)

OWEN—That's good, my boy. Only a fortnight, now, isn't it?

LEONORA—That's all, Isaiah.

OWEN—Well, there'll be nothing to stop you then. The first

test is always the hardest, when you've changed your mode of life. Afterwards, you can do anything you want. No temptation from the old life has any power over you.

JULIAN—Is that the text of this week's sermon, Isaiah?

OWEN—I don't mean to preach to you, my boy.

LEONORA—What have you been doing, Isaiah?

OWEN—I've been walking, and thinking about my sermon.

JULIAN—I thought you'd been to the pictures.

OWEN—I leave that to you, Davy.

LEONORA—It would really do you a world of good to go to the pictures, now and again. I'm sure you don't have half enough pleasure in your life.

OWEN—I have pleasure enough with my boy back.

LEONORA—But you lead such a model life, in that dear little dairy downstairs. I have a vision of you, Isaiah, sitting there peacefully, surrounded by fresh eggs and glasses of milk.

JULIAN—Watered.

OWEN—Don't say that, Davy.

JULIAN—Oh, you're awfully difficult, Isaiah. I was only joking.

OWEN—I don't like your jokes.

JULIAN—Oh, very well.

For a moment the silence is embarrassing. Owen moves over to the writing table to add a few thoughts to his sermon. Soon his interest in Leonora and Julian has returned. He would know about Leonora's business, which has been falling off. He would know about Julian's extravagance in paying nearly fifteen shillings for a tie he is wearing.

"I'd rather wear a bootlace than pay so much," insists Owen. "You're much too extravagant, my boy. What will you do when your money's gone?"

"I'll settle that when the time comes," answers Julian.

"But, my boy, you can't go over the abyss with your eyes open. What did you do with the ten pounds I gave you a fortnight ago?"

"I shouldn't be surprised if I spent it."

"I'm not rich, my boy. Ten pounds is a lot of money to me."

"You'll be paid back, Isaiah."

A telegram has come for Julian. It is from Dulcimer. Julian is quite excited about it. Dulcie's back from Silver Gates. He must have had a marvelous time there. Silver Gates is the country place Julian is hoping a bit wistfully to buy for Leonora one day. Leonora is amused by such optimism.

Owen, listening, is moved to read them something from the Bible. It's about the ungodly.

" 'I've seen the wicked in great power and spreading himself like a green bay tree!' " fervently intones Owen. " 'Yet he passed away, and, lo, he was not; yea, I sought him, but he could not be found!' "

It is an impressive thought to Owen. " 'Yet he passed away and, lo, he was not,' " he repeats, sonorously.

"Isaiah, you're a barbarian," charges Julian. "You belong to the Old Testament. I'm going to keep out of your way. I shall never buy another tie as long as I live."

Owen is worried about Julian. He wishes his son would come to chapel and hear him preach. Then he would know the power that is in him. Owen is interested in putting the fear of God in Julian. He hopes he and Leonora can keep Julian away from Dulcimer. Occasionally his conscience gives him a turn.

"I don't want an excuse for my act," Owen explains. "There is none in the eyes of God. I was a drunkard and I gave my boy away because someone wanted him and could pay me for him. I must have been blind drunk when I signed the document. And, do you know," he adds, naïvely, "from the moment I got the money I became a different man and everything flourished."

"Like a green bay tree," smiles Leonora.

Sometimes Owen is puzzled as to who are the ungodly and who aren't. He would not have had his dairy if it had not been for the money he had from Dulcimer fifteen years ago. He has been a better man since then.

Leonora believes it would be better if Owen were to talk more freely to Julian about what he has done. It might make it easier for Julian to understand and to sympathize with him.

"You can't just suddenly appear out of nowhere and say, 'Here I am, my boy. I'm your father,' and expect him to have any feeling for you. You must have patience, Isaiah."

"Sometimes I can hardly believe that he is my boy. We're so entirely different. We're so entirely different. You know, Leo, sometimes I would stand outside Dulcimer's house just to see David come out. I'd hide behind a tree and wait—and they would come out together, arm in arm, and walk up the road . . . then . . . (*Slight pause.*) Ah, well, let's have some music, shall we?"

Owen has gone to the harmonium and is playing "Tone Botel,"

an old Welsh air, with deep feeling. Julian, coming back, is stirred by the music. Something out of his past moves him as he listens. . . .

Trump has arrived with an invitation from Mr. Dulcimer for Julian and Leonora to dine with him that evening. He is looking forward to the meeting eagerly. Julian, too, is excited at the prospect. A dinner with Dulcie is much more important than the studying he had expected to do that evening. Nor does he want to go alone. He wants Leonora to go, too.

"How does Dulcie, as you call him, justify his existence?" demands Owen, when Trump has gone. "You don't like to have me talk about him, do you?" he adds as Julian shrugs his shoulders.

JULIAN—It doesn't really matter very much.

OWEN—Doesn't it?

JULIAN—I don't expect you to understand a man like Dulcie, Isaiah.

OWEN—I can see what he's up to. He wants you back with him.

JULIAN—Don't be silly. He knows very well I'm going to be married. It's only natural that he should ask Leo and me to dinner, after being away for three months.

LEONORA—He might have waited a few days.

JULIAN—Don't you understand, either, Leo? What on earth is the matter with you two? (*Pause.*)

OWEN—Davy, you've been happy here, haven't you, Davy?

JULIAN (*after a slight pause*)—Of course I have.

OWEN—Don't go back, Davy. Don't go back to that man. He's evil, I tell you. He only means to corrupt you. . . .

JULIAN—Oh, stop it, for God's sake. . . .

OWEN (*interrupting*)—I won't stop, do you hear? I won't stop.

JULIAN (*has turned away.* OWEN *takes hold of him fiercely*)—Keep your hands off me.

OWEN (*swinging him around*)—Listen to me. You're going to do as I say for once. You're not going to his house tonight. Do you understand that? You're going to stay here—where you belong—with me. That man shall never see you again.

JULIAN (*quietly*)—You know, Isaiah, I admire your ability to combine moral superiority with a genius for trade. It must be very satisfying to be able to despise someone with whom you once drove such an advantageous bargain. How much was it—

something like five hundred pounds, wasn't it?

OWEN—I'd have done better if I'd killed you.

JULIAN—Why didn't you? (OWEN *relaxes his hold. He looks piteously at* LEO, *takes his hat, and walks out.* JULIAN, *walking up and down, mutters.*) The whole thing is too ridiculous. (*Stops in front of* LEONORA.) Look here, Leo, you're not going to be silly about it, too, are you? (LEONORA *is silent. He continues to walk up and down.*) Good God! I don't know what you people are thinking about. It's maddening for people to act this way.

Perhaps Leonora would like him to ring up Dulcimer and get out of the dinner? Perhaps she is jealous of Dulcimer! It would be rather absurd if she were. Can't she understand what it means that Dulcimer wants to see him?

"Don't you see that I have won, Leo?" Julian demands, a little excitedly. "Don't you see?—He knows well that I can get along without him! And he didn't think I could! Well, I've shown him that I can, haven't I? . . . I knew that he was just testing me. He thought that I'd come running back to him. He's a little frightened now. He's afraid he's going to lose me. Now do you understand, Leo? He wants to be friendly because he has no one else, and I've meant a good deal to him. Don't you see how easy it's going to be, Leo, when I ask him for an allowance tonight?"

"You've told me all along you wanted to make your own money."

"I can't help it. I've got to do something. I can't go about as I have been doing—I'm not used to it, that's all, and there's no reason why I shouldn't go to Dulcie. After all, I lived with him for fifteen years. He does owe me something. Don't you think he knows it? Why do you think he asked us to come to dinner tonight if not to give me an allowance? He knows I need it, Leo. Just as well as I do."

He will never be able to make any money, Julian is now convinced. What's so terribly noble about being a vet? Certainly Leonora could not have thought he ever wanted to be one? He's not suited to it anyhow. The most important thing now is that he and Leonora can get married tomorrow. Now he will be able to give Leonora the infirmary he had promised her.

LEONORA—You seem so sure that Dulcimer will give you an allowance. What if he refuses?

JULIAN (*taking her in his arms*)—He won't refuse, Leo.

LEONORA—But if he does?

JULIAN—He can't. Not now. (*Smiles secretly.*) Not so long as he wants to see me.

LEONORA—I think I will go with you, Julian.

JULIAN—I knew you would. I don't like him, really, any more than you do. After dinner, Leo, I want you to invent some engagement or other and leave me to tackle him. I couldn't do it with you there.

LEONORA—No, of course not. All right. I'll clear out early.

JULIAN—Splendid. Now you must go home and dress. And put on your prettiest frock. I want you to look your very best tonight, Leo. Come along.

The curtain falls.

It is eight o'clock the same evening at Mr. Dulcimer's flat. There are bowls of roses everywhere and the doors into the roof garden are open. There are two tables set for dinner in different parts of the room. Mr. Dulcimer is seated at one, Leonora and Julian at the other.

"The arrangement is one of Mr. Dulcimer's jokes, but it serves to isolate Julian and Leonora from him. It amuses Julian, but it has embarrassed Leonora just a little, although she has entered into the spirit of it. The dinner has been excellent. Throughout it, Mr. Dulcimer has communicated with Julian and Leonora by note, conveyed by Trump, who acts up to Mr. Dulcimer's whim by posing as a magnificent maître d'hôtel."

Leonora is conscious that Mr. Dulcimer has been watching her closely. Julian has entered into the game and played up to his guardian. Now Mr. Dulcimer calls the maître d'hôtel, and sends a note to Julian's table. Julian reads it and laughingly scribbles a reply.

"Shall we have to go on playing this game all evening?" Leonora would know. "I'm beginning to feel self-conscious now. It's gone on too long, and I know he's watching me. He's been watching me all the time."

"He used to spring all sorts of surprises on me when I was a boy, and see how I reacted to them," explains Julian. "It was his idea of education. It did smarten one up."

An exquisite ice pudding is served, shaped like a small rose tree in bloom, the roses made of strawberry ice. It is almost too exquisite to cut, but Trump assures Leonora the management likes to have visitors pick the flowers. Julian remembers that when he was there in the old days there was a fine old brandy— That would be 1796, Trump recalls.

Now Dulcimer has ventured the liberty of sending the roses from his table to the lady at the other table with his compliments, and Leonora has accepted them gracefully. Then Julian, at her suggestion, calls the maître d'hôtel and asks him for his bill. Also a check form. And that breaks the spell.

Julian bursts into roars of laughter as Mr. Dulcimer gives up, shaking him heartily by the hand and greeting Leonora pleasantly. It has, Leonora agrees, been a marvelous game and Mr. Dulcimer is pleased.

"It's a great relief from the obvious and monotonous," says he. "They are the ghosts that haunt modern civilization. Nowadays everybody does everything and nobody does it well. I can't join in the great display of uninspired competence, so I contrive little originalities of my own."

Julian has gone to the roof garden to fetch Dulcimer's cigarette holder and Leonora and Dulcimer are prepared for a summing up of their respective campaigns. Leonora is still confident that she will win, and Mr. Dulcimer, assuming that she means by that that she will marry Julian, is quite willing to admit she will. Hearing of the effort Mr. Owen is making to be a real parent to Julian, Mr. Dulcimer is even prepared to help that cause along.

"You really must disabuse yourself of this notion that I wish to detain him," says Dulcimer firmly. "It's simply that I don't suddenly expose sensitive hot-house plants to harsh winds, not even when you're the Lady of the Garden. I took a certain amount of risk in doing what I did."

All that he has done, Mr. Dulcimer repeats, is to be thorough in his test of their love. Now he is glad to hear that Julian is making progress with the foot and mouth disease and that he has a purpose in life. If he (Dulcimer) had given Julian the allowance he had asked for three months ago it might have undermined him.

"At every crisis in Julian's life I want to be behind him with just that bias in the right direction that a real father never seems able to give. You can't believe that, can you?" asks Dulcimer.

"I should like to believe it very much," answers Leonora.

It is hard for Mr. Dulcimer to believe that Leonora dislikes him as heartily as he feels she does. Yet he knows just when she decided to dislike him.

"Oh, dear!" sighs Mr. Dulcimer. "Why wasn't I born ordinary? Ordinary people aren't accused of casting spells. I know what it is," he adds indignantly. "You'd have liked a nice suburban wooing. High tea and then the upper circle at 'Cavalcade.' I'm sorry I don't know how to go about it."

Julian is back but without the cigarette holder. And in whatever state of mind he may find Leonora and Dulcimer, he is both comfortable and happy. With another dash of brandy he sinks into one of the larger chairs entirely content.

"Isn't it extraordinary, Mr. Dulcimer, the effect your chairs have on Julian," says Leonora. "I do hope you will give us a few for our flat."

Leonora is leaving them. She has a sick dog to look after. Horrifying thought to Mr. Dulcimer. Julian persuades her to stay at least for coffee. Dulcimer, to prove how really ordinary he can be, asks Trump to turn on the wireless. Soon Julian has begged Leonora to dance with him. The sight is a little disturbing to Mr. Dulcimer. He thinks he will have a look for his cigarette holder himself. It must be on the roof.

When they discover that they are alone Julian must know all that Dulcie had said to Leonora. She has little that is encouraging to report, but Julian is still confident he will bring his guardian around.

"I have a feeling he's watching us," whispers Leonora as they resume dancing.

"Darling, what a bogey you make of him."

"I don't trust him. I don't think he cares what you have, unless you come to live with him again."

"I'll never do that, Leo."

"Do you love me enough?"

"I love you enough to do anything."

"I don't want you to be charming, Julian. I want to know." Leonora has moved out of Julian's arms, but Julian has brought her back again. "Take care!" she warns, glancing anxiously at the roof garden.

"Oh, rot! Let him see that we mean business!"

They are in the midst of a long embrace when Dulcimer returns from the roof garden and switches off the radio.

Now Leonora is really leaving them. She would ring Julian up before she goes to bed if she thought it would not disturb his father. Let her ring him at Dulcimer's, suggests Julian. He will be staying on for a time.

Dulcimer has turned down some of the lights and is at the piano playing softly when Julian comes back from putting Leonora in the lift. The effect is pleasing. To Julian there is something in Dulcie's playing Chopin that brings out the peacefulness of the room. At the moment it seems quite magical. Recalls a bit of poetry which Dulcimer recites.

"Sounds and sweet airs that give delight, and hurt not
. . . . and then in dreaming
The clouds, methought, would open, and show riches
Ready to drop upon me; that when I waked, I cried to
dream again."

Julian has fallen back upon the sofa. He is feeling the heat of the room. "I haven't been used to anything soft for such a long time," he explains. "I feel as if I were drowning."

"You were always very imaginative," recalls Dulcimer. "Sit down again. I won't play any more if my playing makes you swoon."

In the talk that follows Julian is willing to confess that he has missed everything terribly. He is glad to be back. He even enjoyed the freak dinner.

Dulcimer is not pleased. He had thought with a touch of formality he could reassure them of his kindly interest. It had not worked that way.

"What a fool I've been!" he all but shouts. "An ill-mannered fool. To start a game and then refuse to play it out! You wanted to go. But then you found that the prison door wasn't really open! Like the captives in the Bastille, you reached the last corridor, only to run into your jailer's arms!"

Dulcimer has worked himself up into a fine passion. Julian is half amused and half alarmed.

"You know quite well that I didn't think anything of the kind!" he says. "I was thankful to get back here, and hated not being able to talk to you all through dinner. Please sit down, and as I said before, don't act!"

DULCIMER—At least you can never say that I kept you against your will, even though I have no respect for natural ties.

JULIAN—I've had an eye-opener over them, I can assure you. Do let me enjoy myself a little bit! I'm going back to natural ties soon enough!

DULCIMER (*interested and inwardly curious*)—Do you find they count for much?

JULIAN—More than I expected. I suppose that's because he's

my father. I suppose he got a footing inside me during those first eight years.

DULCIMER (*indignantly*)—He never bothered about you at all.

JULIAN—Well, there it is! He's utterly impossible but he exists. And then, of course, I have some strange affinity with him over the past. He plays those ghastly Welsh hymns, and I listen to them, and something happens to me. I don't know what it is.

DULCIMER—Some of those melodies are extraordinarily fine.

JULIAN—It isn't anything esthetic. It isn't even pleasure. It calls from somewhere far off and makes me feel that I belong to something very old. I thought what a contrast it was just now. You at the piano, and father at the harmonium. But they both speak. Now let's forget old Camden Town.

DULCIMER—I should like you to have been at Silver Gates this time. I took your advice about the music room. It now faces the swimming pool.

JULIAN—I always told you it ought to be there.

DULCIMER—You were right. I've had the pool floodlighted! Now at night, the box hedges enclose a lagoon of deep Mediterranean blue. Ruinously expensive.

JULIAN—Marvelous! (*Remembering.*) I mean—how exquisite! (*They laugh.*)

DULCIMER—We must give a fancy-dress bathing party. Venetian, and very slippery. (*All the time he is watching* JULIAN *closely.*)

JULIAN—And while you're splashing in the moonlight, I shall be sweating in Camden Town.

Dulcimer was glad to hear from Leonora, he says, that Julian has made so good a start with his work. Glad that he now has a purpose in life and lives simply, with neither cars nor other luxuries to distract him.

"How would you like to give some dog an emetic?" demands Julian.

"I should hate to give anyone an emetic," admits Dulcimer, quickly. "I could never get into the right frame of mind. But then, I haven't the call! Your father isn't preparing to be a vet, too, is he? What an ideal home life, if he were!"

It occurs to Dulcimer that if Julian would come with him for a holiday to Margherita it would help him with his exams. He could bring his books along. He could bring Leo, too, if he wanted to. But Julian is afraid Leo would never leave the business, not after she had given up so much time to him. And he is reluctant to admit it would be easy for him to tear himself away from her for a week or two.

Now, with some effort, Julian has brought himself to the question that has been in his mind from the first. He has never asked Dulcie for anything much before, and now he finds it difficult to put a request into words. But won't Dulcie reconsider his decision about the allowance?

DULCIMER—*Supposing* I do reconsider my decision?

JULIAN (*eagerly*)—Then that would make everything all right. I don't want to be idle. I never have been idle. I like having something to do all the time. You see, my idea is to live in the country, away from all this that I can't afford. But we'd hope to visit you sometimes, Dulcie, and you'd visit us, wouldn't you?

DULCIMER—You think you could endure the country—always?

JULIAN—Oh, I'd like to run kennels or something of the kind. I haven't the slightest intention of vegetating. . . . We've got all sorts of schemes. We'd run polo ponies, too.

DULCIMER—What sum of money do you think would make all that possible?

JULIAN—It would take a good bit, I suppose, but . . .

DULCIMER—It's no good underestimating that. By the time you'd bought your house and equipped it with livestock, you'd have spent the best part of four or five thousand pounds.

JULIAN—I suppose we might, Dulcie, but after that three hundred a year would be enough. It isn't much, and we'd have a home and security, and I should be delivered forever from this nightmare of daily bread.

DULCIMER—It almost seems a pity I didn't make you a plumber.

JULIAN—I rather wish I had been taught something. (DULCIMER *is silent.*) What are you thinking, Dulcie?

DULCIMER—I was thinking that six months hence, or a year hence, you'll find that your allowance isn't enough and that your menagerie doesn't pay, and you'll come and ask for more.

JULIAN—I promise you, I'll never ask you for another penny.

DULCIMER—Like the tiger, you'll have tasted blood, and you'll be greedy to taste more.

JULIAN—Then you mean that you won't help me?

DULCIMER (*looking at him gravely*)—I can't give you any money, Julian. (JULIAN *watches him.*)

JULIAN (*after a moment*)—Dulcie.

DULCIMER (*turning 'round*)—Well?

JULIAN—You want me to be happy, don't you?

DULCIMER (*fiercely*)—Want you to be happy? You've always been happy. I've made you happy.

JULIAN—I know you have, Dulcie, I know you have. But I must go on, Dulcie. You see that, don't you? You've got to help me. I can't just stand still.

DULCIMER—You must be as you are. You must develop naturally. Listen, Julian, there is nothing to be ashamed of, or disappointed over in not being able to earn a living. You aren't made that way, that's all. I delivered you forever from what you call "the nightmare of daily bread." You have a home and security that nothing can take from you, and you won't recognize it.

JULIAN—I want to get married, I tell you.

DULCIMER—For goodness' sake, don't be strident.

JULIAN—I can't always pick and choose my words, just to please you.

DULCIMER—I'm not complaining of your language. I only ask you not to shout.

JULIAN—You seem to think that what is soft and expensive and luxurious is everything. (*He sits again.*)

DULCIMER (*quickly*)—And, don't you? Haven't you proved it tonight? Haven't the last three months proved it? What matters to you most is to be comfortable, to have pleasant rooms and pleasant meals, and money in your pocket. You have tried the other thing and hated it, haven't you? (JULIAN *is silent.*) Very well, then. Be honest with yourself. Don't try to be some other person. Be Julian Dulcimer.

Julian's excited protest that he is not Julian Dulcimer makes little impression upon his foster father. The fact that he may have been stirred by a few Welsh hymns means little to Dulcimer. Let Julian protest as he will he still cannot be two people at the same time. He cannot be Julian Dulcimer and a married man. It is quite natural, agrees Dulcimer, that he should want to include Leonora in his scheme, but unfortunately there isn't room for her. Let him protest as much as he likes, the fact remains that if Julian persists in marrying Leonora she will have to keep him. Let him pretend for a while that he is what is known as a breadwinner, in the end he will come to depend on his wife. All his dreams of what he is going to do will crumble into dust the first morning he doesn't want to get up, or fancies a day in town.

"You think you know me, but you're wrong!" protests Julian, vehemently.

DULCIMER—Very well, then, go and get married. Disregard your temperament, your disposition, your everything that cries out against it. Beat out a living from the world and fashion a home for your wife, and live in it, and be happy ever after. Can you do it?

JULIAN—Yes, yes, I can.

DULCIMER—Can you say, "Leonora comes before everything else. I don't care what I do and where I live so long as she is with me"? Of course you can't. But you haven't the courage to admit, and it's only a fool who won't admit his own limitations. (*A silence.*) However, I suppose that your silence means that you do not recognize them, so we won't use any more harsh names. You're not really the fool you're trying so hard to be.

JULIAN—By God, I'm not. I'm not fool enough to be one thing, and that is your slave.

DULCIMER—Don't be ridiculous.

JULIAN—You call me ridiculous. I'm not ridiculous. You think my life is yours to do with as you please, but it isn't. I'm going to do what I like. I'm not going to listen to you. I was never your son, anyhow. I was something that you had made, that you liked to look at, because it was something you could never be. I think I detest you now, everything about you, your luxury and your beastly superior air. I shall live where I like, and how I like, and you can go to hell. (*Phone starts to ring.*)

DULCIMER—Prove it. Now's your chance. Tell her—you little canting fool. You couldn't do without luxury for a second. What you are feeling is a childish revulsion against yourself. You wanted to be noble and romantic, and you're disappointed because you can't be. Self-loathing is always painful, but fortunately one outgrows it. Tell her—(*pointing to phone*) that I won't help you, and that you'll fight your way to her through poverty and struggle and self-denial. Go. Tell her. (JULIAN *walks to the phone, puts out his hand for the receiver, then draws back and falls on the couch in a fit of weeping.* DULCIMER *smiles, then goes to the bell and rings it. The phone continues to ring.* TRUMP *enters.*) Get Mr. Julian's room ready, please.

TRUMP—Very good, sir. (*He glances at the phone, then at* DULCIMER, *then goes.*)

The phone continues to ring as

THE CURTAIN FALLS

ACT III

At 11 o'clock next morning, a bright, fresh morning, Mr. Dulcimer is at his writing desk giving orders to Trump. They are going abroad. They will be away about six months. They will take sanctuary first at Margherita and after that will probably move about. They will be starting that night, and Trump will make the usual traveling arrangements.

By the time Julian arrives in an elaborate dressing gown Mr. Dulcimer is gayly caroling "O Sole Mio."

Julian is less gay than Mr. Dulcimer. He will be glad to get away, he admits. Glad to get away anywhere so long as it is somewhere new. He would like to get into the car and start at once, but Mr. Dulcimer has other plans.

"I think everything points to a very good lunch somewhere, and then a little shopping," he says. "A super-lunch and then a little agreeable spending in Bond Street or thereabouts. We won't come home until it is time to start."

Julian feels that he must see Leo. He would not be content to write to her. He must talk with Leo.

"Don't be too hard on yourself," advises Mr. Dulcimer, lightly. "Six months' probation before you make up your mind is not an unreasonable request."

"I've got to make Leo see it that way," answers Julian.

A moment later Trump is in to announce that Miss Yale has arrived and would like to see Mr. Julian. She is waiting in the hall.

Dulcimer passes Leonora as she comes through the door. He hopes, he tells her, that she will not scold Julian. They had sat up very late the night before, and hadn't the heart to disturb her. He is smiling as he leaves them.

Julian does not have to tell Leonora that he could not do anything to change Dulcimer's attitude. She can tell that from looking at Dulcimer. She has come to tell Julian that his father had been terribly upset. He had sat up all night. Now he has come with her. He is standing outside in the street, staring up at Dulcimer's apartment. Julian can see him from the window.

"I couldn't get a penny out of him, Leo," Julian explains, going back to his evening with Dulcimer.

"I knew that was why you didn't answer the phone," admits Leonora. "Let's not think about money any more!" she pleads. "I'm sick of it, aren't you? Let's get married now—at once and damn the money. I've got enough for two, with a squeeze."

JULIAN—But, darling, I can't let you do that.

LEONORA—Why not? You won't mind scrimping a bit with me, will you?

JULIAN—It's lovely of you to suggest it, Leo, but—

LEONORA—Darling, don't be silly. It won't be for long anyhow. Something'll turn up. Let's clear out of here, shall we? Don't look so worried, darling. You won't have to take any exams. Everybody who's got a job hasn't passed an exam.

JULIAN—I suppose one can always tout notepaper round to people's front doors.

LEONORA—We've not come to that yet. You'll feel far more confident of yourself when you're married to me.

JULIAN—Leo, I can't marry you.

LEONORA—Julian.

JULIAN—Not yet. I couldn't come and live on you. I should be miserable every minute of the time.

LEONORA (*lightly*)—Darling, you're not turning me down, are you? It's a firm offer.

JULIAN—Of course I'm not turning you down. It's just unthinkable to me, that's all. You can't imagine what a drag I should be.

LEONORA—Darling, don't go on apologizing for yourself. I can see all the drawbacks perfectly well.

JULIAN—I'm not apologizing, but I can't pretend any more, Leo. You don't realize what hell it's been for me these past months. When you've lived the way I have for so many years you just can't give it up.

LEONORA—Of course not. If you don't want to.

JULIAN—The moment I came back here, everything began to get hold of me again. I tried to fight it but it was too strong. I suppose one must be as one is made. You don't know what it means to me to sleep in a comfortable bed again, with decent sheets.

LEONORA—Do you think you're the only one who likes a comfortable bed?

JULIAN—I hate and detest everything that's cheap and ugly

and second-rate.

LEONORA—So does everyone else. But most of them care how they get their luxury and who gives it to them and the price they have to pay for it. You don't seem to care at all so long as you get it.

JULIAN—I don't think I do care. Not much.

LEONORA—It's not very pleasant for me to hear you say that.

JULIAN—I can't help it. I've done my best. But I can't change myself.

LEONORA—You haven't tried.

JULIAN—You can't say that, Leo. I have tried. Can't you see that it's the thought of you that's been making me so desperately miserable.

LEONORA—You don't know what the words mean. You haven't any feelings, not real feelings. If you cared anything for me, if you'd ever cared, you'd have chucked all this to the winds, really chucked it, and not just gone a little way off and hankered after it all the while. But I was a fool and I imagined there was something in you, something that hadn't a chance to get out, and that my love would set it free. My love! I ought to have known last night when you didn't answer, that you'd succumbed to all this again . . . and to him.

Furthermore Leonora is convinced that Julian doesn't want to marry her, or anyone else. It is difficult for her to understand why he should persist so in playing with the idea that he wants her. Still Julian insists that she is wrong. He will come back to her as soon as he has been away for a little while—

Dulcimer is back and has sent Julian to complete his toilet. Dulcimer is free to admit to Leonora that the comedy is finished. He is glad she is able to accept the inevitable so philosophically.

"There is something infinitely pathetic in the way you have set yourself up against me," says Dulcimer, when Leonora would spurn his pity. "Even now that you've failed I feel that you would like to have a real tilt at me."

LEONORA—I've made no secret of what I've thought of you, how utterly I've loathed and despised you. Yet even now I'm wondering how you dare to destroy Julian as you have done. Why couldn't you have let him go? What can he mean to you?

DULCIMER—Everything that's worth having! Youth and charm and companionship. I admit the claims of these indefinable things. I must have them.

LEONORA—And yet, I doubt if he really cares any more for you than he does for me. He stays with you for the sake of what you can give him. If we were both penniless, he'd come to me.

DULCIMER—You're welcome to think so. We can't put it to the proof. But I can see what brought you together. You're both dreamers, idealists.

LEONORA—You have no conscience at all, have you—

DULCIMER—I didn't adopt him to please my conscience, if I have one, or to give him what was best for him. My aim was to make him like, and to be unable to do without, what was best for me. That makes you open your eyes wide, doesn't it?

LEONORA—I should like Julian to hear you.

DULCIMER—You see, I'm not like you good people, with one eye on an ideal and the other on reality, with a feverish urge towards goodness and then a degraded relapse towards what your natures clamor for insistently. I am a hedonist and I glory in it. I know exactly what I want out of life and I get it.

LEONORA—You get what you want simply because you can pay for it. It wouldn't take much to wipe you out. Another convulsion in the world and you'd vanish tomorrow.

DULCIMER—Certainly. It gives you pleasure to contemplate it, doesn't it? I admit that money isn't the rock it used to be. But I like to have it to use. I like the power of money. I have created comfort and beauty and constant change of scene out of money. As you admit, he's coming back to me because I've made him a better offer. You can only offer him your love, with the so-called "demands" made by love, another foolish, futile little marriage. . . .

Leonora is laughing, but Dulcimer refuses to permit this to anger him. Leonora is defiant. She has not given up. Dulcimer shall not have Julian, not until Julian knows exactly what Dulcimer is doing to him.

It is a defiance that arouses Dulcimer. He is stating his position with vehemence now. She may rest assured that the repulsion that Leonora feels for him is mutual. She may believe that she still has a foothold in his affairs, but she has not. Nor ever will have. She has had her chance and has failed. From now on she will cease to interfere either with him or with Julian, and he trusts she will have the good taste to leave his house as quietly as she came in.

Leonora has no intention of leaving until she has seen Julian. Dulcimer would call Trump to show her out. Trump's response is immediate and agitated. There is a gentleman—

The gentleman is William Owen, who now pushes his way into the room past the protesting Trump. Owen has come for his son. He will not take the proffered hand of Dulcimer. He is not there to bandy words. He wants his son and he intends to have him.

Dulcimer would be patronizingly suave. The Owen attitude amuses him. Also he is busy and he does not care to be bothered further. Mr. Owen, being a business man as well as a prophet, must realize that the contract he made fifteen years ago still holds.

"There was nothing in that contract, Mr. Dulcimer, that gave you the right to corrupt my boy!" shouts Owen.

"Oh, nonsense!"

"Yes, nonsense. But once I take him out of your hands, he'll forget all about you! He'll forget the easy way, the soft and corrupt way, and he'll curse you as I have cursed you!"

"I was afraid I'd over-estimated your common sense," drawls Dulcimer. "The prophet *is* stronger than the milkman."

Again Dulcimer would hurry Owen and Leonora out of his house. Trump announces that the car is at the door. Then Julian comes hurrying in. He has been sitting in the car for five minutes waiting for Dulcie. The sight of Leonora and Owen is a great surprise to him. He wants to know what they are doing there. Owen would have a talk with Julian. Leonora urges Julian to listen. Julian turns from them.

"Believe me, David, I'm speaking to you from my heart," pleads Owen. "I'm your father and I tell you this man is wicked. He wants to corrupt you as he corrupted me. Don't let him do it. Don't let him destroy your soul and make you suffer all your life. Get away from him now, while there's still time."

"I'll be glad to get away from all of you," shrills Julian. "I'm sick and tired of being ordered about by each one of you in turn. I'd like to go away by myself and find out who I really am and what I really want to do."

Leonora—Why don't you, Julian? We'll help you to do it.

Owen—That's what we want, Davy. We want you to go.

Dulcimer—Unfortunately, Julian has already decided. He has already chosen. He knows perfectly well what he wants and where his happiness lies.

Leonora—Please, please, Julian. . . .

Dulcimer—Don't let them torment you with their miserable

misgivings. . . .

OWEN—Go, my boy. . . .

DULCIMER—I delivered you from them long ago. . . . (JULIAN *stands still, his eyes brightly wretched. With difficulty he looks from one to the other.*) Why can't you leave him alone? Why do you insist upon making him miserable?

OWEN—Dulcimer, I want you to tell him to go. And be quick about it. (DULCIMER *laughs softly.*) Tell him, Dulcimer.

DULCIMER—What shall I tell him?

OWEN (*menacingly*)—Do as I say, Dulcimer.

DULCIMER—Now you're just getting tiresome, Mr. Owen.

OWEN—Davy, are you going?

JULIAN—Oh, leave me alone! Please! All of you!

LEONORA—Darling. . . .

OWEN (*stands stiffly, his hand below his pocket, staring at* JULIAN)—Davy!

JULIAN—I can't. . . . I can't. . . .

DULCIMER—There, now are you satisfied?

OWEN—Yes! Now I'm satisfied! Now! (*Pulls revolver out of pocket. A shot rings out and* DULCIMER *falls dead.* OWEN *speaks with deep emotion.*) Now you're free, Davy. At last!

The curtain falls.

Three weeks later, late in the afternoon, Trump is arranging the newspapers as he was in the first scene. A fire is burning in the grate and over the mantelpiece a death mask of the late Mr. Dulcimer is conspicuously hung.

A moment later Julian hurries in. He is expecting Miss Yale. He is also anxious about Trump. He wishes Trump would stay on. Trump would be glad to serve Mr. Julian as a bachelor—but "a married establishment means women servants." Trump would not like that.

Julian's greeting of Leonora is cordial rather than affectionate. It has been almost a week since he has seen her, she has been so busy at the infirmary.

Julian, too, has had a tiresome day going over all sorts of things with his solicitors and signing a lot of beastly papers.

"That's one of the penalties of an inheritance," smiles Leonora. "Has he really left you everything?"

"Oh, absolutely—every last penny, and the house at Margherita in Italy and Silver Gates."

"I only knew what I had read in the newspapers."

"That was hardly my fault. I've had the feeling you've been

avoiding me lately."

Leonora evades a direct answer. She has been out to the prison to see Julian's father, she reports. She had found Isaiah awfully quiet, but happy in a way.

"Poor old Isaiah!" mutters Julian. "Do you suppose he'll ever be completely rational?"

"Do you still believe he killed Dulcimer because he was mad?"

"Everybody else seemed to—judge, jury, and all the rest of them. If they hadn't been convinced it was some sort of religious mania they would have hanged him."

Julian doesn't know what he is going to do with Owen's dairy. Put it up for sale, probably, though he wouldn't touch a penny of the money.

"It's yours by law, just as much as Dulcimer's is," suggests Leonora.

"What on earth is the matter with you, Leo?" demands Julian, trying to take hold of her.

"Don't touch me, Julian," she protests sharply, backing away.

JULIAN—You're being fantastic, Leo! First we couldn't be married because I hadn't the money, and now you're being difficult because I have got it.

LEONORA—I've begun to have an enormous respect for Dulcimer. He knew you better than I did. He told me that you came back to him because he could make you a better offer.

JULIAN—It's horrible of you to tell me that.

LEONORA—Do you realize, Julian—in some manner you've got rid of your guardian, you've got rid of your father—and now you'll find yourself getting rid of me.

JULIAN—That's not true, Leo, you know it's not true. I love you as much as ever.

LEONORA—That's not enough—

JULIAN—I want to marry you.

LEONORA—Then prove it— Tell the solicitors you don't want Dulcimer's money—throw it in their smug faces—and I'll marry you now!!! (JULIAN *is silent.*) I'm afraid there is nothing more to be said. I expect I'm well out of it.

As she moves towards the door Leonora pauses a moment beneath the death mask of Dulcimer.

"I don't wonder he is smiling," she says, and is gone.

Julian calls Trump excitedly. He wants brandy. He takes one drink and then another.

"Are you alone for tea, sir?" asks Trump.
"Yes. Miss Yale has gone."

TRUMP—I wonder, sir, would you permit me to withdraw my "notice"?

JULIAN—You would like to stay, Trump?

TRUMP—Very much, sir.

JULIAN—I hope I shall keep you for life, Trump. You understand me. You understand my ways.

TRUMP—Thank you, sir. (TRUMP *turns to go.* JULIAN *takes out cigarettes.*)

JULIAN—Oh, Trump.

TRUMP—Yes, sir?

JULIAN—Have you the lighter?

TRUMP—Certainly, sir. (*Brings lighter to him and lights cigarette. Stands away as* JULIAN *puffs on cigarette.*) By the by, sir, the flowers have come from Silver Gates.

JULIAN—Have they? Do you think I ought to do them now, Trump?

TRUMP—The room does look rather naked, sir.

JULIAN—Perhaps I ought.

TRUMP—I'll fetch you the flowers, sir. (*Exit* TRUMP.)

JULIAN—Thank you, Trump. (*The death-mask continues to smile. Gradually all the lights fade, leaving only a pin spot on the death-mask and the end of* JULIAN'S *cigarette.*)

THE CURTAIN FALLS

THE PLAYS AND THEIR AUTHORS

"Mary of Scotland." A drama in three acts by Maxwell Anderson. Copyright, 1933, by the author. Copyright and published, 1934, by Doubleday, Doran & Co., Inc., Garden City, N. Y.

Maxwell Anderson has been so consistent a contributor to the volumes of the year book that readers are probably familiar with the facts of his playwrighting career. He was born in Atlantic, Pa. He is the son of a minister. He was a university professor before he was an editorial writer, first for several Pacific Coast papers and later for the New York *Globe* and the New York *World*. He turned seriously to playwrighting after he helped Laurence Stallings with "What Price Glory?" and earned sufficient return from that success to permit him to give up journalism. His first play, "White Desert," had been produced a year or so before and failed. Last year he won the Pulitzer prize with "Both Your Houses." His successes have included "Saturday's Children" and "Elizabeth the Queen." He has done quite a bit of writing for the motion pictures.

"Men in White." A drama in three acts by Sidney Kingsley. Copyright, 1933, by the author. Copyright and published, 1933, by Covici, Friede & Co., New York.

Sidney Kingsley is a mere infant compared with most of the playwrights who appear in these pages. He was born in New York twenty-seven years ago and "Men in White" is his first play to be produced. He wrote it as far back as 1930 and sold it, or sold options on it, which amounts to the same thing, no less than five times at $500 the option before the Group Theatre finally managed a production. He was graduated from Cornell University in 1928, and got his urge for playwrighting from fussing around with the Cornell Dramatic Club.

"Dodsworth," a comedy in three acts by Sidney Howard, from the novel of the same title by Sinclair Lewis. Copyright, 1933, by the authors. Copyright and published, 1934, by Harcourt, Brace & Co., New York.

Last year Sidney Howard crashed the pages of "The Best Plays" with two dramatic exhibits, "Alien Corn" and "The Late Christopher Bean." This year he came within an ace of doing so again with "Dodsworth" and "Yellow Jack." He has been represented in two previous volumes, with "They Knew What They Wanted" in the issue of 1924-25 and with "The Silver Cord" in 1926-27. His career, therefore, is also fairly well known to readers of these records. He is a Californian (Oakland, 1891). He was a University of California graduate in 1915 and was studying drama with Prof. Baker at Harvard when he heard the call to go to Europe and shoot a couple of enemies. When they signed the Armistice he was in command of a combat squadron in the air service. At the moment he is in Maine writing another play. Perhaps two plays.

"Ah, Wilderness!" A comedy in three acts. Copyright, 1933, by the author. Copyright and published, 1933, by Random House, N. Y.

Eugene O'Neill is another of the consistently successful contributors to this year book of the American drama. He started with "Beyond the Horizon" in the first issue (1919-20), and has been represented in seven of the fifteen issues since then. He won the Pulitzer prize with "Beyond the Horizon," "Anna Christie" and "Strange Interlude." He is the son of James O'Neill, the "Count of Monte Cristo" of the old trouping days, was born in New York and is 46 years old.

"They Shall Not Die." A drama in three acts by John Wexley. Copyright, 1933, by the author. Copyright and published, 1934, by Alfred A. Knopf, New York.

John Wexley goes into his sophomore year as a contributor to "The Best Plays" with the inclusion this year of "They Shall Not Die." As a freshman playwright he qualified with "The Last Mile," the most impressive of the prison reform documents in play form that so far has been written. He is a radical by instinct and a wanderer of the world by inclination. He was born, brought up and educated in New York, and is now in his early thirties. He has been a worker through a succession of jobs, including that of acting. He is a nephew of Maurice Schwartz, head of the Yiddish Art Theatre, on his mother's side, and has often played in Yiddish in the companies of his uncle. He has also played in English with Eva Le Gallienne's Civic Repertory company and with Leo Bulgakov. In addition to "The Last Mile" he is the author of "Steel," a propaganda play that failed of popular support.

"Her Master's Voice." A comedy in three acts by Clare Kummer. Copyright, 1933, by the author. Copyright and published, 1934, by Samuel French, Inc., New York.

Clare Kummer was a composer of songs before she was a writer of plays. That sweeping high-note hit of other years called "Dearie" was hers. It was in 1912 that she tried her hand at fashioning a comedy under the expert guidance of the late Sydney Rosenfeld. A few years later she wrote "Good Gracious Annabelle," which was a success under Arthur Hopkins' direction, and after that "A Successful Calamity," which William Gillette played. She was born Clare Beecher and is willing to accept Henry Ward Beecher and Harriet Beecher Stowe as famous kinfolk. Her daughter Marjorie married Roland Young, who this year did his bit toward killing the mother-in-law joke by helping with the success of "Her Master's Voice."

"No More Ladies." A comedy in three acts by A. E. Thomas. Copyright, 1933, by the author.

Albert Ellsworth Thomas, shortened to "A E" by his associates and to "Tommy" by his friends, achieved the distinction among newspaper men of being known as a star reporter of the old *Morning Sun* in New York when being a star reporter meant more than it has meant since. He took to playwrighting some years before he scored his first success with a comedy called "Her Husband's Wife" in 1910. His successes after that included "The Rainbow" and "Come Out of the Kitchen." He wrote the comedy entitled "Just Suppose" that introduced Leslie Howard and Geoffrey Kerr to the American theatre in 1920. His less successful plays have included, in recent years, "Embers," "Her Friend the King" and "Vermont." He is gracefully approaching the early sixties, was born in Chester, Mass., summers at his farm in Mulberry Bend,

Wakefield, R. I., and does a good bit of European traveling when the mood is on and funds are in.

"Wednesday's Child." A comedy in three acts by Leopold Atlas. Copyright, 1933, by the author. Copyright and published, 1934, by Samuel French, Inc., New York.

Leopold Atlas was born in 1907 in New York, which also takes in Brooklyn, where he lives at present. He studied playwrighting for two years with Professor George P. Baker at Yale, 1927-29, and had a short play produced in the Baker workshop called "L." Since then "L" has been played by the dramatic class at Dartmouth, by the Comsomolakaya Theatre of the Soviet republic, by the Workers' Theatre in New York and at the University of Rochester. He has done some newspaper work and free-lance writing. "Wednesday's Child" was written in 1930, sold three times on option and finally produced in 1934, as hereinbefore recorded. Of recent months he has been accepting salary checks and gaining experience in Hollywood.

"The Shining Hour." A drama in three acts by Keith Winter. Copyright, 1933, by the author. Copyright and published, 1934, by Doubleday, Doran & Co., Inc., Garden City, N. Y.

Keith Winter is a young Oxonian who took to writing with what may truthfully be described as a vengeance soon after leaving college. He wrote "The Rats of Norway" as a novel and discovered it was a play. It came to the attention of the London actress, Gladys Cooper, and won for him the friendship and respect of Noel Coward. His second play, "The Ringmaster," will be done in America next season by Mr. Coward. His third play, which was "The Shining Hour," was taken over by Miss Cooper, in association with the Canadian actor, Raymond Massey, and brought by them first to Canada and then to New York, where it was immediately successful. He was born in Aber, North Wales, twenty-seven years ago.

"The Green Bay Tree." A comedy in three acts by Mordaunt Shairp. Copyright, 1933, by the author. Copyright and published, 1933, by the Baker International Play Bureau, Boston, Mass.

Mordaunt Shairp was born in the village of Totnes, South Devon, England, in 1887. He was educated at St. Paul's school and Lincoln College, Oxford, by which institution he was given his B.A. He has written several plays, including "The Offense," in 1925, "The Bend in the Road," 1927, "The Crime at Blossom's," 1929. "The Green Bay Tree," which was a London success, came along in 1932. He has been an assistant master at University College School and an extension lecturer to the Universities of Oxford and London. "The Green Bay Tree" is his first play to reach America.

PLAYS PRODUCED IN NEW YORK

June 17, 1933—June 16, 1934

(Plays marked with asterisk were still playing June 16, 1934)

THE GHOST WRITER

(24 performances)

A play in three acts by Martin Mooney. Produced by F. Richard Hopkins and Walter Heyer at the Masque Theatre, New York, June 19, 1933.

Cast of characters—

Mike....................Tom Fadden
Kitty....................Mary Arden
Mrs. Klein....................Clare Woodbury
Peggy Winston....................Peggy Conklin
Bill Harkins....................Hal Skelly
Joe Gordon....................William Frawley
Jimmie Higgins....................George Sweet
Claire Castell....................Ara Gerald
Burke....................Arthur J. Wood
Edwin Preece....................Louis Morrell
Mrs. Winston....................Madeline Grey
A. H. McGee....................Frederick G. Lewis
Dan Clayton....................Robert Pitkin
Duffy....................Anthony Blair
Betty....................Lynn Eswood
Jay Barnes....................Griffin Crafts

Acts I, II and III.—The Carnegie Plaza Apartments, New York City.

Staged by Jo Graham; settings by Cirker and Robbins.

Bill Harkins, gone broke trying to land as a writer of pieces for the magazines, reduced to living in the storeroom of an apartment building and deeply in love with Peggy Winston, accepts an assignment to write a novel for A. H. McGee, a popular but worn-out best seller. The same day he is put in jail for non-payment of alimony. In jail he writes the novel. McKee dies. Peggy, publishing a discarded manuscript of Bill's under another assumed name, presents him to the publishing world as a hit and McKee's publishers want him to go on writing, but not under his own name.

A CHURCH MOUSE

(9 performances)

A comedy in three acts by Ladislaus Fodor. Revived by Chamberlain Brown at the Mansfield Theatre, New York, June 26, 1933.

Cast of characters—

Chapple....................................Mr. Harold Bolton
Baron Thomas Von Ullrich...................Mr. Horace Braham
Olly Frey..................................Miss Paula Stone
Count Von Talheim..........................Mr. William Ingersoll
P. J. Jackson..............................Mr. Florenz Ames
Baron Frank Von Ullrich....................Mr. John Drew Colt
Susie Sachs................................Miss Louise Groody
Act I.—Private office of the president of the Vienna Bank, Vienna. Acts II and III.—Apartment in a hotel in Paris.
Staged by Robert Lively and Jack Barnes; settings by George Allgier.

"A Church Mouse" was produced originally by William A. Brady at the Playhouse, New York, October 12, 1931, with Ruth Gordon and Bert Lytell in the leading rôles. A Chicago company was headed by Louise Groody and Ernest Glendinning. "Best Plays 1931-32."

SHADY LADY

(30 performances

A musical comedy in two acts by Estelle Morando, revised by Irving Cæsar; music and lyrics by Sam H. Stept, Bud Green, Jesse Greer, Stanley Adams. Produced by Harry Meyer at the Shubert Theatre, New York, July 5, 1933.

Cast of characters—

Richard Brandt.............................Charles Purcell
Tracy......................................Harold Webster
Geoffrey Benson............................Max Hoffmann, Jr.
Francine...................................Audrey Christie
Clarisse...................................Phyllys Cameron
Sonia......................................Vivian Vernon
Al Darcy...................................Lester Allen
Peggy Stetson..............................Louise Kirtland
Millie Mack................................Helen Kane
Lulu Stetson...............................Helen Raymond
Taxi Driver................................William Meader
Ladies of the Ensemble: Kay Cameron, Lauretta Brislin, Joan Connor, Marie Felique, Rita Jason, Gladys Keating, Jeanette Lea, Jean Lawrence, Beth Reynolds, Janice Winter, Dorothy Van Hest.
Gentlemen of the Ensemble: Maurice Ash, Dick Langdon, Tully Millett, Ed Murray, Emmet O'Brien, Bruce Riley.
Acts I and II.—Studio of Richard Brandt's Summer Home on Long Island.
Staged by Theodore Hammerstein; settings by Tom Adrian Cracraft; dances and ensembles by Jack Donohue.

Richard Brandt, artist, has a commission to do the murals for a Shady Lady night club. He collects a variety of models, including Millie Mack, recently paroled from Bedford reformatory, who is to pose for studies in the nude. Millie, being tough, causes considerable trouble until it is discovered near midnight that she, too, has a heart of gold.

STRAY LEAVES

(2 performances)

A play in three acts by Robert Ewing. Produced by The Avocational Art Club at the Chanin Auditorium, New York, June 28, 1933.

Cast of characters—

Leon Trowbridge....................................Thomas Leahy
Sylvia Trowbridge....................................Sylvia Leigh
Webster....................................George Sartin
Ross Hamilton....................................Leonard Asher
Leonard Birch....................................Charles Stuart Edwards
Castano....................................Giulio Giuliano
Clyde Fletcher....................................James Nelson
June Trowbridge....................................Louise Kirby
Reporter....................................Michael Green
Mr. Simpson....................................Jack Davis
Mrs. Oglethorpe....................................Helen McGrail
Acts I, II and III.—Home of Leon Trowbridge in New York City.
Staged by Carl Johnson.

Leon Trowbridge, son of a famous author, cannot write. Ross Hamilton, his college pal and fellow student in the classes of dear old Professor Birch, can write but cannot sell what he writes. When the boys need money to help old Professor Birch out of a mess, and Leon needs a reputation to make good with his girl, Leon puts his name to a novel written by Ross and it wins a Pulitzer prize. After which Leon is tortured by his conscience, Ross is tortured by jealousy and the audience is tortured by the suspense until confessions set all things right.

JOHN FERGUSON

(54 performances)

A drama in four acts by St. John Ervine. Revived by O. E. Wee and J. J. Leventhal at the Belmont Theatre, New York, July 10, 1933.

Cast of characters—

John Ferguson....................................Augustin Duncan
Sarah Ferguson....................................Lucy Beaumont
Andrew Ferguson....................................Angus Duncan
Hannah Ferguson....................................Lillian Savin
James Cæsar....................................Edward Favor
Henry Witherow....................................Howard Hall
"Clutie" John McGrath....................................Barry Macollum
Sam Mawhinney....................................P. J. Kelly
Sergeant Kernaghan, R.I.C....................................Arthur Mack
Acts I, II, III and IV.—Kitchen of a Farm House in County Down, Ireland.
Staged by Augustin Duncan.

The first production of "John Ferguson" in America was that given by the New York Theatre Guild at the Garrick Theatre May 13, 1919. Later it was transferred to the Fulton Theatre, achieving a total run of 177 performances. In 1928 the play was revived at the Masque Theatre, again with Augustin Duncan in the chief rôle. "Best Plays 1919-20; 1927-28."

DANGEROUS CORNER

(90 performances)

A drama in three acts by J. B. Priestley. Revived by Wee and Leventhal at the Waldorf Theatre, New York, July 17, 1933.

Cast of characters—

Maud Mockridge....................................Olive Reeves-Smith
Olwen Peel....................................Eden Gray
Freda Chatfield....................................Agnes George
Betty Whitehouse....................................Helen Walpole
Charles Stanton....................................Jack Hartley
Gordon Whitehouse....................................Warren Ashe
Robert Chatfield....................................Gavin Muir
Acts I, II and III.—Living Room of the Chatfield Home, on the Hudson.
Staged by Jane Wheatley.

"Dangerous Corner," produced in October, 1932, completed a run of twenty-six weeks in April. ("Best Plays of 1932-33.") Revived with above cast July 17, 1933.

THE BOHEMIAN GIRL

(11 performances)

An opera in three acts and seven scenes by Michael Balfe. Revived by The Aborn Opera Company at the Majestic Theatre, July 27, 1933.

Cast of characters—

Count Arnheim....................................Allan Waterous
Little Arline....................................Patricia Roe
Florestein....................................Maurice Lavigne
Buda....................................Frances Baviello
Thaddeus....................................Roy Cropper
Devilshoof....................................Detmar Poppen
Captain of the Guard....................................Norman Van Emburgh
Queen of the Gypsies....................................Marie Bard
Arline....................................Ruth Altman
A Gypsy....................................Hobson Young
Major Domo....................................John Willard
Chorus: Nobles, Soldiers, Gypsies, Retainers and Peasants

Act I.—Château of Count Arnheim, in Austria. Act II.—Scene 1—On the Road to the Gypsies' Encampment. 2—The Encampment. 3—Road to the Fair. 4—A Square in Pressburg. 5—The Hall of Justice. Act III.—Reception Room in the Château of Count Arnheim.

Staged by Milton Aborn; dances by Albertina Rasch.

"The Bohemian Girl," sung first in London in 1843 and in New York in 1844, was last revived the season of 1918-19 by the Society of American Singers.

GOING GAY

(25 performances)

A comedy in a prologue and three acts by William Miles and Donald Blackwell. Produced by Select Theatres Corporation at the Morosco Theatre, New York, August 3, 1933.

Cast of characters—

Ann Appleton....................................Diane Bourget
Daisy Appleton....................................Edith King
Benny....................................Charles Halton
Pullman Porter....................................Richard N. Gregg
Ridges....................................Homer Barton
T. Courtland-Smith....................................Walter Kingsford
Bing....................................Barnett Parker
Mrs. Smith....................................Thais Lawton
George Smith....................................George Walcott
H.R.H. The Grand Duchess Pukalschik....................................Rita Vale
Bradford Ward Williams....................................Alan Marshall
Footman....................................Chase Adams

Prologue—On the Train en Route to Providence. Acts I and II.—At the Smiths' in Newport. Act III.—Bedroom Occupied by Daisy at the Smiths'.

Staged by Donald Blackwell.

Ann Appleton, daughter of Daisy Appleton, one of Broadway's flashier actresses, is in love with George Smith of the Newport Smiths. Daisy, seeking to promote the marriage, visits the Smiths with her daughter. Daisy vamps the men, astounds the women and finally is forced to use all her stage tricks to keep a couple of men out of her bed and in the closet, where they take turns hiding. Late in the evening George and Ann announce their marriage.

TOMMY

(24 performances)

A comedy in three acts by Howard Lindsay and Bertrand Robinson. Revived by Wee and Leventhal at the Forrest Theatre, New York, August 7, 1933.

Cast of characters—

Mrs. Wilson....................................Marguerite Merrill
Bernard....................................Alan Bunce
Marie Thurber....................................Janet McLeay
Mrs. Thurber....................................Maida Reade
Mr. Thurber....................................Harlan Briggs
David Tuttle....................................Seth Arnold
Tommy Mills....................................Charles Eaton
Judge Wilson....................................Geo. L. Graves
Acts I, II and III.—The Living Room of the Thurber Home.
Staged by Alan Bunce; settings by Karle T. Amend.

Marie Thurber loves Tommy Mills, but insists she isn't going to marry him just to spite the family. Whereupon her Uncle David schemes to throw discredit upon Tommy and Marie flies to the boy's defense. The play was produced originally in January, 1927, with Peg Entwistle playing Marie, William Janney the Tommy rôle and Sidney Toler Uncle Dave. Alan Bunce was also the Bernard of the original cast.

PIRATES OF PENZANCE

(8 performances)

An operetta in two acts by W. S. Gilbert, music by Arthur Sullivan. Revived by Milton Aborn at the Majestic Theatre, New York, August 7, 1933.

Cast of characters—

Richard....................................Herbert Waterous
Samuel....................................Allen Waterous
Frederic....................................Roy Cropper
Major-General Stanley....................................Frank Moulan
Edward....................................William Danforth
Mabel....................................Ruth Altman
Kate....................................Mabel Thompson
Edith....................................Frances Moore
Isabel....................................Frances Baviello
Ruth....................................Vera Ross
General Stanley's Daughters, Pirates, Policemen, etc.
Act I.—A Rocky Seashore off Cornwall. Act II.—Ruined Abbey (Moonlight).
Staged by Milton Aborn.

"Pirates of Penzance" was last sung in New York in June, 1931, when it was revived by the Civic Light Opera Company with Howard Marsh singing Frederic and Vivian Hart, Mabel; Moulan, Danforth and Waterous cast as above.

YEOMEN OF THE GUARD

(8 performances)

An operetta in two scenes by W. S. Gilbert, music by Arthur Sullivan. Revived by Milton Aborn at the Majestic Theatre, New York, August 14, 1933.

Cast of characters—

Sir Richard Cholmondeley........................Frederic Persson
Colonel Fairfax..Roy Cropper
Sergeant Meryll..................................Herbert Waterous
Leonard...Allen Waterous
Jack Point...Frank Moulan
Wilfred Shadbolt...............................William Danforth
Elsie Maynard...Ruth Altman
Phœbe...Laura Ferguson
Dame Carruthers ....Vera Ross
Kate..Frances Moore
First Yeoman...Hobson Young
Second Yeoman.....................................Frederick Grieve
First Citizen.......................................Harrison Fuller
Headsman.................................Norman Van Emburgh
Chorus of Yeomen of the Guard, Gentlemen, Citizens, etc.
Scenes 1 and 2—Tower Green, London. Time: 16th Century.
Staged by Milton Aborn.

Last previous revival of "Yeomen of the Guard" was made by Mr. Aborn in May, 1933.

LOVE AND BABIES

(7 performances)

A comedy in three acts by Herbert P. McCormack. Produced by Morris Green and Frank McCoy at the Cort Theatre, New York, August 22, 1933.

Cast of characters—

Roddy...Ernest Truex
Nona..Linda Watkins
Carl..Glenn Anders
Vera..Ruth Weston
The Pollywog..By Himself
Acts I, II and III.—A Modern Apartment in New York City, the Home of Roddy and Nona.
Staged by Frank McCoy; settings by Tom Adrian Cracraft.

Roddy and Nona are married and childless by reason of Roddy's dislike of babies. Carl and Vera are married and devoted to a 7-months-old infant. Nona invites Carl and Vera to bring their Pollywog for a visit, thinking with a baby in the house Roddy will acquire a normal parental urge. Failing in this she is ready to choose a free lance father for her child. Roddy decides to do his part.

A PARTY

(45 performances)

A play in three acts by Ivor Novello. Produced by William A. Brady and Samuel Nirdlinger at the Playhouse, New York, August 23, 1933.

Cast of characters—

Powys....Wilfred Jessop
Alice....Margaret Anderson
Mrs. Mumford....Nelly Malcolm
Gloria Mumford....May Marshall
Fay Strube....Olive Reeves-Smith
Arthur Fowle....Kenneth Treseder
Esme Riddle....Winifred Harris
Eva....Brenda Forbes
Clutter....Edward Broadley
Harley Angel....Reginald Carrington
Mrs. MacDonald....Mrs. Patrick Campbell
Mrs. Lynch....Jane Corcoran
Miranda Clayfoot....Lora Baxter
Sir Philip Bay-Clender (Bay)....Edward Crandall
Lady Bay-Clender (Rosie)....Margot Stevenson
Lord Ellerton (Guy)....J. W. Austin
Widdy....Paddy Reynolds
Lily....Betty Linley
Johnnie McLewis....E. H. Bender
Leo Beers....Leo Beers
Cecilia Loftus....Cecilia Loftus
Lucille Manners....Lucille Manners
Betsy Culp....Betsy Culp
Doctor Fargeon....Charles Dalton
Guests at the Party: Elizabeth Dewing, Mary Heberden, Florence Pierson, Helen Glenn, Dan Thew Wright, Arthur Porter, Storrs Haynes.

Acts I, II and III.—Party at Studio After a Fashionable First Night.

Staged by Anthony John; settings by Livingston Platt.

Miranda Clayfoot is the popular favorite of the theatre in London. Following one of her more fashionable first nights she gives a party at her studio to which the town's celebrities are invited. Among them Mrs. MacDonald, a star of other days. Guests also include Sir Philip Bay-Clender and his bride. Sir Philip had been a lover of Miranda's. She is trying to win him back. Mrs. MacDonald discovers the intentions of Miranda and takes a hand in defeating them. The two actresses exchange insults and go to breakfast.

COME EASY

(23 performances)

A comedy in three acts by Felicia Metcalfe. Produced by Elizabeth Miele at the Belasco Theatre, New York, August 29, 1933.

Cast of characters—

Mrs. Ward...Helen Lowell
Sammy Ward..David Morris
Mr. Daye..George Henry Trader
Pamela Ward...Claire Carleton
Tobie Drake...Bruce Evans
Marcia Ward..Nancy Sheridan
Count Riccardo di Lucca...........................Edward Raquello
Miss Victoria Ward....................................Alice Fischer
Rita Davis..Joan Clive
Clyde Massey..Guy Standing, Jr.

Acts I, II and III.—Living Room of the Ward Family in Baltimore.

Staged by Milton Roberts; settings by Philip Gelb.

Marcia Ward, returning from the wedding of one of her rich friends, brings the Count di Lucca with her. The improvidence of her family is embarrassing. The Count is in love with Marcia and does not mind. Tobie Drake, who had been sweet on Marcia, seeks to expose Di Lucca as a fake. His campaign is seemingly successful until Di Lucca flies to Washington to fetch proofs of his identity and returns with his determination still fixed on marrying Marcia.

THE BLUE WIDOW

(29 performances)

A comedy in three acts by Marianne Brown Waters. Produced at the Morosco Theatre, New York, August 30, 1933.

Cast of characters—

Cynthia Talbot..Helen Flint
Doris Darrow..Roberta Beatty
Ellen...Claire Stratton
Betsy Martin..Eleanor King
Nicky Martin...Harold Conklin
Jay Berton...Don Beddoe
Bently Keith..Sam Wren
Tony Talbot...Albert Van Dekker
Willie Hendricks..Queenie Smith
Horace Jones...Ralph Locke

Acts I, II and III.—Living Room of the Talbot Home in Darien, Conn.

Staged by Harold Winston.

Willie (short for Wilhelmina) Hendricks appeals to the sympathies of her old friend, Cynthia Talbot, and is invited to make the Talbot summer place her temporary home. Willie, as a house guest, excites the sympathies of all the men, attached and unattached, because of her pretty helplessness and the fact that she is, as she reports, a recently bereaved widow. Only one member of the party knows her for a cheat and he doesn't tell. Not until Willie is about to elope with Tony Talbot. Threatened revelations cause Willie to take Horace Jones, a sex-conscious millionaire, instead.

CRUCIBLE

(8 performances)

A drama in three acts by D. Hubert Connelly. Produced by Huban Plays, Inc., at the Forrest Theatre, New York, September 4, 1933.

Cast of characters—

Rosemary Adair....Genevieve Paul
Carmella....Betty Cardoza
Tom Deering....Spencer Kimbell
Mother Darragh....May Gerald
Joe Manson....Don Costello
Arlo Borsad....Edwin Redding
Turido, "The Fang"....Juan Varro
Jerry Ryan....John Wheeler
"Speed"....Ralph Cullinan
John Evans....Dan Carey
"Monk"....William Evans
"Little Hymie"....Clifford Mack
"Red" McKean....Earl Redding
William Nelan....Glen Beveridge
Doctor Henry Flood....Wayne Nunn
Frederick Hilton....Lawrence Grattan
A Prisoner....Harry E. Allen
Matthew Burke....Gordon Hamilton
Mrs. Bond....Laurie McVicker
Harold Bond....Spencer Bentley
Jacob Grobber....Jed Cogert
Adele Del Roy....Annabelle Williams
W. Le Roy Swifton, 2nd....Walter Vaughn
James Lowden....Tom Bennett
Danny Deering....Robert Capron
Charles Harmon....Bertram Millar
Policemen, Turnkeys, "Trusties," Keepers

Acts I and III.—Rosemary's Apartment. Act II.—A Corner of the Tombs, New York.

Staged by Guy Bragdon; settings by Amend Studios.

Joe Mason, an honest guard at the Tombs, is driven by the kidnaping of his young son, to do the bidding of Arlo Borsad, known in the underworld as "The Blight." Mason helps smuggle guns to prisoners in the Tombs with which they shoot their way to freedom. Mason's conscience tortures him until he jumps off a roof. "The Blight" is finally exposed and most of the good people in the story are rewarded with marriage or something.

THE SELLOUT

(5 performances)

A comedy in three acts by Albert G. Miller. Produced by Drama Craftsmen at the Cort Theatre, New York, September 6, 1933.

Cast of characters—

John C. Matthews.................................Robert Conness
B. O. Adams.................................Herbert Dobbins
Ernest Hunter.................................Charles Harrison
Emily Burke.................................Jane Seymour
Mrs. Wilfred Robbins.................................Minnie Dupree
Charles Maguire.................................Frank Dae
Big Mike Angelino.................................Robert H. Gordon
Vito.................................Jack Rigo
Elaine Rivers.................................Ruth Thomas
Henry Cornell.................................John Grattan
George Apple.................................Warren Parker
Irving.................................A. M. Griffith
The Man With the Kettle-Drum.................................Geo. Weston
Abe (Frogface) Matz.................................Harry Bellaver

Acts I and III.—Conference Room of the "Francis R. Gates" Advertising Agency. Act II.—Radio Studio of the "Acme Recording Co."

Staged by Ashley Miller.

Mrs. Wilfred Robbins inherits an advertising agency from her husband and undertakes to run it in keeping with her higher moral and social standards. She is soon convinced that what the agency needs is a really good beer account. Getting a beer account auditions for a radio program are held which expose the extravagances of that particular racket. The audition is broken up by gangsters interested in a rival beer. Mrs. Robbins is finally moved to marry one gangster and sell the other a part interest in the business, thus making the rival gunmen partners.

MURDER AT THE VANITIES

(207 performances)

A musical mystery play by Earl Carroll and Rufus King; music and lyrics by John Green, Edward Heyman, Richard Meyers, Ned Washington, Victor Young, Herman Hupfeld, John J. Loeb and Paul Francis Webster. Produced by Earl Carroll at the New Amsterdam Theatre, New York, September 8, 1933.

Cast of characters—

Charles....Charles Ashley
Liane Ware....Pauline Moore
Mr. Martin....Frank Kingdon
Mr. Kerrick....Lew Eckles
Inspector Ellery....James Rennie
Miss Jones....Naomi Ray
Cornish....Amby Costello
Manger....Al Webster
Officer Johnson....Walker Thornton
Walter Buck....Billy House
Hope....Beryl Wallace
Madame Tanqueray....Jean Adair
Biggers....William Fay
Jack Purdy....Robert Cummings
Noomhouse....William Balfour
Sonya Sonya....Olga Baclanova
Hulda....Lisa Silbert
Siebenkase....Bela Lugosi
Scrubwoman....Barbara Winchester
Billy Slade....Ben Lackland
Mrs. Foreman....Martha Pryor
Fred Bernie....James Coughlin
Doris....Mickey Braatz
Vila....Villi Milli
Elsie....Elsie Rossi
Greeves....Charles G. Johnson
Scrubwoman....Helena Rapport
Moore....Edwin Vickery
Tom....F. X. Mahoney
Fred....Wiley Adams
Scrubwoman....Eileen Burns
Winchester....Phil Sheridan
Mack....Ben Lewis
Williams....F. Raymond
A Bostonian....Al Lee
Another Bostonian....Samuel Shaw
Woods Miller....Woods Miller
Una Vilon....Una Vilon
The Blottos....Mackie & Lavallie
The Dancers....Lewis & Van
The Skater....Paul Gerrish

Acts I and II.—Stage and Dressing Rooms of a Metropolitan Theatre During a Performance of "The Vanities."

Staged by Earl Carroll; dialogue staged by Burk Symon and Eugene Conrad.

A showgirl is discovered murdered during a "Vanities" performance. While the show goes on Police Inspector Ellery and his aids search for the murderer back stage discovering, after following numerous false scents and bumping into another killing or two, that the wardrobe lady did it in the hope of promoting the professional standing of her daughter.

THE MOUNTAIN

(4 performances)

A melodrama in four acts by Carty Ranck. Produced by the Provincetown Playhouse Guild Association at the Provincetown Theatre, New York, September 11, 1933.

Cast of characters—

"Mammy" Goodson.....Clara Thropp
Sally Holson.....Elizabeth Malone
Molly McIntyre.....Lois Jesson
Tom Holston.....William Lovejoy
Zeke Holston.....John Nicholson
Lon Bracken.....Ulric Collins
Jim McIntyre.....John Parrish
Nick Godwin.....John Burke
Samantha McIntyre.....Gertrude Fowler
Joe Wilkes.....Richard Warner
Thad Barker.....Jules Oscare
Wes Stevens.....Royal Dana Tracy
Clerk of the Court.....William Smith
A Mountaineer.....David Yerzy

Acts I, II, III and IV.—A Small Town in Breathitt County, Ky.
Staged by Fred Eric; settings by Stanley Fort and Roy LaPaugh.

Zeke Holston has been running the politics and feuding with the McIntyres of a Breathitt county town for twenty or thirty years. His son Tom goes away to college, comes home with book larnin', gets himself elected public prosecutor and falls in love with Molly McIntyre. When Zeke engineers the shooting of another of the McIntyre clan Tom is called to prosecute him. He is saved the trouble of forcing a conviction upon his father when Samantha McIntyre shoots and kills Zeke.

HEAT LIGHTNING

(44 performances)

A drama in three acts by Leon Abrams and George Abbott. Produced by Abbott-Dunning, Inc., at the Booth Theatre, New York, September 15, 1933.

Cast of characters—

Myra.....Emily Lowry
A Wife.....Maud B. Sinclair
Everett.....Eddie Acuff
A Husband.....William Wadsworth
Olga.....Jean Dixon
Steve.....Coburn Goodwin
George.....Robert Gleckler
Jeff.....Robert Sloane
First Hitch-Hiker.....Gail De Hart
Second Hitch-Hiker.....Geraldine Wall
Mrs. Ashton.....Joan Carr
Mrs. Tifton.....Leonore Sorsby
Chauffeur.....Joseph Downing
A Mexican Family.....Joseph Rivers, Irene Castellanos, Carmen Castellanos, Dolores Sierra, Emilio Sierra

Acts I, II and III.—Lunch Room of a Filling Station in an Auto Camp on a Highway Crossing the Southwest Desert.
Staged by George Abbott; settings by Cirker and Robbins.

Olga and her sister Myra have gone from Oklahoma to a location at the edge of the Arizona desert and opened a gas station and lunch room. Among their customers a year later is "Tuffy" George, an Oklahoma bad man from whom Olga was trying to escape. George is being hunted by the law for a recent bank holdup. He decides to stay the night with Olga, rob her safe and continue his run for the border. Before he can quite make it Olga shoots him through the stomach.

DOUBLE DOOR

(143 performances)

A melodrama in three acts by Elizabeth McFadden. Produced by H. C. Potter and George Haight at the Ritz Theatre, New York, September 21, 1933.

Cast of characters—

Avery....................Alice May Tuck
Telson....................Frothingham Lysons
Louise....................Barbara Shields
William....................George H. Quinby
Anne Darrow....................Aleta Freel
Caroline Van Bret....................Anne Revere
Victoria Van Bret....................Mary Morris
Mr. Chase....................George R. Taylor
Detective....................Elbert Gruver
Mortimer Neff....................Granville Bates
Rip Van Bret....................Richard Kendrick
Dr. John Sully....................Ernest Woodward
Lambert....................William Foran

Acts I, II and III.—Living Room of Van Bret House, New York.
Staged by H. C. Potter; settings by Rollo Wayne and Mary Merrill.

Victoria Van Bret, fanatically devoted to the Van Bret name and Van Bret traditions, has dominated the lives of her younger sister Caroline and their half brother, Rip, since the death of their father. When Rip marries Anne Darrow Victoria tries by every means to break up the marriage. Threatened with defeat she risks murder by locking Anne in the Van Bret vault and leaving her there to smother. The family attorney, helped by Caroline, is able finally to break Victoria.

HOLD YOUR HORSES

(88 performances)

A musical comedy in two acts and nineteen scenes by Russel Crouse and Corey Ford based on play by the authors and Charles

Beahan; music and lyrics by Russell Bennett, Robert A. Simon, Lois Alter, Arthur Swanstrom, Ben Oakland and Owen Murphy. Produced by Producing Associates at the Winter Garden, New York, September 25, 1933.

Cast of characters—

Mike.....Rex Weber
Charles Rector.....Walter Armin
Flash Ricardo.....Douglas Gilmore
Dolly Montague.....Frances Upton
Diamond Jim Brady.....Jack Howard
Anna Held.....Frances Ford
Lillian Russell.....Phyllis Carroll
Gwen Fordyce.....Inez Courtney
Kid Hogan.....Tom Patricola
John L. Sullivan.....Edwin Guhl
Boss Donovan.....Edward J. McNamara
Alan Donovan.....Stanley Smith
Spike Ahearn.....W. K. Brady
Dan Guiness.....Jack Morrissey
Big Bill Haenckle.....C. E. Smith
Nervy Nat.....Jimmy Fox
Hold-Up Man.....R. J. Mulligan
Broadway Joe.....Joe Cook
Marjory Ellis.....Ona Munson
Magnolia (the Horse).....{Jack Burleigh / Ernest Recco}
Felix.....Joey McKeon
Frothingham.....Dave Chasen
Peanut Vendor.....Charles Senna
Luigi.....Jack Anthony
Guiseppe.....Harry Rogers
Bartender at Nigger Mike's.....Walter Palm
Irving Berlin.....Lehman Byck
Patron at Nigger Mike's.....Clarence Harvey
Steve Brody.....Eugene Winchester
Ambrose McGillicuddy.....George Schiller
First Chorus Girl.....Margie Finley
Second Chorus Girl.....Emeeta Casanova
Third Chorus Girl.....Hene D'Amur
Fourth Chorus Girl.....Dorothy Drum
First Croupier.....Jack Byrne
Dick Canfield.....Jack Howard
Dowager.....Maurine Holmes
Three-Card Monte Man.....Eugene Winchester
Al Smith.....Dick Wallace
Kid Hogan's Second.....Olaf Olsen
Mr. Milquetoast.....Jimmy Fox
Stenographer.....Margie Finley
G. A. R. Veteran.....Clarence Harvey
Committeeman.....Donnell O'Brian

Act I.—Scene 1—Rector's. 2—Private Dining Room at Rector's. 3—Outside Rector's. 4—Central Park Outside Lion House. 5—Nigger Mike's in the Bowery. 6—Dressing Room at Casino Theatre. 7—Backstage Casino Theatre. 8—Stage Casino Theatre. 9—Canfield's Gambling House. 10—Union Square. 11—Ballroom in Waldorf Astoria Hotel. Act II.—Scene 1—Coney Island. 2—Outside Flea Circus, Coney Island. 3—At Flea Circus. 4—Central Park. 5—Mayor's Office. 6—The Chase Up Broadway. 7—In Front of Flatiron Building. 8—The Subway.

Staged by R. H. Burnside and John Shubert; dances by Bob Alton; ballets by Harriet Hoctor; settings by Russell Patterson.

Broadway Joe, one of the most popular of the old kebbies, is picked by the political bosses to head an opposition mayoralty ticket. The bosses expect to elect Joe's opponent and divide a subway grab. Joe gets himself elected by the artful dodge of campaigning for his opponent and refuses to sign the subway bill so long as there are cabmen and horses that need feeding.

* MEN IN WHITE

(311 performances)

A drama in three acts by Sidney S. Kingsley. Produced by The Group Theatre, Sidney Harmon and James R. Ullman at the Broadhurst Theatre, New York, September 26, 1933.

Cast of characters—

Dr. Gordon....Luther Adler
Dr. Hochberg....J. Edward Bromberg
Dr. Michaelson....William Challee
Dr. Vitale....Herbert Ratner
Dr. McCabe....Grover Burgess
Dr. Ferguson....Alexander Kirkland
Dr. Wren....Sanford Meisner
Dr. Otis (Shorty)....Bob Lewis
Dr. Levine....Morris Carnovsky
Dr. Bradley (Pete)....Walter Coy
Dr. Crawford (Mac)....Alan Baxter
Nurse Jamison....Eunice Stoddard
Mr. Hudson....Art Smith
James Mooney....Gerrit Kraber
Laura Hudson....Margaret Barker
Mr. Smith....Sanford Meisner
Mrs. Smith....Ruth Nelson
Dorothy Smith....Mab Maynard
Barbara Dennin....Phœbe Brand
Dr. Cunningham....Russell Collins
First Nurse....Paula Miller
Nurse Mary Ryan....Dorothy Patten
Orderly....Elia Kazan
Mr. Houghton....Clifford Odets
Mr. Spencer....Lewis Leverett
Mrs. D'Andrea....Mary Virginia Farmer
Second Nurse....Elena Karam

Act I.—Scene 1—Staff Library, St. George's Hospital. 2—Mr. Hudson's Room. 3—Children's Ward. 4—George Ferguson's Room. Act II.—Scene 1—Board Room. 2—Staff Library. 3—Corridor. 4—Operating Room. Act III.—George Ferguson's Room.

Staged by Lee Strasberg; settings by Mordecai Gorelik.

See page 76.

KULTUR

(10 performances)

A play in three acts by Adolf Philipp. Produced by J. J. Vincent at the Mansfield Theatre, New York, September 26, 1933.

Cast of characters—

Schmid....................................Hans Hansen
Hertha....................................Arlien Marshal
Olga....................................Charlotte Reynolds
Mrs. Koerner....................................Madeline Grey
Hans....................................Alan Ward
Professor Koerner....................................Charles Coburn
Professor Brunner....................................Bennett Southard
Alfreda....................................Kathleen Lowry
Baron von Werner....................................Craig Ward
Von Zuder....................................Lester Alden

Acts I, II and III.—Living Room of Professor Christian Koerner in a Large European Capitol.

Staged by J. J. Vincent and Charles Coburn; settings by Tom Adrian Cracraft.

During a social and political upheaval in a large European capital which might easily have been Berlin, Professor Koerner, noted surgeon and lecturer at the University, is dismissed because it is discovered that his great grandfather was a Jew. The name had been successively changed from Cohen to Korn and from Korn to Koerner. But when the new Chancellor, who is rabidly opposed to Jews, is injured in an automobile accident he insists that Professor Koerner shall perform the necessary operation. A blood transfusion proving necessary, the donor chosen is Hans Schmid, who, it transpires when it is too late, is also of Jewish descent. The Chancellor recovers and is greatly improved in matters of reasonableness and tolerance with the mixture of Jewish blood in his veins.

AMOURETTE

(22 performances)

A comedy in three acts by Clare Kummer. Produced by Leo Peters and Leslie J. Spiller at the Henry Miller Theatre, New York, September 27, 1933.

Cast of characters—

Amsey Tucker....................................Arthur Aylsworth
Drusilla Thorpe....................................Mildred Natwick
Abbie Hole....................................Marie Pettes
Hiram Hallowell....................................Byron McGrath
Amourette Tucker....................................Francesca Bruning
Evie Vale....................................Clara Mahr
Alan Wylie....................................Charles Coleman
Amos Todd....................................William Lynn
Enoch Chappell....................................Frederick Kaufman
Larkin Tucker....................................Tom Morrison
Mrs. Belle Morrow....................................Frances Halliday
Peleg Bossert....................................Fred Sumner
Gandy Hasp....................................James P. Houston

Act I.—Amsey Tucker's Bedroom in Tuckerton, Mass. Act II.—Amourette's Room in Duxbury. Act III.—Peleg Bossert's Inn.

Staged by Leo Bulgakov; settings by S. Syrjala.

Amourette Tucker, wearying of the dull life of Tuckerton, Mass., rebels and runs away to Duxbury in search of adventure. On the same coach with her (the time is 1840) is the Rev. Hiram Hallowell, young and deeply in love with Amourette. Putting two and four together, Amsey Tucker, Amourette's father, decides that Hiram must have seduced Amourette and should be forced to marry her. After following the suspected pair to Duxbury and back Amsey learns it isn't true, and Amourette marries Parson Alan Wylie.

* SAILOR, BEWARE!

(311 performances)

A comedy in two acts and eight scenes by Kenyon Nicholson and Charles Robinson. Produced by Courtney Burr at the Lyceum Theatre, New York, September 28, 1933.

Cast of characters—

Mattie Matthews....Horace MacMahon
Wop Wilchinski....George Heller
Spud Newton....Ross Hertz
Barney Waters....Edward Craven
Luther Reed....Bradford Hatton
Peewee Moore....Don Rowen
Herb Markey....Murray Alper
Chester "Dynamite" Jones....Bruce Macfarlane
Jake Edwards....Larry Fletcher
Lieut. Loomis, U.S.N....Paul Huber
Texas Patton....Rod Maybee
Ruby Keefer....Ann Winthrop
Bernice Dooley....Ann Thomas
Hazel De Fay....Ruth Conley
Dode Bronson....Josephine Evans
Humpty Singer....Edgar Nelson
Louie....John Bard
Billie "Stonewall" Jackson....Audrey Christie
Señor Gomez....Harry Hornick

Act I.—Scenes I and 4—Compartment 108, Aboard U.S.S. "Dakota," Panama Bay, C.Z. 2 and 5—Patio of the Idle Hour Café, Panama City. 3—Billie's Room. Act II.—Scene 1—Nearby Beach. 2—Compartment 108. 3—Billie's Room.

Staged by Kenyon Nicholson; settings by P. Dodd Ackerman.

Chester Jones of the U.S.S. "Dakota" has been nicknamed "Dynamite" because all manner of defenses, especially feminine, crumble before his attack. Billie Jackson, hostess at the Idle Hour Café, Panama City, is called "Stonewall" by her friends because of her complete success in blocking all attacks upon her honor. When "Dynamite" meets "Stonewall" the issue is definitely drawn. Gobs on the "Dakota" and hostesses at the Idle Hour lay bets as to which of the two will be the first to surrender. At a moment when both, having fallen legitimately in love with each other, are willing to admit defeat Lieutenant Loomis, U.S.N., fearing a general scandal, calls all bets off. Which makes Billie very, very sorry for Dynamite.

* AS THOUSANDS CHEER

(304 performances)

A musical revue in two acts by Irving Berlin and Moss Hart, music and lyrics by Edward Heyman and Richard Myers. Produced by Sam H. Harris at the Music Box Theatre, New York, September 30, 1933.

Principals—

Marilyn Miller	Clifton Webb
Helen Broderick	Ethel Waters
Leslie Adams	Hal Forde
Jerome Cowan	Harry Stockwell
Thomas Hamilton	Hamtree Harrington
Peggy Cornell	Harold Murray

Charles Weidman Dancers: Letitia Ide, Jose Limon, Helen Bache, Debby Coleman, Paula Yasgour, Robert Gorham, Harry Joyce, William Matons.

Staged by Hassard Short; settings by Albert Johnson; dances arranged by Charles Weidman; orchestra directed by Frank Tours.

AH, WILDERNESS!

(289 performances)

A play in four acts by Eugene O'Neill. Produced by The Theatre Guild, Inc., at the Guild Theatre, New York, October 2, 1933.

Cast of characters—

Nat Miller....................George M. Cohan
Essie....................Marjorie Marquis
Arthur....................William Post, Jr.
Richard....................Elisha Cook, Jr.
Mildred....................Adelaide Bean
Tommy....................Walter Vonnegut, Jr.
Sid Davis....................Gene Lockhart
Lily Miller....................Eda Heinemann
David McComber....................Richard Sterling
Muriel McComber....................Ruth Gilbert
Wint Selby....................John Wynne
Belle....................Ruth Holden
Nora....................Ruth Chorpenning
Bartender....................Donald McClelland
Salesman....................John Butler

Act I.—Sitting Room of Miller Home in a Large Small-town in Connecticut. Act II.—Dining Room. Act III.—Scene 1—Back Room of a Bar in a Small Hotel. 2—Miller Sitting Room. Act IV.—Scenes 1 and 3—Miller Sitting Room. 2—Strip of Beach.

Staged by Philip Moeller; settings by Robert Edmond Jones.

See page 159.

AN UNDESIRABLE LADY

(24 performances)

A play in three acts by Leon Gordon. Produced by the author in association with W. Herbert Adams at the National Theatre, New York, October 9, 1933.

Cast of characters—

Charles Fennick....................Lee Baker
Sally Marsh....................Nancy Carroll
Henry Welsh....................Donald Campbell
Miss Wales....................Miriam Battista
Horton....................John Boyd
Rockett....................Jack Easton
Adams....................Leo Kennedy
Hagan....................W. W. Shuttleworth
Brett....................Edward Leiter

Act I.—Law Offices of Fennick & Welsh in a Middle Western City. Acts II and III.—Cabin in the North.
Staged by Leon Gordon; settings by P. Dodd Ackerman.

Sally Marsh, about to be brought to trial a second time for the murder of a former companion, is faced with probable conviction because of new witnesses uncovered for the state. Charles Fennick, her middle-aged attorney, in love with Sally and fearful for her future, suggests an elopement before trial and a hideaway until the law forgets. Sally and Fennick later find themselves snowed in for the winter in the Canadian wilds. Brett, alleged trapper, joins their camp and completes the triangle. Sally and Brett carry on a love affair which Fennick is not supposed to see because of snow blindness. Fennick recovers his sight, exposes Brett as an officer of the law and Sally takes the rest of the veronal.

THE PURSUIT OF HAPPINESS

(252 performances)

A comedy in three acts by Alan Child and Isabelle Louden (Mr. and Mrs. Lawrence Langner). Produced by Laurence Rivers, Inc., at the Avon Theatre, New York, October 9, 1933.

Cast of characters—

Meg....................Dennie Moore
Mose....................Oscar Polk
Captain Aaron Kirkland....................Charles Waldron
Colonel Mortimer Sherwood....................Hunter Gardner
Prudence Kirkland....................Peggy Conklin
Comfort Kirkland....................Eleanor Hicks
Max Christman....................Tonio Selwart
Thaddeus Jennings....................Raymond Walburn

Two Sons of Liberty	R. G. Kirchner David Hart
Reverend Lyman Banks	Seth Arnold

Acts I, II and III.—Parlor of the Kirkland Farm, Westville, Connecticut.

Staged by Miriam Doyle; settings by Livingston Platt.

Max Christman, a Hessian soldier escaping from the British, makes his way to the Connecticut farm of Aaron Kirkland. He is eager to join the Colonials in their enjoyment of life, liberty and the pursuit of happiness. He falls in love with Prudence Kirkland, and she with him, though she is affianced to Thaddeus Stevens, sheriff. Prudence gives Max a bundling date—bundling being the old Colonial custom that permitted a young woman and the lad who came sparkin' her to jump into bed with their clothes on and thus keep warm without burning more firewood. They are discovered by Thaddeus and the village dominie, a strict Puritan. Scandal threatens but love prevails.

HER MAN OF WAX

(14 performances)

A comedy in three acts by Julian Thompson, adapted from the German of Walter Hasenclever. Produced by Lee Shubert at the Shubert Theatre, New York, October 11, 1933.

Cast of characters—

Guard	Kermit Miller
First Lady	Florence Arlington
Second Lady	Jane Farrell
General Du Marais	John E. Wheeler
Guide	Harold de Becker
Josephine Delmar	Lenore Ulric
Lola Valette	Louise Kirtland
Napoleon	Lloyd Corrigan
Landru	Courtney White
Mussolini	Frank Marino
General Louis L'Oiseaux	Moroni Olsen
Margot	Jane Farrell
Jacot	Raymond Bramley
Henri	Clarence Rock
A Waiter	Walden Boyle
Le Brun	Mortimer H. Weldon
Mons Swartz	Albert Gloria
Le Femme de Chambre	Florence Arlington
First Reporter	Rodrick Benton
General Courot	George Anderson
Captain of the Guard	Carl Benton Reid
Commissioner of Police	Jules Epailly
Second Reporter	Martin Abbott
Third Reporter	Richard Bengali
Senator Buvette	Robert C. Long
Chairman of the Conference	Louis Casavant
Professor Zolney	Leslie King
English Delegate	Albert Froom
American Delegate	George Lessey
Scandinavian Delegate	Frederic Persson

Latvian Delegate....................................Boris Korlin
Chinese Delegate....................................H. L. Donsu
Italian Delegate....................................E. J. Varny
Philip....................................Kenneth Patterson
Soldiers, Delegates, Cameramen, Figures of History, Tourists, Sightseers, Children, Students, Crowds: Jack Fago, Kermit Miller, Don Shelton, Claude Tahlmore, Theodore Pezman, Ted Edwin, Cleland Davis, Josephine Morse, Ada Curry, Eleanor Franco, Dorothy Daniels, Gulda Ross, Mary Ackley, Dorothy Zorn, Hilda Hayword Howe, Richard Ross, Emmett Martine and Alfredo de Luca.

Act I.—Scene 1—Musée Grevin, Paris; 2—Apartment of Josephine Delmar at the Hotel Ritz. Act II.—Josephine's Apartment. Act III.—Scene 1—Disarmament Conference, Paris; 2—Musée Grevin.

Staged by Arthur Lubin; settings by Arthur Segal.

Josephine Delmar, motion picture actress assigned to play Josephine in a forthcoming picture, spends so much of her time studying the waxen image of Napoleon at the Musée Grevin that her interest develops into love and she imagines her love brings Napoleon to life. She sees him step down from his niche and invites him to visit her in her apartment. After a night with Josephine Napoleon attends a disarmament conference, lectures the world representatives on their failures, and returns to the Musée. Josephine's friends find her still gazing rapturously at the wax Napoleon when they come to take her home.

CHAMPAGNE, SEC

(113 performances)

An operetta in three acts adapted by Alan Child (Lawrence Langner) with lyrics by Robert A. Simon, from "Die Fledermaus" by Johann Strauss. Revived by Dwight Deere Wiman and Lawrence Langner at the Morosco Theatre, New York, October 14, 1933.

Cast of characters—

Alfred....................................George Trabert
Adele....................................Helen Ford
Rosalinde....................................Peggy Wood
Von Eisenstein....................................George Meader
Dr. Blind....................................William J. McCarthy
Falke....................................Joseph Macaulay
Frank....................................John Barclay
Ida....................................Olive Jones
Prince Orlofsky....................................Kitty Carlisle
Frosh....................................John E. Hazzard
A Dancer....................................Paul Haakon
Second Dancer....................................Eleanor Tennis
Footmen, Guests, Ladies of the Ballet: Claire Miller, Carol Chandler, Pierce Hearn, David Rogers, Bruce Norman, Gudrun Ekelund, Nina Dean, Nellilew Winger, Betty Quay, Glenn Darwin, Don English, Samuel Mendel, Alan M. MacCracken, Wilfried Klamroth, Ronald Jones, John Thomas.

Act I.—Scene 1—Von Eisenstein's Garden, Vienna. 2—Interlude. 3—Rosalinde's Boudoir. Act II.—Grand Salon in the Palace of Prince Orlofsky. Act III.—A Jail.
Staged by Monty Woolley; settings by Jo Mielziner.

Von Eisenstein has been ordered to jail for a tax violation. Falke, his friend, suggests that as a proper farewell they attend a gay party of chorus girls on the way to jail. Falke, being a practical joker, also invites Mrs. Eisenstein and the housemaid, Adele, with whom Eisenstein has been on something more than speaking terms. At the party there are excited discoveries and temperamental explosions. Eisenstein finds jail a restful place after all.

THE SCHOOL FOR HUSBANDS

(116 performances)

A comedy in two acts adapted in rhyme by Arthur Guiterman and Lawrence Langner with music by Edmond W. Rickett, from a play by Molière. Produced by the Theatre Guild at the Empire Theatre, New York, October 16, 1933.

Cast of characters—

Sganarelle....Osgood Perkins
Ergaste....James Jolley
Street Vendor....Parker Steward
Lisette....Flora Le Breton
Ariste....Stuart Casey
Valere....Michael Bartlett
Leonor....Joan Carr
Isabelle....June Walker
Lysander....George Macready
Sylvester....Lewis Martin
1st Lackey....Francis Tyler
2nd Lackey....William Miley
Street Dancers....Doris Humphrey and Charles Weidman
Bear....Marcus Blechman
1st Girl....Janice Joyce
2nd Girl....Dorothea Petgen
3rd Girl....Lee Whitney
4th Girl....Virginia Marvin
Pierrot....Parker Steward
Columbine....Doris Humphrey
Harlequin....Charles Weidman
Magician....Robert Reinhardt
3rd Lackey....John Cherry
1st Bravo....George Macready
2nd Bravo....Lewis Martin
Magistrate....Stanley Harrison
Notary....Horace Sinclair
Link Boy....Kenneth Bostock

BALLET INTERLUDE

THE DREAM OF SGANARELLE

Adapted from the Ballet of "Le Mariage Force" (Originally danced by His Majesty Louis XIV and his court, the 29th day of January, 1664)

Cast of characters—

Sganarelle....................................Osgood Perkins
Athenee.......................................Janice Joyce
Psyche..Doris Humphrey
Solomon.......................................Lewis Martin
Socrates......................................Horace Sinclair
1st Egyptian..................................Ada Korvin
2nd Egyptian..................................Eleanor King
Dancing Master................................Charles Weidman
Tircis..Stuart Casey
Olympians: Ernestine Henock, Adad Korvin, Katherine Manning, Hyla Rubin, Marcus Blechman, George Bockmann, Kenneth Bostock, Jack Cole.

Acts I, II and Interlude.—A Square in Paris.

Staged by Lawrence Langner; settings by Lee Simonson; choreography by Doris Humphrey and Charles Weidman.

Molière's ancient tale of the two brothers, Sganarelle and Ariste, who inherited young wards and hoped to marry them. Sganarelle kept his ward, Isabelle, under lock and key. Ariste gave Leonore every freedom. So Isabelle deceived Sganarelle and married Valere, while Leonore remained true to Ariste.

TEN MINUTE ALIBI

(89 performances)

A mystery play in three acts by Anthony Armstrong. Produced by Crosby Gaige and Lee Shubert at the Ethel Barrymore Theatre, New York, October 17, 1933.

Cast of characters—

Hunter..Joseph Spurin-Calleia
Philip Sevilla................................Sebastian Braggiotti
Betty Findon..................................Daphne Warren-Wilson
Colin Derwent.................................Bramwell Fletcher
Sir Miles Standing............................Oswald Yorke
Inspector Pember..............................Reynolds Denniston
Sergeant Brace................................John Williams

Acts I, II and III.—Philip Sevilla's Flat in Bloomsbury.

Staged by Herman Shumlin; settings by Watson Barratt.

Colin Derwent learns that the girl he has loved from childhood, Betty Findon, is about to bolt with Philip Sevilla, a rotter if there ever was one. Derwent threatens Sevilla and is laid low with a drugged cigarette. While he is drugged Derwent dreams that he has murdered Sevilla and established a perfect alibi. Awaking he puts the dream into practice and, after threatened failure and considerable suspense, it works.

KEEPER OF THE KEYS

(23 performances)

A drama in three acts by Valentine Davies from an Earl Derr Biggers' novel. Produced by Sigourney Thayer at the Fulton Theatre, New York, October 18, 1933.

Cast of characters—

Don Holt..........Roy Roberts
Kathleen Ireland..........Ruth Easton
Dr. Frederick Swan..........Romaine Callender
Inspector Charlie Chan..........William Harrigan
Ah Sing..........Dwight Frye
Dudley Ward..........Fleming Ward
Luis Romano..........Aristides De Leoni
John Ryder..........Howard St. John
Ellen Landini..........Roberta Beatty
Michael Ireland..........Robert Lynn
Cash Shannon..........Warren Parker
Seth Leahy..........Elwood K. Thomas

Acts I, II and III.—Hunting Lodge of Dudley Ward, Pineview, Lake Tahoe, Nevada.

Staged by Sigourney Thayer; settings by Donald Oenslager.

Dudley Ward, once the husband of Ellen Landini, prima donna, believes that she has borne him a son whom she is concealing from him. He summons Charlie Chan, Honolulu's favorite police inspector, two other former Landini husbands as well as the current number. They meet at Ward's hunting lodge in Nevada. The first day Landini is shot on the balcony. The second day one of the husbands is shot on the portico. The third day, or shortly thereafter, Charlie Chan uncovers Ward as the man behind the gun.

THE CURTAIN RISES

(61 performances)

A comedy in three acts by B. M. Kaye. Produced by Morris Green and Frank McCoy at the Vanderbilt Theatre, New York, October 19, 1933.

Cast of characters—

Poldi..........Helen Salinger
Thona Landorf..........Millicent Hanley
Rudolf Dortman..........G. Albert Smith
Elsa Karling..........Jean Arthur
Arny Zander..........Bertram Thorn
Wilhelm Meissinger..........Kenneth Harlan
Franz Kermann..........Donald Foster

Acts I, II and III.—Studio Room of Elsa Karling, Vienna.

Staged by Ernest Truex; settings by Yellenti.

Elsa Karling, a spinster at thirty, determines to buy romance and a touch of happiness by engaging Wilhelm Meissenger, the town's matinée idol, to teach her acting. Wilhelm, not impressed, sends his understudy, Franz Kermann. Franz and Elsa rehearse "Romeo and Juliet." Wilhelm's leading woman is stricken and Elsa has a chance to serve as understudy. This experience reveals to her that it is Franz she loves and not Wilhelm.

THE GREEN BAY TREE

(166 performances)

A drama in three acts by Mordaunt Shairp. Produced by Jed Harris at the Cort Theatre, New York, October 20, 1933.

Cast of characters—

Trump....................................Mr. Leo G. Carroll
Mr. Dulcimer....................................Mr. James Dale
Julian Dulcimer....................................Mr. Laurence Olivier
Leonora Yale....................................Miss Jill Esmond
William Owen....................................Mr. O. P. Heggie

Acts I and III.—Mr. Dulcimer's Flat in Mayfair. Act II.—Scene 1—Mr. Owen's House in Camden Town. 2—Mr. Dulcimer's Flat.

Staged by Jed Harris; settings by Robert Edmond Jones.

See page 381.

LET 'EM EAT CAKE

(90 performances)

A musical comedy in two acts by George S. Kaufman and Morrie Ryskind; music by George Gershwin; lyrics by Ira Gershwin. Produced by Sam H. Harris at the Imperial Theatre, New York, October 21, 1933.

Cast of characters—

Gen. Adam Snookfield, U. S. A....................................Florenz Ames
Trixie Flynn....................................Grace Worth
A. Flunkey....................................David Lawrence
Francis X. Gilhooley....................................Harold Moffatt
Mrs. Gilhooley....................................Alice Burrage
Louis Lippman....................................Abe Reynolds
Mrs. Lippman....................................Grenna Sloane
Senator Carver Jones....................................Edward H. Robins
Mrs. Jones....................................Vivian Barry
Senator Robert E. Lyons....................................George E. Mack
Mrs. Lyons....................................Consuelo Flowerton
Matthew Arnold Fulton....................................Dudley Clements
Mrs. Fulton....................................Mary Jo Matthews
Mary Wintergreen....................................Lois Moran
John P. Wintergreen....................................William Gaxton

Chief Justice of the Supreme Court....................Ralph Riggs
Alexander Throttlebottom............................Victor Moore
Kruger..Phillip Loeb
President of the Union League Club...................Ralph Riggs
Uncle William.................................W. F. J. Robertson
Pete...Hazzard Newberry
Lieutenant...George Kirk
John P. Tweedledee...............................Richard Temple
Secretary ....Charles Conklin
The Misses Kay Adams, Ruth Adams, Peggy Bancroft, Gail Darling, Olgene Foster, Yvonne Gray, Peggy Green, Viola Hunter, Jessica Worth, Kathleen Ayres, Alyce Downey, Enes Early, Louise Estis, Dorothy Graves, Ethel Hampton, Pat Hastings, Evelyn Hannons, Amalie Ideal, Kay Lazell, Betty Lee, Terry Lawlor, Ruth Porter, Baun Sturtz, Martha Tibbetts, Bobbette Walker and Wanda Wood.
The Messrs. Bruce Barclay, Robert Burton, Paul Brachard, Tom Curley, Gordon Clark, Leon Dunar, Bryan Davis, Vance Elliott, Michael Forbes, Charles Flower, David Gross, Don Hudson, Tom Harris, David Lawrence, Martin Leroy, Robert Lewis, Ed Loud, Al LeFebevre, Richard Neely, Martin Sheppard, Harold Sternberg, Morris Tepper, Norman Van Emberg, John Walsh, Ray Clarke, Charles Conklin, Frank Gagen, Phil King, Hazzard Newberry, Fred May, Victor Pullman and Steward Steppler.

Act I.—Scene 1—Main Street. 2—White House. 3—Union Square. 4—New Store. 5—Union League Club. 6—Bar. 7—On to Washington. 8—Outside the White House. Act II.—Scene 1—Blue House. 2—Ball Park. 3—Tribunal. 4—Jail. 5—Guillotine.

Staged by George S. Kaufman; dances and ensembles by Von Grona and Ned McGurn; settings by Albert R. Johnson.

A continuation of the adventures of President John P. Wintergreen and Vice-President Alexander Throttlebottom of "Of Thee I sing." Running for reëlection they are defeated. Wintergreen organizes a revolution with the help of Kruger of Union Square. The army is drawn in by being promised the war debts. Mary Wintergreen does nicely as the designer and manufacturer of the blue shirts and blouses adopted by the revolutionists. In the end the country's problems are rested on the outcome of a baseball game between the nine justices of the Supreme Court and the nine foreign representatives of the League of Nations. Throttlebottom is the umpire. A wrong decision against the home team sends him to the guillotine, a gift from France.

HER MASTER'S VOICE

(224 performances)

A comedy in two acts and five scenes by Clare Kummer. Produced by Max Gordon at the Plymouth Theatre, New York, October 23, 1933.

Cast of characters—

Queena Farrar...................................Frances Fuller
Mrs. Martin................................Elizabeth Patterson
Ned Farrar.......................................Roland Young
Craddock.......................................Francis Pierlot

Aunt Min....................................Laura Hope Crews
Mr. Twilling....................................Frederick Perry
Phœbe..Josephine Williams
Act I.—Living Room of the Farrars' House, Homewood, New Jersey. Act II.—Sleeping Porch of Aunt Min's Home at Dewellyn.
Staged by Worthington Miner; settings by Raymond Sovey.

See page 256.

MOVE ON, SISTER

(7 performances)

A drama in five scenes by Daniel N. Rubin. Produced by A. H. Woods at the Playhouse, New York, October 24, 1933.

Cast of characters—

Eugene Greer................................Ernest Glendinning
Dr. Sage....................................Robert Harrison
Dr. London..............................Edward L. Davenport
Miss Morse....................................Kathryn March
Stick..Robert W. Craig
Phil Sibley....................................Carrol Ashburn
Burt Travers ....Frank Shannon
Reverend Dr. Ray Vogus.........................Harry Davenport
Alva Haury....................................Moffat Johnston
Paul Cromer...................................Harland Tucker
Mrs. Ott......................................Marion Willard
Alice Drave.......................................Fay Bainter
Mrs. Bell.....................................Jessie Graham
Brill...Harry Hanlon
Thurson..John T. Doyle
Scene 1—Private Room in a Hospital. 2 and 3—Living Room in Greer's Home. 4 and 5—Study in Paul Cromer's Home.
Staged by A. H. Van Buren; settings by P. Dodd Ackerman.

Eugene Greer, capitalist, dying, sends for his worst enemy, the radical Paul Cromer, as the only man he can trust. Greer, having loved and deserted Alice Drave in his youth, learning his desertion drove her to prostitution, wants to make amends by leaving Alice his money. Cromer accepts the trust. After Greer dies all his hypocritical associates, expecting to be named in the will, fight Cromer and Alice. The lower courts sustain them and throw out the new will. The Supreme Court reverses the order.

SPRING IN AUTUMN

(41 performances)

A comedy in three acts adapted by Blanche Yurka and Nene Belmonte from the Spanish of Gregorio Martinez Sierra. Produced by Arthur J. Beckhard at the Henry Miller Theatre, New York, October 24, 1933.

Cast of characters—

Pura....................Mildred Natwick
Manolo....................Hugh Rennie
Pepe....................Thomas Fisher
Madame Elena Alcara....................Blanche Yurka
Agustina Bastida....................Helen Walpole
Juan Manuel Lorenzana....................Charles C. Leatherbee
Ramirez....................George Spelvin
Don Enrique Bastida....................Richard Hale
Justa....................Esther Dale
Miguel....................Andrei Salama
Jack Brennan....................James Stewart
Dame Sarah Hutt....................Daisy Belmore
Fifi....................Helen Huberth
Dmitri Alexei....................Paul Dane
Don Sebastian de la Fresneda....................Wyrley Birch

Act I.—Elena's Apartment in Madrid. Acts II and III.—Enrique's House in Andalucia.

Staged by Bretaigne Windust; settings by Jarin Scenic Studio.

Mme. Elena Alcara, a highly temperamental prima donna, separated from her husband, Don Enrique Bastida, for years, agrees to return to the Bastida home to lend an air of respectability to the domestic situation so her daughter, Agustina, may become engaged to Manolo, a catch of the neighborhood. During the visit Elena is swarmed upon by a troupe of her former music hall friends. She is merry-making with them, standing on her head and singing a bar from Puccini at the same time, when the village padre calls and catches her so. A new scandal threatens but is averted.

THE WORLD WAITS

(30 performances)

A drama in three acts by George F. Hummel. Produced by Frank Merlin at the Little Theatre, New York, October 25, 1933.

Cast of characters—

Jenks (Cook)....................Victor Beecroft
Burroughs (Radio Operator)....................Millard Mitchell
Collins (Correspondent)....................Neil McFee
Royce (Assistant to Hawkins)....................Philip E. Truex
Johansen (Dog Driver)....................John Fredrik
Hellman (Meteorologist)....................Mitchell Harris
Williams (Geologist)....................Eric Kalkhurst
Hawkins (Surveyor and Second in Command)......Charles Quigley
McKenzie (Doctor)....................Joseph King
Hartley (Commander)....................Blaine Cordner
Frensen (Dog Driver)....................Hans Sandquist
Kelly (Second Aviator)....................Donald Gallaher
Brice (First Aviator)....................Reed Brown, Jr.
Donahue (Carpenter)....................Russell Morrison
McGregor (Dog Driver)....................Charles Gerrard

Acts I, II and III.—Camp of the Hartley Expedition in the Antarctic.

Staged by Frank Merlin; settings by Arne Lundborg.

Commander Hartley continues successfully in command of the Hartley expedition to the South Pole until a series of crises develop. Then he is much better at sending high-sounding messages to the States by radio than he is at meeting the emergency. When death to one of his men results from his ill-advised orders and there is need of new counsel and a firmer hand in the conduct of the expedition Brice, first aviator, takes charge and Hartley is deposed. When the relief ship arrives Brice turns the command back to Hartley. "You're a national hero," he says. "You take the ticker tape."

THREE AND ONE

(77 performances)

A comedy in three acts adapted by Lewis Galantiere and John Houseman from the French of Denys Amiel. Produced by William Harris, Jr., at the Longacre Theatre, New York, October 25, 1933.

Cast of characters—

Doris Grey....................................Edith Van Cleve
Arthur Valois....................................Paul McGrath
Charles Valois....................................Brian Donlevy
Mathard....................................Harold West
Lois Valois....................................Ruth Shepley
Yvonne Dallier....................................Lillian Bond
Paul Valois....................................John Eldredge
A Servant....................................Lucien Self

Acts I and III.—Living Room in Louis Valois' Country Place near Paris. Act II.—Charles' Room.

Staged by William Harris; settings by Livingston Platt.

Arthur, Charles and Paul Valois are sons of Lois Valois, dancer. Each was born of a different father. Each inherits the characteristics of his sire. Arthur is a broker, Charles is an athlete, Paul is a poet. Lois Valois invites Yvonne Dallier for the week end. All the boys try for Yvonne. She likes Arthur for his business acumen and Paul for his charm, but she entertains Charles in her room. Lois considers that Charles has played his half brothers a dirty trick. Next morning she insists that Yvonne shall be packed off to Paris and that she and her three sons shall go on a holiday jaunt to the Italian lakes.

A DIVINE DRUDGE

(12 performances)

A drama in three acts by Vicki Baum and John Golden. Produced by John Golden at the Royale Theatre, New York, October 26, 1933.

Cast of characters—

Markus....................................Ralf Belmont
Frau Klapstuhl....................................Josephine Hull
Liza....................................Mady Christians
Herr Alkott....................................Frank Monroe
Niko....................................Walter Abel
Lungaus....................................Victor Kilian
Mayor....................................Roman Bohnen
Karl Kruppe....................................Minor Watson
Lania....................................Tamara Geva
Kid Pauker....................................Gerald Kent
Putsch....................................James Lane
Reiffeisen....................................John Blair

Acts I, II and III.—In the Village of Lohwinckel.
Staged by John Golden; settings by Jo Mielziner.

For years on years Liza slaved with her husband, Niko, a struggling physician in a small German town. Niko, absorbed by his practice and his studies, overlooked Liza's devotion. An automobile accident brings Karl Kruppe, big business man from Berlin, and several others into Liza's home for treatment. She is flattered by the love of Herr Kruppe and runs away to Weisbaden with him. When she comes home she finds Niko depressed and miserable because of the failure of his greatest experiment. Liza decides Niko needs her more than she needs Herr Kruppe and happiness.

GIVE US THIS DAY

(3 performances)

A drama in three acts by Howard Koch. Produced by Francis I. Curtis and Richard Myers at the Booth Theatre, New York, October 27, 1933.

Cast of characters—

Matt Strong....................................Harlan Briggs
Eva Strong....................................Eva Condon
Brad Strong....................................Harry Gresham
John Strong....................................Ralph Theadore
Nora Strong....................................Ann Dere
Jane Strong....................................Eleanor Phelps
Mark Strong....................................Paul Guilfoyle
Anne Strong....................................Zamah Cunningham
Miriam Brandon....................................Linda Watkins
Wes Carnwright....................................J. Anthony Hughes

Mr. Sedgwick....................................Joaquin Souther
Mark Strong as Child..............................Edward Ryan
Miriam Brandon as Child............................June Meier
Acts I, II and III.—Strong Family Home in the West Seventies, New York City.
Staged by Arthur Sircom; settings by Cleon Throckmorton.

Grandpa Strong died and left $200,000 to Grandma Strong. Grandma Strong lived for many years surrounded by greedy and impatient relatives. One cast-off daughter died in poverty waiting. One granddaughter took a lover because she could not afford marriage. Mark Strong, Grandma's favorite, gave up a career and Miriam Brandon, whom he loved, to please Grandma. Worn down by his own defeats and his relatives' miseries Mark finally hurries Grandma out by firing off a revolver under her pillow. She dies of shock and leaves all her money to Mark. Conscience smitten, Mark divides it among the greedy relatives and kills himself.

THE FAMILY UPSTAIRS

(3 performances)

A comedy in three acts by Harry Delf. Revived by Leonard Doyle at the Biltmore Theatre, New York, October 27, 1933.

Cast of characters—

Joe Heller..Thos. W. Ross
Emma Heller..Helen Carew
Willie Heller......................................Gilbert Morgan
Louise Heller......................................Florence Ross
Annabelle Heller...................................Marjorie Jane
Charles Grant......................................Leonard Doyle
Mrs. Grant..Elsa Ryan
Miss Calahan..Eileen O'Day
Acts I, II and III.—Parlor of the Heller Apartment.
Staged by Leonard Doyle.

Emma Heller, eager to marry off her daughter Louise, spoils all Louise's chances by her interference. Finally Joe Heller, Louise's father, takes a hand, there is a family explosion, and one romance is mended. The play was produced originally by Sam H. Harris in August, 1925, with Walter Wilson as Joe, Clare Woodbury as Emma and Ruth Nugent as Louise Heller.

EIGHT BELLS

(17 performances)

A drama in three acts by Percy G. Mandley. Produced by A. C. Blumenthal at the Hudson Theatre, New York, October 28, 1933.

Cast of characters—

Collister..Philip Tonge
Carl..Alfred Kappeler
Marjorie..Rose Hobart
Ormrod..John Buckler
Gerhardt..Siegfried Rumann
Dale...Colin Clive
Ashworth..Harrison Brockbank
Zimmerman......................................Henry Von Zynda
Schill..Richard Hughes
Klotz..Joseph Singer
Pancho..Wayne Nunn
Rastello..John Fraser
Snider..David Hughes
Pedro..Eric West
Yetts...Donald Bruce
Nalo...S. B. Pink
Volotsky...Paul Dietz
Oscar..Walter Dressel

Acts I, II and III.—Aboard Full-rigged Ship "Combermere."
Staged by Frank Gregory; settings by Cleon Throckmorton.

Dale, having married the owner's daughter, is master of the sailing ship "Combermere." His chief mate, Ormrod, having loved the present Mrs. Dale for years, resents his captain's attitude toward his wife and toward his crew. The animosity leads to a fight or two while the ship is becalmed. When a passing steamer wigwags news of Germany and England going to war there are other things to think of. Six German members of the crew, rebelling against being taken back to England to be interned and insisting on being put ashore at Rio, start a mutiny that results in the death of Dale and the victory of Ormrod in quelling the mutiny and taking charge of both the ship and Mrs. Dale.

UNDER GLASS

(8 performances)

A comedy in three acts by Eva Kay Flint and George Bradshaw. Produced by William B. Friedlander at the Ambassador Theatre, New York, October 30, 1933.

Cast of characters—

Janie..Clara Palmer
Terry...Pacie Ripple

Tony Pell.....Ross Alexander
Stephanie Pell.....Ethel Barrymore Colt
John Douglas.....Robert Keith
William Schuyler.....Boyd Irwin
Mari Fielding.....Leona Maricle
Edward B. Ransome.....Harry Shannon

Acts I, II and III.—Center Room in the House of William Schuyler, New York.

Staged by William Friedlander; settings by Karle Amend.

Tony and Stephanie Pell, briefly married, have got on each other's nerves to such an extent that trivial invitations bring on a series of violent quarrels. They decide upon a two months' vacation, Stephanie going to Arizona and Tony to Nova Scotia. At which time William Schuyler, Stephanie's father, suggests that the trouble is caused by inexperience and ignorance. Neither Tony nor Stephanie knows anything of life. Tony should take a mistress, among other things. Which Tony does. Takes Mr. Schuyler's mistress. This drives Stephanie to Reno, where she acquires a divorce and a marriageable lawyer. At 11 P.M. Tony and Stephanie make up.

THUNDER ON THE LEFT

(31 performances)

A fantasy in three acts by Jean Ferguson Black from the novel by Christopher Morley. Produced by Henry Forbes at the Maxine Elliott Theatre, New York, October 31, 1933.

Cast of characters—

THE PLAY

Martin.....Frank Thomas, Jr.
Bunny.....Jeanne Dante
Joyce.....Ethel Delveccio
Phyllis.....Edna Hagan
Ruth.....Patricia Goodwin
Ben.....Eugene Low

THE INTERLUDE

Phyllis Granville.....Katharine Warren
George Granville.....Louis Jean Heydt
Martin.....James Bell
Sylvia.....Mary McQuade
Rose.....Charita Bauer
Lizzie.....Cele McLaughlin
Ruth Brook.....Eleanor Audley
Ben Brook.....Otto Hulett
Joyce Clyde.....Hortense Alden

The Play—Porch of the Richmond Home, Dark Harbor. The Interlude—Act I.—Porch. Act II.—Lawn in Front of the House. Act III.—Inside the House.

Staged by Anton Bundsmann; settings by Aline Bernstein.

At his tenth birthday party Martin is worried about growing up. He would, if he could, like to take a peek into the future to see what being grown-up is like. He makes a wish on the cake and when he and his guests blow out the candles they all go out at once, which makes the wish come true. Twenty years pass. Martin is visiting Phyllis, who has grown up and married George Granville. Joyce, who was at the party, is also there and in love with George. Martin is rather disgusted with the way his old friends carry on as grown-ups. Finally, after several adventures, he is glad to return to childhood.

IT PAYS TO SIN

(3 performances)

A comedy in four scenes by Johann Vaszary, adapted from the Hungarian by Louis Macloon and George Redman. Produced by Louis Macloon at the Morosco Theatre, New York, November 3, 1933.

Cast of characters—

Rita Dreyfuss.................................Frances Woodbury
Dr. David Janossy.................................Leon Waycoff
Max Mariska.................................Martin Burton
Nurse.................................Jean Benedict
Mitzi Hofer.................................Ginger Pearson
Greta Kasda.................................Jane Starr
Maid.................................Francelia Waterbury
Waiter.................................Jules Charmette
Groner.................................Edmund Dalby
Folkes.................................Caryl Gillin
Horvat.................................Joe Fields
A Gentleman of Intoxication.................................George Shutta
A Gentleman of Annoyance.................................Edward Walters
Margot.................................Olga Rosenova
Zoltan Keleti.................................Victor Sutherland
Butler.................................Clyde Armstrong

Scene 1—Office of Dr. David Janossy in Vienna. 2—Greta's Sitting Room. 3—Moulin Rouge. 4—Bedroom in Zoltan Keleti's Apartment.

Staged by Monty Collins; settings conceived by Clive A. Rickabaugh and painted by Peter J. Donigan.

Greta Kasda, being unemployed and hungry, answers the advertisement of Dr. Janossy, who would study the reactions of an unmarried mother during her months of expectancy. Greta is able to lie herself out of a preliminary examination and convince the doctor that her condition is what he expected. By the time exposure threatens the doctor is in love with her and eager to carry on his investigations with the blessings of the church.

THOROUGHBRED

(25 performances)

A comedy in three acts by Doty Hobart. Produced by Theodore Hammerstein and Denis Du-For at the Vanderbilt Theatre, New York, November 6, 1933.

Cast of characters—

John Collins....................Thurston Hall
Henry....................John Lynds
Doctor Patten....................Clyde Fillmore
Mrs. Patricia (Petie) Westervail....................Florence Reed
Richard (Rickey) Westervail....................Harry Ellerbe
Alex....................Charles Stepaneck
Gloria Joy....................Louise Glover
Clarissa Van Horne....................Hilda Spong
Sylvia Van Horne....................Lillian Emerson
Mary Westervail....................Claudia Morgan
Tommy Farnsworth....................Jerry Norris
Hickson....................John Daly Murphy

Acts I, II and III.—The Long Island Home of the Westervails.
Staged by Theodore Hammerstein; settings designed by William Warren and painted by Joseph Teichner Studios.

Petie Westervail, born of a long line of turf followers, has her own ideas of breeding, both in the line of animals and humans. A good common strain is certain to strengthen the purest blood line she reasons. Her conviction is strengthened by her success with her own children, who were fathered by Collins, the Westervail butler, after the failure of Mr. Westervail to be blessed with paternity. Petie also enters her filly, Lady Jane, in the Futurity knowing that she is not eligible, having been sired by a superior work horse. Discovery of both conspiracies threatens Petie with scandal, but she faces the exposé and wins out. Lady Jane captures the Futurity without the Jockey Club discovering the cheat and Petie marries Collins.

DOCTOR MONICA

(16 performances)

A drama in three acts by Marja M. Szczepkowska, adapted from the Polish by Laura Walker. Produced at the Playhouse, New York, November 6, 1933.

Cast of characters—

Anna....................Gale Sondergaard
Monica....................Alla Nazimova
Elsa....................Beatrice de Neergaard

Acts I, II and III.—Anna's Studio in Vienna.
Staged by Dmitri Ostrov; settings by Raymond Sovey.

Dr. Monica, eager for motherhood, submits herself to a critical operation, the success of which will permit her to bear children. During the time she is in hospital and convalescent she dismisses her husband and lives with Anna, an architect, where she is visited by Elsa, a young woman in trouble, who hopes that Dr. Monica will help her be rid of an unwanted child. Monica, out of hospital greatly weakened, discovers that her husband is the father of Elsa's child. She would throw herself from a high window but is saved by Anna, who confesses a similar experience with men. Women, it is concluded, are silly to permit the male sex to completely dominate their lives.

IS LIFE WORTH LIVING?

(12 performances)

A comedy in three acts by Lennox Robinson. Produced by Harry Moses at the Masque Theatre, New York, November 9, 1933.

Cast of characters—

Lizzie Twohig.................................Octavia Kenmore
Helena.................................Mary Ricard
Eddie Twohig.................................John McCarthy
Mr. John Twohig.................................Whitford Kane
Hector de la Mare.................................Jerome Lawlor
Constance Constantia.................................Margaret Wycherly
Mrs. Annie Twohig.................................Mary Maddock
Peter Hurley.................................Ralph Cullinan
Michael.................................John Mackesy
John Hegerty.................................Neill O'Malley
William Slattery.................................Byron Russell
Tom Murray.................................Lawrence C. O'Brien

Acts I, II and III.—A Private Sitting Room in the Seaview Hotel.
Staged by Lennox Robinson; settings by Cleon Throckmorton.

John Twohig, proprietor of the Seaview Hotel and Casino at Inish, an obscure seacoast village in Ireland, decides to import a dramatic repertory company headed by Hector de la Mare and Constance Constantia for a season of intellectual drama. The actors stage plays by Chekov, Ibsen, Tolstoy, Strindberg, et al., and soon the villagers, grown self-conscious, are immersed in fogs of doubt and self-analysis. Attempted suicides, attempted murders, blighted love affairs follow in Inish until Twohig, grown panicky, throws out the actors and brings in a circus. Then Inish returns to normal.

DOROTHY SANDS

(6 performances)

A series of sketches entitled "Our Stage and Stars." Presented at the Little Theatre November 11, 1933.

Sketches and Impersonations—

"The Contrast," by Royall Tyler, first American comedy, John Street Theatre, 1787.

"Adelgitha," played by troupers in frontier states, 1820.

"Little Nell and the Marchioness," as played by Lotta Crabtree.

"Captain Jinks of the Horse Marines," as played by Ethel Barrymore in 1901.

Torch songs of the eighties, as Lillian Russell might have presented them at Tony Pastor's.

"The Easiest Way," as played by Frances Starr in 1909. Greta Garbo, Theda Bara, and May West as Meta Hari taking the papers away from the young officer in the movies.

I WAS WAITING FOR YOU

(8 performances)

A comedy in three acts by Melville Baker, adapted from the French of Jacques Natanson. Produced by Edward Choate at the Booth Theatre, November 13, 1933.

Cast of characters—

Maître d'Hôtel....................................Charles Maillard
Waiter....................................Kenneth Berry
Edouard....................................Joshua Logan
Gaston Marchezais....................................Myron McCormick
Gigolo....................................William E. Blake
Jean Favieres....................................Bretaigne Windust
Madeleine Jadain....................................Vera Allen
Young Man....................................Harry Selby
Young Girl....................................Iris Whitney
Doorman....................................James Moreno
M. Marle....................................Frederick Roland
Marise....................................Margaret Swope
Colette Lausay....................................Helen Brooks
Pierre Fromelin.................................... Glenn Anders
Elderly Man....................................Clarence Bellair
Elderly Woman....................................Myra Brooks
Chambermaid....................................Beverly Sitgreaves
Maid....................................Freda Altman

Act I.—A Bar in a Parisian Restaurant. Act II.—Bedroom in a Hotel in Orleans. Act III.—Madeleine Jadain's Apartment in Paris.

Staged by Arthur J. Beckhard; settings by Jo Mielziner.

Jean Favieres, artist, grows restless in the spring, which distresses his mistress, Madeleine Jadain. Colette Lausay, attractive mademoiselle, wearies lightly of the attentions of her aging patron, Pierre Fromelin. When Jean and Colette meet it is a case of curiosity at first sight, followed by confirmations that lead to what appears to be love. Madeleine and Pierre, who had been more than friends in the old days, learn the truth in time and decide to go on as happily as may be, leaving the young people to their own adventures.

* ROBERTA

(255 performances)

A musical comedy in two acts adapted by Otto Harbach from a novel by Alice Duer Miller; music by Jerome Kern. Produced by Max Gordon at the New Ambassador Theatre, New York, November 18, 1933.

Cast of characters—

Billy Boyden....................................George Murphy
John Kent....................................Raymond E. Middleton
Sophie Teale....................................Helen Gray
Huckleberry Haines' Orchestra....................California Collegians
Huckleberry Haines....................................Bob Hope
Mrs. Teale....................................Roberta Beatty
Aunt Minnie (Trade Name, Roberta)....................Fay Templeton
Stephanie....................................Tamara
Angele....................................Bobette Christine
Lord Henry Delves....................................Sydney Greenstreet
Mme. Nunez (Clementina Scharwenka)....................Lyda Roberti
Ladislaw....................................William Hain
Mme. Grandet....................................Marion Ross
Luella....................................Nayan Pearce
Marie....................................Mavis Walsh
M. Leroux....................................Ed Jerome
Sidonie....................................Berenice Alaire
The Buyer....................................Gretchen Sherman
The Flower Girl....................................Virginia Whitmore
The Bartender....................................William Torpey
The Singer at Café Russe....................................George Djimos
The Proprietor of Café Russe....................Stanislaw Sarmatoff
California Collegians: Lou Wood, Herb Montei, Ray Adams, Alan Jones, Neil Wood, Rene Du Plessis, Fred MacMurray.

Prologue: Fraternity House at Haverhill College, U. S. A. Act I.—Scene 1—Roberta's Paris Office. 2—Fitting Room at Roberta's. 3—Corridor. 4—Show Room. Act II.—Scene 1—Roberta's Office. 2—Willie's American Bar. 3—Roberta's Employees' Entertainment. 4—Wardrobe at Roberta's. 5—Café Russe, Paris.

Staged by Hassard Short; settings by Clark Robinson; dances arranged by John Lonergan.

John Kent, all-American fullback, inherits the modiste's shop of his Aunt Minnie, known professionally as Roberta of Paris, France. John doesn't want a modiste's shop but agrees to take it in partnership with Stephanie, Aunt Minnie's assistant, because he likes Stephanie. As it turns out, after misunderstandings, Stephanie is really a Russian princess, which is an extra thrill for John when she agrees to marry him.

* SHE LOVES ME NOT

(248 performances)

A comedy in two acts dramatized by Howard Lindsay from a novel by Edward Hope. Produced by Dwight Deere Wiman and Tom Weatherly at the 46th Street Theatre, New York, November 20, 1933.

Cast of characters—

Curley Flagg.......................................Polly Walters
Mugg Schnitzel.....................................Harry Bellaver
J. B...Ralph J. Locke
A Stenographer.....................................Gerrie Worthing
Paul Lawton..John Beal
Buzz Jones...Burgess Meredith
Henry Broughton....................................Philip Ober
Phillip Laval......................................Frederic Voight
Marshall Mercer....................................John T. Dwyer
Midge Mercer.......................................Florence Rice
Baldy O'Mara.......................................Jack Byrne
A Housekeeper......................................Caroline Morrison
A Jailer...Nelson West
A. Augustus McNeal.................................Charles O. Brown
J. Thorval Jones...................................Jerome Daly
Mrs. Arbuthnot.....................................Frances Brandt
Frances Arbuthnot..................................Jane Buchanan
Joseph Arkle.......................................Randall O'Neil
Abram Liebowitz....................................Harold P. Flick
A Camera Man.......................................Robert Bentzen
Assistant Camera Man...............................Andy Anderson
Assistant Camera Man...............................DeLancey Cleveland
Charles M. Lawton..................................John M. Kline
A Stenographer.....................................Helen Buck
Senator Gray.......................................Allan Allen
A Mother...Maude Odell
A Father...Edward M. Favor

Acts I and II.—Philadelphia, Princeton, New York City, Detroit and Washington.

Staged by Howard Lindsay; settings by Raymond Sovey.

Curley Flagg, a dancer in a Philadelphia night club, is witness to a gang murder. Knowing the police will be after her as a material witness she throws a cloak over her dancing costume and rides as far on a bus as her money will take her, which turns out to be close to Princeton College. Hungry and uncomfortable, she crawls through a dormitory window into the room of Paul Lawton and asks for help. Paul gallantly agrees to help Curley and asks the three other seniors in his entrance to lend a hand. They dress Curley in a suit of pajamas, cut her hair and introduce her as a younger brother. Trying to get her a job they arouse a moving picture concern, which results in an army of camera men and directors descending on Princeton, a grand publicity story, a job for Curley and threatened expulsion for the boys.

BIRTHRIGHT

(7 performances)

A drama in three acts by Richard Maibaum. Produced by Irving Barrett and Robert Rossen at the 49th Street Theatre, New York, November 21, 1933.

Cast of characters—

Jakob Eisner....................................Montagu Love
Joseph....................................Edgar Stehli
Leopold....................................Herbert Warren
Freeda....................................Julio Brown
Hugo....................................Courtney White
Alfred....................................David Leonard
Minna....................................Thais Lawton
Dr. Walter Federmann....................................Milano Tilden
Elga....................................Rose Burdick
Clara....................................Sylvia Field
Willi....................................Alan Bunce
Hilda....................................Charlotte Reynolds
Max....................................Alan Gould
Friedrich Lowenberg....................................Harold Elliot
Kurt Strasser....................................Don Beddoe
Abram....................................Charles P. Burrows
Karl....................................Hayden Roike
Erik Phlaum....................................Harry Levian
Nazi Shock Troopers: Jay Addison, Stephen Courtleigh, Joseph Grant, Dennis Gurney, Don Shelton and Larry Williams.
Acts I, II and III.—Parlor of Jakob Eisner's House in Charlottenburg, Suburb of Berlin.
Staged by Robert Rossen; settings by Cleon Throckmorton Studios.

The family and kin of Jakob Eisner are torn asunder by the rise to power of Chancellor Hitler in Germany. Willi, the grandson, college student, becomes actively hostile. Friedrich Lowenberg, engaged to Clara Eisner, is forced to return to the Nazi forces and break his engagement. Kurt Strasser, nastiest of the Nazis, is shot by Willi, whom he has come to arrest. Willi is executed for the murder. The Eisners are left forlornly fighting for their right to live peaceably in the country that has been their homeland for generations.

GROWING PAINS

(29 performances)

A comedy by Aurania Rounerol. Produced by Arthur Lubin at the Ambassador Theatre, New York, November 23, 1933.

Cast of characters—

George McIntyre....................................Junior Durkin
Mrs. McIntyre....................................Leona Hogarth
Professor McIntyre....................................Ralph Freud

Terry McIntyre....................................Jean Rouverol
Brian....................................Johnny Downs
Dutch....................................Charles Eaton
Omar....................................Leo Needham
Pete....................................John O'Shea
Hal....................................Garrett Starmer
Mrs. Patterson....................................Mary Horne Morrison
Elsie Patterson....................................Olive Corn
Prudence....................................Joan Wheeler
Jane....................................Georgette McKee
Patty....................................Lili Zehner
Miriam....................................June Cox
Sophie....................................Pauline Meyers
Traffic Officer....................................Eddie Acuff
Alice....................................Anna Erskine
Eddie ....William Courtleigh, Jr.
Sally....................................Claire McQuillen
Clay....................................Emmett Rogers
Helen....................................Patricia Morrison
"Spats"....................................Philippe de Lacy
Mary Ann ....Lorraine Hayes
Slim....................................Murry Rhyness
Margie....................................Jacqueline Rusling
Vivian....................................Beverly Phalon
Rascal....................................."Stingy Bossifer"

Acts I, II and III.—Patio of the McIntyre Residence in Southern California.

Staged by Arthur Lubin; settings by Herbert Moore.

Terry McIntyre, 16, is fearfully in love with Brian, her neighbor, and distressed that Brian doesn't seem to know it. George McIntyre, 17, has no regular attachments until he acquires white flannels and catches a glimpse of Prudence, a cute trick and flirty, recently come to town. The McIntyres give a party. Ice cream runs low. George goes for more with the flivver, runs past a traffic light in his eagerness to get back to Prudence, sasses the traffic officer and is arrested. Practically everybody is hours older and wiser by 11 o'clock that evening.

THE DRUMS BEGIN

(11 performances)

A drama in three acts by Howard Irving Young. Produced by George Abbott and Philip Dunning at the Shubert Theatre, New York, November 24, 1933.

Cast of characters—

Emile Moreau....................................Pierre de Ramey
Andre Roussel....................................Walter Abel
Dominique....................................William Wadsworth
Victor....................................Oliver Barbour
Jacques....................................Juan Varro
Gaston Corday....................................Jose Ruben
Batiste....................................C. C. Charles
Albert....................................Harry Cooke
Karl Hoffman....................................Kent Smith
George Patterson....................................William Foran
Curtis....................................F. Cliff Jewell

Feodor Dobinsky....................................Lionel Stander
Rosie....................................Ingeborg Tillisch
Starling....................................Joseph Downing
Philippe....................................William Shea
Schenck....................................Alf Weinberger
Kammerich....................................Charles Wagenheim
Ludwig Von Tappen....................................Moffat Johnston
Pierrette....................................Alice Reinheart
Jackie....................................Alexander Lewis
Valerie Latour....................................Judith Anderson
J. A. Higgins....................................Robert Gleckler
Sound Man....................................J. Ascher Smith
Charlotte....................................Mathilde Baring

Act I.—Scene 1—Battle Trench, Somewhere in France. 2—Office in Paris. Act II.—Scene 1—Courtyard of the Château de Sarnac. 2—Balcony of an Apartment in Paris. 3 and 4—Hall of the Château de Sarnac. Act III.—Scene 1—Bedroom in the Château. 2—Corner of a French Garden.

Staged by George Abbott; settings by Cirker and Robbins.

Andre Roussel is the leading man in a French version of a film to be called "No More War." There are to be both French and German versions of the picture. Valerie Latour, a French actress who speaks German, doubles the part of the leading woman. Andre falls desperately in love with Valerie, and she with him. As the making of the picture proceeds it is discovered that Valerie, as the Countess de Sarnac, was a German spy during the war. Andre is shocked painfully by the discovery of his true love's treachery. Valerie goes out of his life after denouncing all men, and particularly all military men, for their hypocrisies. There will always be wars so long as such as they continue to defend greed in terms of patriotism. Even now the drums begin—

THE DARK TOWER

(57 performances)

A melodrama in three acts by Alexander Woollcott and George S. Kaufman. Produced by Sam H. Harris at the Morosco Theatre, New York, November 25, 1933.

Cast of characters—

Hattie....................................Margaret Hamilton
Martha Temple....................................Margaret Dale
Ben Weston....................................William Harrigan
Damon Wells....................................Basil Sydney
Daphne Martin....................................Leona Maricle
Jessica Wells....................................Margalo Gillmore
Barry Jones....................................John Griggs
Dr. Kendall....................................John T. Doyle
Marcus Blaine (alias Stanley Vance)....................................Ernest Milton
A Taxi Driver....................................Charles Romano
Max Sarnoff....................................Anton Stengel
Patsy Dowling....................................Beatrice Blinn
A Bellboy....................................William MacFadden
William Curtis....................................Porter Hall

Acts I and III.—Martha Temple's House in East 40th Street,

New York. Act II.—Scene 1—The House. 2—Max Sarnoff's Suite at the Waldorf.
Staged by the authors; settings by Jo Mielziner.

Jessica Wells, the most promising ingénue lead of her day, is preparing a return to the stage from which mental disturbances, stemming from an unfortunate marriage with one Stanley Vance, have kept her removed. She is happy in the support of her brother Damon, the best character actor of his day. On the eve of the production of "The Dark Tower" Stanley Vance returns from the supposedly dead. He had been in jail under an assumed name. Immediately he resumes his vicious hypnotic control of Jessica, who falls again into a decline. Stanley, conscious of the trouble he is causing, offers to be bought off. Max Sarnoff, a foreign producer, considers taking an option on the play and Jessica. Stanley visits Sarnoff at the Waldorf and is stabbed to death. Sarnoff vanishes. The police give up. Sarnoff reappears, but only privately. He is brother Damon disguised. "The Dark Flower" goes on.

MARY OF SCOTLAND

(248 performances)

An historical drama in three acts by Maxwell Anderson. Produced by The Theatre Guild, Inc., at the Alvin Theatre, New York, November 27, 1933.

Cast of characters—

Jamie	Cecil Holm
Monk	William Jackson
John Knox	Moroni Olsen
Tammas	Jock McGraw
James Hepburn, Earl of Bothwell	Philip Merivale
A Page	Maurice F. Manson
Chatelard	Edward Trevor
Mary Stuart	Helen Hayes
Duc de Chatelherault	Leonard Willey
Mary Beaton	Mary Michael
Mary Seton	Helen Shea
Mary Livingstone	Deane Willoughby
Mary Fleming	Cynthia Rogers
Elizabeth Tudor	Helen Menken
Lord Burghley	George Coulouris
Lord Darnley	Anthony Kemble-Cooper
Lord Douglas	Edgar Barrier
David Rizzio	Philip Leigh
James Stuart, Earl of Moray	Wilton Graff
Maitland of Lethington	Ernest Lawford
Lord Huntley	Charles Dalton
Lord Morton	Stanley Ridges
Lord Erskine	George Coulouris
Lord Throgmorton	Ernest Cossart
Lord Ruthven	Leonard Willey
Lord Gordon	Philip Foster
Graeme	Maurice F. Manson

A Warder....................................Quentin Anderson
Act I.—Scene 1—Pier at Leith. 2—Queen Elizabeth's Study at Whithall. 3—Hall in Mary Stuart's Apartments at Holyrood House. Act II.—Scene 1—Holyrood House. 2—Queen Elizabeth's Study. 3—Dunbar Castle. Act III.—Carlisle Castle, England.
Staged by Theresa Helburn; settings by Robert Edmond Jones.

On June 2 Helen Hayes was succeeded by Margalo Gillmore as Mary and Stanley Ridges took over the rôle of Bothwell so Philip Merivale could return to England for the summer. The supplementary engagement continued for two weeks. See page 29 for digest of play.

THE SCORPION

(8 performances)

A melodrama in three acts by Bernard J. McOwen. Produced by Maris Productions at the Biltmore Theatre, New York, November 27, 1933.

Cast of characters—

Captain Roger Owen....................................Leslie Austen
First Lieut. Stuart Duncan....................................J. Malcolm Dunn
Second Lieut. Neil Lambert....................................Allen Nourse
Surg. Maj. Lawrence Linton....................................Fredk. Forrester
Trooper Hawley....................................Harry Sothern
El Emir Safi El Quertassi....................................Douglas Gerard
Illyana Lortay-Randall....................................Annette Margulies
Zuleika....................................Beatrice Allen
Acts I, II and III.—In the Sudan.
Staged by J. Bernard Steele.

Illyana Lortay-Randall, crossing the Sudan in a plane, drops into upon the officers of a British mess. They, not having seen a white woman for a year or more, are disturbed no end. Illyana is doing quite well enslaving Capt. Roger Owen when she succumbs to "a wolf in sheik's clothing" named El Emir. After which it transpires that Illyana is really the wife of Surgeon Major Linton, who is vastly surprised at his wife's carryings on and not very sorry when she is poisoned by a jealous native woman.

STRANGE ORCHESTRA

(1 performance)

A comedy in three acts by Rodney Ackland. Produced by Charles Hopkins and Raymond Moore at the Playhouse, New York, November 28, 1933.

Cast of characters—

Vera Lyndon....................................Cecilia Loftus
George....................................Gerald Oliver-Smith
Val...Harry Ellerbe
Esther Lyndon..............................Helen Trenholme
Freda.....................................Mary Newham-Davis
Laura...Valeria Cossart
Jimmie.....................................Robert C. Conway
Gordon Lyndon...............................Leslie Denison
Jenny Lyndon...................................Edith Barrett
Peter...Ian Emery
Sylvia...Patricia Calvert

Acts I, II and III.—Hall of Vera's Flat near Chelsea in London.
Staged by Charles Hopkins; settings by Robert Redington Sharpe.

Vera Lyndon, a slovenly but kindly person, runs a boarding house of sorts in the Chelsea district of London. Her daughter Jenny, having been told by the specialists that she will be blind within a few months, decides to live life at its fullest during the wait. She is deceived by a professional seducer named Peter who robs her of her jewels and runs away the night Jenny is stricken blind. The boarders convince Jenny that Peter is dead, but after he has been taken by the police Peter escapes and comes back to Jenny for more money. She gives him the money and faints.

PEACE ON EARTH

(First engagement 126; second, 18 performances)

A drama in three acts by George Sklar and Albert Maltz. Produced by The Theatre Union at the Civic Repertory Theatre, New York, November 29, 1933.

Cast of characters—

Laurie Owens.......................................Julia Colin
Peter Owens.....................................Robert Keith
Jo Owens.......................................Ethel Intropidi
Walter McCracken.............................Clyde Franklin
Prof. Frank Anderson......................Walter Vonnegut
Mary Bonner.....................................Allace Carroll
Stephen Hamill.................................John Boruff
Bob Peters.......................................Fred Herrick
Policeman......................................Jack Williams
Dean Walker..................................Charles Esdale
Fred Miller.......................................Victor Kilian
Primo..John Brown
Lena..Caroline Newcombe
Speed..Elliot Fisher
Mike...David Lesan
Ann..Mara Tartar
Rose...Millicent Green
Ryan...Earl Ford
Flynn...Donald A. Black
Krauss..Frank Tweddell
Max..John Boruff
Kemmerich......................................Jack Williams
Fenning..David Kerman
Company Guard....................................Paul Stein

Henry Murdoch....James MacDonald
Dr. Carl Kelsey....John Brown
President Howard....Halliam Bosworth
Miss Ellen Bancroft....Caroline Newcombe
John Andrews....Alvin Dexter
Bishop Parkes....Thomas Coffin Cooke
Marjorie Howard....Allace Carroll
Bill Prentice....Frank Tweddell
Charlie Wilcox....Earl Ford
Biff Morris....Donald A. Black
Harry Boynton....Charles Thompson
The Guard....Fred Herrick
The Cop....David Lesan
The Messenger....Jules Garfield
The Judge....Charles Esdale
The District Attorney....John Brown
Attorney Gordon....Frank Tweddell
Radio Announcer....John Boruff
The Blues Singer....Mara Tartar
Also David Gray, Ralph Steves, John Caraway, Sigmund Salomon, George Russell, Joe Connors, George Nafely, A. W. Biberman, W. Washington, Mary George, Carl Carlsen, and Harry Constantine.

Act I.—Scene 1—Living Room of the Owens Home. 2—Green. 3—Owens Home. 4—Warehouse. 5—Dock. Act II.—Scene 1—Room in the Faculty Club. 2—Owens Home. 3—University Campus. Act III.—Prison.

Staged by Robert B. Sinclair, assisted by Michael Blankfort; settings by Cleon Throckmorton.

Peter Owens, economy professor in an Eastern university is drawn to the contemplation of a strike of longshoremen who refuse to load munitions for the next war. His best friend is shot down by the police seeking to break up the strike. Peter becomes deeply involved on the side of the workers, is accused of a killing at a mass meeting on the college campus and sentenced to be hanged for murder. In his cell he day dreams the outstanding events of his harried and muddled life. Outside the jail bands are playing and men are marching to the war he had striven so desperately to avert.

BLACKBIRDS OF 1933

(25 performances)

A revue in two acts by Nat N. Dorfman, Mann Holiner and Lew Leslie; lyrics and music by Mann Holiner, Alberta Nichols, Joseph Young, Ned Washington, and Victor Young. Produced by Sepia Guild Players, Inc., at the Apollo Theatre, New York, December 2, 1933.

Principals engaged—

John Mason
Lionel Monagas
Speedy Smith
Slappy Wallace
Brady Jackson
James Thomas Boxwill
Henry Williams
Edith Wilson
Eddie Hunter
Worthy & Thompson

Kathryn Perry — Mary Mathews
Blue McAllister — Cecil Mack's Choir
Pike Davis' Continental Orchestra. Gretchen Branche, Louise Madison, Phil Scott, Al Richard.
Staged by Lew Leslie; settings by Mabel A. Buell.

* TOBACCO ROAD

(233 performances)

A drama in three acts by Jack Kirkland, based on a novel by Erskine Caldwell. Produced by Anthony Brown at the Masque Theatre, New York, December 4, 1933.

Cast of characters—

Jeeter Lester..Henry Hull
Dude Lester ....Sam Byrd
Ada Lester..................................Margaret Wycherly
Ellie May...Ruth Hunter
Grandma Lester.................................Patricia Quinn
Lov Bensey..Dean Jagger
Henry Peabody....................................Ashley Cooper
Sister Bessie Rice...............................Maude Odell
Pearl..Reneice Rehan
Captain Tim..Lamar King
George Payne...Edwin Walter
Acts I, II and III.—Farm of Jeeter Lester, Situated on a Tobacco Road in the Back Country of Georgia.
Staged by Anthony Brown; settings by Robert Redington Sharpe.

Jeeter Lester, representing poor white trash in his particular section of Georgia, is the shiftless, poverty-stricken, no-account head of what is left of the Lester clan. His one consuming conviction is that he is entitled to continue living on the land his fathers have rented before him. His discouragement is complete when the banks take the land away from him. His son has married a lustful neighbor for the chance of running her automobile, which he finally runs over his mother and kills her. His youngest daughter has run away to replace the oldest daughter who has abandoned her husband. His mother has wandered into the woods and is probably dead. Jeeter is too tired to dig graves.

ALL GOOD AMERICANS

(40 performances)

A comedy in three acts by Laura and S. J. Perelman. Produced by Courtney Burr at the Henry Miller Theatre, New York, December 5, 1933.

Cast of characters—

A French Man.....................................Charles Angelo
A French Girl.......................................Renee Cartier

A French Girl....................................Doris Laurey
Jimmy....................................George Todd
Cassie Bond....................................Mary Philips
Noble Smart....................................Charles Henderson
Metzger....................................Frank Rowan
Julie Gable....................................Hope Williams
Moses....................................Johnny Gubelman
Ham Farnsworth....................................Eric Dressler
Miss Moorhead....................................Paula Bauersmith
Pat Wells....................................Fred Keating
Rex Fleming....................................Coburn Goodwin
Bar Man....................................Harry C. Anderson
A Flower Woman....................................Louza Riane
A Rug-Seller....................................Henry De Koven
Johnny Chadwick....................................James Stewart
A French Man....................................C. Francois Barrere
A Colored Girl....................................Hazel Curry
Mary-Louise Porter....................................Janet McLeay
Ginsberg....................................Hilda Bruce
Concierge....................................Michelette Burani
A French Gentleman....................................George Spelvin
Lucy Starkweather....................................Marie Adels
George Palfrey....................................LeRoi Operti
Mrs. Greenspan....................................Helena Rapport
Mr. Bond....................................Willard Dashiell
A Bystander....................................Joseph P. Harris
A Gendarme....................................Claude Burani

Act I.—Jimmy's Bar, Rue de Montparnasse, Paris. Acts II and III.—Julie Gable's Studio, Rue Boissonnade, Paris.

Staged by Arthur Sircon; settings by Mordecai Gorelik.

Julie Gable, designer, stationed in Paris, is fond of Pat Wells, writer, with whom she has carried on a desultory love affair for two or three years. Pat prefers Julie to all his other women friends, but will not ask her to marry him because of a consuming sense of his own unworthiness. When Julie decides to marry a New Rochelle man and Pat takes up with Mary-Louise Porter, a touring Texan, their affairs are brought to a crisis. They decide to cleave unto each other instead.

JEZEBEL

(32 performances)

A drama in three acts by Owen Davis. Produced by Katharine Cornell and Guthrie McClintic at the Ethel Barrymore Theatre, New York, December 19, 1933.

Cast of characters—

Miss Sally....................................Cora Witherspoon
Uncle Billy....................................Lew Payton
General Rand....................................Frederic Worlock
Daphne....................................Frances Creel
Bap....................................Alston Burleigh
Sam Orton....................................Leo Curley
Julie Kendrick....................................Miriam Hopkins
Mammy Winnie....................................Laura Bowman
Lulu....................................Blois Jackson
Zulu....................................Anita Jackson
Messy-Ann....................................Rena Mitchell

Dick Ashley....................Joseph Cotten
Allan Dorsey....................Henry Richards
Buck Buckner....................Gage Clarke
Preston Kendrick....................Reed Brown, Jr.
Ted Kendrick....................Owen Davis, Jr.
Amy Kendrick....................Helen Claire
Jean Labich....................Bjorn Koefoed
Joe Staley....................Clem Wilenchick
Sheriff's Deputies.................... { William Richardson / Gilbert McKay }
A Doctor....................Harold Martin
Servants, Field Hands: Ida Brown, Ruth Boyd, Romaine Johns, Henry May, James Waters, Joseph Maxwell, Ray Yeates.

Acts I, II and III.—Twin Oaks Plantation, Louisiana.

Staged by Guthrie McClintic; settings by Donald Oenslager.

Julie Kendrick of the Louisiana Kendricks had at one time been very much in love with her cousin, Preston Kendrick. They quarreled violently. Julie went to Europe to forget. For three years she lived excitingly. Realizing she could not conquer her love for Preston she returned to the old plantation prepared to humble herself by asking his forgiveness. Preston is forgiving, but he is also married. Julie's ungovernable jealousy again conquers her. She schemes to have Preston drawn into a duel with the best shot in the county. Preston's brother Ted takes this quarrel off his hands and kills the best shot. Thereafter the yellow fever scourge invades the Kendrick district. Preston is smitten. Julie goes to the pesthouse with him and sends his wife back up north.

THE LOCKED ROOM

(8 performances)

A melodrama in two acts by Herbert Ashton, Jr. Produced by M. S. Schlesinger and William B. Friedlander at the Ambassador Theatre, New York, December 25, 1933.

Cast of characters—

John Burgess....................Morton Flamm
Anna....................Valerie Bergere
Harvey....................Harold Kennedy
Charles Burgess....................Lawrence Keating
Alice....................Ruth Sheppard
Ralph Burgess....................Robert Sloane
Josephine Burgess....................Jane Kim
Mary Burgess....................Nena Sinclair
John Burgess, Jr....................Jonathan Hole
Edward Parker....................Walter Gilbert
Ryan....................Robert Gleckler
Dr. Morrison....................Harmon MacGregor
Tommy....................Sam J. Park

Acts I and II.—Room in the Home of John Burgess, New York City.

Staged by William B. Friedlander; settings by Amend.

John Burgess is found murdered in a room of which the one door is locked on the inside and into which there are no windows. The investigation of the suspects, who include practically all members of the family, is somewhat complicated by the appearance of Edward Parker, an investigator for the insurance company in which Mr. Burgess carried his largest policy. Parker and Ryan, from police headquarters, work together until the end of the play is in sight. Then Ryan turns on Parker and there is an unexpected exposure revealing the use of a new kind of infernal machine.

THE LAKE

(55 performances)

A drama in three acts by Dorothy Massingham and Murray Macdonald. Produced by Jed Harris at the Martin Beck Theatre, New York, December 26, 1933.

Cast of characters—

Mildred Surrege....................Frances Starr
Williams....................J. P. Wilson
Lena Surrege....................Blanche Bates
Henry Surrege....................Lionel Pape
Marjorie Hervey ....Roberta Beatty
Stella Surrege....................Katharine Hepburn
Ethel....................Esther Mitchell
Cecil Hervey....................Geoffrey Wardwell
John Clayne....................Colin Clive
Maude....................Mary Heberden
Stoker....................Edward Broadley
Stephen Braite....................Philip Tonge
Dolly Braite....................Wendy Atkin
Jean Templeton....................Audrey Ridgwell
Anna George....................Vera Fuller-Mellish
Mrs. George....................Rosalind Ivan
Miss Kurn....................Florence Britton
Miss Marle....................Elizabeth Townsend
Mrs. Hemingway....................Eva Leonard-Boyne
Mr. Hemingway....................Douglas Garden
Dennis Gourlay....................O. Z. Whitehead
Lady Stanway....................Constance Pelissier
Sir Philip Stanway....................Reginald Carrington
Captain Hamilton....................James Grainger
Miss White....................Lucy Beaumont
Lady Kerton....................Elliott Mason

Acts I and III.—Drawing Room of Mildred Surrege's Country House in England. Act II.—Corner of the Marquee in the Grounds.
Staged by Jed Harris; settings by Jo Mielziner.

Stella Surrege, daughter of the well-to-do Henry Surrege of England, is unhappy in her home, which is dominated completely by Mildred Surrege, her utterly shallow and selfish mother. Seeking release from boredom Stella falls desperately in love with Cecil Hervey, a married neighbor. Cecil, accustomed to a parasitical existence, would make Stella his mistress, but not his wife.

Stella thereafter engages herself to a man of her mother's choice, John Clayne. During the three months of her engagement she comes to love John. The day of the wedding she confesses her love and proposes that they steal away from the reception. The car in which they are escaping skids into an artificial lake with which Mrs. Surrege has destroyed the beauty of the landscape. John is killed. Stella escapes. For days she contemplates suicide and is apparently still of two minds as she starts for the lake at the play's end.

THE FIRST APPLE

(53 performances)

A comedy in three acts by Lynn Starling. Produced by Lee Shubert at the Booth Theatre, New York, December 27, 1933.

Cast of characters—

Sylvia Carson.......................................Irene Purcell
Gilbert Carey.......................................Conrad Nagel
Henry.......................................A. J. Herbert
Hester Glenn.......................................Spring Byington
Archy Glenn.......................................Dudley Hawley
Evangeline Carson.......................................Nana Bryant
Helen Travers.......................................Beatrice Swanson
Calvin Barrow.......................................Albert Van Dekker
Miss Merkle.......................................Edmonia Nolley

Prologue—Street in Greenwich Village. Acts I, II and III.—Living Room in the Carsons' Summer Home, New Jersey.
Staged by Bela Blau; settings by Arthur Segal.

Sylvia Carson and Gilbert Carey are caught in a rainstorm in Greenwich Village and make for the same doorway. In the doorway Gilbert starts a pleasant conversation which is so reassuring to Sylvia that she agrees to go to his apartment to dry out and listen to a little Brahms. Sylvia stays much longer than she planned. Thereafter she suffers such twinges of conscience that she promptly engages herself to another man. Even after Gilbert searches her out and insists that he really intended marriage from the first it takes her some time to make up her mind. In the end she returns to Gilbert and gives the other man to her mother.

THE LOVES OF CHARLES II

(23 performances)

A repertory of dramatic sequences and character sketches by Cornelia Otis Skinner. Presented at the 48th Street Theatre, New York, December 27, 1933.

Character Sketches—

The Eve of Departure
Hotel Porch
Being Presented
Lynch Party

"The Loves of Charles II—"

Henrietta Maria
A Dutch Trollop
Lady Castlemaine
Louise de Queroalle
Nell Gwyn
Catharine of Braganza

Staged by Cornelia Otis Skinner.

YOSHE KALB

(4 performances)

A drama in two acts adapted by Fritz Blocki from a dramatization by Maurice Schwartz in Yiddish of a book by I. J. Singer. Produced by Daniel Frohman at the National Theatre, New York, December 28, 1933.

Cast of characters—

First Young Man	Harry Morrison
Second Young Man	Libbey Charney
Third Young Man	Jack Arnold
Zisha	M. Farman
Jacob	David Kortchmar
Moisha	John Wexley
Leibush	Robert Harris
Rachmanivke Rabbi	Manart Kippen
Motye Godol	John Burke
Reb Melech	Fritz Leiber
Israel Avigdor	John Moore
Gedaliah	David Sorin
Berl	Morris Belawsky
Gittel	Ethel Wilson
Hannah-Leah	Helen Waren
Fayge-Haye	Kate Pierce Roemer
Serele	Mildred Van Dorn
Mechele	Mark Schweid
Pinchas	Louis Krugman
Leah	Florence Fair
Naum	Horace Braham
Palthiel	Charles Mansfield
Malkele	Erin O'Brien Moore
Eidele	Jeanne Wardley
Psachya	Robert Harris
Yankel	John Burke
Red-headed Beggar	Curtis Karpe
Hunchbacked Beggar	Martin Cravath
Blind Beggar	Robert Davis
Koona	Norman C. Hammond
Zivyah	Joanne Myers
Reb Schachne	Boyd Irwin
Abush	Joseph Singer
Dobbe	Julia Dorn
Reb Mayerl	Mark Schweid
The Rabbi of Cracow	Henry Herbert
The Rabbi of Dinaburg	Manart Kippen

The Rabbi of Lizhan................................Lou Polan

Acts I and II.—Austria and Russian Poland. Act I.—Scenes 1 and 17—Before the Curtain. 2—Carlsbad. 3, 6, 10 and 18—Home of Reb Melech. 4—Living Room in Reb Melech's Home. 5—Courtyard of Reb Melech. 7—Before the Portals of the Synagogue. 8—Interior of the Synagogue. 9—Courtyard on a Side Street. 11—Room in Home of Malkele. 12—Reb Melech's Room in Przemysl. 13—Reb Melech's Room in Nyeshever. 14—Living Room in Serele's Home in Nyeshever. 15—In the Forest. 16—Before the Synagogue. Act II.—Scene 1—Ancient Synagogue in Biala Gura. 2—House of Chona, the Sexton. 3—Home of Reb Mayerl, Biala Gura. 4—Street in Biala Gura. 5—Cemetery of Biala Gura. 6 and 9—Before the Curtain. 7—Home of Nyeshever Rabbi. 8—Before the Portals of the Synagogue. 10—The Synagogue in Nyeshever.

Staged by Maurice Schwartz; settings by Alex Chertov.

Reb Melech, an aging rabbi, at 68 decides to marry for the third time. Before he can satisfy the rabinnical law he must marry off his daughter. To do this he forces a protesting fellow rabbi to agree to the marriage of his son, Naum, with Serele, daughter of Reb. Naum, a student, takes no interest in Serele but is drawn to Malkele, his new and amorous mother-in-law. Naum and Malkele sin in the forest and Naum, conscience-stricken, becomes a wanderer, finally losing his mind and becoming known as Yoshe, the simpleton. Married by force to the foolish daughter of a gravedigger, Yoshe makes his way back to Reb Melech's house and attempts to reëstablish his identity before a rabbinical court. After a three-day trial the rabbis disagree and Naum resumes his wandering.

BIG HEARTED HERBERT

(154 performances)

A comedy in three acts adapted by Sophie Kerr and Anna Steese Richardson from a story by Sophie Kerr. Produced by Eddie Dowling at the Biltmore Theatre, New York, January 1, 1934.

Cast of characters—

Herbert Kalness................................J. C. Nugent
Robert Kalness................................Norman Williams
Elizabeth Kalness................................Elisabeth Risdon
Martha................................Dorothy Walter
Herbert Kalness, Jr................................David Morris
Alice Kalness................................Betty Lancaster
Andrew Goodrich................................Alan Bunce
Amy Lawrence................................Marjorie Wood
Jim Lawrence................................George Lessey
Mr. Goodrich................................Forrest Orr
Mrs. Goodrich................................Gertrude Fowler
Mr. Havens................................Guy Dennery
Mrs. Havens................................Claudia Carlstedt

Acts I, II and III.—Combination Living Room and Dining Room of the Kalness Home, Indiana.

Staged by Dan Jarrett.

Herbert Kalness was mean-minded and tight-fisted. A boastful self-made man who did not realize how badly the job had been finished. Herbert refuses to let his son go to college. He hates colleges. His son shall come into the factory and make plumbers' supplies. Herbert refuses to let his daughter Alice marry Andrew Goodrich, because Andrew is a Harvard man. Herbert insults all the Goodriches. He is a plain man and wants plain people around him. When Herbert invites his best customer to dinner Mrs. Kalness determines to make it plain with a vengeance. She strips the house of its decorations and cooks Irish stew. She and Alice get into gingham and do their own serving. Herbert is cured.

HALFWAY TO HELL

(7 performances)

A mystery melodrama in three acts by Crane Wilbur. Produced by Elizabeth Miele in association with M. Van R. Schuyler at the Fulton Theatre, New York, January 2, 1934.

Cast of characters—

Captain Zebulon Brant............................Carlton Macy
Dr. Potter............................Austin Fairman
Soo Song............................Van Lowe
Martha Brant............................Lida McMillan
Christopher Brant............................Mitchell Harris
Elsie Brant............................Ann Mason
Edward Brant............................Grant Richards
Ruth Allen............................Katherine Locke
Tony Allen............................Richard Ewell
Bonnie McGee............................Mabel Kroman
Lefty Adams............................Robert Williams
Lieutenant Kelton............................Guy Standing, Jr.
Gabe Jarvis............................John Regan

Acts I, II and III.—Captain Brant's Bedroom on the Upper Floor and The Lounge on the Lower Floor of a Converted Lighthouse.
Staged by Crane Wilbur; settings by Philip Gelb.

Capt. Zebulon Brant, hi-jacker and pirate, having accumulated a fortune, finds himself outward bound with a bad heart. He buys Halfway Island and invites his eight Brant heirs to visit him there. Soon they are squabbling over what they hope to get and murder is done mysteriously. One old lady is stabbed. One mean-mannered brother is hatcheted. The remaining six suffer a variety of narrow escapes. Captain Zeb dies finally, but not until they have discovered a wax duplicate of his emaciated form in a chest. It was he, we suspect, who did the killing.

THE WOODEN SLIPPER

(5 performances)

A comedy in three acts by Samson Raphaelson. Produced by Dwight Deere Wiman at the Ritz Theatre, New York, January 3, 1934.

Cast of characters—

Conductor.................................Mortimer H. Weldon
Antoinette.....................................Alice Reinheart
Andre..Ross Alexander
Julie Zigurny....................................Dorothy Hall
Michael Hajos...................................John Halloran
Adele Zigurny...................................Cecilia Loftus
Ina Zigurny......................................Ruth Altman
Otto Zigurny....................................Montagu Love
Lushka..Dorothy Drake
August...Clarence Bellair
Mortimer Pavlicek...............................Lionel Stander
A Woman...Marjorie Hollis
Another Conductor...............................M. H. Bender
Albert...John Philliber
Pierre..Richard Enbach
Katy...Jonatha Jones
Madame Boyer................................Alice Belmore Cliffe
Alexander Dudot..................................Hale Norcross

Act I.—Scene 1—Train Leaving Paris. 2—The Zigurny Home in Budapest. 3—Train Leaving Budapest. Act II.—Kitchen in Paris. Act III.—The Zigurny Home.

Staged by Samson Raphaelson; settings by Raymond Sovey.

Julie Zigurny, daughter of famous stage folk in Budapest, is in Paris studying for the stage and in love with Michael Hajos. Michael, visiting Budapest, forgets Julie and takes on her handsomer sister. Julie, discovering the deception, meets Andre, a handsome and proud young chef and feels comforted in his presence. Refusing to go on with her acting she takes a job as kitchen maid in Andre's kitchen. Just as he begins to notice her she is discovered and taken home. Again the Zigurnys try to make an actress of Julie. The night she plays Desdemona Andre is in the audience. He rushes to Julie to tell her of his renewed devotion and his conviction that she is great. Everybody else thinks she is terrible. So Julie quits the stage and becomes a cashier in Andre's new restaurant, living happily and well fed forever after.

THE GODS WE MAKE

(13 performances)

A comedy in three acts by G. H. McCall and S. Bouvet de Lozier. Produced by John Cameron, Inc., at the Mansfield Theatre, New York, January 3, 1934.

Cast of characters—

Mado Glendon....................Ara Gerald
Merle Cavendish....................John Blair
Dick Webster....................Lloyd Hughes
Jimmy Laurelton....................Frank M. Thomas
Annette....................Eve Casanova

Acts I, II and III.—Merle's Living Room in a Pent-House Apartment in Park Avenue, New York.

Staged by John Cameron; settings by Cleon Throckmorton.

Merle Cavendish is a rich widow in love with Dick Webster, an unhappy stockbroker whose wife refuses to divorce him. Merle and Dick therefore live contentedly in sin for five years. When the panic strikes them Merle sacrifices her fortune to save Dick from bankruptcy. At the end of the sacrifice another man tries to get Dick messed up with another woman so he (the other man) can inherit Merle. The conspiracy is defeated.

ZIEGFELD FOLLIES

(182 performances)

A musical revue in two acts, lyrics by E. Y. Harburg, sketches and tunes by Vernon Duke, Samuel Pokrass, Billy Hill, H. I. Phillips, Fred Allen, Harry Tugend, Ballard McDonald and David Freedman. Presented by Mrs. Florenz Ziegfeld (Billie Burke) at the Winter Garden Theatre, New York, January 4, 1934.

Principals engaged—

Fannie Brice	Willie Howard
Jane Froman	Everett Marshall
Patricia Bowman	Eugene Howard
Vilma Ebsen	Buddy Ebsen
Betzi Beaton	Victor Morley
Judith Barron	Don Ross
Ina Ray	Brice Hutchins
Eve Arden	Jacques Cartier
Preisser Sisters	The Vikings

Staged by Edward C. Lilley; dances by Robert Alton; settings by Watson Barrett and Albert R. Johnson.

OLIVER OLIVER

(11 performances)

A comedy in three acts by Paul Osborn. Produced by Dwight Deere Wiman at the Playhouse, New York, January 5, 1934.

Cast of characters—

Gertrude....................Jolyn Fabing
Constance Oakshot....................Ann Andrews

Carl Bridgewater....................................Hugh Rennie
Williamson...Henry Vincent
Judith Tiverton................................Alexandra Carlisle
Phyllis..Helen Brooks
Oliver Oliver................................Bretaigne Windust
Justin Stock....................................Thomas Chalmers
Acts I, II and III.—Room in Constance's Country House.
Staged by Auriol Lee; settings by Raymond Sovey.

Constance Oakshot, out of funds after having gone through three inheritances from three husbands, is hoping to marry her practically useless son Oliver to Phyllis Tiverton, who has money in her own right. Judith, Phyllis' mother, is resentfully opposed to the match. Oliver, being sensitive, refuses to be used to further his mother's conspiracy. Phyllis deliberately engages herself to another man. Oliver deliberately urges the match. In the end Phyllis and Oliver, in love all the time, come to an understanding and Constance snares herself an Ohio banker.

A DIVINE MOMENT

(9 performances)

A play in three acts by Robert Hare Powel. Produced by Peggy Fears at the Vanderbilt Theatre, New York, January 6, 1934.

Cast of characters—

Miss Attica Taylor............................Charlotte Granville
Martin...Royal Stout
Admiral Standish..............................William Ingersoll
Rodney Taylor.....................................Tom Douglas
Sarah..Dulce Fox
Boatswain Klatz, U.S.N..........................Allen Kearns
Cynthia Raeburn...................................Peggy Fears
Gordon Raeburn....................................Roy Gordon
Pinkie...Milly June
Frank Wardman...................................John Carmody
Footman..A. N. Andrews
Act I.—Miss Taylor's Room. Act II.—Her Garden. Act III.—A Room at Wardman's.
Staged by Rowland Leigh; settings by P. Dodd Ackerman.

Cynthia Raeburn, unhappily married, strolls from a Newport party into the garden of a neighboring home. Meets Rodney Taylor, a handsome young man who had previously rescued her from a dance with her drunken host. Indulges a moment of romance, loving and being loved. Rodney takes her to his aunt, the owner of the garden. The old lady assumes that Cynthia is Rodney's choice of a wife and sleeps contentedly. Cynthia is forced to confess her marriage to Rodney and return to the party and her husband.

DAYS WITHOUT END

(57 performances)

A modern miracle play in four acts by Eugene O'Neill. Produced by The Theatre Guild, Inc., at the Henry Miller Theatre, New York, January 8, 1934.

Cast of characters—

John.....Earle Larimore
Loving.....Stanley Ridges
William Elliott.....Richard Barbee
Father Baird.....Robert Loraine
Elsa.....Selena Royle
Margaret.....Caroline Newcombe
Lucy Hillman.....Ilka Chase
Herbert Stillwell.....Frederick Forrester
Nurse.....Margaret Swope

Act I.—John Loving's Office in the Offices of Elliott & Co., New York City. Act II.—Living-room of the Loving Duplex Apartment. Act III.—Scene 1—The Living-room. 2—John Loving's Study. Act IV.—Scene 1—The Study and Elsa's Bedroom. 2—Section of the Interior of a Church.

Staged by Philip Moeller; settings by Lee Simonson.

John Loving, chief protagonist of "Days Without End," is played by two actors, John representing the real man, Loving his other and baser self. John has become embittered with life and resentful of religion. He had prayed earnestly for help at the death of his parents and the prayers had gone unanswered. He had turned atheist. Having married he made a god of Love. His baser self led him into a betrayal of that love. Now he would write a novel and tell all. Outlining the story to his uncle, a priest, and his wife he includes the incident of his hero's betrayal of love. The wife recognizes the story and knows the truth. The shock throws her into a fever from which she is likely to die. In this last extremity John turns again to the church. His sin is forgiven, his baser self collapses at the foot of the cross, the wife recovers.

RE-ECHO

(5 performances)

A drama in three acts and a prologue by I. J. Golden. Produced by Carol Sax at the Forrest Theatre, New York, January 10, 1934.

Cast of characters—

Richard Lord.....Thurston Hall
Henry.....Leonard Mence
Harriet Lord.....Florence Walcott

Grace Manning.....................................Phyllis Povah
John Lord.....................................Harry Davenport
Tom Lord.....................................George Walcott
Bob Harrison.....................................Charles Holden
James Kavanaugh.....................................Walter D. Greene
James.....................................Chisholm Beach

Acts I, II and III.—Living-room of Richard Lord's Residence on Fifth Avenue, New York City.

Staged by Carol Sax; settings by Louis Kennel.

Richard Lord, one of the world's great bankers, had wanted to be a writer and a dreamer in his youth. His father whipped the notion out of his mind. Richard Lord, married and successful, takes the same course with his own son, Tom, when Tom wants to write poetry. In the end Richard Lord is a sadly defeated man, having lost two wives and one son through his selfish determination to have his own way.

COME OF AGE

(35 performances)

A dramatic fantasy in three acts by Clemence Dane, music by Richard Addinsell. Produced by Delos Chappell at the Maxine Elliott Theatre, New York, January 12, 1934.

Cast of characters—

Boy.....................................Stephen Haggard
Shadow of Death.....................................Frederick G. Lewis
Woman.....................................Judith Anderson
Man.....................................John W. Austin

Friends of the Woman.....................................{ Edna James, Clara Palmer, Dorothy Johnson, Mabel Gore, Virginia Volland, Katherine Tracy, Helen Wills, Alice Swanson, Malcolm Soltan, Jeremy Bowman, Judd Carrel, Harold Webster, Wheeler Dryden, Ralph Stuart }

Singer for the Woman.....................................Dorothy Johnson
River Music.....................................Helen Wills
Singer for the Boy.....................................Ralph Stuart
An Entertainer.....................................Muriel Rahn

Acts I, II and III.—In London.

Staged by Clemence Dane; settings by James Reynolds.

Thomas Chatterton, who died a suicide's death in 1770 to be immortalized later as one of the world's poetic geniuses, is here imagined to have struck a bargain with Death and to have been permitted to return to earth for a reprieve that shall give him time to come of age. On earth, in the London of the present, he meets and loves the mistress of a fellow tenant of the same flat building. His love flourishes until he is disgusted through an adventure with a cocktail party. His reprieve is ended. He returns to keep his compact with Death.

FALSE DREAMS, FAREWELL

(25 performances)

A drama in three acts and thirty-three scenes by Hugh Stange. Produced by Frank Merlin at the Little Theatre, New York, January 15, 1934.

Cast of characters—

Radio Voice	Kirk Ames
Mr. Sims	Walter O. Hill
Executive Officer Jones	Charles Quigley
Mr. Mackaye	Homer Barton
Miss Rhinebeck	Adora Andrewes
Dr. Hartley	Arthur Stenning
Ship News Reporters	John Frederik Elizabeth Weston James McColl
Camera-Man	Ben Delano
Joe	Frank Lawrence
A Deck Steward	Leslie Urbach
Murray Fineman	Dave Leonard
Irving Silvers	Henry Lase
Palmerly Harte	Edward Forbes
Josie	Shiela Trent
Edward Duncan	Clarence Derwent
Two Passengers	Thyrza Sturges Marianne Mosner
Masha	Natasha Boleslavsky
Ida Jarrett	Helen Raymond
Christopher Jarrett	Millard Mitchell
Daniel T. Moore	John Daly Murphy
Bishop Bliss	Royal Dana Tracy
Dr. Hayden	Eric Kalkhurst
Faith Baldy	Frieda Inescort
Eugene Cabot	Glenn Anders
Two Passengers	Ralph Nelson Dorothy Lowell
Steward Blythe	Harry Green
Bingham Baldy	Blaine Cordner
Joan Arden	Claudia Morgan
Eleanor Cabot	Lora Baxter
Captain Sackett	Clyde Fillmore
A Cabin Steward	Larry Regan
Radio Operator McBride	Neil McFee
Ship's Officer	Robert Burtt

Acs I, II and III.—On Board the S.S. "Atlantia."
Staged by Frank Merlin; settings by Arne Lundborg.

The S.S. "Atlantia," 80,000 tons, is sailing on her maiden voyage. Edward Duncan, president of the company owning the "Atlantia," is determined she shall break the crossing record by at least twelve hours. If she fails to do so the company, unable to float another loan, will be bankrupt. Captain Sackett, knowing the ship to have sprung certain plates on her trial trips, would refuse to attempt the record if he were not desperately in need of money. The "Atlantia" springs a leak and goes down carrying with it a varied assortment of passengers whose private lives and problems are revealed in a series of short dramatic sketches.

WEDNESDAY'S CHILD

(56 performances)

A drama in two acts and nine scenes by Leopold Atlas. Produced by Potter and Haight at the Longacre Theatre, New York, January 16, 1934.

Cast of characters—

Ray Phillips....................Walter N. Greaza
Kathryn Phillips....................Katharine Warren
Bobby Phillips....................Frank M. Thomas, Jr.
Lenny....................Robert Mayors
Herbert....................Stanton Bier
Georgie....................Joie Brown, Jr.
Joie....................Harry Clancy
Alfred....................Lester Lonergan, 3rd
Howard Benton....................Walter Gilbert
Mr. Proctor....................George Pembroke
Judge....................Harry Hanlon
Mr. Keyes....................Alfred Dalrymple
Clerk....................Leonard M. Barker
Carrie....................Sally Hodges
Louise....................Cele McLaughlin
Miss Chapman....................Mona Bruns
Dr. Stirling....................Wyrley Birch
Chic Nevins....................Richard Jack

Act I.—Scene 1—The Phillips Dining-room. 2—Corner of a Back Lot. 3—Phillips Sun Parlor. 4—Boardwalk Along the Sea. 5—Courtroom. Act II.—Scene 1—Benton Living-room. 2—Phillips Dining-room. 3—Phillips Sun Parlor. 4—Bobby's New Room.

Staged by H. C. Potter; settings by Tom Adrian Cracraft.

See page 317.

MAHOGANY HALL

(21 performances)

A drama in three acts and six scenes by Charles Robinson. Produced by John R. Sheppard, Jr., at the Bijou Theatre, New York, January 17, 1934.

Cast of characters—

Cassie....................Daisy Belmore
Eric....................John Lucas
Tangie....................Florence McGee
Diana....................Charlotte Andrews
The Professor....................Eduardo Ciannelli
Madame Paris....................Olga Baclanova

Steve....William Foran
Marge....Paula Bauersmith
Victoire....Chas. La Torre
Babette....Beatrice Pons
Dolores....Isis Brinn
Lialia....Frances Sage
Lighthouse....Cliff Hicks
Fitz....Wayne Nunn
The Major....Gordon Nelson
The Deacon....Charles Angelo
The Commissioner....Marion Green
Miss Hall....Ann Dere
Smith....H. H. McCollum
Hector....Arthur Griffen
Brown....Benedict MacQuarrie
Barnes....Anthony Blair
Jones....Erik Walz
Black....Mark Preston
Piano Tuner....William Dorbin

Acts I, II and III.—Mahogany Hall.
Staged by Eduardo Ciannelli; settings by Thomas Farrar.

Madame Paris, who has been the landlady of many famous bagnios the world over, finds herself in love with the professor who plays her piano in the house she has established in Washington, D. C. The professor, however, being a superior sort, cannot return the madame's love, in which disappointment she determines to give up Mahogany Hall and go back to Europe. Thus are the young ladies of her establishment released to follow those impulses toward a more normal life that many of them were denied so long as Mme. Paris was determined to continue the business.

AND BE MY LOVE

(4 performances)

A comedy in three acts by Lewis Galantiere and John Houseman. Produced by Maurice Colbourne and Barry Jones at the Ritz Theatre, New York, January 18, 1934.

Cast of characters—

Louise....Rita Vale
Lawrence Brooke....Barry Jones
George Barlow....Ronald Simpson
Maier....Maurice Colbourne
Mary....Virginia Tracy
David....Fred Forrest
Jane Barlow....Lily Cahill
Lypyate....Lambert Larking
Florence....Hancy Castle
Elsa Frost....Renee Gadd

Acts I and III.—Lawrence Brooke's Sitting-room. Act II.—Jane Barlow's Drawing-room.
Staged by Maurice Colbourne; settings by David Homan.

Lawrence Brooke, a Casanova of the teacups, is pursued by many women, including Jane Barlow. When he meets Jane's young niece, Elsa Frost, he finds one to whom his every glance is something less than devastating. With his campaign for Elsa's love a failure, Lawrence must be content with her promise that she may bring her pet dog to call on him after she is married.

JOHN BROWN

(2 performances)

An historical drama in three acts by Ronald Gow. Produced by George Abbott at the Ethel Barrymore Theatre, New York, January 22, 1934.

Cast of characters—

Annie Brown....................................Whitney Bourne
Mrs. John Brown....................................Alma Kruger
Ellen Brown....................................Edna Hagan
Owen Brown....................................Harry M. Cooke
Salmon Brown....................................Buford Armitage
Uncle Jeremiah....................................Harold Gould
Watson Brown....................................Robert Foulk
Bell....................................Betty Kendall
Oliver Brown....................................Oliver Barbour
Martha....................................Iris Whitney
John Brown....................................George Abbott
Shields Green....................................Walter Price
A Slave-Owner....................................Charles McClelland
John Kagi....................................John Emery
Stevens....................................Alfred Webster
A Sentry....................................J. Ascher Smith
T. W. Higginson....................................Herbert Yost
Frederick Douglass....................................Ernest R. Whitman
Colonel Lewis Washington....................................Tom Morgan
A Telegraph Operator....................................William Shea
A Virginia Militiaman....................................Eddie Acuff
J. P. Gallagher of the *New York Herald*....................................James Lane
Colonel Robert E. Lee....................................William Corbett

Act I.—John Brown's Home at North Elba, in the Adirondacks. Act II.—The Kennedy Farm in Maryland near the Virginia Border. Act III.—Scene 1—The Fire Engine Shed at Harper's Ferry on the Virginia Bank of the Potomac. 2—The Telegraph Office. 3—John Brown's Home at North Elba.

Staged by George Abbott; settings by Cirker and Robbins.

John Brown, home from the free state wars in Kansas, organizes the expedition into Virginia with the object of taking the government arsenal at Harper's Ferry, arming the Negroes and wiping out slavery in the South. He is taken by the federal forces under Col. Robert E. Lee and turned over to the civil authorities to be executed. The family hears of the failure of the enterprise and the hanging of old John while still carrying on at the farm in North Elba, N. Y.

NO MORE LADIES

(162 performances)

A comedy in three acts by A. E. Thomas. Produced by Lee Shubert at the Booth Theatre, New York, January 23, 1934.

Cast of characters—

Dickens....................John Bramall
Oliver Allen....................Bradley Cass
Mrs. Fanny Townsend....................Lucile Watson
Jacquette....................Miriam Battista
Mrs. Anderson Townsend....................Mary Sargent
Mr. Anderson Townsend....................Edward Fielding
Sheridan Warren....................Melvyn Douglas
Marcia Townsend....................Ruth Weston
Stafford....................Boyd Davis
James Salston....................Rex O'Malley
Diana....................Nancy Ryan
The Earl of Moulton....................Louis Hector
Teresa German....................Marcella Swanson

Act I.—New York Apartment of the Townsends. Acts II and III.—Living-room of the Warrens, Southampton, L. I.
Staged by Harry Wagstaff Gribble; settings by Watson Barratt.

See page 292.

MACKEREL SKIES

(23 performances)

A drama in two acts by John Haggart. Produced by George Bushar in association with John Tuerk at the Playhouse, New York, January 23, 1934.

Cast of characters—

Anna....................Florence Edney
Elizabeth....................Carol Stone
Hobson....................Glenn Coulter
Valentine Struthers....................Lillian Gahagan Corey
Sophie....................Cora Witherspoon
Elsa....................Violet Kemble Cooper
Max Schurman....................Max Figman
Timothy Lord....................John Griggs
David Gerard....................Charles Trowbridge
Mr. Kubeck....................Tom Powers

Acts I and II.—An Upstairs Sitting-room of the Gerard Mansion on Upper Fifth Avenue, New York.
Staged by John Roche; settings by Aline Bernstein.

Elsa Gerard had been the wife of an Austrian Prince and had taken as her lover a gifted peasant living on the estate. Later she had married an American broker who made it possible for her to try for a career as a singer. She had failed in this. When her daughter Elizabeth, the child of the peasant, grew to womanhood it was evident she had inherited a great voice from her father. Elsa, jealous for fear Elizabeth will enjoy the career her mother has missed, tries to prevent the girl's advance. The peasant father turns up as a wealthy wheat broker in Chicago and makes it possible for Elizabeth to gain her heart's desire, an appearance at the opera, and also the young man she loves, Timothy Lord.

BY YOUR LEAVE

(37 performances)

A comedy in three acts by Gladys Hurlbut and Emma Wells. Produced by Richard Aldrich and Alfred de Liagre, Jr., at the Morosco Theatre, New York, January 24, 1934.

Cast of characters—

Ellen Smith....................................Dorothy Gish
Mrs. Gretchell....................................Josephine Hull
Winifred....................................Esther Dale
Miss Whiffen....................................Elizabeth Bruce
Henry Smith....................................Howard Lindsay
Frances Gretchell....................................Cynthia Rogers
David Mackenzie....................................Kenneth MacKenna
Freddy....................................Ernest Glendinning
Andree....................................Elizabeth Love
1st Bell Boy....................................Henry Fox
2nd Bell Boy....................................Thomas Hayes

Acts I and III.—Living-room in the Home of the Henry Smiths in a Suburb of New York. Act II.—Scene 1—Hotel Bedroom in New York City. 2—Hotel Sitting-room in Another Hotel in New York City.

Staged by Alfred de Liagre, Jr.; settings by Jo Mielziner.

Henry Smith resents his approach toward middle age, and would disprove it. To his wife Ellen he proposes a week's vacation from their suburban home, each to take half the savings account and do whatever he or she wants to do, with no questions asked on the return home. Henry's week is devoted to a series of stag parties and one embarrassing adventure with an efficient Titian comforter sent by Lonely Hearts, Inc., at Henry's request. Ellen's week is devoted to a shopping spree and frequent teas with a handsome explorer. When the explorer pleads that they let romance take its course the last night Ellen agrees to stay and manages to satisfy Henry's troubled questioning later. The Smiths are content with their home and their years after that.

WHATEVER POSSESSED HER

(4 performances)

A farce in three acts by Hardwick Nevin. Produced by Raymond Moore at the Mansfield Theatre, New York, January 25, 1934.

Cast of characters—

Burchard Bangs....................................Pierre Watkin
Sellers..Stapleton Kent
Genevieve Trubee..................................Flora Campbell
Henry...Joseph Allen
Eddie..Percy Kilbride
Millicent Bangs.........................Catherine Calhoun Doucet
Phœnix Greggs......................................Richard Whorf
A Young Reporter...................................Philip Huston
Jerome Mortimer......................................Otto Hulett
May Moss..Constance McKay
Arthur Strong....................................Gordon Richards
Wiley...Frederic Forman
Mr. Hallett...................................George Henry Trader
Ted..Edward Ryan
Hastings McElway....................................Ronald Drew
His Secretary......................................Edward Fuller
Guests of the Theatre, Ushers, Firemen: Alice Dowd, Jacqueline Green, Betty Parsons, Caroline Allen, Dorothy Bayley, Barbara Heggie, Dorothy Adams, Ellen Spencer, Gertrude Augarde, Ruth Miller, Lois Scales, Peter Barrik, Lyn Howe, Richard Glyer, Richard Allen, Richard Dana, Charles Koren, Paul Ballantyne, Joan Barbee-Lee, Robert Warfield, John Kelsey, Harry Hutchinson, William Tobin.

Acts I and III.—Interior of a Barn on the Bangs' Estate. Act II. —Living-room of the Bangs' Household.

Staged by Arthur Sircom; settings by Eugene C. Fitsch.

Millicent Bangs, thinking to improve the culture of her own particular country side, decides to turn the Bangs barn into a theatre. The actors engaged arrive from New York a week too soon, rehearsals are confused and comic and the first performance distressful. Then Millicent Bangs decides to take a long rest from art, and her husband is greatly pleased.

THE JOYOUS SEASON

(16 performances)

A comedy in three acts by Philip Barry. Produced by Arthur Hopkins at the Belasco Theatre, New York, January 29, 1934.

Cast of characters—

Francis Battle......................................Eric Dressler
Theresa Farley Battle.................................Jane Wyatt
Martin Farley......................................Jerome Lawler
Patrick...Barry Macollum
Hugh Farley..Alan Campbell
Ross Farley..John Eldredge
Monica Farley...................................Florence Williams
John Farley.......................................Moffat Johnston
Edith Choate Farley.................................Mary Kennedy
Christina Farley.....................................Lillian Gish
Nora...Kate Mayhew
Sr. Aloysius..Mary Hone

Acts I, II and III.—Living-room of the Farley House on Beacon Street, Boston.

Staged by Arthur Hopkins; settings by Robert Edmond Jones.

The Farleys, an old Boston family, have left the ancestral farm, Good Ground, and are living in the Beacon Street district, which has become fashionable. Their Sister Christina, who went into the church when she was quite young, has been summoned to confer with the family regarding certain provisions in the paternal Farley's will giving her the choice of either property. Sister Christina, stopping off on one of her missions, finds the family beset by problems, mostly spiritual. After she has straightened out the marital difficulties of one sister, set a radical brother back in the path and saved another sister from a foolish act she goes back to the church, leaving the decision about the property to the spiritually rehabilitated family.

HOTEL ALIMONY

(16 performances)

A comedy adapted by A. W. Pezet from a farce by Adolf Philipp and Max Simon. Produced by Irving P. Franklin and Donald M. Stoner at the Royale Theatre, New York, January 29, 1934.

Cast of characters—

Kate Ryan....................Eve Farrell
Ni-Tong....................Peter Goo Chong
Jim Ryan....................John Henry McKee
Peter Thorpe....................James Shelburne
Roger Woods....................Robert Emmett Keane
Mildred Thorpe....................Nancy Evans
Mrs. Hopkins....................Edna Archer Crawford
Dorothy Fulton....................Marjorie Dille
A House Porter....................Frank Coletti
John Bromford 2nd....................Roland Bottomley
Arthur Nathan....................Sheldon Leonard
Jenkins....................Stanley De Wolfe
Mike....................Alf Helton
Sam Cohen....................Muni Diamond
Wilbur Warren....................Wylie Adams
Charles Dudley....................Norman Duggan
Al Gordon....................Bert Wilcox
Montague....................Denis Gurney
Jake Lippskovitch....................Martin Noble
William Collins....................Harrison Brockbank
Deputy Sheriff O'Connor....................Tom Dillon
Henry C. Carter....................Desmond Gallagher
Stella Gordon....................Jeanette Fox-Lee
Mary Saunders....................Winifred Law

Act I.—Scene 1—Living-room and Alcove Bedroom of Peter Thorpe's Greenwich Village Apartment. 2—Law Office of John Bromford 2nd. Act II.—Scenes 1 and 3—Warden's Office and Reception Room County Jail. 2—Prisoners' Recreation Room, County Jail. Act III.—Scene 1—Peter Thorpe's Apartment. 2 and 4—Warden's Office and Reception Room. 3—Prisoners' Recreation Room.

Staged by A. W. Pezet and Irving P. Franklin; settings by P. Dodd Ackerman.

Peter Thorpe, composer of musical comedies, agrees to a divorce from his wife Mildred and, because he is in funds at the time, submits to $300 weekly alimony. When his income fails he is slapped into the alimony jail. There he discovers a racket that includes the renting of private cells, the sale of various privileges, a poker game conducted by a professional gambler whose wife has him regularly committed and various other evils. Needing an arranger to help him with his music, Peter has an old pal framed so they may work together. Reforms are promised in the end.

AMERICAN—VERY EARLY

(7 performances)

A comedy in three acts by Florence Johns and Wilton Lackaye, Jr. Produced by Wilton Lackaye, Jr., at the Vanderbilt Theatre, New York, January 30, 1934.

Cast of characters—

Nippy Andrews....................................Lynn Beranger
Hub Tilson..Edward Favor
Winafred Proctor..................................Florence Johns
Victoria Buzzer...................................Harriet Sterling
Ezra Buzzer.......................................John Ravold
Sylvanus Sperry...................................Harry Tyler
Canary Twist......................................Edith Tachna
Tom Courtney......................................Alexander Clark
Birdsie Littlefield...............................Vincent York
Hulda...Georgette Spelvin
A Mother..Lulu Mae Hubbard
Her Little Boy....................................Bobby Hess
Annie McCall......................................Florence Auer
Mrs. Preston G. Polk..............................Marion Warring-Manley
F. Millard Hopewell...............................James Seeley
Lawrence Proctor..................................Grant Mills
Mrs. Mortemore Santly.............................Helen Royton
A Farmer..John P. Brawn
A Collector.......................................Jeanne De Me

Acts I, II and III.—Dining-room of "The Old Cadoo Place," Botsville, at the Foot of the Berkshires.

Staged by Wilton Lackaye, Jr.; settings by Nicholas Yellenti.

Nippy Andrews and Winafred Proctor go into the business of selling antiques in Connecticut. Trying to run an honest business they find themselves being tricked by the natives. Turning hard, Winafred makes up as a grandmother and Nippy poses as her granddaughter. They turn the tables on the natives and the snooty summer residents and make a success of the business. This wins Winafred a $10,000 bet with her husband, with whom she had quarreled over the question of her business ability.

ALL THE KING'S HORSES

(120 performances)

A romantic musical comedy in two acts by Frederick Herendeen; music by Edward A. Horan. Produced by Harry L. Cort and Charles H. Abramson by arrangement with E. Steuart-Tavant at the Shubert Theatre, New York, January 30, 1934.

Cast of characters—

Kessel...Robert O'Conner
Albert...Arthur F. Otto
A Patron.......................................Manart Kippen
Loli...Frances Thress
Baron Koritz...................................Frank Greene
King Rudolph of Langenstein....................Jack Edwards
Con Conley.....................................Andrew Tombes
Donald McArthur................................Guy Robertson
Sherry Shannon.................................Doris Patston
Joseph...Louis Morrell
Count Ergard Regitard Batthy...................Russell Hicks
Countess Putkammer.............................Betty Starbuck
Queen Erna of Langenstein......................Nancy McCord
A Mother.......................................Edna West
A Father.......................................Howard Morgan
A Spinster.....................................Blanche Lytell
Ladies in Waiting: Doris Anderson, Helen Ryan, Virginia Davies, Etna Ross, Gertrude Hogan, June Tempest, Joan Orner, Frances Thress, Naida Pahl, Mora Vordkin, Winnie Duncan, Dorothy Koster.
Peasants from the Southern Province: Frank Augustyn, Einar Holt, Leonard Rogall, Harold Freeman.

Act I.—Scene 1—Andre Kessel's Barber Shop. 2—In Front of the Palace. 3—A Room in the King's Quarters. 4—The Royal Bed Chamber. Act II.—Scene 1—The Morning Room in the Palace. 2—In Front of the Palace. 3—The Royal Gardens.

Staged by Jose Ruben; settings by Herbert Ward.

Donald McArthur, internationally popular film star, is touring Europe with his publicity agent, Con Conley. In the royal barber shop of Langenstein they meet King Rudolph, come to have his hair cut, and discover that without his chin whiskers Rudolph looks enough like Donald to be his twin brother. This gives the king an idea. He will go to Paris for a fortnight and leave Donald to reign secretly in his place. Donald accepts the job, not knowing that there is a Queen Erna who left the king on their wedding night and lives three hundred miles away. Donald, talking to his subjects over the radio, does a bit of crooning, which brings Erna to the palace to find out what has changed the king. She stays the fortnight, sings many duets and is very happy until Donald goes back to America.

A HAT, A COAT, A GLOVE

(13 performances)

A drama in three acts adapted by William A. Drake from the German of Wilhelm Speyer. Produced by Crosby Gaige and D. K. Weiskopf at the Selwyn Theatre, New York, January 31, 1934.

Cast of characters—

Jerry Hutchins....................Lester Vail
Ann Brewster....................Isabel Baring
A Man....................A. E. Matthews
Felicia Mitchell....................Nedda Harrigan
John Walters....................Philip Van Zandt
Secretary....................Helen Wynn
Robert Ross....................Boyd Irwin
Judge Breed....................George Alison
Court Attendant....................Charles G. Johnson
James Gardiner....................Horace Casselberry
Clerk....................George W. Williams
Court Stenographer....................Henry Brent
Henrietta C. Jones....................Claire Woodbury
Sergeant Whalen....................D. J. Carew
Tommy Harris....................Oscar Berlin

Act I.—Jerry Hutchins' Studio Apartment, New York City. Act II.—Private Office of John Walters. Act III.—Court of General Sessions.

Staged by Crosby Gaige and Robert C. Fischer; settings by Aline Bernstein.

Jerry Hutchins fishes Ann Brewster out of the East River the night she tried to commit suicide. Takes her to his rooms, keeps her the night, tries to interest her in living next day. Ann isn't interested. Jerry goes in search of help from his mistress, Felicia Mitchell. While he is gone Felicia's husband comes in search of Jerry, finds Ann trying to shoot herself, struggles for the revolver and Ann is accidentally killed. Jerry is arrested for the murder. Felicia pleads with her husband to defend her lover. He agrees on promise she will come back to him if the lover is freed. At the trial the husband, Robert Mitchell, is able to confound the jury by proving that a hat, coat and glove figuring in the evidence fit him quite as well as they fit Jerry. Jerry is acquitted. Felicia sticks to her bargain.

THEODORA, THE QUEAN

(5 performances)

A comedy in three acts by Jo Milward and J. Kerby Hawkes. Produced by Jo Graham at the Forrest Theatre, New York, January 31, 1934.

Cast of characters—

Crier....................Hitous Gray
Klytemnestra....................Lina Abarbanell
Ahgrah....................Harriet Freeborn
Chandra....................Sarat Lahiri
Cici....................Julia Colin
Tavianus....................Tom Fadden
Guard....................Robert Anderson
Hypatius....................Horace Braham
Antonina....................Carla Gloer
Hatu....................Rex Ingram
Theodora....................Elena Miramova
Belisarius....................Paul Everton
Paul....................Raymond Jones
Marcus....................Raymond Bramley
Father Sebastian....................Lester Alden
Justinian....................Minor Watson

Act I.—Scenes 1 and 3—Theodora's Dressing Room Beneath the Circus, Byzantium. 2—Dungeon Under the Royal Palace. Act II.—Upper Terrace of Theodora's House. Act III.—Theodora's Dressing Room.

Staged by Jo Graham; settings by Yellenti.

"Quean," meaning harlot, Theodora is the most desired of the ladies appearing in a circus in ancient Byzantium. She sells her favors for pearls and rubies until she meets Justinian, who is in a fair way to become Emperor. For Justinian, Theodora decides to lead practically a virtuous life. Then Prince Hypatius plots to seize the throne and offers to make Theodora Empress if she will give Justinian what Mae West might describe as the boot. Theodora sticks to Justinian.

THE WIND AND THE RAIN

(119 performances)

A drama in three acts by Merton Hodge. Produced by George Kondolf and Walter Hart at the Ritz Theatre, New York, February 1, 1934.

Cast of characters—

Anne Hargraves....................Rose Hobart
Mrs. McFie....................Mildred Natwick
Gilbert Raymond....................Alexander Archdale
John Williams....................Lowell Gilmore
Charles Tritton....................Frank Lawton
Paul Duhamel....................Edward Raquello
Jill Mannering....................June Blossom
Roger Cole....................Charles Campbell
Peter Morgan....................Albert Whitley

Acts I, II and III.—Students' Study at Mrs. McFie's in Edinburgh.

Staged by Walter Hart; settings by Philip Gelb.

Charles Tritton arrives at Edinburgh for five years at the university from which to get his medical degree. In London he has left Jill, his fiancée, and his mother, for both of whom he is very homesick. In Edinburgh he meets Anne Hargreaves who comes to take the place of both mother and sweetheart in Charles' life. At the end of the five years Charles finds that he cannot go on without Anne. He tells Jill so in London and goes back to Edinburgh to get Anne.

BIOGRAPHY

(First engagement 267. Return 16. Total 283)

A comedy in three acts by S. N. Behrman. Return engagement presented by The Theatre Guild, Inc., at the Ambassador Theatre, New York, February 5, 1934.

Cast of characters—

Richard Kurt....................................Shepperd Strudwick
Minnie....................................Josephine Deffry
Melchior Feydak....................................Arnold Korff
Marion Froude....................................Ina Claire
Leander Nolan....................................Jay Fassett
Warwick Wilson....................................Norman Stuart
Orrin Kinnicott....................................Charles Richman
Slade Kinnicott....................................Gertrude Flynn

Acts I, II and III.—Marion Froude's Studio in New York City.
Staged by Philip Moeller; settings by Jo Mielziner.

See "Best Plays of 1932-33."

NO QUESTIONS ASKED

(16 performances)

A comedy in three acts by Anne Morrison Chapin. Produced by John Golden at the Masque Theatre, New York, February 5, 1934.

Cast of characters—

Evelyn....................................Emma Bunting
Noel Parker....................................Barbara Robbins
Richard Gorham....................................Milo Boulton
Sonny Raeburn....................................Ross Alexander
Pet Walsh....................................Spring Byington
Mary....................................Barna Ostertag
Willie Parker....................................Charles Lawrence
Ernie Dulaney....................................Brian Donlevy
Harriet Wells....................................Margery Garrett
Miss Kubec....................................Dorothy Vernon
Dr. King....................................Joseph King
Mrs. Gorham....................................Kate McComb

Act I.—Scene 1—A Staten Island Ferry. 2—Sonny Raeburn's Penthouse, Park Avenue, New York. Acts II and III.—The Penthouse.

Staged by John Golden and Edward Goodman; settings by P. Dodd Ackerman.

Noel Parker, having quarreled with her lover, Richard Gorham, because he refuses to leave his mother and marry her, tries to throw herself off a Staten Island ferry boat. She is pulled back by Sonny Raeburn, a rich young alcoholic of Park Avenue. Sonny takes Noel to a few night clubs to cheer her up and next day they are married. Three months later Sonny has quit drinking and Noel knows she is going to have Richard Gorham's baby. When Gorham and his mother pester Noel, Sonny learns the truth, goes back to the drink, and in a struggle for a revolver is shot in the arm. Sober again, Sonny asks Noel to stay on as his wife and no questions asked.

AFTER SUCH PLEASURES

(23 performances)

A series of comedy vignettes derived from Dorothy Parker's book of the same name by Edward F. Gardner. Produced by A. L. Jones at the Bijou Theatre, New York, February 7, 1934.

Principals engaged—

Shirley Booth
Enid Markey
Ackland Power
Felicia Sorel
Henriette Caperton
Mary Farrell
Blossom McDonald
Don Shelton
Lea Penman
Al and Lee Reiser
Taylor Gordon
Vernon Biddle
Kathleen Chase

Vignettes.—1—A Young Lady from Paris. Dusk Before Fireworks. Here We Are. 2—Impressions of a Supper Club. 3—You Were Perfectly Fine. Glory in the Daytime. The Mantle of Whistler.

Staged by Edward F. Gardner.

BROOMSTICKS, AMEN!

(41 performances)

A drama in three acts by Elmer Greensfelder. Produced by Thomas Kilpatrick at the Little Theatre, New York, February 9, 1934.

Cast of characters—

Herman Hofnagel....Byron McGrath
Crista Hofnagel....Helen Huberth
Frieda Sulzbach....Jane Seymour
Minna Hofnagel....Jean Adair
Emil Hofnagel....William Von Schoeller
Otto Strumpkopf....Victor Kilian
Rika Uffelman....Margaret Mullen
Vincent Lambert....K. Elmo Lowe

Gansdilliger....................................Jules Epailly
Acts I, II and III.—Living-room of the Hofnagels' Cottage in Pennhimmel, a "Pennsylvania-Dutch" Village.
Staged by Arthur J. Beckhard; settings by Tom Adrian Cracraft.

Emil Hofnagel is a leading hex doctor of Pennhimmel, Pa., and a power in a community that is still devoted to the pow-wow practitioners. Crista Hofnagel, his daughter, marries Vincent Lambert, the young medical student who seduced her, and brings him to the Hofnagel home to start his practice. Emil hates doctors, believing them agents of the devil. When Crista's child is a few months old it is seized with a quinsy for which its father would inject anti-toxin. Emil, convinced by signs that his son-in-law has bewitched the house, shoots him in the arm to prevent his treating the baby. The baby dies and Emil is taken in charge by the state's attorney for questioning. For Crista's sake the young doctor decides to stay on and continue his fight against the hexers.

SING AND WHISTLE

(74 performances)

A comedy in three acts by Milton Herbert Gropper. Produced by Gropper and Truex at the Fulton Theatre, New York, February 10, 1934.

Cast of characters—

Sylvia Jillson....................................Sylvia Field
Frank Jillson....................................Ernest Truex
Carole Dickens....................................Dorothy Mathews
Hugo Dickens....................................Donald Macdonald
Acts I, II and III.—Jillsons' Apartment.
Staged by Ernest Truex; settings by Cleon Throckmorton.

Frank Jillson was sweet on Carole Dickens before she married Hugo. Sylvia Jillson is still a little jealous of Carole and Hugo Dickens is so fed up with hearing Frank Jillson's virtues cited that he purposes to lay the Jillson ghost once for all. The Dickenses spend a week end with the Jillsons. Hugo Dickens and Sylvia Jillson deliberately leave the suspected pair together. Frank and Carole share a bottle of brandy and a Murphy bed between them, but not until after the brandy has made them so drowsy the only thing they can think of is sleep. Hugo and Sylvia come back from the movies to find Frank and Carole cured of whatever it was that ailed them.

A SUCCESSFUL CALAMITY

A comedy in two acts by Clare Kummer. Revived by Paul Gilmore at the Cherry Lane Theatre, New York, October 12, 1933.

Cast of characters—

Henry Wilton, a millionaire who longs to spend a quiet evening at home....Paul Gilmore
Emma Wilton, his young second wife....Virginia Gilmore
Marguerite, his daughter....Marjorie Andre
Eddie, his son....James Canty
George Struthers, Marguerite's fiancé....Tom Dunne
Clarence Rivers, another fiancé....Harry Forbes
Julia Parkington, Eddie's fiancée....Julia Johnson
Connors, the butler....William Galloway
Pietro Rafaelo, an Italian portrait painter....Earle Tuttle
Dr. Brodie, the family physician....Leroy Miller
John Belden, Wilton's partner....Alexander Speight
Albertine, Mrs. Wilton's maid....Marie Chiquet
Acts I and II.—Living-room in Mr. Wilton's Home, New York.
Staged by Paul Gilmore.

Mr. Gilmore and his daughter Virginia have conducted a season of revivals and new play experiments at the Cherry Lane Theatre, tucked away in a cozy corner of Greenwich Village, for five years, playing seven nights a week, summer and winter. The current season has been devoted to two plays. "Strictly Dishonorable" was revived October 3 and played until February 11. February 12 "A Successful Calamity" took its place and was played through the remainder of the season. This Kummer comedy, relating the ruse of a millionaire who pretended to be broke to test the loyalty of his family, was originally produced by Arthur Hopkins in 1917, at the Booth Theatre, New York, with William Gillette as Henry Wilton and Estelle Winwood playing his wife, Emma.

THE SHINING HOUR

(121 performances)

A drama in three acts by Keith Winter. Produced by Max Gordon at the Booth Theatre, New York, February 13, 1934.

Cast of characters—

Judy Linden....Adrianne Allen
Hannah Linden....Marjorie Fielding
Henry Linden....Cyril Raymond
Mickey Linden....Derek Williams
Mariella Linden....Gladys Cooper
David Linden....Raymond Massey
Acts I, II and III.—Living-room in Elizabethen Farmhouse in Yorkshire.
Staged by Raymond Massey; settings by Aubrey Hammond.

See page 352.

RICHARD OF BORDEAUX

(38 performances)

A tragedy in two parts by Gordon Daviot (Agnes Mackintosh). Produced by Dennis King and William Mollison at the Empire Theatre, New York, February 14, 1934.

Cast of characters—

A Page, Maudelyn	Andrew Cruickshank
Another Page	Jack Benwell
Richard II	Dennis King
Anne of Bohemia, his Queen	Margaret Vines
Duke of Gloucester, Thomas of Woodstock	Hugh Buckler
Duke of Lancaster, John of Gaunt	Charles Bryant
Sir Simon Burley	A. G. Andrews
Duke of York	Alexander Frank
Michael de la Pole	Lionel Hogarth
Earl of Arundel	Montagu Love
Robert de Vere, Earl of Oxford	Francis Lister
Mary Bohun, Countess of Derby	Olive Reeves Smith
Agnes Launcekron	Elizabeth Cerf
Henry, Earl of Derby, Bolingbroke	Henry Mollison
Thomas Mowbray, Earl of Nottingham	John Buckler
Sir John Montague	Charles Romano
John Maudelyn	Andrew Cruickshank
Edward, Earl of Rutland, Aumerle	Michael Pearman
A Waiting Woman	Virginia Pierce
Thomas Arundel, Archbishop of Canterbury	Cyril Chadwick
First Page	Jack Benwell
Second Page	Everett Ripley
Lord Derby's Page	Charles Bellin
Doctor	Milano Tilden

Part I.—Scene 1—A Corridor in the Royal Palace at Westminster. 2—The Council Chamber in the Palace. 3—A Room in the Palace. 4—A Pavilion in the Garden of the Royal Palace at Eltham. 5—A Room in the Tower of London. Part II.—Scenes 1 and 2—A Room in the Royal Palace of Sheen. 3—A Gallery Overlooking the Great Hall at Westminster. 4—A Room in the Lodgings of the Earl of Derby in Paris. 5—Courtyard of Conway Castle. 6—A Room in the Tower of London.

Staged by William Mollison; settings by P. Dodd Ackerman.

Richard II, in his nineteenth year, is rebelling earnestly against the domination of his uncle guardians, particularly that of the Duke of Gloucester. Richard, being an effeminate youth of ideals strange to the fighting British, would spend the treasury on tournaments at home rather than on foreign wars. He is favored in this by his wife, the gentle Anne of Bohemia, and his best friend, Robert de Vere. The nobles beat Richard and his ideals down. Then for a time his personal popularity and honesty of purpose wins him standing with the people. He is revenged on his enemies until, Anne dead of the plague, and Robert de Vere dead in exile, Richard overplays his luck by confiscating the Lancastrian estates and is forced into abdication, the crown going to Henry, Earl of Derby.

QUEER PEOPLE

(12 performances)

A comedy in three acts by John Floyd dramatized from a novel by Carroll and Garrett Graham. Produced by Galen Bogue at the National Theatre, New York, February 15, 1934.

Cast of characters—

John Grew....................................Willard Dashiell
Mrs. Grew....................................Clara Palmer
Eunice Stair, "Miss Mississippi"....................Colleen Cooper
Edward Worth....................................Frank Allworth
Rosie....................................Sylvia Manners
Gladys....................................Ruth Lee
Bellboy....................................James Fallon
Theodore Anthony White, "Whitey"....................Hal Skelly
Jane Wilson....................................Gladys George
Henry McGinnis....................................Frank Otto
Frank Carson....................................Dwight Frye
Johnny Rocco....................................Walter Fenner
Ricardo Roque...................................."Peppy" D'Albrew
Mandu....................................Frank de Silva
Gilbert Vance....................................Arthur Pierson
Joe Greet....................................Leonard Lord
"Peanuts" Oliver....................................Milly June
Milton Hoffberger....................................Lawrence Keating
Albert Blynn....................................William Roselle
Louise Bagshaw....................................Edna Mears
Dorothy Irving....................................Helen Claire
Monica Mercedes....................................Kay Carlin
Reatha Clore....................................Nita Naldi
Bartender....................................Wesley Givens
Sammy Schmaltz....................................Jerry Hausner
"Pop" Schmaltz....................................Harry Vokes
Ruth Schmaltz....................................Marga Herden
Fanny....................................Billie Kemp
Madame Frankie Lee....................................Flavia Arcaro
Sol Snifkin ....Herbert Heywood
Mr. Pappadoulous....................................J. Arthur Young
Fanna Wong Yong....................................Ming Soy
A Policeman....................................Frank Allworth
A Policeman....................................W. W. Shuttleworth
Turnkey....................................James Levers
Sheriff....................................Joseph Burton
Brady....................................Charles O'Connor
A Hotel Porter....................................Walter Kevan

Act I.—Scene 1—Observation Platform of the Santa Fe Train "The Chief" Enroute West. 2—Jane Wilson's Bedroom at the Hotel Major in Hollywood. 3—Living Room of Gilbert Vance's Home in Hollywood. Act II.—Scene 1—The Bar in the Banquet Hall of the Ambassador Hotel, Los Angeles. 2—The Banquet Hall of the Ambassador Hotel, Los Angeles. 3—Reception Room of Madame Frankie Lee's Studio. 4—The Patio of Whitey and Jane's Beach House, Santa Monica, California. Act III.—Scene 1—Whitey's Cell in the Los Angeles County Jail. 2—Jane Wilson's Bedroom at the Hotel Major in Hollywood. 3—Observation Platform of "The Chief" Enroute East.

Staged by Melville Burke; settings by P. Dodd Ackerman.

Theodore Anthony White, a newspaper man weakened by publicity, tries to save Dorothy Irving from the pawing embraces of Albert Blynn, lecherous motion picture director, and fails. His further adventures include a succession of souses from most of which he is rescued by Jane Wilson, a tough girl but in love with "Whitey," the bum.

LEGAL MURDER

(7 performances)

A melodrama in three acts by Dennis Donoghue. Produced by A. J. Allen Productions at the President Theatre, New York, February 15, 1934.

Cast of characters—

Rastus Johnson.......................................Baby Kid
Ben.......................................Rudolph Europe
Med.......................................Maxwell Jones
Scotty.......................................Glen McKay
Dixie Mary.......................................Marian McLaughlin
Joe Green.......................................William Clifford
Paul Claver.......................................Richard Freye
June.......................................Marjorie Warfield
Ma Jackson.......................................Aimee Leslie
Sam Jackson.......................................Zeb Jones
Roy.......................................Alfonzo Ashley
Smitty.......................................Earl Pillard
Ned.......................................Alonzo Settles
Liza.......................................Betty Jennings
Rev. Daniels.......................................Hayes Pryor
Frog.......................................Robert Lee
Judge.......................................Burt Cartwright
Defense Attorney.......................................David Krotchman
Prosecuting Attorney.......................................W. E. Triplett

Acts I, II and III.—In a Southern State.
Staged by S. Jay Kaufman.

In this version of the Scottsboro case the nine colored boys are first shown as happy neighbors who decide to go to Chicago in search of a job as radio singers. They hop a freight car. Soon their car is invaded by two white girls and two white men. One white man pulls a gun and orders the colored boys off the train. The boys rush the white men, knocking them out. The girls are unharmed. Next train stop a sheriff appears and the boys are arrested. The tougher of the two girls invents a wild story of the colored boys' attack. Follows the trial in which the first boy charged with rape and his Jewish New York attorney are made sport of by both a biased court and a biased populace.

FOUR SAINTS IN THREE ACTS

(First engagement 32. Return, 16. Total 48)

An opera in four acts by Gertrude Stein; music by Virgil Thomson. Produced by Harry Moses at the 44th Street Theatre, New York, February 20, 1934.

Cast of characters—

Commere....................................Altonell Hines
Compere....................................Abner Dorsey
St. Theresa I..........................Beatrice Robinson-Wayne
St. Theresa II.................................Bruce Howard
St. Ignatius...............................Edward Matthews
St. Chavez.......................................John Diggs
St. Settlement..........................Bertha Fitzhugh Baker
St. Ferdinand..............................Leonard Franklin
St. Plan...............................Randolph Robinson
St. Stephen......................................David Bethe
St. Cecilia......................................Kitty Mason
St. Giuseppe..............................Thomas Anderson
St. Anselmo...............................Charles Spinnard
St. Sara..................................Marguerite Perry
St. Bernardine................................Flossie Roberts
St. Absalon...................................Edward Batten
St. Answers..................................Florence Hester
St. Eustace...................................George Timber

Male Saints: Harold Des Verney, William Holland, Cecil Murray, William O'Neill, Paul Smellie, Andrew Taylor.

Female Saints: Charlotte Alford, Dorothy Bronson, Josephine Gray, Lena Halsey, Sadie McGill, Assotta Marshall, Olga Maillard, Cordelia Patterson, Jessie Swan, Eva Vaughn, Alma Dickson.

Dancers: Card Lynn Baker, Elizabeth Dickerson, Mable Hart, Floyd Miller, Maxwell Baird, Billie Smith.

Prelude—A Narrative of Prepare for Saints. Act I.—Avila: St. Theresa Half Indoors and Half Out of Doors. (First Entr'acte.) Act II.—Might It Be Mountains If It Were Not Barcelona. (Second Entr'acte.) Act III.—Barcelona: St. Ignatius and One of Two Literally. Act IV.—The Saints and Sisters Reassembled and Reënacting Why They Went Away to Stay.

Staged by John Houseman; settings by Florine Stettheimer and Kate Drain Lawson; chorus trained by Eva Jessye. Music conductor, Alexander Smallens.

An unintelligible libretto set to a pleasant musical score, sung and spoken by a colored cast in a cellophane setting representing a visionary Spain.

THEY SHALL NOT DIE

(62 performances)

A drama in three acts by John Wexley. Produced by The Theatre Guild at the Royale Theatre, New York, February 21, 1934.

Cast of characters—

Mr. Lawrence..............................Carroll Ashburn
Cooley...William Lynn
Henderson..................................John L. Kearney
Red...Tom Ewell
St. Louis Kid.................................Fred Herrick
Blackie.....................................Frank Woodruff
Sheriff Wren................................Ralph Theadore
Jeff Vivian.................................Ralph Sanford
Lewis Collins......................................Bob Ross
Jackson.................................C. Ellsworth Smith
Charley..................................George C. Mantell
Hillary..Derek Trent
Smith..Hugh Rennie

Walter Colton....................................William Norton
Virginia Ross....................................Linda Watkins
Lucy Wells....................................Ruth Gordon
Luther Blakely....................................Hale Norcross
Benson Allen....................................L. M. Hurdle
Roberts....................................George R. Hayes
Purcell....................................Alfred Brown
Walters....................................Bryant Hall
Warner....................................Grafton Trew
Heywood Parsons....................................Al Stokes
Roy Wood....................................Allan Vaughan
Andy Wood....................................Joseph Scott
Morris....................................Joseph Smalls
Moore....................................Frank Wilson
Killian....................................Eddie Hodge
Oliver Tulley....................................Robert Thomsen
Doctor Thomas....................................George Christie
Captain Kennedy....................................Frederick Persson
Sergeant Ogden....................................Ross Forrester
Mrs. Wells....................................Helen Westley
Tommy....................................Edward Ryan, Jr.
Young Man....................................Tom Ewell
Russell Evans....................................Dean Jagger
Guard....................................James Young
Principal Keeper....................................Charles Henderson
Lowery....................................Carroll Ashburn
William Treadwell....................................Will Jackson
Rev. Wendell Jackson....................................Fred Miller
Warden Jeffries....................................Leo Curley
Rokoff....................................Louis John Latzer
Att'y General Cheney....................................St. Clair Bayfield
2nd Guard....................................Robert Porterfield
Mrs. Parsons....................................Teddy Browne
Mr. Parsons....................................K. Browne Cooke
Mrs. Wood....................................Georgia Burke
Mrs. Purcell....................................Cecil Scott
Mr. Purcell....................................Robert J. Lawrence
Mrs. Williams....................................Catherine Francis
Sheriff Nelson....................................Erskine Sanford
Constable....................................Albert West
Nathan G. Rubin....................................Claude Rains
Johnny....................................Hugh Rennie
Mr. Harrison....................................Frank Wilson
Frank Travers....................................Anthony Douglas Gregory
Judge....................................Thurston Hall
Doctor Watson....................................Robert J. Lawrence
Attorney-General Dade....................................Ben Smith
Jury Commissioner Crocker....................................Ralph Sanford
Clerk of Court....................................Albert West
Seth Robbins....................................Harry Hermsen
Circuit Solicitor Slade....................................Carl Eckstrom
Lynching Mob, White Hoboes, Soldiers, Court Guards, etc.: Irene Bevans, Orrin Burke, George A. Cameron, Angus Duncan, Jack Flynn, Vallejo Gantner, Marshall Hale, Eddie Hodge, Alexander Jones, William H. Malone, Edward Mann, George C. Mantell, Grace Mills, Frank Phillips, Robert D. Phillips, Dorothy E. Ryan, Phil S. Michaels, Jack Stone, Jerome Sylvon, Ben Vivian, Charles Wellesley, John Wheeler, Betty Oakwood, George Carroll.

Prologue and Epilogue—Somewhere in a Southern State. Act I.—Jail in Cookesville, Alabama. Act II.—Scenes 1 and 3—Home of Lucy Wells in Humbolt, Alabama. 2—Negro Death-Cell in Pembroke Prison, Alabama. Act III.—Scene 1—Offices of Nathan G. Rubin in New York City. 2—Court-Room in Dexter, Alabama.

Staged by Philip Moeller; settings by Lee Simonson.

See page 203.

* DODSWORTH

(131 performances)

A comedy in three acts by Sidney Howard based on a novel by Sinclair Lewis. Produced by Max Gordon at the Shubert Theatre, New York, February 24, 1934.

Cast of characters—

Samuel Dodsworth....Walter Huston
A Sales Manager....Arthur Uttry
A Publicity Man....Nolan Leary
A Secretary....Alice Griswold
Henry E. Hazzard....Charles Halton
Fran Dodsworth....Fay Bainter
Thomas J. Pearson, called "Tubby"....Harlan Briggs
Mrs. Pearson, called "Matey"....Ethel Jackson
Emily McKee....Ethel Hampton
Harry McKee....Merwin Williams
A Jewish Gentleman....Nick Adams
A Second Jewish Gentleman....William Morris
Clyde Lockert....John Williams
An American Lady....Beatrice Maude
A Second American Lady....Marie Falls
An American....Bert Gardner
His Wife....Lucille Fenton
Edith Cortright....Nan Sunderland
A Steward....Charles Christensen
A Second Steward....Ivan Miller
A Barman....Jay Wilson
A. B. Hurd....Hal K. Dawson
Renee de Penable....Leonore Harris
Arnold Israel....Frederic Worlock
Kurt von Obersdorf....Kent Smith
A Cashier....J. H. Kingsberry
An American Mother....Maric Falls
Her Daughter....Betty Van Auken
An American Tourist....Frank W. Taylor
His Wife....Myrtle Tannehill
"Junior," His Son....Charles Powers
Information Clerk....Ralph Simone
A Second American Tourist....Marie Mallon
Baroness von Obersdorf....Marie Ouspenskaya
Teresa....Flora Fransioli

Act I.—Scene 1—Office of President of Revelation Motor Company, Zenith. 2—Dodsworth's Library. 3—Smoke Room of S.S. "Ultima." 4—Dodsworth Suite at the Ritz, London. Act II.—Scene 1—Dodsworth Suite at the Ritz, Paris. 2—Office of President of Revelation Motor Company. 3—Garden of Villa Doree, Montreaux. 4—Dodsworth's Library, Zenith. 5—Dodsworth Suite at the Ritz, Paris. Act III.—Scenes 1 and 3—Dodsworth Suite at the Adlon, Berlin. 2—Office of the American Express Company, Naples. 4—Villa Cortright at Posilipo, Naples. 5—Smoke Room of S.S. "Ultima," Bremen.

Staged by Robert Sinclair; settings by Jo Mielziner.

See page 115.

RAGGED ARMY

(2 performances)

A drama in three acts by Beulah Marie Dix and Bertram Millhauser. Produced by Crosby Gaige at the Selwyn Theatre, New York, February 26, 1934.

Cast of characters—

Harriett Stockwell..............................Alice Ann Baker
Cordelia Page..............................Irby Marshal
Priscilla Moody..............................Lalive Brownell
Frances Lovejoy..............................Ann Dere
Hannah..............................Mathilde Baring
Tim Page..............................Johnny Downs
Emma Hallowell..............................Justine Wayne
Alethea Page..............................Emily Lowry
William Page..............................Thomas Chalmers
Pat Halloran..............................Roy Roberts
Henry Stockwell..............................Lee Baker
Geoffrey Carver..............................Lloyd Nolan
James Tripp..............................Edwin Vickery
Eliot Lovejoy..............................Fleming Ward
Edward Hallowell..............................Roy Gordon
Nick Rubini..............................Byron Shores
Sandy McGregor..............................Richard Bartel
Nathan Littlefield..............................Forrest Taylor
Malachi Tripp..............................Philip Van Zant
Etienne D'Aulney..............................William Dorbin

Acts I, II and III.—Living Room in Ancestral Home of the Pages, an Old Colonial Family in Dunbury, a New England Town.
Staged by Crosby Gaige; settings by Raymond Sovey.

The William Pages, mill owners of Dunbury, Mass., are organizing a pageant in celebration of the battle of Dunbury and the part taken therein by their illustrious ancestors of Washington's army. In Dunbury the Page millhands are on strike and threatening to organize a parade of protest to break up the pageant. Coming from New York is Geoffrey Carver, direct descendant of General Timothy Page of the Continentals. Carver is to impersonate his famous ancestor. The imaginations of the younger Pages, Tim and Alethea, are fired by the approach of Carver. They see him coming at the head of a detachment of Washington's ragtag and bobtail Continentals risen from their graves in the Dunbury burying ground. Into the Page living room he bursts in a thunderstorm and calls all his pretty ancestors to account. His heart is with the "bohunks" striking in the town and not with these Sons and Daughters of the Revolution. The visitation strengthens the younger generation's resolve to do something about the strike.

WHEN IN ROME

(7 performances)

A farce comedy in three acts by Austin Major. Produced by George Smithfield and Austin Major at the 49th Street Theatre, New York, February 27, 1934.

Cast of characters—

Fabius .... Herbert Weber
Spartacus .... Laurence O'Sullivan
Abraham .... Lee Sanford
Petronius .... Frank Jaquet
Aurelia .... Mabel Kroman
Remus .... Robert Toms
Catiline .... Kenneth Daigneau
Fulvia .... Charlotte Reynolds
Cicero .... C. Edwin Brandt
Marcellus .... Frank Rothe
Lydia .... Louise Latimer
Augustus .... Garland Kerr
Tiberius .... Maurice Freeman
Act I.—The Forum. Acts II and III.—Catiline's Club.
Staged by Austin Major; settings by Nicholas Yellenti.

Catiline, grown strong and brutal on the meats of political power on which he feeds, would Tammanyize Rome, defy Cicero, the orator, and all decent citizens, elope with Lydia, the vestal virgin, and in effect tell the world to go hang. But in the end Cicero is able to organize the forces of fusion and comparative decency and put Catiline temporarily in his place.

TOO MUCH PARTY

(8 performances)

A farce comedy in three acts by Hiram Sherman. Produced by the Metropolitan Players at the Masque Theatre, New York, March 5, 1934.

Cast of characters—

Hagar .... Warda Howard
Brian Smith .... Philip Truex
Judy .... Janet McLeay
Lettice .... Maude Richmond
Kenneth .... Reed McClellan
Falba Twentyman .... Mady Correll
Edith Barstow .... Claire Grenville
Daniel .... Pierre Watkin
Agnes .... Viola Swayne
Judge Everett .... George Alison
Acts I, II and III.—Home of Daniel Dean in a Middle Western City.
Staged by William B. Friedlander.

Lettice Dean, shallow and ambitious and socially dominated by Edith Barstow, is campaigning for the position of probationary officer in her district. During her activities as a social worker her daughter Judy is seduced, her son Kenneth takes up forging checks in a speakeasy and her husband Daniel loses interest in his home. Falba Twentyman, on the trail of Kenneth, takes charge of the situation and brings the family through, marrying Kenneth.

YELLOW JACK

(79 performances)

A dramatic history in one act by Sidney Howard in collaboration with Paul de Kruif. Produced by Guthrie McClintic at the Martin Beck Theatre, New York, March 6, 1934.

Cast of characters—

NEW YORK: Today

Harkness....Robert Shayne
A Laboratory Assistant....Jock Munro

LONDON: January, 1929

Stackpoole....Geoffrey Kerr
An Official of the Kenya Colony Government....Colin Hunter
A Major of the Royal Air Force....Francis Compton
Laboratory Assistants....Bernard Jukes, Lloyd Gough
Kim....Kim

WEST AFRICA: June, 1927

Chambang, a Native Laboratory Assistant....Jack Carr
Adrian Stokes, of the West African Yellow Fever Commission, Rockefeller Foundation....Charles Gerard
Kraemer } of the Rockefeller Foundation { Wylie Adams
Harkness } { Robert Shayne

CUBA: Summer and Fall of 1900

O'Hara } Privates, M.C., U. S. A. { James Stewart
McClelland } { Edward Acuff
Busch } { Samuel Levene
Brinkerhof } { Myron McCormick
Miss Blake, Special Nurse in Charge of the Yellow Fever Ward....Katherine Wilson
Orderlies.... { Clyde Walters
{ Frank Stringfellow
Walter Reed, Major, M.C., U. S. A. ....John Miltern
Members of the American Yellow Fever Commission in Cuba:
James Carroll....Barton MacLane
Aristides Agramonte....Eduardo Ciannelli
Jesse W. Lazear....Robert Keith
Colonel Tory, of the Marine Hospital Corps....Richie Ling
William Crawford Gorgas, Major, M.C., U. S. A....George Nash
Major Cartwright....Robert Shayne
Roger P. Ames, Asst. Surgeon, M.C., U. S. A....Harold Hoffat
Dr. Carlos Finlay....Whitford Kane
William H. Dean, Private, U. S. A....Millard Mitchell
An Army Chaplain....Lloyd Gough
A Commissary Sergeant....Wylie Adams
Soldiers, Orderlies, Laboratory Assistants, Doctors, etc.

LONDON: September, 1929

Stackpoole....Geoffrey Kerr

A Laboratory Assistant............................Bernard Jukes
Staged by Guthrie McClintic; settings by Jo Mielziner.

A dramatic transcription of the record contained in the chapter devoted to Walter Reed and the researches by which he eventually located the fever-breeding mosquito in Cuba, taken from Paul de Kruif's "The Microbe Hunters." The action, beginning in London, 1929, and in South Africa, 1927, traces the work of the scientists, Stackpoole and Harkness, tying it in with the work of Reed in Cuba, and the heroic sacrifices of his loyal assistants, Drs. Lazear, Carroll and Agramonte. The good work of the volunteers, O'Hara, McClelland, Busch and Brinkerhof, is featured.

* THE DRUNKARD

(100 performances)

A melodrama in five acts by H. S. Smith. Revived by the Fifty-fifth Street Group, Inc., at the American Music Hall, New York, March 10, 1934.

Cast of characters—

Mrs. Wilson.......................................Vera G. Hurst
Mary, her daughter............................Dortha Duckworth
Squire Cribbs....................................Robert Vivian
Edward Middleton..................................Hal Conklin
William Dowton...................................Charles Jordan
Agnes, his sister..............................Katherine Hirsch
Farmer Gates....................................Herbert Shelley
Farmer Stevens.....................................James Coyle
Landlord..Alfred Regali
Bar Fly..Stan Huff
Bar Fly..Sandy Strouse
Julia..June Mura
Arden Rendelaw...................................George Mura
Boy...Master Bracken

Act I.—A Cottage. Act II.—A Barroom. Act III.—In a Wood. Act IV.—On Broadway. Act V.—The cottage.
Staged by Harry Bannister; settings by Franklyn Geramia Ambrose.

"The Drunkard" was first produced in 1843 by P. T. Barnum, "The Price of Humbugs," in what he called "A Moral Lecture Room" in his American Museum in New York. It was rediscovered in 1926 with a lot of old manuscripts stored in Berkeley, California. Revivals were staged in Berkeley, Carmel and San Francisco, and later in a number of American cities. "The Drunkard, or the Fallen Saved" was the full title. The story is of a young man who, through drink, brought disgrace upon himself, his wife and his angel child, and was later reformed.

THE PERFUMED LADY

(40 performances)

A comedy in three acts by Harry Wagstaff Gribble. Produced by O. E. Wee and Jules J. Leventhal at the Ambassador Theatre, New York, March 12, 1934.

Cast of characters—

Catharine Pellett....................Helen Brooks
Homer Pellett....................Ben Lackland
Shaler, Inc....................Thomas Bate
Thora Donnelle....................Marjorie Peterson
Warren Pascal....................Brian Donlevy
Eva Mordecai....................Ollie Burgoyne
Janice McNish....................June Martel
Hans Platt....................Carl Johan

Acts I, II and III.—Apartment in a Converted "Brown Stone Front," Occupied by Warren and Homer, New York City.
Staged by Harry Wagstaff Gribble; settings by Watson Barratt.

Warren Pascal, engaged to Catharine Pellett of Rochester, is taking time out for social investigations in New York. He buys his stenographer two bits of lingerie and invites her to his apartment to collect them. That same day Catharine arrives unexpectedly and finds both lingerie and the stenographer. It takes another hour and a good deal of leaping for Warren to hurdle several delicate situations and convince Catharine that she is still the girl.

WRONG NUMBER

(12 performances)

A comedy in three acts by Eloise Keeler. Produced by the Intimate Theatre Group at the Provincetown Theatre, New York, March 13, 1934.

Cast of characters—

Victor Morrison....................William Bonelli
Benvenuto Morrison....................Whitner Bissell
Caroline Morrison....................Dorothy South
Anna....................Helen Bliss
Rowena Lankershim....................Genevieve Belasco
Ceringa Morrison....................Patricia Martin
William A. Becker....................William S. Phillips
King Karson....................Alan Floud
1st Furniture Mover....................Fred Smith
2nd Furniture Mover....................John Mortensen
Stevens....................Harold Bassage
Mrs. Becker....................Elsa Ryan

Acts I and II.—Living Room of the Morrison Home. Act. III.—Dinette of the Morrison Flat.
Staged by John F. Grahame; settings by Alexander Maissel.

Caroline Morrison is a flighty matron who goes in for fads and faddists. Her newest is King Karson, numerologist, who induces Caroline to sell practically everything in order to put herself right with the science of numbers and then runs away with the money. Doubtless Caroline was cured in the end.

* NEW FACES

(109 performances)

A revue in two acts conceived and assembled by Leonard Sillman; lyrics and sketches by Viola Brothers Shore, Nancy Hamilton and June Sillman; music by Warburton Guilbert, Donald Honrath, Martha Caples, James Shelton and Morgan Lewis. Presented by Charles Dillingham at the Fulton Theatre, New York, March 15, 1934.

Principals engaged—

Leonard Sillman
Imogene Coca
Nancy Hamilton
Louise Lynch
Hildegarde Halliday
Dorothy Kennedy Fox
Frances Dewey
Billy Haywood
Charles Walter
James Shelton
Roger Stearns
O. Z. Whitehead
Henry Fonda
Edith Sheridan
Kenneth Bates
Helen O'Hara
Jean Briggs
Peggy Hovenden
Mildred Todd
Edward Potter
Gordon Orme
Allen Handley
Cliff Allen
Marvin Lawler
Jeanne Palmer
Harry Peterson
Gustave Schirmer
Reeder Boss
Reed McClelland
Beverly Phalon
Sandra Gould
Moyne Rice

Staged by Elsie Janis; settings by Sergei Soudeikine.

ANOTHER LOVE

(16 performances)

A comedy in three acts by Jacques Deval; translated and adapted by George Oppenheimer. Produced by Milton Stiefel and Frank Lewis at the Vanderbilt Theatre, New York, March 19, 1934.

Cast of characters—

Henriette....................Iris Whitney
Fernand du Bois....................Raymond Walburn
Simone du Bois....................Mary Servoss
Cesar Poustiano....................Romaine Callender
Stassia Poustiano....................Suzanne Caubaye
Uncle Emile....................France Bendtsen
Aunt Valerie....................Ethel Strickland
Etienne du Bois....................Alfred Corn
M. Sasselin....................William Webb Robertson

Acts I, II and III.—Living Room of the Du Bois.
Staged by Milton Stiefel.

Etienne du Bois, son of Fernand du Bois, pompous, lecherous and shallow floor walker at the Galeries Lafayette, seeks to protect his mother by writing and telephoning complaints to his father's employers concerning papa's philanderings. His success is considerable, and is later made more or less complete when he is able to take Stassia Poustiano, a new mistress, away from the old gentleman. Etienne's mother then realizes that her son is no longer her baby and thinks to keep him at home more by choosing her maids wisely.

THE PURE IN HEART

(7 performances)

A drama in four scenes by John Howard Lawson with incidental music by Richard Myers. Produced by Richard Aldrich and Alfred de Liagre at the Longacre Theatre, New York, March 20, 1934.

Cast of characters—

Pa Sparks....................Joseph Allenton
Annabel Sparks....................Dorothy Hall
Iceman....................Owen Martin
Johnnie Sparks....................Peter Donald, Jr.
Ma Sparks....................Janet Young
Postman....................Scott Moore
Edwina Raleigh....................Ara Gerald
Otto Bauer....................C. H. Davis
Hinkle....................Larry Bolton
Joe....................Charles S. Howard
Matt Swann.................... Harold Vermilyea
Homer Edwards....................Charles C. Leatherbee
Broderick....................Michael Gray
Dr. Martin Goshen....................Tom Powers
Faith McCarthy....................Zelma Tiden
Larry Goshen....................James Bell
James B. Mellon....................Joaquin Souther
A Singer....................Frances Langford
Wilkes....................Scott Moore
1st Detective....................Michael Gray
2nd Detective....................Owen Martin
Albertina Rasch Girls: Mary Mascher, Ruth Bond, Rita Horgan, Patti Heaton, Amalie Ideal, Peggy Dell, Mary Phillips.

Prologue—Sparks Home, Middleville. Scene 1—Theatre, New York City. 2—Dr. Goshen's Apartment. 3—Theatre. 4—Room in a Lodging House.

Staged by Edward Massey; dances by Albertina Rasch; settings by Jo Mielziner.

Annabel Sparks, restless and unhappy in her Middleville home, runs away to New York, her heart set upon a career. Invading a theatre Annabel agrees to make whatever sacrifice may be demanded of her in exchange for a job. The director favors her for a time. Next she turns to the playwright. Finally she discovers her true love in Larry Goshen, a convict, out of jail but hunted for one or two accidental murders. Annabel and Larry, still pure in heart, seeking to escape, are shot down by the police.

THE SHATTER'D LAMP

(37 performances)

A drama in three acts by Leslie Reade. Produced by Hyman Adler, for Comesy Productions, Inc., at the Maxine Elliott Theatre, New York, March 21, 1934.

Cast of characters—

Professor Fritz Opal............................Guy Bates Post
Sophie..Effie Shannon
Karl Opal.......................................Owen Davis, Jr.
Dr. Hans Muller.................................Moffat Johnston
Elisabeth Muller..............................Katherine Stewart
Louisa Muller...................................Jane Bramley
Roman...Horace Braham
Johannes von Rentzau............................John Buckler
First Storm Trooper.............................Walden Boyle
Second Storm Trooper............................Jack Arnold
Storm Troopers: Gilbert Squarey, Simeon Greer, Paul Thorne, Walter Dressel, Milton Luban.
Acts I, II and III.—Lounge of the Opal House in Small University Town in South Germany.
Staged by Hyman Adler; settings by Watson Barratt.

Karl Opal, son of a gentle university professor, is engaged to marry Louisa Muller, daughter of an old, old friend of the family. When the storm troopers take charge of the town in which the Opals and Mullers live Karl hopes to join them. He is thrown out on discovery that Sophie Opal, his mother, is a Jewess. For eight hundred years her family has been honored in Germany, but "The Leader" will have none of them. In the resulting tragedy Louisa deserts Karl, Sophie Opal kills herself and Professor Opal is shot by the troopers. At the crisis of the tragedy word comes that because his oldest son was killed in the war, "The Leader" has agreed to let Professor Opal retain his place at the university.

GENTLEWOMAN

(12 performances)

A comedy in three acts by John Howard Lawson. Produced by the Group Theatre in association with D. A. Doran, Jr., at the Cort Theatre, New York, March 22, 1934.

Cast of characters—

Connie Blane....................................Claudia Morgan
Elliott Snowden.................................Lewis Leverett
Havens..Russell Collins
Dr. Lewis Golden..............................Morris Carnovsky
Mrs. Stoneleigh.............................Zamah Cunningham

Gwyn Ballantine....................................Stella Adler
Colonel Richard Fowler............................Roman Bohnen
Rudy Flannigan.....................................Lloyd Nolan
Vaughn...Neill O'Malley
Hattie..Frances Williams

Act I.—Drawing Room of Ballantine House, New York. Act II.—Gwyn's Sitting Room. Act III.—Scene 1—Apartment on Tenth Street, New York. 2—Drawing Room of Ballantine House.

Staged by Lee Strasberg; settings by Mordecai Gorelik.

The night Elliott Snowden introduces Rudy Flannigan to Gwyn Ballantine, Gwyn's broker husband kills himself. The Ballantines have for generations represented the higher socialites of New York. Rudy is a rough fellow with some literary gifts who hates the pretenses of society. Six weeks later Gwyn, in a grand burst for freedom, goes to live with Rudy. Six months later Rudy has deceived her and decided they still are definitely of two worlds. Gwyn does not tell him she is carrying his child for fear it might impose an added burden of obligation upon him.

ONE MORE HONEYMOON

(17 performances)

A farce in three acts by Leo F. Reardon. Produced by John Nicholson and Ned Brown at the Little Theatre, New York, March 31, 1934.

Cast of characters—

Chuck McAffee....................................Charles Harrison
Richard I. Mason.................................Burford Hampden
Ramona St. Clair....................................Sally Starr
Nancy Devore.......................................Ann Butler
Wanda Rutledge....................................Alice Fleming
Henry Rowland...................................George Pembroke
Pookeelocodeekasomoko..........................Will H. Philbrick
Miss Rutherford...................................Almira Sessons
Charles Lummus....................................Harry Hanlon

Acts I, II and III.—Richard Mason's Sherman Arms Hotel Apartment in New York.

Staged by John Nicholson; settings by Amend Studios.

Richard Mason, facing bankruptcy as the heir to a bug exterminator business, is about to kill himself when he is importuned by Wanda Rutledge, a rich and amorous widow some years his senior, to marry her and solve his troubles. They marry, the honeymoon is in Iceland, where the nights are long and cold. Richard brings home an Eskimo with a fishoil preparation for bug removal. Wanda, wearied by her Icelandic honeymoon, is eager to have her husband give up the exterminator business. They quarrel. Separation threatens until the Eskimo's fishoil makes everybody rich. Then they start another honeymoon.

HOUSE OF REMSEN

(34 performances)

A drama in three acts by Nicholas Soussanin, William J. Perlman and Marie Baumer. Produced by Nicholas Soussanin at the Henry Miller Theatre, New York, April 2, 1934.

Cast of characters—

Vivienne Remsen (as a child)........................Joy Lange
Clara Collins..Leota Diesel
Clyde Remsen (as a child)........................Raymond Roe
Marsten..John Hendricks
Mabel Crooks..Julia Bruner
John Crooks..Karl Swensen
Harriett Langdon..Ellen Lowe
Charles Langdon..Houston Richards
Arthur Remsen..James Kirkwood
Laura Remsen..Francesca Bruning
Leslie Stokes..Albert Van Dekker
Dr. Mansfield..Edgar Stehli
Clyde Remsen (later)..Ben Starkie
Vivienne Remsen (later)........................Francesca Bruning
Lona Banner..Virginia Curley

Act I.—Scenes 1, 2 and 4—Living-room of the Remsen Home on Long Island. 3—Room in a Hospital. Acts II and III.—Remsen Home.

Staged by Nicholas Soussanin; settings by the Vail Studios.

Arthur and Laura Remsen are happy in their home life with their two small children, Clyde and Vivienne, until Leslie Stokes, who had been a suitor for Mrs. Remsen's hand before she married Remsen, tries to wiggle his way back into her life. Stokes and Mrs. Remsen are in an automobile accident which results in the death of Laura and the serious injury of Stokes. Finding an incriminating letter in his wife's effects Remsen goes to the hospital to face Stokes, who is not expected to live, to learn of which Remsen child he is the confessed father. Stokes tells him it is the boy Clyde. For the next ten years Remsen hates and is cruel to Clyde. Stokes returns to confess that he had lied to protect his daughter. It is Vivienne who is illegitimate. Clyde is as pure as a Harvard man can be.

PEACE ON EARTH

(First engagement 126; second engagement 18 performances)

"Peace on Earth" played at the Civic Repertory Theatre from November 29, 1933, to March 17, 1934, and reopened March 31, 1934, at the 44th Street Theatre with the following cast—

Laurie Owens..Hilda Reis
Peter Owens..Maurice Wells

Jo Owens..Ethel Intropidi
Walter McCracken..................................John Boruff
Prof. Frank Anderson........................Walter Vonnegut
Mary Bonner.......................................Allace Carroll
Stephen Hamill.......................................David Gray
Bob Peters..Jules Garfield
Dean Walker....................................Charles Esdale
Fred Miller.....................................Clem Wilenchick
Primo..John Brown
Lena..Alice Brooks
Speed..Charles Thompson
Mike..David Lesan
Ann...Mara Tartar
Rose..Millicent Green
Ryan...Earl Ford
Flynn...Donald A. Black
Krauss..Frank Tweddell
Max...David Lesan
Fenning..David Kerman
Company Guard...Paul Stein
Henry Murdoch................................James MacDonald
Dr. Carl Kelsey.......................................John Brown
President Howard.............................Halliam Bosworth
Miss Ellen Bancroft..................................Alice Brooks
John Andrews.......................................Alvin Dexter
Bishop Parkes..............................Thomas Coffin Cooke
Marjorie Howard...................................Allace Carroll
Bill Prentice.....................................Frank Tweddell
Charlie Wilcox..Earl Ford
Biff Morris......................................Donald A. Black
Harry Boynton................................Charles Thompson
The Guard.......................................Abner Biberman
The Cop..David Lesan
The Messenger.....................................Jules Garfield
The Judge.......................................Charles Esdale
The District Attorney...............................John Brown
Attorney Gordon.................................Frank Tweddell
Radio Announcer.................................David Kerman
The Blues Singer....................................Mara Tartar

The cast of the original production of "Peace on Earth" will be found on pages 465-466.

THE MIKADO

(24 performances)

Operetta in two acts by W. S. Gilbert; music by Arthur Sullivan. Revived by S. M. Chartock at the Majestic Theatre, New York, April 2, 1934.

Cast of characters—

The Mikado of Japan..........................William Danforth
Nanki-Poo..Roy Cropper
Ko-Ko..John Cherry
Pooh-Bah..Herbert Waterous
Yum-Yum..Hizi Koyke
Pitti-Sing...Vivian Hart
Peep-Bo..Laura Ferguson
Katisha...Vera Ross
Pish-Tush..Allen Waterous

Act I.—Courtyard of Ko-Ko's Official Residence. Act II.—Ko-Ko's Garden.

Staged by Lee Daly; settings by Franklyn Ambrose.

The only changes in the cast of this revival and that of the last previous performance (April, 1933) were in the characters. Here John Cherry took over the rôle of Ko-Ko previously sung by Frank Moulan, Vivian Hart replaced Ethel Clarke as Pitti-Sing, and Laura Ferguson was the Peep-Bo in place of Mabel Thompson.

MOOR BORN

(63 performances)

A drama in five parts by Dan Totheroh. Produced by George Bushar and John Tuerk at the Playhouse, April 3, 1934.

Cast of characters—

Charlotte Emily Anne	The Three Brontës	Frances Starr Helen Gahagan Edith Barrett

Rev. Patrick Brontë................................Thomas Findlay
Branwell Brontë....................................Glenn Anders
Tabby..Beverly Sitgreaves
Martha...Grace Francis
Christopher..Arling Alcine

Parts 1, 2, 3, 4 and 5—Narrow Hallway and Sitting Room of the Parsonage at Haworth, Yorkshire, England. Time, 1845-48.
Staged by Melvyn Douglas; settings by Louis Kennel.

The Brontës are living in the parsonage at Haworth. Charlotte is just back from Brussels. Emily and Anne have been caring for the Reverend Patrick, their father, and Branwell, their gifted but dissipated brother, now a victim of liquor and opium and much brooding on his failure to achieve fame as a genius. Charlotte discovers her sisters' gifts as poets and publishes a book of verse, the sisters taking the name of Bell to save the face of their unhappy brother. The verse volume leads to Charlotte's writing of "Jane Eyre," Anne's "Agnes Grey" and Emily's "Wuthering Heights." Branwell and Emily die. The Brontës are temporarily at loose ends.

BRAIN SWEAT

(5 performances)

A comedy in three acts by John Charles Brownell. Produced by James Montgomery and Henry R. Stern at the Longacre Theatre, April 4, 1934.

Cast of characters—

Henry Washington...................................Billy Higgins
Carrie Washington..................................Rose McClendon

Charlie Washington.................................Barrington Guy
The Rev. Elisha Tatum..........................A. B. Comathiere
Angie Johnson ....Pearl Wright
Jake Johnson......................................Dick Campbell
Lucy...Viola Dean
Laura...Marie Young
Flatfoot Mobly.................................Andrew Tribble
Mr. Covington....................................E. J. Blunkall

Shrimp Jones Orchestra and Russell Wooding's Choir.

Acts I, II and III.—Home of Henry Washington in a Small Town on the Mississippi River.

Staged by Robert Ober.

Henry Washington, finding a pamphlet on psychology the day he is fired by the steamboat company, learns the only way he can hope to make the most of his mental powers is to relax and give his brain a chance to function. Henry relaxes for two years, while his wife and son support him. Carrie, the wife, disgusted finally, wishes Henry would go drown himself. Henry agrees to oblige. They find his hat on the river brink and, after two days, give him a grand funeral. Henry comes home from a trip to Memphis and eventually dumbfounds everybody with the success of his latest project.

PIRATES OF PENZANCE

(16 performances)

An operetta in two acts by W. S. Gilbert; music by Arthur Sullivan. Revived by S. M. Chartock at the Majestic Theatre, April 9, 1934.

Cast of characters—

Richard.......................................Herbert Waterous
Samuel..Allen Waterous
Frederic...Roy Cropper
Major-General Stanley.............................John Cherry
Edward.......................................William Danforth
Mabel..Vivian Hart
Kate..Frances Baviello
Edith...Laura Ferguson
Isabel...Olga Schumacher
Ruth...Vera Ross

Act I.—Rocky Seashore off Cornwall. Act II.—Ruined Abbey.

Staged by Lee Daly; musical director, J. Albert Hurley; settings, Franklyn Ambrose.

The last previous revival was that of the Aborn Opera Company in August, 1933, with practically the same cast. Frank Moulan was then the Stanley and Mabel Thompson the Mabel Stanley.

WIFE INSURANCE

(4 performances)

A comedy in three acts by Frederick Jackson. Produced by Langdon Productions, Inc., at the Ethel Barrymore Theatre, New York, April 12, 1934.

Cast of characters—

Marion Langdon....................................Ilka Chase
Gregory Langdon...........................Kenneth MacKenna
Lulu...Helen Huberth
Diane Chadwick...............................Lillian Emerson
Morgan Chadwick...................................Walter Abel
Leonard Drummond...........................Harvey Stephens

Acts I, II and III.—Drawing Room of Langdon's Apartment, Gracie Square, New York City.

Staged by Arthur J. Beckhard; settings by William H. Mensching Studio.

Marion Langdon, discouraged after five years of marriage because her husband has acquired the habit of taking her for granted, determines to do what she can to excite his jealousy. Flirting with Leonard Drummond, a popular woman's novelist, she forces Drummond to sit out the night with her until Langdon gets home. Langdon is only mildly excited, but accepts with grace Drummond's advice that all men should pay more attention to their wives if they hope to insure their loyalty.

H.M.S. "PINAFORE"

(16 performances)

An operetta by W. S. Gilbert; music by Arthur Sullivan. Revived by S. M. Chartock at the Majestic Theatre, New York, April 16, 1934.

Cast of characters—

The Right Hon. Sir Joseph Porter, K.C.B.............John Cherry
Captain Corcoran..............................Allen Waterous
Ralph Rackstraw...................................Roy Cropper
Dick Deadeye...............................William Danforth
Bill Bobstay ....Herbert Waterous
Josephine...Vivian Hart
Little Buttercup (Mrs. Cripps).......................Vera Ross
Hebe...Laura Ferguson
Sailors: Messrs. Harrison Fuller, Francis Clarke, John Cardini, Siegfried Langer, John Willard, Lloyd Ericson, Hobson Young, Sidney Dunay, Thomas Green, John Bast, Allen Ware, Walter Bartholomew, John Eaton and Frank Benedict.
First Lord's Sisters, Cousins and Aunts: Misses Caroline Cantlin, Doris Snyder, Charlotte LaRose, Elizabeth Kerr, Geraldine Olive, Margaret Walker, Celia Schiffren, Frances Baviello, Olga Schumacher, Eleanor Gilmore, Barbara Martsin, Beatrice Pons,

Doris Reed, Jean Chase, Margaret Henzel and Lauretta Brislin.
Scene—Deck of H.M.S. "Pinafore," off Portsmouth, England.
Staged by Lee Daly; musical director, J. Albert Hurley.

Last previous revival by the Aborn Civic Light Opera Company in the spring of 1933.

TRIAL BY JURY

(16 performances)

An operetta by W. S. Gilbert; music by Arthur Sullivan. Revived by S. M. Chartock at the Majestic Theatre, New York, April 16, 1934.

Cast of characters—

The Learned Judge....................................John Cherry
Foreman of the Jury............................Herbert Waterous
The Defendant.......................................Roy Cropper
Counsel...Allen Waterous
Usher..William Danforth
Plaintiff..Vivian Hart
Jurors: Messrs. Harrison Fuller, Francis Clarke, John Cardini, Siegfried Langer, John Willard, Lloyd Ericson, Hobson Young, Sidney Dunay, Thomas Green, John Bast, Allen Ware, Frank Murray, Walter Bartholomew, John Eaton and Frank Benedict.
Bridesmaids: Misses Caroline Cantlin, Doris Snyder, Charlotte LaRose, Elizabeth Kerr, Geraldine Olive, Margaret Walker, Celia Schiffren, Frances Baviello, Olga Schumacher, Eleanor Gilmore, Barbara Martsin, Beatrice Pons, Doris Reed, Jean Chase, Margaret Henzel and Lauretta Brislin.
Scene—Court of Exchequer.
Staged by Lee Daly; musical director, J. Albert Hurley.

Last previous revival by Aborn Civic Opera Company in April, 1933.

* STEVEDORE

(71 performances)

A drama in three acts by Paul Peters and George Sklar. Produced by the Theatre Union, Inc., at the Civic Repertory Theatre, April 18, 1934.

Cast of characters—

Florrie..Millicent Green
Bill Larkin..Jack Hartley
Sergeant..Jack Daley
Bobo Valentine..................................Carrington Lewis
Rag Williams....................................Alonzo Fenderson
Angrum..Ray Yeates
Lonnie Thompson......................................Jack Carter
Joe Crump.......................................G. I. Harry Bolden
Steve..Frank Gabrielson
Binnie..Georgette Harvey
Ruby Oxley..Edna Thomas
Sam Oxley..Al Watts

Uncle Cato....................................William C. Elkins
Jim Veal....................................Leigh Whipper
Blacksnake....................................Rex Ingram
Walcott....................................Dodson Mitchell
Mike....................................Robert Caille
Detective....................................Jack Williams
Lem Morris....................................Neill O'Malley
Marty Fox....................................Jack Williams
Al Regan....................................Frank Gabrielson
Charley Freeman....................................Irving Gordon
Mitch....................................Jack Hartley
Pons....................................Robert Caille
Cop....................................Jack Williams
Bertha Williams....................................Susie Sutton
Mose Venable....................................William C. Elkins
Nanny....................................Gena Brown
Sherman....................................Arthur Bruce
Neighbors, Wharf Hands, Policemen and Mitch's Gang: Roy Gillespie, Dewey Armstrong, Wm. Myers, I. Peters, Cal Bellaver, Henry Moy, Emely Patterson, Esther Hall, C. M. Davis.

Act I.—Scene 1—Backyard. 2—Police Station. 3—Binnie's Lunch-room. 4—Office of Oceanic Stevedore Co. 5—Stuyvesant Dock. Act II.—Scene 1—Union Headquarters. 2—Stuyvesant Dock. 3—Binnie's Lunch-room. Act III.—Scene 1—Bertha Williams' Attic. 2—Courtyard.

Staged by Michael Blankfort and Irving Gordon; settings by Sointu Syrjala.

Florrie, a white girl, quarrels with and is beaten by her lover, Bill Larkin. When her husband answers her cry for help she swears she was attacked by a black man. The blacks of the neighborhood are rounded up and the attack fastened finally on rebellious Lonnie Thompson, a dock worker of better than average intelligence bent on defending the Negro race against the brutalities and injustices of the whites. The Dock company would frame Lonnie. He escapes the law and inspires the Negroes of his neighborhood to barricade the end of the alley and fight off a white trash mob that is organized to burn the quarter.

* ARE YOU DECENT

(68 performances)

A comedy in three acts by Crane Wilbur. Produced by Albert Bannister in association with George L. Miller at the Ambassador Theatre, New York, April 19, 1934.

Cast of characters—

Peggy Witherspoon....................................Zamah Cunningham
Edwards....................................Royal Stout
Dolly Van Etten....................................Beatrice Hendricks
Harry Van Etten....................................A. J. Herbert
Antonia Wayne....................................Claudia Morgan
Bill Adams....................................Eric Dressler
Keith Darrell....................................Lester Vail

Acts I, II and III.—Aboard the House-boat "Antonia," Anchored off the Connecticut Shore.

Staged by Dmitri Ostrov.

Antonia Wayne, being both open and maternally minded, conceives it to be her womanly right to become a mother without benefit of matrimony. In selecting a father for her prospective child she tries to make a choice between Keith Darrell, who loves and wants to marry her, and Bill Adams, who is merely eager to be accommodating. On the advice of Antonia's mother Keith pretends to agree to Antonia's plan. In the processes of consummation Antonia decides that perhaps marriage is wisest after all.

BROADWAY INTERLUDE

(12 performances)

A comedy in three acts by Achmed Abdullah and William Almon Wolff, based on a novel by Faith Baldwin and Achmed Abdullah. Produced by Theodore Hammerstein and Denis Du-For at the Forrest Theatre, New York, April 19, 1934.

Cast of characters—

Ben Levi....................Hans Hansen
Jack Griggs....................Robert Lynn
Katherine Healy....................Claire Whitney
Maid....................Margot Allaine
Grant Thompson....................Robert Emmett Keane
Sally Cameron....................Sally Starr
Deane Powers....................Neil Moore
Robert Foster....................Arthur Pierson
Julius Beck....................Paul Everton
Rita Andre....................Suzanne Caubaye
Graham Steele....................Leslie Dennison
MacDonald Norris....................Peter Whitman
Ruth Hoyt....................Janice Dawson
Mary Bronson....................Dorothy Knapp

Acts I, II and III.—Studio Penthouse Atop the Grant Thompson Theatre.

Staged by Theodore Hammerstein; settings by Karle Amend.

Grant Thompson (a thinly veiled caricature of the late David Belasco) is a Broadway producer of admitted eccentricities. In accepting a play written by Robert Foster he agrees to rewrite it on a split royalty basis highly advantageous to Grant Thompson, and to produce it with Foster's fiancée, Sally Cameron, in the chief rôle, providing Sally's career continues to interest him. During the rehearsal period Foster becomes gradually aware of the producer's intentions and withdraws his play and his sweetheart, leaving Thompson in search of a new manuscript and a new skirted inspiration.

LATE WISDOM

(2 performances)

A comedy in three acts by Nathan Sherman. Produced by Mark Newman at the Mansfield Theatre, New York, April 23, 1934.

Cast of characters—

Willison....................Walter O. Hill
Vincent Truex....................Carleton Young
Nancy Jackson....................Miss Franc Hale
Frank Dutton....................Jay Fassett
Albert Goodright....................Horace Casselberry
Steve Whitman....................Eric Kalkhurst

Acts I, II and III.—Office of Frank Dutton.

Staged by Nathan Sherman; settings by Walter Street and Samuel L. Tabor.

Frank Dutton, big rubber man at 41, engages Nancy Jackson as a new secretary and immediately takes a new interest in life. Dutton is married and the father of two daughters. Nancy is engaged to marry a personable young man. Defying these barriers Nancy seeks to comfort her employer with the result that Dutton acquires a belated wisdom and is cured while Nancy loses her fiancé.

UNION PACIFIC

(4 performances)

An American ballet drama in one act and four scenes by Archibald MacLeish; music by Nicolas Nabokoff, based on folk songs; orchestration by Edward Powell; choreography by Leonide Massine. Produced by the Monte Carlo Ballet Russe and S. Hurok at the St. James Theatre, New York, April 25, 1934.

Principals—

Irina Baronova	Eduard Borovansky
Joseph Dolotin	Andre Eglevsky
David Lichine	Leonide Massine
Sonia Ossato	Vania Psota
Yurek Shabelevsky	Tamara Toumanova
Paul Petroff	Jan Hoyer

Dancers: Alexandroff, Branitzka, Canon, Coudine, Dunkan, Fedorova, Haskin, Ismailoff, Katcharoff, Kosloff, Kiddon, Kirsova, Matouchevsky, Martinez, Nelidova, Strogova, Tarakanova, Wayne, Verchinina, Valentinoff.

Scene 1—Railroad Right-of-Way East of Promontory Point. 2—Right-of-Way West of Promontory Point. 3—The Big Tent. 4—Right-of-Way at Promontory Point.

Staged by W. de Basil; ballet by Leonide Massine; settings by Albert Johnson; costume designing Irene Sharaff.

The repertory of the Ballet Russe also included revivals of "Le Beau Danube," "Petrouchka," "Les Presages," "Les Sylphides," "Scuola di Ballo," "Jeux d'Enfants," "Beach," "Prince Igor," "Cotillon," "Three Cornered Hat," "Les Matelots," "Carnaval," and "Nocturne."

OTHER DANCE DRAMAS

The Jooss Ballet, a German troupe of twenty actor-dancers under the leadership of Kurt Jooss, presented by the Metropolitan Musical Bureau, Inc., gave forty-eight performances at the Forrest Theatre, New York, beginning October 31, 1933. Directed by F. C. Coppicus; musical director, Fritz Cohen. The program for the season included a satire, "The Green Table," a burlesque, "Seven Heroes," "The Big City," "A Spanish Pavane," and a romance "Ball in Old Vienna." Principals were Frida Holst, Liza Czobel, Elsa Kohl, Mascha Lidolt, Lola Botka, Ruth Harris, Maria Kindlova, Rudolf Pescht and Ernst Uthoff.

A company of eight Russian actor-dancers under the leadership of Serge Lifar were presented by the Metropolitan Musical Bureau, Inc., at the Forrest Theatre, New York, November 5, 1933. Directed by F. C. Coppicus. Their program included "Le Spectre de la Rose," "L'Apres-Midi d'un Faune," and "La Chatte" by Balanchine. Principals—Olga Adabache, Lycette Darsonval, Roman Jasinsky, S. Kochanowsky, T. Slavinsky, V. Karnetzky, L. Matlinsky and S. Bausloff.

A group of 14 Hindus under the leadership of Uday Shan-Kar were presented by the Hurok Music Bureau, Inc., at Carnegie Hall, New York, October 21, 1933. Principals—Shan-Kar, Limke and Kanak Lata. The program included "Burmese Impressions," "Snanum," "Ganga Puja," and "The Dance of the Snake Charmer."

IOLANTHE

(8 performances)

An operetta in two acts by W. S. Gilbert; music by Arthur Sullivan. Revived by S. M. Chartock at the Majestic Theatre, April 30, 1934.

Cast of characters—

Lord Chancellor.................................William Danforth
Earl of Mountararat..............................Frederic Persson

Earl of Tolloller....................................Roy Cropper
Private Willis....................................Herbert Waterous
Strephen....................................Allen Waterous
Queen of the Fairies....................................Vera Ross
Iolanthe....................................Dean Dickens
Celia....................................Frances Baviello
Leila....................................Eleanor Gilmore
Fleta....................................Olga Schumacher
Phyllis....................................Vivian Hart

Act I.—Arcadian Landscape. Act II.—Palace Yard, Westminster.
Staged by Lee Daly; music directed by J. A. Hurley.

Last previous revival by the Aborn Civic Light Opera Company, July, 1931.

JIGSAW

(49 performances)

A comedy in three acts by Dawn Powell. Produced by the Theatre Guild, Inc., at the Ethel Barrymore Theatre, New York, April 30, 1934.

Cast of characters—

Rosa....................................Virginia Tracy
Porter....................................Albert Bergh
Bell Boy....................................James York
Mrs. Letty Walters....................................Cora Witherspoon
Del Marsh....................................Ernest Truex
Claire Burnell....................................Spring Byington
Nathan Gifford....................................Eliot Cabot
Frank Mason....................................Charles Richman
Julie....................................Gertrude Flynn
Mrs. Finch....................................Helen Westley
Ethel Mason....................................Babel Kroman
Simpson....................................Sheppard Strudwick

Acts I and II.—Living Room of Claire Burnell's Furnished Penthouse in the Hotel Harwich. Act III.—The Terrace.
Staged by Philip Moeller; settings by Lee Simonson.

Claire Burnell and Del Marsh have practically been living together in New York for the better part of fifteen years. The arrangement is made possible by the fact that Mrs. Burnell is a divorcee and Mr. Marsh's wife prefers to stay on in Baltimore. The year Julie Burnell comes home from her convent training in France matters become a little complicated. Julie helps solve them by attaching herself to the newest of her mother's flirtations, a young man named Nathan Gifford. Julie takes Nathan away from mother and the Burnell-Marsh arrangement is resumed.

LOVE KILLS

(15 performances)

A drama in three acts by Ida Lublenski Ehrlich. Produced by the author at the Forrest Theatre, New York, May 1, 1934.

Cast of characters—

Douglas Cameron..Marion Green
Robert Barton..Harry Hanlon
Harry Deming...John Parrish
Pearl Barton...Vivian Giesen
Arthur Coyle...Bram Nossen
A Doctor...Hendrick Joyner

Act I.—Scenes 1 and 3—Room in a Hotel. 2—Robert Barton's Home. Act II.—Scene 1—Room in a Hotel. 2—Douglas Cameron's Home. Act III.—Scenes 1 and 2—Hotel Room.
Staged by Percival Vivian.

Pearl Barton marries Douglas Cameron, millionaire, to save her father's bank. Years later she is pursued by a man who had once saved her from a fate more exciting and frequently less satisfying than death. Her husband refuses to believe Pearl is as good as she says she is and she is forced to return to the arms of another lover. He tires of her and she jumps out of a very high window.

THE LADY FROM THE SEA

(15 performances)

A drama in five acts by Henrik Ibsen. Revived by Nathan Zatkin at the Little Theatre, New York, May 1, 1934.

Cast of characters—

Boletta..Rose Keane
Hilda..Margaret English
Lyngstrand...Richard Whorf
Dr. Wangel...Moffat Johnston
Arnholm..Roman Bohnen
Ellida...Mary Hone
The Stranger...Clem Wilenchick

Act. I.—Scene 1—Veranda of Dr. Wangel's Home. 2—The Garden. Act II.—A Hilltop Overlooking the Fiord. Act III.—Remote Corner of the Garden. Act IV.—A Room in the House. Act V.—The Garden.
Staged by John Houseman; settings by Donald Oenslager.

"The Lady from the Sea" was produced in New York in 1911 by the Drama Players with Hedwig Reicher and Donald Robertson playing Ellida and Dr. Wangel. It was the opening play in Eleanor Duse's repertory on her last tour in 1923. She died in Pittsburgh. It was revived again by the Actors' Theatre in March, 1929, with Blanche Yurka and Edward Fielding in the leading rôles.

PICNIC

(2 performances)

A play in three acts by Gretchen Damrosch. Produced by Arthur J. Beckhard at the National Theatre, New York, May 2, 1934.

Cast of characters—

Philip....................Marvin Kline
Wallace....................Fred Leslie
Helene....................Jean Adair
Larson....................Jan Ulrich
Lois....................Esther Dale
Robert....................Percy Waram
Mona....................Olive Corn
Mademoiselle....................Frieda Altman
Guba....................Millard Mitchell
Vera....................Joanna Roos
Mr. Mooney....................Hugh Rennie

Act I.—Living Room in the Country House of Robert. Acts II and III.—A Hillside Meadow.
Staged by Kaye Lowe; settings by P. Dodd Ackerman.

Philip, who lives in Westchester and comes of an old, old family now being slowly disintegrated by the economic crises, has taken sympathetically to Communism through meeting Vera, one of the most successful of soapbox orators. Vera, pursued by the police, is given shelter by Philip in Westchester. It is her first contact with sunshine, fresh air and the bourgeoisie. She falls in love with Philip's Uncle Robert, a Wall Street softie. After a picnic in the country Uncle Robert decides to go back to town with Vera. Vera thinks they might marry later.

THE CHOCOLATE SOLDIER

(13 performances)

An operetta in three acts by Rudolph Bernauer and Leopold Jacobson based on George Bernard Shaw's "Arms and the Man." American version by Stanislaus Stange; music by Oscar Strauss. Revived by Charles Purcell and Donald Brian at the St. James Theatre, New York, May 2, 1934.

Cast of characters—

Nadina....................Bernice Claire
Aurelia....................Olivia Martin
Mascha....................Lauretta Brislin
Bummerli....................Charles Purcell
Captain Massakroff....................Detmar Poppen
Colonel Casimir Popoff....................John Dunsmure
Major Alexius Sparidoff....................Parker Steward

Lucca.......................................Theo Van Tassle
Stephan.......................................Frank Worden
Act I.—Nadina's Sleeping Apartment in Popoff's House. Acts II and III.—Garden of Popoff's House.
Staged by Alonzo Price.

"The Chocolate Soldier" was first produced in New York by F. C. Whitney at the Lyric Theatre in September, 1909, with Ida Brooks Hunt as Nadina. It was revived in December, 1921, at the Century, by the Shuberts, with Tessa Kosta and Donald Brian in the leading rôles, and again at the Jolson Theatre the following year with Alice McKenzie and Charles Purcell.

BITTER SWEET

(16 performances)

An operetta in three acts by Noel Coward. Revived by the Messrs. Shubert at the 44th Street Theatre, New York, May 7, 1934.

Cast of characters—

ACT I

SCENE ONE

The Marchioness of Shayne.......................Evelyn Herbert
Dolly Chamberlain.......................Mary Wrick
Lord Henry Jekyll.......................Herbert Weber
Vincent Howard.......................Cameron York
Lady Shayne's House in Grosvenor Square. Time—1934.

SCENE TWO

Sarah Millick.......................Evelyn Herbert
Carl Linden.......................Allan Jones
Mrs. Millick.......................Elizabeth Crandall
Hugh Devon.......................Henry Rabke
The Millick House, Belgrave Square. Time—1875.

SCENE THREE

Sarah Millick.......................Evelyn Herbert
Carl Linden.......................Allan Jones
Mrs. Millick.......................Elizabeth Crandall
Hugh Devon.......................Henry Rabke
Lady Devon.......................Ethel Morrison
Sir Arthur Fenchurch.......................Victor Casmore
Victoria.......................Martha Boyer
Harriet.......................Marion Carlisle
Gloria.......................Beatrice Berenson
Honor.......................Ruth Adams
Jane.......................Anna Werth
Effie.......................Beulah Blake
The Marquis of Steere.......................Jay Conley
Lord Edgar James.......................Samuel Thomas
Lord Sorrel.......................Brian Davis
Mr. Vale.......................Jack Richards
Mr. Bethel.......................Harold Abbey
Mr. Proutie.......................Trueman Gaige
Four Footmen.........Earl Mason, Leon Sabater, Martin Shepherd
Don Drew

The Butler..Jack Fago
Guests, Musicians, etc.

The Ballroom of the Millick House in Belgrave Square. Time—1875.

Act II

SCENE ONE

Sari Linden..Evelyn Herbert
Carl Linden..Allan Jones
Manon (La Crevette)..Hannah Toback
Lotte..Carol Boyer
Freda..Beatrice Berenson
Hansi..Marion Carlisle
Gussie..Kay Simmons
Captain August Lutte..Leonard Ceeley
Herr Schlick..Victor Casmore

Herr Schlick's Café in Vienna. Time—1880.

SCENE TWO

Herr Schlick's Café, a few hours later.

Act III

SCENE ONE

Madame Sari Linden..Evelyn Herbert
The Marquis of Shayne..Clyde Kelly
Lady James..Marion Carlisle
Mrs. Proutie..Beatrice Berenson
Mrs. Bethel..Beulah Blake
Lady Sorrel..Ruth Adams
Mrs. Vale..Anna Werth
The Duchess of Tenterton..Martha Boyer
Lord James..Samuel Thomas
Mr. Proutie..Trueman Gaige
Mr. Bethel..Harold Abbey
Lord Sorrel..Brian Davis
Mr. Vale..Jack Richards
The Duke of Tenterton..Frank Grinnell
The Hon. Hugh Devon..Henry Rabke
Mrs. Devon..Frances Marion Comstock
Vernon Craft..Cameron York
Cedric Ballantyne..Brian Davis
Bertram Sellick..Frank Grinnell
Lord Henry Jade..Jack Richards
Accompanist..Theodore Schnyder

Drawing Room of The Marquis of Shayne's House in London. Time—1895.

SCENE TWO

Dolly Chamberlain..Mary Wrick
Vincent Howard..Cameron York
The Marchioness of Shayne..Evelyn Herbert

Lady Shayne's House in Grosvenor Square. Time—1934.

Staged by Edward J. Scanlon; settings by Watson Barratt; music directed by Pierre Dereeder.

"Bitter Sweet" was a November, 1929, success at the Ziegfeld Theatre, New York, with Evelyn Laye and Gerald Nodin, supported by an English company.

THESE TWO

(8 performances)

A drama in three acts by Lionel Hale. Produced by Leslie J. Casey and James W. Liddle at the Henry Miller Theatre, New York, May 7, 1934.

Cast of characters—

Tom Rowlands.....A. E. Matthews
Miss Butterworth.....Hilda Spong
Simon More.....Bramwell Fletcher
Mr. Gregory.....Edward Emery
Celia Desmond.....Helen Chandler
Fay Carlile.....Kay Strozzi
Taxi Driver.....Egbert Jones
Acts I, II and III.—In a London Flat.
Staged by A. E. Matthews.

Tom Rowlands and Simon More are a couple of bachelors occupying the same flat in London. Simon is desperately in love with Celia Desmond. Celia throws him over temporarily for a former love. When she discovers that she is to bear the first lover a child and he will not marry her she confesses to Simon and he takes on the responsibility. After they are married on the records only a year Celia is more in love with Simon than he with her. Soon Simon is seeking other women and Celia is contemplating suicide. Tom Rowlands, as a friendly advisor, does what he can for all parties, but that isn't much.

* THE MILKY WAY

(47 performances)

A comedy in three acts by Lynn Root and Harry Clork. Produced by Sidney Harmon and James R. Ullman at the Cort Theatre, New York, May 8, 1934.

Cast of characters—

Spider.....William Foran
Speed McFarland.....Brian Donlevy
Anne Westley.....Gladys George
Gabby Sloan.....Leo Donnelly
Burleigh Sullivan.....Hugh O'Connell
Mae Sullivan.....Emily Lowry
Eddie.....John Brown
Willard.....Edward Emerson
Wilbur Austin.....Bernard Pathe
Acts I, II and III.—Speed's Room in Apartment Hotel in West Fifties in New York City.
Staged by William W. Schorr; settings by Sointu Syrjala.

Burleigh Sullivan is a milkman. His sister Mae is a cigarette girl in a night club. Burleigh is waiting to take Mae home the night Speed McFarland, middleweight champion, gets tight and tries to make up to Mae. There is a fight. Burleigh is a practiced ducker, having trained as an artful dodger, with his head through a canvas, at state fairs. He ducks all the blows struck and McFarland is knocked out by his own trainer. McFarland's manager, thinking it was Burleigh, insists on training the milkman, building him up with fixed fights and putting him in a match with McFarland for a grand haul. But Burleigh butts his way to a victory even with McFarland. If his sister had not bet on him he never could have bought the dairy.

I, MYSELF

(7 performances)

A drama in three acts by Adelyn Bushnell. Produced by Malcolm L. Pearson and Donald E. Baruch at the Mansfield Theatre, New York, May 9, 1934.

Cast of characters—

Annette Trent....................................Eleanor King
Alice Trent....................................Regina Wallace
Arthur Hanlon................................Edmund MacDonald
David Martin.....................................Frank Wilcox
Bill Trent..................................Charles Trowbridge
Harry Stimpson..............................Harry M. Cooke
Dan O'Brien....................................Walter Baldwin
Andrews..William Bonelli
Jerry..Larry Bolton
Connelly....................................Robert J. Mulligan
Charlie Trent..................................Warren Trent
Squinty Anderson..............................Frank Roberts
Jim Kallock..David Bern
Mike Butler.....................................Frank Verigun
Osgood Williams................................Martin Howe
Reverend MacDonald..........................David Hughes
Merrifield.......................................William David
Women Guests: Edith Speare, Muriel Wright, Alice Dowd, Constance Brown.
Quartet: Eddie Brennan, William Zinell, George Hughes, Norvin Mack.

Acts I, II and III.—Home of Bill Trent in a New England City.
Staged by Charles Hopkins; settings by Tom Adrian Cracraft.

Bill Trent, an unsuccessful lawyer who sells life insurance on the side, realizes that he is a failure. Overhears both his wife and his daughter admit as much. Decides that, because of a $50,000 life insurance policy he has been secretly carrying, he is worth more to them dead than alive. Doesn't want to put the stigma of his suicide upon them. Hires a tramp, himself a failure, to shoot him and make it look like the work of burglars.

After he is shot Bill's ghost comes back and tries to get through to his wife to comfort her at the funeral and later to protect her when she is accused of his murder. Looks bad for the wife until the tramp decides to confess.

* EVERY THURSDAY

(44 performances)

A comedy in three acts by Doty Hobart. Produced by Wee and Leventhal, Inc., at the Royale Theatre, New York, May 10, 1934.

Cast of characters—

Mr. Thomas Clark....................George Carleton
Mrs. Thomas Clark....................Ann Dere
Sadie....................Queenie Smith
Raymond Clark....................Leon Janney
Fern Adams....................Tucker McGuire
Dr. Adams....................Frederick Forrester
Ferguson....................Jack Davis
Florence Amelia Elizabeth Lowell....................Sheila Trent
Acts I, II and III.—Living Room in the Clark Home in a Small Town not far from Springfield, Mass.
Staged by Theodore Viehman; settings by Ackerman Studio.

Sadie works for the Clarks every Thursday. The Clarks' son, Raymond, is seventeen years old and growing fast. While his mother and father are away Raymond picks up a femme du pave and brings her home for a drink of gin and a gay evening. Sadie, realizing her responsibilities, substitutes for the street girl. When her relations with young Raymond are discovered she tearfully agrees to leave and also to marry the chauffeur next door.

COME WHAT MAY

(23 performances)

A drama in two acts by Richard F. Flournoy. Produced by Hal Skelly at the Plymouth Theatre, New York, May 15, 1934.

Cast of characters—

Chet Harrison....................Hal Skelly
Eve Hayward....................Mary Philips
Fred Hayward (as a boy)....................Stanton Bier
Dr. Hughes....................Granville Bates
Mrs. Hayward....................Sara Perry
Billy Harrison (as a boy)....................Robert Mayors
Fred Hayward (as a young man)....................Robert Sloane
John Hayward (as a boy)....................Harry Clancy
Billy Harrison (as a young man)....................Alfred Corn
Reed Benton....................W. W. Shuttleworth

Mary Wiley..Nancy Evans
John Hayward (as a young man)................John Bennethum

Act I.—Scene 1 (1896)—Yard of Hayward Home. Scenes 2 (1897), 3 and 4 (1898), 5 (1899)—Sitting Room of Hayward Home. Act II.—Scenes 1 (1906), 2 (1907), 3 (1917), 4 (1918)—Sitting Room of Hayward Home. Scene 5 (1928)—Yard of Hayward Home.

Staged by Leo Bulgakov; settings by Clement M. Williams.

Chet Harrison and Eve Hayward are married; Chet is called to the Spanish-American war; Eve bears him a son; Eve's brother takes lightly to drink; Chet loses his job; Chet loses his insurance; Chet and Eve lose their son in the Great War. In 1928 they have settled peacefully to a contemplation of their old age with $10,000 in the local bank. The world, says Chet, has grown old and sensible. There is nothing for them to fear.

* INVITATION TO A MURDER

(37 performances)

A mystery melodrama in three acts by Rufus King. Produced by Ben Stein at the Masque Theatre, New York, May 17, 1934.

Cast of characters—

Walter Channing...............................William Valentine
Estelle Channing..........................Daphne Warren-Wilson
Horatio Channing.............................Humphrey Bogart
Martin...James Shelburne
Pedro...Juan Varro
Peter Thorne....................................Sherling Oliver
Lorinda Channing...........................Gale Sondergaard
Doctor Linton..Walter Abel
Jeanette Thorne....................................Jane Seymour
Mr. Dickson..Edgar Charles
Detective Sergeant Selbridge.......................Walter Plinge

State Troopers, Police Officials, Plainsclothesmen, etc.

Acts I, II and III.—The Great Hall of the Channing Estate on the Coast of Southern California.

Staged by A. H. Van Buren; settings by Robert Barnhart.

Lorinda Channing, excessively proud of her old Spanish family, has taken the Channing fortune and converted it back into golden treasure, which is the way it was established by the pirate Channings of old. Convinced that one of her ratty relatives is seeking to poison her she plans to trap him by taking a drug that will permit her to simulate death, as Juliet did, and come to life after the poisoner has revealed himself. The doctor who is part of her conspiracy discovers a map to the hidden treasure clasped in her hands and decides to let her die while he is making himself rich. Lorinda is too smart. She comes back to life and puts them in their places.

THE ONLY GIRL

(16 performances)

A musical comedy in three acts by Henry Blossom, derived from Frank Mandel's comedy "Our Wives"; music by Victor Herbert. Revived by the Messrs. Shubert at the 44th Street Theatre, New York, May 21, 1934.

Cast of characters—

Alan Kimbrough (Kim)........................Robert Halliday
Sylvester Martin (Corksey)........................Billy Taylor
John Ayer (Fresh)........................Richard Keene
Andrew McMurray (Bunkie)........................Robert Emmett Keane
Ruth Wilson........................Bettina Hall
Saunders........................George Meader
Birdie Martin........................Betzi Beaton
Margaret Ayer........................Dorothy Dare
Jane McMurray........................Louise Kirtland
Patricia La Montrose (Patsy)........................Neila Goodelle
Ruby........................Frances Foley
Violet........................Evelyn Bonefine
Viola........................Louise Joyce
Paula........................Antoinette Bartlett
Pearle........................Louise Ryan
Renee........................Grena Sloan
Diana........................Sylvia Roberts
Aimee........................Ulita Torgerson

Acts I, II and III.—Living Room of Kimbrough's Apartment, New York City.

Staged by R. H. Burnside.

Alan Kimbrough is the last one of a quartet of bachelors to succumb to the lure of the feminine sex. He makes a stand against Ruth Wilson, a composer with whom he is collaborating in the writing of an opera. In the end love conquers practically all. "The Only Girl" was produced originally by Joe Weber in New York at the Thirty-ninth Street Theatre in November, 1914. It was revived in San Francisco the season of 1932-33.

FURNISHED ROOMS

(15 performances)

A comedy drama in three acts by Ragnhilde Bruland. Produced by Edgar Allen at the Ritz Theatre, New York, May 29, 1934.

Cast of characters—

Frank Foster........................John F. Morrissey
Rose Gordon........................Ronnie Madison
John Maher........................Billy M. Greene
Adele Willis........................Violet Barney
Tom Carney........................Huntly Weston
Billy........................Spencer Bentley

Ann Hadley....................................Vicki Cummings
Margie Kelly....................................Valerie Raemier
Marie....................................Liana Grey
Joe....................................Jay Young
Paul Menti....................................Clarence Rock
Robert Foster....................................Frank Reyman
Officer....................................Jack Willis

Acts I and III.—A Second Floor Bedroom in a Rooming House in the West 50 Streets, New York. Act II.—Scene 1—Parlor on the First Floor. 2—Second Floor Bedroom.

Staged by Russell Morrison.

Ann Hadley, coming to New York in search of a job, advances her last $6 as rent for a furnished room. Frank Foster, who owns the house, forces his attentions upon Ann. Frank Foster's son Robert comes home from college and falls in love with Ann and she with him. She hesitates to tell him about his father but Bob finds out. Father is finally shot by one of his former victims, Adele Willis, who had been his mistress for fifteen years.

WHILE PARENTS SLEEP

(16 performances)

A comedy in three acts by Anthony Kimmins. Produced by William A. Brady in association with Leon M. Lion at the Playhouse, New York, June 4, 1934.

Cast of characters—

Mrs. Hammond....................................Winifred Harris
"Nanny"....................................Jane Corcoran
Colonel Hammond....................................Lionel Pape
Vintcent....................................May Marshall
Neville Hammond....................................Alan Marshal
Lady Cattering....................................Ilka Chase
Jerry Hammond....................................Charles Romano
Bubbles Thompson....................................Jane Bramley

Acts I, II and III.—Drawing Room of the Hammond House in Eccleston Square, London.

Staged by William Brady; settings by Robert Barnhart.

Neville Hammond, who is something of an Army snob, brings his friend Lady Cattering home to have dinner and spend the night. His younger brother, Jerry, a Navy boy, picks up Bubbles Thompson at a dance and insists that she come home with him, also for dinner and the evening. Lady Cattering is a bit uppish with Bubbles Thompson, so when Bubbles finds Neville and her ladyship trying to hide out on the sofa at 2 in the morning it gives her a fairish chance to be even. Colonel and Mrs. Hammond luckily sleep all through the second act.

* CAVIAR

(12 performances)

A romantic musical comedy in two acts by Leo Randole; music by Harden Church; lyrics by Edward Heyman. Produced by Patrick A. Leonard at the Forrest Theatre, New York, June 7, 1934.

Cast of characters—

Jeannine	Violet Carlson
Messenger	George Gordon
A Manicurist	Mitzi Garner
Another Manicurist	Amalie Ideal
A Masseuse	Gene Ashley
Another Masseuse	Tully Millet
A Pedicure	Kai Hansen
A Hairdresser	Nonie Dale
Facialist	Mary Mascher
Another Facialist	George Hunter
Midinette	Drina Hill
Elena	Nanette Guilford
Jack	Billie Leonard
Helen	Don Connolly
Count Chipolita	Walter Armin
Wallace	Hugh Cameron
Carol	Franklyn Fox
Maid	Alice Dudley
Sailor	Jack Cole
Organ Grinder	Walter Armin
Tesore Mio	Herself
Carabinieri	Joseph Olney
Dimitri	George Houston
Pavel	Dudley Clements
Wassili	John J. Walsh
A Reporter	Frank Coletti
An English Sailor	Tully Millet
A French Sailor	George Hunter
An American Sailor	Gene Ashley
A Turkish Detective	Ed Loud
Moofty	Joseph Long
Lenotcha	Drina Hill
Ray	Ray Miller

Act I.—Scene 1—Eleana's Boudoir—Venice. 2—Curtains. 3—Venice. Act II.—Scene 1—A Suite in a Hotel—Constantinople. 2—A Street in Constantinople. 3—A Russian Cabaret.

Staged by Clifford Brooke; dances by Lonergan; settings by Steele Savage.

Elena, an American prima donna studying in Europe, agrees at the insistence of her managers to marry Dimitri, a Russian Prince, who shall be blindfolded and agree to leave her immediately following the ceremony. Dimitri is to be paid for the sacrifice of his title and Elena is to get the benefit of the publicity. After the wedding Elena discovers Prince Dimitri to be the handsome tenor who has been singing under her balcony. She changes her mind about having the marriage dissolved and finally induces her Prince to stay put.

* KYKUNDOR

(41 performances)

A native African dance-opera by Asadata Dafora. Produced by Mr. Dafora at the Little Theatre, New York, June 10, 1934.

Cast of characters—

Bridegroom..Asadata Dafora
Bride ....Musu Esmai
Witch Doctor..Abdul Essen
Witch Woman..Mirammu
Otobone..Rimeru Shikeru
Agunda Dancer..Matta
Chief Burah..Tuguese
Eboe (Eccentric Dancer)..Alala
Drummers: Abrodun Salakox, Uno Eno, Sakor Jar, Ezebro Ejiho.
The Action Takes Place in an African Maiden Village.
Staged and designed by Asadata Defora.

Asadata Dafora (Horton), whose great-great-grandfather was sold as a slave into Nova Scotia, gained fame as an authority on the tribal songs and dances of Africa. Putting his knowledge to use he composed an opera based on the native rites of courtship and marriage, including a variety of associated ceremonies. "Kykundor" or "The Witch Woman" was first produced obscurely in New York by the Unity Theatre Group and attracted the attention of New York's leading authorities on the dance. Outgrowing the scene of its early performances in a hall in East 23d Street after thirteen performances the African opera was moved to the auditorium of the City College for four performances, then to the Chanin Auditorium, fifty floors above street level in the Chanin Building, for fifteen showings, and finally to the Little Theatre, where it was still playing when this record was closed.

PUPPET SHOWS, ETC.

During the season puppet shows were given by the Teatro Dei Piccoli at the Hudson Theatre, continuing for a run of forty-four performances.

Tony Sarg presented his Marionette troupe in adaptations from the Uncle Remus stories and a production of "Alice in Wonderland" during the Easter holidays at Carnegie Hall.

Sue Hastings' Marionettes performed at the Plaza Theatre Christmas week.

The Marionette Guild presented "The Emperor Jones" at the Provincetown Theatre during the Christmas holidays.

During the holidays the Theatre Guild sponsored a production of Robert Reinhardt's "Matinées of Magic" at the Guild Theatre.

Clare Tree Major gave three matinées of "The Five Little Peppers" at the Roerich Theatre.

A performance of "The Adventures of Ola" at the Heckscher Theatre was given under the auspices of the Henry Street Settlement.

In January at the Barbizon Plaza Margo Sanger gave a series of dramatic sketches. At the Forty-eighth Street Theatre Miriam Elgas presented a series of classic Hebrew sketches.

Thirteen performances of Lillian Mortimer's "No Mother to Guide Her" were offered by a cast of fifteen midgets at what was formerly the President Theatre during the Christmas holidays. Lester Al Smith was the producer and C. Swayne Gordon the director.

STATISTICAL SUMMARY

(Last Season Plays Which Ended Runs After June 17, 1933)

Plays	*Number Performances*	*Plays*	*Number Performances*
Another Language (return)	89	Goodbye Again	216
(including original run)	433	June Moon (revival)	49
Biography	267	Music in the Air	342
(including return)	283	One Sunday Afternoon	322
Both Your Houses	120	Shooting Star	16
Climax, The	15	Take a Chance	243
Gay Divorce	248	Tattle Tales	28

LONG RUNS ON BROADWAY

To June 16, 1934

Plays	*Number Performances*	*Plays*	*Number Performances*
Abie's Irish Rose	2,532	Street Scene	601
Lightnin'	1,291	Kiki	600
The Bat	867	Blossom Time	592
The Ladder	789	Show Boat	572
The First Year	760	The Show-off	571
Seventh Heaven	704	Sally	570
Peg o' My Heart	692	Strictly Dishonorable	557
East Is West	680	Good News	551
Irene	670	The Music Master	540
A Trip to Chinatown	657	The Boomerang	522
Rain	648	Blackbirds	518
The Green Pastures	640	Sunny	517
Is Zat So	618	The Vagabond King	511
Student Prince	608	The New Moon	509
Broadway	603	Shuffle Along	504
Adonis	603	Bird in Hand	500

PULITZER PRIZE WINNERS

"For the original American play performed in New York which shall best represent the educational value and power of the stage in raising the standard of good morals, good taste and good manners."—The Will of Joseph Pulitzer, dated April 16, 1904.

In 1929 the advisory board, which, according to the terms of the will, "shall have the power in its discretion to suspend or to change any subject or subjects . . . if in the judgment of the board such suspension, changes or substitutions shall be conducive to the public good," decided to eliminate from the above paragraph relating to the prize-winning play the words "in raising the standard of good morals, good taste and good manners."

The committee awards to date have been:

1917-18—Why Marry? by Jesse Lynch Williams
1918-19—None
1919-20—Miss Lulu Bett, by Zona Gale
1920-21—Beyond the Horizon, by Eugene O'Neill
1921-22—Anna Christie, by Eugene O'Neill
1922-23—Icebound, by Owen Davis
1923-24—Hell-bent fer Heaven, by Hatcher Hughes
1924-25—They Knew What They Wanted, by Sidney Howard
1925-26—Craig's Wife, by George Kelly
1926-27—In Abraham's Bosom, by Paul Green
1927-28—Strange Interlude, by Eugene O'Neill
1928-29—Street Scene, by Elmer Rice
1929-30—The Green Pastures, by Marc Connelly
1930-31—Alison's House, by Susan Glaspell
1931-32—Of Thee I Sing, by George S. Kaufman, Morrie Ryskind, Ira and George Gershwin
1932-33—Both Your Houses, by Maxwell Anderson
1933-34—Men in White, by Sidney Kingsley.

PREVIOUS VOLUMES OF BEST PLAYS

Plays chosen to represent the theatre seasons from 1909 to 1934 are as follows:

1909-1919

"The Easiest Way," by Eugene Walters. Published by G. W. Dillingham, New York; Houghton Mifflin Co., Boston.

"Mrs. Bumpstead-Leigh," by Harry James Smith. Published by Samuel French, New York.

"Disraeli," by Louis N. Parker. Published by Dodd, Mead and Co., New York.

"Romance," by Edward Sheldon. Published by the Macmillan Co., New York.

"Seven Keys to Baldpate," by George M. Cohan. Published by Bobbs-Merrill Co., Indianapolis, as a novel by Earl Derr Biggers; as a play by Samuel French, New York.

"On Trial," by Elmer Reizenstein. Published by Samuel French, New York.

"The Unchastened Woman," by Louis Kaufman Anspacher. Published by Harcourt, Brace and Howe, Inc., New York.

"Good Gracious Annabelle," by Clare Kummer. Published by Samuel French, New York.

"Why Marry?" by Jesse Lynch Williams. Published by Charles Scribner's Sons, New York.

"John Ferguson," by St. John Ervine. Published by the Macmillan Co., New York.

1919-1920

"Abraham Lincoln," by John Drinkwater. Published by Houghton Mifflin Co., Boston.

"Clarence," by Booth Tarkington.

"Beyond the Horizon," by Eugene G. O'Neill. Published by Boni & Liveright, Inc., New York.

"Déclassée," by Zoe Akins.

"The Famous Mrs. Fair," by James Forbes.

"The Jest," by Sem Benelli. (American adaptation by Edward Sheldon.)

"Jane Clegg," by St. John Ervine. Published by Henry Holt & Co., New York.

"Mamma's Affair," by Rachel Barton Butler.
"Wedding Bells," by Salisbury Field.
"Adam and Eva," by George Middleton and Guy Bolton.

1920-1921

"Deburau," adapted from the French of Sacha Guitry by H. Granville Barker. Published by G. P. Putnam's Sons, New York.
"The First Year," by Frank Craven.
"Enter Madame," by Gilda Varesi and Dolly Byrne. Published by G. P. Putnam's Sons, New York.
"The Green Goddess," by William Archer. Published by Alfred A. Knopf, New York.
"Liliom," by Ferenc Molnar. Published by Boni & Liveright, New York.
"Mary Rose," by James M. Barrie.
"Nice People," by Rachel Crothers.
"The Bad Man," by Porter Emerson Browne. Published by G. P. Putnam's Sons, New York.
"The Emperor Jones," by Eugene G. O'Neill. Published by Boni & Liveright, New York.
"The Skin Game," by John Galsworthy. Published by Charles Scribner's Sons, New York.

1921-1922

"Anna Christie," by Eugene G. O'Neill. Published by Boni & Liveright, New York.
"A Bill of Divorcement," by Clemence Dane. Published by the Macmillan Company, New York.
"Dulcy," by George S. Kaufman and Marc Connelly. Published by G. P. Putnam's Sons, New York.
"He Who Gets Slapped," adapted from the Russian of Leonid Andreyev by Gregory Zilboorg. Published by Brentano's, New York.
"Six Cylinder Love," by William Anthony McGuire.
"The Hero," by Gilbert Emery.
"The Dover Road," by Alan Alexander Milne.
"Ambush," by Arthur Richman.
"The Circle," by William Somerset Maugham.
"The Nest," by Paul Geraldy and Grace George.

1922-1923

"Rain," by John Colton and Clemence Randolph.

"Loyalties," by John Galsworthy. Published by Charles Scribner's Sons, New York.

"Icebound," by Owen Davis. Published by Little, Brown & Company, Boston.

"You and I," by Philip Barry. Published by Brentano's, New York.

"The Fool," by Channing Pollock. Published by Brentano's, New York.

"Merton of the Movies," by George Kaufman and Marc Connelly, based on the novel of the same name by Harry Leon Wilson.

"Why Not?" by Jesse Lynch Williams.

"The Old Soak," by Don Marquis. Published by Doubleday, Page & Company, New York.

"R.U.R.," by Karel Capek. Translated by Paul Selver. Published by Doubleday, Page & Company.

"Mary the 3d," by Rachel Crothers. Published by Brentano's, New York.

1923-1924

"The Swan," translated from the Hungarian of Ferenc Molnar by Melville Baker. Published by Boni & Liveright, New York.

"Outward Bound," by Sutton Vane. Published by Boni & Liveright, New York.

"The Show-off," by George Kelly. Published by Little, Brown & Company, Boston.

"The Changelings," by Lee Wilson Dodd. Published by E. P. Dutton & Company, New York.

"Chicken Feed," by Guy Bolton. Published by Samuel French, New York and London.

"Sun-Up," by Lula Vollmer. Published by Brentano's, New York.

"Beggar on Horseback," by George Kaufman and Marc Connelly. Published by Boni & Liveright, New York.

"Tarnish," by Gilbert Emery. Published by Brentano's, New York.

"The Goose Hangs High," by Lewis Beach. Published by Little, Brown & Company, Boston.

"Hell-bent fer Heaven," by Hatcher Hughes. Published by Harper Bros., New York.

1924-1925

"What Price Glory?" by Laurence Stallings and Maxwell Anderson.

"They Knew What They Wanted," by Sidney Howard. Published by Doubleday, Page & Company, New York.

"Desire Under the Elms," by Eugene G. O'Neill. Published by Boni & Liveright, New York.

"The Firebrand," by Edwin Justus Mayer. Published by Boni & Liveright, New York.

"Dancing Mothers," by Edgar Selwyn and Edmund Goulding.

"Mrs. Partridge Presents," by Mary Kennedy and Ruth Warren.

"The Fall Guy," by James Gleason and George Abbott.

"The Youngest," by Philip Barry. Published by Samuel French, New York.

"Minick," by Edna Ferber and George S. Kaufman. Published by Doubleday, Page & Company, New York.

"Wild Birds," by Dan Totheroh. Published by Doubleday, Page & Company, New York.

1925-1926

"Craig's Wife," by George Kelly. Published by Little, Brown & Company, Boston.

"The Great God Brown," by Eugene G. O'Neill. Published by Boni & Liveright, New York.

"The Green Hat," by Michael Arlen.

"The Dybbuk," by S. Ansky, Henry G. Alsberg-Winifred Katzin translation. Published by Boni & Liveright, New York.

"The Enemy," by Channing Pollock. Published by Brentano's, New York.

"The Last of Mrs. Cheyney," by Frederick Lonsdale.

"Bride of the Lamb," by William Hurlbut. Published by Boni & Liveright, New York.

"The Wisdom Tooth," by Marc Connelly. Published by George H. Doran & Company, New York.

"The Butter and Egg Man," by George Kaufman. Published by Boni & Liveright, New York.

"Young Woodley," by John Van Druten. Published by Simon and Schuster, New York.

1926-1927

"Broadway," by Philip Dunning and George Abbott. Published by George H. Doran Company, New York.

"Saturday's Children," by Maxwell Anderson. Published by Longmans, Green & Company, New York.

"Chicago," by Maurine Watkins. Published by Alfred A. Knopf, Inc., New York.

"The Constant Wife," by William Somerset Maugham. Published by George H. Doran Company, New York.

"The Play's the Thing," by Ferenc Molnar and P. G. Wodehouse. Published by Brentano's, New York.

"The Road to Rome," by Robert Emmet Sherwood. Published by Charles Scribner's Sons, New York.

"The Silver Cord," by Sidney Howard. Published by Charles Scribner's Sons, New York.

"The Cradle Song," translated from the Spanish of G. Martinez Sierra by John Garrett Underhill. Published by E. P. Dutton & Company, New York.

"Daisy Mayme," by George Kelly. Published by Little, Brown & Company, Boston.

"In Abraham's Bosom," by Paul Green. Published by Robert M. McBride & Company, New York.

1927-1928

"Strange Interlude," by Eugene G. O'Neill. Published by Boni & Liveright, New York.

"The Royal Family," by Edna Ferber and George Kaufman. Published by Doubleday, Doran & Company, New York.

"Burlesque," by George Manker Watters. Published by Doubleday, Doran & Company, New York.

"Coquette," by George Abbott and Ann Bridgers. Published by Longmans, Green & Company, New York, London, Toronto.

"Behold the Bridegroom," by George Kelly. Published by Little, Brown & Company, Boston.

"Porgy," by DuBose Heyward. Published by Doubleday, Doran & Company, New York.

"Paris Bound," by Philip Barry. Published by Samuel French, New York.

"Escape," by John Galsworthy. Published by Charles Scribner's Sons, New York.

"The Racket," by Bartlett Cormack. Published by Samuel

French, New York.

"The Plough and the Stars," by Sean O'Casey. Published by the Macmillan Company, New York.

1928-1929

"Street Scene," by Elmer Rice. Published by Samuel French, New York.

"Journey's End," by R. C. Sheriff. Published by Brentano's, New York.

"Wings Over Europe," by Robert Nichols and Maurice Browne. Published by Covici-Friede, New York.

"Holiday," by Philip Barry. Published by Samuel French, New York.

"The Front Page," by Ben Hecht and Charles MacArthur. Published by Covici-Friede, New York.

"Let Us Be Gay," by Rachel Crothers. Published by Samuel French, New York.

"Machinal," by Sophie Treadwell.

"Little Accident," by Floyd Dell and Thomas Mitchell.

"Gypsy," by Maxwell Anderson.

"The Kingdom of God," by G. Martinez Sierra; English version by Helen and Harley Granville-Barker. Published by E. P. Dutton & Company, New York.

1929-1930

"The Green Pastures," by Marc Connelly (adapted from "Ol' Man Adam and His Chillun," by Roark Bradford). Published by Farrar & Rinehart, Inc., New York.

"The Criminal Code," by Martin Flavin. Published by Horace Liveright, New York.

"Berkeley Square," by John Balderstone. Published by the Macmillan Company, New York.

"Strictly Dishonorable," by Preston Sturges. Published by Horace Liveright, New York.

"The First Mrs. Fraser," by St. John Ervine. Published by the Macmillan Company, New York.

"The Last Mile," by John Wexley. Published by Samuel French, New York.

"June Moon," by Ring W. Lardner and George S. Kaufman. Published by Charles Scribner's Sons, New York.

"Michael and Mary," by A. A. Milne. Published by Chatto & Windus, London.

"Death Takes a Holiday," by Walter Ferris (adapted from the Italian of Alberto Casella). Published by Samuel French, New York.

"Rebound," by Donald Ogden Stewart. Published by Samuel French, New York.

1930-1931

"Elizabeth the Queen," by Maxwell Anderson. Published by Longmans, Green & Co., New York.

"Tomorrow and Tomorrow," by Philip Barry. Published by Samuel French, New York.

"Once in a Lifetime," by George S. Kaufman and Moss Hart. Published by Farrar and Rinehart, New York.

"Green Grow the Lilacs," by Lynn Riggs. Published by Samuel French, New York and London.

"As Husbands Go," by Rachel Crothers. Published by Samuel French, New York.

"Alison's House," by Susan Glasgow. Published by Samuel French, New York.

"Five-Star Final," by Louis Weitzenkorn. Published by Samuel French, New York.

"Overture," by William Bolitho. Published by Simon & Shuster, New York.

"The Barretts of Wimpole Street," by Rudolf Besier. Published by Little, Brown & Company, Boston.

"Grand Hotel," adapted from the German of Vicki Baum by W. A. Drake.

1931-1932

"Of Thee I Sing," by George S. Kaufman and Morrie Ryskind; music and lyrics by George and Ira Gershwin. Published by Alfred Knopf, New York.

"Morning Becomes Electra," by Eugene O'Neill. Published by Horace Liveright, Inc., New York.

"Reunion in Vienna," by Robert Emmet Sherwood. Published by Charles Scribner's Sons, New York.

"The House of Connelly," by Paul Green. Published by Samuel French, New York.

"The Animal Kingdom," by Philip Barry. Published by Samuel French, New York.

"The Left Bank," by Elmer Rice. Published by Samuel French, New York.

"Another Language," by Rose Franken. Published by Samuel French, New York.

"Brief Moment," by S. N. Behrman. Published by Farrar & Rinehart, New York.

"The Devil Passes," by Ben W. Levy. Published by Martin Secker, London.

"Cynara," by H. M. Harwood and R. F. Gore-Browne. Published by Samuel French, New York.

1932-1933

"Both Your Houses," by Maxwell Anderson. Published by Samuel French, New York.

"Dinner at Eight," by George S. Kaufman and Edna Ferber. Published by Doubleday, Doran & Co., Inc., Garden City, New York.

"When Ladies Meet," by Rachel Crothers. Published by Samuel French, New York.

"Design for Living," by Noel Coward. Published by Doubleday, Doran & Co., Inc., Garden City, New York.

"Biography," by S. N. Behrman. Published by Farrar & Rinehart, Inc., New York.

"Alien Corn," by Sidney Howard. Published by Charles Scribner's Sons, New York.

"The Late Christopher Bean," adapted from the French of Rene Fauchois by Sidney Howard. Published by Samuel French, New York.

"We, the People," by Elmer Rice. Published by Coward-McCann, Inc., New York.

"Pigeons and People," by George M. Cohan.

"One Sunday Afternoon," by James Hagan. Published by Samuel French, New York.

WHERE AND WHEN THEY WERE BORN

Abbott, George ....Hamburg, N. Y. 1895
Abel, Walter ....St. Paul, Minn. 1898
Aborn, Milton ....Marysville, Cal. 1864
Adams, Maude ....Salt Lake City, Utah 1872
Adler, Stella ....New York 1904
Aherne, Brian ....King's Norton, England ..1902
Akins, Zoe ....Humansville, Mo. 1886
Alexander, Katherine ....Arkansas 1901
Alexander, Ross ....Brooklyn, N. Y. 1904
Allanby, Peggy ....New York 1905
Allen, Adrianne ....Manchester, England 1907
Allen, Viola ....Huntsville, Ala. 1869
Ames, Robert ....Hartford, Conn. 1893
Ames, Winthrop ....North Easton, Mass. 1871
Anders, Glenn ....Los Angeles, Cal. 1890
Anderson, Judith ....Australia 1898
Anderson, Maxwell ....Atlantic City, Pa. 1888
Andrews, Ann ....Los Angeles, Cal. 1895
Anglin, Margaret ....Ottawa, Canada 1876
Anson, A. E. ....London, England 1879
Anspacher, Louis K. ....Cincinnati, Ohio 1878
Arliss, George ....London, England 1868
Arthur, Julia ....Hamilton, Ont. 1869
Astaire, Fred ....Omaha, Neb. 1899
Atwell, Roy ....Syracuse, N. Y. 1880
Atwill, Lionel ....London, England 1885

Bainter, Fay ....Los Angeles, Cal. 1892
Baker, Lee ....Michigan 1880
Bankhead, Tallulah ....Huntsville, Ala. 1902
Banks, Leslie J. ....West Derby, England 1890
Barbee, Richard ....Lafayette, Ind. 1887
Barrett, Edith ....Roxbury, Mass. 1904
Barrie, James Matthew ....Kirriemuir, N. B. 1860
Barry, Philip ....Rochester, N. Y. 1896
Barrymore, Ethel ....Philadelphia, Pa. 1879
Barrymore, John ....Philadelphia, Pa. 1882

Barrymore, Lionel .... London, England 1878
Bates, Blanche .... Portland, Ore. 1873
Baxter, Lora .... New York 1907
Beatty, Roberta .... Rochester, N. Y. 1900
Beecher, Janet .... Chicago, Ill. 1884
Behrman, S. N. .... Worcester, Mass. 1893
Ben-Ami, Jacob .... Minsk, Russia 1890
Bennett, Richard .... Cass County, Ind. 1873
Bennett, Wilda .... Asbury Park, N. J. 1894
Berlin, Irving .... Russia 1888
Best, Edna .... Sussex, England 1900
Binney, Constance .... Philadelphia, Pa. 1900
Blackmer, Sidney .... Salisbury, N. C. 1896
Boland, Mary .... Detroit, Mich. 1880
Bondi, Beulah .... Chicago, Ill. 1892
Bordoni, Irene .... Paris, France 1895
Brady, Alice .... New York 1892
Brady, William A. .... San Francisco, Cal. 1863
Brady, William A., Jr. .... New York 1900
Braham, Horace .... London, England 1896
Brian, Donald .... St. Johns, N. F. 1877
Brice, Fannie .... Brooklyn, N. Y. 1891
Broadhurst, George H. .... England 1866
Broderick, Helen .... New York 1891
Bromberg, J. Edward .... Hungary 1903
Bryant, Charles .... England 1879
Buchanan, Jack .... England 1892
Buchanan, Thompson .... Louisville, Ky. 1877
Buckler, Hugh .... Southampton, England ... 1886
Burke, Billie .... Washington, D. C. 1885
Burton, Frederick .... Indiana 1871
Byington, Spring .... Colorado Springs, Colo. ... 1898
Byron, Arthur .... Brooklyn, N. Y. 1872

Cagney, James .... New York 1904
Cahill, Lily .... Texas 1885
Cahill, Marie .... Brooklyn, N. Y. 1871
Calhern, Louis .... New York 1895
Cantor, Eddie .... New York 1894
Campbell, Mrs. Patrick .... England 1865
Carle, Richard .... Somerville, Mass. 1871
Carlisle, Alexandra .... Yorkshire, England 1886
Carminati, Tullio .... Zara, Dalmatia 1894

Carpenter, Edward Childs .....Philadelphia, Pa. 1871
Carr, Alexander ....Russia 1878
Carroll, Earl ....Pittsburgh, Pa. 1892
Carter, Mrs. Leslie ....Lexington, Ky. 1862
Catlett, Walter ....San Francisco, Cal. 1889
Cawthorne, Joseph ....New York 1868
Chandler, Helen ....Charleston, N. C. 1906
Chaplin, Charles Spencer ......London 1889
Chase, Ilka ....New York 1900
Chatterton, Ruth ....New York 1893
Cherry, Charles ....England 1872
Christians, Mady ....Vienna, Austria 1907
Churchill, Burton ....Toronto, Can. 1876
Claire, Ina ....Washington, D. C. 1892
Clarke, Marguerite ....Cincinnati, Ohio 1887
Cliffe, H. Cooper ....England 1862
Clifford, Kathleen ....Charlottesville, Va. 1887
Clive, Colin ....St. Malo, France 1900
Coburn, Charles ....Macon, Ga. 1877
Coghlan, Gertrude ....England 1879
Coghlan, Rose ....Petersborough, England ...1850
Cohan, George M. ....Providence, R. I. 1878
Cohan, Georgette ....Los Angeles, Cal. 1900
Colbert, Claudette ....Paris 1905
Collier, Constance ....Windsor, England 1882
Collier, William ....New York 1866
Collinge, Patricia ....Dublin, Ireland 1894
Collins, José ....London, England 1896
Colt, Ethel Barrymore ....Mamaroneck, N. Y. 1911
Colt, John Drew ....New York 1914
Conklin, Peggy ....Dobbs Ferry, N. Y. 1912
Connolly, Walter ....Cincinnati, Ohio 1888
Conroy, Frank ....London, England 1885
Cook, Joe ....Evansville, Ind. 1890
Cooper, Gladys ....Lewisham, England 1888
Cooper, Violet Kemble ....London, England 1890
Cornell, Katharine ....Buffalo, N. Y. 1900
Corrigan, Emmett ....Amsterdam, Holland 1871
Corthell, Herbert ....Boston, Mass. 1875
Cossart, Ernest ....Cheltenham, England 1876
Courtenay, William ....Worcester, Mass. 1875
Courtleigh, William ....Guelph, Ont. 1869
Coward, Noel ....England 1899

Cowl, Jane	Boston, Mass.	1887
Craven, Frank	Boston, Mass.	1880
Crews, Laura Hope	San Francisco, Cal.	1880
Crosman, Henrietta	Wheeling, W. Va.	1865
Crothers, Rachel	Bloomington, Ill.	1878
Cumberland, John	St. John, N. B.	1880
Dale, Margaret	Philadelphia, Pa.	1880
Dalton, Charles	England	1864
Daly, Blyth	New York	1902
Danforth, William	Syracuse	1869
Daniels, Frank	Dayton, Ohio	1860
Davis, Owen	Portland, Me.	1874
Davis, Owen, Jr.	New York	1907
Dawn, Hazel	Ogden, Utah	1891
Day, Edith	Minneapolis, Minn.	1896
De Angelis, Jefferson	San Francisco, Cal.	1859
Dean, Julia	St. Paul, Minn.	1880
De Cordoba, Pedro	New York	1881
Dillingham, Charles B.	Hartford, Conn.	1868
Dinehart, Allan	Missoula, Mont.	1889
Dixey, Henry E.	Boston, Mass.	1859
Dixon, Jean	Waterbury, Conn.	1905
Dodson, John E.	London, England	1857
Doro, Marie	Duncannon, Pa.	1882
D'Orsay, Lawrence	England	1860
Dressler, Eric	Brooklyn, N. Y.	1900
Dressler, Marie	Cobourg, Canada	1869
Drew, Louise	New York	1884
Duncan, Augustin	San Francisco	1873
Dunn, Emma	England	1875
Dunning, Philip	Meriden, Conn.	1890
Dupree, Minnie	San Francisco, Cal.	1875
Edeson, Robert	Baltimore, Md.	1868
Eldridge, Florence	Brooklyn, N. Y.	1901
Ellis, Mary	New York	1900
Elliston, Grace	Wheeling, W. Va.	1881
Ellinger, Desirée	Manchester, Vt.	1895
Elliott, Gertrude	Rockland, Me.	1874
Elliott, Maxine	Rockland, Me.	1871
Eltinge, Julian	Boston, Mass.	1883
Emery, Gilbert	Naples, New York	1875

Emerson, John	Sandusky, Ohio	1874
Errol, Leon	Sydney, Australia	1881
Ervine, St. John Greer	Belfast, Ireland	1883
Fairbanks, Douglas	Denver, Colo.	1883
Farnum, William	Boston, Mass.	1876
Farrar, Geraldine	Melrose, Mass.	1883
Faversham, William	Warwickshire, England	1868
Fenwick, Irene	Chicago, Ill.	1887
Ferber, Edna	Kalamazoo, Mich.	1887
Ferguson, Elsie	New York	1883
Field, Sylvia	Allston, Mass.	1902
Fields, Lew	New York	1867
Fields, W. C.	Philadelphia, Pa.	1883
Fischer, Alice	Indiana	1869
Fiske, Minnie Maddern	New Orleans, La.	1867
Fontanne, Lynn	London, England	1882
Forbes, Robertson, Sir J.	London, England	1853
Foster, Claiborne	Shreveport, La.	1899
Foster, Norman	Richmond, Ind.	1907
Foster, Phœbe	New Hampshire	1897
Foy, Eddie, Jr.	New Rochelle, N. Y.	1906
Franklin, Irene	St. Louis, Mo.	1878
Frederick, Pauline	Boston, Mass.	1884
Friganza, Trixie	Cincinnati, Ohio	1870
Frohman, Daniel	Sandusky, Ohio	1850
Gahagan, Helen	Boonton, N. J.	1902
Garden, Mary	Scotland	1876
Gaxton, William	San Francisco, Cal.	1893
Gaythorne, Pamela	England	1882
George, Grace	New York	1879
Gerald, Ara	New South Wales	1902
Gillette, William	Hartford, Conn.	1856
Gillmore, Frank	New York	1884
Gillmore, Margalo	England	1901
Gish, Dorothy	Massillon, Ohio	1898
Gish, Lillian	Springfield, Ohio	1896
Gleason, James	New York	1885
Glendinning, Ernest	Ulverston, England	1884
Golden, John	New York	1874
Gottschalk, Ferdinand	London, England	1869
Granville, Charlotte	London	1863

Greenstreet, Sydney ....England 1880
Grey, Katherine ....San Francisco, Cal. 1873
Groody, Louise ....Waco, Texas 1897

Haines, Robert T. ....Muncie, Ind. 1870
Hale, Louise Closser ....Chicago, Ill. 1872
Hall, Bettina ....North Easton, Mass. 1906
Hall, Laura Nelson ....Philadelphia, Pa. 1876
Hall, Natalie ....North Easton, Mass. 1904
Hall, Thurston ....Boston, Mass. 1882
Hamilton, Hale ....Topeka, Kansas 1880
Hampden, Walter ....Brooklyn, N. Y. 1879
Hanson, Gladys ....Atlanta, Ga. 1887
Harding, Lyn ....Newport, England 1867
Harrigan, William ....New York 1893
Harris, Sam H. ....New York 1872
Harrison, Richard B. ....London, Ontario 1864
Hayes, Helen ....Washington, D. C. 1900
Hazzard, John E. ....New York 1881
Hedman, Martha ....Sweden 1888
Heggie, O. P. ....Australia 1879
Heming, Violet ....Leeds, England 1893
Hepburn, Katharine ....Hartford, Conn. 1907
Herbert, Evelyn ....Brooklyn, N. Y. 1900
Herne, Chrystal ....Dorchester, Mass. 1883
Hobart, Rose ....New York 1906
Hodge, William ....Albion, N. Y. 1874
Hopkins, Arthur ....Cleveland, Ohio 1878
Hopkins, Miriam ....Bainbridge, Ga. 1904
Hopper, de Wolf ....New York 1858
Hopper, Edna Wallace ....San Francisco, Cal. 1874
Holmes, Taylor ....Newark, N. J. 1872
Howard, Leslie ....London, England 1890
Hull, Henry ....Louisville, Ky. 1893
Hunter, Glenn ....Highland Mills, N. Y. 1896
Huston, Walter ....Toronto 1884
Hutchinson, Josephine ....Seattle, Wash. 1898

Inescort, Frieda ....Hitchin, Scotland 1905
Irving, Isabel ....Bridgeport, Conn. 1871
Irwin, May ....Whitby, Ont. 1862

Janis, Elsie ....Delaware, Ohio 1889
Joel, Clara ....Jersey City, N. J. 1890

Johann, Zita ....Hungary 1904
Jolson, Al ....Washington, D. C. 1883
Johnston, Moffat ....Edinburgh, Scotland 1886

Kaufman, George S. ....Pittsburgh, Pa. 1889
Keane, Doris ....Michigan 1885
Keith, Robert ....Scotland 1899
Kelly, Walter C. ....Mineville, N. Y. 1875
Kennedy, Madge ....Chicago, Ill. 1890
Kerrigan, J. M. ....Dublin, Ireland 1885
Kerr, Geoffrey ....London, England 1895
Kershaw, Willette ....Clifton Heights, Mo. 1890
Kingsford, Walter ....England 1876
Kirkland, Alexander ....Mexico City 1904
Kosta, Tessa ....Chicago, Ill. 1893
Kruger, Alma ....Pittsburgh, Pa. 1880
Kruger, Otto ....Toledo, Ohio 1895

Lackaye, Wilton ....Virginia 1862
Larimore, Earl ....Portland, Oregon 1899
Larrimore, Francine ....Russia 1898
La Rue, Grace ....Kansas City, Mo. 1882
Lauder, Harry ....Portobello, England 1870
Lawrence, Gertrude ....London 1898
Lawton, Thais ....Louisville, Ky. 1881
Lean, Cecil ....Illinois 1878
Lederer, Francis ....Karlin, Prague 1906
Le Gallienne, Eva ....London, England 1900
Leiber, Fritz ....Chicago, Ill. 1884
Leontovich, Eugenie ....Moscow, Russia 1894
Levey, Ethel ....San Francisco, Cal. 1881
Lewis, Mabel Terry ....London, England 1872
Lillie, Beatrice ....Toronto, Canada 1898
Logan, Stanley ....Earlsfield, England 1885
Loraine, Robert ....New Brighton, England ...1876
Lord, Pauline ....Hanford, Cal. 1890
Lorraine, Lillian ....San Francisco, Cal. 1892
Lou-Tellegen ....Holland 1881
Love, Montagu ....Portsmouth, Hants 1877
Lowell, Helen ....New York 1866
Lunt, Alfred ....Milwaukee, Wis. 1893

Mack, Andrew ....Boston, Mass. 1863
Mack, Willard ....Ontario, Canado 1873

Mackay, Elsie	London, England	1894
MacKellar, Helen	Canada	1896
Marlowe, Julia	Caldbeck, England	1870
Marshall, Herbert	London, England	1890
Massey, Raymond	Toronto, Canada	1896
Matthews, A. E.	Bridlington, England	1869
Matthison, Edith Wynne	England	1875
Maude, Cyril	London, England	1862
McClintic, Guthrie	Seattle, Wash.	1893
McIntyre, Frank	Ann Arbor, Mich.	1879
Meek, Donald	Glasgow, Scotland	1880
Meighan, Thomas	Pittsburgh, Pa.	1879
Melba, Nellie	Melbourne, Australia	1866
Menken, Helen	New York	1901
Mercer, Beryl	Seville, Spain	1882
Merivale, Philip	Rehutia, India	1886
Miller, Gilbert	New York	1884
Miller, Marilyn	Findlay, Ohio	1898
Mitchell, Grant	Columbus, Ohio	1874
Mitchell, Thomas	Elizabeth, N. J.	1892
Mitzi (Hajos)	Budapest	1891
Moore, Grace	Del Rio, Tenn.	1901
Moore, Victor	Hammonton, N. J.	1876
Moran, Lois	Pittsburgh, Pa.	1909
Morgan, Claudia	New York	1912
Morgan, Helen	Danville, Ill.	1900
Morgan, Ralph	New York City	1889
Morris, Mary	Boston	1894
Morris, McKay	San Antonio, Texas	1890
Muni, Paul	Lemberg, Austria	1895
Nagel, Conrad	Keokuk, Iowa	1897
Nash, Florence	Troy, N. Y.	1888
Nash, Mary	Troy, N. Y.	1885
Nazimova, Alla	Crimea, Russia	1879
Nielsen, Alice	Nashville, Tenn.	1876
Nolan, Lloyd	San Francisco, Cal.	1903
Nugent, J. C.	Miles, Ohio	1875
Nugent, Elliott	Dover, Ohio	1900
O'Connell, Hugh	New York	1891
Olcott, Chauncey	Buffalo, N. Y.	1862
O'Neill, Eugene Gladstone	New York	1888

O'Neill, Nance ....Oakland, Cal. 1875
Overman, Lynne ....Maryville, Mo. 1887

Painter, Eleanor ....Iowa 1890
Pawle, Lenox ....London, England 1872
Pemberton, Brock ....Leavenworth, Kansas 1885
Pennington, Ann ....Philadelphia, Pa. 1898
Perkins, Osgood ....Boston, Mass. 1892
Philips, Mary ....New London, Conn. 1901
Pickford, Mary ....Toronto 1893
Pollock, Channing ....Washington, D. C. 1880
Post, Guy Bates ....Seattle, Wash. 1875
Power, Tyrone ....London, England 1869
Powers, James T. ....New York 1862
Pryor, Roger ....New York City 1901

Quartermaine, Leon ....Richmond, England 1876

Rains, Claude ....London, England 1889
Rambeau, Marjorie ....San Francisco, Cal. 1889
Rathbone, Basil ....Johannesburg 1892
Reed, Florence ....Philadelphia, Pa. 1883
Rennie, James ....Toronto, Canada 1890
Revelle, Hamilton ....Gibraltar 1872
Richman, Charles ....Chicago, Ill. 1870
Ring, Blanche ....Boston, Mass. 1876
Ring, Frances ....New York 1882
Robson, May ....Australia 1868
Ross, Thomas W. ....Boston, Mass. 1875
Royle, Selena ....New York 1905
Ruben, José ....Belgium 1886
Rumann, Siegfried ....Hamburg, Germany 1879
Russell, Annie ....Liverpool, England 1864

Sanderson, Julia ....Springfield, Mass. 1887
Sands, Dorothy ....Cambridge, Mass. 1900
Santley, Joseph ....Salt Lake City 1889
Sawyer, Ivy ....London, England 1897
Scheff, Fritzi ....Vienna, Austria 1879
Schildkraut, Joseph ....Bucharest, Roumania 1896
Scott, Cyril ....Ireland 1866
Segal, Vivienne ....Philadelphia, Pa. 1897
Selwyn, Edgar ....Cincinnati, Ohio 1875
Serrano, Vincent ....New York 1870

Shannon, Effie	Cambridge, Mass.	1867
Shepley, Ruth	New York	1889
Sherman, Lowell	San Francisco, Cal.	1885
Sherwood, Robert Emmet	New Rochelle, N. Y.	1896
Sidney, George	New York	1876
Sidney, Sylvia	New York	1910
Sinclair, Arthur	Dublin, Ireland	1883
Sitgreaves, Beverly	Charleston, S. C.	1867
Skelly, Hal	Allegheny, Pa.	1891
Skinner, Cornelia Otis	Chicago	1902
Skinner, Otis	Cambridgeport, Mass.	1857
Smith, Ben	Waxahachie, Texas	1905
Smith, Queenie	New York	1898
Sondergaard, Gale	Minnesota	1899
Sothern, Edward H.	New Orleans, La.	1859
Spong, Hilda	Australia	1875
Stahl, Rose	Montreal, Canada	1872
Standing, Sir Guy	London	1873
Starr, Frances	Oneonta, N. Y.	1886
Stone, Fred	Denver, Colo.	1873
Stone, Dorothy	New York	1905
Strudwick, Sheppard	North Carolina	1905
Sullavan, Margaret	Norfolk, Va.	1910
Sydney, Basil	London	1894
Taliaferro, Edith	New York	1892
Taliaferro, Mabel	New York	1887
Tanguay, Eva	Middletown, Conn.	1878
Taylor, Laurette	New York	1884
Tearle, Conway	New York	1878
Tell, Alma	New York	1892
Tell, Olive	New York	1894
Terris, Norma	Columbus, Kansas	1904
Thomas, Augustus	St. Louis, Mo.	1859
Thomas, John Charles	Baltimore, Md.	1887
Tobin, Genevieve	New York	1901
Tobin, Vivian	New York	1903
Toler, Sidney	Warrensburg, Mo.	1874
Tone, Franchot	Niagara Falls, N. Y.	1907
Truex, Ernest	Red Hill, Mo.	1890
Tynan, Brandon	Dublin, Ireland	1879
Ulric, Lenore	New Ulm, Minn.	1897

Varesi, Gilda	Milan, Italy	1887
Victor, Josephine	Hungary	1891
Waldron, Charles	New York	1877
Walker, June	New York	1904
Walker, Charlotte	Galveston, Texas	1878
Walter, Eugene	Cleveland, Ohio	1874
Warfield, David	San Francisco, Cal.	1866
Warwick, Robert	Sacramento, Cal.	1878
Ware, Helen	San Francisco, Cal.	1877
Waterous, Herbert	Flint, Mich.	1863
Webb, Clifton	Indiana	1891
Weber, Joseph	New York	1867
Welford, Dallas	Liverpool, England	1874
Westley, Helen	Brooklyn, N. Y.	1879
Westman, Nydia	White Plains, N. Y.	1906
Whiffen, Mrs. Thomas	London, England	1845
White, George	Toronto, Canada	1890
Whiteside, Walker	Logansport, Ind.	1869
William, Warren	Aitkin, Minn	1896
Williams, Hope	New York City	1901
Wilson, Francis	Philadelphia, Pa.	1854
Wiman, Dwight Deere	Moline, Ill.	1895
Winwood, Estelle	England	1883
Witherspoon, Cora	New Orleans, La.	1891
Wood, Peggy	Brooklyn, N. Y.	1894
Wright, Haidee	London, England	1868
Wycherly, Margaret	England	1883
Wyndham, Olive	Chicago, Ill.	1886
Wynward, Diana	London, England	1906
Wynn, Ed.	Philadelphia, Pa.	1886
Young, Roland	London	1887
Yurka, Blanche	Bohemia	1893
Zabelle, Flora	Constantinople	1885
Ziegfeld, Florenz, Jr.	Chicago, Ill.	1867

NECROLOGY

June 17, 1933—June 16, 1934

Aborn, Milton, producer, 69. Famous for revivals of Gilbert and Sullivan operas; impresario in Boston and with B. F. Keith several years; founded Aborn Light Opera Company with brother Sargent in 1899. Born Marysville, Calif.; died New York City, November 12, 1933.

Arbuckle, Roscoe (Fatty), actor and director, 46. Began career in vaudeville; member Famous Players Organization, 1917-1921; appeared with Charles Chaplin, Mabel Normand; prominently cast in "Brewster's Millions," "Dollar-A-Year-Man," "Life of the Party," "The Round-Up," etc.; directed films under name of William Goodrich. Born San Jose, Calif.; died New York City, June 29, 1933.

Bahr, Hermann, playwright, 70. Wrote many plays including "The Concert," "The Master" and "Josephine"; was responsible for introduction of Shaw's plays into Germany. Born Linz, Austria; died Munich, Germany, January 15, 1934.

Baird, Dorothea, actress, 60. Original "Trilby" in Sir Herbert Tree's production, 1895; original "Mrs. Darling" in "Peter Pan"; toured England as understudy for Ellen Terry; married H. B. Irving. Born Teddington, England; died Broadstairs, Kent, England, September 24, 1933.

Booth, Hope, actress, 55. Played in Daniel Frohman stock company and with Mrs. Fiske; married and divorced Rennold Wolf, dramatic critic of the New York *Morning Telegraph*. Born Toronto, Canada; died New York City, December 18, 1933.

Cahill, Marie, actress, 63. Popular as musical comedy comedian; début in Hoyt's "A Tin Soldier"; played in Augustin Daly and George W. Lederer productions; married and starred by D. V. Arthur. Born Brooklyn, New York; died New York City, August 23, 1933.

Cline, Maggie, actress, 77. Musical comedy singer of the nineties; famous in vaudeville; won national fame singing "Throw Him Down, McCloskey," "Nothing Too Good for the Irish" and "McNulty Carved the Duck." Born Haverhill, Mass.; died Fair Haven, New Jersey, June 11, 1934.

Cody, Lew, actor, 47. Starred in "The Whirl of the World" before becoming a pioneer in pictures; started with Bessie Barriscale in "Mating"; more recently in "Beyond Victory," "What a Widow" and "X Marks the Spot"; married Dorothy Dalton and Mabel Normand. Born Waterville, Maine; died Hollywood, Calif., May 31, 1934.

Collins, Sewell, playwright and producer, 57. Cartoonist, newsman, magazine writer for *Life, Collier's Weekly,* Chicago *Tribune;* drama critic for New York *Journal;* decorated by Great Britain for war work as Chief Intelligence Officer for United States in England; plays include "Miss Patsy," "Just Like a Woman" and "9:45" (with Owen Davis); produced "Outward Bound." Born Denver, Colorado; died London, England, February 15, 1934.

Cook, Madge Carr, actress, 77. Professional career covered half a century; began in England at 3 in "Macbeth"; retired in 1910 after road tour of "If I Had Money"; played name part in "Mrs. Wiggs of the Cabbage Patch"; mother of Eleanor Robson Belmont. Born Yorkshire, England; died Syosset, L. I., September 20, 1933.

De Cisneros, Eleanor, singer, 53. First American singer in Metropolitan Opera Company without previous European training; chosen by d'Annunzio to create rôle in "La Figlia di Jorio"; sang at Covent Garden, London; La Scala in Milan and with Melba's opera company in Australia. Born New York City; died New York City, February 3, 1934.

Du Maurier, Sir Gerald, actor, playwright and producer, 61. Son of the author of "Trilby"; played in New York in 1896 in "The Dancing Girl," "Hamlet," "The Seats of the Mighty," "The Red Lamp," "Trilby," "King Henry IV" and "Brewster's Millions"; wrote "A Royal Rival"; knighted in 1922. Born Hampstead, England; died London, April 11, 1934.

Ediss, Connie, actress, 62. English comedienne; toured United States between 1896 and 1920; played in "The Shop Girl," "Girl Behind the Counter," "The Arcadians," etc.; last American appearance, New Haven, in "Oh, Uncle!" Born Brighton, England; died London, April 18, 1934.

Gemier, Firmin, actor and producer, 68. Director for ten years of Odeon Theatre, Paris; founded Shakespeare Society of France; introduced Eugene O'Neill to France with "Anna Christie"; brought own troupe to New York for three weeks' season 1924. Born Aubervilliers, France; died Paris, November 26, 1933.

Glass, Montague Marsden, author and playwright, 56. Creator of "Potash and Perlmutter" in both story and plays; best known comedies "Business Before Pleasure," "Why Worry?" "Object Matrimony" and "Abe and Mawruss." Born Manchester, England; died Westport, Conn., February 3, 1934.

Greene, Clay M., actor and playwright, 83. Author of Santa Clara "Passion Play" and some seventy-eight other stage works including "M'liss," "Sharps and Flats," "Wang" and "The Weavers." Born San Francisco, Calif.; died San Francisco, September 5, 1933.

Guinan, Mary Louise Cecelia (Tex), actress and entertainer. Started career as heroine of cowboy two-reel pictures; drifted into vaudeville and musical comedy; became famous as singing hostess at New York night clubs. Born Waco, Texas; died Vancouver, B. C., November 5, 1933.

Hale, Louise Closser, actress and author, 60. Wrote "Mother's Millions" in which May Robson starred; appeared in "Candida," "Beyond the Horizon," "Miss Lulu Bett," "Peer Gynt" and many other plays; screen performances included "White Sister," "Dinner at Eight," "Shanghai Express" and "Another Language." Born Chicago, Ill.; died Los Angeles, Calif., July 26, 1933.

Harrison, Duncan, playwright and manager, 72. Wrote "The Paymaster" in which Maude Adams, then known as Moyne Sullivan, made her professional début, and "Honest Hearts and Willing Hands" in which John L. Sullivan starred; major in the United States Army. Born Toronto, Canada; died New Rochelle, New York, March 13, 1934.

Harrold, Orville, opera tenor, 55. Discovered by Oscar Hammerstein as member of "Pump House Gang"; first appearance in "Social Whirl"; reputation expanded in vaudeville, grand opera and radio. Born Muncie, Indiana; died Norwalk, Conn., October 23, 1933.

Hawkins, Anthony Hope, playwright and novelist, 70. Plays included "The Prisoner of Zenda," "The Adventure of Lady Ursula," "Pilkerton's Peerage," etc. Born London; died Walton, Surrey, July 8, 1933.

Illington, Margaret, actress, 52. Won success in "The Two Orphans," "The Lion and the Mouse," "The Thief," "His House in Order," "Mrs. Leffinwell's Boots" and "Kindling"; last appearance in "A Good Bad Woman"; married and separated from Daniel Frohman; married Major Bowes. Born

Bloomington, Ill., died Miami Beach, Florida, March 11, 1934.

Kahn, Otto, theatre and arts patron, 68. Director and once chairman of the Metropolitan Opera Association; active in affairs of the theatre and motion picture industry; instrumental in bringing to this country Diaghileff's Russian Ballet, Copeau's Theatre du Vieux Columbier, Stanislawsky's Moscow Art Theatre, Max Reinhardt's Repertory Company featuring "The Miracle" and Messager's Orchestre du Conservatoire. Born Mannheim, Germany; died New York City, March 29, 1934.

Kester, Paul, playwright, 62. Writer of romantic plays from 1892 to 1920; first play, "Countess Roudino," produced at 22 with Minnie Maddern Fiske in title rôle; among other plays "Sweet Nell of Old Drury," "When Knighthood Was in Flower" and "Dorothy Vernon of Haddon Hall." Born Delaware, Ohio; died Lake Mohegan, New York, June 20, 1933.

Klauber, Adolph, actor, producer and dramatic critic, 54. Drama critic of New York *Times* for many years; produced "Nighty Night," "Scrambled Wives," "The Emperor Jones," "Diff'rent," etc.; married Jane Cowl. Born Louisville, Ky.; died Louisville, December 7, 1933.

Lardner, Ring, author and humorist, 48. Started writing career as sports editor of Chicago *Inter Ocean* going later to Chicago *Tribune;* wrote short stories for *Saturday Evening Post* and other magazines; sketches and lyrics for Ziegfeld "Follies"; wrote "Elmer the Great"; co-author with George Kaufman of "June Moon." Born Niles, Michigan; died East Hampton, L. I., September 25, 1933.

Link, Adolf, actor, 81. Début in America 1881 at the Thalia Theatre on the Bowery, New York; won success as Toni in "The Student Prince of Heidelberg." Born Budapest, Hungary; died New York City, September 24, 1933.

Mack, Charles (Charles E. Sellers), comedian, 46. Of black-face comedy team of Moran and Mack, known as the "Two Black Crows"; appeared in Ziegfeld "Follies," Earl Carroll's "Vanities" and George White's "Scandals"; well known in vaudeville. Born White Cloud, Kansas; died Mesa, Arizona, January 11, 1934.

Mantell, Bruce, actor, 24. Son of Robert Bruce Mantell and Genevieve Hamper; father carried him on stage at age of 2 in "Merchant of Venice"; with Walter Hampden in "Cyrano." Born Atlantic Highlands, New Jersey; died Hollywood, Calif., October 24, 1933.

Mayhew, Stella, actress, 59. Vaudeville and musical comedy star; professional début as child in "Rip Van Winkle"; with Weber and Fields in "Show Girl," "Fritz in Tammany Hall" and "High Jinks"; starred in "Swanee River"; played in "Hit the Deck"; married Billie Taylor, comedian. Born Pittsburgh, Pa.; died New York City, May 2, 1934.

Moses, Montrose Jonas, critic, editor and author, 55. Wrote "The American Dramatist," "Famous Actor Families in America," "Henrik Ibsen," "Maurice Maeterlinck," "The Fabulous Forrest" and translated the "Passion Play of Oberammergau"; married Lucille Herne, daughter of James A. Herne. Born New York City; died New York City, March 29, 1934.

Parker, Henry Taylor, critic, 67. For many years drama and music critic of the Boston *Transcript;* two years with New York *Globe.* Born Boston, Mass.; died Boston, March 29, 1934.

Payton, Corse, actor and producer, 65. Trouped for years through West as "World's best bad actor"; produced over 300 plays in 15 years in Brooklyn, originating the 10-20-30 scale of prices; Mark Pickford, the Gish sisters, Fay Bainter, Richard Bennett, Ernest Truex and others played in his company. Born Centreville, Iowa; died Brooklyn, February 23, 1934.

Percival, Walter C., actor and playwright, 46. Known for vaudeville sketch, "King for a Night"; wrote "Someone in the House" (with George Kaufman); "Among Those Present" and "The Choice." Born Chicago, Ill.; died Hollywood, January 28, 1934.

Reid, Francis Ellison, press agent, 67. Represented Liebler & Co., Charles Frohman, Klaw and Erlanger and many others for 30 years. Born Lancaster, Pa.; died New York City, October 3, 1933.

Rogers, Louise Mackintosh, actress, 68. Pioneer stage and screen actress. Prominent in stock companies of the West. Died Beverly Hills, Calif., November 1, 1933.

Ryley, Madeline Lucette, actress and playwright, 75. Best remembered for "An American Citizen," "Christopher, Jr.," and "Mice and Men"; one time prima donna in light operas. Born London, England; died London, February 21, 1934.

Seymour, William, actor and director, 82. Played with John

Wilkes Booth in 1864; with Joseph Jefferson, Edwin Booth, Charlotte Cushman, Lawrence Barrett and John McCollough; stage manager for Boston Museum, 1879-1888; stage director for Charles Frohman and George C. Tyler for many years. Born New York City; died Plymouth, Mass., October 2, 1933.

Shipman, Louis Evan, playwright, 69. Author of "The Crisis," "D'Arcy of the Guards," "The Crossing," "Poor Richard," etc.; editor of *Life* for two years; married Lucile Watson. Born Brooklyn, New York; died Bourg-en-Vexin, France, August 2, 1933.

Silverman, Sime, editor and publisher, 61. Edited and published *Variety*, profession's favorite news weekly, for thirty years. Born Cortland, New York; died Hollywood, September 22, 1933.

Skelly, Hal, comedian, 43. Toured in musical comedy and minstrels in China, Japan and America following several years in circus started at fifteen; first big success Skid in "Burlesque"; last theatrical venture production of "Come What May"; played in "Fiddlers Three," "Night Boat," "No, No, Nanette," etc. Born Allegheny, Pa.; died West Cornwall, Conn., June 16, 1934.

Sothern, Edwin Hugh, actor, 74. Son of Edward A. Sothern, famous early American actor; started with Boston Museum stock company; under management of Daniel Frohman from 1885 to 1896, playing many famous comedy rôles including those of "The Highest Bidder," "Lord Chumley," "The Dancing Girl," "Captain Letterblair," etc.; starred with his first wife, Virginia Harned; later married and toured with Julia Marlowe in Shakespearian repertoire. Born New Orleans, La.; died New York City, October 28, 1933.

Summerville, Amelia (Amelia M. Shaw), comedienne, 71. Prominent in musical comedies of the eighties and nineties; début at 7 in "The Pet of the Petticoats"; appeared in "The Black Crook," "Adonis" (with Henry Dixey), "The Glass Slipper" and "The Gingham Girl"; also in vaudeville, stock and pictures. Born Kildare, Ireland; died New York City, January 21, 1934.

Sutro, Alfred, playwright, 70. Author of more than thirty plays; translated many of Maurice Maeterlinck's plays; won first recognition with "The Walls of Jericho"; last dramatic offering here, "John Gladye's Honor" in 1928. Born London, England; died London, September 11, 1933.

Tashman, Lilyan, actress, 34. Début in "Follies of 1917"; subsequently in "The Gold Diggers," "The Garden of Weeds," etc.; success in pictures in "Camille," "So This Is Paris," "The Trial of Mary Dugan," "Golddiggers," and "Frankie and Johnnie"; married Edmund Lowe. Born Brooklyn, New York; died New York City, March 21, 1934.

Urban, Joseph, artist, architect and scene designer, 61. Noted for modern stage designing, especially for Ziegfeld Follies and Metropolitan Opera House; won citations in Austria and Russia; last work direction of color and lighting of Chicago Century of Progress. Born Vienna, Austria; died New York City, July 10, 1933.

Wilstach, Frank Jenners, author and manager, 68. At various times represented de Wolf Hopper, Sothern and Marlowe, Viola Allen, Mrs. Leslie Carter and William Faversham; assistant to Will H. Hays as censor of United States cinema advertising and publicity; author of "Book of Similes." Born Lafayette, Indiana; died New York City, November 28, 1933.

THE DECADES' TOLL

(Players of Outstanding Prominence Who Have Died in Recent Years)

	Born	*Died*
Aborn, Milton	1864	1933
Bacon, Frank	1864	1922
Belasco, David	1856	1931
Bernhardt, Sarah	1845	1923
Coghlan, Rose	1851	1932
Crabtree, Charlotte (Lotta)	1847	1924
Crane, William H.	1845	1928
De Koven, Reginald	1861	1920
De Reszke, Jean	1850	1925
Ditrichstein, Leo	1865	1928
Drew, John	1853	1927
Du Maurier, Sir Gerald	1873	1934
Duse, Eleanora	1859	1924
Fiske, Minnie Maddern	1865	1932
Galsworthy, John	1867	1933
Goodwin, Nathaniel	1857	1920
Hawtrey, Sir Charles	1858	1923
Herbert, Victor	1859	1924
Lackaye, Wilton	1862	1932
Mantell, Robert Bruce	1854	1928
Miller, Henry	1858	1926
Morris, Clara	1848	1925
O'Neill, James	1850	1920
Patti, Adelina	1843	1919
Rejane, Gabrielle	1857	1920
Russell, Lillian	1861	1922
Shaw, Mary	1860	1929
Smith, Winchell	1862	1933
Sothern, Edwin Hugh	1859	1933
Terry, Ellen	1848	1928
Ziegfeld, Florenz	1869	1932

INDEX OF AUTHORS

Abbott, George, 432, 541, 542
Abdullah, Achmed, 518
Abrams, Leon, 432
Ackland, Rodney, 464
Adams, Stanley, 421
Addinsell, Richard, 479
Akins, Zoe, 538
Allen, Fred, 476
Alsberg, Henry G., 541
Alter, Lois, 434
Ames, Christine, 24
Amiel, Denys, 449
Anderson, Maxwell, 5, 8, 22, 29, 415, 463, 537, 541, 542, 543, 544, 545
Andreyev, Leonid, 539
Ansky, S., 541
Anspacher, Louis Kaufman, 538
Archer, William, 539
Aristophanes, 22
Arlen, Michael, 541
Armstrong, Anthony, 443
Ashton, Herbert, Jr., 469
Atlas, Leopold, 317, 418, 481

Baker, Melville, 457, 540
Balderstone, John, 543
Baldwin, Faith, 518
Balfe, Michael, 423
Barrie, J. M., 539
Barry, Philip, 11, 317, 486, 540, 541, 542, 543, 544
Baum, Vicki, 450, 544
Baumer, Marie, 511
Beach, Lewis, 540
Beahan, Charles, 434
Behrman, S. N., 21, 492, 545
Belmonte, Nene, 448
Benelli, Sem, 538
Bennett, Russell, 434
Berlin, Irving, 6, 438
Bernauer, Rudolph, 523
Besier, Rudolf, 544
Biggers, Earl Derr, 444, 538
Black, Jean Ferguson, 7, 453
Blackwell, Donald, 424
Blocki, Fritz, 472
Blossom, Henry, 530
Bolitho, William, 544
Bolton, Guy, 539, 540
Bradford, Roark, 543
Bradshaw, George, 452
Bridgers, Ann, 542
Browne, Maurice, 543
Browne, Porter Emerson, 539
Brownell, John Charles, 513
Bruland, Ragnhilde, 530
Bushnell, Adelyn, 527
Butler, Rachel Barton, 539
Byrne, Dolly, 539

Caesar, Irving, 421
Caldwell, Erskine, 8, 467
Capek, Karel, 540
Caples, Martha, 507
Carroll, Earl, 5, 430
Casella, Alberto, 544
Chapin, Anne Morrison, 492
Child, Alan, 439, 441
Church, Harden, 532
Clork, Harry, 526
Cohan, George M., 538, 545
Colton, John, 540
Connelly, D. Hubert, 429
Connelly, Marc, 537, 539, 540, 541, 543
Cormack, Bartlett, 542
Coward, Noel, 524, 545
Craven, Frank, 539
Crothers, Rachel, 539, 540, 543, 544, 545
Crouse, Russel, 433

Dafora, Asadata, 15, 533
Damrosch, Gretchen, 523
Dane, Clemence, 11, 317, 479, 539
Davies, Valentine, 444
Daviot, Gordon, 12, 352, 496
Davis, Owen, 9, 468, 537, 540
De Kruif, Paul, 13, 504
Delf, Harry, 451
Dell, Floyd, 543

Deval, Jacques, 507
Dix, Beulah Marie, 502
Dodd, Lee Wilson, 540
Donoghue, Dennis, 498
Dorfman, Nat N., 466
Drake, William A., 490, 544
Drinkwater, John, 538
Duke, Vernon, 476
Dunning, Philip, 542

Ehrlich, Ida Lublenski, 521
Elgas, Miriam, 534
Emery, Gilbert, 539, 540
Ervine, St. John, 422, 538, 543
Ewing, Robert, 422

Fauchois, Rene, 545
Ferber, Edna, 541, 542, 545
Ferris, Walter, 544
Field, Salisbury, 539
Flavin, Martin, 23, 543
Flint, Eva Kay, 452
Flournoy, Richard F., 528
Floyd, John, 497
Fodor, Ladislaus, 421
Forbes, James, 538
Ford, Corey, 433
Franken, Rose, 544
Freedman, David, 476

Galantiere, Lewis, 449, 482
Gale, Zona, 537
Galsworthy, John, 539, 540, 542
Gardney, Edward F., 493
George, Grace, 539
Geraldy, Paul, 539
Gershwin, George and Ira, 7, 445, 537, 544
Gilbert, W. S., 14, 425, 426, 512, 514, 515, 516, 520
Glaspell, Susan, 537, 544
Gleason, James, 541
Gogol, 24
Golden, I. J., 478
Golden, John, 450
Goldoni, 25
Gordon, Leon, 439
Gore-Brown, R. F., 545
Goulding, Edmund, 541
Gow, Ronald, 483
Graham, Carroll and Garrett, 497
Granville-Barker, Harley, 539
Granville-Barker, Helen and Harley, 543

Green, Bud, 421
Green, John, 430
Green, Paul, 76, 537, 542, 544
Greensfelder, Elmer, 493
Greer, Jesse, 421
Gribble, Harry Wagstaffe, 505
Gropper, Milton Herbert, 494
Guilbert, Warburton, 507
Guiterman, Arthur, 5, 6, 442
Guitry, Sasha, 539

Hagan, James, 545
Haggart, John, 484
Hale, Lionel, 526
Hamilton, Nancy, 507
Harbach, Otto, 7, 458
Harburg, E. Y., 476
Hart, Moss, 6, 438, 544
Harwood, H. M., 545
Hasenclever, Walter, 440
Hastings, Sue, 534
Hawkes, J. Kerby, 490
Hecht, Ben, 543
Herbert, Victor, 21, 530
Herendeen, Frederick, 489
Heyman, Edward, 430, 438, 532
Heyward, DuBose, 542
Hill, Billy, 476
Hobart, Doty, 455, 528
Hodge, Merton, 12, 352, 491
Holiner, Mann, 466
Honrath, Donald, 507
Hope, Edward, 8, 459
Horan, Edward A., 489
Houseman, John, 449, 482
Howard, Leslie, 26
Howard, Sidney, 12, 13, 22, 25, 115, 416, 501, 504, 537, 541, 542, 545
Hughes, Hatcher, 537, 540
Hummel, George F., 448
Hupfeld, Herman, 430
Hurlbut, Gladys, 485, 541

Ibsen, Henrik, 20, 522

Jackson, Frederick, 515
Jacobson, Leopold, 523
Johns, Florence, 488

Katzin, Winifred, 541
Kaufman, George S., 7, 8, 445, 462, 537, 539, 540, 541, 542, 543, 544, 545

Kaye, B. M., 444
Keeler, Eloise, 506
Kelly, George, 537, 540, 541, 542
Kennedy, Mary, 541
Kern, Jerome, 7, 458
Kerr, Sophie, 10, 473
Kimmins, Anthony, 531
King, Rufus, 430, 529
Kingsley, Sidney, 29, 76, 415, 435, 537
Kirkland, Jack, 8, 467
Koch, Howard, 450
Kummer, Clare, 7, 256, 417, 436, 446, 495. 538

Lackaye, Wilton, Jr., 488
Langner, Lawrence, 5, 6, 439, 441, 442
Langner, Mrs. Lawrence, 439
Lardner, Ring W., 543
Lawson, John Howard, 13, 508, 509
Leslie, Lew, 466
Levy, Benn W., 545
Lewis, Morgan, 507
Lewis, Sinclair, 12, 115, 416, 501
Lindsay, Howard, 8, 425, 459
Loeb, John J., 430
Lonsdale, Frederick, 541
Louden, Isabelle, 439
Lozier, S. Bouvet de, 475

MacArthur, Charles, 543
MacDonald, Murray, 9, 470
MacIntosh, Agnes, 12, 352, 496
MacLeish, Archibald, 519
Macloon, Louis, 454
Maeterlinck, Maurice, 23
Maibaum, Richard, 460
Major, Austin, 503
Maltz, Albert, 9, 203, 465
Mandley, Percy G., 452
Marquis, Don, 540
Massine, Leonide, 519
Massingham, Dorothy, 9, 470
Maugham, William Somerset, 539, 542
Mayer, Edwin Justus, 541
McCall, G. H., 475
McCormack, Herbert P., 426
McDonald, Ballard, 476
McFadden, Elizabeth, 433
McGuire, William Anthony, 539
McOwen, Bernard J., 464
Metcalfe, Felicia, 428
Middleton, George, 539
Miles, William, 424
Miller, Albert G., 430
Miller, Alice Duer, 458
Millhauser, Bertram, 502
Milne, Alan Alexander, 539, 543
Milward, Jo, 490
Mitchell, Thomas, 543
Molière, 5, 6, 23, 442
Molnar, Ferenc, 539, 540, 542
Mooney, Martin, 420
Morando, Estelle, 421
Morley, Christopher, 7, 453
Mortimer, Lillian, 534
Murphy, Owen, 434
Myers, Richard, 430, 438, 508

Nabokoff, Nicolas, 519
Natanson, Jacques, 457
Nevin, Hardwick, 485
Nichols, Alberta, 466
Nichols, Robert, 543
Nicholson, Kenyon, 437
Novello, Ivor, 427

Oakland, Ben, 434
Obey, Andre, 22
O'Casey, Sean, 543
O'Neill, Eugene, 5, 6, 10, 21, 25, 28, 29, 159, 317, 416, 438, 478, 537, 538, 539, 541, 542, 544
Oppenheimer, George, 507
Osborn, Paul, 476

Parker, Dorothy, 493
Parker, Louis N., 538
Perelman, Laura and S. J., 467
Perlman, William J., 511
Peters, Paul, 9, 203, 516
Pezet, A. W., 487
Philipp, Adolf, 435, 487
Phillips, H. I., 476
Podrecca, Vittorio, 21
Pokrass, Samuel, 476
Pollock, Channing, 540, 541
Powel, Robert Hare, 477
Powell, Dawn, 5, 14, 521
Powell, Edward, 519
Priestley, J. B., 423

Ranck, Carty, 431
Randole, Leo, 532
Randolph, Clemence, 540
Raphaelson, Samson, 475
Reade, Leslie, 509
Reardon, Leo F., 510
Redman, George, 454
Reinhardt, Robert, 534
Reizenstein, Elmer, 538
Rice, Elmer, 543, 544, 545
Richardson, Anna Steese, 10, 473
Richman, Arthur, 539
Rickett, Edmond W., 442
Riggs, Lynn, 544
Robinson, Bertrand, 425
Robinson, Charles, 437, 481
Robinson, Lennox, 456
Root, Lynn, 526
Rosenblatt, Martin S., 23
Rouverol, Aurania, 22, 460
Rubin, Daniel N., 447
Ryskind, Morrie, 7, 445, 537, 544

Sands, Dorothy, 457
Sanger, Margo, 534
Sarg, Tony, 534
Schwartz, Maurice, 472
Selver, Paul, 540
Selwyn, Edgar, 541
Shairp, Mordaunt, 381, 418, 445
Shakespeare, 25
Shaw, George Bernard, 25, 523
Sheldon, Edward, 538
Shelton, James, 507
Sherman, Hiram, 503
Sherman, Nathan, 519
Sherriff, R. C., 543
Sherwood, Robert Emmet, 542, 544
Shore, Viola Brothers, 507
Sierra, Gregorio Martinez, 448, 542, 543
Siftons, The, 76
Sillman, June, 507
Sillman, Leonard, 507
Simon, Max, 487
Simon, Robert A., 6, 434, 441
Singer, I. J., 472
Skinner, Cornelia Otis, 17, 471
Sklar, George, 9, 203, 465, 516
Smith, H. S., 505
Smith, Harry James, 538
Soussanin, Nicholas, 511
Speyer, Wilhelm, 490
Stallings, Laurence, 29, 415, 541
Stange, Hugh, 480
Stange, Stanislaus, 523
Starling, Lynn, 471
Stein, Gertrude, 12, 498
Stept, Sam H., 421
Stewart, Donald Ogden, 544
Strauss, Johann, 441
Strauss, Oscar, 523
Sturges, Preston, 543
Sullivan, A. S., 14, 425, 426, 512, 514, 515, 516, 520
Swanstrom, Arthur, 434
Szczephkowska, Marja M., 455

Tarkington, Booth, 538
Thomas, A. E., 11, 292, 417, 484
Thompson, Julian, 440
Thompson, Virgil, 12, 498
Totheroh, Dan, 14, 513, 541
Treadwell, Sophie, 543
Tugend, Harry, 476
Turney, Katherine, 26

Underhill, John Garrett, 542

Van Druten, John, 541
Vane, Sutton, 540
Varesi, Gilda, 539
Vaszary, Johann, 454
Vollmer, Lulu, 540

Walker, Laura, 455
Walters, Eugene, 538
Warren, Ruth, 541
Washington, Ned, 430, 466
Waters, Marianne Brown, 428
Watkins, Maurine, 542
Watters, George Manker, 542
Webster, Paul Francis, 430
Weitzenkorn, Louis, 544
Wells, Emma, 485
Wexley, John, 5, 203, 416, 499, 543
Wilbur, Crane, 474, 517
Wilde, Oscar, 22
Williams, Jesse Lynch, 537, 538, 540
Wilson, Harry Leon, 540
Winter, Keith, 12, 352, 418, 495
Wodehouse, P. G., 542
Wolff, William Almon, 518

Woollcott, Alexander, 8, 462

Young, Howard Irving, 8, 461
Young, Joseph, 466
Young, Victor, 430, 466
Yurka, Blanche, 448

Zilboorg, Gregory, 539

INDEX OF PLAYS AND CASTS

Abie's Irish Rose, 536
Abraham Lincoln, 538
Adam and Eva, 539
Adonis, 536
Adventures of Ola, The, 534
After Such Pleasures, 493
Ah, Wilderness!, 5, 6, 21, 25, 26, 27, 29, 115, 159, 416, 438
Alice in Wonderland, 5, 17, 534
Alien Corn, 17, 25, 416, 545
Alison's House, 537, 544
All Good Americans, 27, 467
All the King's Horses, 17, 489
Amaco, 23
Ambush, 539
American—Very Early, 488
Amourette, 7, 256, 436
And Be My Love, 482
Angel, 17
Animal Kingdom, The, 544
Anna Christie, 416, 537, 539
Annina, 17
Another Language, 535, 544
Another Love, 507
Arabella, 24
Are You Decent?, 517
Arms and the Man, 523
As Husbands Go, 544
As Thousands Cheer, 6, 438
Autumn Crocus, 17, 21, 26

Bad Man, The, 539
Ball in Old Vienna, 520
Ballet Russe, 519
Barretts of Wimpole Street, The, 5, 20, 25, 544
Bat, The, 536
Beach, 520
Beau Danube, Le, 520
Beggar on Horseback, 540
Behold the Bridegroom, 542
Bend in the Road, The, 419
Berkeley Square, 543
Beyond the Horizon, 416, 537, 538
Big City, The, 520
Big Hearted Herbert, 10, 17, 473
Bill of Divorcement, A, 11, 539
Biography, 17, 21, 26, 492, 535, 545
Bird in Hand, 536
Birds, The, 22
Birthright, 460
Bitter Harvest, 26
Bitter Sweet, 524
Blackbirds, 536
Blackbirds of 1933, 466
Blossom Time, 536
Blue Widow, The, 428
Bohemian Girl, The, 423
Boomerang, The, 536
Both Your Houses, 29, 415, 535, 537, 545
Bourgeois Gentilhomme, Le, 23
Brain Sweat, 513
Bride of the Lamb, 541
Brief Moment, 545
Broadway, 536, 542
Broadway Interlude, 518
Broomsticks, Amen!, 493
Brothers Karamazov, The, 22
Burlesque, 542
Burmese Impressions, 520
Butter and Egg Man, The, 541
By Your Leave, 485

Candida, 5, 20, 25
Carnaval, 520
Cavalcade, 24
Caviar, 532
Champagne, Sec, 6, 441
Changelings, The, 540
Chatte, La, 520
Chicago, 542
Chicken Feed, 540
Chocolate Soldier, The, 523
Choir Singer, The, 256
Church Mouse, A, 421
Circle, The, 539
Clarence, 538
Climax, The, 535
Come Easy, 428
Come of Age, 11, 317, 479
Come Out of the Kitchen, 417

Come What May, 528
Constant Wife, The, 542
Coquette, 542
Cotillon, 520
Counsellor-at-Law, 26
Count of Monte Cristo, 416
Cradle Song, The, 542
Craig's Wife, 537, 541
Crime at Blossom's, The, 419
Criminal Code, The, 543
Crucible, 429
Curtain Rises, The, 6, 17, 19, 444
Cynara, 352, 545

Daisy Mayme, 542
Dance Dramas, 519-520
Dance of the Snake Charmer, The, 520
Dancing Mothers, 541
Dangerous Corner, 17, 423
Dark Tower, The, 8, 462
Days Without End, 5, 10, 159, 317, 478
Death Takes a Holiday, 544
Deburau, 539
Déclassée, 538
Design for Living, 545
Desire Under the Elms, 541
Devil Passes, The, 545
Dinner at Eight, 17, 19, 20, 545
Disraeli, 538
Divine Drudge, A, 7, 450
Divine Moment, A, 477
Doctor Monica, 455
Dodsworth, 12, 26, 115, 416, 501
Doll's House, A, 5, 20, 26
Double Door, 6, 26, 27, 433
Dover Road, The, 539
Drums Begin, The, 8, 461
Drunkard, The, 25, 27, 505
Dulcy, 539
Dybbuk, The, 541

Easiest Way, The, 538
East Is West, 536
Eight Bells, 452
Elizabeth Sleeps Out, 26
Elizabeth the Queen, 415, 544
Embers, 417
Emperor Jones, The, 534, 539
Enemy, The, 541
Enter Madame, 539
Escape, 542
Every Thursday, 528

Fall Guy, The, 541
False Dreams, Farewell, 480
Family Upstairs, The, 451
Famous Mrs. Fair, The, 538
Fan, The, 25
Firebrand, The, 541
First Apple, The, 471
First Mrs. Fraser, The, 543
First Year, The, 536, 539
Five Little Peppers, 534
Five-Star Final, 544
Fledermaus, Die, 6, 441
Follies, 10, 476
Fool, The, 540
Four Saints in Three Acts, 12, 498
Front Page, The, 543
Furnished Rooms, 530

Ganga Puja, 520
Gay Divorce, 17, 535
Gentlewoman, 14, 509
Ghost Train, The, 26
Ghost Writer, The, 420
Girls in Uniform, 18
Give Us This Day, 450
Gods We Make, The, 475
Going Gay, 424
Good Gracious Annabelle!, 7, 256, 417, 538
Good News, 536
Goodbye Again, 535
Goose Hangs High, The, 540
Grand Hotel, 544
Great God Brown, The, 11, 541
Green Bay Tree, The, 6, 26, 381, 418, 445
Green Goddess, The, 539
Green Grow the Lilacs, 544
Green Hat, The, 541
Green Pastures, The, 536, 537, 543
Green Table, The, 520
Growing Pains, 22, 25, 460
Grumpy, 22
Gypsy, 543

Hairy Ape, The, 26
Halfway to Hell, 474
Hamlet, 17, 21, 26, 352
Hat, a Coat, a Glove, A, 490
He Who Gets Slapped, 539
Heat Lightning, 432
Hedda Gabler, 5, 17, 20, 26
Hell-Bent fer Heaven, 537, 540
Her Friend, the King, 417

Her Husband's Wife, 417
Her Majesty the Widow, 17
Her Man of Wax, 25, 440
Her Master's Voice, 7, 26, 115, 256, 417, 446
Hero, The, 539
Hold Your Horses, 6, 17, 434
Holiday, 543
Hotel Alimony, 487
House of Connelly, The, 76, 544
House of Remsen, 511
Human Side, The, 24

I, Myself, 527
I Was Waiting for You, 457
Icebound, 537, 540
In Abraham's Bosom, 537, 542
Inspector General, 24
Invitation to a Murder, 14, 529
Iolanthe, 14, 520
Irene, 536
Is Life Worth Living?, 456
Is Zat So?, 536
It Pays to Sin, 454
It Takes a Frenchman, 23

Jane Clegg, 538
Jest, The, 538
Jeux d'Enfants, 520
Jezebel, 9, 468
Jigsaw, 5, 14, 521
John Brown, 11, 317, 483
John Ferguson, 422, 538
Jooss Ballet, 520
Journey's End, 76, 543
Joyous Season, The, 11, 317, 486
June Moon, 535, 543
Just Suppose, 417

Keeper of the Keys, 444
Kiki, 536
Kingdom of God, The, 543
Kultur, 435
Kykundor, or Witch Woman, 15, 533

L, 418
Ladder, The, 536
Lady from the Sea, The, 522
Lake, The, 9, 470
L'Apres-Midi d'un Faune, 520
Last Mile, The, 203, 416, 543
Last of Mrs. Cheyney, The, 541
Late Christopher Bean, The, 22, 26, 416, 545
Late Wisdom, 519
Left Bank, The, 544
Legal Murder, 498
Let 'Em Eat Cake, 7, 445
Let Us Be Gay, 543
Let Who Will Be Clever, 24
Lightnin', 536
Liliom, 539
Little Accident, 543
Locked Room, The, 469
Louder Please, 26
Love and Babies, 426
Love Chiselers, 26
Love Kills, 521
Loves of Charles II, 17, 471
Low and Behold, 26
Loyalties, 540
Lucrece, 22

Macbeth, 21, 26
Machinal, 543
Mackerel Skies, 484
Mahogany Hall, 481
Malia, 22
Mamma's Affair, 539
Marionettes, 534
Mary of Scotland, 5, 8, 26, 29, 115, 415, 463
Mary Rose, 539
Mary the 3d, 540
Master Builder, The, 5, 20, 26
Matelots, Les, 520
Matinees of Magic, 534
Memory, 26
Men in White, 6, 25, 28, 29, 76, 115, 415, 435, 537
Merry Wives of Windsor, The, 22
Merton of the Movies, 540
Michael and Mary, 543
Mikado, The, 14, 512
Milky Way, The, 14, 526
Minick, 541
Miss Lulu Bett, 537
Monte Carlo Ballet Russe, 17
Moon and Sixpence, The, 24
Moor Born, 14, 513
Mountain, The, 431
Mourning Becomes Electra, 544
Move On, Sister, 447
Mrs. Bumpstead-Leigh, 538
Mrs. Partridge Presents, 541
Murder at the Vanities, 5, 430
Music in the Air, 17, 21, 535
Music Master, The, 536

Nest, The, 539
New Faces, 13, 26, 507
New Moon, The, 536
Nice People, 539
Night over Taos, 22
1931, 76
No More Ladies, 11, 14, 26, 292, 417, 484
No More War, 8
No Mother to Guide Her, 534
No Questions Asked, 492
Nocturne, 520

Of Thee I Sing, 7, 446, 537, 544
Offense, The, 419
Old Homestead, The, 159
Ol' Man Adam an' His Chillun, 543
Old Soak, The, 540
Oliver Oliver, 476
Olympia, 256
On the Cuff, 26
On Trial, 538
Once in a Lifetime, 544
One More Honeymoon, 510
One Sunday Afternoon, 26, 535, 545
Only Girl, The, 21, 530
Othello, 12, 115
Our Stage and Stars, 457
Our Wives, 530
Outward Bound, 540
Overture, 544

Paris Bound, 542
Party, A, 427
Peace on Earth, 9, 203, 465, 511
Peg o' My Heart, 536
Pelleas and Melisande, 23
Perfumed Lady, The, 505
Petrouchka, 520
Piccoli, Teatro dei, 21, 534
Picnic, 523
Pigeons and People, 545
Pinafore, 14, 515
Pirates of Penzance, 14, 425, 514
Playboy of the Western World, 24
Play's the Thing, The, 542
Plough and the Stars, The, 543
Porgy, 542
Presages, Les, 520
Prince Igor, 520
Pure in Heart, The, 13, 508
Pursuit of Happiness, The, 6, 27 115, 439

Queen's Husband, The, 256
Queer People, 497

Racket, The, 542
Ragged Army, 502
Rain, 536, 540
Rainbow, The, 417
Rats of Norway, The, 418
Rebound, 544
Reckless Preface, 14
Re-Echo, 478
Reunion in Vienna, 544
Richard of Bordeaux, 12, 17, 19 352, 496
Richelieu, 17, 21, 26
Ringmaster, The, 418
Road to Rome, The, 542
Roberta, 7, 458
Romance, 538
Romeo and Juliet, 5, 20, 25
Royal Family, The, 542
R.U.R., 540

Sailor, Beware!, 6, 17, 21, 26, 437
St. Joan, 25
Sally, 536
Salome, 22
Saturday's Children, 415, 542
School for Husbands, The, 5, 6, 442
Scorpion, The, 464
Scuola di Ballo, 520
Sellout, The, 430
Servant in the House, The, 17, 21, 26
Seven Heroes. 520
Seven Keys to Baldpate, 538
Seventh Heaven, 536
Shady Lady, 421
Shan-Kar Ballet, 520
Shatter'd Lamp, The, 509
She Loves Me Not, 8, 21, 459
Shining Hour, The, 12, 17, 26, 115 352, 418, 495
Shooting Star, 535
Shore Acres, 159
Show Boat, 22, 536
Show-Off, The, 536, 540
Shuffle Along, 536
Silver Cord, The, 416, 542
Sing and Whistle, 494

Six Cylinder Love, 539
Skin Game, The, 539
Snanum, 520
Spanish Pavane, A, 520
Spectre de la Rose, Le, 520
Spring in Autumn, 7, 448
Steel, 417
Stevedore, 9, 203, 516
Strange Interlude, 11, 416, 537, 542
Strange Orchestra, 464
Stray Leaves, 422
Street Scene, 536, 537, 543
Streets of New York, The, 27
Strictly Dishonorable, 495, 536, 543
Student Prince, 536
Successful Calamity, A, 256, 417, 495
Sunny, 536
Sun-Up, 540
Swan, The, 540
Sylphides, Les, 520

Take a Chance, 17, 21, 27, 535
Tarnish, 540
Tattle Tales, 535
Ten Minute Alibi, 6, 17, 26, 443
Theodora, the Quean, 490
There's Always Juliet, 26
These Two, 526
They Knew What They Wanted, 416, 537, 541
They Shall Not Die, 5, 26, 203, 416, 499
Thoroughbred, 455
Three and One, 449
Three Cornered Hat, 520
Thunder on the Left, 7, 453
Ticket-of-Leave Man, The, 27
Tobacco Road, 8, 467
Tommy, 425
Tomorrow and Tomorrow, 544
Too Much Party, 503
Trial by Jury, 14, 516
Trip to Chinatown, A, 536
Twentieth Century, 22

Unchastened Woman, The, 538
Under Glass, 452
Undesirable Lady, An, 439
Union Pacific, 519

Vagabond King, The, 536
Vanities, Earl Carroll's, 5
Vermont, 417

We, the People, 545
Wedding Bells, 539
Wednesday's Child, 11, 26, 115, 317, 418, 481
What Price Glory?, 29, 415, 541
Whatever Possessed Her, 485
When in Rome, 503
When Ladies Meet, 545
While Parents Sleep, 531
Whispering Gallery, The, 26
White Cargo, 26
White Desert, 415
Why Marry?, 537, 538
Why Not?, 540
Wife Insurance, 515
Wild Birds, 541
Wind and the Rain, The, 12, 115, 352, 491
Wings over Europe, 543
Wisdom Tooth, The, 541
Witch Woman, The, 533
Wooden Slipper, The, 475
World Waits, The, 7, 448
Wrong Number, 506

Yellow Jack, 13, 416, 504
Yeomen of the Guard, 426
Yoshe Kalb, 20, 26, 472
You and I, 540
Young Woodley, 541
Youngest, The, 541